Routledge Handbook of Transnational Criminal Law

Certain types of crime are increasingly perpetrated across national borders and require a unified regional or global response to combat them. Transnational criminal law covers both the international treaty obligations which require states to introduce specific substantive measures into their domestic criminal law schemes, and an allied procedural dimension concerned with the articulation of inter-state cooperation in pursuit of the alleged transnational criminal.

The *Routledge Handbook of Transnational Criminal Law* provides a comprehensive overview of the system which is designed to regulate cross-border crime. The book looks at the history and development of the system, asking questions as to the principal purpose and effectiveness of transnational criminal law as it currently stands. The book brings together experts in the field, both scholars and practitioners, in order to offer original and forward-looking analyses of the key elements of the transnational criminal law.

The book is split into several parts for ease of reference:

- Part I, fundamental concepts surrounding the international regulation of transnational crime.
- Part II, procedures for international cooperation against alleged transnational criminals including jurisdiction, police cooperation, asset recovery and extradition.
- Part III, substantive crimes covered by transnational criminal law analysing the current legal provisions for each crime.
- Part IV, the implementation of transnational criminal law and the effectiveness of the system of transnational criminal law.

With chapters from over 25 authorities in the field, this handbook will be an invaluable reference work for students and academics and for policy makers with an interest in transnational criminal law.

Neil Boister is a Professor at the University of Waikato, New Zealand and is the author of *An Introduction to Transnational Criminal Law* (2012).

Robert J. Currie is Associate Professor at the Schulich School of Law, Dalhousie University, Canada and is the co-author (with Joseph Rikhof) of *International and Transnational Criminal Law* 2ed (2013).

"This handbook is a very timely and important contribution to the literature on transnational crime, covering key dimensions of this emerging area of law and policy. Both jurisdictional and procedural aspects of the topic are covered as well as aspects of its implementation in global, regional and domestic state practice. Incisive analysis from leading scholars and practitioners in the field of transnational criminal law combine to make this an invaluable reference."

Dr Robin Warner, Australian National Centre for Ocean Resources and Security (ANCORS), University of Wollongong, Australia

Routledge Handbook of Transnational Criminal Law

Edited by Neil Boister and Robert J. Currie

LONDON AND NEW YORK

First published 2015
by Routledge

2 Park Square, Milton Park, Abingdon, Oxon OX14 4RN
711 Third Avenue, New York, NY 10017, USA

Routledge is an imprint of the Taylor & Francis Group, an informa business

First issued in paperback 2017

British Library Cataloguing in Publication Data
A catalogue record for this book is available from the British Library

Library of Congress Cataloging-in-Publication Data
A catalog record has been requested for this book

ISBN: 978-0-415-83712-5 (hbk)
ISBN: 978-1-138-08441-4 (pbk)

Typeset in Bembo
by RefineCatch Limited, Bungay, Suffolk

Contents

Contributors

Jay L. Batongbacal is a lawyer from the Philippines, and holds the degrees of Master of Marine Management and Doctor in Jurisprudential Science, both from Dalhousie University in Canada. Since 1997, he has done work in maritime affairs, including community-based fisheries management, coastal resource management, marine environment protection, maritime boundaries, high seas fishing, offshore energy, seafaring and shipping. He was legal advisor to the Philippine delegation that successfully pursued the Philippines' claim to a continental shelf beyond 200 nautical miles in the Benham Rise Region before the Commission on the Limits of the Continental Shelf. He is presently an Assistant Professor at the University of the Philippines College of Law, and concurrently Director of the Institute for Maritime Affairs and Law of the Sea of the U.P. Law Center.

Neil Boister is Professor in the Te Piringa Faculty of Law, University of Waikato, New Zealand. A graduate of the universities of Natal and Nottingham, he has held academic positions in South Africa, the UK and New Zealand, where he has taught transnational criminal law, international criminal law, criminal law, evidence and criminology. His principal research interest is the suppression of transnational crime through international law. His PhD from the University of Nottingham resulted in the publication of *Penal Aspects of the UN Drug Conventions* (Kluwer, 2001). He has written numerous pieces exploring transnational criminal law more generally beginning with 'Transnational Criminal Law?' (2003) 14(5) *European Journal of International Law* 953–976. In 2012 he published *An Introduction to Transnational Criminal Law* (OUP). He works as a consultant on issues in transnational criminal law. In 2014 he was awarded a Friedrich Wilhelm Bessel Research Award by the Humboldt Foundation in Germany in recognition of his work in this field.

Lindsay Buckingham is currently a Principal Legal Officer with the Transnational Crime and Corruption Branch, Australian Government Attorney-General's Department. Within the Australian Government she has worked across a range of transnational crime law and policy issues, including leading Australia's engagement in mechanisms under the United Nations criminal justice system, and delivering technical assistance programs to support partner countries' implementation of transnational crime obligations under international legal instruments. She has also worked as a Solicitor with the Child Protection Practice Group of the New South Wales Crown Solicitor's Office. Lindsay has previously worked as a consultant on child sex tourism, trafficking in persons and migrant smuggling projects with the United Nations Office on Drugs and Crime, Regional Centre for East Asia and the Pacific, and with the International Labour Organization's Project to Combat Trafficking in Children and Women in the Greater Mekong Subregion. She holds a combined Bachelor of Arts and Laws (Hons) from Macquarie University, and a Master of Laws from the University of Sydney.

Anthony E. Cassimatis BA LLB (Hons) (*Qld*) LLM (Cantab) PhD (Qld) is an Associate Professor in the TC Beirne School of Law, University of Queensland. His doctoral thesis, which examined human rights-related trade measures under international law, was published by Martinus Nijhoff in 2007. He teaches administrative law and public international law, is a fellow and member of the executive of the Centre for Public, International and Comparative Law at the University of Queensland and is the chairperson of the Red Cross's Queensland International Humanitarian Law Committee. He is the author or co-author of three books and numerous articles and book chapters on public international law, administrative law and legal advocacy. He has been academic coordinator of teams representing the Law School in the Philip C. Jessup International Law Moot Court Competition over many years, including teams that have won the Jessup Moot World Championship in Washington DC (2005 and 2014). Anthony was a Visiting Fellow at the Lauterpacht Centre for International Law at Cambridge University in 2007.

Vivienne Chin is a criminal justice professional with more than 25 years of experience in the security and justice sectors, having worked in a range of organizations beginning with the Security Intelligence Service of the Government of Singapore; the Commonwealth Secretariat, London; the Commonwealth Magistrates' and Judges' Association, London; and currently as an Associate of a United Nations affiliated research institute in Vancouver, The International Centre for Criminal Law Reform and Criminal Justice Policy. Vivienne has focused her work on the promotion of the rule of law and good governance, human rights, peace-building, criminal justice reform and policy development, as well as institution-building in post-conflict societies. This includes programmes to assist the effective human rights-based implementation of international standards and norms and international treaties, in particular those relating to counter-terrorism, transnational organised crime, human trafficking and smuggling, women's rights and violence against women, corruption, juvenile justice, youth at risk, crime prevention, prison reform and the social reintegration of young and adult offenders.

Roger S. Clark is a graduate of Victoria University in New Zealand (BA, LLD) and of Columbia Law School in New York (LLM, JSD), and is Board of Governors Professor at Rutgers Law School, Camden, New Jersey. He has written widely on international law, human rights and criminal law. He was a member of the United Nations Committee on Crime Prevention and Control between 1986 and 1990. In 1995 he represented the Government of Samoa in arguing the illegality of nuclear weapons before the International Court of Justice. Since 1995, he has represented Samoa in the negotiations to create the International Criminal Court, including the Rome Conference in 1998 when the treaty setting up the Court was finalized, in subsequent meetings of the Preparatory Commission for the Court, the Court's Special Working Group on the Crime of Aggression, and at the 2010 Review Conference on the Court in Kampala, Uganda.

Robert J. Currie (of the Bar of Nova Scotia) is Associate Professor and Director of the Law and Technology Institute at the Schulich School of Law, Dalhousie University, where he teaches International Criminal Law, Criminal Law, Evidence, Advocacy and Civil Procedure. Prior to his academic appointment he had a litigation practice at a leading Atlantic Canadian firm. He is a member of the Executive Board of the Canadian Council on International Law and Vice-President of the Law Reform Commission of Nova Scotia. Professor Currie specializes in the area of international and transnational criminal law, and his publications on this subject have been cited by the Supreme Court of Canada and other Canadian courts. The first edition of his book, *International and Transnational Criminal Law* (second edition, Toronto: Irwin, 2013, now co-authored with Joseph Rikhof), was shortlisted for the Walter Owen Book Prize for Outstanding Canadian Legal Literature in 2011.

Yvon Dandurand, a criminologist, is a member at the School of Criminology and Criminal Justice at the University of the Fraser Valley (British Columbia, Canada) and a Senior Associate of the International Centre for Criminal Law Reform and Criminal Justice Policy (Vancouver), a United Nations affiliated institute. He specializes in comparative criminal law and criminal justice research and was involved in numerous criminal justice reform and capacity-building projects in Canada and abroad, including several projects and studies in the areas of organized crime, human trafficking, witness protection, corruption, counter-terrorism, crime prevention, policing and corrections. He has been involved in several projects to facilitate and monitor the implementation of international criminal law conventions. He has developed performance indicators and other monitoring mechanisms in the areas of child protection, juvenile justice, organized crime and corruption. He recently served as the senior consultant for the United Nations Rule of Law Indicators Project developed for the UN Department of Peacekeeping Operations and the UN Office of the High Commissioner on Human Rights.

Catherine E. Drummond LLB (Hons), BA (UQ), GDip Legal Practice (Distinction) (ANU) is admitted as a solicitor in Queensland, Australia, and is currently a trainee with the Public International Law and International Arbitration Group at an international law firm in Paris. She has worked in domestic criminal prosecution, criminal defence, as Associate to the President of the Queensland Court of Appeal, and in Chambers at the United Nations International Criminal Tribunal for Rwanda. She was also a guest lecturer and tutor in Public International Law at the University of Queensland and a member of the Australian Red Cross International Humanitarian Law Advisory Committee for Queensland. In 2014, Catherine commenced her LLM as a General Sir John Monash Scholar at Cambridge University.

Anne T. Gallagher AO (BA, LLB, MIntL, PhD) is a lawyer, practitioner, teacher and scholar with an established reputation in international affairs, most particularly human rights and the administration of criminal justice. As a United Nations official she led the UN inter-agency delegation that participated in the drafting process for both the migrant smuggling and trafficking in persons protocols. She has continued to be closely involved in the evolution of the international legal framework around these issues while also working on the front line with governments in South East Asia to develop more effective criminal justice responses. An independent and award-winning scholar, she has been recognized by the US Government as 'the leading global authority on the international law of human trafficking'. She is the lead author of *The International Law of Migrant Smuggling*, published by Cambridge University Press in 2014.

William Gilmore is Emeritus Professor of International Criminal Law at the University of Edinburgh, Scotland. An international lawyer by background, he has written extensively on various aspects of transnational criminal law and cooperation in criminal matters. He has been the legal scientific expert to MONEYVAL, the FATF-style regional body for Europe, since its creation in late 1996. In that capacity he has been extensively involved in the evaluation of numerous jurisdictions, from Russia to the Vatican/Holy See, for compliance with international AML/CFT standards. He has been a Member of the Board of Directors of the Cayman Islands Monetary Authority since 2006.

Henning Grosse Ruse-Khan is a University Lecturer in Intellectual Property Law at the Faculty of Law at the University of Cambridge and a Fellow at King's College, Cambridge. A Fellow at the Lauterpacht Centre for International Law and Centre for Intellectual Property and Information Law, he also holds positions as external researcher at the Max Planck Institute for Intellectual Property and Competition Law in Munich and at the Centre for International Sustainable Development Law. He teaches IP and WTO Law at Cambridge and at the Centre for International Intellectual Property Studies, Strasbourg, and the Munich Intellectual Property Law Centre. A member of the editorial board of the *International Review of Intellectual Property and Competition Law* and co-founder of the international IP network at the Society of International Economic Law, his research and teaching focuses on international intellectual property protection and development issues, world trade and investment law, as well as on interfaces among distinct legal orders in international law. In addition, he advises international organizations and NGOs as well as developing and developed country governments on international IP, WTO and investment law issues.

Douglas Guilfoyle is a Reader in Law at the Faculty of Laws, University College London, where he teaches the international law of the sea and international criminal law. He is the author of *Shipping Interdiction and the Law of the Sea* (2009) and numerous articles on Somali piracy and maritime security and law enforcement. He has acted as a consultant on piracy and maritime security issues to the Contact Group on Piracy off the Coast of Somalia (Working Group 2), the Foreign Affairs Committee of the House of Commons and the UN Office on Drugs and Crime. He holds graduate degrees from the University of Cambridge, where he was a Gates Scholar, and undergraduate degrees from the Australian National University.

Joanna Harrington is a Professor in the Faculty of Law and an Associate Dean in the Faculty of Graduate Studies and Research at the University of Alberta in Canada. She has combined an academic career, specializing in constitutional law and international law, with experience as a legal adviser, serving from 2006 to 2008 as the Scholar-in-Residence with the Legal Affairs Bureau of Canada's then Department of Foreign Affairs and International Trade. She has represented Canada at international negotiations at the United Nations, the Organization of American States, and the Assembly of States Parties to the Rome Statute of the International Criminal Court. Her consultancy experience includes work with the Canadian Human Rights Commission and the United Nations Development Programme, as well as work with defence counsel in transnational criminal matters. She received her PhD in Law from the University of Cambridge, where she was a Tapp Scholar.

John Hatchard is a Barrister and Professor of Law at the Buckingham Law School and Visiting Professor at the Open University. He is also a senior research fellow at the School of Oriental and African Studies. He has held senior academic positions at universities in the United Kingdom, United States, Australia, Zambia and Zimbabwe. He has also served as Chief Mutual Legal Assistance Officer at the Commonwealth Secretariat and was a Senior Fellow at the British Institute for International and Comparative Law. He has published extensively in the area of criminal law, criminal justice and evidence, constitutional law and human rights, with particular reference to the Commonwealth and Anglophone Africa. He is the author of, among other books, *Combating Corruption: Legal Approaches to Supporting Good Governance and Integrity in Africa* (Edward Elgar, 2014); *Comparative Constitutionalism and Good Governance in the Commonwealth* (with Muna Ndulo and Peter Slinn, Cambridge University Press, 2005) and *Corruption and the Misuse of Public Office* (with Colin Nicholls, Tim Daniel and Alan Bacarese, Oxford University

Press, 2006, second edition 2011). He is a member of the Editorial Board of the *Journal of Commonwealth Law and Legal Education* and serves on the Editorial Advisory Board of the *Denning Law Journal*. For many years he was Editor of *Commonwealth Legal Education*, Editor of the *Corruption Case Law Reporter* and Joint Editor of the *Journal of African Law*.

Saskia Hufnagel is a qualified German legal professional and accredited specialist in criminal law. She currently works as Lecturer in Criminal Law at Queen Mary University of London. She previously worked as a Research Fellow at the Australian Research Council Centre of Excellence in Policing and Security, Griffith University, Australia, and was a Leverhulme Fellow at the University of Leeds. Her main research areas encompass law enforcement cooperation in Asia, North America, the EU and Australasia, comparative constitutional and human rights law with a focus on terrorism legislation and emergency management and the policing of art crime. Her monograph *Policing Cooperation Across Borders: Comparative Perspectives on Law Enforcement within the EU and Australia* was published by Ashgate in 2013. Saskia was awarded an LLM (2004) and a PhD in Law (2011) by the Australian National University.

Bernard Leroy is a retired High Court Judge, currently Director of the International Institute of Research Against Counterfeit Medicines (IRACM) in France. In his professional career, he was an investigating judge specializing in drug cases – Evry High Court (1979–1988); in charge of legal and international affairs – French National Drug Coordination (1988–1990); senior Legal Advisor – United Nations Office on Drugs and Crime (UNODC) (1990–2010); and Deputy General Prosecutor – Versailles Court of Appeal (2010–2013). He was a member of the French delegation in 1988 for the final negotiations of the United Nations Convention against Illicit Traffic in Narcotic Drugs and Psychotropic Substances. As manager of the UNODC Legal Assistance Programme (LAP) set up to help Member States to ratify and implement the 1988 Convention, he designed, drafted and disseminated, for the first time in the UN system, specific model laws that have been used by many States, and provided in-site assistance from 1990 to 2010, to more than 100 governments on request in Africa, North and South America, Asia and Europe. He established and implemented national and regional programmes to train judges and prosecutors, in order to optimize the application of the legislation adopted by their States. In 2014, he was elected to the International Narcotics Control Board (INCB) for a five-year term.

Carole McCartney is a Reader in the School of Law at Northumbria University. Previously senior lecturer in criminal law and criminal justice at the University of Leeds and Bond University, Queensland, Australia, she has written on Australian justice, innocence projects, miscarriages of justice, policing cooperation, and DNA, forensic science and criminal justice more widely. She established an Innocence Project at the University of Leeds in 2005, and was project manager for the Nuffield Council on Bioethics report 'The Forensic Uses of Bio-information: Ethical Issues' and the Nuffield Foundation project 'The Future of Forensic Bioinformation'. She has also run projects on forensic science education and forensic regulation and recently completed an EU Marie Curie international research fellowship (2009–2012) on 'Forensic Identification Frontiers'. She currently teaches and researches in the areas of criminal law, criminal evidence and forensic science.

Valsamis Mitsilegas is Professor of European Criminal Law, Director of the Criminal Justice Centre and Head of the Department of Law at Queen Mary University of London. From 2001 to 2005 he was legal advisor to the House of Lords European Union Committee. He is a regular consultant to EU institutions, governments, parliaments and NGOs on matters related to EU

Justice and Home Affairs law, security and human rights. He is a member of two Commission Expert Groups, the Commission Expert Group on EU Criminal Policy and the Commission Expert Group on Needs on Data on Crime. Professor Mitsilegas is Principal Investigator in a transnational research project on European Union responses to environmental crime funded by the Commission's FP7 Programme. He is Co-Coordinator of the European Criminal Law Academic Network (ECLAN) and the author of three books and over seventy articles and chapters spanning the fields of EU criminal law, immigration and asylum law, legal responses to transnational crime and terrorism and the relationship between globalization, security and human rights. His monographs include *Money Laundering Counter-measures in the European Union* (Kluwer, 2003) and *EU Criminal Law* (Hart, 2009).

Charles Monteith is admitted both as a Solicitor and as a Higher Court Advocate in England and Wales. He is Head of Legal and Case Consultancy at the International Centre for Asset Recovery (ICAR) in the Basel Institute on Governance. Prior to this he worked as Counsel in the White Collar group of international law firm White & Case. He is an expert on due diligence enquiries, risk assessment, corporate investigations, and on the governance and compliance implications of the UK Bribery, Fraud and Proceeds of Crime Acts. Prior to that, he was Head of Assurance at the UK Serious Fraud Office (SFO), where he was a leading policy maker and a key architect of the UK Bribery Act. He was on the Law Commission's Bill Advisory Group. He has been involved in such high-profile cases as *BAE, Mabey Johnson, Balfour Beatty* and *Oil for Food*. He is peer reviewer for the OECD Working Group on Bribery, and has assisted with country reviews under the UNCAC. He has also designed and implemented serious economic crime and anti-corruption training *inter alia* for Ghana, Nigeria and Zambia. A regular speaker at high-level anti-corruption, corporate compliance, securities fraud, money laundering and white-collar crime conferences, he has authored many articles and edited and contributed to leading publications such as *Modern Bribery* (Cambridge University Press 2012) and *Emerging Corruption Trends* (Basel Institute 2013).

Tom Obokata is Professor of International Law and Human Rights at Keele Law School. He has extensive experience of research into human trafficking and has published widely on the topic, including his monograph, *Trafficking of Human Beings from a Human Rights Perspective: Towards a Holistic Approach* (2006). He also actively engages in consultancy activities, providing expert advice for governmental, non-governmental and international organizations. In the past, he served as an expert for bodies such as the UK Parliamentary Joint Committee on Human Rights, Northern Ireland Assembly All Party Group on Human Trafficking, European Union and International Organization for Migration.

Pedro Gomes Pereira is senior asset recovery specialist at the Basel Institute for Governance's International Centre for Asset Recovery (ICAR). A lawyer and a member of the Brazilian Bar Association, while attending law school, Pedro joined the Brazilian central authority for mutual legal assistance, where he assisted authorities around the world in coordinating their international strategies and obtaining evidence in order to effectively combat organized crime, corruption and money laundering. Upon completing his studies, Pedro directed his professional activities in asset recovery to supporting local and foreign authorities in sensitive cases involving high-ranking government officials and private entrepreneurs. He also developed strategies tracing and seizing the proceeds of crime in these cases. Before joining ICAR, Pedro was the Acting General Coordinator for Mutual Legal Assistance and Asset Recovery in the Brazilian Ministry of Justice. He has participated in a number of fora on asset recovery assistance at both national and international level.

Christopher Ram is a lawyer and criminologist who has been employed as Legal Counsel at the Canada Department of Justice since 1989, apart from 1999 to 2003, when he was employed by the United Nations Office on Drugs and Crime as a crime prevention expert. He specializes in matters relating to transnational crime and the effects of globalization on crime, including jurisdictional law and the use of international law, domestic law and non-legal responses to the problem. He has served as a cybercrime expert for Canadian delegations to the G7/G8, the Commonwealth, the UN Commission on Crime Prevention and Criminal Justice and several UN crime congresses, and was responsible for cybercrime and related matters for the UN Office on Drugs and Crime from 1999 to 2003. He served as the Rapporteur for the UN open-ended intergovernmental expert group on economic fraud and the criminal misuse of identity from 2004 to 2007 and is currently the Rapporteur for the UN open-ended intergovernmental expert group on cybercrime.

Sławomir Redo, Dr hab. (Law/Criminology, Poland) is a retired former Senior Crime Prevention and Criminal Justice Expert at the UN Office on Drugs and Crime, and is a visiting lecturer at the University of Vienna. He has been involved in various UN capacities in technical assistance projects implementing the UN law against organized crime, in crime prevention cooperation between developing countries, in urban crime prevention, in the abolition of the death penalty, in crime prevention and civilian private policing, in the virtual forum against cybercrime, in online crime prevention and criminal justice education for the international rule of law, and in intercultural training skills in justice and security sector reform worldwide. He is the author of more than sixty publications on various crime and justice issues, mostly covering UN law and practice. In particular, he is the author of several books, including *Blue Criminology: The Power of United Nations Ideas to Counter Crime Globally* (HEUNI, Helsinki 2012) and *Organized Crime and its Control in Central Asia* (Office of International Criminal Justice, Sam Houston State University, Texas, USA, 2004). He is co-editor of *For the Rule of Law: Criminal Justice Teaching and Training across the World* (Helsinki–Seoul 2008), the *Global Crime and Justice Report* (OUP, New York 1999), and *Women and Children as Victims and Offenders: Background – Prevention – Reintegration: Suggestions for Succeeding Generations* (Springer Verlag, 2015).

Ben Saul is Professor of International Law and an Australian Research Council Future Fellow at the University of Sydney. Ben has expertise on international counter-terrorism law, human rights, the law of armed conflict, and international criminal law. He has published 10 books, 75 scholarly articles, and hundreds of other publications and presentations, and his research has been used in national and international courts. He is author of *Defining Terrorism in International Law* (OUP, 2006) and co-author of *The International Covenant on Economic, Social and Cultural Rights: Commentary, Cases and Materials* (OUP, 2014). Ben has taught law at Oxford, at the Hague Academy of International Law and in China, India, Nepal and Cambodia, and has been a visiting professor at Harvard Law School. Ben practises as a barrister in international and national courts, has advised various United Nations bodies and foreign governments, has delivered foreign aid projects, and often appears in the media. He has a doctorate in law from Oxford and honours degrees in Arts and Law from Sydney.

Andreas Schloenhardt is Professor of Criminal Law in the School of Law at The University of Queensland in Brisbane, Australia and a Visiting Professor at the Faculty of Law, Department of Criminal Law and Criminology at the University of Vienna, Austria. He is also a consultant to the United Nations Office on Drugs and Crime (UNODC) and a guest professor at the University of St Gallen, Switzerland. His principal areas of research include criminal law, organized crime, migrant smuggling, trafficking in persons, narco-trafficking, terrorism, criminology, and immigration and refugee law. He is the author of many books and journal articles and his work is frequently cited by other scholars, in government reports, and judicial decisions, including the High Court of Australia. His recent work focuses on organized crime legislation and international efforts to prevent and suppress migrant smuggling and trafficking in persons.

James Sheptycki is a Professor of Criminology in the Department of Social Science at York University, Toronto, Canada. He has published widely on criminological topics including organized crime, money laundering, transnational policing and comparative criminology. His recent book, written with Ben Bowling (King's College, London) and entitled *Global Policing* was published by Sage in 2012. In 2011 he published a collection of essays titled *Transnational Crime and Policing*, in the *Pioneers in Contemporary Criminology Series* (London: Ashgate). He edited a special issue of *Criminology and Criminal Justice* concerning guns, crime and social order (Vol. 9 No. 3, 2009) with Adam Edwards and, together with Andrew Goldsmith, he edited a major collection of essays titled *Crafting Transnational Policing* (2007, Oxford: Hart Publishing). Broadly speaking, he is interested in the intersection of governance, crime, policing and the global system.

John A.E. Vervaele is full-time Professor of Economic and European Criminal Law at Utrecht Law School (the Netherlands) and Professor of European Criminal Law at the College of Europe in Bruges (Belgium). He is vice-president of the AIDP, in charge of the scientific coordination of the world organization for criminal law. The main topics in his research field are white collar crime, European Union Law, mutual legal assistance, standards of due process of law, procedural safeguards and human rights, comparative economic and financial criminal law, and terrorism and criminal procedure. He has realized a lot of research in these areas, for both Dutch departments and European institutions, and has also worked as a consultant for them. He regularly teaches as a visiting professor at foreign universities, in Europe, the United States, Latin America and China.

Arianna Visconti, whose PhD was in Italian and Comparative Criminal Law (2008), is Assistant Professor in Criminal Law in the Università Cattolica del Sacro Cuore of Milan. She is a senior member of CSGP ('Federico Stella' Centre for Research on Criminal Justice and Policy) in the same university, and coordinates its research groups on offences against cultural heritage (she edited, with S. Manacorda, *Beni culturali e sistema penale*, Milan, 2013) and on law and literature (she is editor, with G. Forti and C. Mazzucato, of *Giustizia e letteratura I*, Milan, 2012, and *Giustizia e letteratura II*, Milan, 2014). Her other publications and studies cover defamation law, legal protection of reputation and 'reputational sanctions', theory of punishment, white-collar and organizational crimes, bribery, corruption and offences against Public Administration. She is also a lecturer in the UCSC Higher School of Specialization in Legal Professions.

Rob White is Professor of Criminology in the School of Social Sciences at the University of Tasmania, Australia. He has published widely in the areas of criminology and youth studies. Recent books include *Environmental Harm: An Eco-Justice Perspective, Transnational Environmental Crime: Toward an Eco-Global Criminology*, and *Green Criminology: An Introduction to the Study of Environmental Harm*.

Foreword

Evidently, there are certain historic roots to international crime *writ large* and international cooperation, including notably the concept of extradition which can be traced to antiquity. However, if you carefully examine practice, until quite recently, crime was generally regarded and addressed as a local matter – local in commission, in effect, in reaction. And it follows that priorities and policy in the criminal law sphere were driven almost exclusively by domestic and local imperatives.

But the last few decades have brought remarkable change to the criminal law landscape in our ever shrinking 'global village' – a term coined by Canadian author Marshall McLuhan. Sadly, some of this has been driven by horrific atrocities which have brought the concepts of international crime – whether by its commission or by its nature – to the forefront, driving significant efforts towards justice and bringing an end to impunity. We have seen the advent of international criminal tribunals and the birth of the International Criminal Court. These advances represent momentous progress for humanity and have appropriately garnered much attention, including in the writings of practitioners and academics alike.

Interestingly though, while less prominent on the world stage, the most fundamental and widespread transformation – the real 'internationalization' of criminal law – has been through the rise of transnational crime and the measures developed, particularly through international efforts and initiatives, to address it.

It is our reality today that a significant portion of serious criminal activity is transnational in nature in some way. Many crimes are committed transnationally, have a cross-border effect or require international measures for evidence to be gathered or suspects to be brought to justice. The proceeds of criminal activity are moved in sophisticated ways around the world. And this phenomenon is not limited in its geographic reach. Almost no part of the world is left untouched by the rise of the transnational component of crime, though its manifestations may vary widely. This reality of the changed face of the criminal threat has led to remarkable developments and advancement in how we define crime and respond to it – procedurally and substantively. It has also influenced the evolution of criminal law policy and has shaped the development of priorities at the international, regional and domestic levels.

As a criminal law practitioner who has dabbled in the field at both the national and international levels, I am often struck by the lack of clarity which exists about the concept of transnational criminal law, especially in my own mind! I like to think this is attributable to the fact that over the past 30 years there has been a literal explosion – crimes, concepts, principles, practices and measures – in this field. New crimes have been established and the definitions of existing crime expanded in response to the endless ingenuity of those who perpetrate crime. International instruments have been agreed, successively improving the measures to address crime with each round of negotiation. Procedural mechanisms – extradition, mutual assistance, law enforcement cooperation, cross-border asset confiscation, joint investigations – have expanded and been redefined. And all of this has occurred at relatively 'breakneck' speed in contrast to the pace of progress in many other contexts of international or even domestic law.

For those caught up in trying to implement it, there has been limited opportunity for reflection. And the overall 'system' which has developed can best be described kindly as a patchwork and, less kindly, as chaotic. It is a scheme the evolution which has been driven by crisis and necessity as opposed to policy and planning.

The result is that, for academics and practitioners alike, the field of transnational crime and the responses to it are increasingly difficult and challenging to navigate. Whether one categorizes it as a subset of the broader subject of international criminal law or considers it as a 'stand-alone' concept, I believe there is consensus that transnational criminal law is a subject matter crying out for compilation, reflection and considered discourse.

It is with this background that I am delighted to introduce this *Handbook of Transnational Criminal Law*, which provides a comprehensive, focused and methodical reflection on transnational criminal law. I am certain that a grateful audience of academics, criminal law practitioners, policy makers and legislators will join me in welcoming it.

An immediate and obvious advantage of the *Handbook* is that it will have broad appeal for varied reasons to different readers. For those who teach and write in this area it will be an invaluable reference point. Practitioners will have a concise but substantive tool which will provide critical background information to interpret the relevant treaties and related legislation and to give context to individual cases. The same is true for policy makers and legislators called upon to implement the international instruments or to enhance domestic regimes by using best practice and accepted measures from the international sphere. And for those of us who labour at the international level, it highlights past achievements and sets important goals for future work.

In essence, to replicate the phrase used by Neil Boister in his contribution, to all these different audiences the book will bring 'transnational criminal law clearly into view'.

The book canvasses concepts and regulation, procedure and substance. The survey of underlying concepts and 'regulatory' regimes is an important and comprehensive one which considers the basic principles, as well as the contributions of the United Nations and regional bodies. It is refreshing to see proper emphasis on the latter – the part played by regional groupings and institutes – given their increasingly important role. This part of the *Handbook* also gives much-needed attention to the human rights component of transnational criminal law instruments – the progression of thinking over time and the challenges that remain.

All the key components of procedure are addressed including a clear and precise discussion of the complex world of jurisdiction. Being a self-identified 'international cooperation geek' and having spent many years in practice in that field, I am particularly pleased to see the excellent review on modern extradition, mutual assistance and the complicated world of asset confiscation. And importantly, the far-reaching and often overlooked area of police cooperation receives rare notice and consideration.

Finally, the impressive survey of the various forms of transnational crime cannot be over-emphasized. I was a member of the Canadian delegation for the negotiation of the Transnational Organized Crime Convention, and one of the most striking points of the early discussions was the complete lack of agreement on the definition or 'face' of transnational organized crime. It is the reality which drove the adoption of the formula used to define the scope of application in the Convention and led to the inclusion of Protocols. From this practical experience I know that it is not possible to produce a compendium of transnational crime; and even if you did, it would be outdated before it was printed. In that context, one of the accomplishments of this *Handbook* is the excellent, in-depth survey of some of the most significant transnational crime/criminal activity, including those subjects which were ultimately identified for the Protocols and areas such as the environment and cultural property which do not receive sufficient attention. Through its content the *Handbook* brings together, in one place, detailed examinations of the prominent forms of transnational crime and the legal frameworks associated with the same.

On a personal note, I am happy to see the prominence accorded throughout the text to the work of my former office, the United Nations Office on Drugs and Crime, given its unique role in the field of transnational criminal law. Not only has this been in the form of pioneering work in past decades, but also the contribution of the term 'transnational crime' by one of its predecessor organizations – the Crime Prevention and Criminal Justice Branch. I cannot help but give special notice to colleagues from UNODC – present and former – who have contributed their direct and practical experience to the *Handbook*.

Since the closing days of the last century, we have seen technological advances which make our world a much smaller place. This has created a global atmosphere which is highly conducive for progress but also serves as a great 'incubator' for transnational crime and criminal groups. The challenges to an effective response are multiple and complex. It appears clear that improvement in suppressing transnational crime – let alone success – will come only with a coordinated international response that includes the adoption of treaty provisions and implementation of best practice, along with efficient measures for international cooperation. We are a long way from achieving that goal. However, this *Handbook of Transnational Criminal Law* represents a positive step forward on the right path. With its accumulated wealth of information and the contributions from academics and practitioners alike, it provides a much-needed resource to guide future progress in responding to the urgent threat posed by transnational crime and criminals, in our ever shrinking world. I can enthusiastically endorse it to a waiting audience.

Kimberly Prost
Ombudsperson
United Nations Security Council Al-Qaida Sanctions Committee

Acknowledgements

The editors are very grateful to Judge Kimberly Prost for taking the time from her busy schedule to write the Foreword. We are also grateful to Erika Schollum for carrying out an initial copy-edit of the work and Mel Dyer, Ian Howe, Mark Sapwell and everyone else from Routledge, with whom it has been a pleasure to work. We remain responsible for all the errors that may be found in the book.

Abbreviations

ACTA	Anti-Counterfeiting Trade Agreement
ACTIP	ASEAN Convention on Trafficking in Persons
AFSJ	Area of Freedom, Security and Justice
AML	anti- money laundering
AMMTC	ASEAN Ministerial Meeting on Transnational Crime
APGML	Asia/Pacific Group on Money Laundering
ARIS	Asset Recovery Intelligence System
ASEAN	Association of South East Asian Nations
ASI	Anti-Slavery International
AU	African Union
AUCPCC	African Union Convention on Preventing and Combating Corruption
BCN	biological, chemical or nuclear weapons
Benelux	Belgium Netherlands Luxembourg
BMR	(EU) Border Measures Regulation
CBD	Convention on Biological Diversity
CCAMLR	Commission for the Conservation of Antarctic Living Marine Resources
CCPCJ	(UN) Commission on Crime Prevention and Criminal Justice
CEDAW	Convention on the Elimination of All Forms of Discrimination against Women
CFATF	Caribbean Financial Action Task Force
CFT	countering the financing of terrorism
CICAD	Inter-American Drug Abuse Control Commission.
CITES	Convention on International Trade in Endangered Species of Wild Fauna and Flora
CJEU	Court of Justice of the European Union
CND	(UN) Commission on Narcotic Drugs
CoE	Council of Europe
COP	Conference of the Parties
CoSP	Conference of States Parties
COSPOL	Comprehensive Operational Strategic Planning for the Police
CRC	Convention on the Rights of the Child
CS	civil society
DELC	(UNEP) Division of Environmental Law and Conventions
DOJ	(US) Department of Justice
DPA	Department of Political Affairs
DPKO	Department for Peacekeeping Operations

DSU	(WTO) Dispute Settlement Understanding
EAG	Eurasian Group (on money laundering)
EAW	European Arrest Warrant
EBN	economic benefit of noncompliance
ECHR	European Convention on Human Rights
ECOSOC	(UN) Economic and Social Council
ECOWAS	Economic Community of West African States
ECT	environmental courts and tribunals
ECtHR	European Court of Human Rights
EEW	European Evidence Warrant
EEZ	exclusive economic zone
EIO	European Investigation Order
ELOs	Europol Liaison Officers
EMMI	Euregional Multimedia Information Exchange
EP	European Parliament
EPICC	Euregional Police Information Coordination Centre
EPPO	European Public Prosecutors Office
ESAAMLG	Eastern and Southern Africa Anti-Money Laundering Group
EU	European Union
EUCFR	EU Charter of Fundamental Rights
Eurojust	EU Agency for Criminal Justice
Europol	European Police Agency
EUTR	European Union Timber Regulations
FAST	Federation Against Software Theft
FATF	Financial Action Task Force
FCPA	(US) Foreign Corrupt Practices Act
FDA	(US) Food and Drug Administration
FIU	Financial Intelligence Unit
Frontex	European Border Security Office
FSRBs	FATF Style Regional Anti- money Laundering Bodies
FTAs	free trade agreements
G8	Group of Eight Industrialised Nations
GA	(UN) General Assembly
GAFISUD	The Financial Action Task Force on Money Laundering in South America
GATT	General Agreement on Tariffs and Trade
GIABA	Inter Governmental Action Group against Money Laundering in West Africa
GMOs	genetically modified organisms
GRECO	Group of States against Corruption
HCFCs	hydrochlorofluorocarbons
HSC	High Seas Convention
HVTs	High Value Targets
IACAC	Inter-American Convention against Corruption
IAIS	International Association of Insurance Supervisors
IATG	International Ammunition Technical Guidelines
ICAR	International Centre for Asset Recovery
ICC	International Criminal Court
ICCPR	International Covenant on Civil and Political Rights

ICCWC	International Consortium Combating Wildlife Crime
ICESCR	International Covenant on Economic, Social and Cultural Rights
ICIR	(Rwanda) International Commission of Inquiry
ICJ	International Court of Justice
ICPC	International Criminal Police Commission
ICRC	International Committee of the Red Cross
ICRG	International Co-operation Review Group
ICTR	International Criminal Tribunal for Rwanda
ICTY	International Criminal Tribunal for the former Yugoslavia
IGO	inter-governmental organisation
IHL	international humanitarian law
ILC	International Law Commission
ILPA	(Australia) Illegal Logging Prohibition Act
IMF	International Monetary Fund
IMO	International Maritime Organization
INCB	International Narcotics Control Board
INECE	International Network for Environmental Compliance and Enforcement
Interpol	International Criminal Police Organization
IP	intellectual property
IPOS	Intellectual Property Office of Singapore
IPR	intellectual property rights
IPT	Intellectual Property Theft
ISACS	International Small Arms Control Standards
ISPAC	International Scientific and Professional Advisory Council
ISPs	internet service providers
ITTA	International Tropical Timber Agreement
ITTO	International Tropical Timber Organization
ITU	International Telecommunications Union
IUU	illegal, unreported and unregulated (fishing)
JCE	joint criminal enterprise
JHA	justice and home affairs
JHTs	Joint hit Teams
JIT	Joint Investigation Team
LIBE	(European Parliament) Committee on Civil Liberties, Justice and Home Affairs
LN	League of Nations
MARPOL	International Convention for the Prevention of Pollution from Ships
MEA	Multilateral Environment Agreement
MENAFATF	Middle East and North Africa Financial Action Task Force
MERCOSUR	Mercado Común del Sur (Southern Common Market)
MERs	Mutual Evaluation Reports
MESICIC	Mechanism for the Implementation of the Inter-American Convention against Corruption
MLA	mutual legal assistance
MLAT	mutual legal assistance treaty
MONEYVAL	The Council of Europe Committee of Experts on the Evaluation of Anti-Money Laundering Measures and the Financing of Terrorism
MoU	Memorandum of Understanding

MPAA	Motion Picture Association of America
MR	mutual recognition
NCBs	National Central Bureaus
NCCTs	non- cooperating countries and territories
NeBeDeAgPol	Chiefs of Police in the border regions of The Netherlands, Belgium and Germany
NESTs	National Environmental Security Task Forces
NGO	non-governmental organisation
NRA	(US) National Rifle Association
OAS	Organization of American States
ODS	ozone-depleting substances
ODSR	(Canada) Ozone-depleting Substances Regulations
OECD	Organisation for Economic Cooperation and Development
OEPA	Canadian Environmental Protection Act
OHCHR	Office of the High Commissioner for Human Rights
OIC	Organisation of Islamic Cooperation
OLAF	European Anti-Fraud Office
OSCE	Organisation for Security and Cooperation in Europe
PCIJ	Permanent Court of International Justice
PD	prisoner's dilemma
PEPs	politically exposed persons
PG	Public Goods
RICO	Racketeer Influenced and Corrupt Organizations Act
RSPCA	Royal Society for the Prevention of Cruelty to Animals
SAARC	South Asian Association for Regional Cooperation
SADC	Southern African Development Community
SARPCCO	Southern African Regional Police Chiefs Cooperation Organisation
SARs	Suspicious Activity Reports
SCSL	Special Court for Sierra Leone
SDOMD	SAARC Drug Offences Monitoring Desk
SEC	(US) Securities and Exchange Commission
SFO	(UK) Serious Fraud Office
SIS	Schengen Information System
SIT	Special Investigative Technique
SOFAs	Status of Forces Agreements
STOMD	SAARC Terrorist Offences Monitoring Desk
TCLC	transnational criminal law convention
TEU	Treaty on European Union
TFEU	Treaty on the Functioning of the European Union
TIP	trafficking in persons
TOC	transnational organized crime
TRIPS	(WTO Agreement on) Trade-Related Aspects of Intellectual Property Rights'
UG	Ultimatum Game
UNCAC	UN Convention against Corruption
UNCLOS	UN Convention on the Law of the Sea
UNCND	UN Commission on Narcotic Drugs
UNDCP	UN Drug Control Programme

UNEP	United Nations Environment Programme
UNESCO	UN Educational, Scientific and Cultural Organisation
UNHCR	UN High Commissioner for Refugees
UNICRI	UN Interregional Crime and Justice Research Institute
UNIDROIT	International Institute for the Unification of Private Law
UNODC	UN Office on Drugs and Crime
UNOWA	UN Regional Office For West Africa
UNTOC	UN Convention against Transnational Organized Crime
UPR	Universal Periodic Review
USPTO	US Patent and Trademark Office
VCRs	video cassette recorders
WACI	West African Coast Initiative
WCO	World Customs Organisation
WGB	Working Group on Bribery
WHO	World Health Organization
WMD	weapons of mass destruction
WTO	World Trade Organization

Introduction

Goal and definition

This *Handbook* is a collection of short chapters by experts in their particular fields on the legal regimes that make up transnational criminal law. It is not dedicated to the criminology of transnational organised crime, the policy responses to transnational crime, or the study of transnational law enforcement.[1] Although the chapter authors in differing degree touch on many of these topics, it is primarily a book about the legal rules, both the international frameworks and the national implementing legislation, that make up the normative skeleton of the system that attempts to suppress harmful activity that crosses borders or threatens to do so.

The notion that certain norms and institutions dealing with transnational crime relate to each other in a loose system is a premise of the investigation of the system of transnational criminal law. One of the main purposes of gathering these chapters together is to try to clarify what transnational criminal law is, in order to bring this system of law into focus. Those who enforce these rules or study their policy provenance or social consequences often say very little about the rules themselves. This book aims to correct that imbalance. Transnational criminal law still adheres to the modernist notion that crime is a technical problem amenable to technical solutions developed and implemented by technical specialists working for the state. However, the tools are normative rather than scientific – general proscriptions on behaviour and prescriptions for procedure are given normative flesh by technical specialists through the high-church doctrine of international legal cooperation and the low-church doggerel of police cooperation.

We have not been prescriptive about the foundational concept, transnational criminal law. The concept of transnational criminal law is in a nascent phase; many of the chapter authors, while concerned with the legal response to transnational crime, do not share a common vision of transnational criminal law. However, the *Handbook* does try to drive a wedge between the material discussed by the various authors of the constituent chapters of this *Handbook*, and international criminal law in a strict sense. There is little here about crimes such as aggression, war crimes, crimes against humanity or genocide, except discussion of situations where transnational criminal law is weak and can be effectively complemented by

---

1   See, for examples, F. Allum and S. Gilmour (eds), *The Routledge Handbook of Transnational Organized Crime*, Abingdon: Routledge, 2012; P. Reichel and J.S. Albanese (eds), *Handbook of Transnational Crime and Justice* (2nd edn), Thousand Oaks, CA: Sage Publications, 2014; J.R. Richards, *Transnational Criminal Organizations, Cybercrime and Money Laundering: A Handbook for Auditors, Law Enforcement Officers, and Financial Investigators*, Boca Raton, FL: CRC Press, 1999.

prosecution for these crimes in international tribunals. We recognise that the difference between international criminal law in this strict sense and transnational criminal law is contestable – genocide and human trafficking arguably sit on the same political continuum – but our point is that both the political actors engaged in responding and the institutional means of response are distinct. The driver of transnational criminal law is the practical difficulty of overcoming the limitations of sovereignty through cooperation against harmful activity that affects a given state but occurs in part or whole beyond the state's territory. This cooperation occurs in different forms, but the two main modes are substantive and procedural cooperation.

Organisational structure of the *Handbook*

This *Handbook* brings together authors writing on their own specific areas of expertise – substantive transnational crime or procedure – within a structure that tries to sew their work together into a systematic whole. These chapters constitute short introductions to each specialist area. In a reverse of the usual order of examination, this book sets out the procedural modes for cooperation among states in regard to transnational crime generally, then examines specific substantive crimes in which these procedural modes are used (and, in addition, examines specific forms of cooperation peculiar to those crimes).

Part I of the book, however, is dedicated to introductory matters. It deals with concepts and different levels of regulation. The opening chapter by Neil Boister is on the concept of transnational criminal law. It suggests an inherently dualistic structure for transnational criminal law determined mainly by the clash between sovereign concerns about control of crime and about territorial integrity, but also explores other areas of transnational law-making, the rise of soft transnational criminal law, and the lack of a coherent set of principles to guide the application of justice in the transnational criminal arena. Chapter 2, Rob Currie's chapter on human rights in transnational criminal law, focuses on the tension between effective cooperation in crime suppression and protecting the human rights of those individuals caught up in it. He examines how the 'silos' of transnational criminal law and international human rights law have begun to break down in recent decades, but explores how integration of procedural protections for investigated/accused persons has been piecemeal and subject to resistance by states. Chapter 3 is meant as an antidote to rule fixation. Examining transnational crime from an interdisciplinary perspective, James Sheptycki seeks to dissolve the assumptions on which much of the law examined in this book is built and to show that social and political scientists have exposed the contested nature of concepts like 'transnational crime'. His message is that those concerned with the system of transnational criminal law should understand that the concepts in the family of transnational crime – which serve as the subjects of many of the chapters of this book – are not value neutral but are rather terms of governance. Focusing on the institutional development of the system, Sławomir Redo illustrates in Chapter 4 that historical experience in drug control, suppression of the slave trade and then more recently transnational organised crime has resulted in certain modes of cooperation being adopted at different times in the incremental and piecemeal evolution of the system. In what is essentially a history of the UN's involvement in the suppression of transnational crime, he also asks some philosophical questions about the fundamental possibilities of effective coordination against transnational crime. Chapter 5 by Valsamis Mitsilegas, the final contribution to the introductory part of the book, explores the regional dimension of transnational criminal law-making. Given its prominence in the field, it is not surprising that development within Europe through the Council of Europe and then the European Union is the main subject.

However, he also examines the regional activities of organisations like the Financial Action Task Force (FATF) to show how the regional underpins the global in the taking of significant steps against transnational crime.

Part II of the book is dedicated to modes of procedural cooperation commonly used in the suppression of transnational crime. As noted, this is deliberate on our part: discussing them first avoids meaningless repetition of general procedural forms of cooperation in each chapter discussing substantive crimes, and suggests that these procedural modes of cooperation are in fact the main technical goals of the system. Chapter 6, Roger Clark's chapter on jurisdiction, covers some of the most important principles underpinning transnational criminal law. Using the 2010 Beijing Convention on the Suppression of Unlawful Acts Relating to International Civil Aviation as an explanatory device, Clark analyses how the obligations and entitlements regarding the exercise of jurisdiction by states are typically laid out in the context of suppression conventions. Police cooperation is critical for most enforcement action against transnational crime, and in Chapter 7 Saskia Hufnagel and Carole McCartney place personal contacts at the heart of police cooperation. Although they sketch the international framework provided by the suppression conventions, within the Council of Europe and in the more advanced EU measures, they note that officers will take advantage of whatever choice of measures is available to them as a platform for cooperation. They make the point that the establishment of policing networks outside governance and accountability frameworks leads to inevitable questions about supervision and human rights adherence. In Chapter 8, John Vervaele examines the more formal modes of legal assistance in the transnational gathering of evidence to be used at trial. Concerned with the foundational procedures for this mode of cooperation, he shows how mutual legal assistance is shifting in some regions to mutual recognition. Yet still the problems remain the same – too much concern with the necessity of satisfying the prescripts of domestic authority, too little concern with either helping other states or ensuring justice through defence rights. In Chapter 9 on asset recovery, Charlie Monteith and Pedro Pereira concentrate not on the international structure enabling this procedure, but on the practical problems involved in working with these procedures to achieve recovery. They ponder the steps in the investigation process, emphasising the problems of establishing jurisdiction, of planning an investigation and gathering information, of managing the evolving flow of information, and establishing the personal trust necessary to bring the process to a successful conclusion. The final chapter in Part II, Joanna Harrington's exposition on extradition in Chapter 10, illustrates the difficulties of finding general agreement on this, the thorniest issue in transnational criminal law. The focus of her short history of the law of extradition is on the nature of the obligations that states undertake in order to extradite, controversial exceptions to these obligations such as the political offence exception, and the attempts to establish exceptions to these exceptions such as the carve-out in some agreements from the political offence exception in regard to terroristic offences.

Part III of the book turns to substantive crimes. These crimes are grouped according to the nature of the activity undertaken rather than the interest harmed, because what distinguishes transnational crime is not so much the level of harm threatened but the peculiar difficulties involved in enforcing the law extraterritorially occasioned by the transnational nature of the conduct involved.

The first section deals with migration and exploitation crimes. In Chapter 11, Tom Obokata traces the early roots of human trafficking, but his main focus is on the substance of the Human Trafficking Protocol, which he measures against the yardstick of the 3P obligations – prevention, prosecution and protection – and finds it to be wanting. He advocates strongly that these inadequacies must be supplemented by human rights law, a point that can be made more generally about transnational criminal law as a whole. In Chapter 12 Anne Gallagher discusses the fairly recent shift to criminalisation of migrant smuggling through the Migrant Smuggling Protocol in order to stem unauthorised immigration. She places this apparently novel regime in its broader context of rights and obligations relating to migrants in human rights law, the law of the sea and refugee law, and shows how these older rules serve to restrain state response to migrant smuggling. In Chapter 13, Lindsay Buckingham points out the congruities and incongruities of the process of criminalisation of child sex tourism through human rights treaties protecting children's rights such as the Convention on the Rights of the Child and its Optional Protocol. She illustrates that what has resulted are strong obligations to criminalise internal and transnational sex tourism, but what is absent is the institutional infrastructure now common in UNODC-administered treaties to review implementation of these promises.

The second section of Part III is devoted to commodity crimes, arguably the most basic forms of transnational criminality. The most prominent of these and arguably the keystone of transnational criminal law are the crimes enforcing drug prohibition. In Chapter 14, Bernard Leroy describes the evolution of the system of international drug control from its roots in the response to the Chinese opium problem, through the concerns of the League period with regulating licit production and supply of drugs to prevent diversion, to the more recent concern with suppression of the illicit traffic. He emphasises limitation of licit production and supply for medical and scientific purposes, and criticises various developments that threaten to undermine the integrity of prohibition such as harm reduction and legalisation. In Chapter 15, Catherine Drummond and Anthony Cassimatis examine the legal standards governing illicit and lawful transfers of small arms and light weapons, highlighting the links between lawful and unlawful behaviour in this regard. The major failing in this area has been the inability to regulate the licit trade so as to prevent diversion into the illicit traffic, something which they point out has been remedied by the recently negotiated Arms Trade Treaty. A form of trafficking which has been given fairly heavy media exposure recently, trafficking in cultural property, is, according to Arianna Visconti in Chapter 16, an area of law plagued with uncertainty and ambiguity. This is reflected in the grey market for antiquities and the penal minimalism of the international responses that have been developed since 1945. While the conventions include provisions aimed at fighting cultural property trafficking, she illustrates that they lean heavily towards indirect obligations to take measures to protect or vindicate private rights in cultural property. Against the background of detailed descriptions of the damage caused by the illegal trade and trafficking of natural resources, in Chapter 17 Rob White provides an overview of the transnational environmental crimes that involve theft and/or trafficking of vulnerable resources including illegal, unregulated and unauthorised fishing, illegal logging and the traffic in protected species. His fundamental point is that the key international environmental instruments designed to protect species are only very broadly penal in nature because they do not detail substantive offences, punishments or modes of procedure in the suppression of these crimes. In Chapter 18 Jay Batongbacal discusses the steps taken both internationally and domestically to criminalise all forms of dumping of pollution. The chapter traverses a number of these areas – the control of marine dumping under MARPOL and London, terrestrial pollution under Basel, atmospheric pollution under Montreal – with reference to implementing criminal and administrative laws from a selection of states, to illustrate the nature and scope of dumping of pollution as a transnational environmental crime. In Chapter 19, Henning Grosse Ruse-Khan examines the controversial issue of criminalisation of transnational intellectual property (IP) violation and the failure to achieve normative consensus in this regard. Pointing out the differing rationales for criminalisation (protection of property versus safety and quality of the product) and the territorial nature of IP protection, he examines the faltering efforts through TRIPS to achieve criminalisation of IP violation globally, and the attempts by states with strong IP lobbies to step way beyond TRIPS through the ACTA agreement, the gold standard for IP protection through criminalisation.

The third section of substantive offences deals with crimes that fall under a broad heading, facilitative and organisational crimes – crimes that in some way make possible transnational criminal activity. In Chapter 20, Bill Gilmore is at some pains to point out the relative novelty of the global criminalisation of money laundering through the agency of the 1988 Vienna Convention. He sets out the rationale for the offence as a response to an attempt to go after the money and his initial focus is on the criminalisation provisions of Article 3 of the 1988 Convention as a radical departure from previous law, but he also points to the allied procedural mechanisms for asset forfeiture which in many ways were the main target. He shows how subsequent treaties built on this precedent, and how they evolved in an interplay with the soft law of the FATF's recommendations. In Chapter 21, John Hatchard traces the evolution of international measures against corruption, the key facilitative transnational crime. He shows how they are characterised by a proliferation of offences, uneven measures for international cooperation against corruption, and the slow growth in attention in regard to the monitoring of implementation of these rules. His main subject is the UNCAC, which as he notes provides for guidance in regard to prevention and for obligations on asset recovery, perhaps its most important feature. In Chapter 22 on piracy and the SUA offences, Douglas Guilfoyle examines one of the earliest crimes that can be characterised as an extra-national method for facilitating other criminal activities (robbery and violence). Using the recent proliferation of anti-piracy efforts arising from the upswing in activity by Somali pirates as a springboard, he explores the historically confused development of the crime of piracy arising from state practice, and the gaps that were to some extent filled by the SUA Convention (and its 2005 Protocol) which, as Guilfoyle compellingly demonstrates, provides more coherent and effective suppression obligations in many respects. Cybercrime is at the cutting edge of facilitative transnational crimes because the use of digital devices makes possible other crimes, but as Chris Ram makes clear in Chapter 23, it raises many familiar problems of definition, jurisdiction and law enforcement. Because of the amorphous nature of the concept he engages in an extensive discussion of the struggle to demarcate the offence with a workable definition. His history of the efforts to regulate charts forerunner legislation, the slow emergence of the Budapest Convention and the debate around a global instrument. The chapter analyses the substances of the crimes themselves and also touches on cybercrime's most difficult issue, the enforcement of jurisdiction, where the choice despite arguments otherwise is starkly between consent or violation. Ben Saul's Chapter 24 examines the politically fraught treaty and domestic provisions for the suppression of terrorism. After establishing that the roots of the offence lie in the nineteenth century's ambivalent response of states to political violence, where a balance was achieved between exceptional measures and safeguards against abuse, he develops the theme that this balance has slowly been upset by subsequent efforts against terrorism. His account sets out the struggle around definition of the crime and the use of the sectoral treaties as a functional response, the failure to draft a comprehensive international treaty, and the UN Security Council's eruption into quasi-legislative mode criminalising terrorism. In Chapter 25, Andreas Schloenhardt examines the UN Convention against Transnational Organised Crime, which is, he suggests, the most significant milestone not so much in the fight against organised crime as in the fight against criminal organisations. His main focus is on the substantive provisions for criminalisation and the definition of an organised criminal group, which relies extensively on the definition of serious crimes as those carrying a penalty of four years' or more deprivation of liberty in domestic law. Schloenhardt's survey reveals that the authors of the convention neither agreed on what transnational organised crime is nor revealed any genuine desire to understand the organisation and operation of organised crime.

Part IV of the book, dedicated to implementation, consists of just one chapter, Chapter 26 on implementation of the system by Yvon Dandurand and Vivienne Chin. Their verdict is that more than a century of treaty-making in an attempt to suppress transnational crime has produced very poor results. Exploring the barriers to implementation, effective machinery for reporting implementation and compliance, and mechanisms for assessment, they conclude that international cooperation may be the goal, but it is not the reality. Their discussion of the highly complex reasons for this reveals a range of significant technical and political barriers, poor monitoring and a lack of any real consequence for non-compliance.

Thematic structure

Each of these chapters is by nature of the subject matter unique and reflects the author's own views. However, at the risk of over-generalisation, we suggest that a number of different thematic concerns reveal themselves.

- One of the concerns of the authors is to identify and examine the normative agendas that determine the kind of cooperation that eventuates in regard to the suppression of certain activities. While some accept the rhetoric of global consensus in the suppression of all forms of transnational criminal activity, others expose the push by certain states for ever heavier penal responses to certain activities, and the tense and unpredictable dynamics this can produce.
- If there is a dominant theme to this book, it is the highlighting of the turn to criminalisation at a transnational level as a first, not last, resort. Various authors examine not just the definition of the criminal activity or process with which they are concerned, but the process of coming to that definition. They expose, for example, that many of the substantive crimes are defined in an expansive way to reach beyond transnational conduct (they do not insist on a transnational element) to purely domestic activity, and examine why this expansive choice has been made. A technical issue which is highlighted less frequently is the tendency of some offences to depend on special or ulterior forms of intention, in order to distinguish the behaviour as more serious than common crimes and thus deserving of inclusion within these special legal regimes.
- Another identifiable theme is the establishment of international cooperation as a goal and as a reality. Many of the chapters expose the tension between broad lowest common denominator multilateralism and narrower bases for agreement on stronger criminal sanctions and extensive obligations to cooperate, which are then imposed through access to markets, aid and so forth, on third states. Many of these chapters expose the disjunction between the rigidity of the law, and the informality of the practice of transnational law enforcement.
- A prominent concern is to identify the institutional forms cooperation has taken and the reasons why this has occurred. One of the questions the book prompts is that if these distinct areas of transnational criminal activity are so heterogenous, then why has the response of transnational criminal law been so homogenous? These chapters suggest that an explanation can be found in the necessity of separating lawful from unlawful behaviour

through legal definition, the limited options available for formalising international co-operation (particularly if it is to be broadly based), the continuity of expertise, the entrenchment of certain kinds of institutional forms, and perhaps path-dependency.

Restriction on length has made it difficult for the chapters in this book to scrutinise a number of areas deserving of closer study. They do not test the factual claims made to justify criminalisation, or examine the effectiveness of implementation, or confront the technically driven decontextualisation of suppression activity from existing relevant legal rules and obligations. The certainty of transnational criminal law is offered, and grasped, as a solution to uncertainty about the actual nature of the factual threat, about implementation, and about the quality of the justice it metes out.

In the end, however, this book picks up the ragged ends of the cloth from which all this law was spun, and offers the argument that if this field was ever properly labelled 'international criminal law', that time is well past. We suggest that, despite the blurriness of the boundaries and the confusion as to goals and outcomes, there is something distinct, systemic and fascinating to be observed here. The work of all of the authors here is offered as a jumping-off point, into a stream whose course is rapid and unpredictable.

Part I
Concepts and regulation

1

The concept and nature of transnational criminal law

Neil Boister

Introduction

'Transnational criminal law' describes a category of domestic crimes established through treaty obligations in multilateral conventions such as the 1988 Vienna Convention[1] – the so-called 'treaty crimes'[2] or 'crimes of international concern'.[3] States enforce their own criminal laws, thus expressing their sovereignty; and yet because of sovereignty, they must rely on the sovereignty of other states if they are to enforce their laws against transnational criminals that operate extraterritorially. Through the crime suppression conventions states parties embrace tortious or delictual treaty obligations to criminalise the activities specified in those conventions and to adopt procedural provisions that enable them to cooperate with other states which seek to establish and exercise jurisdiction over the criminals concerned.

The label transnational criminal law provides a doctrinal match for the criminological term transnational crime, while making it possible to distinguish this category of criminal law from international criminal law in a strict sense, i.e. that criminal law applicable in international criminal tribunals where individual criminal responsibility is directly applied under international law. The orthodox view was that crimes with a transnational element fell within international criminal law in an undifferentiated sense.[4] Although transnational

1 United Nations Convention against Illicit Traffic in Narcotic Drugs and Psychotropic Substances, 20 December 1988, 1582 UNTS 95; in force 11 November 1990.
2 See N. Boister, 'Transnational Criminal Law?', *European Journal of International Law,* 2003, vol. 14, p. 953; N. Boister, *An Introduction to Transnational Criminal Law*, Oxford: Oxford University Press, 2012, pp. 13–23.
3 The term used by M.C. Bassiouni, 'An Appraisal of the Growth and Developing Trends of International Criminal Law', in J. Dugard and C. van den Wyngaert (eds.), *International Criminal Law and Procedure*, 1996, Aldershot: Dartmouth, p. 85.
4 See M.C. Bassiouni, 'The Sources and Content of International Criminal Law: A Theoretical Framework', M.C. Bassiouni (ed.), *1 International Criminal Law: Crimes*, Ardsley on Hudson: Transnational, 2nd edn, 1999, p. 13 et seq.

criminal law was originally used in a much broader sense to include all forms of criminal law with an international dimension, including international criminal law in the strict sense,[5] this narrower sense is now fairly well accepted.[6]

The view taken here is that there is a distinct 'system' of transnational criminal law, with a distinct normative existence. Its principal distinguishing feature is its indirect nature, which contrasts with the direct nature of international criminal law, a reflection of the fact that it protects limited transnational values and interests and that, unlike international criminal law, it does not serve as an instrument of a Grotian community of states where communitarian values dominate but is at most an instrument of a loosely aligned Vattelian society of states where sovereignty and self-interest are the dominant values and laws of coordination the result.[7] The degree of coordination varies from crime to crime, depending on the threat of harm or actual harm perceived to be offered by the particular conduct concerned, balanced against complex factors such as vested societal interests in carrying out that conduct and the spatial impact of the conduct.

This chapter explores the concept of transnational criminal law by trying to identify its sources and delimit its boundaries. The first part examines the basic elements of the concept. The second part examines whether transnational criminal law can accurately be termed a legal system. The third section asks whether it is possible to expand the transnational legal space. The fourth part considers whether transnational criminal law is a pluralist legal order. The final section asks who benefits from transnational criminal law.

The basic elements of the concept of transnational criminal law revisited

The starting point is the notion of transnational crime, a term coined by the UN Crime Prevention and Criminal Justice Branch to 'identify certain criminal phenomena transcending international borders, transgressing the laws of several states or having an impact on another country'.[8] This concept has been developed in Article 3 on the 'Scope of Application' of the United Nations Convention against Transnational Organized Crime (UNTOC),[9] which applies the Convention to a range of offences 'transnational in nature', that are:

> committed in more than one State; (b) . . . committed in one State but a substantial part of its preparation, planning, direction or control takes place in another State; (c) . . . committed in one State but involves an organised criminal group that engages in criminal activities in more than one State; or (d) . . . committed in one State but has substantial effects in another State.

---

5   A. Eser and O. Lagodny (eds), *Principles and Procedures for a New Transnational Criminal Law*, Freiburg im Breisgau: Max Planck Institute, 1992, generally.

6   See R. Cryer, 'The Doctrinal Foundations of International Criminalization' in M.C. Bassiouni (ed.), 1 *International Criminal Law: Sources, Subjects and Contents*, Dordrecht: Nijhoff, 3rd edn, 2008, p. 108; R. Cryer, H. Friman, D. Robinson and E. Wilmshurst, *An Introduction to International Criminal Law and Procedure*, Cambridge: Cambridge University Press, 2nd edn, 2010, p. 5; R.J. Currie, *International and Transnational Criminal Law*, Toronto: Irwin, 2010, p. 19; C. Kreβ, 'International Criminal Law' in R. Wolfrum (ed.), *Max Planck Encyclopedia of Public International Law: online edition*, 2009 update, para. 6.

7   Boister, 'Transnational Criminal Law?', pp. 967–974.

8   G. Mueller, 'Transnational Crime: Definitions and Concepts', in P. Williams and D. Vlassis (eds), *Combating Transnational Crime*, Milan/London: ISPAC/Frank Cass, 2001, p. 13.

9   Opened for signature 16 December 2000, 2225 UNTS 209; in force 29 September 2003.

Evidence of such a transnational element provides what Nadelmann terms a 'transnational hook'[10] used to convince states that they should participate in a multilateral convention aimed at suppressing the particular activity by criminalising it. These 'suppression conventions' and resultant domestic law and practice together create distinct 'global prohibition regimes' on drugs, money laundering, corruption and so forth.

Is a crossborder element in the definition of the transnational crimes in these conventions necessary? Somewhat paradoxically, the answer is no. The suppression conventions include within their scope behaviour that (i) actually crosses borders or (ii) has substantial effects in other states. Nadelmann's critical insight is that the practice of states as reflected in the suppression conventions (iii) also includes local crime that has only the most tenuous potential extraterritorial impact but which is of transboundary moral concern sufficient to include this behaviour within the scope of treaty obligations obliging its criminalisation.[11] As Scott points out, transnational issues also include:

> phenomena not involving physical acts or events across borders that are nonetheless understood by relevant participants and/or observers as 'transnational' situations because of how the issue has come to be constructed by interacting normative (legal, policy, and moral) discourses as transcending . . . national frontiers.[12]

When Philip Jessup coined the term 'transnational law' he was concerned with a legal space that included actions and events that transcended boundaries.[13] 'Transnational criminal law' conjoins the criminological term 'transnational crime' with Jessup's term 'transnational law'. It is concerned with governance of transnational criminal actions. It involves the indirect suppression by international law through domestic penal law of criminal activities that have (i) actual or (ii) potential transboundary effects or (iii) transboundary moral impacts. Article 3(2) of the 1988 Vienna Convention's obligation on states parties to criminalise the possession and purchase of drugs for non-medical and scientific purposes (i.e. use) is an example of such a cosmopolitan moral concern, generating a legal norm.

Transnational criminal law as a system

The definition of transnational criminal law offered here fits within what Scott has termed 'transnational legalized traditionalism'.[14] It takes Jessup's 'law which regulates actions or events that transcend national frontiers' and includes within its scope those transnational crime-focused public international laws (mainly the rules in the suppression conventions placing obligations on states to enact criminal laws and procedures against transnational crime) and domestic laws (the national criminal laws that implement those treaty obligations), considered both independently and in combination. Describing transnational criminal law as a system suggests a hierarchical system of legal norms with an identifiable legislative source. Yet as defined it consists in an autonomous set of international treaty norms and many

---

10 E. Nadelmann, 'Global Prohibition Regimes: The Evolution of Norms in International Society', *International Organisation*, 1990, vol. 44, p. 479, p. 482.
11 Ibid., p. 525.
12 C. Scott, '"Transnational Law" as Proto-Concept: Three Conceptions', *German Law Journal*, 2009, Vol. 10, p. 859, p. 864.
13 P.C. Jessup, *Transnational Law*, New Haven: Yale University Press, 1956, p. 2.
14 See Scott, 'Transnational Law', pp. 868–872.

autonomous sets of domestic criminal norms with quite distinctive points of authority. Is it more apt to describe transnational criminal law as a non-hierarchical normative area or as a fixed system of norms of similar content, type and purpose?[15] The answer to this question requires a closer look at the horizontal international and vertical national components of transnational criminal law.

The international component: ordering states

The 'horizontal' component of transnational criminal law that orders states not individuals is found within international law. There is no general customary obligation on states to coop- erate against crime (although there is no reason in principle why a custom could not be estab- lished that obliges states to enact a specific offence in national law).[16] Rather states promise to suppress specific crimes in their national laws when they become party to the crime suppres- sion conventions. The legal subject is the state; the remedy for breach is not criminal penalty but state responsibility. States come under pressure from their citizens to coordinate their positions using international law when the efficacy of the system of criminal law under which they live is put into question by the commission of an offence; sympathy for or even horror at conduct within other states does not usually achieve this result.[17]

The consensus of the signatories to these conventions is managed on an ongoing basis through regular meetings of the parties. In theory this permits amendment but this is rare, and incremental normative development occurs within the various prohibition regimes that develop around suppression of a particular activity by periodic negotiation of new treaties. These new treaties frequently borrow agreed substantive and procedural innovations already adopted in older treaties concerned with different crimes. For example, the obligation to criminalise money laundering pioneered in Article 3(1)(b) and (c) of the 1988 Vienna Convention was included in Article 6 of the 2002 UN Convention on Transnational Organized Crime and is now a stock feature of new suppression conventions. Such transfers are rationalised on the basis that the provisions deal either with common features of, or appropriate responses to, different types of crime. This 'normative sharing' gives a similar architecture to many of the conventions, and transposed nationally into domestic law makes for familiar-looking domestic law, thus increasing the integrity of transnational criminal law as a whole. But the international norms do not always determine national norms in a linear fashion; national, regional and global norms interact in a complex and dynamic fashion.

A horizontal international component is a necessary condition of transnational criminal law. What of the horizontal diffusion of criminal law norms from state to state without the agency of a suppression convention?[18] They are not part of transnational criminal law if they

---

15 Ibid.
16 In this regard *US v Arjona* (1887) 120 US 479 appears to establish a customary obligation to punish counterfeiting – see R.S. Clark, 'Reflections on International Criminal Law and Jurisdiction', *Criminal Law Forum*, 2011, vol. 22, p. 519, p. 520, n. 2. There may arguably be a *ius cogens* obligation on non-states parties to the Convention against Torture and Other Cruel, Inhuman or Degrading Treatment or Punishment, 10 December 1984, 1465 UNTS 85, in force 26 June 1987, to enact an offence of torture derived in content from the convention offence.
17 A. Chehtman, *The Philosophical Foundations of Extraterritorial Punishment*, Oxford: Oxford University Press, 2010, p. 78.
18 A common feature of legal development – see W. Twining, *General Jurisprudence*, Cambridge: Cambridge University Press, 2009, pp. 250–251.

are simply the unilateral borrowings by states of norms to address purely national issues rather than issues of transnational conduct, effect or concern, because in that case they are absolutely parochial in nature and do not involve two or more states coordinating their repressive responses. It is arguable, however, that as soon as states coordinate their positions an international ordering exists. In other words, it is the transnational transfer of the norm and the shared purpose of the states involved which distinguishes transnational criminal law; the actual mode of transfer can be a formal legal obligation – a treaty – or some more informal agreement to do so. It is submitted, however, that the agreement must have some legal form – whether multilateral convention, bilateral treaty or soft law – because without it there is no legal framework to these sovereign relations. They are international relations, not law. In actuality, the formal treaty-making methods of a nineteenth-century 'civilised' international society have endured as the main form in which states coordinate their responses to transnational crime.

Domestic offences subject to some form of extraterritorial jurisdiction or international procedural arrangements like extradition or mutual legal assistance are problematic because of the presence of a transnational dimension. Currie's solution is to refer to these 'crimes under domestic law which involve, in some way, more than one state' as 'transnational crimes of domestic concern', which he distinguishes from 'transnational crimes of international concern' falling under transnational criminal law.[19] It is perhaps more accurate to describe the former as national crimes subject to transnational criminal procedures, because coordination through international law does not involve making acts crimes, even indirectly, but is limited to procedural cooperation – or perhaps to label it by its more common name – the law of international cooperation in criminal matters.[20]

The necessity of an international component, however, does not mean that we are really talking about international criminal law, except in the broad sense of criminal law with an indirect international law dimension. The obvious distinctions from international criminal law in a strict sense are that: (i) the right to criminalise remains with the state and unlike international criminal law[21] there is no individual penal responsibility under international law; and (ii) the right to adjudicate remains with the state and there is no international jurisdiction. We lazily talk of the 'crimes' in the suppression conventions but they are not crimes, only obligations to enact crimes couched in broad terms and highly conditioned on compatibility with the general structure and basic principles of the enacting state's domestic law. Nor is there delegation of jurisdiction over transnational crimes to an international criminal court of any kind.[22] States exercise only their own criminal jurisdiction over transnational crimes. While international criminal law suggests a hierarchical legal order established by an international community in order to suppress actions subject to universal opprobrium or threatening the security of the international community,[23] transnational

---

19 Currie, *International and Transnational Criminal Law*, pp. 19–20. His category is in fact broader, including those crimes over which the state takes jurisdiction under qualified/extended territoriality.

20 See Kreβ, 'International Criminal Law', para. 6

21 Art. 25(2), Rome Statute of the International Criminal Court, 17 July 1998, 2187 UNTS 90, in force 1 July 2002.

22 See, for example, Art. 1 of the Rome Statute.

23 See principle 3 of the 'Report of the UNWCC summarising the elements of Crimes Against Humanity in Eight Principles' in UNWCC, *History of the United Nations War Crimes Commission*, London: HMSO, 1948.

criminal law is the product of a non-hierarchical order of formally equal centres of legal authority based on reciprocity, equality and sovereign consent.[24] International criminal law may be trying to shake free of its roots in national law and become autonomously supra-national both in substance and process; but transnational criminal law lags behind, a burden too great for the international community to hoist and one which many states are for pragmatic reasons opposed to it hoisting: they prefer to rely on their own highly developed national criminal justice systems to suppress transnational crime.[25]

Certain extradite or prosecute provisions in the suppression conventions, not of the type triggered by an extradition request which adheres to the model of state coordination, but of the Hague Hijacking Convention[26] type obliging a state party only on the basis that it does not extradite that person, suggest a crime that serves a broader international community interest – perhaps an international crime; but there is an absence of state practice accepting this.[27] The distinction between criminal law emanating from an international community and one in which international law serves as an instrument for coordinating sovereign positions is perhaps better reflected (and understood) by the German distinction of *Internationales Strafrecht* from *Völkerstrafrecht*, the French distinction of *droit pénal international* from *droit international pénal*, and the Spanish distinction of *derecho penal internacional* from *derecho internacional penal*.[28] Continental legal systems correctly identify the criminalising entity as the state.

The two main purposes of the suppression conventions are (a) substantive criminalisation and (b) procedural cooperation.

Substance

The development of a suppression convention has a clear purpose – the suppression through criminal law of certain harmful activities of transnational nature, effect or concern. Consider, for example, preambular paragraph 3 of the 2001 Council of Europe Convention on Cybercrime:[29]

> Convinced of the need to pursue, as a matter of priority, a common criminal policy aimed at the protection of society against cybercrime, *inter alia*, by adopting appropriate legislation . . .

Preambular paragraphs of this kind seldom mention criminalisation specifically, choosing rather to use verbs like 'combating' crime. Yet obligations to criminalise within suppression conventions are a common transnational legislative tool, with roots back into the nineteenth century.

---

24 See R.A. Falk, 'International Jurisdiction: Horizontal and Vertical Conceptions of Legal Order', *Temple Law Quarterly*, 1959, vol. 32, p. 295.
25 I am grateful to Robert Currie for pointing this out.
26 Art. 4(2), Hague Convention for the Suppression of Unlawful Seizure of Aircraft, 16 December 1970; 860 UNTS 105, in force 14 October 1971.
27 Kreβ, 'International Criminal Law', para. 8.
28 See R. Cryer, H. Friman, D. Robinson and E. Wilmshurst, *An Introduction to International Criminal Law and Procedure*, Cambridge: Cambridge University Press, 2010, p. 6.
29 Budapest, 23 November 2001, ETS No 185, in force 1 July 2004.

Obligations to criminalise usually set out a number of material conduct, consequence and/ or circumstance elements coupled with appropriate mental elements. As the system has evolved there has been a shift from definition of the conduct of individual criminals to definition of criminogenic transnational activities, places, situations and organisations, as states struggle to control these spaces and forms. Yet while in some offences transnational conduct is required in the substantive definition of an 'offence', in the main it is excluded so as to enable the laying down of criminal offences that apply to intra- as well as inter-state conduct. When it is required, such as in Article 3(1) of the 1997 Convention on Combating Bribery of Foreign Public Officials in International Business Transactions,[30] which provides that 'bribery of a foreign public official shall be a punishable offence', the transnational element in the definition of a crime is both substantive and also jurisdictional, because it implies an obligation on a state party to establish jurisdiction over activities that occur extraterritorially.

The range of these obligations has been quite broad, from suppressing repugnant conduct heavily invasive of human rights such as trading in slaves[31] to actions *mala prohibitum* such as manufacturing tobacco without a licence.[32] There may arguably be a thicker cosmopolitan consensus to criminalise the former than the latter, but this does not explain why criminalisation of highly repugnant forms of behaviour such as weapons trafficking is much more limited in scope than criminalisation of more innocuous forms of behaviour such as money laundering. Differences of this kind can only be understood through a contextual analysis of the political, social and economic forces that have shaped criminalisation of the particular form of conduct.

In regard to the mental elements of culpability, older provisions such as Article 3 of the 1929 International Convention for the Suppression of Counterfeiting Currency[33] seldom mention *mens rea* – the only mention is 'intentional' participation in paragraph 4 – but more recent provisions such as Article 3(1) of the 1988 Vienna Convention expressly require intention. Offences directed at preventive preemptive criminalisation, such as those in recent anti-terrorist conventions, depend decreasingly on evidence of harmful conduct and place a greater emphasis on special intent.

Procedure

The other main function of the suppression conventions is to make provision for effective procedural cooperation among the states parties in regard to the various 'offences' they contain. These procedural regimes either oblige or permit states parties to establish both territorial and extraterritorial jurisdiction over these 'offences' and then to enforce that jurisdiction through policing and adjudication.

Criminalisation under transnational criminal law is in many ways primarily a means to the establishment of extraterritorial jurisdiction, an instrument to apply the enforcement power of the state against alleged transnational criminals located in other jurisdictions. The

---

30 18 December 1997, 37 ILM 1; in force 15 February 1999.
31 See Art. 1(1) and (6) of the 1926 Slavery Convention, Geneva, 60 LNTS 253; in force 9 March 1927.
32 See Art. 14(1)(a) of the 2012 Protocol to Eliminate Illicit Trade in Tobacco Products, opened for signature 10 January 2013, available at UNTS, http://treaties.un.org/doc/source/signature/2012/CN699E.pdf (accessed 13 November 2013).
33 20 April 1929, [1929] PITSE 3; in force 22 February 1931.

territorial state's interest in enforcement of its laws abroad may lead it to seek to convince the extraterritorial state to permit it to establish its extraterritorial jurisdiction over the particular offence. The suppression conventions provide a multilateral vehicle for the extraterritorial state to agree to permit extraterritorial jurisdiction in regard to specific crimes on recognised grounds.[34] It implicitly agrees to act on the enforcing state's behalf through its own procedural apparatus. Even when the requested state refuses to extradite an alleged offender and on the *aut dedere aut judicare* principle establishes and enforces its own criminal jurisdiction, it still acts on behalf of the other state where the harm was done.

While some of the procedural provisions commonly found in a suppression convention are directed at increasing the efficiency of domestic prosecution, most – extradition, legal assistance, police cooperation – are directed towards international cooperation. They rely heavily on the existing system of regional and bilateral treaties for criminal cooperation between states available against all serious crime. These provisions make it possible for the states parties to apply their laws to help other parties, not to apply the laws of other parties. The extent of the enforcement power granted in a suppression convention will depend on its subject matter. As Clark points out after reviewing the extensive powers for extraterritorial enforcement jurisdiction at sea in the 1884 Convention for the Protection of Submarine Cables[35] (compared to the absence of such powers in regard to other crimes *malum in se* involving homicide):

> Do not underestimate the randomness in all of this: one might think that killing someone is worse than damaging a piece of wire (albeit an expensive one) and others probably ought to be able to board and investigate homicides, but the treaty dealt with cables, not dead people.[36]

The national component: ordering individuals

The 'vertical' component in transnational criminal law involves domestic criminalisation of the specified conduct of individuals and the enactment of allied procedures and provisions for cooperation in regard to those individuals by the states parties to the particular suppression convention. These national criminal laws constitute the goal of the system because they enable suppression of criminal activities domestically, and transnational cooperation in the suppression of criminal activity. The state is left to criminalise and enforce because it is the most effective unit to take these steps; there is no supra-national unit available to do so – only other states.

Methods of implementation vary widely. Some states take legislative action independently of the treaty obligation.[37] Others make the necessary domestic changes before actually

---

34 Chehtman, *Philosophical Foundations*, p. 75.

35 14 March 1884, TS 380, in force 1 May 1888.

36 See R.S. Clark, 'Reflections on International Criminal Law and on Jurisdiction' (2012), p. 13, available at http://camlaw.rutgers.edu/sites/camlaw/files/International%20Criminal%20Law%20 %20Reflections_0.pdf> (accessed 1 April 2014).

37 For example, the United States enacted the Trafficking Victims Protection Act 2000 in the same year as the Protocol to Prevent, Suppress and Punish Trafficking in Persons, Especially Women and Children, supplementing the United Nations Convention against Transnational Organized Crime, 15 November 2000, 2237 UNTS 319, in force 9 September 2003, but out of domestic concerns not international obligation – see S.E. Merry, 'Sex Trafficking and Global Governance in the Context of Pacific Mobility', *Law, Text, Culture*, 2011, vol. 15, p. 187, p. 200.

ratifying the treaty in question. Some directly transpose the treaty formulations. Others do so indirectly, decoding the essence of the norm to fit national structures, principles and existing criminal laws.[38] The suppression conventions provide a normative outline, but so much space is given to national discretion in implementation as to undo any claim to codification. What results can be characterised as 'conformal' national law, an idiosyncratic representation of different features or elements of the conventions in a number of different pieces of national legislation. These domestic changes are isolated in separate sectors. They do not result in the holistic development of the whole criminal justice systems of all participating states. Political difficulty makes it impossible to agree to general changes to fundamental concepts such as the general principles of criminal law.

The transversal relationship between the vertical and horizontal components

Although distinct in source (agreement v national legislative authority), nature (tortious v criminal) and in terms of subjects (states v individuals), the horizontal international and vertical national components of transnational criminal law can be said to be 'transversal' in combination. To put it another way, the ordering of states at an international level indirectly orders individuals at a national level.

The degree of coordination within particular prohibition regimes has evolved as transnational criminal law has itself evolved through different phases of interstate order. There has, however, been a clear tendency towards a tighter, more punitive system as the policy goal has shifted from the Durkheimian solidarity of the early period (where the emphasis was almost entirely on regulation of licit activity to avoid diversion) to the more recent emphasis on crime control and the Hobbesian problem of order.[39]

Expanding the transnational legal space?

Is there more to transnational criminal law than this synthesis of international obligation and national criminal law? Important national judicial decisions such as *Liangsiriprasert v US*,[40] where the Privy Council held that effects-based jurisdiction could be established over an inchoate conspiracy that had no actual impact on the territory of the state establishing jurisdiction,[41] have normative effects elsewhere.[42] The international provisions for effects jurisdiction in the suppression conventions enable this kind of normative transferability. Is there a dimension to transnational criminal law composed, at least in part, of what Jessup classed as 'other rules' autonomous from international and national sources of legislative authority?[43]

Transnational legal theory seeks to break assumptions like those implicit in the concept of transnational criminal law about the nexus of state and law or the nexus of territory and law. Scott's notion that transnational law also includes 'transnationalized legal decisionism' suggests that transnational criminal law may also consist in national and international

---

38 C. Nowak, 'The Internationalization of Polish Criminal Law: How Polish Law Changed Under the Influence of Globalization', *Crime, Law and Social Change,* 2013, vol. 59, p. 139, p. 144.

39 See in this regard generally D. Garland, *The Culture of Control: Crime and Social Order in Contemporary Society,* Chicago: University of Chicago Press, 2001, p. 102.

40 1990 (2) All ER 866.

41 Ibid., p. 878.

42 See in English law *R v Sansom* [1991] 2 All ER 145.

43 See Scott, 'Transnational Law', pp. 873–875.

decisions (diplomatic, administrative, judicial etc.) made about a particular transnational criminal situation. The last thirty years have seen a proliferation of transnational law enforcement networks composed of non-state actors which engage in normative activity directed at states and at individuals. The normative actions of IGOs like the Financial Action Task Force (FATF), for example, often appear detached from any justifying legislative national or international source.[44] Central bankers and securities commissions,[45] transnational corporations,[46] non-governmental organisations,[47] together with select 'transnationalised' national law enforcement agencies that behave like non-state actors,[48] all enjoy within transnational interstices some measure of de facto independence to suggest, interpret and sometimes make rules in their areas of expertise. Does this mean that the neat transversal structure of transnational criminal law described above is dissolving into multiple nodes of unrecognisable legal authority unjustified by any participatory process?[49]

In answering this question it should not be ignored that these actors work within legal frameworks. The suppression conventions provide a space for governance, within which these actors try to hammer out tighter obligations on states and thus indirectly on individuals. Take for example, Recommendation 3 of the 2012 FATF Recommendations: 'Countries should criminalise money laundering on the basis of the Vienna Convention and the Palermo Convention.'[50] It provides a tool to enforce existing treaty obligations and through elastic interpretation to extend those obligations.

As an instrument of 'soft' power, however, 'soft' transnational criminal law such as the FATF's recommendations is remarkably independent and hard-edged. Recommendation 4 provides, for example, that 'Countries should consider adopting measures that allow such proceeds or instrumentalities to be confiscated without requiring a criminal conviction (non-conviction based confiscation)', whereas non-conviction-based forfeiture is only indirectly suggested in the conventions themselves. For proselytisers of globalisation like the OECD,

---

44 See generally K.S. Blazejewski, 'The FATF and its Institutional Partners: Improving the Effectiveness and Accountability of Transgovernmental Networks', *Temple International and Comparative Law Journal,* 2008, vol. 22, p. 1.

45 See e.g. Basel Committee on Banking Supervision (BCSB), International Association of Insurance Supervisors (IAIS) and International Organisation of Securities Commissions (IOSCO), *Initiatives by the BCBS, IAIS and IOSCO to Combat Money Laundering and the Financing of Terrorism,* June 2003, available at http://www.bis.org/publ/joint05.pdf (accessed 1 November 2013).

46 See e.g. the anti-tobacco smuggling agreements signed between major tobacco products manufacturers such as Philip Morris International and the European Anti-Fraud Office (OLAF), which contain a wealth of normative content, available at http://ec.europa.eu/anti_fraud/investigations/eu-revenue/cigarette_smuggling_en.htm (accessed 1 November 2013).

47 See e.g. Transparency International's work as the UNCAC Coaltion Secretariat, a coalition of more than 300 NGOs working to pressure state compliance with the UNCAC – see http://www.transparency.org/whatwedo/activity/our_work_on_convention (accessed 13 November 2013).

48 See e.g. the US Drug Enforcement Agency – see generally E.A. Nadelmann, *Cops Across Borders: The Internationalization of U.S. Criminal Law Enforcement,* University Park, Pennsylvania: Pennsylvania State University Press, 1993, p. 189 et seq.

49 See U. Sieber, 'Legal Order in a Global World – The Development of a Fragmented System of National, International and Private Norms' in A. von Bogdany and R. Wolfrum (eds), *Max Planck Yearbook of United Nations Law,* 2010, vol. 14, p. 1, pp. 17–19.

50 The FATF Recommendations: International Standards on Combating Money Laundering and the Financing of Terrorism and Proliferation, FATF, 2012, available at http://www.fatf-gafi.org/media/fatf/documents/recommendations/pdfs/FATF_Recommendations.pdf (accessed 1 April 2014).

soft law of this kind is faster and cheaper to make than treaty law and is thus more adaptive. In addition, it can be combined with fairly coercive name and shame tools to ensure implementation, while the suppression conventions only have very weak powers for enforcement of implementation. A further dimension of this soft power, of which FATF Recommendation 4 on civil forfeiture also provides an example, is its reliance on administrative and regulatory penalties that avoid the *ne bis in idem* rule, impose a milder degree of censure less likely to draw public attention, and involve less formal process and less rigorous standards of proof. Their penal nature obscured, these civil provisions increase coercive public power, while eroding individual rights and executive accountability.

The transnational normative space may be expanding, but these norms are directed at states rather than individuals and the state still mediates these expressions of authority. Thus transnational criminal law retains its transversal structure; it is only that the participants in the horizontal level include non-state entities.

It is doubtful whether the expansion of a transnational legal space signals the triumph of the functional ends of transnational criminal law over its national (statist) origins. The activities of criminal justice IGOs such as the UN Office of Drugs and Crime, for example, reflect state rather than their own interests.[51] Indeed, the opposition is false: the dominant state interest is in the function of suppressing crime. Both the softening and 'civilising' of transnational criminal law indicate not the diminution of state power, but its growth.

Transnational criminal law as a pluralist legal order

Treaty relations, national criminal laws, 'other' norms of transnational origin make for a confusion of normative orders with diffuse law-making authorities. Can it be called a system?

One response is simply to ignore issues of systematicity. At a general level Zumbansen suggests that 'transnational law' is best conceived of as a methodological lens through which to study the transformation of a plurality of national legal institutions as they extend their operations into the transnational legal space.[52] Used in the same way, transnational criminal law provides a valuable lens for revealing what the terms 'international criminal law' and 'crimes of international concern' obscure. It permits avoidance of the fruitless searches for the supra-national connotations associated with the former term, while revealing the nature of the criminal activity and normative space not revealed by either term. It enables a clearer focus on the peculiar social, political, economic and normative contexts in which different transnational crimes emerge and are implemented. It helps to reveal the nature of the social construction of prohibition regimes, the structured diffusion of legal norms through socialisation processes that rely on emulation, persuasion, manipulation or coercion.

In plotting this diffusion, scholarship on legal pluralism provides a useful magnifier. Legal pluralism is the 'situation in which two or more legal systems coexist in the same social field.'[53] Using a pluralist framework allows the capture of the dialectical and iterative interplay

---

51 Revealed, for example, in the donation by states of funds for earmarked special projects rather than into the general purpose funding, allowing donors to dictate the direction of UNODC activity – see http://www.unodc.org/unodc/donors/index.html (accessed 1 April 2013).

52 P. Zumbansen, 'Defining the Space of Transnational Law: Legal Theory, Global Governance and Legal Pluralism', *Transnational Law and Contemporary Problems*, 2012, vol. 21, p. 305, p. 307, p. 312, p. 330.

53 S.E. Merry, 'Legal Pluralism' in *Law and Society Review*, 1988, vol. 22, p. 869, p. 870.

among normative communities not revealed by rigidly territorialist or positivist visions of legal authority.[54] Transnational criminal law can be understood as an area or field within transnational legal pluralism that only becomes fully visible if domestic legal systems are examined with a view to identifying their transnational features. Interstate, state and non-state systems for the suppression of crimes overlap, governing the same compound normative situation. Thus, for example, when someone engages in the act of money laundering within a particular state's territorial jurisdiction, her action may engage the extraterritorial jurisdiction of more than one state and be the kind of situation contemplated by the obligations contained in a suppression convention. Each state will proceed using its own selection of jurisdictional principles and its own version of the money-laundering offence (given the absence of an operative principle of *ne bis in idem* in these situations, she may be proceeded against multiple times). However, given the provenance of the crime in Article 3(1) of the 1988 Drug Trafficking Convention, that legislation is likely to exhibit marked similarities. A closer examination of the history of law reform in each state in regard to money laundering is likely to reveal a web of links between states leading all the way back to the first formulation of the offence in section 1956 of the United States' Money Laundering Control Act.[55] Only a thorough investigation of the history of particular norms in particular contexts, and the dialectical way in which they have been constituted and reconstituted under the influence of other norms whether by radical reform or by incremental adjustment and reinterpretation,[56] will expose these extraterritorial influences and make it possible to judge the weight of their impact. The lens of transnational criminal law thus reveals that alleged criminals are members of multiple normative communities, local, territorial, extraterritorial and non-territorial in nature.[57]

Cui bono?

Transnational criminal law has never been entirely about the notion that effective criminalisation and cooperation makes for effective suppression of crime. Its cultural and political authority can appear suspect, chiefly because of scepticism about which states benefit from it and for what purpose. An interventionist element was present, as Mazower notes, for example, 'in Britain's use of abolitionism to legitimise its aggressive policing of the high seas to Facist Italy's cynical rationalisation of its invasion of Ethiopia in 1935 as an intervention in the name of civilization to suppress the slave trade'.[58] Transnational criminal law is not usually reliant on hard power of the kind exhibited through illegal rendition of alleged terrorists. It more normally depends on multilateral treaty obligations with a strongly developmental nature. But as Mazower also comments, 'development has always been about making a safer world for those doing the developing . . .'.[59] Development of a cooperating state's laws within the framework of transnational criminal law serves a kaleidoscope of aims from the parochial to the cosmopolitan. Some crimes, such as that under Article 1 of the Optional Protocol to the Convention on the Rights of the Child on the Sale of Children, Child Prostitution and Child

---

54 P.S. Berman, *Global Legal Pluralism: A Jurisprudence of Law Beyond Borders*, Cambridge: Cambridge University Press, 2012, p. 25.
55 Title 18 USC §1956.
56 Merry, 'Legal Pluralism', p. 889.
57 Berman, *Global Legal Pluralism*, p. 11.
58 M. Mazower, *Governing the Word: The History of an Idea*, Allen Lane: London, 2012, pp. 395–396.
59 Mazower, *Governing the World*, p. 373.

Pornography[60] involving the suppression of 'child exploitation material', appear to reflect a more broadly shared norm.

However, no crime is the product of perfect consensus. The leaders of transit states through which migrants are trafficked may, for example, be less concerned about the human rights of those trafficked and more concerned that developed states are using these laws to prevent immigration.[61] In the main transnational crimes tend to be more particularist than universalist because transnational criminal law is founded in the collective interest of the individuals within a state in having a system of criminal laws in force within that state and projecting that power abroad when that interest is threatened or harmed by transnational activities. States use the prohibition regimes to seek the cooperation of other states in overcoming the territorial limits on their own coercive power. They endeavour to convince other states that this interest is mutual and that they should reform their domestic laws to suppress these threats internally and make it possible to cooperate internationally.[62] Yet as Nye cautions, in international relations '[c]ontrary to some rhetorical flourishes, interdependence does not mean harmony. Rather, it often means unevenly balanced mutual dependence.'[63]

The imbalance within transnational criminal law arises out of the greater capacity of some states to project their self-interest. Historically Western states and, in particular, Great Britain in the nineteenth century and the United States in the twentieth century, have driven its development to suit their interests, using their national legislation as models for treaty provisions and thus for law reform in other states.[64] It has been used to de-nationalise and then re-nationalise criminal law norms in a unidirectional process of normative diffusion from developed to developing states. At a macro level developed states often provide the legal models for suppression conventions.[65] The 'forerunner' legislation for the OECD Anti-Bribery Convention,[66] for example, is the US Foreign Corrupt Practices Act.[67] Delmas-Marty comments:

> Many international conventions providing for the rapprochement of domestic criminal systems in various areas linked to globalisation, such as bribery, money laundering, organised crime and terrorism, have been drafted on the initiative of the United States and generally result in the transplant of the American Model.[68]

60 GA Res. 54/263, Annex II, 54 UN GAOR Supp. (No. 49) at 6, UN Doc. A/54/49, vol. III (2000), entered into force 18 January 2002.
61 P. Lloyd, B. Simmons and B. Stewart, 'Combating Transnational Crime: The Role of Learning and Norm Diffusion in the Current Rule of Law Wave', in M. Zürn, A. Nollkaemper and R. Peerenboom (eds), *Rule of Law Dynamics: In an Era of International and Transnational Goovernance*, Cambridge: Cambridge University Press, 2012, p. 159.
62 B.M. Yarnold, 'The Doctrinal Basis for the International Criminalization Process' in M.C. Bassiouni (ed.), *I International Criminal Law: Crimes,* 2nd edn, Ardsley on Hudson: Transnational, 1999, p. 31.
63 J.S. Nye, 'Soft Power', *Foreign Policy*, 1990, vol. 80, p. 153, p. 158.
64 See generally P. Andreas and E. Nadelman, *Policing the Globe: Criminalization and Crime Control in International Relations*, New York: Oxford University Press, 2006, p. 105.
65 See S. Silbey, '1886 Presidential Address: "Let Them Eat Cake": Globalization, Postmodern Colonialism, and the Possibilities of Justice', *Law and Society Review,* 1997, vol. 31, p. 207, p. 221.
66 Convention on Combating Bribery of Foreign Public Officials in Transnational Business Transactions, 17 December 1998, 37 ILM 1 (1998); in force 5 March 2002.
67 15 US § 78dd-1 et seq.
68 M. Delmas-Marty, *Ordering Pluralism: A Conceptual Framework for Understanding the Transnational Legal World*, trans. Naomi Norberg, Oxford and Portland: Hart, 2009, p. 107.

It is unsurprising that this happens – experts from Western states are familiar with their own policies and laws and usually have neither the time nor inclination to examine the merits of competing approaches (if they exist). These legal blueprints are fleshed out at meso- and micro-levels through the 'technology transfer' of policy, domestic model laws, practical know-how, administrative arrangements and institutions. Intergovernmental organisations like the UNODC and FATF play an important support and intermediary role in this regard.

Negative externalities (other crimes, threats and financial burdens to the state, corruption and so forth) and concern for the rule of law makes states receptive to these norms.[69] In many cases it is domestic policy to extra-territorialise this law, and technical assistance is used as an inducement. However, Western influence in shaping transnational criminal law arises out of more than just the accessibility of this forerunner legislation, or its prestige, or more broadly shared legal traditions.[70] Negotiating by threat and developing treaty-violation-based sanctions through naming and shaming or withdrawal of aid also serve as inducements for participation.

There is a democratic deficit in the development of transnational criminal law. First, the drafting and conclusion of the suppression convention itself – an exercise in executive 'foggy' power – reifies the global legitimacy of the suppression of the transnational crime through the consent of nominally equal but substantively unequal negotiating parties. For one thing, states have an incentive to join the regime because transnational criminal law strengthens state power through more substantive criminal laws and greater procedural powers. Second, legitimisation of these norms through legislative institutions ignores the many inducements for local political elites to comply. The process of legislative implementation is frequently characterised by a lack of transparency, ignorance, political incapacity to resist diplomatic pressure, and a complete absence of democracy at a national level.

The resistance of states to these donations depends on a range of factors including the lack of domestic legal capacity, the recalcitrance of local political elites, the basic incompatibility of underlying value systems and criminal laws, and the national margin of appreciation permitted by the suppression conventions which differs from regime to regime. In a few instances they directly repudiate the regime itself. Thus, for example, while some US commentators are satisfied with the level of order in the drug-trafficking regime,[71] President Evo Morales of Bolivia considers the drug prohibition regime to be a failure.[72] As noted above, however, donor states have more recently overcome some of the formal barriers of sovereignty by shifting their attention away from a treaty-based system to more informal rules and norms that are less sovereignty bound: soft law.

Ironically, compliance with hegemonic demands makes transnational criminal law more systematic, with the hegemon as the centre of authority. However, the negative consequences of compliance for developing states include the potential distortion of their legal systems (e.g.

---

69 See Lloyd *et al.*, 'Combating Transnational Crime' p. 164, p. 165.

70 Conditions for transferability of legal norms isolated by A. Watson, 'Legal Change: Sources of Law and Legal Culture', *University of Pennsylvania Law Review,* 1982, vol. 131, p. 1121, p. 1147.

71 See S.M. Patrick, 'International Efforts not up to Combating Criminals, Shows CFR Interactve', Council of Foreign Relations, 10 July 2012, available at http://www.cfr.org/international-crime/international-efforts-not-up-combating-criminals-shows-cfr-interactive/p28684, accessed 1 June 2013.

72 Opening statement at the 56th Session of the UN Commission on Narcotic Drugs, UN Centre Vienna, 12 March 2012, available on CND Blog, http://www.cndblog.org/search/label/plenary%20sessions?updated-max=2013-03-12T14:59:00%2B01:00, accessed 29 May 2014.

up-to-date transnational crime legislation flanked by colonial-era criminal codes). Moreover, the impact of using these new laws at the behest of other states may overburden the already creaking criminal justice systems of developing states (e.g. Kenya's struggle to cope with Somali pirates).[73] Finally, suppression of supply-side activities in their jurisdictions can have considerable negative impacts (e.g. the war on drugs in Mexico)[74] without any reciprocal suppression of demand in developing states. Much about the development of transnational criminal law smacks of modernism, the notion that behaviour around the suppression of crime should converge on forms of social organisation dictated by the needs of modern industrial societies, and that the principal difficulty is overcoming the cultural relativism of domestic criminal laws. A transnational criminal law that remains part of the Western *mission civilisatrice*, enforcing the contingent, parochial morality of its authors, is of questionable effectiveness and doubtful legitimacy.

How can it be ensured that states cooperate against the truly harmful but do not subordinate themselves and become instruments of other states or of interest groups within those states in crime suppression to which they do not authentically subscribe? For Delmas-Marty a system like transnational criminal law should hover somewhere between world disorder (a disorder of states of equal status and capacity in relationships of horizontal 'coordination' based on reciprocity, which seldom achieves efficiency, in this case in suppressing transnational crime) and an externally imposed order (a hegemonic vertical relationship that attempts to 'unify' the systems of subordinate states but which is illegitimate and inefficient because it is resisted by states) in a middle ground that she terms 'ordered pluralism', where states accept a vertical relationship to a set of principles rather than other states – a system of 'harmonisation'.[75] These principles would have to govern the process of substantive criminalisation and procedural cooperation in the suppression of transnational crime. A transnational criminal law governed by such a clear set of principles would be a mosaic of systems which do not necessarily conform to a particular model but are compatible because they are consistent with governing principles in such a way that their systemic nature is clear.[76]

Work on a set of principles for transnational criminal law has already begun,[77] but a number of suggestions can be made in regard to the establishment of such a set of principles. First, the development of transnational criminal policy should be governed by an outcomes-based principle that tests each new policy to ensure a measurable equal benefit for all. Second, the governance of transnational criminal law should adhere to a precautionary principle: a willingness to question criminalisation/procedural cooperation as an appropriate response to certain practices. Third, the deep grammar of the extant transnational criminal law (principles of material and mental culpability, participation in crime and so forth),[78] a product of dominant common law states, should be reshaped to provide an incontestable set of

---

73 See generally J. Gathii, 'Kenya's Piracy Prosecutions', *American Journal of International Law*, 2010, vol. 104, p. 416.

74 See C.A. Bloom, 'Square Pegs and Round Holes: Mexico, Drugs and International Law', *Houston Journal of International Law*, 2012, vol. 34, p. 345.

75 Delmas-Marty, *Ordering Pluralism*, p. 14, p. 17 et seq.

76 Ibid., p. 46.

77 See the work of Sabine Gless to identify the general principles underpinning transnational criminal law – see http://tcl.ius.unibas.ch (accessed 12 November 2013). The latest iteration of this project was published in a special issue of the *Utrecht Law Review* (2013, vol. 9, no. 4), entitled 'Law Should Govern: Aspiring General Principles of Transnational Criminal Justice'.

78 See Boister, *Introduction*, p. 125.

grammatical principles. Fourth, the regulatory concept – coordination or cooperation in procedural matters – should be re-engineered to preserve the flexibility needed at a national level to adjust to the international obligations[79] (e.g. functional equivalence, mutual recognition, graded compatibility etc.).[80] Finally, legality and the protection of human rights should be recognised as the governing framework. Systems of extraterritorial enactment and enforcement of criminal laws run into problems of legality (certainty, fair warning, fair labelling, the individualisation of guilt and so forth)[81] in imposing criminal proscriptions on individuals in other states who may have no warning of the criminality of their actions, and operates in zones beyond the protection of domestic constitutional orders. Although the suppression conventions do make occasional direct reference to human rights,[82] this is usually under domestic law[83] and there is little direct reference to the international human rights instruments.[84]

Bringing transnational criminal law clearly into view

Transnational criminal law should be seen as a whole. If it is not, many of its features are lost to sight. The programmatic nature of the development of the system is obscured. The taint of an overarching Western influence is lost. The systemic absence of concern for legality and human rights is hidden. When these systemic features are overlooked, it makes the essential reform of this system, which should start with agreement on a basic system of principles to govern transnational criminal law, extremely difficult.

79 Delmas-Marty, *Ordering Pluralism*, p. 159.
80 Ibid., p. 161.
81 Art. 11(2) of the Universal Declaration of Human Rights, GA Res 2174 (III), UN Doc A/810, 71, 10 December 1948.
82 See, for example, Art. 30(5) of the United Nations Convention against Corruption, New York, 31 October 2003, 2349 UNTS 41, in force 14 December 2005.
83 See, for example, Art. 16(13) of the UNTOC.
84 An exception is the rights of victims under Art. 2(b) of the Trafficking Protocol.

2

The protection of human rights in the suppression of transnational crime

Robert J. Currie

Introduction

By 1974 the transnational criminal law regime examined in this book was well under way.[1] Building on earlier treaties dealing with such diverse subject matter as undersea cables and counterfeiting, crime suppression conventions had been and were being negotiated to deal with crimes that, while they were not yet being called 'transnational',[2] raised enforcement difficulties best solved by inter-state cooperation. The 1963 Tokyo Aircraft Convention[3] had contemplated organizing principles for dealing with concurrent jurisdiction over crimes as well as extradition between party states, both of which had been operationalized by the Hague Convention[4] and Montreal Convention.[5] More anti-terrorism suppression conventions would appear later in the decade, and Interpol's facilitation of police cooperation was in full swing. In that year, Professor M. Cherif Bassiouni took note of these developments and expressed concern about the disconnect between this international penal cooperation regime, on the one hand, and international human rights law, on the other. It appeared that states were becoming eager to craft international law instruments to aid their efforts in the fight against crime, but the level of cooperation required did not extend to the provision of basic procedural protections for the individuals being investigated and prosecuted.[6]

---

1 The historical developments up to that point are tracked in Professor Clark's classic essay: R. Clark, 'Offenses of International Concern: Multilateral State Treaty Practice in the Forty Years since Nuremburg', *Nordic Journal of International Law,* 1988, vol. 57, p. 49.
2 The phrase 'transnational crime' appears to have been coined around 1975 by Professor Gerhard Mueller; see M.C. Bassiouni and E. Vetere, *Organized Crime: A Compilation of UN Documents 1975–1998,* Ardsley, NY: Transnational, 1998 at xxxi, n. 19.
3 14 September 1963; 704 UNTS 219, in force 4 December 1969.
4 Convention for the Suppression of Unlawful Seizure of Aircraft, 16 December 1970; 860 UNTS 105, in force 14 October 1971.
5 Convention for the Suppression of Unlawful Acts against the Safety of Civil Aviation, 23 September 1971; 974 UNTS 177, in force 26 January 1973.
6 M.C. Bassiouni, 'An Appraisal of the Growth and Developing Trends of International Criminal Law', *Revue International de Droit Penal,* 1974, vol. 45, p. 405 at pp. 427, 429.

Nearly thirty years later, Professor Neil Boister took up the subject in a study of what human rights protections existed in the body of transnational criminal law instruments as it then stood, as well as in the cooperative machinery that it contained and was supplemented by, such as extradition and mutual legal assistance.[7] He observed that there was both progress and room for concern; progress because the human rights issue was clearly on the table during the negotiation of more modern suppression conventions, but room for concern because such protections as made it into the treaties were vaguely worded and left a great deal of room for state discretion and accommodation only of the human rights obligations which a particular state had already taken on. 'The elementary point', he observed, 'is that many parties to the suppression conventions may implement their obligations under the suppression conventions but may not be subject to effective international human rights obligations.'[8]

This chapter will illustrate that the protection of human rights in transnational criminal law is captured in B.B. King's famous lyric: 'Same old story, same old song / Goes all right 'til it goes all wrong.'[9] It will argue that the disconnect raised by Bassiouni forty years ago remains an issue in transnational criminal law. It will look at the history, analyze the issues in methodological terms and survey what progress has been made, but ultimately conclude that, for all but the most heinous human rights abuses, it is difficult to discern obligations that are meaningful or effective and bind large pluralities of states. This will be shown to be due both to the diffusion of international human rights law itself and to the lack of political will on the part of governments to bring the suppression of transnational crime and human rights protection into alignment.

Which rights, and whose?

It is important for this discussion to locate human rights law within the transnational criminal law system. The suppression conventions represent the operationalizing in international law of what Nadelmann influentially called 'global prohibition regimes',[10] an effort to coordinate crime suppression efforts among networks of like-minded states. The starting point, then, is that this is fundamentally an anti-crime system, not one designed to protect human rights.[11] Human rights are fundamentally enjoyed *vis-à-vis* the state and the goal of international human rights law is to both require and prohibit particular forms of state interaction with individuals. While crimes obviously have victims, the victimization is normally not properly classed as a human rights abuse; if an organized crime gang steals my car for re-tooling and sale overseas, I am a victim of transnational crime but have not had my rights breached. This is in contrast to international criminal law *stricto sensu*, where the criminalization regime is often described as a way of promoting human rights norms and deterring governments and

---

7 N. Boister, 'Human Rights Protection in the Suppression Conventions', *Human Rights Law Review*, 2002, Vol. 2, p. 199 ('Protection').

8 Ibid., p. 218.

9 'Same Old Story (Same Old Song)' by Will Jennings and Joe Sample, from the record *B.B. King: Take It Home* (MCA 1970).

10 E. Nadelmann, 'Global Prohibition Regimes: The Evolution of Norms in International Society', *International Organisation*, 1990, vol. 44, p. 479.

11 See, e.g., *B010 v Canada (Minister of Citizenship & Immigration)*, 2013 FCA 87 at para. 82 (Can Fed Ct App), per Dawson JA: 'In view of the stated purpose of the [Transnational Organized Crime] Convention, neither it nor the [Human Trafficking] Protocol can readily be characterized as international human rights instruments.'

state officials from breaching them. Such crimes as genocide or crimes against humanity most often are perpetrated by or with the involvement of state actors, and it is therefore unsurprising and doctrinally sound to see the Genocide Convention or the Torture Convention characterized as a human rights treaty.[12] So far as transnational criminal law goes, while there may be 'a duty on states to protect individuals from transnational crime',[13] that duty is not primarily based in human rights law.[14]

This is not to say, of course, that there are no exceptions or that transnational criminal law has no protective impact on the rights of individuals. As Lindsay Buckingham outlines later in this book,[15] the criminalization of child sex tourism and assorted other crimes against children originates not from the usual crime suppression treaty stable, but by way of the UN CRC and its Optional Protocol, the latter of which has all of the usual hallmarks of a suppression convention.[16] Thus, this particular skein of transnational criminal law is expressly contemplated as part of an overall package of human rights protections for children. As will be seen, however, this is an exceptional situation. Accordingly, the focus here will be essentially on civil rights, particularly those which pertain to detention, treatment of the individual and trials – and specifically, those rights which might protect (or not protect) from mistreatment an individual who is the target of a law enforcement investigation into a transnational criminal matter.

Protection of human rights in the suppression conventions

As much as the transnational criminal law system is about corralling states into creating common prohibitions of conduct,[17] co-ordinating jurisdiction[18] and establishing inter-state cooperative machinery,[19] it is also a vehicle for what Andreas and Nadelmann have described as norm or moral entrepreneurialism, i.e. a system for some states to proselytize particular forms of morality so as to create broadly based criminalization.[20] This is important because the norm which is being transplanted may bring with it impacts, sometimes harsh, on the human rights of various players within the involved states and not just the targets of investigation and prosecution. As Boister has it:

> Transnational criminal law threatens human rights in many ways. Drug laws may threaten the property rights of innocent farmers caught up in drug eradication operations

---

12 See e.g. M. Freeman and G. van Ert, *International Human Rights Law*, Toronto: Irwin, 2004, p. 132.
13 N. Boister, *An Introduction to Transnational Criminal Law*, Oxford: Oxford University Press, 2012, p. 21.
14 It is sometimes argued that the international human rights law treaties oblige states actively to protect individuals against rights breaches by both the states and private individuals; see V. Padmanabhan, 'To Transfer or Not to Transfer: Identifying and Protecting Relevant Human Rights Interests in Non-Refoulement', *Fordham Law Review*, 2011, vol. 80, p. 73, at pp. 102–107. Moreover, one could argue that Article 2 of the ICCPR obliges states to ensure there are legal structures in place to realize their rights and to provide remedies for breaches, and thus perhaps a crime suppression regime is required (I am grateful to Gib van Ert for this observation). Such an already diffuse norm becomes more so if one attempts to translate it into an obligation to enter into cooperative arrangements with other states.
15 See Chapter 13.
16 As described by Neil Boister in Chapter 1.
17 See Chapter 1.
18 See Chapter 6.
19 See Chapters 7 to 10.
20 See P. Andreas and E. Nadelmann, *Policing the Globe: Criminalization and Crime Control in International Relations*, Oxford: Oxford University Press, 2006.

involving the use of herbicides. Innocent bank account holders may find their privacy violated by inspection of bank records. Trafficked humans may be subject to detention as illegal aliens rather than treated as the victims of crime.[21]

The extent to which such issues arise obviously depends on the substantive and procedural criminal machinery which a state party to a suppression convention uses to implement its obligations. Yet as explored below, just as the conventions impose very little in the way of obligatory human rights protections for the investigated or accused, still less is there anything that might mitigate the harshness of the enforcement mechanisms. The exceptional cases are the instruments designed to combat human trafficking and child sex tourism, which often have victim protection obligations of various sorts.[22] In the overall system, however, the emphasis is very much on the prosecutorial side.

This is compounded by states sometimes using the very fact that a suppression treaty is in play as a justification for watering down protections that might exist in their legal orders, or even for imposing tougher consequences than would ordinarily be the case. This is a double-edged sword, since on the one hand the goal of the suppression regimes overall is to create a climate in which as broad a group of states as possible treats the conduct in question as not just a criminal offence, but a serious one. On the other hand, however, are states which run too freely with whatever flexibility they feel the presence of the convention provides. This is particularly and notoriously the case with the international drug control regime under the 1988 Vienna Narcotics Convention,[23] which has been acknowledged as being unapologetically and 'deliberately draconian in character'.[24] So, for example, a South African court justified limitations on various constitutional rights by according weight to the relevant provisions of the Vienna Convention;[25] and an Indonesian court refused to find that execution for drug trafficking violated the right to life under Article 6(2) of the International Covenant on Civil

---

21 Boister, *Introduction*, pp. 21–22.
22 There is a debate regarding whether a crime control model is the best way to deal with human trafficking, as well as the effectiveness of the human rights protections that exist in the relevant conventions; see E. Bruch, 'Models Wanted: The Search for an Effective Response to Human Trafficking', *Stanford Journal of International Law*, 2004, vol. 40, p. 1, and Chapter 11 in this volume.
23 Discussed in Chapter 14.
24 *Commentary on the United Nations Convention Against Illicit Traffic in Narcotic Drugs and Psychotropic Substances, 1988*, New York: United Nations, 1988, at p. 144. Space does not permit me to take up the interesting topic of the role played by the UN's crime control and human rights agencies in this mix, the 'Vienna v Geneva' matrix. It is worth noting here that the UNODC, initially focused heavily on crime suppression, has lately stressed the importance of human rights protection within criminal suppression efforts (see UNODC, *UNODC and the Promotion and Protection of Human Rights* (2012), available at http://www.unodc.org/documents/justice-and-prison-reform/UNODC_Human_rights_position_paper_2012.pdf (accessed 28 April 2014). This has brought it into conflict with the INCB; see LSE !deas, *Governing the Global Drug Wars* (2012), available at http://www.lse.ac.uk/IDEAS/publications/reports/SR014.aspx (accessed 28 April 2014), particularly the contributions by Barrett and Csete. In Chapter 13 of this book, Lindsay Buckingham offers the intriguing observation that the child exploitation transnational criminal law regime's emergence from the UN's human rights stable has had implications for the effectiveness of monitoring and implementation.
25 *Director of Public Prosecutions v Bathgate*, 2000 (1) SACR 105 (CPD). Boister refers to another case from South Africa where a court 'made much of the obligation to criminalise simple possession of illicit drugs under the drug conventions, seemingly unaware of the fact that these conventions specifically provide for constitutional limitation of the obligation' (Boister, 'Protection,' at p. 209, n. 49).

and Political Rights (ICCPR) based on the dubious holding that drug crimes constituted the 'most serious' crimes for which the death penalty was lawful – comparable to genocide.[26] While the inter-state cooperation angle is discussed more fully in the next section, this same dynamic can be observed in the willingness of states to accommodate harsher penalty in partner states than their own domestic laws would allow. So, for example, Canada's extradition law takes no account of the exponentially tougher narcotic sentencing laws of the United States – the state with which it does the vast bulk of its extradition business – despite the fact that many American sentences would be considered cruel and unusual punishment if they were levelled in Canada.[27]

The backdrop, then, is an uneven one in terms of how willing states are to allow foreign-sourced prohibition regimes, even those arrived at via treaty negotiations, to impact upon the human rights of their populations. This is reflected as well in a certain permissiveness as to how the treaty obligations are implemented into national laws, reflecting of course the traditional respect for local criminal law chauvinism but accepting the cooperation obligations at the cost of control over or input into how implementation is executed.

This is very clear from the human rights protection provisions themselves. Or, at least as regards the older treaties, the lack of them: Bassiouni's remarks in 1974 certainly arose from the fact that at that time one would have searched the extant suppression conventions (such as the Hague and Montreal Conventions, or the slightly later 1979 Hostages Convention[28]) in vain for any hint of an explicit human rights protection. In his 2002 article, Boister compared the 1988 United Nations Convention against Illicit Traffic in Narcotic Drugs and Psychotropic Substances (Vienna Convention), concluded in 1988,[29] with the UN Transnational Organized Crime Convention (UNTOC), concluded in 2000.[30] The Vienna Convention, he noted, contains no particular protections, but instead 'incorporate[s] human rights protections by reference to the constitutional protections available in the domestic law of the parties'.[31] The more contentious penal provisions and some of the procedural provisions (e.g. those around extradition) are made subject to the 'constitutional principles and basic concepts' or 'basic principles' of a party state's system, which provides some avenues for domestic protections to block particular parts of the treaty and for states to incorporate some of the traditional grounds for refusal of cooperation.[32] Article 5(8) provides some protection for the rights of 'bona fide third parties' as part of the overall obligations regarding confiscation, but the details are all left to the state and its domestic law.[33] Article 14(2) makes reference to states respecting 'fundamental human rights' when engaged in illicit crop prevention and eradication that is required under this provision, though without any detail or even a definition. Beyond this, he noted, '[t]here is little more.'[34]

26 *Sianturi and ors v Indonesia*, Constitutional Review, Nos 2, 3/PUU-V/2007 (23 October 2007).
27 See *United States v Ferras*, 2006 SCC 33.
28 International Convention Against the Taking of Hostages, New York, 17 December 1979, 1316 UNTS 205.
29 Vienna, 20 December 1988, 1582 UNTS 95; in force 11 November 1990.
30 The United Nations Convention against Transnational Organized Crime, 15 November 2000, 2225 UNTS 209, in force 29 September 2003.
31 Boister, 'Protection', p. 208.
32 Canvassed in more detail below.
33 Boister, 'Protection,' p. 210.
34 Ibid., p. 211.

Turning to the UNTOC, the situation with the substantive provisions was even more dire than with those of the Vienna Convention, as fewer of the provisions were left subject to national legal orders – and where it happened it seemed designed to accommodate domestic criminal law theories (e.g. making conspiracy offences optional for states which do not subscribe to this kind of inchoate liability) rather than any limitations a state party might wish to place on a treaty obligation. This suggested 'that the pressure for unqualified adherence is growing and that limitation is being replaced by an all or nothing approach to legal obligation'.[35] The situation was much the same for many of the law enforcement provisions (e.g. confiscation assistance and law enforcement between states), though the orthodox bases for refusal for extradition and mutual legal assistance were left intact and the cooperation obligations were subject to existing bilateral treates of states parties. As with the Vienna Convention, the obligations regarding confiscation and seizure were to be implemented in such a way as to respect the rights of 'bona fide third parties',[36] though all of this was left to be defined under the laws of the states parties themselves.

Strides were made, however, with the inclusion of certain defense-oriented protections of the sort notably absent from the Vienna Convention and earlier treaties. Article 11(3), dealing essentially with procedures for bail, requires 'due regard to the rights of the defence', and similar approaches were taken to mutual legal assistance,[37] witness protection[38] and victim assistance and protection.[39] Moreover, the extradition provisions at Article 16(13) included the following somewhat enigmatic paragraph:

> Any person regarding whom proceedings are being carried out in connection with any offences to which this Article applies shall be guaranteed fair treatment at all stages of the proceedings, including enjoyment of all the rights and guarantees provided by the domestic law of the State Party in the territory of which that person is present.

The UNODC's guide for legislative implementation of the UNTOC indicates[40] that this provision had the modest but nonetheless significant goal of ensuring that state parties actually had procedural provisions in place that would provide 'fair treatment' in extradition; which, given the hoped-for global ratification of the convention, would not necessarily otherwise be the case. However, as Boister pointed out, it left a great deal unclear: was it lawful for states from whom extradition was requested to even consider whether there were issues with procedural fairness in the requesting state, which would depart from the traditional practice of 'non-inquiry'?[41] If so, was potential lack of 'fair treatment' a ground for refusal of extradition? And how was 'fair treatment' ('a non-standard term in a human rights sense'[42]) to be interpreted, beyond the provision's explicit inclusion of the rights and guarantees in either state's domestic law, and particularly because the *travaux préparatoires* were opaque on the issue?

---

35 Ibid., p. 212.
36 UNTOC, Arts 12 and 13.
37 Article 18.
38 Article 24(2).
39 Article 25(3).
40 UNODC, *Legislative Guides for the Implementation of the United Nations Convention Against Transnational Organized Crime and the Protocols Thereto*, New York: United Nations, 2004, p. 203.
41 Discussed below.
42 Boister, 'Protection', p. 215.

Boister suggested that the injection of the 'human rights issue' into the UNTOC was explicable in two ways: 1) an increased sensitivity of some states to accepting obligations which might violate their human rights obligations, arising from the development of the '*Soering* principle' (discussed below);[43] and 2) the fact that human rights protections had been introduced into two anti-terrorism conventions which had been negotiated concurrently with (though separately from) the TOC Convention.[44] The latter point deserves a brief look. Article 14 of the 1998 International Convention for the Suppression of Terrorist Bombings (Terrorist Bombing Convention)[45] (and the identically worded Article 17 of the 2000 International Convention for the Suppression of the Financing of Terrorism (Terrorist Financing Convention)[46]) contained a more robust 'fair treatment' obligation:

> Any person who is taken into custody or regarding whom any other measures are taken or proceedings are carried out pursuant to this Convention shall be guaranteed fair treatment, including enjoyment of all rights and guarantees in conformity with the law of the State in the territory of which that person is present and applicable provisions of international law, including international law of human rights.

This provision is of broader application than Article 16(13) of the UNTOC, in that it applies to the entire procedure of any case which is undertaken 'pursuant to' the treaties, rather than just extradition. It also makes explicit reference to international human rights law as a standard of measure for a state's actions, though of course this is qualified by the word 'applicable'. The oddness of the discrepancy between suppression conventions so close in time was possibly explained, as Boister pointed out, by concern among the parties negotiating the terrorism conventions around the inherently political nature of the crime and the fact that the 'political offence' exception for extradition was being barred; '[t]he lack of similar political alarm' could explain why Article 16(13) of the TOC Convention contained 'a watered down version' of this language.[47] Another possible explanation, of course, is the ad hoc and uncoordinated way in which the suppression conventions have been negotiated, where the diplomats sent to negotiate on behalf of a state are not necessarily briefed on earlier or concurrent developments.

In any event, despite there being more meat on the bones of some treaty-based human rights obligations than others, over a century of negotiating suppression conventions and recent attention to human rights concerns amounts to no more than this: apart from the symbolic and/or political value of explicitly linking crime suppression and human rights in more recent treaties, in those treaties states are only obliged to be bound by any human rights obligations that arise from their own laws, or under international human rights law treaties to which they are already parties. This was the crux of Boister's argument in his 2002 article, which contained several variations on this comment:

> [T]hese provisions are vague . . . [and] the detail of these defence rights is not provided by the convention itself; domestic or general international human rights law provides

---

43 Ibid., p. 217.
44 Ibid., pp. 215–216.
45 15 December 1997, 2149 UNTS 256, in force 23 May 2001.
46 New York, 9 December, 1999, 2178 UNTS 197, in force 10 April 2002.
47 Boister, 'Introduction', p. 216, n. 73.

them. This indicates an acceptance of continued large-scale variation of these rights in national law.[48]

It also indicates, one might add, mandatory acceptance of situations where there are no, or no meaningful, human rights protections in the national laws, but nonetheless makes it very difficult – if not impossible – to avoid the substantive, procedural and cooperation obligations. States have agreed to abide by their own visions of human rights protection, but the suppression conventions themselves contain no well-defined obligations, and little suasion.

While one might wonder about such a detailed rehearsal of Boister's arguments from an article more than a decade old, I have done so not just out of admiration for its scholarly quality but for efficiency reasons; apart from some minor technical details, the state of the law and politics is essentially the same in 2014 as it was in 2002. This is quite effectively illustrated by an examination of the newest suppression convention,[49] the Beijing Convention on the Suppression of Unlawful Acts Relating to International Civil Aviation,[50] formulated in 2010 to replace the Montreal Convention. In Chapter 6 of this book, Professor Clark uses this treaty as a vehicle for illustrating the typical jurisdictional regime of a suppression convention, and describes it as 'state of the art'. While this is true for the law enforcement machinery contained in the Beijing Convention, I know Professor Clark will forgive me for saying that the human rights protections in it are old hat. This is to say, the treaty hits the high mark for human rights protection within the body of a suppression convention as established in the two terrorism conventions described above, as it contains the same provisions – the identical 'fair treatment' clause in Article 11, and an extradition/mutual legal assistance exception for discrimination in Article 14. Stasis. The interests of states negotiating the treaties, or at least the way in which they perceive those interests, do not seem to have changed. Nor, of course, is there anyone at the negotiating table pushing the issue on behalf of the accused person.

Silos, *Soering* and September 11th

The next task is to look at the question from the other side of the lens: what impact do states' international human rights law obligations have on their transnational criminal law obligations – particularly those relating to cooperation which have grown up parallel to, and to some extent interacting with, the suppression conventions? The conventions themselves contain provisions dealing with extradition, mutual legal assistance and law enforcement cooperation, the function of which is to create a legal basis for cooperation between state parties to the conventions which require it. However, it is expected that many states will have their own existing bilateral and regional cooperation networks of first resort and will

---

48 Ibid., p. 215.
49 Support can also be found by examining the Council of Europe Convention on Cybercrime, CETS No 185 (2001), the human rights provisions of which have been the subject of criticism (M. Miquelon-Weismann, 'The *Convention on Cybercrime*: A Harmonized Implementation of International Penal Law: What Prospects for Procedural Due Process?', *John Marshall Journal of Information Technology and Privacy Law*, 2005, vol. 23, p. 329). The difference is that the EU states which are the main parties of the treaty are also subject to the European Convention Human Rights, a point made in the next section of this chapter. However, the Convention is open to non-EU parties, and has several at the moment, including the United States.
50 Not yet in force. Available at http://legacy.icao.int/DCAS2010/restr/docs/beijing_convention_multi.pdf (accessed 28 April 2014).

keep the suppression convention machinery as subsidiary. This existing network of treaties has a troubled history with international human rights law, which must be examined in order to properly understand the current state of the protection of human rights in transnational criminal law.

As is well known, the story begins with extradition,[51] historically a creature of international law and executive discretion. States engaged in extradition have always had some interest in protection of individuals on their territories, and thus developed the traditional protections in the form of bases for refusal by the requested state, which are still found in extradition treaties throughout the world: non-discrimination, double criminality, specialty, political offence and (for common law states) the requirement of a prima facie case.[52] However, individuals did not have standing to invoke these protections, which were inter-state entitlements. While domestic courts had some supervisory powers over extradition, these tended to be driven by the 'rule of non-inquiry', that courts will not inquire into the rule of law or level of human rights protection in the requesting state, as these are matters best left to the executive. Much the same was the case with mutual legal assistance,[53] which was coming online as a law enforcement cooperation method by the 1980s.

A great deal of the modern development of these treaty mechanisms took place post-World War II, and it was during this era that international human rights law challenged the view that the individual was only an object of international law; state activities could be contested on the basis that individuals had rights *vis-à-vis* governments. Some of the central human rights protections were against state excesses in criminal process, and individuals slowly gained standing in this arena. However, at the international level, the view among states was that these two bodies of law – international human rights law on the one hand and the law of international criminal cooperation on the other – existed largely in splendid isolation from each other. Human rights laws and obligations were essentially territorially limited, and governments did not bear hard legal obligations regarding what might happen to an individual who was the target of the inter-state criminal cooperation.

This was most troublesome in situations where there were two cooperating states, one of which adhered to international human rights standards and the other of which did not and perhaps had a very spotty human rights record. While it might have been viewed as unfortunate that a person would, say, be extradited to face harsh conditions, an unfair trial, torture or death, it was not the extraditing state which was violating applicable human rights norms and therefore it had no legal duty to refuse to extradite. Such matters were better handled by the discretionary political decision-making at the ministerial, inter-governmental level. This is not to say that state practice in transnational criminal cooperation did not evolve at all commensurately with international human rights norms; the UN Model Treaty on Extradition, for example, showed growing state tolerance for refusal to extradite for death penalty offences, among others.[54] However, it was the extradition treaties themselves, and how they reflected the policy preferences of states, from which the obligations came. Human rights law and transnational criminal cooperation remained in separate silos.

---

51 See Chapter 10 in this volume.
52 See generally W. Gilmore, 'The Provisions Designed to Protect Fundamental Human Rights in Extradition and Mutual Legal Assistance Treaties' in Commonwealth Secretariat, *International Co-operation in Criminal Matters: Balancing the Protection of Human Rights with the Needs of Law Enforcement*, London: Commonwealth Secretariat, 2001.
53 See Chapter 8 in this volume.
54 UN Doc A/RES/45/116 (1990), as amended UN Doc A/RES/52/88 (1997).

This mutual exclusivity came under significant attack in the late 1980s and early 1990s in a series of remarkable decisions by both international human rights bodies and domestic courts. The legal point was that by extraditing to a state where certain fundamental human rights were threatened, a requested state engaged (and could violate) its treaty-based human rights obligations. The most significant was the decision of the European Court of Human Rights in *Soering v United Kingdom*,[55] where the court ruled that 'the decision by a Contracting State to extradite a fugitive may give rise to an issue under Article 3 [of the European Convention on Human Rights (ECHR)], and hence engage the responsibility of that State under the Convention'.[56] Soering, a German national, had appealed the United Kingdom's acquiescence to an extradition request from the United States on murder charges in Virginia, which were subject to the death penalty. The court found that the conditions that would be faced by Soering when on death row in Virginia would constitute 'inhuman or degrading treatment or punishment' within the meaning of Article 3 of the Convention, and thus extradition would breach the United Kingdom's obligation to proscribe such conduct. This was even though the extraditing state was not directly involved in whatever treatment would be faced by the fugitive, but 'by reason of its having taken action which has as a direct consequence the exposure of an individual to proscribed ill-treatment'.[57] Accordingly, even though complying with its international human rights obligations would obviously have an impact outside that state, this did not amount to extending extraterritorial jurisdiction.[58]

The *Soering* principle, then, holds that under international law states engage their human rights obligations when they engage in international criminal cooperation that affects an individual's fundamental human rights. This vindicates the central idea behind international human rights law that human beings have some capacity to enjoy rights autonomously as subjects – rather than objects – of international law.[59] Outside the ECHR space, the *Soering* principle was applied to the ICCPR by the UN Human Rights Committee in several cases involving Canada. Kenneth Ng petitioned the Committee and argued that, by extraditing him to the US, Canada had violated his rights under Articles 6 (right to life) and 7 (prohibition of cruel, inhuman, or degrading punishment or treatment) of the ICCPR. The Committee held that in extraditing an individual to face a 'real risk' of violations of their rights, Canada could incur responsibility for violating the ICCPR,[60] and that it had done so

---

55 Series A, No. 161 (1989). See also the decision of the Supreme Court of the Netherlands in *The Netherlands v Short*, reprinted in (1990) 29 ILM 1375.

56 *Soering*, ibid. at para. 91. Conceptually this line of argument originated in what is usually referred to as the 'non-*refoulement* obligation' in Article 33 of the Convention Relating to the Status of Refugees, 28 July 1951, 189 UNTS 150 (1951), in force 22 April 1954, and Article 3 of the United Nations Convention Against Torture, 10 December 1984, 1465 UNTS 85 (1984), in force 26 June 1987. Under these provisions states were prohibited from sending an individual to face persecution or torture, respectively. The *Soering* principle represented a breakthrough because, while the non-*refoulement* obligations explicitly dealt with the sending of the individual, the Court found that the sending state would be implicated *in the actual mistreatment* that was the subject of the otherwise territorially limited prohibition. So, the UK would breach the prohibition on 'inhuman or degrading treatment or punishment', not because it was administering the treatment, but because by sending Soering to the US it was actively facilitating it.

57 *Soering*, ibid.

58 Ibid., at para. 86.

59 S. Williams, 'Human Rights Safeguards and International Cooperation in Extradition: Striking the Balance', *Criminal Law Forum* 3 (1992) p. 191 at p. 222.

60 *Ng v Canada* (1993), Comm. No. 469/1991, UN Doc CCPR/C/49/D/469/1991, at para. 14.2. See also *Cox v Canada* (1994), Comm. No. 539/1993, UN Doc CCPR/C/52/D/539/1993.

with regard to Ng, since the technique of execution by gas asphyxiation that he faced constituted cruel and unusual punishment in violation of Article 7.[61] Ten years later, the Committee again ruled against Canada in the case of Roger Judge,[62] a convicted American murderer who escaped from prison and fled to Canada, from where he was deported in 1998. The Committee found that, by this time, international law developments had moved along sufficiently that an abolitionist state, such as Canada, had an obligation not to expose an individual to a real risk of the death penalty being imposed, whether via deportation or extradition.[63] Accordingly, Canada had violated Judge's right to life under Article 6 of the ICCPR.

The birth and development of the *Soering* principle had a galvanizing effect on human rights lawyers and NGOs all over the world, who defended or intervened in proceedings using this new argument as sword or shield. Governments began to engage with the issue, sometimes reluctantly, but with a realization that the increasing amount of crime with transnational aspects meant that the protection of the individual in criminal cooperation was likely to be a front-burner issue.[64] The European Court of Human Rights itself developed its own *Soering* jurisprudence, focusing in particular on torture. The academic literature was expanding.[65]

However, the 9/11 attacks on New York and Washington, and the shock and horror that accompanied them dampened the enthusiasm for aligning criminal cooperation with human rights standards, particularly among governments but also in civil society. The idea of ensuring procedural protections for people facing criminal – and now, increasingly, national-security-oriented – cooperation between governments was subordinated to fighting the terrorist threat. As the public record shows,[66] a number of democratic and human rights-oriented states (led by the United States but including many others) began to subvert this idea. People were apprehended and moved around in secret, without legal process, and the world became familiar with the phrase 'extraordinary rendition'.[67] Most chillingly, individuals were taken to 'dark sites' or notoriously abusive states to ensure they could not get access to courts, could be tortured in secret, and so that there would be no impediments to sharing the information gleaned from them between governments.

The shockwaves of these terrible attacks had propelled us out of a criminal cooperation system where human rights protections were evolving, into a new milieu where national security and suppression of terrorism was the trump card that beat every other hand, the end

---

61 Ibid. at para. 16.4. And see *Kindler v Canada* (1993), Comm. No. 470/1991, UN Doc CCPR/C/48/D/470/1991.

62 *Judge v Canada* (2003), Comm. No. 829/1998, UN Doc. CCPR/C/78/D/829/1998 [*Judge*].

63 Ibid., at para. 10.4.

64 For example, the collection of papers in Commonwealth Secretariat, above note 52 (Gilmore), emerged from a conference at which the enforcement authorities in the Commonwealth states came together in 1998 to consult on this topic.

65 J. Dugard and C. van den Wyngaert, 'Reconciling Extradition with Human Rights', *American Journal of International Law*, 1998, vol. 92, p. 187; S. Williams, 'Human Rights Safeguards'; V. Nanda, 'Bases for Refusing International Extradition Requests – Capital Punishment and Torture', *Fordham International Law Journal*, 2000, vol. 23, p. 1369; R.J. Currie, 'Human Rights and International Mutual Legal Assistance: Resolving the Tension', *Criminal Law Forum*, 2000, vol. 11, p. 143.

66 Open Society Justice Initiative, *Globalizing Torture: CIA Secret Detention and Extraordinary Rendition*, New York: Open Society Foundations, 2013.

67 See L. Sadat, 'Extraordinary Rendition, Torture and Other Nightmares from the War on Terror', *George Washington Law Review*, 2007, vol. 75, p. 1200.

that seemed to justify every means. As Philippe Sands commented, 'the events of 11 September 2001 became a catalyst for the systematic disregard of established international rules on human rights, the treatment of combatant prisoners and the use of military force around the world . . .'[68] And with the rights of alleged terrorists everywhere went the rights of all alleged transnational criminals.

Civil society fought through this dark time and pressed the case,[69] to the point where we are probably back to a situation where constructive and sensible dialogue can be had about how we calibrate two very important goals: cooperation between states to suppress crime, perhaps particularly terrorism, and threats to national security; but doing so in a way that allows us to preserve the fundamental human integrity of those whom we are prosecuting. Yet the resistance continues, spearheaded by the very governments which entered into obligations under international human rights law. The protections in the suppression convention obligations, as we have seen, are paltry, and neither extradition and mutual legal assistance treaties nor human rights treaties are being renegotiated to provide any explicit linkage.

Conclusion: the state of play and current issues

There is no doubt that the *Soering* principle has left an indelible mark on the law of inter-state criminal cooperation. Yet the challenge for an individual seeking to invoke a *Soering*-type approach in a particular case is twofold: convincing governments that there is such a link between the state's cooperation activities and its human rights obligations; and convincing courts to apply such a principle as law. This is easier in the ECHR space,[70] the birthplace of *Soering* itself, due to the direct applicability of the treaty in the law of party states. The debate in the ECHR's cases,[71] as well as in those of party states,[72] tends to be around whether the fate to be met by the individual is a sufficiently egregious human rights violation to put the co-operating state in breach of its human rights obligations.

Outside Europe, and particularly within the ICCPR network of states, the situation is more ephemeral, and more troubled. There are certainly bilateral treaty provisions. For those states which have taken on international human rights law treaty obligations, there are some protective interpretations of those treaties[73] that are definitely having an impact on transnational criminal cooperation practice. That said, hard rules are difficult to come by. There is no unity about either whether or how the human rights treaty applies to cooperation. There is state practice, either through bilateral relations or because states accept a *Soering* approach as desirable policy or as a legal obligation under domestic laws (or are forced to by their courts). However, too many states resist the idea that application of human rights standards to

68 P. Sands, *Lawless World: Making and Breaking Global Rules*, rev. edn., London: Penguin, 2006, p. 21.
69 International Commission of Jurists, *Assessing Damage, Urging Action: Report of the Eminent Jurists Panel on Terrorism, Counter-terrorism and Human Rights* (Geneva: International Commission of Jurists, 2009), www.un.org/en/sc/ctc/specialmeetings/2011/docs/icj/icj-2009-ejp-report.pdf (accessed 30 May 2014).
70 Most of the literature on inter-state criminal cooperation focuses on the ECHR regime, in my view simply because there is solid law there to talk about; see e.g. A. Van Hoek and M. Luchtman, 'Transnational Cooperation in Criminal Matters and the Safeguarding of Human Rights', *Utrecht Law Review*, 2005, vol. 1, p. 1.
71 See e.g. *Harkins and Edwards v United Kingdom*, ECHR 2012.
72 See e.g. *Kapri v The Lord Advocate representing The Government of the Republic of Albania*, [2013] UKSC 48.
73 Such as the decisions of the Human Rights Committee mentioned above.

their criminal cooperation is obligatory *from an international law point of view* for there to be hard norms. Even democratic, human-rights-loving states resist attempts to apply such rules.[74] To be clear, it is not that states feel unable to refuse to cooperate, that they do not take into account the views of the Human Rights Committee or the Torture Committee, or that they do not attempt to massage cooperation requests in order for them to avoid implication in human rights abuses, as attention to all of these are standard features of state practice. It is that there is little acceptance of an international law obligation to do so. One does not like to be exessively positivist, but in my view, aside from a few exceptions, one searches in vain for anything resembling a solid norm, either treaty-based or customary.[75]

In terms of what hard norms there may be, in a recent article Professor Satterthwaite makes a case (based on a review of: treaties, including the UN Torture Convention; the judgments or views of the European Court of Human Rights, Human Rights Committee, Torture Committee and other UN entities; and some state practice) that states are obliged as a matter of international human rights law to 'refrain from transferring any individual to the custody of a state where he is at a real risk of: torture or ill-treatment; persecution; enforced disappearance; and arbitrary deprivation of life'.[76] Notwithstanding the skepticism expressed above regarding the diffusion outside the ECHR space, this is a fairly defensible account. It is supported by the growing use of 'diplomatic assurances' by requested states as a means of ensuring compliance with these obligations, a practice ratified by the ECtHR,[77] though it tends to focus around torture cases where the cooperation standards are highest and most readily accepted.[78] The fact that such assurances are sought is some evidence that states view compliance as obligatory, though it is indirect evidence at best, not to mention a controversial practice. In any event, outside the context of transferring individuals, there is nothing beyond scattered state practice to evidence any human rights obligations attaching to mutual legal assistance, and still less to policing cooperation.

The simple explanation for this, within the consent-based system of international law, is lack of political will. Many states do not take human rights obligations seriously. Those that do certainly incorporate practices protective of human rights into their transnational criminal cooperation, and within like-minded networks of states these can be robust, but there is

---

74 For example, Canada has refused a plea from the UN High Commissioner for Human Rights to stay a deportation of an individual to Rwanda while the fair trial situation in that state was sorted out (www.theglobeandmail.com/news/national/quebec-court-gives-rwandan-man-one-week-reprieve-from-deportation/article2300166); and has publicly attacked the UN Human Rights Committee as an agenda-driven 'advocacy' organization, rather than an authoritative interpreter of the ICCPR (*Amnesty International Canada v Canada (Chief of Defence Staff)*, 2008 FC 336 at para. 239 (Fed Ct Can)).

75 It is worth noting my own view that fairly widespread state practice seems to indicate a permissive norm to refuse cooperation on human rights grounds; that is, while requesting states are mostly not obliged to refuse, they may do so without breaching the extradition or mutual legal assistance treaty. The problem of potential conflicts between cooperation treaties and human rights treaties was a preoccupation of the literature for some time (see Dugard and van den Wyngaert, 'Reconciling Extradition' and Currie, 'Human Rights and International Mutual Legal Assistance'), but the lack of any notable inter-state disputes on this issue supports my point.

76 M. Satterthwaite, 'The Legal Regime Governing Transfer of Persons in the Fight Against Terrorism' in L. van den Herik and N. Schrijver, eds, *Counter-Terrorism Strategies in a Fragmented International Legal Order: Meeting the Challenges*, Cambridge: Cambridge University Press, 2013, p. 589 at p. 615.

77 *Othman (Abu Qatada) v United Kingdom*, ECtHR 2012.

78 J. Johnston, 'The Use of Torture as a Basis for Refusing Extradition and the Use of Diplomatic Assurances', *International Criminal Law Review*, 2011, vol. 11, p. 1.

continual resistance to a *Soering*-based notion that they are obliged to do so. Of course, one cannot wave a magic wand and create widespread adherence to international human rights law. There is some force to the argument that a certain margin of flexibility is required for effective transnational cooperation against crime in a diverse world. However, margins of flexibility can exist within rights frameworks that are obligatory overall, yet the stance of even human-rights-adhering states has been to maintain as discretionary a state of affairs as possible, undermining the rule of law. Even what progress has been made over the last few decades is fragile, as the reaction to 9/11 demonstrated. The gains that have been made tend to emerge from litigation, rather than from cooperation. While there is a sense of forward motion, it is slow and its direction is uncertain.

3

Transnational crime: an interdisciplinary perspective

James Sheptycki

Introduction

Transnational crime presents a new object for global governance with law. A key difficulty resides in the definitional ambit of the term. One perspective, legal positivism, suggests that transnational crime consists in those phenomena defined in law as such. That is not the perspective adopted in this chapter. Instead an interdisciplinary perspective is adopted which synthesizes different viewpoints including political, economic, sociological and legal ones. The reason for adopting an interdisciplinary perspective is the contestability of the concept 'transnational crime' and allied terms such as 'transnational organized crime'.[1] These notions exist as components in a language game concerning certain phenomena that are in the process of being designated as objects for global governance. Many concepts are part of this discourse including, *inter alia*, human sex trafficking, human organ trafficking, cyber-crime, crimes against the environment, terrorism, intellectual property theft, piracy, cultural property theft, drug trafficking and so on. All of these terms are abstract analytical categories; they are essentially contested and warrant being placed in inverted commas.

According to Gallie,[2] abstract analytical concepts are evaluative and have an internally complex character which appeals to us on both a psychological and a sociological level. They are open-ended terms, which can be differently applied to differing phenomena in different times and places and their application is, in the basic sense of the word, political. They are 'essentially contested concepts'. When it comes to discussions about the meaning of terms such as these, it is important that all parties to the debate recognize that their own peculiar instantiation of the words is disputed by others and, further, understand the criteria on which

---

1   There are seemingly obvious albeit subtle differences in the terms 'transnational crime' and 'transnational organized crime', both at the connotative and denotative levels of meaning. In this chapter, these definitional subtlties are largely elided. Both terms are essentially contestable. Therefore what is important is to understand them as components in the language game of global governance through law.
2   W.B. Gallie, 'Essentially Contested Concepts', *Proceedings of the Aristotelian Society,* 1956, vol. 56, p. 167.

others' (perhaps repudiating) views are based. Much discussion about the problem of trans-national crime and transnational organized crime risks becoming radically confused because the participants have trouble with the essential contestability of the terms and insist that their own definitions are neutral, self-evident, constant, and proper or commonsensical. This point is of particular importance for legal scholarship because recognizing the essential contest-ability of terms such as 'transnational crime' and (even more so) 'transnational organized crime' brings the politics of law to the fore. This chapter aims to help the reader give due consideration to a variety of approaches to defining the issues. In truth there are actually three problems with the term 'transnational organized crime'. The term 'transnational', the term 'organized', and the term 'crime'.

Beginnings

The etymology of relevant terms is revealing of their contestability. In a thoughtful essay by the Dutch criminologists Petrus van Duyne and Mark Nelemans titled 'Transnational Organized Crime: Thinking in and out of Plato's Cave',[3] the historical evolution of these words within the institutional context of the United Nations is described. On the basis of a content analysis of UN documents and position papers they show how the terminology shifted over a period of several decades beginning in the early 1970s. Initially, the term of art was 'transnational crime' and it signaled a concern about illicit activities or harmful effects of licit capitalist enterprise in countries of the Third World. Van Duyne and Nelemans trace the slow transformation of the policy language into a narrative about illicit markets in drugs and other commodities, signaled by the term 'transnational organized crime', and the attendant disap-pearance of crimes by transnational corporations, white-collar crime and the crimes of corruption participated in by social and political elites. In another essay titled 'Transnational Organized Crime: The Strange Career of an American Concept', Michael Woodiwiss[4] traces the development of the concept of organized crime from its basis in the discourse of American law enforcement circles in the early part of the twentieth century until its mutation into 'trans-national organized crime' in the aftermath of the Cold War during the 1990s. He shows how the discourse of organized crime was useful in building up the apparatus of US federal law enforcement, a project of institution-building that was rather antithetical to certain legal and political norms of American society suspicious of the encroachment of federal state power. In the post-Cold War period, the shift to a concern with transnational organized crime was again useful in legitimating the projection of US law enforcement power onto the global stage.[5] Adam Edwards and Peter Gill have shown how, in the early twenty-first century, in addition to traditional law enforcement agency interest, western security, intelligence and defense agencies have also been reoriented around the trope of transnational organized crime (TOC).[6]

---

3   P.C. Van Duyne and M.D.H. Nelemans, 'Transnational Organized Crime: Thinking in and out of Plato's Cave', in F. Allum and S. Gilmore (eds), *Routledge Handbook of Transnational Organized Crime*, Abingdon: Routledge, 2012, p. 36.
4   M. Woodiwiss, 'Transnational Organized Crime: The Strange Career of an American Concept', in M. Beare (ed.), *Critical Perspectives on Transnational Organized Crime, Money Laundering and Corruption*, Toronto: University of Toronto Press, 2003, p. 1.
5   See also E. Nadelmann, *Cops Across Borders: The Internationalization of US Criminal Law Enforcement*, University Park, PA: Penn State University Press, 1993.
6   A. Edwards and P. Gill, 'The Politics of "Transnational Organized Crime": Discourse, Reflexivity and the Narration of "Threat"', *The British Journal of Politics and International Relations*, 2002, vol. 4, no. 2, p. 245.

According to Woodiwiss,[7] the American conception of organized crime was an oversimplification making the term synonymous with 'the Mafia'. The projection of this term into the discourse concerning transnational crime amounted to the 'dumbing of global discourse':

> making the term 'organized crime' synonymous with gangster or Mafia-type organizations will not help in efforts to combat a problem that is increasingly damaging and destructive but is rarely so structured and never so separate from legitimate institutions as the common use of the term now implies.[8]

As social historians are well aware, the phenomena of organized crime were familiar to citizens of the big American cities from at least the early nineteenth century.[9] Daniel Bell explained organized crime as integral to the American 'way of life'. According to him the pattern of organized criminality in the big American cities emerged from a confluence of factors involving the changing character of the urban 'political machines', the aspirations of immigrant groups to attain the 'American Dream' and 'queer ladders of social mobility' provided by certain vice industries, notably gambling. His narrative account of Big City Crime in America during the twentieth century was aimed at explaining a 'ritual drama' wherein a deep-seated pattern of corruption involving players in the illegal 'rackets', police and politicians is uncovered by reformers who rise to prominence and positions of political power only to be again 'swallowed up in the insatiable maw of corruption'.[10] 'Obviously', he concluded, 'the simple moralistic distinction between "good guys" and "bad guys" so deep at the root of the reform impulse, bears little relation to the role of organized crime in American society.'[11] For Mark Haller, the organization of crime was really about *illegal entrepreneurship*, and central to the functioning of the illicit economy were systemic relationships between illegal business, police and politicians.

Frequently cited work by Alan Block and William Chambliss gives a sense of why and how the Mafia image came to dominate conceptions of organized crime in America. Social historians had uncovered the functional symbiosis between the illicit 'underworld' and the 'upper world' populated by social, political and business elites. In an essay titled 'History and the Study of Organized Crime',[12] Block argued that the Mafia conspiracy theory condenses a highly complex phenomenon into a narrative format that hides some things while projecting other convenient 'truths'. Picturing organized crime as a bureaucracy and the organized criminals as 'protobureaucrats' is 'the lawman's favorite: the ladder of conspiracy with each rung integrated in a series leading to the master conspirator'.[13] Seeing organized crime as a hierarchy is not merely a projection of the lawman's institutional world (although it certainly is that). The portrait of Mr Big is also, conveniently, the picture of a cultural outsider. Bereft of an awareness of the social embeddedness of informal patron–client networks, and the interconnections between the corrupt denizens of the 'upper world' and the criminality of

---

7 Woodiwiss, 'Transnational Organized Crime', p. 4.
8 Ibid., p. 4.
9 D. Bell, 'Crime as an American Way of Life', *Antioch Review*, 1953, vol. 13, p. 131; M.H. Haller, 'Illegal Enterprise: A Theoretical and Historical Interpretation', *Criminology*, 1990, vol. 28, p. 207.
10 Bell, 'Crime as an American Way of Life', pp. 131–132.
11 Ibid.
12 A.A. Block, 'History and the Study of Organized Crime', *Journal of Contemporary Ethnography*, 1978, vol. 6, no. 4, p. 455.
13 Ibid., p. 466.

the 'under world' that are part-and-parcel of organization of crime in big American cities, the term 'organized crime' becomes a kind of cover-up. In his classic work *On the Take: From Petty Crooks to Presidents*, Chambliss observed that 'organized crime really consists of a coalition of politicians, law enforcement people, businessmen, union leaders and (in some ways least important of all) racketeers'.[14] According to him, of these groups it was actually 'the politicians who . . . have had the ultimate and most important practical control of organized crime'.[15] Chambliss revealed that it is not an accident that the topic of corruption is left out whenever the subject of organized crime becomes a matter of public attention and public policy in America. Rather than acknowledging the connections between national elites, local political machines and law enforcement to the organization of crime in America, the Mafia-conspiracy conception of organized crime makes corruption invisible. Chambliss showed that the mythology of the Mafia is not fictive; it is merely misleading.

Why is this important? The answer lies in a sociological analysis provided by Dwight Smith, Jr in an essay titled 'Mafia: The Prototypical Alien Conspiracy' originally published in 1976.[16] On the basis of a socio-historical analysis of three cases of 'alien conspiracy' – the first two being the 'Illuminati Conspiracy' and the 'Red Scare', the third being the 'Mafia conspiracy' – Smith suggested that there was a reoccurring cultural fixation of great significance for American public policy: the 'recurring apprehension that somewhere "out there" is an organized, secret, alien group that is poised to infiltrate our society and to undermine our fundamental democratic beliefs'.[17] At a general level, Smith's analysis suggests that threatening alien conspiracy theories exhibit three common characteristics or conditions. First, there has to arise a widespread sense of social unease and anxiety threatening to a given community's traditions, institutions and boundaries. This ontological precariousness is fertile soil for psychological projection and moralizing that is all too easily pronounced against cultural outsiders. Importantly, it also provides the basis for justifying the building of social institutions, or the buttressing of already existing ones. Enter the second element in the equation: the moral entrepreneur. A moral entrepreneur, or several of them, must act to focus public attention onto a perceived threat that can be plausibly linked with these anxieties and fears. Such entrepreneurship is undertaken because it upholds the interests of those who espouse it. These crusaders act in the way that they do because it allows them to manufacture the institutional basis of their own power. A third factor is critical to successfully doing so. There must be available to the moral entrepreneur a set of facts, or presumed facts, usable as supporting evidence concerning the conspiracy claims.

When it comes to the Mafia conspiracy myth, Smith's theory holds that the valorization of the term 'Mafia' provided the pretext for building up the national apparatus of US federal law enforcement. This included, but was not limited to, the Federal Bureau of Investigation and Federal Bureau of Narcotics (now the Drug Enforcement Agency). Federal institution-building in the United States was, according to Smith, problematic for two reasons. First, it 'led to a group of strategies that do not effectively address the problems of illicit enterprise'.[18] Second, and more importantly,

---

14 W. Chambliss, *On the Take: From Petty Crooks to Presidents*, Bloomington, IN: Indiana University Press, 1978, p. 9.
15 Ibid., p. 9.
16 D.C. Smith, Jr., 'Mafia, the Prototypical Alien Conspiracy', *Annals of the American Academy of Political and Social Science*, January 1976, vol. 423, no. 1, p. 75.
17 Ibid., p. 76.
18 Ibid., p. 87.

though ostensibly aimed at destroying organized crime, those strategies have themselves been more threatening to this country than the illicit behavior they were supposed to control. They have been threatening on two counts. First, they have affected law enforcement beyond the confines of organized crime control; second they have had a significant impact on the corruption of justice in the United States.[19]

Thus established, and continuing thereby to live through the myth, America had to endure the reality it supposed.

The crucial year in the constitution of 'that strange American concept', to use Michael Woodiwiss' turn of phrase, was 1967, which saw the publication of the results of the United States President's Task Force on Organized Crime. A well-known academic criminologist named Donald Cressey was one of its most influential members. Based on his experience with the Task Force, he was the first academic criminologist to attempt a systematic study of organized crime in his seminal book *Theft of a Nation*.[20] Cressey elaborated on the division of labor in the American Mafia by making metaphorical use of military ranks alongside Italian terminology and references to familial ties.[21] As those who have watched the 1972 American drama *The Godfather* know well, Cosa Nostra families are each headed by a boss, or *il capo* (literally 'the head'), and beneath each boss is a *sotto capo* (literally 'under the head'). Neither is involved in direct criminal activity. To communicate to the working level of the illicit enterprise, bosses work through channels of communication by way of a *capporegima* – the 'head of the régime', in effect a lieutenant. Beneath the 'lieutenant' are 'deputy lieutenants', and the 'rank-and-file' 'soldiers' at the bottom of the hierarchy do most of the hands-on dirty work. This language was largely popularized through works of fiction, but academic criminology gave it an added degree of verisimilitude.[22] Cressey concluded that although such a sketch of the organization of the Mafia is

> a gross oversimplification of the complex inferences which can be made about La Cosa Nostra norms from observation of one structural position, it does show that the social scientist can create data on organized crime by reasoning from the known to the inaccessible, just as the archeologist creates data . . . the social scientist . . . can comfortably make the assumption that 'in the long run' the action scene which he has created by inference can be directly observed.[23]

In this way, the English language gained scientific affirmation for a particular way of talking about organized crime as Mafia-type crime. From Cressey's work onward the criminological literature concerning organized crime is enveloped in this conceptualization and, according

19 Ibid., pp. 87–88.
20 D. Cressey, *Theft of a Nation: The Structure of Organized Crime in America*, New York: Harper and Row, 1967.
21 D. Cressey, *Criminal Organization: Its Elementary Forms,* New York: Harper and Row, 1972.
22 Mario Puzo, author of *The Godfather*, learned the tales upon which it is based during his prior career as a writer of pulp fiction for men's magazines with titles like *True Action* and *Swank*. He drew heavily on his family heritage in Campania, Italy and his youth in gritty mid-town Manhattan in the 1930s and 1940s. E. Homberger, 'Mario Puzo: Author of the Godfather, the Book the Mafia Loved', *The Guardian*, Monday, 5 July 1999.
23 D.R. Cressey, 'Methodological Problems in the Study of Organized Crime as a Social Problem', *Annals of the American Academy of Political and Social Science*, 1967, vol. 374, p. 101, p. 112.

to Alan Block, it tends to suffer from 'historical naïveté'.[24] Too much writing on the subject amounts to a naïve propagation of the Mafia Myth in which 'the connection between the term organized crime and the supposed alien conspiracy . . . runs so deep . . . that employment of it [the term organized crime] increasingly implies acceptance of a conspiracy'.[25] Obviously there is some real substance underlying organized crime discourse. It does not have to imply that all organized crime is Italian Mafia-type organized crime. 'Unfortunately', Block argues, 'it is not enough to point out examples of historical naïveté and insensitivity with the admonishment for care and attention to historical methods.'[26]

Understanding historical change in the terminology concerning the organization of crime gives a good sense of the contestability of the terms involved. There is more to this historical evolution than can be conveyed in this short essay.[27] However, the reader can begin to appreciate that the labeling of something as 'organized crime' or 'transnational crime' or 'transnational organized crime' is not a neutral or scientific decision. All concepts are somebody's concepts, and the historical record shows that these particular abstract analytical categories are harnessed to particular institutional interests.

This point is nicely summed up by Jude McCulloch in an essay somewhat provocatively titled 'Transnational Crime as a Productive Fiction'.[28] McCulloch argues that discourses concerning the threat of transnational organized crime and the threat of global terrorism function as rhetorical justifications for the transformation and extension of the coercive capacities of states. They are a 'productive fiction'. She points out that the countermeasures common to TOC talk and to counter-terrorism discourse are ineffective and counterproductive, and goes on to systematically show how the language concerning organized crime and terrorism has served the development, maintenance and extension of social, political and economic hierarchies between and within states. It is not *just* that the concept of transnational organized crime and like terms are *social* constructions; they are *political* constructions. The security paradigm arising from the fear and anxiety created around TOC talk provides the mechanisms for political elites to 'deal' with their enemies while neutralizing the censure of human rights discourse and it has allowed stronger actors within the global system to pursue political and economic agendas unimpeded.

Realism

The probably, too brief, discussion of the previous section served to establish that abstract concepts like 'transnational crime' and 'transnational organized crime' are always components in language games in which power relations between players shape outcomes. The conclusion from this is that observable facts are formulated discursively as social and political constructs. For some people organized criminality is self-evidently a real problem and any theoretical discussion about the meaning of terms is an unwelcome side-show. Yet careful observers are alive to the difficulties in operationalizing a term like 'transnational crime' even if they remain comfortable in the assumption that, in the final analysis, it is a real thing. In short, most criminological discussion concerning transnational crime and transnational

---

24 Block, 'History and the Study of Organized Crime', p. 457.
25 Ibid., p. 470.
26 Ibid., p. 464.
27 See J. Sheptycki, *Historical Perspectives: Transnational Organized Crime, A Sage Major Works Collection Vol. 1*, London: Sage, 2014.
28 J. McCulloch, 'Transnational Crime as a Productive Fiction', *Social Justice*, 2007, vol. 34, no. 2, p. 19.

organized crime adopts a tacitly 'realist' position. Realists, whether they refer to themselves as such or not, aim to draw accurate pictures of the phenomena they problematize. Realists aim to produce coherent explanations of these phenomena and they also, although not always, aim to produce pragmatic policy recommendations about what is to be done. Criminologists do not often emphasize their ontological assumptions because it is as if that were to state the obvious. When it hits you, transnational organized crime is as real as a falling rock. And yet, there are many debates, influences and approaches to the realistic understanding of what constitutes transnational crime or transnational organized crime and quite a bit of disagreement. Any survey of the literature on organized and transnational organized crime confronts a somewhat bewildering array of interests and concerns. Observing this, there is at least some room for questioning the epistemological status of the terminology. Like 'crime', the moon may be a real object but astronomers, astronauts and astrophysicists describe it differently. Likewise, economists, political scientists, sociologists, social-policy experts and (of course) lawyers describe the reality of transnational crime differently.

Let us look briefly at some examples of criminological realism concerning transnational organized crime.[29] Louise Shelley's 'Unraveling the New Criminal Nexus'[30] and 'Anticipating Organized and Transnational Crime' by Roy Godson and Phil Williams[31] can be usefully read in tandem. These essays are good contemporary examples of typical criminological realist thinking concerning the problem of transnational organized crime. Shelley mounts a powerful case for transnational organized crime to be a central problem for global governance. She argues for a multi-pronged approach involving, among other things, coordinated international intelligence and law enforcement campaigns, development of legal tools to aid in combating organized crime, journalistic efforts to expose the activities of transnational criminals, and the integration of economic development strategies into efforts to prevent transnational organized crime.[32] According to her, the problem is not 'that of a single, monolithic, international organized crime network', but rather one of a 'multiplicity of politically and economically powerful crime groups operating both regionally and globally'.[33] These 'interlinked networks'[34] include the possibility of a 'nexus between transnational crime and terrorism'. These groups 'benefit from weak law enforcement in their home countries' while at the same time they 'depend on the structures of established states to move their commodities, launder their funds, and create a market for their goods'.[35]

Godson and Williams consider a number of models for describing the nature of the problem. The first of these are a group of 'political models'.[36] The weak states model suggests that opportunities for crime arise because of poor state capacity and lack of legitimacy.[37] Connectedly, there are many instances of 'strong states becoming weak', which provide

---

29 Again it needs to be stressed that much more could be said about realist interpretations of the problem of transantional crime. See J. Sheptycki, *Realist Perspectives on Organized and Transnational Organized Crime: A Sage Major Works Collection Vol. 3*, London: Sage, 2014.
30 L. Shelley, 'Unraveling the New Criminal Nexus', *Georgetown Journal of International Affairs*, 2005, vol. 6, no. 1, p. 5.
31 R. Godson and P. Williams, 'Anticipating Organized and Transnational Crime', *Crime, Law and Social Change*, 2002, vol. 37, p. 311.
32 Shelley, 'Unraveling the New Criminal Nexus', pp. 10–11.
33 Ibid., p. 12.
34 Ibid., p. 8.
35 Ibid., p. 9.
36 Godson and Williams, 'Anticipating Organized and Transnational Crime', pp. 315–322.
37 Ibid., p. 316.

incubators of organized crime. This happens when strong authoritarian regimes move through a period of 'dual transition' – from authoritarianism to democracy and from a centrally controlled economy to freer markets. They illustrate this model by reference to the dissolution of the USSR and the case of Mexico after the breakdown of one-party rule in the 1980s.[38] In both instances there was organized crime during the authoritarian period which became much more virulent as the strong states became weak. Political modeling along these lines is taken to suggest that democratic states with functioning governmental capacity and high levels of political legitimacy are 'crime resistant states'.[39] They also describe two closely related economic models in relation to organized crime.[40] On the one hand are markets for illicit goods and services which are subject to the laws of supply and demand and are governed by the profit motive. On the other are models of economic organization for capitalizing on factors such as new product opportunities, product dominance in the market, profit margins, competition, risk management and so on.[41] These economic models provide the basis on which to speculate about the nature of business opportunities and the strategies that different groups of criminal entrepreneurs adopt to maximize profit.[42]

Williams and Godson go on to outline three social models that depict the transnational organization of crime. First, *cultural* models concern patron–client relations, family and kinship ties. Second, *ethnic* models look at group loyalty based on shared language and other ethnic characteristics. They speculate that 'ethnically-based criminal networks are . . . difficult to penetrate since they have inbuilt defense mechanisms provided by their language and culture'.[43] Third, *social network* models describe 'webs of influence linking criminals'.[44] Williams and Godson argue that 'networks are sophisticated organizational structures that are well suited for criminal activities', because they are 'flexible and adaptable', 'resistant to disruption', 'capable of expansion', and they can extend across boundaries, for example 'between licit and illicit sectors of the economy'. Networks can also draw in 'politicians, bureaucrats, judges and law enforcement agents who are susceptible to bribery'.[45] These models can be hybridized and combined in various ways. Williams and Godson do so in order to open up a discussion about 'appropriate preventive, defensive or mitigating strategies'.[46]

Petrus van Duyne and Maarten van Dijck are less easily impressed by the knowledge base upon which these realist accounts rest. The knowledge base is what is known in police circles as 'organized crime threat assessments', and in their essay 'Assessing Organised Crime: The Sad State of an Impossible Art' they examine in close detail how these kinds of survey attempt to measure, assess and otherwise account for organized crime.[47] The threat assessments and other policy papers circulating in various policy arenas and European governmental arenas reveal 'little scientific and methodological discipline and much art'[48] and they go on to

---

38 Ibid., p. 317.
39 Ibid., p. 320.
40 Ibid., p. 320.
41 Ibid., pp. 324–325.
42 Ibid., p. 328.
43 Ibid., p. 331.
44 Ibid., p. 331.
45 Ibid., pp. 332–333.
46 Ibid., p.311.
47 P. van Duyne and M. van Dijck, 'Assessing Organised Crime: The Sad State of an Impossible Art', in F. Bovenkerk and M. Levi (eds), *The Organised Crime Economy: Essays in Honour of Alan Block,* New York: Springer, 2007, p. 101.
48 Ibid., p. 101.

caricature them as exhibiting, *inter alia*, impressionist, expressionist, magical realist and pop art styles. The literature 'is very extensive and has a complex appearance, [but] the centre of the debate simply circulates around a few imprecise words'.[49] Thus, in law enforcement 'threat assessments' there is a 'curtain of smoke' behind which there is very little real substance.[50] The problem is not that transnational crime phenomena cannot be studied with scientific rigour. It is just that the work is not done by disinterested scientific observers:

> Assessing 'organised crime' is not a neutral undertaking carried out by detached researchers. Most of the time, it is carried out by law enforcement agencies, which have an interest in its outcome. Particularly when these agencies are also tasked to fight organised crime, they have an understandable incentive to report (what they think are) serious threats. After all, they are doing a serious job. It is certainly not far fetched to state that the agency's own ranking correlates with the seriousness of its reported threats. Between agencies we even observed a kind of 'threat competition': who has the biggest threat?[51]

That is why so much of the available literature, which purports to present a pragmatic view of the transnational crime problem and what needs to be done about it, 'will not function as support tools for strategic decision making, but as justifying texts for decisions taken in other settings'.[52] When it comes to 'serious organised crime' and similar terms, the best thing to do is 'delete for research purposes' since 'this word string will merely serve conversational and political purposes.'[53] Van Duyne and van Dijck advocate thinking scientifically about the organization of crime. Essentially they think that by looking at the way social actors interact with their environment in the manufacture of specific types of criminal opportunity is the way forward for a scientifically engaged, empirical and realistic approach to the issues. The economics of protection rackets differ from the economic provision of prohibited substances, organized prostitution is different from organized theft of 'high end' vehicles, art and antiques theft has unique organizational features, as does match-fixing of sporting and racing events, and the economic and political crimes of the 'upper world' are different again. The forms and principles of criminal cooperation, the differing manifestations of criminal entrepreneurial conduct, the shape and functioning of different kinds of criminal division of labour suggest heterogeneity. Understanding this leads to sensible researchers 'declaring the organized crime concept redundant', thus saving 'time and energy for more fruitful intellectual endeavors'.[54]

The categories of 'transnational crime', 'transnational organized crime', 'serious organized crime' and so on form a family of resemblance. The core constituent term in this familial set is the concept of 'crime' but they are subject to intense political activity, especially under conditions of transnationalization when many different institutional interests vie for primacy in defining them. It is therefore difficult for social scientists to strictly adopt van Duyne's and van Dijck's recommendation. A couple of classic essays, one from a political science and one an economic point of view, give clues as to why this is the case. Charles Tilly's famous essay

---

49 Ibid., p. 106.
50 P. van Duyne and M. van Dijck, 'Assessing Organised Crime: the Sad State of an Impossible Art', in F. Bovenkerk and M. Levi (eds), *The Organised Crime Economy: Essays in Honour of Alan Block*, New York: Springer, 2007, p. 110.
51 Ibid., pp. 104–105.
52 Ibid., p. 108.
53 Ibid., p. 115.
54 Ibid., p. 121.

entitled 'War Making and State Making as Organized Crime' advances the analogy that the modern state is akin to a 'protection racket'.[55] On the basis of a historical analysis of European state-making, he argues that

> a portrait of war makers and state makers as coercive and self-seeking entrepreneurs bears a far greater resemblance to the facts than do its chief alternatives: the idea of a social contract, the idea of an open market in which operators of armies and states offer services to willing consumers, the idea of a society whose shared norms and expectations call forth a certain kind of government.[56]

To a political realist, banditry, piracy, gangland rivalry, policing and war-making all belong on the same continuum; the line between extortion and taxation, between protection racket and police force is blurred and the legitimacy of state government is a question of democratic accountability won but never granted. The economist Frederick Lane largely concurs in his brilliant essay concerning the 'Economic Consequences of Organized Violence'.[57] Quoting St Augustine – 'without justice, what is government but a great robbery?'[58] – Lane argued that, being monopoly providers, states exert powerful effects on the economic order of human relations, with consequences for social order as a whole. Police and extortionists should, in theory, be distinguishable from each other because, while the latter promise to render a benefit to none but themselves, the former promise the benefit of protection and to protect the rights of people – even against police. Economic realist thinking about the role of force in the maintenance of markets gives rise to paradoxes because the protection on offer is often protection against violence threatened by the protector in the securitization of a monopoly of violence against rival protectors. Confronting this paradox de-centers the criminological predispositions in thinking about the 'reality of organized crime' and both Lane and Tilly, albeit in very different ways, raise questions about the role of the state.

The state is a central pivot in the conjunction of criminal opportunity[59] and this is especially evident in the context of the global system.[60] Under transnational conditions awareness of the role of systemic corruption in enabling transnational crime became difficult to avoid. According to Manuel Castells, as world capitalism entered the new phase of 'informational capitalism', new planetary-wide patterns of organization – the global 'networked society' – made possible new institutional connections between actors in legitimate social, political and economic institutions including secretive interlinkages with illicit activity.[61] Hence transnational crime is the natural efflux of the global social system.

---

55 C. Tilly, 'War Making and State Making as Organized Crime', in P.B. Evans, D. Rueschemeer, and T. Skocpol (eds.), *Bringing the State Back In,* Cambridge: Cambridge University Press, 1985, p. 169.
56 Ibid.
57 F.C. Lane, 'Economic Consequences of Organized Violence', *Journal of Economic History,* 1958, vol. 18, p. 401.
58 Ibid., p. 416.
59 M. Beare, 'Corruption and Organized Crime: Lessons from History', *Crime, Law and Social Change,* 1997 vol. 28, p. 155; W.J. Chambliss, 'State-Organized Crime – The American Society of Criminology, 1988 Presidential Address', *Criminology,* 1989, vol. 27, no. 2, p. 183; D.L. Rothe and D.O. Friedrichs, 'The State of the Criminology of Crimes of the State', *Social Justice,* 2006, vol. 33, no. 1, p. 147.
60 B. Bowling and J. Sheptycki, *Global Policing,* London: Sage, 2012; J. Sheptycki, *Transnational Crime and Policing,* London, Ashgate – Pioneers in Contemporary Criminology Series, 2011.
61 M. Castells, *The Information Age: Economy, Society and Culture Vol III: End of the Millennium,* Oxford: Basil Blackwell, 1998.

While globalization opens up new vistas for criminology, the complexity of the transnational condition entails that a strictly criminological lens is insufficient to bring everything into adequate focus. David Nelken's and Michael Levi's essay 'The Corruption of Politics and the Politics of Corruption' makes this abundantly clear.[62] Corruption has been simply defined by Transparency International as 'the abuse of entrusted power for private gain',[63] but things are more complicated than this allows. As Nelken and Levi point out, both corruption and anti-corruption 'can serve to undermine (or extend) the legitimacy of politicians, [political] parties and the State'.[64] Further, perceptions of what constitutes 'corruption' are culturally relative, and there can even be 'noble cause corruption'.[65] Thus, 'corruption creates its own "normative" patterns, [and] anti-corruption campaigns may even function as a "lawless" force destroying existing order'.[66] Appreciating corruption as a 'force destroying social order' taps into a fundamental connotative meaning of the word, since the term derives from the Latin *corruptus*, from a verb meaning to abuse or destroy. Corruption is a deviation from orthodox belief or practice and often signals the dying off of a social institution: the fall of the Roman Empire has been attributed to the corruption of Roman virtue. Antithetical and contradictory as it may seem, Nelken and Levi regard the manifestation of corruption and anti-corruption as co-dependent:

> The deterioration in political and administrative service which results from the privileged access offered to their clients leads others to seek their own privileged routes, and so the cycle of corruption spirals. In the same way, a cycle of mutual dependence between politicians and organized criminals can develop.[67]

The expansion of corruption and the knee-jerk implementation of anti-corruption programs are part of an interlinked cycle in which law features as a tool in the hands of the relatively powerful, implicating the governmental apparatus in the ongoing problem:

> The enforcement of laws involving corruption and white-collar crime, often enacted on a tide of popular resentment in harness with a need for political élites to re-legitimate the State, often involves major intrusions into civil liberties, which may have broader social consequences. Precisely because there are seldom any complainants, even where the corrupt extort money from business people or the public, corruption may be seen as an opportunity for policing agencies to develop proactive strategies: but this gives powerful élites the opportunity to target selectively their political opponents (or those who refuse to pay bribes/make political 'donations' to the 'right' party) for 'sting' operations or intensive tax reviews, while leaving 'friendly' parties alone.[68]

Ultimately it is on issues of power inequalities that debates about the use of law for controlling corruption twist and turn. Nelken and Levi's thesis can be condensed into a number of solid

---

62 D. Nelken and M. Levi, 'The Corruption of Politics and the Politics of Corruption', *Journal of Law and Society*, 1996, vol. 23, no. 1, p. 1.
63 See Transparency International, 'What is the Corruption Perceptions Index?', available at www.transparency.org/cpi2011/in_detail (accessed 2 August 2013).
64 Nelken and Levi 'The Corruption of Politics and the Politics of Corruption', p. 2.
65 Ibid., p. 3.
66 Ibid., p. 3.
67 Ibid., p. 4.
68 Ibid., p. 9.

points. Law can be used by the relatively powerful in a given social order to protect corrupt practice. Law can be deliberately designed so as to make it impossible to prosecute even obviously malign power holders. Substantive law may only target the most crude and obvious exchanges of money for favors, while remaining blind to more subtle and pervasive forms of corruption. The rules of procedural law may make it difficult to mount prosecutions against élite persons; for example rules to protect privacy may be used to mask nefarious acts from legal purview. Political élites can act to ensure that the functional resourcing for policing against crimes of the powerful is inadequate to the task, perhaps by diverting those resources onto policing those in a weaker class position, hence the nifty title of Jeffrey Reiman's classic book *The Rich Get Richer, the Poor Get Prison*.[69] Finally there is the political control route, which 'refers to the ability of élites to frustrate investigations that threaten them and their allies or, alternatively, to press prosecutions against their political opponents'.[70]

Viewing 'the State' as the defender of legitimate social and political order and political élites as subservient to an abstraction like 'rule of law' becomes debatable when faced with the possibility of 'inner political power holders' mounting 'symbolic displays of action' in order to mask secretive, corrupt and criminal 'business as usual'.[71] Criminality and political economy can become intertwined in coalitions of power interests through corruption, fraud and racketeering, and this can happen in democracies just as it can in autocracies and totalitarian states. Ultimately, Nelken and Levi show that, when corruption becomes functional for social power, the politics of corruption can be played out through attempts to suppress scandal and it can also form part of the routines involved in the circulation of élite power.

Law

The genesis and application of the terminology in which the language game of 'transnational crime' is played out raises interesting points of discussion in the sociology of law. Insofar as this language game is pursued within the discourse of law it is one that is constituted as a set of legal power tools. That is to say, as the phenomenon 'transnational crime' and its various sub-categories – such as human sex trafficking, human organ trafficking, cyber-crime, transnational crimes against the environment, terrorism, intellectual property theft, piracy, cultural property theft, drug trafficking and so on – are conceptualized in legal terms they become objects of governance. Objectification in terms of legal discourse turns these phenomena into particular kinds of objects subject to the disciplinary control of particular kinds of institution in particular ways.

The transnational crime of 'intellectual property theft' (IPT) is a telling illustration of this. The new concept of 'seed piracy' was made possible by an innovation in US patent law, in a decision of the United States Supreme Court in *Diamond v Chakrabarty*.[72] Historically patents were only granted to things that were useful, novel and non-obvious and that could not be found in nature. *Diamond v Chakrabarty* found that 'anything under the sun that is made by man', including genetically altered microorganisms, could be patentable. The ability to patent

---

69 J.H. Reiman, *The Rich Get Richer, the Poor Get Prison*, New York: Wiley and Sons, 1979.
70 D. Nelken and M. Levi, 'The Corruption of Politics and the Politics of Corruption', p. 10.
71 Ibid., p. 11.
72 *Diamond v Chakrabarty*, 447 US 303; 1980, cited in K. Aoki, 'The Stakes of Intellectual Property Law', in D. Kennedy (ed.), *The Politics of Law: A Progressive Critique,* New York: Basic Books, 1998, p. 259.

genes produced new forms of property, which in principle could be stolen. In order to preserve their intellectual property rights (IPRs), the large corporations who own the patents have moved to forbid the practice of seed saving; that is, keeping back a portion of the harvest for next year's planting. Seed saving has been transformed into seed piracy.[73] Policing seed piracy has been documented in a variety of jurisdictions around the world, notably India. Private detectives gather information, intelligence and evidence while lawyers undertake prosecutions and also monitor farmers' fields once they have been convicted of seed piracy in the courts. A hybrid of both public and private forms of policing controls the activities of farmers and enforces the privatization of nature. Intellectual property rights are a form of ruling with law. The example of seed piracy shows how these new legal tools challenge, and ultimately undermine, ancient agricultural practices like seed saving, seed cleaning and seed trading between independent producers.[74]

The idea of intellectual property theft is manifest in other spheres where, interestingly, the term 'piracy' has again been brought into the language. Another manifestation of this is so-called 'movie piracy' or 'music piracy'. Majid Yar's essay 'The Global "Epidemic" of Movie "Piracy": Crime-wave or Social Construction?' offers a telling perspective on a transnational crime unique to the 'information age'.[75] With movie and music 'piracy', publically funded law enforcement agencies around the world have been drafted into policing a new kind of private property. Yar asks if this 'epidemic' of crime is a 'crime wave' or if it is 'socially constructed' as such. He observes that 'globalization, socio-economic "development" and innovation in information technology help to establish the conditions for expanded production and consumption of "pirate" audio-visual goods', but the 'epidemic' is the 'product of shifting legal regimes, lobbying activities, rhetorical maneuvers, criminal justice agendas, and "interested" or "partial" processes of statistical inference'.[76]

It is not an accident that the term 'piracy' has been attached to these phenomena as they are articulated in popular legalese. Legalese is normally thought of as an obfuscating form of legal writing which, although precise, has the effect of preventing easy comprehension by laypersons. In this instance intellectual property law is given urgency and familiar ease in popular parlance by designating IPT as *piracy*. The IPT case is made more easily in a climate predisposed to skepticism when dramatic connotations are grafted onto the terminology. Designating the free acquisition of digitally recorded entertainment through systems of user trading 'piracy' turns a mundane act into a sensational one. Similarly, turning the ancient practice of seed saving into 'seed piracy' allows for the criminalization of relatively powerless farmers and creates an apparatus for policing the interests of transnational agribusiness corporations. These examples show how the designation of forms of transnational crime in legal terms allows for a form of ruling with law. Law is a double-edged sword, however, and the seeds of resistance to the powerful interests encoded in the terms of intellectual property law can be seen in the concept of 'bio-piracy' – a quasi-legal term which refers to the harvesting and patenting of natural remedies by the pharmaceutical industry. This too might be

73 M. Laffey and J. Weldes, 'Policing and Global Governance', in M. Barnett and R. Duvall (eds), *Power in Global Governance*, Cambridge: Cambridge University Press, 2005, p. 59.
74 V. Shiva, *Stolen Harvest: The Hijacking of the Global Food Supply*, London: Zed Books, 2000.
75 M. Yar, 'The Global "Epidemic" of Movie "Piracy": Crime-wave or Social Construction?', *Media, Culture and Society*, 2005, vol. 27, no. 5, p. 677.
76 Ibid., p. 691.

considered a crime and efforts to suggest that it is further illustrated the contestability of the umbrella notion of 'transnational crimes'.[77]

Sea piracy offers another example of how the designation of transnational crime in the terms of legal discourse is essentially contestable. In 2008 and 2009 a crime panic emerged in the western media about the activities of Somali 'pirates' off the Aden peninsula on the east coast of Africa.[78] Coastal fishermen whose livelihoods were disappearing quickly due to commercial exploitation by factory fishing vessels flying foreign flags sought redress.[79] They did so by attempting to 'tax' oil tankers sailing through their waters in what was interpreted by the flag-states of those vessels as piracy and kidnap. In their defense, Somalis pointed to the effects of toxic waste dumping and factory fishing off their shores, effectively arguing that they were extending their sovereignty within the 200-mile offshore limit. In this instance the power of western media to define what was transpiring as 'sea piracy' papered over the conflict. This act of labeling unambiguously designated one party as a criminal aggressor and another as victim in a twenty-first-century manifestation of transnational crime discourse. Among other things, this meant that the naval vessels policing the pirates protected not only oil tankers, but also vessels illegally dumping toxic waste and overfishing the waters.

The interdisciplinary study of transnational crime offers many more examples of the essential contestability of its terms. The so-called 'war on drugs' is the most historically well-known case.[80] Human organ trafficking is an even more dramatic example.[81] Cyber-crime[82] produces yet another case study. White-collar crime, money laundering and other forms of economic crime also present a rich vein of evidence concerning the essential contestability of

---

77 A. Johns, *Piracy: The Intellectual Property Wars from Gutenberg to Gates*, Chicago: University of Chicago Press, 2009, p. 4; L. Orsenigo, G. Dosi and M. Mazzucato, 'The Dynamics of Knowledge Accumulation, Regulation and Appropriability in the Pharma-biotech Sector: Policy Issues', in M. Mazucato and G. Dosi (eds), *Knowledge Accumulation and Industry Evolution,* Cambridge: Cambridge University Press, 2006, p. 402, pp. 406–408; J. van Wijk, 'Terminating Piracy or Legitimate Seed Saving? The Use of Copy Protection Technology in Seeds', *Technology Analysis and Strategic Management*, 2010, vol. 16, no. 1, p. 121.

78 Bowling and Sheptycki, *Global Policing*, pp. 107–108.

79 Some scholars have even suggested that illegal fishing and overfishing might by labelled as 'organized crime'. H. Österblom, A. Constable and S. Fukumi, 'Illegal fishing and the Organized Crime Analogy', *Perception*, 2011, vol. 6, no. 7, p. 261.

80 E. Nadelmann, 'US Drug Policy: A Bad Export', *Foreign Policy*, 1988, vol. 70, p. 83; E. Nadelmann, 'Think Again: Drugs', *Foreign Policy*, 2007, vol. 162, p. 24; J. Sheptycki, 'The "Drug War": Learning from the Paradigm Example of Transnational Policing', in J. Sheptycki (ed.), *Issues in Transnational Policing*, London: Routledge, 2000, p. 210.

81 F. Ambagtsheer, D. Zaitch and W. Welmar, 'The Battle for Human Organs: Organ Trafficking and Transplant Tourism in a Global Context', *Global Crime*, 2013, vol. 14, no. 1, p. 1; L.P. Francis and J.G. Francis, 'Stateless Crimes, Legitimacy and International Criminal Law: The Case of Organ Trafficking', *Criminal Law and Philosophy*, 2010, vol. 4. no. 3, p. 283; G. Geis and G.C. Brown, 'The Transnational Traffic in Human Body Parts', *Journal of Contemporary Criminal Justice*, 2008, vol. 24, no. 3, p. 212.

82 J. Grieve, *Organized Crime in the Digital Age*, London: London Metropolitan University, John Grieve Centre for Policing and Community, and BAE Systems Detica, 2012; R. McCusker, 'Transnational Organised Cyber-Crime: Distinguishing Threat from Reality', *Crime, Law and Social Change*, 2006, vol. 46, nos 4–5, p. 257; J. Sheptycki, 'Technocrime, Criminology and Marshall McLuhan', in S. Leman-Langlois (ed.), *Technocrime: Policing and Surveillance*, Abingdon: Routledge, 2012, pp. 133–150; A.C. Yen, 'Western Frontier or Feudal Society: Metaphors and Perceptions of Cyberspace', *Berkeley Technology Law Journal*, 2002, vol. 17, no. 4, p. 1232.

the terms of transnational crime.[83] The advent of 'green criminology' and the discovery of 'crimes against the environment' is yet another.[84] Human trafficking, human smuggling, sex trafficking and sex tourism are all categories of transnational crime with highly emotive levels of connotative meaning and they too denote issues areas of great complexity and conflict – and the language is, again, made up of abstract analytical categories which are essentially contestable.[85]

These issue areas in transnational criminology, as well as others, present occasions to test the claims to analytical neutrality of our terms which we ignore at great cost. Unfortunately all of the possible issue areas cannot be fully discussed in a short essay.[86] Transnational crime presents an important object for global governance with law. Legal positivism suggests that transnational crime consists simply in those phenomena defined in law as such. The interdisciplinary criminological perspective adopted here has served to highlight the essential contestability of the 'transnational crime' concept and all others with which it shares a family resemblance. As stated at the outset of this chapter, these terms exist as components in a language game concerning certain phenomena that are in the process of being designated as objects for global governance, and, as has been shown here, that this process is political, conflictual and contested.

Conclusion

Looking at the discourse concerning transnational crime and transnational organized crime from a critical and interdisciplinary perspective has shown why it is that the official language systematized in international legal instruments such as the Palermo Convention[87] is, despite

83 M. Levi and D. Middleton, 'The Role of Solicitors in Facilitating "Organized Crime": Situational Crime Opportunities and their Regulation', *Crime, Law and Social Change*, 2005, vol. 42, nos. 2–3, p. 123; M. Levi, 'The Media Construction of White Collar Crimes', *British Journal of Criminology*, 2006, vol. 46, p. 1037; M. Levi, 'Suite Revenge? The Shaping of Folk Devils and Moral Panics about White-Collar Crimes', *British Journal of Criminology*, 2009, vol. 49, no. 1, p. 48; M. Levi and P. Reuter, 'Money Laundering', in M. Tonry (ed.), *Crime and Justice: A Review of Research*, 2006, vol. 34, Chicago: Chicago University Press, p. 289.

84 L. Bisschop, 'Out of the Woods: The Illegal Trade in Tropical Timber and a European Trade Hub', *Global Crime*, 2012, vol. 13, no. 2, p. 191; D. Brack and G. Hayman, *International Environmental Crime: The Nature and Control of Environmental Black Markets*, London: Royal Institute of International Affairs, Chatham House, 2002; N. South and P. Beirne, *Green Criminology*, Aldershot: Ashgate, 2006; R. Walters, 'Eco Mafia and Environmental Crime', in K. Carrington, M. Ball, E. O'Brien and J. Tauri (eds), *Crime, Justice and Social Democracy: International Perspectives*, London: Palgrave MacMillan, 2013, p. 281; R. White, 'Environmental Crime in Global Context: Exploring the Theoretical and Empirical Complexities', *Current Issues in Criminal Justice*, 2005, vol. 16, no. 3, p. 271; R. White, 'Depleted Uranium, State Crime and the Politics of Knowing', *Theoretical Criminology*, 2008, vol. 12, no. 1, p. 31; R. White, 'Toxic Cities: Globalising the Problem of Waste', *Social Justice*, 2009, vol. 35, no. 3, p. 107; R. White, 'Environmental Victims and Resistance to State Crime Through Transnational Activism', *Social Justice*, 2010, vol. 36, no. 3, p. 46.

85 K.F. Aas, *Globalization and Crime*, London: Sage; 2007; K.F. Aas, '"Crimmigrant Bodies" and Bona Fide Travellers: Surveillance, Citizenship and Global Governance', *Theoretical Criminology*, 2011, vol. 15, no. 3, p. 331; K.F. Aas and M. Bosworth, *The Borders of Punishment: Migration, Citizenship and Social Exclusion*, Oxford: Oxford University Press, 2013.

86 For a fuller examination see J. Sheptycki, *New Perspectives: Bringing the State Back In: A Sage Major Works Collection Vol. 4*, London: Sage, 2014.

87 The United Nations Convention against Transnational Organized Crime, 15 November 2000, 2225 UNTS 209, in force 29 September 2003.

any superficial appearance of definitional exactitude, essentially contestable. Few observers doubt that there are human activities that are harmful and thereby may be rightly labeled criminal, and that some of these activities may be transnational and/or organized in their manifestation. However, following the now classic proposition established by the labeling theorists – that the category of 'the criminal' is that which people so label[88] – defining something as 'transnational crime' or 'transnational organized crime' is not an altogether neutral and scientific decision. Formal designation as such is seldom a scientific exercise. More probably it comes as part of a policy process in which certain institutional interests are at play, which suggests that the coming into being of 'transnational crime' as an object of study has not been a disinterestedly academic matter of purely scientific inquiry. It is the phenomenological tension between realist and social-constructionist points of view which makes the study of transnational crime and its sister concepts so perturbing and ultimately underlies the contestability inherent in the terminology. For some people organized criminality is self-evidently a real problem and any theoretical discussion about the parameters of the term's meaning is unwelcome. As the analysis pursued here has shown, there are inherent difficulties in operationalizing terms like 'transnational crime' and (even worse) 'transnational organized crime', and this is especially so when it is done in legal discourse because such designations have practical consequences. Critical theorists point out that abstract concepts are always components in language games in which power relations between players shape outcomes and, therefore, that all observable facts are social and political constructs. The language for talking about 'transnational crime' and allied terms is not a neutral medium that conveys ideas independently formed. It is an institutionalized structure of meanings that channels thought and action in certain directions. It is also frequently camouflaged by its co-articulation with other concepts – security, human rights, and other emotive terms bearing moral meanings that bespeak protective action and noble motive. Before legal practitioners accept the central categories that constitute the language of transnational crime, they would do well to critically evaluate those terms. Otherwise the implementation of transnational criminal law in the effort to suppress transnational crime is likely to have paradoxical effects in terms of justice, fairness and so on. But abstract analytical categories like justice and fairness are themselves essentially contested, so perhaps the clearest lesson here is that, when it comes to terms like 'transnational crime', legal theory confronts the politics of law in a raw form.

---

88 D.E. Downes and P.E. Rock, *Understanding Deviance: A Guide to the Sociology of Crime and Rule-Breaking*, Oxford: Oxford University Press, 2007.

4

The United Nations criminal justice system in the suppression of transnational crime

Sławomir Redo

Introduction

This chapter seeks to cast light on the development of United Nations law against transnational crime. The most important feature of this complex process is the legislative transformation of international concern into binding UN treaty obligations to supress transnational crime. In the context of obligations such as those for countering trafficking in drugs and people, and regulating firearms control, this chapter demonstrates the legally nuanced growth of that international concern, examining various roles including state and non-state actors in that process. The content of 'international concern' is broad and vague. Clearly, however, it includes human rights and/or security concerns that may or may not offend fundamental moral values of the international community. Yet in all cases, a transnational offence has an actual or potential harmful effect across national borders.[1]

Drawing on the history of international action against crime and drugs (1840–2013),[2] this chapter begins by reviewing certain penal developments related to the five UN drug and crime control treaties (1961–2003), the process that before the First World War yielded the international criminalization of trafficking in people and before the Second World War the criminalization of illicit trafficking in narcotic drugs. In the over 170-year history of international action against drugs and crime, the UN's authentic involvement in international crime suppression has been relatively limited. It has only been involved in penal treaty action against drugs for sixty years and in other transnational crime treaties for just over a decade. Barring additional specific authorization for the organization to do more, the UN does little more to counter transnational crime other than through its token role under Article 102 of

---

1 N. Boister, 'Transnational Criminal Law?', *European Journal of International Law*, 2003, vol. 14, p. 953, pp. 967–977.
2 See further S. Redo, *Blue Criminology: The Power of United Nations Ideas to Counter Crime Globally. A Monographic Study*, Helsinki: HEUNI, 2012. The UN Crime Prevention and Criminal Justice Programme credits its historical origin to the International Penitentiary Congress (Frankfurt, Germany, 1846). However, in 1840 the World Anti-Slavery Convention had already been organized in London by Quakers.

the UN Charter naming the Secretariat as registrar of every treaty and international agreement.

In the UN treaty-base, there are about 60 binding treaties with penal provisions among some 500 altogether (around 12 per cent). One may therefore only very loosely speak about 'the UN Criminal Justice System'; the UNODC holds only a 1 per cent stake (five conventions) in the total number of conventions. Given this, the chapter also covers the treaty involvement of some other UN stakeholders in treaties with penal elements. As a whole this system constitutes a very diversified transnational 'hard' criminal law. These 60 treaties with penal elements constitute approximately 20 per cent of all treaties, agreements or protocols with penal provisions (approximatley 300).[3] Most of the latter are registered with IGOs other than the UN or deposited with single states. Therefore the UN criminal justice system, loose as it is, must be seen against a bigger and quite dispersed picture of international criminal treaty law.

In the penultimate section, the chapter looks at the role of civil society (CS)[4] in suppressing transnational crime. Depending on the treaty mandate, CS may or may not be entrusted with some participatory role in crime prevention and criminal justice implementation, but in one way or another it is relevant to the UN intergovernmental process against transnational crime. This role may be positive, equivocal (ambiguous/positive) or negative.

The chapter concludes with findings and comments on the issue of fundamental human values around which the concept of transnational crime continuously develops, with a view to strengthening the suppression of transnational crime by the UN.

Historical identification of transnational crime

Drug control

The growth dynamics of transnational crime may be unclear,[5] but certainly the progressive development of public international law projected in Article 13(1) of the UN Charter shows the strengthening of controls over it, ultimately through penal measures. This process is very complex. It now formally involves UN control of the licit or illicit production and trade of no fewer than 234 narcotic and psychotropic substances, while about 260 – the so-called 'designer drugs' – are not under that control.[6]

The history of criminalization of illicit cultivation and trade in narcotics reflects the complexity of this process of development. Paradoxically, the scourge of two opium wars against China by Britain (1839–1842/1850–1860) stood in the way of early international penal counteraction to the cultivation, manufacturing and distribution of narcotics. Humiliated by Britain's successful war in defence of drugs, China legalized opium's

---

3   M.C. Bassiouni, *I International Criminal Law: Crimes*, 3rd edn, Leiden: Martinus Nijhoff, 2008, p. 82, pp. 203–233.
4   Alternatively 'civil society organizations', 'global civil society', 'public participation' and 'non-governmental organizations' (NGOs); see Report of the Secretary-General in response to the report of the Panel of Eminent Persons on United Nations-Civil Society Relations, A/59/354 (2004), p. 2, n. 1.
5   It is methodologically very difficult to measure. See further: P. Knepper, 'Measuring the Threat of Global Crime: Insights from Research by the League of Nations into the Traffic of Women', *Criminology*, 2012, vol. 3, pp. 777–778.
6   UNODC, *The Challenge of New Psychoactive Substances*, Vienna: UN, 2013, p. 49.

cultivation and trade. This brought China's currency outflows to a halt, but created a huge source of tax revenue. However, tens of millions of Chinese became addicted to the drug. Twenty-seven per cent of the adult male population used it annually, 'a level of mass addiction never equalled by any other nation'.[7]

The British Government, unaware of opium's detrimental health consequences,[8] denounced China's opposition to the opium trade. Disregarding China's opposition,[9] in his role as British Foreign Secretary, Lord Palmerston defended the drug trade, arguing that China was intent upon the 'promotion of moral habits'.[10] He argued that China had an ulterior motive of stemming its balance of payments deficit by protecting its own market against foreign opium imports. Taking account of the ensuing higher-than-local import drug prices,[11] he declared this a sign of China's weak international competitiveness and poor mercantilism.

While moral and economic motives may indeed have been on a collision course (something echoed in the question of firearms regulation under the United Nations Convention against Transnational Organized Crime or UNTOC[12]), only in 1909 at the Shanghai Commission (a non-plenipotentiary entity) were the first steps taken internationally to institute administrative control over global drug trade, with China and Britain acting in concert.[13] In 1912 in The Hague, the 12 signatories of the Opium Convention[14] imposed administrative limitations on the shipment of narcotic drugs for non-medical purposes.

In 1920 international drug control became part of the Covenant of the League of Nations, and its intergovernmental Opium Advisory Committee (the forerunner of the UN Commission on Narcotic Drugs/CND) was authorized to take over the functions laid down in 1912. Among other things, the Committee was mandated to receive statistical information on opium imports, exports, re-exports, consumption, reserve stocks, etc.

In 1925, the Agreement Concerning the Manufacture of, Internal Trade in, and Use of Prepared Opium established governmental monopoly over the production, import, selling and distribution of opium. In the same year the International Opium Convention[15] introduced measures more definite than those in the Hague Convention for the limitation of the production or manufacture of narcotic substances. It introduced closer supervision of international trade (e.g. periodical reviews of related laws, limitation of ports and other

7 A.W. McCoy, 'From Free Trade to Prohibition: A Critical History of the Modern Asian Opium Trade', *Fordham Urban Law Journal*, 2000–2001, vol. 28, p. 307, p. 320.

8 Until 1926 it was widely used for recreation and dispensed to cure nervous diseases. In China it was used in folk medicine and as an appetite suppressant.

9 Between 1729 and 1858 China prohibited opium in various ways and forms.

10 P. Guedalla, *Palmerston (1784–1865)*, New York and London: G.P. Putnam's Sons 1927, p. 235.

11 H.G. Gelber, 'China as Victim: The Opium War that Wasn't', Harvard University Centre for European Studies Working Paper 136, www.howardscott.net/4/HongKong_A_Colonial_ Heritage/Files/Documentation/Gelber%20on%20the%20Opium%20Wars.pdf (accessed 30 May 2014).

12 15 November 2000, 2225 UNTS 209, in force 29 September 2003.

13 International Opium Commission, *Report of the International Opium Commission*, Shanghai, China, February 1 to February 26, 1909, Vol. I, Minutes of the Proceedings, p. 68. and International Opium Commission, Report of the International Opium Commission, Shanghai, China, February 1 to February 26, 1909, Vol. II, Reports of the Delegation, China, Memorandum on Opium from China, p. 66.

14 23 January 1912, 8 LNTS 187; in force in 23 January 1922.

15 81 LNTS 317; in force 25 September 1928.

localities for coca leaves export/import).[16] The Convention also established the Permanent Central Opium Board (the forerunner of the present International Narcotics Control Board or INCB), composed of experts in their personal capacities, including experts from non-member states of the League of Nations (LN) such as Germany and the United States. This new institutional arrangement to internationally supervise the drug industry introduced a duality that persists in the supervision of international drug control by intergovernmental (CND) and independent bodies (INCB). This is not an easy arrangement for effective drug policy reform[17] in, for example, the question of criminalization of illicit drug consumption, especially of soft drugs. Unlike the INCB, which has a limited authority to check on the compliance of a state with the three UN drug control treaties (it reacts to the reports involving estimated drug needs and drug usage, although it cannot prevent overproduction and thus potential diversion into the illicit traffic), the Opium Board did not even have the authority to question the reliability of submitted statistical returns involving governments' dealings with opium (save in those cases when excessive quantities of drugs were accumulated). On the positive side, the 1925 Convention brought cannabis under international administrative control.

In 1931, the Geneva Narcotics Manufacturing and Distribution Limitation Convention[18] placed cocaine under control and, with opium and its derivatives (morphine, heroin), established more stringent regulations over all of them. The Convention introduced a compulsory governmental estimates system aimed at limiting the world manufacture of drugs to the amounts needed for medical and scientific purposes. These administrative controls led to a fall in governmentally controlled manufacture of opiates and cocaine and to a rise in illegal drug activities by international organized crime syndicates.[19] The 1936 Convention for the Suppression of the Illicit Traffic in Dangerous Drugs[20] focused explicitly on criminalizing drug trafficking (opiates, cannabis, cocaine), but not on drug cultivation, production, manufacture and distribution. In 1961 the Single Narcotic Drugs Convention[21] filled these gaps through Article 36's criminalization of activities from extraction to importation, intentional participation, conspiracy, attempts, preparatory acts and financial operations in connection with these offences. It then opened them to extradition if sufficiently serious.

The development of other crime control treaties

By 1807 Britain had already abolished commerce in slaves. Lord Palmerston, one of the most outspoken anti-slavery crusaders, castigated his own country for engagement in 'the diabolical slave trade',[22] and demanded from Portugal and Brazil that they cease their involvement

---

16 S.K. Chatterjee, *Legal Aspects of International Drug Control*, The Hague, Boston and London: Martinus Nijhoff Publishers, 1981, pp. 117–118.

17 W.B. McAllister, *Drug Diplomacy in the Twentieth Century: An International History*, London: Routledge, 2000, pp. 156–179, pp. 240–246.

18 139 LNTS 301; in force 9 July 1933.

19 McAllister, *Drug Diplomacy in the Twentieth Century*, pp. 120–124; J. Buxton, *The Political Economy of Narcotics: Production, Consumption and Global Markets*, London: Zed Books Limited, 2006, pp. 41–42.

20 198 LNTS 299; in force 26 October 1939.

21 30 March 1961, 520 UNTS 151; in force 13 December 1964. See N. Boister, *Penal Aspects of the UN Drug Conventions*, The Hague: Kluwer Law International, 2001.

22 Quoted in H. Thomas, *The Slave Trade: The Story of the Atlantic Slave Trade: 1440–1870*, New York: Simon & Schuster, 1997, p. 736.

in transatlantic traffic.[23] He may be regarded as an early expounder of Western international moral concerns about the 'guilty traffic among the nations',[24] pressure that eventually resulted in the 1904 Agreement establishing international law enforcement cooperation in countering trafficking in people[25] and the 1910 International Convention for the Suppression of the White Slave Traffic,[26] which contained the first ever multilateral extradition provision.

Although the 1936 Convention was the first to establish certain drug offences as transnational, it was the 1910 Convention that introduced the first ever internationally recognized crime of a transnational nature – the trade in women and girls,[27] and provided for extradition for slave-related offences, in accordance with the conventions already existing between the contracting parties.[28]

The 1936 Convention introduced a new standard extradition clause, according to which states parties which 'do not make extradition conditional on the existence of a treaty or on reciprocity shall as between themselves recognize the offences referred to above as extradition crimes'.[29] That provision was repeated in the original texts of the 1961 Single Convention[30] and the 1971 Convention on Psychotropic Substances.[31] The Single Convention, as amended in 1972,[32] provided for an even newer standard: the possibility of extraditing solely on the basis of the Convention itself if a state party that makes extradition conditional on the existence of a treaty receives a request for extradition from another state party with which it has no extradition treaty.[33] That model was repeated in Article 6 of the 1988 Convention against Illicit Traffic in Narcotic Drugs and Psychotropic Substances,[34] which widened the scope of extraditable offences by including money laundering. Reports on the use of the 1988 extradition provisions are positive.[35]

Another typical provision is found in the Optional Protocol to the Convention on the Rights of the Child on the Sale of Children, Child Prostitution and Child Pornography (2000),[36] which adds that the offences listed in the Protocol shall be deemed to be included as extraditable offences in any extradition treaty existing between states parties. In addition, and in line with Article 13 of the UN Charter stipulating a progressive development of international law, the Protocol also provides that these offences shall be included as extraditable offences in every extradition treaty subsequently concluded between them, in accordance with the conditions set forth in such treaties. Finally, it provides that states parties that do not make extradition conditional on the existence of a treaty shall recognize such offences as

---

23 'We consider Portugal as morally at war with us and if she does not take good care and look well ahead, she will be physically at war with us also'; D. Brown, *Palmerston, A Bibliography*, New Haven: Yale University Press, 2010, p. 240.
24 D. Southgate, *'The Most English Minister': The Policies and Politics of Palmerston*, New York-London: Macmillan/St Martin's Press, 1966, p. 147.
25 18 May 1904, 1 LNTS 83; in force 18 July 1905.
26 4 May 1910, 8 LNTS 278; in force 5 July 1920.
27 Article 1.
28 Article 5.
29 Article 9(2).
30 Article 36(2)(b).
31 21 February 1971, 1019 UNTS 14956; in force 16 August 1976, art. 22(2)(b).
32 Protocol amending the 1961 Single Convention on Narcotic Drugs, 25 March 1972, 976 UNTS 3; in force 8 August 1975.
33 Article 36(2)(b)(ii).
34 20 December 1988, 1582 UNTS 95; in force 11 November 1990.
35 UNODC, *A Century of International Drug Control*, New York: UN, 2009, p. 78.
36 25 May 2000, 2171 UNTS 227; in force 18 January 2002.

extraditable offences between themselves subject to the conditions provided by the law of the requested state.[37]

The full multilateral extradition clause was repeated in the UNTOC in Article 16(4). The United Nations Convention against Corruption (UNCAC) uses different wording but the same idea in Article 44(2),[38] as does the 1970 Convention for the Suppression of Unlawful Seizure of Aircraft.[39] The UNCAC has recently been deemed by the UN Secretariat 'a model for most of the contemporary conventions for the suppression of specific offences'.[40] This may be so regarding general norm-setting for extradition, i.e. in terms of what so far has been or may be achieved, but not in other transnational criminal assistance matters, in which UNTOC is certainly more advanced.

The United Nations and the monitoring of the implementation of transnational crime treaties

The UN takes control

The United Nations is a part of the international arrangements through which its member states develop, adopt and implement treaties and other legal instruments countering transnational crime. The history of drug and crime control treaties shows that for 55 years (1946 to 2000) the UN had a say in drug control and rather little to say on transnational crime control.

The UN was introduced into the drug control system in 1946 through the Protocol Amending the Agreements, Conventions and Protocols on Narcotic Drugs.[41] The Protocol shifted all drug control functions that had been assigned first in 1912 to the Netherlands and in 1920 to the League of Nations. In 1961 the Single Convention on Narcotic Drugs terminated all previous drug control treaties. Recognizing that 'addiction to narcotic drugs constitutes a serious evil and is fraught with social and economic danger to mankind', it replaced them with its own penal provisions against illicit trafficking, and authorized the UN to deal with their implementation.

Even though anti-drug and anti-slavery actions have common historical roots,[42] the UN's mandate over anti-slavery actions did not begin when the UN took over control responsibilities from the League of Nations (LN) on the implementation of the International Convention for the Suppression of Traffic in Women and Children (1921)[43] and on the Circulation of Obscene Publications (1923).[44] Nor did it begin when the UN took over implementing the Convention for the Suppression of the Traffic in Persons and of the Exploitation of the Prostitution of Others (1949).[45] Until 1948, France had been mandated to deal with implementation of the latter two treaties. Only since taking over France's functions in 1948 has the UN, through the Secretariat, administered all drug control instruments. The information

---

37 Article 5.
38 31 October 2003, 2349 UNTS 41; in force 14 December 2005.
39 16 December 1970; 860 UNTS 105; in force 14 October 1971.
40 Survey of multilateral conventions which may be of relevance for the work of the International Law Commission on the topic 'The obligation to extradite or prosecute (*aut dedere aut judicare*)', Study by the Secretariat (2010), A/CN.4/630.
41 11 December 1946, 12 UNTS 179; in force 11 December 1946.
42 A number of anti-slavery activists later became strong anti-opium activists: UNODC, *A Century*, 29.
43 30 September 1921, IX LNTS 415; in force 1922.
44 12 September 1923, XXVII LNTS 213; in force 7 August 1924.
45 21 March 1950, 96 UNTS 271; in force 25 July 1951.

received on the implementation of the newer drug control treaties is published periodically by the Secretariat and sent to all member and non-member states.

Whether or not the letter of a transnational crime convention is followed is another matter. In his 1996 report on Trafficking in Women and Girls,[46] the UN Secretary-General noted the absence of a monitoring body and his concern that the lack of any enforcement mechanism would weaken the implementation and effectiveness of that Convention. In practice the Convention is monitored by the Sub-Commission on the Promotion and Protection of Human Rights of the Human Rights Council and administered by the United Nations Office of the High Commissioner for Human Rights (OHCHR, Geneva, Switzerland). The OHCHR also administers the Optional Protocol on the Sale of Children, Child Prostitution, and Child Pornography, through the Committee on the Rights of the Child (a treaty body of individually elected members). The Committee is authorized to receive states parties' comprehensive reports on the implementation of the Protocol.

The UN has only recently introduced a global state-driven monitoring process. This happened through the adoption in 2000 of the UNTOC and in 2003 of the UNCAC. Both made the UN Secretariat (i.e. UNODC) the entity responsible for their global implementation. In comparison to other legal or logistical arrangements for countering transnational crime, UNTOC – a genuinely in-house treaty – is really a better model for future global transnational crime control conventions.

Two examples support this argument. The first involves the setting by UNTOC of a new normative benchmark for the seriousness of transnational organized crime offences. Unlike preceding UN anti-drug treaties, which leave to domestic legislation and regulation what a 'serious' trafficking offence is, the UNTOC stipulates that 'serious crime' shall mean conduct constituting an offence punishable by a maximum deprivation of liberty of at least four years or a more serious penalty'.[47]

Second, UNTOC has also projected a new arrangement concerning the principles and modalities of its own self-execution. In a new step by the UN and other international organizations,[48] the UNTOC set up a Conference of States Parties for the implementation of the provisions of the convention. In other words, it is not a depository government of a treaty, or, as in the case of UN human rights treaties, a committee of experts in personal capacity, but instead it is a global, biennial, intergovernmental conference that decides how to go about the implementation of UNTOC's substantive provisions.

This change placed the UN Secretariat, and the UNODC in particular, as an essential actor in a recurrent intergovernmental exercise for the first time. Since 2002 the UN Secretariat's independence, even though still professed to be unchanged under the UN Charter's Article 100, has been gradually reduced (through attrition of permanent staff contracts, recurrent regular budget cuts and selective extra-budgetary funding). This impact of *realpolitik* also shows the Secretariat's vulnerability in terms of its essential performance regarding dealing with transnational organized matters, especially as far as treaty business is concerned. A treaty should be independently administered by the UN Secretariat from its regular budget resources. But with permanent contracts for its staff abrogated by the UN General Assembly (GA), 'he who pays the piper calls the tune' and so has the floor. This creates a suspicion that the treaty's implementation may indeed be constricted by budget resources and personnel pressures.

46 'Trafficking in Women and Girls', Report of the Secretary-General (1996), para. 27, pp. 54–55.
47 Article 2 (b).
48 The INCB monitors the three UN drug control conventions, but not as a state-driven process.

Finally, there is one further dimension of the implementation of the UN treaty law – through its model treaty laws. There are two types of model laws: those developed by the UN Secretariat with the help of experts in a personal capacity, and those developed by member states and adopted by the GA. On their face they may not differ between one another in substance, but they do differ in terms of binding force. The former is 'softer' than the latter. The latter enjoys intergovernmental consensus; the former does not.

The United Nations Commission on Crime Prevention and Criminal Justice (Commission) which, in principle, may mandate the UNODC to develop the former, does not really seize itself of the subsequent process of development, which it leaves very much to the Secretariat. Consequently, at the Commission governments may question such laws, discouraging the Secretariat from their development.[49]

State-driven drafting of a model law is different. Before reaching the GA it has fully-fledged intergovernmental involvement and the imprimatur of the Commission and the Economic and Social Council/ECOSOC. The 1990 Model Treaty on Extradition[50] belongs to this group and has been cited in case law. For example, in a case before the Human Rights Committee in which a US capital offender who escaped to Canada was extradited to the United States to face execution, Canada emphasized that it had merely complied with its obligation pursuant to the Canada–US Extradition Treaty of 1976 'which is, we would note, compatible with the UN Model Extradition Treaty'.[51]

One of several differences between such model laws and UNTOC or UNCAC is *de facto* absence of a monitoring mechanism for their implementation. Formally, together with other soft law instruments (approximately 65), the Commission has a mandate to review periodically their 'use and application' (terms considered softer than 'implementation'), but has suspended it because of resource constraints.[52] As long as essential legal institutions such as extradition are a part of a treaty implementation mechanism, this is not a big problem. But when it comes to other soft laws that do not have counterparts in treaty law, it is important that other UN entities take the place of the Commission and carry out that work. This still leaves unmonitored soft law instruments such as the Model Bilateral Treaty for the Return of Stolen or Embezzled Vehicles or the model treaty for the prevention of crimes that infringe on the cultural heritage of peoples in the form of movable property.[53] In these cases there is no second-best choice.

---

49 A mixed arrangement combines the individual–group expert process with an intergovernmental expert group process. The 'pipeline' example of this is the UNODC's project to develop Model Strategies and Practical Measures on the Elimination of Violence against Children in the Field of Crime Prevention and Criminal Justice. Technically initiated in 2013 by an individual expert meeting, the draft text of Strategies will next be considered by the intergovernmental group meeting. Subject to its recommendation it may then be considered and acted upon by the Commission, then the ECOSOC and, if so decided, the GA.

50 UN Doc. GA resolution 52/88.

51 UN Doc. CCPR/C/52/D/539/1993, *Cox v Canada*, Communication No. 539/1993. The revised Model Treaty on Extradition now authorises Member States to refuse extradition absent assurances the death penalty will not be imposed or carried out.

52 S. Redo and M. Platzer, 'The United Nations' Role in Crime Control and Prevention', in P. Reichel and J. Albanese (eds), *Handbook of Transnational Crime and Justice*, London: Sage, 2014, pp. 293–294.

53 Adopted by the Eighth United Nations Congress on the Prevention of Crime and the Treatment of Offenders (Havana, Cuba, 1990), and released as a publication (Sales No. E.91.IV.2, chap. I, sect. B.1, annex). In terms of its legislative mandate, the Congress was not a fully-fledged intergovernmental conference. In contrast, the Model Bilateral Treaty was attached to the ECOSOC resolution 1997/29, annex II something reflected in the lower and upper case lettering of their respective titles.

The implementation of UNTOC is the best example of the essential fieldwork carried out by the UNODC in technical assistance. Numerous training seminars have been organized, including seminars on the question of legal protection of witnesses,[54] money laundering[55] or the tracing, seizure, confiscation and recovery of stolen assets.[56]

Public participation in the system

These highly specialized training seminars are rightly reserved for governments, intergovernmental organizations and institutes of the United Nations Crime Prevention and Criminal Justice Programme network. But the legislative history of the UNTOC reveals instances of involvement of non-governmental organizations in a very sensitive firearm regulation project, and in the development of the Protocol against the Illicit Manufacturing of and Trafficking in Firearms, their Parts and Components and Ammunition[57] (Firearms Protocol). In 1998 and 1999 the US National Rifle Association/NRA (UN NGO) attended four regional training firearm regulation workshops together with government officials.

Public participation in countering transnational crime at the domestic level has been explicitly regulated by Article 13 of UNCAC and Article 31 of UNTOC. The way in which it was done is suggestive of member states' preferences. The most elaborate regulations pertaining to civil society (CS) involvement in the question of implementation are found in the Protocol to Prevent, Suppress and Punish Trafficking in Persons, especially Women and Children, where there are relatively wide social welfare assistance provisions.[58] There are rather basic provisions for public participation in the Protocol against the Smuggling of Migrants by Land, Sea and Air[59] (for personnel training) and they are completely absent from the Firearms Protocol – a telling example of an area where governments did not want CS to be locally active.

In regard to UN-level public participation in countering transnational crime the picture is more complex. While UNCAC rules of procedure provide for very generous participation (even of non-governmental organizations not in a consultative status with ECOSOC), public participation rules still have not been adopted by states parties to UNTOC, which have also been reluctant so far even to adopt intergovernmental rules of procedure for its implementation.

In regard to public participation in the implementation of the three UN drug control conventions, there is no specific mandate to involve the representatives of CS in the INCB's annual sessions. They may, however, be invited separately for an informal dialogue with INCB members. These devices contrast with those created by the Convention on the Rights of the Child for its independent body – the Committee on the Rights of the Child. In all

---

54 Article 24.
55 Article 7.
56 Articles 12–14.
57 Protocol against the Illicit Manufacturing of and Trafficking in Firearms, Their Parts and Components and Ammunition, supplementing the United Nations Convention against Transnational Organized Crime, New York, 31 May 2001, 2326 UNTS 208, in force 3 June 2005.
58 Protocol to Prevent, Suppress, Punish Trafficking in Persons, Especially Women and Children, supplementing the United Nations Convention Against Transnational Organized Crime, New York, 15 November 2000, 2237 UNTS 319, in force 25 December 2003.
59 Protocol Against the Smuggling of Migrants by Land, Sea and Air, supplementing the United Nations Convention Against Transnational Organized Crime, New York, 15 November 2000, 2241 UNTS 507, in force 28 January 2004.

matters covered by the Convention, it provides NGOs with a clear, well-structured and constructive role in monitoring its implementation, and with a direct reporting right to the General Assembly.[60]

Civil society may also make representations to the General Assembly through its Social, Humanitarian and Cultural Affairs Committee, and, separately, to the Security Council. In both cases the rules of procedure for public participation are not as generous as, for example, in the case of the Convention on the Rights of the Child.

The most comprehensive but parallel avenue for public participation in the implementation of the drug control treaties is paved by ECOSOC Resolution 1996/31.[61] The resolution regulates the terms of participation of non-governmental organizations in consultative status with the ECOSOC in UN business, including international crime and drug control (but not the part involving the INCB because it reports to the CND).

The CND, as a treaty organ for the 1961 and 1971 drug control conventions, and through Article 21 of the 1988 Drug Trafficking Convention, is mandated to analyse the global situation on drug control and make policy recommendations to ECOSOC on changes to enhance the drug control system. In regard to the criminological aspects of drug control and the related transnational crime, CS may speak out at the CND, which by its own Resolution 49/2 has requested NGOs to reflect on their own achievements in the context of reporting on the goals and targets set by the UN General Assembly Special Session on the World Drug Problem (1998) – 'a grave threat to the health and well-being of all mankind'.[62]

Other transnational and conventional crime topics are handled in a similar way by the annually convened Commission on Crime Prevention and Criminal Justice. This intergovernmental body is in charge of the non-treaty mandate of the UN Crime Prevention and Criminal Justice Programme. It receives reports from the Secretary-General on various forms of transnational crime that may or not have a global treaty basis mandated in or for the Programme. Civil society representatives from organizations as diverse as the Quakers and Zonta International attend only as observers.

The Commission's legal actions range from countering illicit trafficking in cultural property, to countering financial flows resulting from criminal activities such as terrorism (most recently as a threat to the tourism sector[63]). It also serves as the preparatory body for the quinquennial UN congresses on crime prevention and criminal justice.[64] At these conferences, which are subsidiary to the Commission, state participants discuss and take action with NGO participation on various rule-of-law topical issues, including those of a transnational criminal nature.

The Human Rights Council also deals with various non-treaty aspects of transnational crime, and the role of CS is very clearly pronounced by its rules of procedure. It is mandated to undertake the Universal Periodic Review (UPR) – the process by which the human rights

---

60 Article 45(a).
61 Consultative relationship between the United Nations and non-governmental organizations (1996), UN Doc. ECOSOC Resolution 1996/31.
62 Recognizing the contribution of civil society in global efforts to address the drug problem in the context of reporting on the goals and targets for 2008 set by the General Assembly at its twentieth special session (2006), UN Doc. E/2006/28; E/CN.7/2006/10, Resolution 49/2.
63 Ways and means of enhancing the effectiveness of international cooperation in countering criminal and terrorist threats and challenges to the tourism sector, including by means of public–private partnership (2013), UN Doc. E/CN.15/2013/9.
64 E.g. the Thirteenth Congress, from 12 to 19 April 2015 in Doha.

records of all 193 UN member states are reviewed once every four years, with the aim of improving the human rights situation on the ground in each state.[65] Although the basis of the UPR is a national report prepared by the state under review, that report is taken together with a compilation of information on the state under review from UN sources and a summary of information submitted by NGOs and other civil society actors. The summaries of UN and other stakeholder information are prepared by the OHCHR.

Times are changing, as, *inter alia*, documented by developments in the role of CS in the UN transnational crime treaties. Formally at least, they are more open and elaborate regarding global and local CS participation than the drug control treaties. But on a broader plane, in each and every treaty the access of CS to its implementation is dependent on the 'sentiment of the house' that results in more or less favourable respective procedural rules. Clearly, as proposed in academia,[66] there should be greater public participation in the development of transnational criminal policy and its transformation into criminal law.

Resolution 1996/31 of ECOSOC called upon the governing bodies of the relevant organizations, bodies and specialized agencies of the UN system to examine the principles and practices relating to their consultations with NGOs and to take action, as appropriate, to promote coherence in the light of its provisions. But this has not yet produced coherence in the rules for CS participation in the two transnational crime control treaties.

The impact of global civil society on the suppression of transnational crime

Three examples will assist in evaluating the influence of NGOs on the prescription and evolution of the United Nations law against transnational crime. Judging them from the standpoint of the United Nations criminal policy and prevention,[67] these examples are positive, equivocal (ambiguous/positive) and negative.

The positive example involves the role of CS in countering human trafficking, in the first of the global social movements, initiated in the 1680s by Pennsylvania Quakers (now a UN NGO). Their considerable US influence started to radiate internationally when in 1787 an anti-slavery campaign arose in Britain. In 1806, Lord Grenville, the British Prime Minster, proposed a ban on the trade to the House of Lords[68] and he introduced domestic prohibition in the 1807 Slave Trade Act. Britain then led other countries to condemn it internationally as 'repugnant to the principles of humanity and universal morality'[69] through a non-binding declaration on the Universal Abolition of the Slave Trade, appended to the Act of the Vienna Congress (1815). Subsequently, anti-slavery groups established the first Peace Societies.[70] In

---

65 Information available from the Office of the UN High Commissioner on Human Rights, www.ohchr.org/EN/HRBodies/UPR/Pages/UPRMain.aspx; see also www.upr-info.org (both accessed 1 April 2014).

66 Boister, 'Transnational Criminal Law?', p. 958.

67 Articles 13 and 55 of the UN Charter and numerous other human rights standards.

68 Slave Importation Restriction Bill. HL Deb 16 May 1806, vol. 7, cc. 227–36, Commons and Lords Hansard, The Official Report of Debates in Parliament, http://hansard.millbanksystems.com/lords/1806/may/16/slave-importation-restriction-bill (accessed 30 September 2013).

69 Declaration Relative to the Universal Abolition of the Slave Trade, 8 February 1815, Consolidated Treaty Series, vol. 63, No. 473.

70 B. Woodward, *Global Civil Society in International Lawmaking and Global Governance: Theory and Practice*, Leiden: Martinus Nijhoff Publishers, 2010, p. 81.

1839, the first European NGO – the British and Foreign Anti-Slavery Society (today Anti-Slavery International/ASI, another UN-recognized NGO[71]) – was created. In Berlin, in 1885, the British Parliament sponsored an international anti-slavery conference.[72] The Conference declared the slave trade to be forbidden under international law, introduced a soft legal norm, the principle of 'native welfare', as a matter of international concern,[73] and paved the way to the aforementioned first inter-governmentally binding agreements of 1904 and 1910.

One might think that the generous UNTOC provisions for NGO involvement in their implementation, particularly as far as countering human trafficking is concerned, provide further evidence of an undisputed progressive development of transnational criminal law and NGO influence upon it. But the sixth session of the Conference of Parties could not agree to a US $28 million estimated budget (2014–2017) for instituting the review mechanism,[74] and hence to the NGOs' role in it. Notwithstanding the absence of these implementation rules, the NGOs working under the UNTOC's umbrella still enjoy considerable support and cooperation from states and the UNODC. Here one may note, for example, the NGO attention given to the impact of anti-trafficking measures on human rights in the world.[75]

The role played by NGOs in influencing United Nations law against drugs has been an equivocal one. The ambiguity involves the argument put forward by certain NGOs that the global 'war on drugs' has not prevented the long-term trend of increasing drug supply and use. According to the partisan argument of the British 'Transform Drug Policy Foundation' (a UN NGO) they result not from drug use itself, but from choosing the punitive enforcement-led approach.[76] Another British NGO 'Count the Costs'[77] argues that the war on drugs actively undermines development and security in many of the world's most fragile regions and states.[78]

Some NGOS have played an initially ambiguous but ultimately positive role through lobbying against punitive law enforcement because of its human rights implications. These NGOs criticized the role of the UNODC in providing unreserved technical assistance to law enforcement operations such as those that resulted in the 'extraordinarily large number of killings'[79] in 2003 in Thailand of drug traffickers and peddlers, and, likewise, the large number of executions of drug offenders in Iran.[80] Eventually, after cumulative

---

71 See further: D. Weissbrodt and Anti-Slavery International, *Abolishing Slavery and its Contemporary Forms*, New York and Geneva: United Nations, 2002.

72 P.P. Hinks, J.R. McKivigan and R.O. Williams, *Encyclopedia of Antislavery and Abolition*, vol. 1, Westport, CT: Greenwood Press, 2007, p. 91.

73 Woodward, *Global Civil Society*, pp. 160–161.

74 Note by the Secretariat on the estimated financial requirements for a mechanism to review the implementation of the Organized Crime Convention and the Protocols thereto, Table 1 (2012), UN Doc. CTOC/COP/2012/14.

75 Global Alliance Against Traffic in Women, *Collateral Damage: The Impact of Anti-Trafficking Measures on Human Rights around the World*, Bangkok, 2007.

76 Transform Drug Policy Foundation, *After the War on Drugs: Blueprint for Regulation*, Bristol 2009.

77 Count the Costs, *The Alternative World Drug Report*, UK, 2012, p. 34.

78 For a review of the argument see H.H. Brownstein, *Contemporary Drug Policy. New Directions in Critical Criminology*, Abingdon and New York: Routledge, 2013, pp. 71–85.

79 'Concluding Observations of the Human Rights Committee: Thailand', UN Doc. CCPR/CO/84/THA No., 8 July 2005, paras 10 and 11.

80 Between 1997 and 2011 an estimated 10,000 drug offenders were executed in Iran – P. Gallahue, R. Gunawan, F. Rahman, K. El Mufti, N.U. Din and R. Felten, *The Death Penalty for Drug Offences: Global Overview 2012, Tipping the Scales for Abolition*, London: International Harm Reduction Association 2012, p. 27.

non-governmental and intergovernmental pressure, in 2012 the UNODC issued a position paper articulating to its offices worldwide their human rights responsibilities and conditions for rendering their field assistance in drug control projects.[81]

In some situations the drawn-out conflicts between NGOs, such as the very divisive and partisan arguments concerning global firearm regulation,[82] provide a negative example of NGO influence on the system. While many local NGOs advocate the implementation of the UNTOC's Firearms Protocol, the NRA – also a UN NGO – not only resents this Protocol and resisted its formulation at the negotiation stage, but also carefully monitors UNODC and US involvement in it. The fact that the United States has neither signed nor ratified the Protocol may be the result of the NRA's 'decisive advantage through its significant influence on the US government'.[83] Behind the constitutional prerogative of a US citizen to the right to bear arms (the prevailing interpretation which prevents the US from joining the Protocol thus far) there is the vested interest of private producers of arms to uphold that prerogative through liberal market regulation.

Philosophical rationalization for prohibitions of transnational evils and international assistance in criminal matters

The philosophical rationale for global laws in regard to transnational crime is not well explored. Ever since the rulers of European cities developed the legal protection of foreign traders through *pax urbis* policies in the early Middle Ages, urbanization seems to have been an engine for 'normative mediation'[84] powering criminal law policies aiming at *pax orbis*. This urban law-finding, now rather overlooked in criminology,[85] was crystallized by the renowned Polish penal anthropologist Juliusz Makarewicz (1872–1955).[86] It accords with the views of Hugo Grotius (1583–1645), who in *De Jure Praedae* ('On the Law of Prize and Booty', 1605/1609)[87] stressed that at the core of any international law developments there are properties shared by all humans on the basis of which their existence may be preserved. Among these properties, self-interest is the first principle of the whole natural order, but there is also man's inclination towards peaceful coexistence with others. Since self-preservation is the obvious fact in social life everywhere, Grotius argued that through *a priori* and axiomatic deduction it was possible to prove logically the specific principles of universal natural law for

---

81 UNODC and the Promotion and Protection of Human Rights, Position Paper, Vienna 2012.

82 For the excerpts from the debate, see M.A. Browne, *The United Nations and 'Gun Control'*, CRS Report for Congress, Congressional Research Service, The Library of Congress, Washington DC, 2005, available at www.fas.org/asmp/resources/govern/109th/CRSRS22108.pdf (accessed 1 April 2014).

83 A. Efrat, *Governing Guns, Preventing Plunder. International Cooperation against Illicit Trade*, Oxford: Oxford University Press, 2012, p. 100.

84 See further M. Acuto, 'City Leadership in Global Governance', *Global Governance*, 2013, vol. 19, p. 481.

85 But see e.g. L.E. Cohen, 'Uncertainty, Cooperation and Crime: Understanding the Decision to Co-offend', *Social Forces*, 1998, vol. 77, p. 155.

86 J. Makarewicz, *Einführung in die Philosophie des Strafrechts auf Entwicklungsgeschichtlicher Grundlage*, Amsterdam: E. J. Bonset, 1967, pp. 273–304.

87 H. Grotius, *De Jure Praedae Commentarius: Commentary on the Law of Prize and Booty*, trans. G.L. Williams, ed. J.B. Scott, Toronto: Oxford University Press, 1950.

human cooperation, independently of their *a posteriori* occurrence in empirical positive law.[88] He deduced four such principles[89] that balance out individual and social interests.

The existence of that core has been mathematically tested and contested through neo-Grotian game theory. Applied to testing human potential for conflict versus cooperation, on the basis of the prisoner's dilemma (PD) game, the mathematician John Nash showed that the optimum strategy was not to cooperate generally. This result was reinforced by repetitious follow-up PD experiments even though it would eventually yield a term of imprisonment half as long again.[90] For many years researchers wondered that, if negative PD outcomes are right, why then do microbes, animals and people still cooperate? A recent study found that only in a 'tit-for-tat' situation (only the opponent's last 'here and now' move) is Nash's abstract model correct. But if one adapts a longer-memory communication strategy (i.e., the players are informed about three prior moves of the opponent) then cooperation prevails.[91] It corroborates Grotius's logical proof of human natural cooperation.

This support is essential because Grotius emphasizes that only relations among individuals that transcend them constitute 'hard law' that grounds universally valid rights and rules in the world. First, this transcendental effect is facilitated by the aforementioned normative mediation of the cities. Two other experimental games (the Ultimatum Game or UG – jointly agreeing on a given sum of money to share – and Public Goods (PG) – committing funds to a joint purpose notwithstanding someone's refusal to contribute), played with randomly selected university students in cities in various regions, yielded, respectively, the most balanced and consistent positive results with regard to a common sense of fairness (UG) and common cause (PG).[92] Second, the subjects' university-level education is not only a methodological point. Interregional results of UG experiments on other groups (tribes living in a rural area) have been at wide variance with one another. In other words, in the case of students living in cities, the results showed that notions of fairness were closer to the modal 50/50 split than in tribal settings, although these notions among various cities were still somewhat different.[93]

These remarkable neo-Grotian findings lead to the following observations. First, they may imply that the notion of fairness is a developmental concept. Consequently, international technical assistance in capacity-building, including in regard to transnational justice, may enhance the understanding of that notion globally and may inform developmental assistance in criminal matters.

Second, they confirm Grotius' argument of a natural sociability instinct among people. In particular, the PG results suggest that the sociability of residents of cities managed with broader public participation involves more tolerance for otherness than in cities where that

---

88 H. van Eikema Hommes, 'Grotius' Mathematical Method', *Netherlands International Law Review*, 1984, vol. 31, no. 1, pp. 98–106.

89 Abstention from taking things of others; obligations to keep agreements, repair the damage and punish the breaches of law (H. van Eikema Hommes, 'Grotius on Natural and International Law', *Netherlands International Law Review*, 1983, vol. 30, no. 1, p. 68).

90 See generally H. Gintis (ed.), *The Bounds of Reason. Game Theory and the Unification of the Behavioral Sciences*, Princeton: Princeton University Press, 2009.

91 C. Adami and A. Hintze, 'Evolutionary Instability of Zero-determinant Strategies Demonstrates that Winning is not Everything', *Nature Communications*, 1 August 2013, 6, http://www.nature.com/ncomms/2013/130801/ncomms3193/full/ncomms3193.html#abstract (accessed 30 September 2013).

92 Gintis, *Bounds of Reason*, p. 58, pp. 79–82.

93 Ibid., p. 58.

participation is limited. That amount of tolerance is shown by a better treatment of those who did not contribute to the common cause.

Third, it may be thus observed that the steady growth of mutual legal assistance in the criminal justice area against evils which offend fundamental values of the international community is not only motivated by the ecumenical belief in fairness, propagated by the UN and like-minded entities, but also by recent mathematical evidence. This can be seen not only in the context of progressing urbanism and higher education, but also in the context of recent PD results (informed interstate cooperation in criminal matters yields better justice outcomes).

Fourth, actions like trafficking in people may indeed be evil in themselves (*mala in se*).

The above 'spontaneous' prohibition contradicts the claim that at abolition the British colonies were less dependent on the import of slaves than other countries, because they had sufficiently large local workforces, and that abolition was therefore in Britain's economic interest, since it would weaken the economic position of its competitors.[94] But this is contradicted by British colonial economic policy of the time, which, adhering to industrial age liberal economic theory, regarded commodities produced under conditions of slavery as inferior to and more expensive than those produced through free labour.[95]

More doubtful is the case of narcotic drug addiction. Whether it is inherently evil has been contested by some CS organizations.[96] They postulate the domestic decriminalization of the consumption and/or possession of soft drugs, as if it was only a moralistic dogma and that addiction to these drugs was not bad in itself but merely prohibited (*mala prohibita*). Decriminalization appears now to be rather an issue of whether or not it contradicts fundamental values of the international community rather than an economic or practical law enforcement issue.

In contrast, stricter global firearm regulation may have a dramatic moral, legal and economic impact on the arms trade and the strengthening of fundamental values of the international community, including the maintenance of peace and security in the world. Indeed, illegal arms trafficking, illicit drug trafficking, the financing of terrorism, cybercrime and trafficking in humans – by virtue of the United Nations Security Council Presidential Statement and resolution[97] – have all been qualified as acts threatening peace and security in the world.

Conclusions

Freud once responded to Einstein[98] that the one sure way of ending war is the establishment, by common consent, of a central control that shall have the last word in every conflict of interests. For this Freud thought two things necessary: the creation of a supreme court of judicature and its investment with adequate executive force. He concluded that the League of Nations, acting as a supreme court, fulfilled the first condition; it did not fulfil the second.

94 L. Thomann, *Steps to Compliance with International Labour Standards: The International Labour Standards, The International Labour Organization (ILO) and the Abolition of Forced Labour*, Heidelberg: Springer 2011, p. 187.

95 J. Chambers, *Palmerston: The People's Darling*, London: John Murray, 2004, p. 204.

96 B. Buzan, *From International to World Society? English School Theory and the Social Structure of Globalization*, Cambridge: Cambridge University Press, 2004.

97 Threats to international peace and security (2010), UN Doc. S/PRST/2010/4; Protection of civilians in armed conflict, UN Doc. S/1674 (2006).

98 A letter from Freud to Einstein, *The UNESCO Courier*, 3, Paris: UNESCO 1993, p. 4, p. 46.

Could the same be said about the United Nations criminal justice system in the suppression of transnational crime? The evidence presented in this chapter documents a steady growth of UN concern over transnational crime accompanied by its more and more incisive treaty-based transformative law. Even if the present executive force of the UN is still rather weak, nonetheless the normative and institutional developments are positive. Thus the fulfilment of the second condition, while still not imminent, is nonetheless emerging. It would be in the best interest of transnational crime control and prevention to invest further in the UN's role in it, so the thus far loose UN criminal justice system can be strengthened.

These positive developments aside, it is not without reason that 'at the very heart of the Organization's mission', as the report of the Secretary-General to the Security Council puts it, is the UN definition of the rule of law, 'consistent with international human rights norms and standards'.[99] They express the universal values or moral mandate of the United Nations. The United Nations' challenge is to live up to these founding values. This entails finding evidence to verify the dogmas of various evils. Even if NGOs offer only partisan evidence in favour of decriminalization of soft drugs, it would be the responsibility of UN member states to independently review such evidence and come to terms with it. Non-partisan knowledge and evidence make the suppression of transnational crime more effective in a changing world with evolving crime prevention and criminal justice standards and norms.

Perhaps then the UNODC, the administrative heart of the institutional system designed to counter transnational crime at global level which assists in the implementation of these norms and standards, will have appropriate capacity to contribute to fulfilling Freud's second condition.

---

99 Report of the Secretary-General on the Rule of Law and Transitional Justice in Conflict and Post-Conflict Societies (2004), para. 6, UN Doc. S/2004/616.

5

Regional organisations and the suppression of transnational crime

Valsamis Mitsilegas

Introduction

The post-Cold War security regime has been characterised by the redefinition and re-prioritisation of security threats and the growing emphasis by governments and international organisations on the need to suppress transnational crime in this context. Global initiatives in the field – such as the 2000 United Nations Convention against Transnational Organised Crime[1] and its Protocols – have been complemented by a series of initiatives taken by regional organisations with the aim of effectively countering transnational crime. The aim of this chapter is to provide an overview of regional initiatives to counter transnational crime, by focusing in particular on three paradigms of regional intervention which the author believes to have been most effective in the field. The chapter will begin by examining supranational integration through a detailed analysis of the work of the European Union in the field of transnational criminal law; it will continue with an analysis of the work of the Council of Europe, both in terms of normative production and in terms of evaluating compliance with its standards; and, before concluding with an overview of other regional initiatives in the field, it will focus on the regional dimension of the work of the Financial Action Task Force (FATF) and explain how a regional approach has enabled the global reach and effectiveness of its 'soft' Recommendations. The various and different aspects and components of regional initiatives to counter transnational crime across the globe will be highlighted, with the chapter focusing in particular on the role of regionalism in developing transnational criminal law, as well as on the measures taken by regional organisations to ensure the effective implementation of the adopted standards.

Supranational regional integration: the case of the European Union

The EU's legal order provides a benchmark for regional integration in regard to legal responses to transnational organised crime, in terms of both the volume and diversity of the measures

---

1   15 November 2000, 2225 UNTS 209, in force 29 September 2003.

adopted and the high standards of compliance and enforcement underpinning EU law. In terms of legislative and governance mechanisms to counter transnational crime, the EU has responded in a threefold manner: by approximating national criminal legislation defining serious criminal offences and imposing criminal sanctions; by facilitating judicial cooperation in criminal matters via the application of the principle of mutual recognition in the field; and by establishing a series of EU criminal justice agencies whose remit includes the fight against transnational crime.[2] The Union legislative *acquis* in the field of substantive criminal law consists at the time of writing of a combination of instruments adopted post-Maastricht (e.g. the Fraud[3] and Corruption in the Public Sector Conventions[4]), post-Amsterdam (a series of Framework Decisions addressing *inter alia* terrorism,[5] organised crime,[6] corruption[7] and drug trafficking[8] as well as a series of directives on money laundering[9]) and post-Lisbon (see the recently adopted directives on human trafficking,[10] sexual exploitation[11] and cyber-crime[12]). The fight against transnational crime is key in the articulation of EU competence to legislate on substantive criminal law in the Lisbon Treaty, with Article 83 of the Treaty of the Functioning of the European Union (TFEU)[13] conferring upon the Union competence to establish 'minimum rules' concerning 'the definition of criminal offences and sanctions' in the areas of 'particularly serious crime with a cross-border dimension' resulting from the nature or impact of such offences or from a special need to combat them on a common basis. These areas of crime are enumerated exhaustively in Article 83(1).[14] On the other hand, Article 83(2) TFEU extends Union competence to define criminal offences and adopt criminal sanctions if the approximation of criminal law proves essential to ensure the effective implementation of a Union policy in an area which has been subject to harmonisation measures.[15] The European Union has thus been at the forefront of adopting substantive criminal law measures to counter transnational crime. The Lisbon Treaty reiterates the Union's priority to tackle serious cross-border crime and provides further impetus for the development of EU legislation in the field.

---

2 V. Mitsilegas, *EU Criminal Law*, Oxford: Hart, 2009.
3 OJ C316/49, 27 November 1995.
4 OJ C195/2, 25 June 1997.
5 See the 2002 Framework Decision on combating terrorism, OJ L164/3, 22 June 2002 as amended in 2008 (OJ L330/21).
6 Framework Decision on organised crime, [2008] OJ L300/42.
7 Framework Decision on corruption in the private sector, OJ L358/2, 31 December 1998.
8 Framework Decision on drug trafficking, OJ L335/8, 11 November 2004.
9 Directive 2005/60/EC on the prevention of the use of the financial system for the purpose of money laundering and terrorist financing, OJ L309/15, 25 November 2005. See also the recent Commission proposal for a Fourth Money Laundering Directive (COM (2013) 45 final).
10 OJ L101/1, 15 April 2011
11 OJ L335/1, 17 December 2011.
12 Directive 2013/40/EU on attacks against information systems, OJ L218/8, 14 August 2013.
13 OJ C83/49, 30 February 2000.
14 Terrorism, trafficking in human beings and sexual exploitation of women and children, illicit drug trafficking, illicit arms trafficking, money laundering, corruption, counterfeiting of means of payment, computer crime and organised crime. The list of these offences may be expanded 'on the basis of developments in crime' by the Council acting unanimously after obtaining the consent of the European Parliament.
15 For an analysis of EU competence on substantive criminal law after Lisbon, see V. Mitsilegas, 'From Securitised to Functional Criminalisation: The Contested EU Competence in Substantive Criminal Law after Lisbon', in D. Acosta and C. Murphy (eds), *EU Security and Justice Law*, Oxford: Hart, 2014.

As regards judicial cooperation in criminal matters, the EU has established a system of cooperation based upon the mutual recognition of judicial decisions at all stages of the criminal process. The principle of mutual recognition goes beyond traditional judicial cooperation by requiring – with limited exceptions – the recognition and execution of judicial decisions produced in one EU Member State by judicial authorities in other Member States under tight deadlines and with a minimum of formality.[16] A raft of third-pillar measures (intergovernmental treaty-based measures rather than supranational EU legislative measures) have been adopted, establishing – at least on paper – a comprehensive system of mutual recognition extending from the pre-trial (recognition of arrest warrants,[17] evidence warrants,[18] freezing orders[19] and decisions on bail[20]) to the post-trial stage (recognition of confiscation orders,[21] decisions on financial penalties,[22] probation orders[23] and decisions on the transfer of sentenced persons[24]). Although no specific EU Framework Decision has been adopted in the field, the Court of Justice has addressed additional reflections of mutual recognition by developing detailed case-law interpreting the principle of *ne bis in idem* as enshrined in Article 54 of the Schengen Implementing Convention, which was incorporated in the EU constitutional order by the Amsterdam Treaty.[25] The principle of mutual recognition has been constitutionalised post-Lisbon, with Article 82(1) TFEU recognising the close link between mutual recognition and judicial cooperation in criminal matters.

Judicial and police cooperation is strengthened by the establishment and work of a series of European Union criminal justice agencies. The first major EU initiative in this context has been the adoption post-Maastricht of a Convention establishing the European Police Office (Europol), which has since been replaced by a post-Amsterdam Decision.[26] The establishment of Europol was followed by the establishment of Eurojust via a 2002 Decision, which has subsequently been amended by a Decision adopted shortly before the entry into force of the Lisbon Treaty in 2009.[27] The main tasks of Eurojust are to coordinate Member States'

---

16 For an analysis of the application of the principle of mutual recognition on criminal matters in the EU, see V. Mitsilegas, 'The Constitutional Implications of Mutual Recognition in Criminal Matters in the EU', *Common Market Law Review*, 2006, vol. 43, p. 1277; and V. Mitsilegas, 'The Limits of Mutual Trust in Europe's Area of Freedom, Security and Justice. From Automatic Inter-state Cooperation to the Slow Emergence of the Individual', *Yearbook of European Law 2012*, vol. 31, p. 319.

17 Framework Decision on the European Arrest Warrant [2002] OJ L190/1.

18 Framework Decision on the European Evidence Warrant [2008] OJ L350/72.

19 Framework Decision on the mutual recognition of orders freezing property or evidence [2003] OJ L196/45.

20 Framework Decision 2009/829/JHA on the application, between Member States of the European Union, of the principle of mutual recognition to decisions on supervision measures as an alternative to provisional detention, OJ L294/20, 11 November 2009.

21 Framework Decision on the mutual recognition of confiscation orders [2006] OJ L328/59.

22 Framework Decision on the mutual recognition of judgments imposing financial penalties [2005] OJ L76/16.

23 Framework Decision 2008/947/JHA on the application of the principle of mutual recognition to judgments and probation decisions with a view to the supervision of probation measures and alternative sanctions, OJ L337/102, 16 December 2008.

24 Framework Decision on the transfer of custodial sentences (sentenced persons) [2008] OJ L327/27.

25 See Cases C-187/01 and C-385/01, *Gozutok and Brugge* ECR [2003] I-1345. For an analysis of the Court's case-law on transnational *ne bis in idem* see Mitsilegas, *EU Criminal Law*, Chapter 3.

26 Council Decision 2009/371/JHA, OJ L121/37, 15 May 2009.

27 Council Decision 2002/187/JHA, OJ L63/1, 6 March 2002, as amended by Council Decision 2009/426/JHA, OJ L138/14, 4 June 2009.

activities in the field of criminal investigations and prosecutions and to provide advice on conflicts of jurisdiction. The mandate of Europol and Eurojust is largely aligned to cover a wide range of areas of serious crime. Their work is complemented by the work of OLAF, the European Anti-Fraud Office, which was established in 1999.[28] The Lisbon Treaty offers a mandate to reform Europol[29] and Eurojust.[30] Importantly, Article 86 TFEU leaves open the possibility of the establishment of a European Public Prosecutor's Office 'from Eurojust', an initiative which may lead to greater centralisation of criminal justice in Europe. New post-Lisbon legislative proposals on Europol, Eurojust and the EPPO have been tabled recently by the European Commission and are at the time of writing under negotiation in Brussels.[31]

What further differentiates the European Union legal order from traditional forms of international cooperation is its supranational character, ensuring the permeation of Union law into the domestic legal orders of EU Member States via the establishment of mechanisms devoted to the maximum enforcement of EU law. The supranational features of the EU legal order can be discerned with regard to the form of EU legislation as well as with regard to the principles underpinning it. The main legal instruments of EU law on transnational crime after the entry into force of the Treaty of Lisbon are Regulations – which have general application and are binding in their entirety and directly applicable in all EU Member States from the date of their publication in the Official Journal of the European Union without the need for any further action at Member State level – and Directives – which are binding as to the result to be achieved upon each Member State to which it is addressed, but leave to the national authorities the choice of form and methods, thus necessitating transposition into the domestic legal orders of Member States.[32] The influence of EU law on national legal orders is thus much more direct than the impact of international treaties, which require ratification at national level.

European Union law provides for a number of important enforcement avenues to ensure its effectiveness. The European Commission, as guardian of the treaties, is empowered to institute infringement proceedings before the Court of Justice against Member States which are deemed not to have implemented EU law promptly or properly and thus to have failed to fulfil their obligations under EU law.[33] This centralised avenue of enforcement is coupled with a number of important mechanisms of decentralised enforcement of EU law. The first such mechanism takes the form of the principle of direct effect, which empowers individuals to invoke and rely upon EU law provisions directly in national courts if EU law has not been implemented or properly implemented in Member States.[34] The principle is not absolute – EU law must be clear, unconditional and sufficiently precise to be invoked in national courts. However, the principle is of immense importance to ensure the full effectiveness of EU law.

---

28 Commission Decision, OJ L136/20, 31 May 1999.
29 TFEU, Article 88.
30 TFEU, Article 85(1) grants the potential to Eurojust in the future to initiate criminal investigations, as well as propose the initiation of prosecutions conducted by competent national authorities. For the potential of Article 85 of the TFEU, see A. Weyembergh, 'The Development of Eurojust: Potential and Limitations of Article 85 of the TFEU', *New Journal of European Criminal Law*, 2011, vol. 2, issue 1, p. 75.
31 Commission proposal for a Europol Regulation (COM (2013) 173 final); Commission proposal for a Eurojust Regulation (COM (2013) 535 final); Commission proposal for the establishment of a European Public Prosecutor's Office (EPPO) (COM (2013) 534 final).
32 On Regulations and Directives, see Article 288 of the TFEU.
33 Articles 258 and 260 of the TFEU.
34 Case 26/62 *Van Gend en Loos* [1963] ECR 13.

While the principle of direct effect cannot be used to aggravate the criminal liability of an individual,[35] it can be used to ensure that an individual derives rights directly from EU law in cases where it is thought that EU law has not been implemented fully or properly. This is particularly the case with regard to legislation such as the directives on the rights of suspects and defendants in criminal proceedings which have been adopted after the entry into force of the Lisbon Treaty.[36] Direct effect is complemented by the principles of indirect effect, according to which national courts are under a duty to interpret domestic law as far as possible in conformity with EU law,[37] and state liability for damages, which obliges states to award compensation for harm caused to individuals by breaches of EU law for which they can be held responsible.[38] These principles are complemented by the principle of primacy of Union law over national law, which – as with the principle of direct effect – was established by the Court of Justice in the 1960s,[39] but which has been recently reaffirmed with regard to EU criminal law post-Lisbon.[40] These principles serve to ensure the effective implementation and enforcement of European Union standards on transnational crime.

In parallel to its establishment and development as a distinct paradigm of supranational regional integration, the European Union has been evolving into a significant global actor, including in the field of transnational criminal law. The European Union has been a distinct actor within the broader European regional framework in the field. It plays an active role in exporting its *acquis* on transnational crime in the context of its enlargement and the accession process this entails, as well as in the context of the development of the European Neighbourhood Policy. As will be seen further below, the European Union is also increasingly speaking with one voice in the development and enforcement of transnational criminal law standards by the Council of Europe.[41] The European Union is also an active participant in the negotiation of international treaties in the field, including the UN Conventions on Transnational Organised Crime and Corruption, and has been a key actor in implementing global standards, including standards set out by the UN Security Council and the Financial Action Task Force (FATF).[42]

Moreover, and in particular post-9/11, the European Union has emerged as a global security actor via the negotiation and conclusion of a number of international agreements with the United States of America. These developments have not been uncontroversial, with a key question being whether the external action by the Union in the field of security and crime compromises, rather than promotes, the values upon which the Union is based, including the protection

---

35 See V. Mitsilegas, 'Article 49 (The Principles of Legality and Proportionality of Criminal Offences and Penalties)', in S. Peers, T. Hervey, J. Kenner and A. Ward (eds), *The EU Charter of Fundamental Rights. A Commentary*, Oxford: Hart, 2014.

36 See: Directive 2010/64/EU on the right to interpretation and translation in criminal proceedings, OJ L280, 26 October 2010, p.1; Directive on the right to information in criminal proceedings, OJ L142/1, 1.6.2012; and Directive on the right to access to a lawyer in criminal proceedings, OJ L294/1, 6 November 2013.

37 Case C-105/03 *Pupino* [2005] ECR I-5285.

38 Cases C-6, 9/90 *Francovich* [1991] ECR I-5357. The principle applies not only to the executive, but also under certain conditions to courts – see Case C-224/01 *Köbler* [2003] ECR I-10239.

39 Case 6/64 *Costa v Enel* [1964] ECR 585.

40 Case C-399/11, *Melloni* (2013) paras 55–59.

41 V. Mitsilegas, 'The EU and the Implementation of International Norms in Criminal Matters', in M. Cremona, J. Monar and S. Poli (eds), *The External Dimension of the Area of Freedom, Security and Justice*, Bern: Peter Lang, College of Europe Studies No. 13, 2011, p. 239.

42 V. Mitsilegas, 'The European Union and the Globalisation of Criminal Law', in *Cambridge Yearbook of European Legal Studies 2009–2010*, vol. 12, p. 337.

of fundamental rights and the rule of law.[43] However, it appears that the transformation of the European Union from a regional to a global actor in the field of transnational crime is here to stay, notwithstanding the legal dilemmas such a role may pose to the EU constitutional order.[44] This is even more so with regard to EU activism within the auspices of the Council of Europe, where the political strength of the EU has resulted in it actually shaping pan-European standards that do not necessarily bind the EU itself.[45] This has been achieved by the insistence of the EU on inserting a series of disconnection clauses (clauses providing that in their relations *inter se* EU members that were party to a multilateral convention would not apply the rules of the convention but specific rules agreed among EU members) to Council of Europe Conventions, a move which has been seen by some as resulting in the fragmentation of international law.[46] However, the insertion of disconnection clauses (which can be explained by the need to ensure the autonomy of EU law) does not alter the fact the EU has been proactive in developing comprehensive standards against transnational crime at the level of the Council of Europe. This focus on the Council of Europe is explained from an EU perspective by the desire to create a pan-European level playing field, including in cases such as anti-corruption law where there is no clear political will for the adoption of detailed internal EU criminal law.[47]

Regional cooperation with an emphasis on compliance: the case of the Council of Europe

The Council of Europe has been a major driver of regional standard-setting in the field of serious and transnational crime, having emerged as a significant norm entrepreneur in the field.[48] The first wave of Council of Europe measures in the field adopted in the early years of the organisation consisted of a number of traditional conventions on judicial cooperation in criminal matters including conventions on extradition[49] and mutual legal assistance in criminal matters.[50] In the absence of express criminal law competence of what was then the

---

43 V. Mitsilegas, 'Transatlantic Counter-terrorism Cooperation and European Values: The Elusive Quest for Coherence', in D. Curtin and E. Fahey, *A Transatlantic Community of Law*, Cambridge: Cambridge University Press, 2014.

44 See in particular the dilemmas raised in the context of terrorist sanctions and the Kadi CJEU litigation – see Mitsilegas, 'The EU and the Globalisation of Criminal Law' and references cited therein and the recent CJEU ruling in *Kadi I*: Joined Cases C-84/10 P, C-593/10 P and C-595/10, *Kadi*) – as well as the dilemmas raised in the context of transatlantic counter-terrorism cooperation: see Mitsilegas, 'Transatlantic Counter-terrorism Cooperation and European Values'.

45 For details see V. Mitsilegas, 'The EU and the Rest of the World: Criminal Law and Policy Interconnections', in M. Evans and P. Koutrakos (eds), *Beyond the Established Orders. Policy Interconnections between the EU and the Rest of the World*, Oxford: Hart, forthcoming.

46 See Mitsilegas, 'The EU and the Rest of the World'; on disconnection clauses more generally, see J. Klabbers, *Treaty Conflict and the European Union*, Cambridge: Cambridge University Press, 2009, p. 222.

47 V. Mitsilegas, 'The Aims and Limits of EU Anti-Corruption Law', in J. Horder and P. Alldridge (eds), *Modern Bribery Law: Comparative Perspectives*, Cambridge: Cambridge University Press, 2013, p. 160.

48 On the Council of Europe as norm entrepreneur more generally, see G. Sasse, 'The Council of Europe as a Norm Entrepreneur: The Political Strengths of a Weak International Institution', in N. Walker and J. Shaw (eds), *Europe's Constitutional Mosaic*, Oxford: Hart, 2011, p. 171.

49 European Convention on Extradition, Paris, 12 December 1957, ETS no. 24; in force 18 April 1960.

50 European Convention on Mutual Legal Assistance in Criminal Matters, Strasbourg, 20 April 1959, ETS no. 30; in force 12 June 1962.

European Community, these conventions constituted the cornerstone of intergovernmental judicial cooperation between Western European countries, including EC Member States. The 1990s transformed the relationship between the Council of Europe and the European Union in a twofold manner: the fall of the Berlin Wall imposed additional demands upon the work of the Council of Europe, while triggering a process of mainly eastward enlargement of the European Union; and at the same time the new political reality in Europe triggered significant constitutional developments at EU level, in particular via the granting to the EU express criminal law competence post-Maastricht.[51]

These constitutional changes have been accompanied by a renewed legislative ambition in the field of transnational criminality by the Council of Europe, via the adoption since the 1990s of a series of comprehensive, avant-garde multilateral conventions covering both substantive and procedural criminal law in areas such as money laundering[52] (followed by a convention on money laundering and terrorist finance[53]), corruption,[54] and the suppression[55] and prevention[56] of terrorism and cyber-crime.[57] The Council of Europe has thus produced a series of detailed and sophisticated legal standards to counter transnational criminality.[58] At the same time, it has acted as a catalyst for the strengthening of the legal framework in the field at both the EU and the global level. At the EU level, membership of the Council of Europe and compliance with Council of Europe standards has acted as a laboratory for membership of the European Union in the context of EU enlargement, with Council of Europe Conventions forming benchmarks with which compliance is required as a criterion of membership of the European Union. Such compliance is also a benchmark in the development of relations between the Union and its neighbours in the context of the European Neighbourhood Policy.[59] Council of Europe measures also serve as EU benchmarks in areas where the European Union is itself reluctant to legislate, such as anti-corruption law.[60] At the global level, the Council of Europe has advanced and strengthened international norms against transnational crime via the adoption of comprehensive and pioneering conventions.[61] Moreover, it is noteworthy that the Council of Europe has legislated in areas where no global consensus has thus far arisen, leading

51 For the background see Mitsilegas, *EU Criminal Law*, chapter 1.
52 Convention on Laundering, Search, Seizure and Confiscation of the Proceeds of Crime, Strasbourg, 8 November 1990, ETS no. 141; in force 1 September 1993.
53 Council of Europe Convention on Laundering, Search, Seizure and Confiscation of the Proceeds from Crime and on the Financing of Terrorism, Warsaw, 16 May 2005, ETS no.198; in force 1 May 2008.
54 Criminal Law Convention on Corruption, Strasbourg, 27 January 1999, ETS no.173; in force 1 June 2002. The Convention is complemented by a Civil Law Convention on Corruption, Strasbourg, 4 November 1999, ETS no.174; in force 1 November 2003.
55 European Convention on the Suppression of Terrorism, Strasbourg, 27 January 1977, ETS no.090; in force 4 August 1978.
56 Council of Europe Convention on the Prevention of Terrorism, Warsaw, 16 May 2005, ETS no.196; in force 1 December 2009.
57 Convention on Cybercrime, Budapest, 23 November 2001, ETS no.185; in force 1 July 2004.
58 For an overview of the evolution of the activities of the Council of Europe in criminal matters, see P. Csonka, 'Organised and Economic Crime (an overview of the Relevant Council of Europe Activities)', in P.J. Cullen and W.C. Gilmore (eds), *Crime sans Frontières: International and European Legal Approaches*, Edinburgh: Edinburgh University Press, 1998, p. 93.
59 Mitsilegas, 'The EU and the Implementation of International Norms in Criminal Matters'.
60 Mitsilegas, 'The Aims and Limits of EU Anti-Corruption Law'.
61 See W.C. Gilmore, *Dirty Money: The Evolution of Money Laundering Counter-Measures*, 4th edn, Strasbourg: Council of Europe Publishers, 2011. See also as regards one of the first conventions in this context H. Nilsson, 'The Council of Europe Laundering Convention: A Recent Example of a Developing International Criminal Law', *Criminal Law Forum*, 1991, vol. 2, p. 419.

to the adoption of comprehensive international conventions in fields such as terrorism and cyber-crime. However, Council of Europe Conventions in the field of transnational crime have been open to the participation of non-European states. A prime example in this context is the Convention on Cyber-crime, where the participation of the United States signals the evolution of a transatlantic enforcement regime despite the fact that a global consensus in favour of this particular form of legislative intervention may be lacking.[62]

The activities of the Council of Europe as regards legal responses to transnational crime have traditionally taken the form of intergovernmental cooperation via the adoption of a series of multilateral conventions. However, in recent years such inter-governmentalism has been supplemented by an innovative approach placing great emphasis on compliance of states with the obligations undertaken under these conventions, going much further than the mere ratification of conventions at national level. In this context, detailed and pioneering processes of evaluation of state action and compliance have been put forward. The first example of innovative compliance mechanisms relates to the mechanisms established within the framework of the Group of States Against Corruption (GRECO). Grounded in the Council of Europe Civil and Criminal Law Conventions on Corruption,[63] GRECO is designed to monitor their implementation by states parties, which are automatically members of GRECO.[64] It works through a process of mutual evaluation and peer pressure. In the evaluation process, a team of experts appointed by GRECO evaluates the particular member state on the basis of written replies to a questionnaire and information gathered in meetings with public officials and representatives of civil society during an on-site visit to the country. The experts' draft report is communicated to the country under scrutiny for comment before submission to GRECO for examination and adoption. Evaluation reports may conclude that legislation and practice complies – or does not comply – with the provisions under scrutiny. Recommendations requiring action within 18 months or observations which members are supposed to take into account but are not formally required to report on, may follow. The compliance procedure involves assessment of the quality of the implementation of a recommendation. Non-compliance results in re-examination within another 18 months. Compliance reports also draw an overall conclusion on implementation, in order to decide whether to terminate the compliance procedure in respect of a particular member. Finally, a special procedure, based on a graduated approach, can be applied to those members whose response to GRECO's recommendations has been found to be globally unsatisfactory.[65]

The potential of the regional evaluation mechanism set out by GRECO to promote anti-corruption standards more broadly is significant. It is noteworthy that membership of GRECO includes the United States, and that other regional organisations such as the Organisation of American States have observer status.[66] Moreover, the GRECO system has

---

62 J. Clough, 'The Council of Europe Convention on Cybercrime: defining "crime" in a digital world', *Criminal Law Forum*, 2012, vol. 23, no. 4, p. 363.

63 'The Group of States against Corruption (GRECO) shall monitor the implementation of this Convention by the Parties' – Criminal Law Convention on Corruption, Article 24; Civil Law Convention on Corruption, Article 14.

64 Articles 32 and 33 of the Criminal Law Convention; Articles 15 and 16 of the Civil Law Convention.

65 Council of Europe, *How Does GRECO Work?*, www.coe.int/t/dghl/monitoring/greco/general/4.%20How%20does%20GRECO%20work_en.asp (accessed 15 January 2014).

66 Council of Europe, *GRECO, Members and Observers*, www.coe.int/t/dghl/monitoring/greco/general/members_en.asp (accessed 15 January 2014).

been internalised to some extent at European Union level. The first EU Anti-Corruption Report (covering 2013), based on existing material from monitoring mechanisms and public data, was released by the European Commission early in 2014.[67]

The MONEYVAL system is another innovative evaluation mechanism based upon peer review set up within the framework of the Council of Europe. It aims at ensuring compliance with Council of Europe anti-money laundering standards.[68] MONEYVAL was established to address in particular the fact that not all Council of Europe members are also members of the Financial Action Task Force on money laundering (FATF).[69] MONEYVAL includes members from Central and Eastern Europe, both EU and non-EU members. The establishment of a specific peer review mechanism for these states serves to ensure that FATF-style peer review through mutual evaluation was applied to FATF non-members in Europe. The MONEYVAL benchmarks are not limited to Council of Europe standards but also include FATF, UN and EU anti-money-laundering standards.[70] The emphasis is on evaluation by experts – some appointed by FATF – with particular knowledge and experience of their domestic anti-money-laundering and terrorist finance regimes. Again questionnaires are followed by on-site country visits aimed at meeting and getting information from practitioners who work in relevant sectors. Development of an evaluation report follows, on which the evaluated country comments. When finally adopted the report provides a summary of the AML/CFT measures in place in the country, makes recommendations on strengthening their system, and sets out the country's levels of compliance with the FATF Recommendations. A detailed follow-up procedure usually commences.[71]

From 'soft' law to global law via regional intervention: the regional dimension of the Financial Action Task Force (FATF)

No analysis of regional initiatives to counter transnational crime would be complete without an examination of the regional dimension of the work of the FATF.[72] The rapid evolution and expansion of the FATF mandate, standards and membership can be attributed to its informal nature[73] and network structure, which aims at flexibility and

---

67 COM (2014) 38 final.
68 Council of Europe, *Committee of Experts on the Evaluation of Anti-Money Laundering Measures and the Financing of Terrorism (MONEYVAL)*, www.coe.int/moneyval (accessed 15 January 2014). For an overview, see W. Rau and J. Ringguth, 'Evaluation in the Framework of the Council of Europe', in A. Weyembergh and S. de Biolley (eds), *Comment Évaluer le Droit Pénal Européen?*, Brussels: Editions de l'Université de Bruxelles, 2006, p. 33.
69 See Gilmore, *Dirty Money*, p. 206.
70 See Article 2(1) fn 1, Statute of the Committee of Experts on the Evaluation of Anti-Money Laundering Measures and the Financing of Terrorism (MONEYVAL), Appendix to Resolution CM/Res(2013)13, adopted by the Committee of Ministers of the Council of Europe, 9 October 2013, available at http://www.coe.int/t/dghl/monitoring/moneyval/About/CMRes(2013)13E.pdf (accessed 12 June 2014).
71 Council Of Europe, *Evaluations: What is the Moneyval Evaluation Procedure?*, www.coe.int/t/dghl/monitoring/moneyval/Evaluations/About_evaluation_en.asp (accessed 15 January 2014).
72 See generally Chapter 20 of this volume.
73 Informal law-making is defined as dispensing with certain formalities traditionally linked to international law having to do with output, process or the actors involved – J. Pauwelyn, 'Informal International Law-making: Framing the Concept and Research Questions', in J. Pauwelyn, R.A. Wessel and J. Wouters (eds), *Informal International Lawmaking*, Oxford: Oxford University Press, 2012, p.13, p. 15.

adaptability.[74] Although the FATF only makes Recommendations, which can be character-ised as 'soft law'[75] in juxtaposition to standards adopted in the form of multilateral interna-tional treaties or supranational EU law, their impact on global law reform in the field has been immense.[76] This impact has been achieved by pairing the adoption of FATF Recommendations with a system of rigorous evaluation of their implementation and compli-ance by FATF members and non-members alike, which takes the form of mutual evaluation and peer review.[77] As a result, the FATF has become a body with selective membership but global reach. The emphasis on the regional dimension has been key in ensuring the achieve-ment of global compliance with FATF standards. This has been achieved in three ways: the expansion of FATF membership to include non-Western countries from key, strategically important regions; the expansion of the FATF system and methodology via the establishment of a series of FATF regional-style bodies; and the inclusion of regional elements in assessing compliance with FATF standards, most notably when extending such assessment beyond FATF members.

The growing importance of the regional dimension is reflected in the evolution of the membership of the FATF, which initially consisted of G7 and related Western countries as well as the European Commission.[78] Since its establishment, FATF membership has expanded significantly to include regional powers such as Russia, China, India, Mexico, Argentina and Brazil.[79] This move reflects the strategic importance of these countries in an era of financial globalisation and the changing balance of power in the global financial and political system. It has been seen as increasing the efficiency and legitimacy of the FATF[80] – with the expan-sion of FATF membership in these terms ensuring the representation of broader national and regional interests beyond a narrow Western perspective. This is particularly relevant as regards the development and adoption of FATF standards.

The importance of the regional dimension in the work of the FATF is also evident in the organisation's criteria for membership. A fundamental criterion for FATF membership is the strategic importance of the jurisdiction, one of the indicators in this context being its regional

---

74 On the network nature of the FATF see A-M. Slaughter, *A New World Order*, Princeton: Princeton University Press, 2004.

75 In the context of the FATF, it can be argued that the regular revision of both mandate and standards has been easier compared to a more formal international organisation. See in this context A. Boyle, 'Some Reflections on the Relationship of Treaties and Soft Law', *International and Comparative Law Quarterly*, 1999, vol. 48, p. 901, p. 903 noting that soft-law instruments are easier to amend or replace than treaties.

76 For further discussion see V. Mitsilegas, 'The EU and the Globalisation of Criminal Law'.

77 M. Levi and W. Gilmore, 'Terrorist Finance, Money Laundering and the Rise and Rise of Mutual Evaluation: A New Paradigm for Crime Control?', *European Journal of Law Reform*, 2002, vol. 4, p. 337.

78 In addition to the participants in the G7 summit establishing the FATF (Canada, France, Germany, Italy, Japan, United Kingdom, United States and the Commission) eight other states (Australia, Austria, Belgium, Luxembourg, Netherlands, Spain, Sweden and Switzerland) were invited to take part – Gilmore, *Dirty Money*, p. 89.

79 See Gilmore, *Dirty Money*. For a more specific regional dimension, see M.R. Machado, 'Similar in their Differences: Transnational Legal Processes Addressing Money Laundering in Brazil and Argentina', in G.C. Shaffer (ed.), *Transnational Legal Ordering and State Change*, Cambridge: Cambridge University Press, 2013, p. 50.

80 R. Hülsse and D. Kerwer, 'Global Standards in Action: Insights from Anti-Money Laundering Regulation', *Organization*, 2007, vol. 14, p. 625.

prominence in efforts against money laundering and terrorist finance. Enhancement of the geographical balance of the FATF is another membership criterion. Full and active membership of a relevant FATF-style regional body is a third membership criterion.[81] In addition to potentially acting as a laboratory for eventual FATF membership, FATF regional-style bodies play a key role in ensuring the global reach of FATF standards. At the time of writing, eight such bodies have been established covering a wide geographical and regional range. These are: the Asia/Pacific Group on Money Laundering (APGML); the Caribbean Financial Action Task Force (CFATF); as mentioned earlier, the Council of Europe Committee of Experts on the Evaluation of Anti-Money Laundering Measures and the Financing of Terrorism (MONEYVAL); the Eurasian Group (EAG); the Eastern and Southern Africa Anti-Money Laundering Group (ESAAMLG); the Financial Action Task Force on Money Laundering in South America (GAFISUD); the Inter-Governmental Action Group against Money Laundering in West Africa (GIABA); and the Middle East and North Africa Financial Action Task Force (MENAFATF).[82] All these regional bodies are entrusted with ensuring their members' compliance with the FATF Recommendations, in particular by organising FATF-style mutual evaluation and peer review processes. In this manner, the standards adopted by the FATF – an ad hoc body with selective membership – are applied via mechanisms of regional cooperation across the globe.

In addition to the importance of the regional dimension in developing, implementing and evaluating compliance with FATF standards, regional elements also play an important role in ensuring the imposition of sanctions for non-compliance with the FATF Recommendations. A key component of the FATF strategy in this context has been to assess and flag up compliance with its Recommendations and evoke sanctions for non-compliance not only as regards its members, but also globally. The initial tool in this context was the compilation of lists of non-cooperative countries and territories (NCCTs), with inclusion in these lists resulting in reputational damage and potentially exclusion from the global financial system.[83] This 'blacklisting' process has since been replaced by a more detailed system of compliance assessment, where reliance on the regional dimension is key. According to the FATF, public identification of non-cooperative jurisdictions has proved to be successful in encouraging them to improve their systems and has resulted in better worldwide compliance with the standards and enhanced international cooperation to counter money laundering, terrorist financing and other related threats.

The work of identifying and engaging with jurisdictions that have strategic deficiencies is carried out by the FATF's International Co-operation Review Group (ICRG), which reviews and monitors a large number of potentially high-risk and non-cooperative jurisdictions around the world. Since 2008, the FATF has issued public statements, three times a year, expressing concerns and calling for particular actions from FATF members and other jurisdictions.[84] Initial referral to the ICRG is based on information on threats, vulnerabilities or particular risks emanating from a specific jurisdiction that comes to the ICRG's attention. Such information includes, but is not exclusively based on, the results of mutual evaluation

---

81 FATF, *About Us: Membership Policy*, www.fatf-gafi.org/pages/aboutus/membersandobservers/fatfmembershippolicy.html (accessed 15 January 2014).

82 FATF, *About Us: FATF Members and Observers*, www.fatf-gafi.org/pages/aboutus/membersandobservers (accessed 15 January 2014).

83 On the NCCT system, see G. Stessens, 'The FATF "Black List" of Non-Cooperative Countries or Territories', *Leiden Journal of International Law*, 2001, vol. 14, p. 199.

84 The FATF has called upon its members and urged all other jurisdictions to strengthen preventive measures and apply effective countermeasures against Iran and the Democratic People's Republic of Korea, since February 2009 and February 2011.

reports (MERs) or the lack of a clear commitment to implementing the FATF standards through non-participation in any of the FATF-style regional bodies. Jurisdictions that are identified as having serious AML/CFT threats and vulnerabilities or posing significant risks are referred to the ICRG for a preliminary or prima facie review conducted by one of the four regional review groups, covering, respectively the Africa/Middle East, the Americas, the Asia/Pacific and the Europe/Eurasia regions. Based upon reports from these groups, the FATF decides whether it should conduct a more in-depth, targeted review of the relevant jurisdiction's strategic AML/CFT deficiencies. The FATF specifically requests high-level political commitment to implement these action plans. On the basis of the results of the ICRG review, jurisdictions may be publicly identified in the FATF Public Statement. The Public Statement identifies two groups of countries, namely jurisdictions in regard to which the FATF calls on its members and non-members to apply countermeasures and jurisdictions in regard to which the FATF calls only on its members to consider the risks arising from the deficiencies associated with the countries. This second category includes jurisdictions that have not made sufficient progress in addressing the deficiencies or have not committed to an action plan developed with the FATF to address the deficiencies.[85]

Other forms of regional integration

The chapter has thus far analysed prominent *fora* of regional cooperation in the suppression of transnational crime, both as regards the volume and content of their normative production and as regards their capacity to ensure the effective implementation of these norms at national level and the compliance of states parties with the standards which have been agreed at EU international level. In addition to these *fora*, a number of further regional initiatives to suppress transnational crime have emerged across the globe. The nature of these initiatives is charac-terised by considerable diversity which reflects different political priorities in different regional configurations as well as – most importantly – the differences in the constitutional nature and constraints of different forms of regional integration. Regional initiatives have emerged in a variety of formats, including the adoption of classical international conventions on aspects of transnational criminal law; the adoption of model laws on transnational crime; the adoption of political action plans and framework programmes of action; the establishment of avenues of judicial and police cooperation in the field of transnational crime; and calls for the strengthening of the institutional framework to counter transnational crime. Regional initiatives in this context have been evolving and growing over time. As with the case of the regional dimension of the work of the FATF, recent years have witnessed the expansion of the geographical and jurisdictional reach of regional initiatives across the world. Moreover, in large regions such as Africa, regional cooperation is also characterised by a further degree of specificity as regards geographical reach (cooperation at sub-regional level), as well as regarding the subject matter (subject-specific initiatives). It is also noteworthy that, as with the initiatives analysed earlier in the chapter, regional cooperation operates largely in synergy and combination with other international organisations and international initiatives.

The Southern Common Market, Mercado Común del Sur (MERCOSUR) is a regional organisation which has been particularly active in developing regional multilateral treaties in the

---

85 See, for example, Financial Action Task force, *Annual Report 2012–2013*, FATF, 2013, p. 26, available at http://www.fatf-gafi.org/media/fatf/documents/brochuresannualreports/FATF%20 Annual%20Report%202012%202013.pdf (accessed 12 June 2013).

field of transnational crime.[86] It has made security a priority.[87] Its member states have concluded a number of international agreements on matters including mutual legal assistance, human trafficking and the establishment of joint investigation teams. The parties to MERCOSUR have also signed a number of cooperation agreements with other non-full member states in the region.[88]

The Association of South East Asian Nations (ASEAN) has also expanded its activities in suppressing transnational crime to include cooperation with neighbouring states in the region. The key ASEAN legislative instrument in the field is the 2007 Convention on Counter-Terrorism, which has been deemed to be a central part of the emerging ASEAN Security Community, coupled with the establishment of ASEAN's database on terrorism and crime which has been linked to Interpol.[89] ASEAN's activities have been extended from terrorism to other areas of transnational crime, with a treaty on human trafficking being under negotiation at the time of writing.[90] The work of ASEAN on transnational crime is led by the ASEAN Ministerial Meeting on Transnational Crime (AMMTC), established in 1997, which takes place every two years. This meeting and the action plans set out therein are extended to further countries in the region,[91] including China[92] and Japan.[93]

86 On the constitutional framework of MERCOSUR see B. Olmos Giupponi, 'International Law and Sources of Law in MERCOSUR: An Analysis of a 20-Year Relationship', *Leiden Journal of International Law*, 2012, vol. 25, p. 707; and J. Vervaele, 'MERCOSUR and Regional Integration in South America', *International and Comparative Law Quarterly*, 2005, vol. 54, p. 387.

87 For an analysis of MERCOSUR as a security actor see A. Oelsner, 'Consensus and Governance in Mercosur: The Evolution of the South American Security Agenda', *Security Dialogue*, 2009, vol. 40, p. 191.

88 See in particular the agreement on mutual legal assistance in criminal matters between the parties to MERCOSUR and Bolivia and Chile, signed on 18.2.2002; the accession of Peru to this agreement, signed on 29.6.2012; the agreement on the trafficking of irregular migrants between the parties to MERCOSUR and Bolivia and Chile, signed on 16.12.2006; and the agreement between parties to MERCOSUR and associated states on the establishment of joint investigation teams, signed on 2.8.2010.

89 See R.C. Severino, 'ASEAN Beyond Forty: Towards Political and Economic Integration', *Contemporary Southeast Asia*, 2007, vol. 29, p. 406; see also J.T. Chow, 'ASEAN Counterterrorism Cooperation since 9/11', *Asian Survey*, 2005, vol. 45, p. 302; and S. Simon, 'ASEAN and Multilateralism: The Long, Bumpy Road to Community', *Contemporary Southeast Asia*, 2008, vol. 30, p. 264.

90 The Joint Statement of the Ninth ASEAN Ministerial meeting on Transnational Crime, Vientiane, Lao PDR, 17 September 2013 called upon the Working Group on Trafficking in Persons to finalise the legally binding ASEAN Convention on Trafficking in Persons (ACTIP), and the Regional Plan of Action to Combat Trafficking in Persons (RPA) and welcomed the creation of a new Working Group on Cybercrime.

91 See the Joint Statement of the 6th Ministerial Meeting Plus Three on transnational crimes (6th AMMTC + 3), 18 September 2013, acknowledging the progress in the efforts to fulfil the transnational crime component of the ASEAN Plus Three Cooperation Work Plan 2007–2017 (point 3).

92 See the Joint Statement of the third ASEAN plus People's Republic of China Minsiterial Meeting on Transnational Crime (3RD AMMTC + CHINA) to commemorate the tenth anniversary of ASEAN–China Ministerial Law Enforcement Cooperation, Vientiane, Lao PDR, 18 September 2013, noting the positive results since the 1st AMMTC + China Consultation in 2009 and the signing of the Memorandum of Understanding between the Association of South East Asian Nations (ASEAN) and the People's Republic of China and on Cooperation in the Field of Non-traditional Security Issues (MoU) in 2004 and its renewal in 2009, noting that developing law enforcement cooperation has been an important part of the ASEAN–China Strategic Partnership (point 2), and establishing the ASEAN Plus China Forum on Law Enforcement Cooperation, in order to provide focused analysis on the various areas of transnational crime in the region, and recommend counter-measures, so as to improve law enforcement capacity (point 6v).

93 See the Joint Statement of the first ASEAN plus Japan Ministerial (1ST AMMTC + JAPAN), Vientiane Capital, Lao PDR, 18 September 2013.

Another regional organisation active in Asia is the South Asian Association for Regional Cooperation (SAARC). The work of the SAARC consists of coordination of members' efforts in the field of transnational crime (see the SAARC Coordination Group of Drug Law Enforcement Agencies, the SAARC Terrorist Offences Monitoring Desk (STOMD) and the SAARC Drug Offences Monitoring Desk (SDOMD)), communication (see the SAARC Conference on Cooperation in Police Matters) and legislation (see the SAARC Convention on Narcotic Drugs and Psychotropic Substances and the SAARC Regional Convention on Suppression of Terrorism and its Additional Protocol).[94]

The adoption of regional legal standards has been key in the work of the Organization of American States (OAS), both via the adoption of multilateral conventions such as the Inter-American Convention Against Corruption[95] and, additionally, by the development of model legislation, including the Model Regulations on Money Laundering.[96] The OAS has established a Technical Group on Transnational Organised Crime and there have been calls for further regional institution-building to counter transnational crime.[97]

A multiplicity of forms of regional integration to address transnational crime has occurred in Africa, where at the same time a number of initiatives for sub-regional cooperation have emerged. Key multilateral conventions in this context have been the African Union Conventions on Preventing and Combating Terrorism[98] and Corruption.[99] In addition to these initiatives, the ECOWAS Regional Action Plan of 2008 confirmed the political commitment to fight drug trafficking and organised crime. It was officially launched in New York in 2009 and places emphasis on criminal justice reform and capacity-building, calling in particular for the establishment of transnational crime units in each country acting as national focal points for international cooperation.[100] These efforts are complemented by the work of the West Africa Coast Initiative (WACI), set up by UNODC, UNOWA/DPA, DPKO and Interpol and mandated to work in synergy to support the implementation of the ECOWAS Regional Action Plan to address the growing problem of illicit drug trafficking, organised crime and drug abuse in West Africa.[101] Another African sub-regional initiative is the Southern African Regional Police Chiefs Co-operation Organisation (SARPCCO), which is working closely with Interpol and was established in 1995; it led to the adoption in 1997 of the SARPCCO Multilateral Cooperation Agreement on Combating Crime within the Region.[102]

---

94 South Asian Association for Regional Cooperation, www.saarc-sec.org/areaofcooperation/detail. php?activity_id=25 (accessed 17 January 2014).
95 N. Boister, *An Introduction to Transnational Criminal Law*, Oxford: Oxford University Press, 2012, pp. 90–91.
96 M.A. Young, *Banking Secrecy and Offshore Financial Centres*, Abingdon: Routledge, 2013, pp. 84–85.
97 See: *Guyana Times*, 'OAS wants to Deal with Transnational Crime', 22 November 2013: 'OAS Secretary General Jose Miguel Insulza has reiterated his call to the hemisphere to move towards the creation within the institution of an entity to coordinate the fight against transnational crime', adding that 'some of the main Conventions have not been signed or ratified by all states in the region and often technical agencies do not liaise with political bodies'.
98 OAU Doc. AHG/Dec. 132 (XXXV) 1999.
99 11 July 2003, 43 ILM 5; in force 5 August 2006.
100 See UNODC, www.unodc.org/westandcentralafrica/en/ecowasresponseactionplan.html (accessed 15 January 2014).
101 On WACI, see http://unowa.unmissions.org/Default.aspx?tabid=841 (accessed 15 January 2014).
102 On SARPCCO, see http://sarpcco.org/index.php/about (accessed 15 January 2014).

Elsewhere in the world, the Pacific Plan for Regional Integration and Cooperation includes a security component consisting of strengthening cooperation in the law enforcement and border security sectors to address terrorism and transnational crime.[103] In addition to calls for greater regional cooperation and information-sharing, part of the plan is to develop model laws on security issues, following up to the Honiara Declaration.[104]

Conclusion: the regional underpinning the global

The recent past has witnessed a plethora of regional initiatives aimed at countering transnational crime. Regional intervention in the field is characterised by diversity and a multi-dimensional approach. Regional organisations have responded to the challenge of transnational crime in a variety of forms, reflecting both political priorities and the degree of regional political and legal integration. These responses range from the adoption of 'classical' multi-lateral treaties to the adoption of model legislation, soft-law measures, action plans, and mechanisms of cooperation and technical assistance on the ground. In a number of regional *fora*, some of these responses (in particular legislative and operational responses) have been combined.

This chapter has attempted to draw attention in particular to three forms of regional integration, which have yielded far-reaching results in terms of standard-setting but also in terms of ensuring effective implementation and compliance.

The first paradigm of regional integration concerns the European Union, where a supra-national system of regional integration has achieved both the adoption of detailed and comprehensive 'hard' legal standards to counter transnational crime as well as – via the compliance mechanisms inherent in EU law – an unparalleled system of monitoring the effective implementation of EU law on transnational crime and full compliance of EU Member States with EU law in the field.

The second paradigm of regional integration concerns the evolving criminal law production by the Council of Europe. Four aspects of action by the Council of Europe render this model of significance in the fight against transnational crime: the adoption of comprehensive and pioneering multilateral conventions in the field of transnational crime; the openness of these conventions to a wide range of states and organisations, including non-European states such as the United States; the ongoing synergy between Council of Europe initiatives and other regional initiatives, in particular those put forward by the European Union; and, perhaps most importantly, the strong emphasis on compliance of state parties with Council of Europe standards, achieved via the adoption of innovative and far-reaching mechanisms of mutual evaluation and peer review.

The third example concerns the regional dimension of the activities of the Financial Action Task Force. What is striking here is how the 'soft law' standards of a body with a selective membership have become the norm and been complied with globally via the use of the

---

103 Pacific Islands Forum Secretariat, Fortieth Pacific Islands Forum, Cairns, Australia, 5–6 August 2009, Forum Communiqué (PIFS (09) 12), Annex C, point e.
104 On the follow-up to the Honiara Declaration, see N. Boister, 'Regional Cooperation in the Suppression of Transnational Crime in the South Pacific', in G. Leane and B. Von Tigerstrom (eds), *International Law Issues in the South Pacific*, Farnham: Ashgate, 2005, p. 35; and N. Boister, 'Transnational Crime in the Pacific', *Journal of South Pacific Law*, 2005, vol. 9, available at http://www.usp.ac.fj/index.php?id=13303 (accessed 12 June 2014).

regional dimension. What these three paradigms of regional integration have in common is the emphasis they place on compliance and the effective implementation of norms, an emphasis which may be valuably transplanted into the work of other regional bodies. At the same time, all three paradigms demonstrate a high level of synergy and cooperation between regional organisations, as well as between regional *fora* and international organisations such as the United Nations. In this manner, action by regional organisations effectively underpins the emergence of a global legal framework to counter transnational crime.

Part II
Procedure

6

Jurisdiction over transnational crime

Roger S. Clark

Introduction

Two good friends invited me to contribute a chapter to their book on transnational criminal law. Looking at the outlines of the chapters and the names of the other contributors, I concluded that it would be a very good, and important, book. The reviewers would surely regard it as a 'significant contribution' to the literature on international and transnational criminal law. *This book.* The editors even provided me with a helpful outline to follow:

> This chapter will make a detailed examination of the manner in which states engaged in the transnational criminal law system assert, and are obliged to assert, prescriptive/legislative jurisdiction over the substantive crimes. It will analyse the jurisdictional principles (mostly originating in customary international law) that appear in the 'suppression conventions', noting the contrasting approaches in different treaty regimes regarding the use of extra-territoriality. It will also examine the use of conditional universal jurisdiction and the linkage between the jurisdictional and cooperation obligations, as well as the establishment (or lack thereof) of mechanisms to resolve conflicting assertions of jurisdiction by party states.

This was right up my alley. Obviously I would have to agree to contribute. But here's the rub: I've written on the topic before, perhaps too much,[1] and sometimes using different terminology for the concepts. How to avoid writing the same thing again? Here is the solution that I came up with: I would wrap the analysis around a treaty, not yet in force, but which I regard as the state of the art in suppression conventions: the Convention on the Suppression of Unlawful Acts Relating to International Civil Aviation.[2] It is an updated version of the 1971

---

1   R.S. Clark, 'Offenses of International Concern: Multilateral State Treaty Practice in the Forty years Since Nuremberg', *Nordic Journal of International Law*, 1988, vol. 57, p. 49; R.S. Clark, 'Some Aspects of the Concept of International Criminal Law: Suppression Conventions, Jurisdiction, Submarine Cables and *The Lotus*', *Criminal Law Forum*, 2011, vol. 22, p. 519; 'International Criminal Law', in D. Patterson and A. Södersten (eds), *The Blackwell Companion to European Law and International Law* (forthcoming 2014).
2   Done at Beijing on 10 September 2010 (hereafter the Beijing Convention).

convention on the same subject,[3] which was in its time a state-of-the-art treaty. Its jurisdictional contents (and, perhaps, striking omissions) will enable me to anchor the discussion on a real live contemporary piece of multilateral state practice, negotiated against the backdrop of over two centuries of suppression conventions, both bilateral and multilateral.[4]

There are, of course, some assumptions made in the outline my editors so kindly supplied. Those assumptions need some early explanation. One assumption is that what I shall call 'categories of jurisdiction' exist; another is that there are certain established 'bases of jurisdiction'.

As to 'categories', the American Law Institute's *Restatement (Third) of the Foreign Relations Law of the United States* draws a distinction that I shall utilize, as follows:

> (a) jurisdiction to prescribe, *i.e.*, to make [a state's] law applicable to the activities, relations, or status of persons, or the interests of things, whether by legislation, by executive act or order, by administrative rule or regulation, or by determination of a court;
> (b) jurisdiction to adjudicate, *i.e.*, to subject persons or things to the process of [a state's] courts or administrative tribunals, whether in civil or in criminal proceedings, whether or not the state is a party to the proceedings;
> (c) jurisdiction to enforce, *i.e.*, to induce or compel compliance with [a state's] laws or regulations, whether through the courts or by use of executive, administrative, police or other nonjudicial action.[5]

My friends the editors hedged their terminological bets a little by describing the first category as 'prescriptive/legislative', thus emphasizing the law-making nature of what we are describing here. In the context of suppression conventions, the prescriptive activity is that of the relevant organ of the state, normally the legislature, in domesticating the treaty obligation into its own penal law.[6] While adjudicative jurisdiction normally goes hand in hand with prescriptive jurisdiction, I shall argue strongly that an important feature of suppression conventions is that

---

3 Montreal Convention for the Suppression on Unlawful Acts against the Safety of Aircraft, 23 September 1971, 974 UNTS 177; in force 26 January 1973. Supplemented by the Protocol for the Suppression of Unlawful Acts of Violence at Airports Serving International Civil Aviation, concluded at Montreal, 24 February 1988, 1589 UNTS 474; in force 21 June 1998. Also done at Beijing on 10 September 2010 was the Protocol Supplementary to the Convention for the Suppression of Unlawful Seizure of Aircraft. The Protocol amends the Hague Convention for the Suppression of Unlawful Seizure of Aircraft (Hijacking), 16 December 1970, 860 UNTS 105; in force 14 October 1971, with similar jurisdictional provisions to those in the 2010 Unlawful Acts Convention. For purposes of exegesis, I found it more convenient to write about the 'clean' text that is the 2010 Unlawful Acts Convention, but a similar analysis could be made of the 1970 Convention as amended in 1970.
4 The earliest suppression provision of which I am aware is Article 20 of the 1794 Treaty of Amity, Commerce and Navigation between Great Britain and the United States ('Jay Treaty'), 52 *Consolidated Treaty Series* 243, which obligated the parties to 'bring to condign punishment' those who assist pirates from the land.
5 American Law Institute, *Restatement of the Law, Third, Foreign Relations Law of the United States* (1987), § 401.
6 The normal expectation of suppression conventions is that the parties will need to adopt new legislation or amend existing law in order to give effect to the relevant convention obligations. Sometimes there will be existing prescriptive work in place so that the main point of the obligations will be one of exercising enforcement jurisdiction and encouraging others to do so. Criminal legislation on land-based assistance to pirates was already in force in both Great Britain and the United States in 1794, so the main expectation of the Jay Treaty, *supra* note 4, may well have been enforcement. *See* Piracy Act 1698 (UK), Section 10 (the source of the reference to 'condign punishment') and First Cong., Sess. II, Chap. IX, Sections 10, 11 and 12 (US).

enforcement jurisdiction is often exercised by a state other than (or perhaps more accurately, in addition to) the state desirous of exercising its prescriptive/adjudicative jurisdiction.

As to 'bases of jurisdiction', or 'jurisdictional principles' as my editors would have it: I start with the analysis in the highly regarded 1935 *Harvard Research in International Law.*[7] Based on an extensive study of State legislative practice,[8] the Harvard researchers isolated a number of widely accepted bases of jurisdiction: territorial jurisdiction,[9] nationality jurisdiction,[10] persons assimilated to nationals,[11] protective (security of the State),[12] protective

7 *Research in International Law Under the Auspices of the Faculty of the Harvard Law School, Drafts of Conventions Prepared for the Codification of International Law, American Journal of International Law (Supplement)*, 1935, vol. 29, 1 (hereinafter *Harvard Draft*). Relevant here is the section on Jurisdiction with Respect to Crime, beginning at p. 443. The study follows the basic format used by the American Law Institute and later the UN International Law Commission of drafting 'black letter' and accompanying research notes and commentary.
8 I do not cavil at my editors' suggestion that this state practice amounts to some sort of customary international law – the legislature can speak for the state in creating customs, just as the executive may.
9 *Harvard Draft* Article 3:

> A State has jurisdiction with respect to any crime committed in whole or in part within its territory.
> This jurisdiction extends to

> (a) Any participation outside its territory in a crime committed in whole or in part within its territory; and
> (b) Any attempt outside its territory to commit a crime in whole or in part within its territory.

Article 4 confirms that for jurisdictional purposes 'a public or private ship or aircraft which has its national character' is treated as part of the national territory. The phrase 'committed in whole or in part within its territory' provides the hook for a discussion of what the *Draft* calls 'subjective' and 'objective' application. As to 'subjective application' the *Draft*, at p. 484, refers to 'the so-called subjective territorial principle which establishes the jurisdiction of the State to prosecute and punish for crime commenced within the State but completed or consummated abroad'. As to 'objective application', the *Draft*, at pp. 487–488, notes 'the so-called objective territorial principle which establishes the jurisdiction of a State to prosecute and punish for crime commenced without the State but consummated within its territory'. The authors add, at p. 488, that 'the same principle has been applied by the Permanent Court of International Justice in the case of the *S.S. Lotus*, where an act or omission within the jurisdiction of one State produced unintended effects within the jurisdiction of another State'.
10 *Harvard Draft*, Article 5:

> A State has jurisdiction with respect to any crime committed outside its territory,

> (a) By a natural person who was a national of that State when the crime was committed or who is a national of that State when prosecuted or punished; or
> (b) By a corporation or another juristic person which had the national characteristic of that State when the crime was committed.

11 *Harvard Draft*, Article 6:

> A State has jurisdiction with respect to any crime committed outside its territory

> (a) By an alien in connection with discharge of a public function which he was engaged to perform for that State; or
> (b) By an alien while engaged as one of the personnel of a ship or aircraft having the national character of that State.

12 *Harvard Draft*, Article 7:

> A State has jurisdiction with respect to any crime committed outside its territory by an alien against the security territorial integrity or political independence of that State, provided that the act or omission which constitutes the crime was not committed in exercise of a liberty guaranteed the alien by the law of the place where it was committed.

(counterfeiting),[13] and universality in respect of piracy.[14] Notably excluded from the black letter of the *Draft* was passive personality jurisdiction, namely 'legislation and practice of those States which assert jurisdiction over offences committed against their nationals abroad by whomsoever'.[15] The authors noted that:

> An important group of States asserts such jurisdiction; others would contest it. Many writers favor it, while others oppose it. . . . It has been vigorously opposed in Anglo-American countries.[16]

In lieu of such a basis of jurisdiction, the *Harvard Draft* offered the opinion that a final provision on 'universal jurisdiction' that it put forward was a more desirable way to achieve the same ends as passive personality jurisdiction (and some other ends as well). This was Article 10, which read:

> A State has jurisdiction with respect to any crime committed outside its territory by an alien, other than the crimes mentioned in Articles 6, 7, 8, and 9, as follows:
>
> (a) When committed in a place not subject to its authority but subject to the authority of another State, if the act or omission which constitutes the crime is also an offence by the law of the place where it was committed, if surrender of the alien for prosecution has been offered to such other State or States and the offer remains unaccepted, and if prosecution is not barred by lapse of time under the law of the place where the crime was committed. The penalty imposed shall in no case be more severe than the penalty prescribed for the same act or omission by the law of the place where the crime was committed.
>
> (b) When committed in a place not subject to the authority of any State, if the act or omission which constitutes the crime is also an offence by the law of a State of which the alien is a national, if surrender of the alien for prosecution has been offered to the State or States of which he is a national and the offer remains unaccepted, and if prosecution is not barred by lapse of time under the law of the State of which the alien is a national.
>
> (c) When committed in a place not subject to the authority of any State, if the crime was committed to the injury of the State assuming jurisdiction, or one of its nationals, or of a corporation or juristic person having its national character.

---

13 *Harvard Draft*, Article 8:

> A State has jurisdiction with respect to any crime committed outside its territory by an alien which consists of a falsification or counterfeiting, or an uttering of falsified copies or counterfeits, of the seals, currency, instruments of credit, stamps, passports, or public documents, issued by that State or under its authority.

14 *Harvard Draft*, Article 9:

> A State has jurisdiction with respect to any crime committed outside its territory by an alien which constitutes piracy by international law.

15 *Harvard Draft* at p. 578.

16 Ibid., pp. 578–579. Times change; not all 'Anglo-American' jurisdictions are so opposed any more. In the Criminal Code Amendment (Offences against Australians) Act 2002, Australia took jurisdiction over murder, manslaughter, intentionally causing serious harm, or recklessly causing serious harm to an Australian citizen or resident of Australia. No knowledge is required on the part of the accused that the victim is an Australian citizen or resident.

(d) When committed in a place not subject to the authority of any State and the alien is not a national of any State.[17]

Insisting upon the advantages of this formulation over the inclusion of a passive personality provision, the authors commented:

> Under the present article, indeed, no less than three groups of States will find practical realization of an asserted competence: first, States asserting a universal jurisdiction over so-called *delicta juris gentium* other than piracy; second, States asserting jurisdiction on the principle of passive personality; and third, States which assert jurisdiction on the principle of universality substantially as herein delimited.[18]

Article 10, and the state practice which it seeks to codify, is a direct ancestor of what my editors call 'conditional universal jurisdiction' or 'extradite-or-prosecute jurisdiction'.

An important feature of the *Harvard Draft* was that the list of bases was not a closed one. Indeed, the black letter provision headed 'Scope of Convention' reads:

> A State's jurisdiction with respect to crime is defined and limited by this Convention; but nothing in its provisions shall preclude any of the parties to this Convention from entering into other agreements, or from giving effect to other agreements now in force, concerning competence to prosecute and punish for crime, which affect only the parties to such other agreements.[19]

This invitation to innovate by treaty is one that has been taken up on many occasions in subsequent suppression conventions. There is another general point here. Modern suppression conventions typically contain a mixture of obligatory and optional bases on which States Parties must or may, as the case may be, exercise jurisdiction. Inserting a particular theory (such as passive personality) into a treaty, whether as a required basis or as an optional one, enhances its legitimacy. Even a party which chooses not to take up an option must be estopped *vis-à-vis* other parties from asserting that the particular theory is unacceptable.

A final introductory thought on the Beijing Convention

As a matter of substance, it greatly expands on the list of proscribed acts contained in its 1971 predecessor. It now includes not only direct sabotage of aircraft and violence to person or property at airports but also various acts with radioactive and other weapons. It also proscribes specifically the September 11 act of using an aircraft in service 'for the purpose of causing death, serious bodily injury, or serious damage to property or the environment'.[20]

With the substance in mind, we can now turn to the jurisdictional aspects of the Convention.

17 *Harvard Draft*, Article 10.
18 *Harvard Draft*, p. 579.
19 *Harvard Draft*, Article 2.
20 Beijing Convention, Article 1(1)(f).

Prescriptive/legislative jurisdiction

Obligatory bases of jurisdiction

The Convention being a typical suppression convention, the parties undertake to exercise their legislative authority to make the offences set forth in the treaty 'punishable by severe penalties'.[21] Each party is required to

> take such measures as may be necessary to establish its jurisdiction over the offences:
>
> (a) when the offence is committed in the territory of that State;
> (b) when the offence is committed against or on board an aircraft registered in that State;
> (c) when the aircraft on board which the offence is committed lands in its territory with the alleged offender still on board;
> (d) when the offence is committed against or on board an aircraft leased without crew to a lessee whose principal place of business or, if the lessee has not such place of business, whose permanent residence is in that State;
> (e) when the offence is committed by a national of that State.[22]

Moreover, and this is the 'conditional universal jurisdiction' provision:

> Each State Party shall likewise take such measures as may be necessary to establish its jurisdiction over the offences set forth in Article 1, in the case where the alleged offender is present in its territory and it does not extradite that person pursuant to Article 12 to any of the States Parties that have established their jurisdiction in accordance with the applicable paragraphs of this Article with regard to those offences.[23]

Subparagraphs (a) and (b) require little exegesis here. They represent simple applications of the principles in Article 3 and 4 of the *Harvard Draft*[24] about territorial jurisdiction and its extension to aircraft and ships registered in the State. Subparagraph (c) is more creative. It is what I have elsewhere called 'landing state jurisdiction'.[25] An assertion of jurisdiction by a port state over events that occurred on a foreign ship on the high seas or on an aircraft prior to landing is not without precedent.[26] But as a treaty matter, and in relation to aircraft, this phrase first appeared in the 1970 Hague Hijacking Convention[27] and the 1971 Montreal Convention. It is a perfect example, is it not, of the application of Article 2 of the *Harvard Draft* that States may enter into 'other agreements' about competence to prosecute for crime. The latter part of Article 2 of the *Harvard Draft* is of interest here. It adds the words 'which affect only the parties to such other agreements'. Here's the catch: is this jurisdictional theory based on the State of

---

21 Ibid., Article 3.
22 Ibid., Article 8(1).
23 Ibid., Article 8(3). In practical terms, the reference here is to States listed in Article 8(1), *supra*, (obligatory grounds to take jurisdiction) and Article 8(2), *infra* (optional grounds).
24 *Supra*.
25 E.S. Podgor and R.S. Clark, *Understanding International Criminal Law*, 2013, 3rd edn, LexisNexis, § 2.05.
26 See e.g. Crimes Act 1961 (New Zealand), Section 8(1)(c) (jurisdiction over acts or omissions of a person who '[o]n board any ship or aircraft, if that person arrives in New Zealand on that ship or aircraft in the course of or at the end of a journey during which the act was done or omitted'.
27 16 December 1970; 860 UNTS 105; in force 14 October 1971.

landing applicable only against a national of another State Party to the Convention or is it applicable *erga omnes*? At some point, the number of parties may become so overwhelming[28] that the treaty provision may be regarded as having entered into international customary law. But in the meantime, the argument is there. Subparagraph (d) is a slight extension of the territorial theory which takes into account one business structure for supplying aircraft in international traffic. Subparagraph (e) is bland, a mere adoption of nationality jurisdiction.

The conditional universal jurisdiction provision is a direct descendant of the *Harvard Draft*'s Article 10 universal jurisdiction provision. It first appeared in essentially its current form in the 1970 Hague Hijacking Convention.[29] It is often called 'extradite or prosecute', *aut dedere aut judicare* or *aut dedere aut prosequi*. The obligation is spelled out further in Article 10 of the Convention, which provides:

> The State Party in the territory of which the alleged offender is found shall, if it does not extradite that person, be obliged, without exception whatsoever and whether or not the offence was committed on its territory, to submit the case to its competent authorities for the purpose of prosecution. Those authorities shall take their decision in the same manner as in the case of any ordinary offence of a serious nature under the law of that State.[30]

The obligation, it will be noted, is not necessarily to bring a case to trial; what is required is that a professional prosecutor makes a good-faith determination on whether to proceed. This is a subsidiary or fallback jurisdiction, conditional on possible negotiation with other states who might wish to exercise jurisdiction. It arises because of the presence of the suspect in the national territory.[31] It is to be compared with the 'pure' form of universal jurisdiction which

---

28 The 1971 Montreal Convention has 188 Parties, an overwhelming representation of the world community surely.

29 *Supra* Article 4. For an exhaustive discussion of examples, see Study by the Secretariat, Survey of multilateral conventions which may be of relevance for the work of the International Law Commission on the topic 'The obligation to extradite or prosecute (*aut dedere aut judicare*)', UN Doc. A/CN.4/630 (2010).

30 Beijing Convention, Article 10.

31 Modest forms of extradite or prosecute made their first appearance in the International Convention for Suppression of Counterfeiting Currency, Geneva, 20 April 1929, 112 LNTS 371. The Convention requires parties to criminalize counterfeiting of foreign currency (primarily on territorial grounds). It adds these obligations:

> In countries where the principle of extradition of nationals is not recognized, nationals who have returned to the territory of their own country after the commission abroad of an offence [under the Convention] should be punishable in the same manner as if the offence had been committed in their own territory, even in a case where the offender has acquired his nationality after the commission of the offence. (Article 8)

And:

> Foreigners who have committed abroad any offence [under the Convention], and who are in the territory of a country whose internal legislation recognizes as a general rule the principle of the prosecution of offences committed abroad, should be punishable in the same way as if the offence had been committed in the territory of that country.
>
> The obligation to take proceedings is subject to the condition that extradition has been requested and that the country to which application is made cannot hand over the person accused for some reason which has no connection with the offence. (Article 9)

These are the provisions that morphed into the extradite-or-prosecute provision in the 1970 Hijacking Convention.

applies to pirates, who are more likely to be captured on the high seas than to be found on land.[32]

Speaking of comparable provisions in the Convention against Torture, the Joint Separate Opinion of Judges Buergenthal, Higgins and Kooijmans in the *Arrest Warrant Case* reads:

> The great treaties on aerial offences, hijacking, narcotics and torture are built on the concept of *aut dedere aut prosequi. Definitionally, this envisages presence on the territory.* There cannot be an obligation to extradite someone you choose not to try unless that person is within your reach.[33]

The Convention against Torture[34] was also at the heart of the case brought by Belgium against Senegal in the International Court of Justice in an endeavour to have Senegal prosecute M. Habré, the former President of Chad, who had sought asylum in its territory. Commenting on the duty to prosecute or extradite in the context of the particular language of the treaty, the Court stated that:

> Extradition is an option offered to the State by the Convention, whereas prosecution is an international obligation under the Convention [owed to other parties to the Convention], the violation of which is a wrongful act engaging the responsibility of the State.[35]

The Court emphasized Senegal's obligation to prosecute, since it had clearly been stalling for some years, but stopped short of saying that the alternative was to extradite *to Belgium.* Belgium was certainly willing to act, but presumably there might be other ways to fulfil the obligation.[36]

Optional bases of jurisdiction

Article 8, paragraph 2 of the Beijing Convention asserts that a State 'may also establish its jurisdiction' over the treaty offences in two situations, '(a) where the offence is committed against a national of that State', and '(b) where the offence is committed by a stateless person whose habitual residence is the territory of that State'. The first is our old friend passive personality jurisdiction. There must still be States that are less than enthusiastic about it, but they have

---

32 A useful way to think of the difference is this: it is hard to base an extradition request on the theory that once the accused is delivered up to the requesting State he can now be 'found' in that State. See *United States v Rezaq*, 134 F.3d 1121 n. 4 (DC Cir. 1998). On the other hand, 'pure' universal jurisdiction may support an extradition request if the treaty contains suitable language. For example, the 1931 United States/United Kingdom Extradition Treaty of 1931, 28 UST 5290, still in force between the United States and about 20 Commonwealth countries, includes in its list of extraditable offences 'piracy by the law of nations'.

33 *Case Concerning the Arrest Warrant of 11 Apr. 2000 (D.R. Congo v. Belgium)*, 2002 ICJ Rep 3, Joint Separate Opinion of Judges Buergenthal, Higgins and Kooijmans, para. 57 (emphasis in original).

34 Convention Against Torture and Other Cruel, Inhuman or Degrading Treatment or Punishment, 10 December 1984, 1465 UNTS 85; in force 26 June 1987.

35 *Questions relating to the Obligation to Prosecute or Extradite (Belgium v Senegal)*, 2012 ICJ Reports p. 422.

36 In August 2012, Senegal and the African Union agreed to establish a special court within the Senegalese justice system with African judges appointed by the AU. In July 2013, Habré was charged with crimes against humanity, war crimes and torture and placed in pre-trial detention. See www. hrw.org/habre-case.

conceded that other States may go ahead and use it. The second harks back to an issue raised by the *Harvard Draft*. It will be recalled that the *Draft* included in its black letter an article dealing with extraterritorial jurisdiction over persons 'assimilated to nationals'.[37] The categories there were 'an alien in connection with discharge of a public function which he was engaged to perform for that State'[38] and 'an alien while engaged as one of the personnel of a ship or aircraft having the national character of that State'. This was as far beyond 'real' nationals as the authors of the *Draft* were prepared to go. In discussing the extent of nationality jurisdiction, they noted that, while a few States assert jurisdiction to prosecute domiciled aliens for crimes committed abroad, the great majority of States assert no such jurisdiction.[39] They added, however, that '[t]he one case in which such an assimilation would be most plausible is the case of persons who are "stateless" . . .'[40] This prescient comment from 1935 has been acted upon in 2010.

Article 8, paragraph 2 carries with it a procedural obligation. Upon ratifying, accepting, approving or acceding to the Convention each State Party is required to 'notify the Depositary [the International Civil Aviation Organization] of the jurisdiction it has established under its national law in accordance with paragraph 2 of Article 8, and immediately notify the Depositary of any change'.[41]

These two provisions in paragraph 2 are quite precise. Article 8 paragraph 4 contains potentially a much more open-ended 'optional' basis, which concedes that even without specific authorization, the classes are not necessarily closed. It provides: 'This Convention does not exclude any criminal jurisdiction exercised in accordance with national law.' What exactly it does in the Beijing Convention is a mystery. This language made its first appearance in the 1963 Tokyo Convention on Offences and Certain Other Acts committed on Board Aircraft.[42] That Convention required the State of registration of aircraft to take jurisdiction over events occurring on those craft ('flag state' jurisdiction for aircraft).[43] The United States had argued in the negotiations that the primary form of jurisdiction in aircraft cases should be that of the place where the aircraft landed. It failed to convince the other negotiators to that effect. But the language about national law was included in the 1963 treaty to save the possibility of exercising 'landing state' jurisdiction, which, indeed, the United States did.[44] In the 1970 Hague Convention, landing state jurisdiction was obligatory, so an identical saving provision[45] may well have protected nationality jurisdiction (which was not included). Yet the

---

37 *Harvard Draft*, Article 6.
38 One engaged as a soldier in a foreign army would be a typical example.
39 *Harvard Draft*, p. 533.
40 Ibid, pp. 533–534. Compare the Australian passive personality legislation, which applies to Australian residents as well as to citizens.
41 Beijing Convention, Article 21(4).
42 14 September 1963; 704 UNTS 219, in force 4 December 1969.
43 The Tokyo Convention is best regarded as a content-free suppression convention. It had become apparent that many States had not exercised their legislative competence to take jurisdiction over what happened on aircraft registered by them. Although these were relatively quiet days for aircraft hijacking, it was already a problem, as were other annoyances such as unruly passengers. The Tokyo Convention also recognizes significant enforcement jurisdiction. In particular all Contracting States are required to take custody of any person arrested by the commander aboard another Contracting State's aircraft. It must immediately make a preliminary inquiry into the facts and notify the State of registration, the State of nationality and any other interested State of the situation. It must promptly report the results of its preliminary inquiry to those States and indicate whether it intends to exercise jurisdiction: Tokyo Convention, Article 13. The expectation is that the other States will be able to decide whether to institute extradition proceedings.
44 See *US v Georgescu*, 723 F Supp. 912 (EDNY 1989).
45 1970 Hague Convention, Article 4 (3).

2010 treaty itself contains both landing state and nationality jurisdiction (Article 8 (1)) which certainly do not now need to be saved. Are there some other cases where the subsection may have some bite? What of a State that now adopts a 'pure' form of universal jurisdiction rather than the 'fallback' version required by the Convention, which depends on presence?[46] Does the broader principle of *The Lotus* still reign? Does that get a boost from the saving provision? Is all permitted unless it is forbidden? Or is paragraph 4 merely mindless repetition of past language?[47]

Enforcement jurisdiction

Many of the nineteenth-century suppression treaties are interesting for the way in which they separate prescriptive jurisdiction from enforcement jurisdiction. Thus, the anti-slave trade treaties that Great Britain entered into with many other players in Europe,[48] the Americas[49] and even Africa[50] usually required the parties to enact penal legislation on a nationality or flag state basis to suppress the trade. On the enforcement front, however, either party could take enforcement measures to free the slaves but needed to hand the slave traders over to the flag or national State for criminal processing.[51] I have written elsewhere about how this pattern plays out in the Submarine Cables Convention of 1884.[52] Thieves, vandals and idiots who

46 On the distinction, see *supra* at notes 23 and 29 to 33.

47 One form of optional jurisdiction that does not appear in the Beijing Convention is 'transferred jurisdiction', where a State typically delegates its prescriptive, adjudicative and enforcement jurisdiction to another State either by treaty or in a one-off action. See generally, Podgor and Clark, *Understanding International Criminal Law*, § 2.05. In the drug area such delegations are legitimated by Article 17 of the 1988 United Nations Convention against Illicit Traffic in Narcotic Drugs and Psychotropic Substances, 1582 UNTS 95. There is significant United States practice in engaging in such transferred jurisdiction, although there is not much American literature explaining it and there is no reference to it in standard American sources. It may be some sort of relative of the *Harvard Draft* Article 10, *supra*.

48 E.g. Additional Convention between Great Britain and Portugal for the Prevention of the Slave Trade, signed at London, 28 July 1817, 67 *Consolidated Treaty Series* 373.

49 E.g. Brazil and Great Britain, Convention for the Abolition of the African Slave Trade, 23 November 1826, 76 *Consolidated Treaty Series* 491; Great Britain and United States, Treaty for the Suppression of the African Slave Trade, 7 April 1862, 125 *Consolidated Treaty Series* 435.

50 See the numerous treaties made by Great Britain with African leaders in the 1840s and 1850s discussed in R.S. Clark, 'Steven Spielberg's *Amistad* and other Things I Have Thought About in the Past Forty Years: International (Criminal) Law, Conflict of Laws, Insurance and Slavery', *Rutgers law Journal*, 1999, vol. 30, p. 371, pp. 427–432.

51 The received wisdom is that slave traders may be tried on the basis of universal jurisdiction. See The Restatement (Third) of the Foreign Relations of the United States (1987) § 404. None of the slave trade treaties, bilateral or multilateral, support that and the United States does not itself exercise such a universal jurisdiction. But see e.g. Crimes Act 1961 (NZ) Section 98 and Vanuatu Penal Code of 1981, section 5 (International Offences). The latter provides:

(1) The criminal law of the Republic shall apply to piracy, hijacking of aircraft, traffic in persons, slave trading and traffic in narcotics committed within or beyond the territory of the Republic. (2) No alien may be tried in the Republic for such an offence committed abroad unless he has been arrested in the Republic and his extradition has not been applied for, and the Public Prosecutor has consented in writing to his prosecution.

An interesting example of purely domestic application of conditional universal jurisdiction.

52 Convention for the Protection of Submarine Cables, signed at Paris, 14 March 1884; French text in 163 *Consolidated Treaty Series*, English Translation in *US Compilation of Treaties in Force*. Discussed in Clark, 'Some Aspects', p. 526.

damage or steal submarine cables may be subject to flag state jurisdiction, with nationality jurisdiction as a fallback. Any party to the treaty may assist in enforcement action.[53] But outside the flag or nationality connection, the other parties have no prescriptive or adjudicative jurisdiction.

Because of the extradite-or-prosecute provisions in modern suppression treaties, this sharing of roles is perhaps not so stark. Nevertheless, there are significant enforcement provisions in the contemporary treaties, which are reflected in the Beijing Convention.

Thus Article 9 provides:

1. Upon being satisfied that the circumstances so warrant, any State Party in the territory of which the offender or alleged offender is present, shall take that person into custody or take other measures to ensure that person's presence. The custody and other measures shall be as provided in the law of that State but may only be continued for such time as is necessary to enable any criminal or extradition proceedings to be instituted.
2. Such State shall immediately make a preliminary enquiry into the facts.
3. Any person in custody pursuant to paragraph 1 of the Article shall be assisted in communicating immediately with the nearest appropriate representative of the State of which that person is a national.
4. When a State Party, pursuant to this Article, has taken a person into custody, it shall immediately notify the States Parties which have established jurisdiction under paragraph 1 of Article 8[54] and established jurisdiction and notified the Depositary under subparagraph (a) of paragraph 4 of Article 21[55] and, if it considers it advisable, any other interested States of the fact that such person is in custody and of the circumstances which warrant that person's detention. The State Party which makes the preliminary enquiry contemplated in paragraph 2 of this Article shall promptly report its findings to the said States Parties and shall indicate whether it intends to exercise jurisdiction.[56]

Some ancillary provisions in the Convention lend further support to the architecture of cooperation created by the Convention. For example, Article 12 states that the offences set forth in the treaty shall be deemed to be included as extraditable offences in any extradition treaty existing between the Parties.[57] When a Party which makes extradition conditional on the existence of a treaty receives a request for extradition from another Party with which it has no extradition treaty, it may consider the Convention as the legal basis for extradition in respect of the offences in the Convention. Extradition shall then be subject to the other conditions provided by the law of the requested State.[58] Parties that do not make extradition conditional on the existence of a treaty are required to recognize the offences in the

---

53 This included a sophisticated and pioneering provision on collecting evidence which is to be forwarded to the State exercising prescriptive/adjudicate jurisdiction. See Clark, 'Some Aspects', pp. 527–528.
54 In principle, this must mean all the parties to the Convention who are obligated to exercise territoriality, 'against or on board' the aircraft, landing state, lessee and nationality jurisdiction. In the real world many of the parties will not in fact have fulfilled this ground level piece of their obligations.
55 These will be examples of the exercise of optional passive personality or stateless person with habitual residence jurisdiction pursuant to Article 8(2) of the Convention.
56 Beijing Convention, Article 9. Recall also the extradite-or-prosecute requirement in Article 10.
57 Article 12(1). The extradition provisions in Article 12 are found in most of the multilateral suppression conventions since they first appeared in Article 8 of the 1970 Hague Hijacking Convention.
58 Article 12(2).

Convention as extraditable offences between themselves subject to the conditions provided by the law of the requested State.[59]

Article 13 is a significant provision that has been appearing in recent treaties.[60] It provides that none of the Convention's offences shall be regarded, for the purposes of extradition or mutual legal assistance, as a political offence or as an offence connected with a political offence or as an offence inspired by political motives. 'Accordingly', the Article adds,

> a request for extradition or for mutual legal assistance based on such an offence may not be refused on the sole ground that it concerns a political offence or an offence connected with political offence or an offence inspired by political motives.[61]

More enforcement obligations are contained in Article 16 of the Convention. It insists, first, that the Parties 'shall, in accordance with international and national law, endeavour to take all practicable measures for the purpose of preventing the offences set forth in Article 1'.[62] It continues that when a flight has been interrupted by commission of one of the treaty offences, 'any State Party in whose territory the aircraft or passengers or crew are present shall facilitate the continuation of the journey of the passengers and crew as soon as practicable, and shall without delay return the aircraft and its cargo to the persons lawfully entitled to possession'.

---

59 Article 12(3). An example of such a situation is the Scheme for Rendition of Fugitive Offenders within the Commonwealth, adopted at a meeting of Commonwealth Law Ministers in 1966 and amended from time to time. It is not a treaty but operates through parallel legislation adopted by the participants.

60 Similar language first appeared in Article 11 of the International Convention for the Suppression of Terrorist Bombings, 15 December 1997, 2149 UNTS 256; in force 23 May 2001. See also International Convention for the Suppression of the Financing of Terrorism, 9 December 1999, 2178 UNTS 197; in force 10 April 2002; International Convention for the Suppression of Acts of Nuclear Terrorism, 13 April 2005, 2445 UNTS 89; in force 7 July 2007, and the International Convention for the Protection of All Persons from Enforced Disappearance of 20 December 2006, UN Doc. A/RES/61/177 (as corrected); in force 23 December 2010. In previous terrorism treaties there was no prohibition against relying on the political offence exception to an extradition requirement. However, the extradite-or-prosecute regime meant that the State refusing extradition on that ground was required to institute proceedings on the conditional universal jurisdiction basis. An earlier model was Article VII of the Convention on the Prevention and Punishment of the Crime of Genocide, 9 December 1948, 78 UNTS 277; in force 12 January 1951. It provided that the offences proscribed in the Convention 'shall not be considered as political crimes for the purpose of extradition', but did not contain an extradite-or-prosecute obligation.

61 Article 13. It may be refused, presumably, on grounds such as nationality or that the custodial State itself plans to prosecute. Note, however, the power to refuse extradition or mutual legal assistance in Article 14 where the requested Party 'has substantial grounds for believing that the request . . . has been made for the purpose of prosecuting or punishing a person on account of that person's race, religion, nationality, ethnic origin, political opinion or gender, or that compliance with the request would cause prejudice to that person's position for any of these reasons'. There may be situations where the custodial State may refuse extradition on such grounds but may nevertheless find it necessary to consider prosecution itself. The same is probably true where return or extradition is refused pursuant to Article 3 of the Convention Against Torture and Other Cruel, Inhuman or Degrading Treatment or Punishment, 10 December 1984, 1465 UNTS 85; in force 26 June 1987 (return or extradition forbidden 'where there are substantial grounds for believing that [the person concerned] would be in danger or being subjected to torture').

62 Article 16(1). See also Article 18, which requires a Party that has reason to believe that one of the offences set forth in Article 1 will be committed to furnish any relevant information in its possession to what it believes to be affected States.

Just as the Convention contains a 'mini-extradition treaty', so does it contain a 'mini-mutual-legal-assistance treaty'. Article 17 obligates Parties to 'afford one another the greatest measure of assistance in connection with criminal proceedings brought in respect of the offences set forth in Article 1.'[63] It adds that 'the law of the State requested shall apply in all cases.'[64] Recognizing that many States now have mutual legal assistance treaties that go into much more detail than this stripped-down obligation does, Article 17 adds that its provisions 'shall not affect obligations under any other treaty, bilateral or multilateral which governs or will govern, in whole or in part, mutual assistance in criminal matters'.[65]

The enforcement provisions conclude with a reporting obligation. Each Party is required, in accordance with its national law, to report to the Council of the International Civil Aviation Organization as promptly as possible any relevant information concerning (a) the circumstances of the offence, (b) action taken to facilitate the onward journey of passengers and crew and recovery of the aircraft, and (c) the measures taken in relation to the offender or the alleged offender and, in particular, the results of and extradition proceedings or other legal proceedings.

Concurrent jurisdiction

An important feature of the Beijing Convention, shared by other modern suppression conventions, is that it contemplates, indeed requires, that there will be concurrent prescriptive and adjudicative jurisdictions available.[66] The expectation is that prosecution will be possible in at least one of them, with conditional universal jurisdiction as the ultimate backup. There will be no safe havens for crimes that are regarded as particularly obnoxious by the international community.

There are two obvious questions that arise, neither of which is addressed in the Beijing Convention. One is whether there is any system of priority among the various bases of jurisdiction; the other is whether there is any relevant doctrine of double jeopardy, or its international equivalent, *ne bis in idem*.

As to the first, some Consular Conventions and most modern Status of Forces Agreements (SOFAs) provide a priority system to deal with situations where two or more parties have concurrent jurisdiction. Thus, in a famous case in the United States where one Belgian mariner killed another aboard a Belgian boat docked in New Jersey, the United States Supreme Court interpreted the relevant Consular Convention as giving priority to New Jersey since the 'peace and tranquility' of the port was affected.[67] As against Belgium's flag state and nationality jurisdiction, New Jersey's territorial jurisdiction prevailed, but only because of the treaty. In the absence of the treaty, who went first could well have depended on who got their hands on the accused first. Such was the situation in *The Lotus*. Since

---

63 Article 17(1).

64 Ibid.

65 Article 17(2).

66 Article 8 contemplates a possible total of eight different places where the exercise of jurisdiction to prescribe is either required or optional. Compare the difficult-enough questions in *The Lotus*, where there were only two possibilities, Turkey and France.

67 *Wildenhus's Case* 120 US 1 (1887). Cf. *United States v Flores*, 289 US 137 (1933), where an American killed another American on a United States vessel 250 miles up the Congo River. Belgium, which might well have had primary jurisdiction, did not prosecute and the United States was free to do so.

M. Demons, the negligent master of the watch, made his way into Constantinople, the Turkish authorities could exercise their jurisdiction first.

In similar vein, the NATO SOFA[68] affords a primary right to exercise jurisdiction to the authorities of the sending State in relation to offences against that State or another member of the forces of that State and to offences arising out of any act or omission done in the performance of official duty. In all other cases, such as rapes or murders of local citizens, the authorities of the host (or 'receiving') State have the primary right to exercise jurisdiction. Such a primary right may, of course, not be actually exercised, or it can be specifically waived, and then the other party may wish to proceed.

No such rules have found their way into the multilateral suppression conventions, including the Beijing Convention, and the matter is left to ad hoc adjustment. The issues surrounding concurrence were discussed briefly in the negotiations that led to the United Nations Convention on Transnational Organized Crime[69] but the difficulties were discounted. The Convention's preparatory work records that it was

> pointed out, however, that concurrent jurisdiction might not be a negative development, as it would indicate the interest of numerous States to deal with specific problems. In addition, conflicts of jurisdiction were rather rare and were invariably resolved at the practical level by an eventual determination of which jurisdiction would be ultimately exercised on the basis of the chances for successful prosecution and adjudication of the particular case.[70]

Some procedural solutions have been offered of late, but they seem more geared to dealing with white-collar and transnational organized crime than with terrorism offences, and these may be as far as the state of international cooperation goes at this point. For example, the Convention on Transnational Organized Crime has a coordination provision. If a State Party exercising jurisdiction under either the mandatory or permissive theories of that Convention has been notified, or has otherwise learned, that one or more other States Parties is conducting an investigation, prosecution or judicial proceeding in respect of the same allegedly criminal conduct, the competent authorities of those States Parties shall, as appropriate, consult with one another with a view to coordinating their actions.[71] To similar effect is the European Union's Council Framework Decision of 2009[72] entitled 'on prevention and settlement of conflicts of exercise of jurisdiction in criminal proceedings'. The Decision insists that there

---

68 Agreement between the Parties to the North Atlantic Treaty regarding the Status of their Forces, 199 UNTS 68 (entered into force 23 August 1953), Article VII (3). For more on the difficult problems of (concurrent) jurisdiction and immunities for 'visiting forces', see R.S. Clark, 'Peacekeeping Forces, Jurisdiction and Immunity: A Tribute to George Barton', *Victoria University of Wellington Law Review*, 2012, vol. 43, p. 77.

69 The United Nations Convention against Transnational Organized Crime, 15 November 2000, 2225 UNTS 209, in force 29 September 2003.

70 Report of the Meeting of the Inter-Sessional Open-Ended Intergovernmental Group of Experts on the Elaboration of a Possible Comprehensive International Convention against Transnational Organized Crime (Warsaw, 2–6 February 1998), UN Doc. C/CN.15/1998/5 (1998).

71 Convention against Transnational Organized Crime, Article 15(5). The paragraph contemplates that the parties may be able to consolidate the case by authorizing one State to exercise jurisdiction transferred from one or more other States. See also Article 21 (encouraging transfer of criminal proceedings).

72 Council Framework Decision 2009/948/JHA.

should be direct consultation between the authorities with a view to 'achieving a consensus on any effective solution aimed at avoiding the consequences arising from parallel proceedings and avoiding waste of time and resources'.[73] The solution 'could notably consist in the concentration of the criminal proceedings in one Member State, for example through the transfer of criminal proceedings'.[74]

As to *ne bis in idem*, the *Harvard Draft* suggested rather emphatically that:

> In exercising jurisdiction under this Convention, no State shall prosecute or punish an alien after it is proved that the alien has been prosecuted in another State for a crime requiring proof of substantially the same acts or omissions and has been acquitted on the merits, or has been convicted and has undergone the penalty imposed, or, having been convicted, has been paroled or pardoned.[75]

I doubt that this confident position is completely supported by subsequent State practice. It is true that the International Covenant on Civil and Political Rights[76] contains a provision that reads:

> No one shall be tried or punished again for an offence of which he has already been finally convicted or acquitted in accordance with the law and penal procedure of each country.[77]

It has, however, been interpreted as applying only to sequential prosecution within a single system and as allowing for the possibility that 'separate sovereignties' might take a different position.[78] Nevertheless, some extradition treaties prevent double jeopardy (unless the accused subsequently travels somewhere else where a different rule applies). The United Nations Model Extradition Treaty has a widely adopted provision which says that extradition 'shall

---

73 Ibid., preambular para. 4.

74 Ibid.

75 *Harvard Draft*, Article 13. It will be noted, however, that the rule applies only to aliens. The commentary, *Harvard Draft*, p. 613, asserts that '[m]ost States apply the principle of *ne bis in idem* in prosecuting their subjects on a nationality principle for offences committed abroad. Certainly it is just and desirable that they should continue to do so. In the present state of international law, however, it would seem inappropriate for a convention on jurisdiction with respect to crime to incorporate limitations on a State's authority over its nationals.'

76 999 UNTS 171.

77 Ibid., Article 14(7). See also the complex *ne bis in idem* provision in Article 20 of the Rome Statute of the International Criminal Court, applicable to the international offences over which that Court has jurisdiction.

78 N. Boister, *An Introduction to Transnational Criminal Law*, Oxford: Oxford University Press, 2012, pp. 226–227; R. Cryer, H. Friman, D. Robinson and E. Wilmshurst, *An Introduction to International Criminal Law and Procedure*, Cambridge: Cambridge University Press, 2007, p. 68 ('cross-border application remains controversial'); *United States v Duarte-Acero*, 208 F.3d 1282 (11th Cir. 2000). Being a federal system, the United States has had some domestic experience with the problem. Note the 'understanding' that it made when ratifying the International Covenant on Civil and Political Rights:

> The United States understands the prohibition upon double jeopardy to apply only when the judgment of acquittal has been rendered by a court of the same governmental unit, whether the Federal Government or a constituent unit, as is seeking the new trial in the same cause.

not be granted' where 'there has been a final judgment rendered against the person in the requested State in respect of the offence for which the person's extradition is requested'.[79]

Ne bis in idem, like many other issues, is best regarded as a work in progress in transnational criminal law.

Conclusion

Transnational suppression treaties have been with us for a couple of centuries. Their jurisdictional structures and contents build upon past precedents. The 2010 Beijing Convention is much more than the current state of the art; it provides a useful prism through which to view all that went before.

---

79 United Nations Model Treaty on Extradition, UNGA Res 45/116 (1990), as amended by UNGA Res 52/88 (1997), Article 3(d).

7

Police cooperation against transnational criminals

Saskia Hufnagel and Carole McCartney

Introduction

This chapter focuses on cross-border law enforcement in the light of international, regional and bilateral legal frameworks. To explain the terminology employed: international frameworks are those that concern a community beyond an established region, such as the UN legislation concerning transnational crime and cooperation or the Council of Europe Conventions (as they go beyond the borders of the European Union (EU)). Regional frameworks are those covering a broad, but legally defined, union of states, where the focus will be on the fight against transnational criminals in the EU. Bilateral and multilateral frameworks are those developed in small regions, such as the Benelux or the Nordic Countries Cooperation, in which very advanced police cooperation mechanisms have developed due to a long common political and cultural history.[1] The first three parts of the chapter give examples of cooperation enforcement practice under the three different types of frameworks. The last part looks critically at some case studies and specific problem areas.

Some of the practices outlined are authorised by international and transnational legislation; others are the result of long-standing practice and historical evolution in border regions. Most of these formal (statutory) and informal practices have arisen from a common cross-border crime problem. Others are the result of membership of a particular multinational group, such as the EU, offering possibilities for advanced multilateral common practices, such as the establishment of Joint Investigation Teams under EU legislation.[2]

---

1 S. Hufnagel, 'Cross-Border Law Enforcement in the Area of Counter-Terrorism: Maintaining Human Rights in Transnational Policing', in C. Walker and A. Masferrer (eds), *Counter-Terrorism, Human Rights and the Rule of Law: Crossing Legal Boundaries in Defence of the State*, Cheltenham: Edward Elgar, 2013, p. 241.
2 See Article 13 EU Council Act of 29 May 2000 Establishing in Accordance with Article 34 of the Treaty on European Union the Convention on Mutual Assistance in Criminal Matters between the Member States of the European Union, [2005] OJ C 197/3; in force 23 August 2005 (2000 Mutual Assistance Convention or simply 2000 Convention).

Police cooperation under international frameworks

At the international level, two forms of law enforcement cooperation mechanism can be distinguished. The first is Interpol, and the second international liaison officers. Both practices are not 'formalised' in that they do not rely on enforceable legislation, but are the main practical cooperation mechanisms between countries that have no special regional, bi- or multilateral cooperation regulation in place. Interpol was the first, and is still today the only prominent international law enforcement cooperation strategy.[3] It was created as the first permanent international body of security cooperation in 1923, and established in Vienna as the International Criminal Police Commission (ICPC).[4] Its aim was the creation of stability in Western Europe after World War I and the Russian Revolution.[5] In 1946, following a short period of German control over the organisation, it was re-established in Paris and emerged, in its current form, after 1989 in Lyon.[6] Interpol, unlike the later Europol, is considered a truly international cooperation mechanism: it is open to all nations of the world to join and currently comprises 190 member countries.[7] Despite the significant reach and prominence of Interpol and its recognition by the UN as an intergovernmental body, it is still not a 'formal' police cooperation initiative as its constitution is not binding and its members are not states but police forces.[8]

In practice, a transnational criminal (one crossing a border (or borders) to offend, or offending in more than one country) would first be pursued by national police forces and if international links were to be established, the relevant liaison officer in the relevant country or countries would become involved via the Interpol National Central Bureau, provided both states are member countries of Interpol. The National Central Bureau (NCB) links national police with the Interpol global network. Typically, NCBs are divisions of a national police agency or investigation service and serve as the contact point for all Interpol activities in the field. The NCBs also contribute to Interpol criminal databases and cooperate together on cross-border investigations, operations and arrests.[9] If the name and nationality of a transnational criminal is known, but not their location, Interpol can issue an international wanted persons alert, often referred to as a 'Red Notice'. This alert is distributed to national police and is accessible generally over the internet.[10]

Interpol, while the most acclaimed international police cooperation mechanism, is informal by nature, as the agreement of police forces to cooperate cannot be enforced. With such an extensive international membership, there also exist diverse policing structures,

---

3 C. Fijnaut, 'International Policing in Europe: Its Present Situation and Future', in J.P. Brodeur (ed.), *Comparisons in Policing: An International Perspective*, Aldershot: Avebury, 1995, pp. 115–116.

4 J. Occhipinti, *The Politics of EU Police Cooperation: Towards a European FBI?*, Boulder: Lynne Rienner, 2003, p. 29.

5 Fijnaut, 'International Policing in Europe: Its Present Situation and Future', p. 116.

6 M. Deflem, *Policing World Society*, Oxford: Oxford University Press, 2002, p. 179; C. Fijnaut, 'Police Co-operation and the Area of Freedom, Security and Justice', in N. Walker (ed.), *Europe's Area of Freedom, Security and Justice*, New York: Oxford University Press, 2004, p. 241.

7 Interpol, *Structure and Governance* available at http://www.interpol.int/About-Interpol/Structure-and-governance/National-Central-Bureaus (accessed 13 March 2013).

8 Its role is, however, recognised in a significant number of suppression and mutual assistance conventions – see http://www.interpol.int/About-Interpol/Legal-materials/Conventions-mentioning-Interpol (accessed 13 April 2014).

9 Ibid.

10 Ibid.

practices and standards, with a greater degree of tolerance of such diversity required than when operating within a more homogenous group of states with similar standards of policing and criminal justice, as well as common value systems (such as the EU). However, Interpol continues to provide a valuable tool in the fight against transnational criminals and growth in its membership is always encouraged to enable police cooperation. In countries that rarely have communications in criminal matters with each other, due to remoteness and differences in crime problems, the Interpol NCBs provide a valuable connection that can be activated when needed.

Another strategy for enabling police and justice cooperation is liaison officers. Before becoming an official device for facilitating police cooperation in many countries, police-to-police cooperation between different nations was often a police 'custom', albeit restricted by sovereignty concerns. In the nineteenth century police action across borders was mostly related to so-called 'political offences' and many covert operations in foreign countries operated as unilateral espionage operations. However, such political policing must have involved at least some bilateral and multilateral contacts between police, for example through the 'personal correspondence system' between police officials and the distribution of alerts relating to wanted suspects.[11]

The initial need for, and establishment of, liaison officers differed according to the historical and political context of each country creating them. In Germany, Sweden and the Netherlands, for example, the appointment of police liaison officers was closely linked to drug law enforcement, and the first officers were posted to Thailand. In Australia, liaison officers were initially posted to Malaysia and their focus was the regulation of migration flows from Vietnam.[12]

Liaison officers have to abide by the national legislation of their home and the host country. They are not part of the police of the receiving state, hence they cannot exercise enforcement powers on foreign territory, so their main task is to exchange information and coordinate investigation efforts.[13] Their deployment can be based on specific bilateral or multilateral treaties and agreements, depending on whether the liaison is deployed to one or more countries or is derived from more general bilateral agreements on diplomatic relations.[14] Beyond the national legislation the activities of liaison officers are also often regulated and facilitated by memoranda of understanding (MoUs). These 'informal' regulations can – in addition to national legislation – determine the scope of the deployment of liaison officers and either limit or broaden their tasks. However, a major advantage of their employment is considered to be the informality with which they can cooperate with other jurisdictions, which lends itself to a conclusion that the legal boundaries of their operations are rather broad.[15]

While outlining the legal frameworks under which law enforcement agencies cooperate in the fight against transnational criminals, international police cooperation strategies appear to

---

11 M. Deflem, *Policing World Society*, p. 47.
12 S. Hufnagel, 'AFP Liaison Officers: Connecting Down Under to the World', in M. den Boer and L. Block (eds), *Liaison Officers: An Analysis of Transnational Policing*, The Hague: Eleven International Publishing, 2013.
13 L. Block, *From Politics to Policing: The Rationality Gap in EU Council Policy-Making*, The Hague: Eleven International Publishing, 2011, p. 166.
14 The use of liaison officers posted abroad by law enforcement agencies of Member States of the European Union is commonly encouraged and facilitated – see Decision 2003/170/JHA, 27 February 2003. The Nordic States also collectively send liaison officers to host States.
15 Block, *From Politics to Policing*, p. 170.

remain governed by a high degree of informality and very few legal constraints. In the case of Interpol, cooperation between 190 state parties would be impossible on a formal level. While two or three states with similar legal systems, policing and human rights standards might agree on binding legal rules to establish shared responsibility, this is less likely for almost all nations of the world working within Interpol. With regard to liaison officers, co-operation has to be governed by informality to increase efficiency. However, a number of legal norms do facilitate police cooperation at the international level. Some examples are the 1929 International Convention for the Suppression of the Counterfeiting of Currency,[16] the United Nations Convention against Corruption (UNCAC),[17] the United Nations Convention against Transnational Organized Crime (UNTOC)[18] and the 1988 Drug Trafficking Convention.[19]

The UNTOC is of particular relevance to international policing today. Article 18 of the Convention specifies that 'Parties are required to afford one another the widest measure of mutual legal assistance in investigations, prosecutions and judicial proceedings in relation to offences covered by the Convention.' Mutual legal assistance can thus be requested for the taking of evidence or statements, service of official documents, searches, seizures, freezing of assets, examining objects and sites, providing information and evidence (Article 18 (a) to (e)). However, limitations exist with regard to domestic law of the requested state party (Article 18 (g)). This means that any law enforcement action that is not provided for in the police proce-dure of the requested party, or prohibited under privacy laws of the requested party, cannot be requested.

With regard to different offences, such as corruption, counterfeiting of currency, drug trafficking or the illicit import, export and transfer of ownership of cultural property, more specific legal provisions have been established in documents separate to the UNTOC. This legislation does not, however, go beyond the rules established in the UNTOC, simply focusing instead on the particular requirements of the different crimes. There are also moves to establish new crimes in specific areas and attach them in protocols to the UNTOC.[20] The only real legal obligation upon law enforcement agencies to cooperate with international counterparts therefore seems to exist for parties to the UNTOC.

Regional legal frameworks – the example of EU legislation

While there exist many EU-level mechanisms promoting cross-border law enforcement coop-eration, the most prominent one by far is Europol.[21] Like the Schengen Convention, the Europol Convention (and since 2010 the Europol Decision) provides a legal framework not

---

16 20 April 1929, 112 LNTS 371; in force 22 February 1931.
17 31 October 2003, 2349 UNTS 41, in force 14 December 2005.
18 15 November 2000, 2225 UNTS 209, in force 29 September 2003.
19 20 December 1988, 1582 UNTS 95; in force 11 November 1990.
20 See, for example, L.V. Prott, 'UNESCO's Influence on the Development of International Criminal Law', in S. Hufnagel and D. Chappell (eds), *Contemporary Perspectives on the Detection, Investigation and Prosecution of Art Crime*, Farnham: Ashgate, 2014, forthcoming.
21 Council Act of 26 July 1995 Drawing up the Convention based on Art. K.3 of the Treaty on European Union on the Establishment of a European Police Office (Europol Convention), [1995] OJ C316/2, as well as its protocols, now Council Decision of 6 April 2009 Establishing the European Police Office, [2009] OJ L121/37; note that the 1995 Convention only entered into force in 1999.

only for police cooperation, but also for operational arrangements. The creation of Europol can be seen as a major surrender of sovereign state powers, for the potential crime reduction and security benefits to be reaped by enhancing police cooperation. Although the mandate and powers of Europol are still subject to contentious debates amongst member states, in particular in relation to possible enforcement powers,[22] the agency is now an integral part of EU policing.

In 2002, Europol's mandate was extended to cover all serious forms of organised crime (including crimes against persons, financial crime and cyber-crime) perpetrated by organised criminals, or where more than one EU member state is directly affected (they have more recently dropped the criteria of 'serious'). Europol Liaison Officers (ELOs), based in The Hague and representing their respective national law enforcement agencies, form bureaux to exchange a range of law enforcement information and intelligence, on either a bilateral or a multilateral basis. They also share information and intelligence with other competent national authorities, such as customs officials and border control agencies. There are also police and judicial cooperation agreements in place with Norway, Iceland, the USA, Switzerland and Croatia. In addition, Eurojust, established in 2002, is tasked with fighting serious crime in the EU by stimulating judicial cooperation and the coordination of investigations and prosecutions, which involve more than one Member State. Eurojust aims to improve cooperation by facilitating international mutual legal assistance in order to make cross-border crime investigations more effective.

The expansion of the Europol mandate included the capacity to initiate investigations and participate in Joint Investigation Teams (JITs).[23] These teams were first mentioned in the EU context in a 1994 Discussion Paper.[24] They were subsequently included in the first draft of the Naples II Convention as an additional method of cooperation that improved upon traditional mutual legal assistance.[25] Consequently, Article 24 of the 1997 EU Convention on Mutual Assistance and Cooperation between Customs Administrations made it possible to establish JITs in the EU context for the first time.[26] In 1999, the German Presidency put forward a proposal to include a provision on JITs in the 2000 Convention.[27] A 2005 report adopted by the European Commission[28] on non-compliance of member states with the 2000 Convention indicates that, until 2005, only Spain was fully compliant with its terms. Though legislation was established, member states did not implement it. The assumption that common legislation always strengthens cross-border law enforcement might therefore not hold true. However, after initial resistance by the member states towards the initiative, a significant number of JITs have been put into practice and, with the assistance of Eurojust, member states seem to increasingly take advantage of this cross-border policing mechanism.

22 V. Mitsilegas, *EU Criminal Law*, Oxford: Hart, 2009, pp. 165–166.
23 See in particular in relation to the expansion of the Europol mandate the 'Danish Protocol' OJ C2 of 6 January 2004, p. 3.
24 Council, Customs Cooperation Working Party, Revision and Updating of the Naples Convention of 7 September 1967 on Mutual Assistance between Customs Administrations, [1994] Doc 8134/94.
25 Council, Customs Cooperation Working Party, Draft Convention on Mutual Assistance Between Customs Administrations in the Internal Market (Naples II), [1994] Doc 8925/94.
26 Convention on Mutual Assistance and Cooperation between Customs Administrations 1997 (Naples II), [1997] OJ C 221/1.
27 Council, Working Party on Mutual Assistance in Criminal Matters (1999), Draft Convention on Mutual Assistance in Criminal Matters, [1999] Doc 6667/99.
28 Commission, *Report from the Commission on National Measures Taken to Comply with the Council Framework Decision of 13 June 2002 on Joint Investigation Teams*, [2005] COM(2004) 858 final [not published in the OJ).

Several European legal frameworks facilitating police and justice cooperation have been established between European states since the 1950s. The earliest include the 1957 European Extradition Treaty[29] and the 1959 European Convention on Mutual Assistance in Criminal Matters adopted by the Council of Europe.[30] The more recent Schengen Convention supplemented this 1959 European Convention on Mutual Assistance, with a view to making it more effective. The Conventions facilitated the establishment of a number of regional strategies, such as the conclusion of the 1962 Benelux Treaty on Extradition and Mutual Legal Assistance in Criminal Matters, NeBeDeAgPol and cooperation in the Meuse–Rhine Euroregion (discussed further below). While not leading to harmonisation of standards and practices between all member states, the Conventions led to the creation of advanced and innovative cross-border enforcement in some European regions.

More recently, the EU adopted the 2000 Mutual Assistance Convention on Criminal Matters.[31] This Convention introduced in its Article 13 a cooperation provision on JITs, and harmonised the use of covert policing techniques, such as controlled deliveries (Article 12), undercover operatives (Article 14) and the interception of telecommunications (Article 18).[32] While the Schengen and the 2000 Mutual Assistance Conventions furthered regional cooperation, they cannot generally be said to have had a harmonising effect. However, the countries that created closer cooperation with neighbouring states under these Conventions demonstrated a considerable willingness to give up sovereign power to enable cooperation.

In the times of the European Community, and today within the EU context, the Schengen Agreement of 1985 and the following 1990 Convention Implementing the Schengen Agreement of 14 June 1985 (Schengen Convention) provided a legislative framework for cross-border enforcement between the European states that became signatories. France, Germany, Belgium, the Netherlands and Luxembourg were the first EU member states to abolish their common borders. The Schengen Agreement did not, however, as is often asserted, mark the commencement of police cooperation in the EU, but was 'the first stage in the creation of legal bases in a still existing grey area of practical cooperation'.[33] It was the Maastricht Treaty of 1992 that formalised policing and judicial cooperation within the 'Third Pillar' of the EU's constitutional framework relating to 'Justice and Home Affairs' (JHA).

An EU Council meeting of October 1999 noted a conclusion drawn by the EU Presidency that:

> People have the right to expect the Union to address the threat to their freedom and legal rights posed by serious crime. To counter these threats a common effort is needed to prevent and fight crime and criminal organisations throughout the Union.[34]

---

29 See European Convention on Extradition, Paris, 13 December 1957, CETS no. 24; in force 18 April 1960.

30 European Convention on Mutual Assistance in Criminal Matters, Strasbourg, 20 April 1959; CETS No. 030; in force 12 June 1962.

31 *Official Journal of the European Union* 2001, C326.

32 See also Article 73 Schengen Convention of 1990.

33 W. Schomburg, 'Are we on the road to a European Law-Enforcement Area? International Cooperation in Criminal Matters: What Place for Justice?', *European Journal of Crime, Criminal Law and Criminal Justice*, 2000, vol. 8, no. 1, p. 1, p. 56.

34 See 'Editorial Comments', *Common Market Law Review*, 1999, vol. 36, no. 3, p. 1119, p. 1120.

The subsequent Amsterdam Treaty of 1999 created an 'Area of Freedom, Security and Justice' (AFSJ), strengthening Europol and continuing the trajectory of expanding legal and judicial cooperation across the EU. Both the Amsterdam Treaty and the Tampere Programme of 1999 laid down more precise provisions for cooperation between EU police authorities. These instruments boosted intergovernmental cooperation within the EU on policing matters. The 2000 Convention on Mutual Assistance in Criminal Matters set out a detailed programme of measures, which introduced a suite of practical tools for enhancing cross-border cooperation, including the introduction of JITs and the European Arrest Warrant, later adding the European Evidence Warrant, and most recently the European Investigation Order.[35]

The Schengen Convention is a broad legal framework that provides considerable scope and latitude for police initiatives. Amongst other measures, it established the Schengen Information System (SIS) and the possibility of cross-border surveillance[36] and pursuit.[37] Title III of the Convention deals with police and security, and more particularly in its Chapter 1[38] with police cooperation. In relation to 'hot pursuit', the Convention confers on member states some flexibility in implementation, which leads to the application of varying degrees of restriction.[39] The impact of the Convention and the measures taken therefore differ from country to country.[40] Some of them are now described in the bilateral and multilateral context. Regional and bi/multilateral police and justice cooperation within the EU cannot be separated. There is a constant interaction between the two.[41]

The Lisbon Treaty, which came into force in December 2009, took the final constitutional step of abandoning the 'three-pillar' structure introduced by the Maastricht Treaty, placing criminal justice policy on an equal footing with other core business at the heart of the EU's activities. Matters concerning justice and home affairs are to be found in the TFEU (Treaty on the Functioning of the EU)[42] and consist of: 1) general provisions; 2) policies on border checks, asylum and immigration; 3) judicial cooperation in civil matters; 4) judicial cooperation in criminal matters; and 5) police cooperation. The changes brought by the Lisbon Treaty impact upon policing and judicial cooperation measures in two important ways. From 1 December 2014, the policing and judicial cooperation measures become subject to the jurisdiction of the Court of Justice (CJEU). This Court assists in interpretation of EU law in cases referred to it by national courts (individuals cannot petition the court). In addition, the EU Commission can now initiate infringement proceedings against EU member states for not implementing measures or doing so incorrectly.

---

35 V. Mitsilegas, 'The Third Wave of Third Pillar Law: Which Direction for EU Criminal Justice?' *European Law Review*, 2009, vol. 34, no. 4, pp. 523–560. See also Chapter 5 in this volume.
36 Article 40.
37 Article 41.
38 Articles 39–47.
39 Article 41.
40 C. Joubert and H. Bevers, *Schengen Investigated: A Comparative Interpretation of the Schengen Provisions on International Police Cooperation in the Light of the European Convention on Human Rights*, Alphen aan den Rijn: Kluwer Law International, 1996, p. 6, pp. 15–17, pp. 538–542.
41 S. Hufnagel, *Policing Cooperation Across Borders: Comparative Perspectives on Law Enforcement within the EU and Australia*, Farnham: Ashgate, 2013.
42 OJ C83/49, 30 February 2000.

Bilateral and multilateral legislation

At the multilateral/bilateral level, law enforcement cooperation agreements include, for example, the Benelux Treaty 1962,[43] the 1969 Cross Channel Intelligence Conference,[44] the Nordic Police and Customs Cooperation[45] and the Police and Customs Cooperation Centres.[46]

Border regions have established cross-jurisdictional cooperation strategies to help counter common crime issues. These can be drug crimes, illegal immigration or a number of other offences prominent in a border situation. Strategies established to counter one crime problem can often be retro-fitted to augment the fight against cross-border crime more generally. Focusing on the EU, several examples of multilateral cooperation practice between member states can be given. Many of them existed long before the EU was established. Others were influenced by EU legislation and implemented into national law.

Regions in the EU where the establishment of cooperation practices and their formalisation through legal frameworks can be observed are, for example, the Benelux countries (Belgium, the Netherlands, Luxembourg), the Meuse–Rhine (M–R) Euroregion, the Nordic countries and the Cross-Channel region (United Kingdom, France, Belgium, the Netherlands). Strategies established encompass, for example, the granting of enforcement powers on foreign territory, joint investigations, information-sharing mechanisms and exchange of evidence. Cooperation between the Benelux countries and the countries forming the M–R Euroregion is based on long-standing collaboration and policing practice, which pre-dated the conclusion of any formal legal frameworks.[47] All countries concerned are also part of the Schengen zone today, enabling further mechanisms of cooperation between member states. One of the first multilateral legal bases for regional cooperation was the 1962 Treaty on Extradition and Mutual Legal Assistance in Criminal Matters concluded between the Benelux countries. Under the Benelux Treaty police from the three jurisdictions cooperated more closely, conducting joint cross-border operations and pursuits.[48] Previously cross-border incursions onto the sovereign territory of another state by law enforcement

---

43 Treaty Concerning Extradition and Mutual Assistance in Criminal Matters between the Kingdom of Belgium, the Grand Duchy of Luxembourg and the Kingdom of the Netherlands, signed 27 June 1962; in force 11 December, as amended by the Protocol Supplementing and Amending the Benelux Treaty Concerning Extradition and Mutual Assistance in Criminal Matters, signed 11 May 1974; in force 1 March 1982.

44 C. Harfield, 'From Empire to Europe: Evolving British Policy in Respect of Cross-Border Crime', *Journal of Policy History*, 2007, vol. 19, p. 180.

45 Convention Between Denmark, Finland, Norway and Sweden Concerning the Waiver of Passport Control at the Intra-Nordic Frontiers, signed on 12 July 1957 (Nordic Passport Convention). Iceland acceded to the Convention on 24 September 1965. The Convention has been amended by an agreement of 27 July 1979, supplemented by the agreements of 2 April 1973 and of 18 September 2000; see, generally, M.E. Kleiven, 'Nordic Police Cooperation', in S. Hufnagel, S. Bronitt and C. Harfield (eds), *Cross-Border Law Enforcement Regional Law Enforcement Cooperation: European, Australian and Asia-Pacific Perspectives*, Abingdon: Routledge, 2012, p. 63.

46 O. Felsen, 'European Police Co-operation: The Example of the German–French Centre for Police and Customs Co-operation Kehl (GZ Kehl)', in S. Hufnagel, S., Bronitt and C. Harfield (eds), *Cross-Border Law Enforcement Regional Law Enforcement Cooperation: European, Australian and Asia-Pacific Perspectives*, Abingdon: Routledge, 2012, p. 73.

47 T. Spapens and C. Fijnaut, *Criminaliteit en Rechtshandhaving in de Euregion Maas-Rijn*, Mortsel: Intersentia, 2005.

48 Articles 26 and 27.

representatives had been regarded as a grave breach of state sovereignty.[49] Police in the three states had, however, already been cooperating closely before the establishment of the treaty.

Before the existence of transnational legislation, police had been using diplomatic channels for cooperation requests, or, in the case of border crossings, the requests had to be formally addressed to the relevant diplomatic and judicial representative before the border could be crossed. Various bureaucratic procedures were perceived by police practitioners to slow down processes and to complicate further cooperation in matters of law enforcement and security.[50] Practitioners therefore tended to circumvent these complicated procedures by resorting to informal means of cooperation.[51] The establishment of the trilateral treaty changed this situation and provided authorisation for de facto practices. In the 1980s the Benelux Treaty contributed to enhancing harmonisation. It became one of the main templates for the Schengen Convention and was formally integrated into the Convention in 1985.[52]

The Benelux countries also form part of another region with strong police cooperation traditions, namely the Meuse–Rhine (M–R) Euroregion. This region encompasses parts of the Netherlands, Belgium and Germany.[53] While not abiding by one legal framework, such as the Benelux Treaty, the states forming the region have established a number of bilateral treaties and agreements, which, together, provide a framework for cooperation without major gaps, supplemented more recently by the provisions of the Schengen Convention.

The M–R Euroregion cooperation has been established to counter specific crime issues in this border area, arising from high population density and high-frequency border crossings in connection with drug trafficking.[54] Police in the region are allowed to cross borders in 'hot pursuit', carry weapons in other jurisdictions, and make use of their weapons when crossing into another jurisdiction.[55] They are also allowed to exercise a limited number of enforcement powers on foreign territory, for example in cases of emergency, and even exchange physical evidence directly with their counterparts.[56] Information exchange within the region takes place directly between domestic criminal investigation departments. The borders and main transport routes are patrolled by Joint Hit Teams (JHTs) consisting of law enforcement personnel from both sides of the border. The police forces in the region have furthermore developed specific institutions facilitating police cooperation and in particular information exchange. The first is EMMI, the Euregional Multimedia Information Exchange; the other is EPICC, the Euregional Police Information Coordination Centre. These are not based on transnational treaties and agreements, but remain purely informal initiatives.

The fact that this advanced cooperation, which clearly incorporates authorisation for the exercise of extraterritorial law enforcement, is based on a multitude of legal frameworks does

---

49 Ibid., p. 26.
50 M. Den Boer, C. Hillebrand and A. Nölke, 'Legitimacy under Pressure: The European Web of Counter-terrorism Networks', *Journal of Common Market Studies*, 2008, vol. 46, no. 1, p. 101.
51 Hufnagel, *Policing Cooperation Across Borders*, p. 182.
52 C. Fijnaut, 'Police Co-operation and the Area of Freedom, Security and Justice', in N. Walker (ed.), *Europe's Area of Freedom, Security and Justice*, New York: Oxford University Press, 2004, p. 241, p. 249.
53 T. Spapens, 'Policing a European Border Region: The Case of the Meuse–Rhine Euroregion', in E. Guild and F. Geyer (eds), *Security versus Justice? Police and Judicial Cooperation in the European Union*, Farnham: Ashgate, 2008, p. 225.
54 Ibid.
55 Prior to these treaties they needed to stop within a certain radius after crossing the border (between the Netherlands and Germany that distance was 10km).
56 Spapens, 'Policing a European Border Region', pp. 226–229.

not seem to hamper its success. On the contrary, practice shows that officers take advantage of the existing choice of measures to achieve best outcomes.[57]

A further practice that is based on a number of bilateral and multilateral treaties and agreements is the Police and Customs Cooperation Centres in the EU. While broadly authorised under the Schengen Convention, there are now close to 40 of these centres, taking a variety of forms, throughout Europe.[58] The Centre chosen as an example here is the German–French Police and Customs Cooperation Centre, the first centre of its kind that was established. Similar to other regional initiatives described above, it had been created to counter particular crime problems in the French–German border region in Strasbourg/Kehl. The Common Centre (or joint commissariat as they are generically known) was established under a bilateral agreement between France and Germany, the Mondorfer Abkommen, in 2000. With regard to practice, German and French police officers patrol the border region together, and both police forces are allowed to conduct 'hot pursuits' across borders. The police agencies, despite differences in organisational structure, have also created innovative ways to share resources, investigate crime together and share information with each other on a day-to-day basis. The close physical location of officers from different nation states and agencies also helps to overcome legal, organisational and cultural differences.[59] The Centre's relevance has now spread beyond the border region and information requests are sent to it by all police agencies of the two countries.

An early initiative, called NeBeDeAgPol, which was part of both the Meuse–Rhine Euroregion and Benelux cooperation, was established by Chiefs of Police in the border regions of the Netherlands, Belgium and Germany in 1969. The NeBeDdeAgPol initiative built upon existing legal bases, such as the Council of Europe (CoE) Treaties, for some of its activities. These included establishing a regional search system, language courses and a radio/telex communications network. It is significant that cooperation did not limit itself to the legal mandates contained in the CoE Conventions.[60] In 1979, NeBeDeAgPol was formalised, moving from an informal network of senior police into a registered non-profit law-enforcement association in order to facilitate cooperation outside of formal government and diplomatic channels.[61] The critical role played by police practitioners in relation to fostering cooperation among EU member states is clear in the evolution of NeBeDeAgPol. This initiative involved the creation, by the police themselves, of their own 'private' working group for the purpose of fostering police cooperation as well as lobbying for reform. Many of the aspirations pursued by NeBeDeAgPol resemble provisions of the later Schengen Convention and were taken into account in its formation.[62]

It is apparent that the first five Schengen states have developed advanced cooperation strategies that involve considerable ceding of sovereign rights under the Schengen Convention. In the regional context in particular, states use the Convention to promote police cooperation. This is also evident in other regions, such as the Nordic countries, although the Schengen

---

57 Hufnagel, *Policing Cooperation Across Borders*, p. 56.
58 Ibid., p. 53.
59 Ibid., p. 52.
60 P. Swallow, 'European Police Cooperation: A Comparative Analysis of European Level Institutional and Organisational Developments and National Level Policies and Structures', PhD Thesis, University of Southampton, 1998, pp. 206–207.
61 Ibid., p. 206.
62 C. Fijnaut, 'The Internationalisation of Criminal Investigations in Western Europe', in C. Fijnaut and H. Hermans, *Police Cooperation in Europe*, Lochem: J.B. van den Brink: 1987, p. 126.

Convention was less influential in the establishment of this cooperation. The Nordic Police cooperation scheme[63] has been labelled 'best practice' in the EU.[64] The Nordic countries had already abolished passport controls at their common borders in 1957 through the Nordic Passport Control Agreement.[65]

Cross-border cooperation strategies in the M–R Euroregion are laid out in the Benelux Cooperation Treaties, which were expanded by the Treaty of Senningen[66] in 2004, the Treaty of Enschede[67] and the Treaty of Prüm[68], as well as several other bilateral agreements. Underlying foundational treaties, like the Benelux Treaty, have already been harmonised within the Schengen Conventions. Other frameworks, like the Treaty of Prüm, have been acceded to by most member states.

Bilateral and multilateral strategies continue to multiply in the field of police cooperation. Supranational legal frameworks facilitate regional cooperation and enhance law enforcement across borders even though they may not be implemented uniformly. A constant interaction takes place between supranational and bi/multilateral initiatives, which ensures continued innovation in the field of EU police cooperation and the further surrendering of sovereign powers by member states. This finding is particularly relevant, as other regions of the world have not developed similar dynamics. In comparison, the United States–Mexico border region[69] and the Southern Chinese seaboard[70] have not had any impact on regional North/South American or Southern Chinese legal frameworks on police cooperation. It might therefore be concluded that it may be that a common value and human rights system is one of the cornerstones for the establishment of formalised cross-border police cooperation.

Many police and justice cooperation strategies do in fact exist between neighbouring states, for example at the Southern Chinese seaboard. These are, however, mainly informal, because of the differences between the states in applying the death penalty, and therefore the clear preference to avoid the assumption of legal regulation of cooperation.[71] By contrast, EU

---

63 The five Nordic countries – Denmark, Finland, Norway, Iceland and Sweden – established close police cooperation in the eighteenth century. In 1952, the Nordic Council was created, and in 1957 a mutual passport agreement was established resulting in the abolition of systemic control at the internal borders between the Nordic countries.

64 *EU Schengen Catalogue, Volume 4, Police Co-Operation: Recommendations and Best Practices* (Council of the European Union, General Secretariat, June 2003), p. 16.

65 Kleiven, 'Nordic Police Cooperation'.

66 Verdrag tussen het Koninkrijk België, het Koninkrijk der Nederlanden en het Groothertogdom Luxemburg inzake grensoverschrijdend politieel optreden (8 juni 2004), available at http://wetten. overheid.nl/BWBV0001717/geldigheidsdatum_12-03-2014 (accessed 3 April 2014).

67 See Verdrag tussen het Koninkrijk der Nederlanden en de Bondsrepubliek Duitsland inzake de grensoverschrijdende politiële samenwerking en de samenwerking in strafrechtelijke aangelegenheden, Enschede, 2 maart 2005, available at http://wetten.overheid.nl/BWBV0001813/AuthentiekNL/VDRTKS828766/TITELIV/Artikel20/geldigheidsdatum_14-04-2014 (accessed 4 April 2014).

68 See Council of EU, http://register.consilium.europa.eu/pdf/en/05/st10/st10900.en05.pdf (accessed 4 April 2014).

69 D. Schneider and C. Gallaher, 'Evaluating and Improving Law Enforcement Cooperation in Combating Mexican Drug Trafficking Organisations', Conference Paper, American Society of Criminology Conference, Chicago, 14 November 2012.

70 S.S.-H. Lo, *The Politics of Cross-Border Crime in Greater China: Case Studies of Mainland China, Hong Kong, and Macao*, Armonk, NY: M.E. Sharpe, 2009.

71 S. Hufnagel, 'Strategies of Police Cooperation along the Southern Chinese Seaboard: A Comparison with the EU', Special Journal Issue on 'Policing the Southern Chinese Seaboard: Histories & Systems in Regional Perspective' forthcoming in *Crime, Law and Social Change*, 2014.

informal strategies, such as NeBeDeAgPol, were incorporated into supranational legal frameworks and became the template for formal cooperation mechanisms. One therefore has to be cautious not to confuse the existence of police cooperation practice with the creation of formal legal frameworks in this area. Where human rights systems differ, police will cooperate as far as they are able to, but they cannot follow a common template. Each case needs to be considered individually, to avoid human rights infringements.

Successes and challenges

It may be undeniable that the policing of cross-border crime demands collaboration between law enforcement authorities from multiple jurisdictions, with an efficient system of information exchange perhaps the bare minimum requirement for such investigations. The collation, sharing and use of policing intelligence across jurisdictions, and cooperation between regional and international law enforcement agencies, is indeed increasingly a central feature of contemporary efforts to ensure 'security' across the globe. More sophisticated cross-jurisdictional police and justice cooperation has also become crucial to many criminal investigations, in particular in the areas of organised crime and terrorism. However, while efforts to facilitate cooperation may be laudable, there remain questions over efficacy, whether there is adequate governance of such cooperation, and whether risks to human rights are properly accounted for operationally. Despite the efforts of legal regulation in the EU context, both European and international policing networks are frequently established outside governance and accountability frameworks. The European Convention on Human Rights is an imperfect tool for ensuring that every signatory country respects human rights, but is a clear point of commonality and a significant, if weak, guarantee that human rights will continue to be a core tenet for all criminal justice systems.

Clearly, while police increase the tools available to them to pursue transnational criminals, they are not always successful, as transnational crime continues to prove profitable for many, and many criminals use border crossing as a successful means of evading detection. However, over the years there have been notable successes, which have reaped significant policing rewards. During 'Operation Golf', Europol and the UK's Metropolitan Police Service worked with a Joint Investigation Team (JIT) from Romania, taking part in a joint operation to rescue 28 Roma children from a child-trafficking ring. A total of 126 individuals were arrested as part of the operation, dismantling a significant organised crime group which spread as far as the UK, Romania, Belgium and Spain. The operation ceased in October 2010 with the charging of individuals with a range of offences including money laundering, child neglect and theft.[72]

Since 2005, Europol has worked with the Synthetic Drugs Group of COSPOL (Comprehensive Operational Strategic Planning for the Police) and in February 2010 their analysis of High Value Targets (HVTs) led to an operation incorporating officers from Belgium, Germany and the Netherlands, targeting suspects planning to set up synthetic drug production process in Belgium. A large illicit drug laboratory was dismantled, with significant quantities of chemicals seized and six suspects arrested. At the same time, Dutch law enforcement seized drugs, including cocaine, large amounts of money and chemicals. These also provided further intelligence links to more illicit laboratories.[73]

---

72 Europol operational successes, available at https://www.europol.europa.eu/content/page/operational-successes-127 (accessed 5 March 2014).
73 See ibid., 'Operation Tex'.

Interpol has many success stories, given its international reach and long history. However, its operations have also sometimes stirred controversy, and the most recent concerns over issues such as possible aircraft hijacking have led to questions over the efficacy of many of its systems for checking stolen and false travel documents, one of its flagship operations. There are many instances where Interpol has led a collaboration of national investigators to lead to the detection of a criminal. In just one example, a Slovak national suspected of raping his daughter in 2012 was arrested in Thailand following cooperation between police in Bratislava and Bangkok through their NCBs. During 'Operation Lionfish' an Interpol-led team with involvement from 34 countries seized nearly 30 tonnes of cocaine, heroin and marijuana in the Caribbean.[74]

In one of their most noted and longest operations, Interpol has worked for years to arrest members of the so-called 'Pink Panther' gang. This highly organised crime group has carried out high-value jewellery robberies around the world. Red Notices were placed on many suspects following a 2007 heist in Dubai, when €11m worth of jewellery was taken. The objective has been to centralise information related to the suspects, who operate globally, identifying the suspects via photos, fingerprints, DNA etc. and matching them with their criminal partners. The 'gang' are estimated to number around 800 individuals, who have taken part in over 300 robberies, netting over €350 million. A Serbian national (using a Bosnian passport) was most recently arrested in Spain as a result of a Red Notice in February 2014.[75]

While such Red Notices have led to significant arrests, their instigation by nation states has led to accusations of political abuse and the facilitation of oppression. A UK organisation, Fair Trials International, has produced a highly critical report, pinpointing cases where individuals have been targeted by governments, who have been able to have Red Notices instigated against individuals with no scrutiny of the credibility of the request. They also point to the steep increase in the numbers of Red Notices being issued since 2008 (when electronic systems were introduced), with more than 8,000 Notices issued in 2013 alone. Countries found to be using the system against political activists include Russia, Sri Lanka, Turkey, Belarus, Indonesia, Iran and Venezuela. These countries can thus ensure that people subject to such notices are unable to travel and are effectively exiled. Examples include a Russian anti-fascist refugee being arrested in Spain at the behest of Moscow authorities, and held in a high-security prison, while a West Papuan freedom fighter who escaped prison in Indonesia was pursued in the UK, where she had been granted asylum. Red Notices can have a dramatic impact upon lives; for example, a 28-year-old British air crew member recently lost her job when she was unable to travel because of a Red Notice, instigated for a small unpaid debt incurred while in the Middle East. While Article 3 of Interpol's constitution forbids any political, military, religious or racial intervention or activities, its systems do not allow for the monitoring of the quality of national-level information, therefore leaving its systems open to potential abuse.[76]

---

74 Interpol website, http://www.interpol.int/News-and-media/Videos/(video_id)/20154 (accessed 12 February 2014).

75 Ibid.

76 Fair Trials International, 'Cases of Injustice', http://www.fairtrials.org/interpol/cases-of-injustice (accesed 4 April 2014).

Conclusion

While neither domestic nor international policing networks are novel, their reach and capabilities continue to expand significantly. Much of the cooperation undertaken by police does not depend upon legal instruments; operational partners cooperate on a daily basis with or without them. Without such instruments, much international cooperation will continue, as will other international obligations. Yet research is only just starting to highlight the potential for difficulties when operationalising novel legal regulations which seek to implement policing strategies that place the cooperation and coordination of policing and sharing of 'intelligence' at the heart of law enforcement. Considering the significant experience of EU member states in police and justice cooperation, this region may provide valuable insight into the formalisation of cooperation beyond the EU region, including in Latin America, Africa and Asia.

Direct law enforcement cooperation, or cross-border evidence exchange, has been increasing for many years, gaining impetus from the terrorist attacks of 9/11.[77] The significant investment of resources in international dissemination of forensic information and police intelligence reflects political belief in their contribution to crime detection and deterrence. The international data-sharing landscape is set to become denser, more complex and more routine, with pressure to cooperate growing and mechanisms multiplying; yet citizens still need assurance that international police cooperation is effective and efficient, while risks of abuse or other potentially harmful effects are minimised. Frequently, the introduction of powers to gather, store, manipulate and share forensic data precedes laws regulating such activity. Even when such laws exist, the diversity of legal instruments across nations, and the interpretation of international treaties and national laws implementing treaties, differ. There ought to be an expectation that the power to gather, store and share forensic intelligence will be 'free from corrupt influence' and used 'only when it is lawful, necessary and proportionate to do so'.[78] Research is thus sorely needed to establish that such cooperation is reaping benefits and not breaching human rights obligations or overstepping policing boundaries. Policing powers cannot go unchecked simply because they are operating at an international level.

77 R. Loof, 'Obtaining, Adducing and Contesting Evidence from Abroad: A Defence Perspective on Cross-border Evidence', *Criminal Law Review*, 2011, p. 40.
78 C. Harfield, 'The Organization of "Organized Crime Policing" and its International Context', *Criminology and Criminal Justice*, 2008, vol. 8, no. 4, p. 483, p. 487.

8

Mutual legal assistance in criminal matters to control (transnational) criminality

John A. E. Vervaele

Concepts and terminology

Mutual legal assistance (MLA) in criminal matters deals with the mechanisms for legal assistance in the gathering of criminal evidence[1] abroad, that is in jurisdictions other than that in which the investigation, prosecution or adjudication has been triggered (investigative or forum jurisdiction). These mechanisms refer not only to processes and timelines, but also to competent authorities and jurisdictional scope (offenses, territories). In civil law countries MLA is mostly defined as judicial cooperation in criminal matters. This terminology indicates that MLA is about cooperation between judicial authorities, the authorities that have competence to investigate, prosecute and adjudicate in criminal matters. It does not, in principle, include mutual assistance between administrative authorities, even if they are dealing with administrative enforcement. The competent judicial authorities for dealing with incoming or outgoing MLA requests are as a rule defined at national level, in line with the design of the domestic administration of justice. This means that in the UK, for example, competent authorities can be police authorities, while these are excluded in most civil law countries. Competent authorities include authorities competent for criminal investigation and prosecution. Courts can be the competent authority to authorize a coercive measure, and in some domestic regimes courts can also order additional investigative measures, even during trial.

Mutual legal assistance is necessary because judicial authorities cannot execute investigative measures outside their state territory, unless provided by international treaties or ad hoc agreements. In civil law countries, investigative authorities need a clear legal basis in order to be competent to exercise investigation. In common law countries, they have the competence to act, even abroad, but their scope of action while abroad is limited to that of a private citizen. They can interview people, but they cannot take investigative action that infringes privacy or that has a coercive or intrusive character (for instance secret surveillance). Mutual legal assistance can be necessary in cases of transnational crime but also in domestic cases with a cross-border dimension. The latter includes those situations when witnesses or suspects are

---

1 The service of process in criminal matters is mostly done through administrative or police cooperation.

abroad, when the evidence is not located in the territory of the forum state, or when criminal assets have been transferred to foreign territory.

The tools of evidence gathering abroad vary from non-coercive measures, such as the exchange of judicial information or voluntary interrogation of experts and witnesses, to very intrusive measures, such as search and seizure, tapping, controlled delivery and undercover surveillance of criminal organizations.

In this contribution I will examine the developments of MLA and highlight the challenges that the system is facing.

MLA: state sovereignty and international obligations (fora and sources)

Under customary international law foreign judicial authorities cannot execute investigative acts in the territory of a foreign state, as this would be an infringement of its sovereignty.[2] This means that states have to agree to afford each other assistance for cross-border gathering of evidence in criminal matters. This can be done on the basis of *letters rogatory*, which can be executed solely on the basis of comity, or through MLA treaties (MLATs) that contain a duty to cooperate. There is, however, no general international law obligation to subscribe to MLATs. The decision to establish formal or informal MLATs is usually based on national sovereignty, although there are legal and political exceptions. The G7/G20 and its related Financial Action Task Force (FATF) have imposed, via non-binding recommendations,[3] a political obligation to sign up to MLATs and implement them. The Security Council has also legally obliged states through Security Resolutions under Chapter VII of the UN Charter to comply with all the UN counterterrorism conventions, independent of status of signature or ratification. Obligations of MLA can also be derived from positive duties under international human rights law, certainly when it comes to the duty to investigate, prosecute, adjudicate and punish core international crimes.

Nation-states have concluded bilateral agreements on extradition since the end of the nineteenth century. A similar set of bilateral MLATs do not exist, but some of the older bilateral extradition treaties include provisions on MLA, though these are limited to the seizure of goods and objects linked to the detention of the person. After World War II there was an increasing national, regional and global interest in the gathering of evidence abroad. At the domestic level states began to recognize the increasing importance of MLA. For example, in 1986 in the UK an interdepartmental working group recommended that the Home Secretary engage in legislative reform in order to provide the UK with easier access to foreign evidence. This resulted in the enactment of the 1990 Criminal Justice International Cooperation Act.[4] Regional organizations, such as the Council of Europe, Organization of American States, European Union, MERCOSUR and ECOWAS, have elaborated specific MLATs. They do have a multilateral character and lay down a specific enhanced regime for MLA in that region. In addition to these regional regimes, states in the region may also subscribe to new generation bilateral MLA regimes with third countries.

At the global level, the UN's increasing involvement in crime prevention and criminal justice, especially in the areas of drugs trafficking, trafficking in human beings, organized

---

2 *SS Lotus Case (France v Turkey)*, 1927 PCIJ, Series A, No. 10.
3 For the most recent set of Recommendations, see FATF, http://www.fatf-gafi.org/topics/ fatfrecommendations/documents/internationalstandardsoncombatingmoneylaunderingandthefin- ancingofterrorismproliferation-thefatfrecommendations.html (accessed 5 February 2014).
4 See http://www.legislation.gov.uk/ukpga/1990/5/contents (accessed 5 February 2014).

crime, terrorism and related money laundering or financing of terrorism, has resulted in topical conventions that also include MLA obligations. The 2000 UN Convention against Transnational Organized Crime (UNTOC)[5] is a good example. Even though there are no specific binding conventions on MLA at UN level, both the UN and other global and regional organizations have elaborated Model Treaties on MLA, such as the UN Model Treaty on Mutual Assistance in Criminal Matters[6] or Legislative Schemes, such as the Scheme relating to Mutual Assistance in Criminal Matters within the Commonwealth (Harare Scheme).[7] Moreover, the UN, sometimes in combination with the IMF, has elaborated specific model provisions for specific areas of crime, which take account of the differences between the common law and civil law legal systems.[8] Finally, the UN, the IMF and the G20 have been very active in the elaboration of international standards of best practices related to specific investigative measures, for instance the freezing and seizure of criminal assets abroad.

Global approach to MLA

MLA and tackling illicit drugs trade: the Vienna Convention

The United Nations Convention against Illicit Traffic in Narcotic Drugs and Psychotropic Substances (1988 or Vienna Convention)[9] is a precursor to what I have called a topical convention dealing with MLA, as it deals with all aspects of control of the illicit narcotics traffic. It contains, beside substantive obligations (offenses and sanctions), not only obligations concerning jurisdiction but also on extradition, transfer of proceedings and MLA. The MLA provisions are not aimed at affecting the existing MLA obligations under any other treaty, but are prescribing minimum obligations related to drugs trafficking offenses. Article 7(1) on MLA imposes upon the signatories the duty to afford one another the widest measure of cooperation. The MLA obligations include the taking of evidence or statements of persons, search and seizure, production orders and assets identification. They do not include Special Investigative Techniques (SITs) such as interception of telecommunications, secret surveillance or covert investigations. However, the Vienna Convention leaves open other forms of MLA that are allowed by the domestic law of the requested party.

Under the Vienna Convention MLA is based on state-to-state cooperation between the central authorities of the executive power. The judicial authorities have no specific role and the subjects (persons concerned) have no rights at all. In terms of Article 7(12), a request shall be executed in accordance with the domestic law of the requested state (*lex locus*), but the law of the requesting state (*lex forum*) can be taken into account to the extent that it is not contrary to the domestic law of the requested state. The requesting state is also obliged to respect the specialty principle, meaning that the requesting state shall not transmit nor use information or evidence furnished by the requested state for investigations, prosecutions or proceedings other than those stated in the request without the prior consent of the requested Party. The

---

5 15 November 2000, 2225 UNTS 209, in force 29 September 2003.
6 Adopted by General Assembly Resolution 45/117, subsequently amended by General Assembly Resolution 53/112, 1990 and amended in 1998, A/RES/53/112.
7 1 August 1986, 12 Commonwealth Law Bulletin (1986) 1118 (as amended in 1990, 2002 and 2005).
8 2009 *Model Provisions on Money Laundering, Terrorist Financing, Preventive Measures and Proceeds of Crime for Common Law Legal Systems*, available at http://www.imolin.org/pdf/imolin/Model_ Provisions_Final.pdf (accessed 5 April 2014).
9 Vienna, 20 December 1988, 1582 UNTS 95; in force 11 November 1990.

Convention also provides for grounds for refusal, based either on formal issues or on substance. The request may be refused if it is likely to prejudice the sovereignty, security, *ordre public* or other essential interest of the requested state. It may also be refused if the requested investigative measure is not available under the domestic law of the requested state with regard to any similar offense or if it would be contrary to the legal system of the requested state. The request can, however, not be refused for reasons of protection of banking secrecy or lack of double incrimination. All refusal grounds are optional; a requested state can always grant MLA if the grounds have not been transposed as mandatory grounds under domestic law.

The Vienna Convention, in Article 9, prescribes a list of obligations under the qualification 'other forms of cooperation'. States are obliged, but only in appropriate cases and if not contrary to domestic law, to establish joint investigation teams. These teams can act only under the authority of the territory of the state concerned and with full respect for its sovereignty. The Vienna Convention does not prescribe, however, the regime of applicable law for the joint investigation team. Article 9 also promotes the exchange of personnel and experts between countries and the posting of liaison officers. Finally, Article 11 deals with controlled delivery. However, all of Article 9's obligations are conditional: on the basis of mutual agreements or arrangements and if permitted by the basic principles of the respective domestic legal systems.

MLA and tackling illicit drugs trade: model laws and model treaties

United Nations model laws were elaborated to assist governments in translating their obligations under international treaties into national legislative provisions. In relation to MLA, they have been elaborated by the UN Office on Drugs and Crime (UNODC) and the UN Drug Control Programme (UNDCP), i.e. in the frame of policy on drugs and crime. In 1990 the UN General Assembly adopted the UN Model Treaty on Mutual Assistance in Criminal Matters.[10] It consists of a quite simple framework, derived from international experience, which can be used as a guide for states negotiating bilateral and multilateral MLATs, in particular when they have to deal with different legal systems and traditions. The framework is based on state-to-state cooperation between central authorities and encourages the widest possible MLA cooperation. The investigative acts requested are limited to the classic ones (taking evidence from persons, search and seizure, production orders, etc.) and do not include SITs, such as electronic surveillance, controlled delivery and undercover surveillance of criminal organizations. The Additional Protocol deals specifically with proceeds of crime.[11] It imposes upon states obligations to locate and trace them, to establish specific financial investigative measures in order to recover them and to foresee forfeiture. However, the obligations are stipulated in very general terms and only binding if permitted by domestic law. The UNDCP updated an MLA Model Bill several times.[12] Although the commentary on the 2000 version of the Model Bill[13] states clearly that one of the aims is to reconcile and

---

10 Annexed to GA Res 45/117 (1990), 14 December 1990, as amended by GA Res 53/112 (1999), 9 December 1998.
11 Optional Protocol to the Model Treaty on Mutual Assistance in Criminal Matters concerning the proceeds of crime (it is attached to the Model Treaty).
12 See, for example, the UNDCP Model Mutual Assistance in Criminal Matters Bill, 1998.
13 UNDCP Model Mutual Assistance in Criminal Matters Bill, 2000, available at http://www.unodc.org/pdf/lap_mutual-assistance_2000.pdf; commentary available at http://www.unodc.org/pdf/lap_mutual-assistance_commentary.pdf (accessed 7 February 2014).

accommodate the differences between legal systems, the Model Bill is clearly geared for common law systems. A similar Model Bill for civil law traditions has not been elaborated.

The 2000 Model Bill contains very detailed provisions both on the MLA procedures and on freezing and confiscation of proceeds of crime. It is of interest that both the evidence-gathering order and search warrant have to be based on a court decision and justified on the basis of proportionality.[14] The court order can also provide for the way in which the evidence is to be obtained in order to give proper effect to the foreign request. However, if this would infringe the law of the requested state, the latter will take precedence and cannot be over-ridden by the terms of the foreign request.[15] It is also of interest that the Bill provides that a person named in the evidence-gathering order may refuse to answer questions or to produce documents or things where the refusal is based on a law currently in force in the requested state, on a privilege recognized by that law, or if the production of evidence would result in committing an offense in the jurisdiction of the requested state.[16] Foreign states can be requested to produce a written declaration to confirm the state of the law in their jurisdiction and such declarations are admissible in the evidence-gathering proceedings. The Model Bill also contains detailed clauses on the privilege for foreign documents (restricted disclosure) in order to preserve the confidentiality and secrecy of documents[17] and on the application of the specialty rule.[18] Astonishingly, the Model Bill does not include grounds for refusal of a request.

The 2000 UN Model Bill on MLA ties in with another UN Model Bill: the 2000 UNDCP Model Foreign Evidence Bill.[19] The latter aims to provide for the admissibility in the forum state of evidence that has been obtained through MLA. It deals mostly with requirements for testimony and with the type of foreign material evidence that may be adduced as evidence in court in the forum state. It includes provisions on exclusion of evidence in case of prejudice to the rights of the defense or to the interest of justice.

From drugs to transnational crime: UNTOC

The UNTOC consolidates the developments made in MLA in the last decades. It does not replace existing or future bilateral or multilateral treaties, but complements them. It imposes broad MLA obligations in relation to investigation and prosecution of transnational offenses and the related freezing, seizure and confiscation of criminal proceeds. These are elaborated in the 30 paragraphs of Article 18: MLA remains based on the classic interstate approach and is dealt with by the central authorities at the executive level. Requests are executed in accordance with the *lex locus*, but the specific rules of the *lex forum* may be applied, if they are not contrary to the domestic law of the requested state. In addition, MLA must also be afforded in the case where the requests relate to legal persons that are criminally liable in the requesting state only. Article 18(3) lists the investigative acts and purposes for which MLA may be requested under the duty to cooperate. This list is a characteristic one, ranging from effecting service of judicial documents, taking evidence or statements from persons to identifying and

14 Clause 8(2) and (3).
15 Clause 8(4).
16 Clause 8(5).
17 Clause 17.
18 Clause 18.
19 Available at UNODC, http://www.unodc.org/pdf/lap_foreign-evidence_2000.pdf; for commentary see http://www.unrol.org/files/lap_foreign-evidence_commentary.pdf (both accessed 5 February 2014).

tracing of objects, assets, etc. for evidentiary purposes. The classic coercive measures, such as search and seizure and the SITs are not mentioned. Article 18(3)(i) mentions, however, 'any other type of assistance that is not contrary to the domestic law of the requested State Party'. If the requested state implements Article 20 it should have the SITs included in its domestic criminal procedure. The UNTOC also includes the spontaneous exchange of information in Article 18(4). It is specified that MLA must respect the specialty rule and the secrecy of certain information. Certain orthodox grounds for refusal are excluded, for instance banking secrecy or fiscal matters. The UNTOC does, however, include established grounds for refusal such as: sovereignty, security, *ordre public* or other essential interests; double incrimination; if investigative action would be excluded in the requesting state for similar offenses; or if it would infringe national domestic law. These remain very wide and heavily based on the architecture of the domestic legal regime of the requested state. They are all, however, optional. The UNTOC also deals with joint investigations in Article 19, but the text is limited to a 'shall consider' and thus does not contain formal obligations.

In 2001 the UNODC elaborated an extensive report on MLA casework and best practices.[20] It contains very detailed recommendations for enhancing the effectiveness of MLA, dealing with the central authorities, the procedures, the time delay, digitalization etc. It is, however, striking that it does not deal with SITs. The document has also been elaborated by experts coming solely from the executive bodies and the law enforcement community. This is perhaps the reason why the document completely avoids aspects of data protection, the specialty rule, defense rights and the standing of suspects and victims under MLA regimes.

From drugs to transnational crime: the 2007 Model Law on MLA

This model law was elaborated by the UNODC Division for Treaty Affairs, Treaty Affairs and Legal Branch, and takes account of UNTOC and the older UN Model Treaties on MLA. The MLA model remains based on state-to-state cooperation and thus on cooperation between central authorities. However, the model law clearly provides for the possibility of spontaneous transmission of information.[21] Although the applicable law is the law of the executing state, the model law contains a very wide *lex forum* principle as all procedures specified in the request of the forum state will be applied unless execution would be contrary to the fundamental principles of the law of that state. In regard to grounds for refusal, the model law provides for two options. The first one is that there is no need to list them as their use is optional and thus leaves much discretion to the executing state. The second one is in line with international treaties on control of crime and sets out the classic grounds for refusal, dealing with sovereignty, security, *ordre public*, etc. Banking secrecy is, however, excluded as such a ground. The model law deals with confidential requests and court orders to limit disclosure of MLA requests or related content or decisions. Persons that illegally disclose such requests, the content of the requests or related decisions in case of confidential requests, may be punished. The model law deals extensively with freezing, seizure and confiscation orders related to criminal assets. It also contains a special section (Part 4) on MLA in relation to computers, computer systems and computer data, dealing with expedited preservation, productions and search and seizure of computer data. It does not, however, deal with SITs or joint investigation teams (JITs).

---

20 UNODC, Report, Informal Expert Working Group on Mutual Legal Assistance Casework and Best Practice, Vienna, 2001, available at http://www.unodc.org/pdf/lap_mlaeg_report_final.pdf (accessed 5 February 2014).
21 Clause 6.

The regional European approach to MLA: the shift from MLA to mutual recognition (MR)

From Council of Europe (CoE) MLA to European Union (EU) MLA

Until the 1999 EU Amsterdam Treaty and the establishment of an Area of Freedom, Security and Justice (AFSJ), the regime for MLA in the European region was laid down in multilateral mother conventions of the CoE. Member States of the EU used regional international public law conventions to gather criminal evidence even within the EU. The historic starting point is without any doubt the CoE's 1959 European Convention on Mutual Assistance in Criminal Matters (ratified by all EU Member States),[22] the related 1978 Additional Protocol to the European Convention on Mutual Assistance in Criminal Matters (ratified by nearly all EU Member States),[23] and the 2001 Second Additional Protocol to the European Convention on Mutual Assistance in Criminal Matters (with a modest ratification rate by EU Member States).[24] The 1959 CoE Convention is the mother convention because it introduced on a multilateral level the MLA duty to cooperate and laid down a model for this cooperation. The 1959 CoE Convention was a worldwide *unicum* and not an obvious development at that stage, as the whole tradition of enforcing criminal law was based on sovereignty and bilateral treaties. The obligation to cooperate is an interstate obligation and the Convention can be qualified as an international convention of an administrative-executive nature, but dealing with a judicial matter. It must be added that the main obligation to cooperate is not always absolute. There are two reasons for this. First of all, many States Parties have made reservations and declarations, which results in a complex patchwork of obligations. Second, the 1959 CoE Convention contains far-reaching grounds for refusal, linked to political, military and tax offenses, but also to sovereignty and public order. Finally, as the Convention is based on interstate cooperation there is a double-track procedure, both in the requesting and in the requested state. That means that a request from a judicial authority must be channeled through the central authorities of the Ministries of Justice and Foreign Affairs both in the requesting and requested countries (diplomatic channel) before arriving on the desk of a judicial colleague in the requested state. These central authorities play a key role and the judicial authorities only trigger and execute requests.

With the deepening of European integration it became clear that there was an increasing need for a proper MLA regime in the EU. Due to a lack of political agreement in the EU as a whole, Belgium, Luxembourg, the Netherlands, Germany and France signed the 1985 Schengen Agreement, which was followed by the Schengen Implementing Convention in 1990, containing provisions (beside migration law, visa policy and police cooperation) on MLA and intended to supplement the 1959 CoE Convention.[25] The Schengen Conventions substantially renewed MLA. They replaced the diplomatic channel by direct cooperation between judicial authorities, which did become competent for deciding, sending, executing and resending. Gradually other EU Member States and non-EU Member States acceded to these agreements and they were integrated into the EU Amsterdam Treaty in 1999.

In 1993 it became possible to include MLA in the EU Maastricht Treaty. However, it ended up in the EU's so-called third pillar, with a strong intergovernmental character. Within

---

22 Strasbourg, 20 April 1959, ETS No. 30; in force 12 June 1962.
23 17 March 1978, ETS 99; in force 12 April 1982.
24 8 November 2001, ETS182; in force 1 February 2004.
25 Schengen Agreement on the Gradual Abolition of Checks at Their Common Borders, 14 June 1985, (1991) 30 ILM 68; Convention Implementing the Schengen Agreement of 14 June 1985, signed 19 June 1990, [2000] OJ L 239/19; in force 1 September 1993.

that framework the CoE conventions were gradually replaced by EU conventions: the 1997 Naples II Convention on Mutual Assistance and Cooperation between Customs Administrations[26] and the 2000 EU Convention on Mutual Legal Assistance in Criminal Matters (2000 MLA Convention).[27] The importance of the 2000 MLA Convention cannot be underestimated. The Convention, inspired by the Schengen Conventions, is conceptually based on direct cooperation between judicial authorities. Direct cooperation between judicial authorities in the EU does not mean that a request from a requesting authority automatically has legal value in the territory of the requested authority. As a rule, these warrants must be converted into a national decision in the requested state through *exequatur* proceedings, against which legal remedies can be used.

The 2000 MLA Convention is also very innovative as far as the investigative tools themselves are concerned. Requests can be sent out to obtain the gathering of evidence through the use of SITs. Article 13 of the 2000 MLA Convention provides the legal basis for the setting up of JITs, composed of judicial, police and/or customs officials of the Member States and even of Europol. The JITs were later developed in a specific framework decision.[28] Finally, requesting authorities can request authorities to apply provisions of their domestic law with the aim of obtaining admissible evidence before the courts of the requesting state. Requested authorities can apply this *lex forum rule* instead of the *lex locus rule*, if it does not contravene the fundamental rules of their legal order. This can be very useful to deal with differences in procedural safeguards and rights of the defense (assistance of a lawyer, judicial authorization etc.) and thus with transnational use of evidence in the EU. It is a way to streamline, within the existing legal frameworks, gathering of evidence and use of evidence, as long as the fundamental rules of the legal regimes allow it.

The 2000 MLA Convention was further enriched in 2001 with an Additional Protocol[29] aiming at further improving MLA in the financial sector. It sets aside bank secrecy and introduces obligations to facilitate the transfer of information on bank accounts and banking operations.

The strengthening of MLA in practice

The EU has not only focused on the drafting of new EU conventions, but has also invested in practical improvements: the establishment of liaison magistrates and the creation of a European Judicial Network. However, only a minority of the EU Member States have established liaison magistrates. They have no operational powers and cannot investigate, but are facilitators. Thanks to both their knowledge of systems and their contacts, they know what has to be done legally and practically to prepare and execute MLA requests. On the other hand the European Judicial Network in MLA[30] has been very successful in establishing a

---

26 23 January 1998, OJ C 24/2.
27 12 July 2000, OJ C 197/3.
28 Council FD of 13 June 2002, OJ L 162/1.
29 Protocol established by the Council in accordance with Article 34 of the *Treaty on European Union to the Convention on Mutual Assistance in Criminal Matters between the Member States of the European Union*, OJ 2001, L326/2.
30 There are several similar regional networks: the Judicial Regional Platforms of Sahel and Indian Ocean Commission Countries, the Commonwealth Network of Contact Persons, the Hemispheric Information Exchange Network for Mutual Legal Assistance in Criminal Matters and Extradition of the Organization of American States, and the Ibero-American Legal Assistance Network (IberRed).

horizontal network between judicial authorities responsible for MLA in the EU Member States and to elaborate good practices, judicial guides, etc.

From MLA to mutual recognition in the EU

The EU Amsterdam Treaty and the special Tampere European Council

In 1999 the European Council organized a special meeting on the AFSJ in Tampere. In the Tampere conclusions mutual recognition (MR) became a cornerstone of judicial cooperation and the aim was to replace all MLA conventions by proper EU MR instruments.[31] The MR concept had been applied by the community legislator in many substantive fields of the internal market with the aim of avoiding detailed harmonization. However, the possibility of extrapolating it to judicial decisions was not that self-evident, as harmonization in the area of criminal procedure and applicable safeguards was minimal or non-existent. In 2000 the European Commission published its Communication on Mutual Recognition of Final Decisions in Criminal Matters.[32] Mutual recognition would apply to both court decisions and pre-trial decisions, as well as orders or warrants to gather evidence or to arrest and surrender suspects.

To what extent is MR different from MLA? The basic idea was that, despite the differences between the procedural regimes in the Member States, they were all party to the European Convention on Human Rights and could thus trust each other. Mutual trust was presupposed and considered sufficient grounds to apply MR, even with little or no harmonization in the field. This means that MR orders or warrants coming from an issuing Member State have legal value in the AFSJ and could thus automatically be executed without an *exequatur* procedure. Legal doubts about the order or warrant, linked to, for instance, the legality of the evidence that served to justify the order or warrant, could only be challenged in the issuing Member State.

In 2002 the Council of Ministers adopted the first MR instrument: the European Arrest Warrant (EAW),[33] replacing the extradition conventions. The EAW was adopted under a fast-track procedure after the 9/11 events and did not include harmonization of investigative acts or procedural safeguards. An EAW, whether meant to bring a suspect to trial or to execute the trial sentence, is based on mutual trust and must thus be recognized and executed, unless mandatory or optional grounds of non-recognition apply. However, the grounds are strongly restricted, compared to the refusal grounds under the MLA extradition treaty, and do not contain grounds that are based directly on a human rights clause.

---

31 See Presidency Conclusion No. 33 of the Tampere special European Council. For in-depth analysis, see J. Ouwerkerk, *Quid Pro Quo? A Comparative Law Perspective on the Mutual Recognition of Judicial Decisions in Criminal Matters*, Cambridge: Intersentia, 2011; A. Suominen, *The Principle of Mutual Recognition in Cooperation in Criminal Matters: A Study of the Principle in Four Framework Decisions and in the Implementation Legislation in the Nordic Member States*, Cambridge: Intersentia, 2011.

32 COM(2000) 495 final, available at http://eur-lex.europa.eu/LexUriServ/LexUriServ.do?uri=CO M:2000:0495:FIN:EN:PDF (accessed 1 April 2014).

33 Council Framework Decision 2002/584/JHA on the *European Arrest Warrant and Surrender Procedure between Member States of 13 June 2002*, OJ 2002 L. 190, p. 1. The decision has been amended by Council Framework Decision 2009/299/JHA of 26 February 2009, OJ 2009 L 81, p. 24.

Mutual recognition and gathering of evidence: free flow of evidence?

After the introduction of the EAW it was time to deal with the replacement of MLA by MR in the area of evidence. In 2003 the European Commission submitted a proposal for a European Evidence Warrant (EEW)[34] that was finally adopted in 2008[35] after difficult negotiations. The EEW was limited to existing evidence and thus interrogations, interception of telecommunications and body searches were excluded from its scope of application. The EEW applies to orders issued by judicial authorities and also to a certain extent to orders issued by administrative law enforcement agencies. In order to issue an EEW the issuing authority must comply with the proportionality principle (using the least intrusive means available) and reciprocity. The latter means that the objects, documents or data can be obtained under the law of the issuing state in a comparable case if they were available in the territory of the issuing state, even though different procedural measures might be used. The EEW also contains complex provisions on double criminality. Germany negotiated a stand-alone position permitting it to make execution subject to verification of double criminality in the case of the offenses relating to terrorism, computer-related crime, racism and xenophobia, sabotage, racketeering and extortion, and swindling. These were offenses for which no double criminality requirement exists in the EAW. Moreover, some of them have been harmonized by EU law. Also, when coercive measures such as search and seizure are ordered, Member States can impose double criminality requirements that go beyond the ones foreseen in the EAW.

The execution of an EEW should, to the widest extent possible and without prejudice to fundamental guarantees under national law, be carried out in accordance with the formalities and procedures expressly indicated by the issuing state. This means that an enlarged concept of *lex fori* is applied. However, Member States are wary of the differences in criminal procedure between themselves and try to protect against dissymmetry between their systems of criminal procedure and legal safeguards. Moreover, the list of grounds of non-recognition or non-execution in Article 13 is very long and all of them are optional. Although the EEW was adopted in 2008, Member States have either not implemented it or do not use it. The most common reason for this lack of enthusiasm was that both practitioners and Member States were not that convinced of its utility. The EEW does not deal with all evidence and leads in practice to very complex procedures. While it was possible to use the EEW for freezing existing evidence, for taking matters further MLA requests were again needed. Practitioners also complain about an overly fragmented and complex regulatory frame.

In the 2009 Stockholm program, the European Council decided that the setting up of a comprehensive system for obtaining evidence in cases with a cross-border dimension, based on MR, should be further pursued. The European Council indicated that the existing instruments in this area constitute a fragmentary regime and that a new approach was needed, based on MR, but also taking into account the flexibility of the traditional system of MLA. It called for a comprehensive system to replace all the existing instruments, including the EEW, covering as far as possible all types of evidence and containing deadlines for enforcement and limiting as far as possible the grounds for refusal.

34 See J.A.E. Vervaele (ed.), *European Evidence Warrant: Transnational Judicial Inquiries in the EU*, Antwerp/Oxford: Intersentia, 2005.
35 Council Framework Decision 2008/978/JHA of 18 December 2008 on the *European Evidence Warrant for the Purpose of Obtaining Objects, Documents and Data for Use in Proceedings in Criminal Matters*, 2008, OJ L 350/72, available at http://eur-lex.europa.eu/LexUriServ/LexUriServ.do?uri=CELEX:32008F0978:EN:NOT> (accessed 1 April 2014).

Draft European Investigation Order (EIO)

Frustrated with the EEW, in 2010 seven Member States submitted a proposal for a directive for a European Investigation Order (EIO).[36] A political agreement was reached in the Council[37] and in December 2013 an amended text was approved by the LIBE-Commission of the European Parliament (EP).[38] The EIO has a horizontal scope and therefore applies to all investigative measures aimed at gathering evidence. The proposed EIO also recognizes that this single regime for obtaining evidence will have to be completed by additional rules for some types of investigative measures, such as the temporary transfer of persons held in custody, hearing by video or telephone conference, obtaining of information related to bank accounts or banking transactions, controlled deliveries and covert investigations. The MR regime of the EIO is certainly not the automatic one envisaged at Tampere. Indeed, something akin to 'double procedurality' or 'double lock' has been introduced. The MR regime does not lead to automatic execution, as Article 2(b) stipulates that the execution must not only be in accordance with the EEW but also with the procedures applicable in a similar domestic case. Issuing authorities may assist in the execution of the EIO (as in the MLA regime), but assistance is also conditional on respect for fundamental principles of the law of the executing state and essential national security interests. *Lex fori* principles do apply[39] unless contrary to the fundamental principles of the law of the executing state.

The EIO has a quite complex system of grounds for non-recognition and non-execution. The executing authority should, wherever possible, use another type of measure if the requested measure does not exist under its national law or would not be available in a similar domestic case (referral to an equivalent measure under domestic law) and should always apply the least intrusive measure (proportionality principle). The issuing authority should therefore ascertain whether the evidence sought is necessary and proportionate for the purpose of proceedings, whether the measure chosen is necessary and proportionate for the gathering of this evidence, and whether, by means of issuing the EIO, another Member State should be involved in the gathering of this evidence. It is interesting that LIBE/EP has obtained the inclusion of a human rights clause in the substantive provisions.[40] Article 2(a) underlines the duty to comply with Article 6 of the Treaty on European Union (TEU)[41] and insists that it include the rights of defense of persons subject to criminal proceedings. Article 10 sets out the grounds of non-recognition or non-execution. In a case where there would be substantial grounds to believe that the execution of the investigative measure contained in the EIO would be incompatible with the executing Member State's obligations under Article 6 TEU and the EU Charter of Fundamental Rights (EUCFR), or in a case where execution would infringe the *ne bis in idem* principle, the recognition or execution of the EIO may be refused. However, these grounds for non-recognition or non-execution are, like all the others, optional and

---

36 Proposal of 29 April 2010 (COPEN 15), initiative of Belgium, Bulgaria, Estonia, Spain, Austria, Slovenia and Sweden.
37 General approach, 21 December 2012, 18918/11, COPEN 369.
38 European Parliament Committee on Civil Liberties, Justice and Home Affairs (LIBE). The text is awaiting approval by the General Assembly of the EP.
39 Draft Article 8(2).
40 Earlier MR instruments referred to human rights only in the preamble.
41 Article 6 TEU imposes the EUCFR as a binding instrument and lays down the legal basis for the application of derived human standards from the European Convention on Human Rights of the Council of Europe and of derived constitutional standards of the common constitutional traditions of the Member States as general principles of EU law.

dependent upon the implementing legislation. The Member States may transform them into mandatory grounds, but may also leave it to the discretion of the judicial authorities.

It is of interest that the EIO may also be requested by a suspected or accused person, within the framework of applicable defense rights and in conformity with national criminal procedure. This option[42] is thus very dependent upon domestic law and can lead to very different situations from one Member State to another. Legal remedies available against an EIO should be at least equal to those available in the domestic case against the investigative measure concerned, including the process being subject to the same time limits. However, substantive reasons for issuing the EIO may only be challenged in the issuing state. Transfer of evidence may be suspended pending decision about the legal remedy.

Bilateral MLATs between the EU and third states

The EU has negotiated a set of bilateral MLATs with third states. In 2010 it signed an MLAT with Japan[43] and with the United States.[44] These MLATs only supplement existing bilateral MLATs between the United States and EU Member States. In the case of Japan there were not that many bilateral MLATs, so the added value is high, but even in case of the United States the added value is high as these MLATs contain modern techniques of evidence gathering including video-conferencing, JITs and financial evidence gathering (identification of bank accounts, financial monitoring etc.). Moreover, the scope includes MLA with administrative law enforcement agencies. Further MLATs with other third states will be concluded in the future.

The setting up of a vertical framework for MLA: Eurojust and the European Public Prosecutor's Office (EPPO)

At the Tampere Council it was also decided to set up Eurojust, in which prosecutors from every Member State (national members) form a College. In 2002, the legal framework for its mission and empowerment was adopted and reflected a strong intergovernmental approach.[45] Eurojust's aims include promoting and improving MLA between the competent national authorities and providing general support to increase the effectiveness of their investigations.[46] Eurojust acts through its national members or through the College. Even in matters entirely within national jurisdiction the national members cannot be considered to be a requesting authority or an operational judicial authority. They remain primarily liaison officers. The powers of the College have been put into stronger terms, but even then it is

---

42 Draft Article 2(a).

43 Agreement between the European Union and Japan on Mutual Legal Assistance in Criminal Matters, OJ L 39/20, 12 February 2010, available at http://ec.europa.eu/world/agreements/prepareCreateTreatiesWorkspace/treatiesGeneralData.do?step=0&redirect=true&treatyId=8341 (accessed 12 June 2014). The agreement entered into force, after ratification by all EU Member States, in 2010.

44 Agreement on Mutual Legal Assistance between the European Union and the United States of America, OJ L 181/34, 19 July 2003, available at http://ec.europa.eu/world/agreements/prepareCreateTreatiesWorkspace/treatiesGeneralData.do?redirect=true&treatyId=5441 (accessed 12 June 2014). The agreement entered into force, after ratification by all EU Member States, in 2010.

45 Decision of the Council, dated 28 February 2002, whereby Eurojust is created to strengthen the fight against serious crime, DOCE 2002 L 63/1.

46 Article 3(1).

legally unclear if they can send out binding MLA requests to the competent authorities of the Member States. Eurojust is mostly involved in the coordination of investigative and prosecutorial action and in organizing and sustaining the JITs. In 2009 the Eurojust Decision was amended[47] in order to achieve greater equivalence powers for the national members in their national legal orders.

Overall, the 2009 reform has been very minimal and mostly limited to access to law enforcement data, and has not resulted in a common set of powers for the national members, even when dealing with MLA or MR in their own legal orders. Moreover, very few Member States have enacted legislation in order to insert the powers for their national member into the national legal order. Many Member States are opposed to the idea of delegated competences for national members, even if they can only act in their own jurisdiction. They are afraid of a body with supranational competences and have put forward constitutional reservations.

The Lisbon Treaty laid down in Article 85 TFEU a new legal basis by which Eurojust is to become a European Agency in the AFSJ and is to gain a new mission. It will remain competent for serious cross-border crime but should also deal with serious crime requiring prosecution on a common basis. It may also initiate investigations, but it is clear from the text that Eurojust cannot become a supranational or federal investigative and prosecutorial office, as all procedural acts must be carried out by competent national authorities. In 2013 the European Commission submitted a proposal for a regulation on the European Union Agency for Criminal Justice (Eurojust).[48] Beside reforms in Eurojust's organizational structure, the proposal also includes new definitions of the operational powers. However, it has not proposed that the powers of the Eurojust College become operational or executive, nor can they be considered as making binding requests or orders. It is interesting, however, that it proposes that the national member should be empowered to issue and execute MLA requests or MR orders in its national jurisdiction. Second, in cases of urgency, the national member will also be able to order all types of investigative measures, including coercive ones. It remains to be seen if these extensions of the powers of the national members will survive negotiation. This proposal suggests that Eurojust has become an EU agency, but that the Commission has not made full use of the potentialities of the legal basis in the Lisbon Treaty, as its autonomous powers to start investigations and to send out MLA requests and MR orders in the AFSJ are poorly elaborated. Eurojust will remain, as it stands, mainly an agency that coordinates the cross-border activities of the law enforcement agencies of the Member States. Thus the only real vertical dimension for MLA is the establishment of the European Public Prosecutor's Office (EPPO). After long discussions, going back to the *Corpus Juris* project[49] and the EU Green paper,[50] the EU Lisbon Treaty included in Article 86 TFEU a legal basis to establish the EPPO. It will be an independent EU body with the authority to investigate and prosecute offenses affecting the Union's financial interests (EU subsidy fraud, EU corruption, EU fraud with custom duties etc.). This material competence could be extended to other

47 Council Decision 2009/426/JHA of 16 December 2008 on the strengthening of Eurojust and amending Decision 2002/187/JHA setting up Eurojust with a view to reinforcing the fight against serious crime.

48 COM(2013) 535 final, http://eur-lex.europa.eu/LexUriServ/LexUriServ.do?uri=COM:2013:05 35:FIN:EN:PDF (accessed 15 January 2014).

49 See M. Delmas-Marty and J.A.E. Vervaele (eds), *Implementation of the Corpus Juris in the Member States*, Vols I–IV, Antwerp/Groningen/Oxford: Intersentia, 2000–2001.

50 COM (2001) 715 final, available at http://eur-lex.europa.eu/legal-content/EN/TXT/PDF/?uri= CELEX:52001DC0715&rid=1 (accessed 12 June 2014).

serious transnational offenses. Adjudication of these criminal cases does, however, remain the exclusive competence of the Member States. In other words, the EPPO will prosecute these cases before national courts of the Member States.

In the summer of 2013 the Commission submitted a draft regulation for the EPPO.[51] The Commission financed an academic study with the aim of elaborating Model Rules[52] for the criminal procedure of the EPPO. These Model Rules strived to establish a fair balance between European-wide powers of the EPPO and the rights of the suspect. In the Commission's draft regulation the EPPO is to be an EU body with a decentralized structure of delegate prosecutors in the Member States. Its task is to direct and supervise investigations, and carry out acts of prosecution. As a rule, the investigations of the EPPO within the Member State should be carried out by the proposed 'European Delegated Prosecutors'. In cases involving several Member States or cases which are of particular complexity, efficient investigation and prosecution may require that the European Public Prosecutor also exercise his/her powers by instructing national law enforcement authorities directly. Although the recitals refer to uniform investigative powers throughout the Union and the proposal states that 'for the purpose of investigations and prosecutions conducted by the European Public Prosecutor's Office (EPPO), the territory of the Union's Member States shall be considered a single legal area in which the EPPO may exercise its competence',[53] it is clear from an overall reading of the text that these powers are fully dependent upon national law and territory.[54] Moreover, the text underlines that all coercive measures that can be ordered or requested by the EPPO as investigative measures are subject to authorization by the competent judicial authority of the Member States where they are to be carried out.[55] If we examine the EPPO proposal, it is doubtful whether the content of what is proposed is in line with the aim of Article 86 TFEU, as it seems that it could have been achieved by upgrading Eurojust under Article 85 TFEU. The *proprio motu* investigative and prosecutorial powers, for which the Public Prosecutor would not need to rely on MLA or MR, are absent from the proposal. Moreover, the whole concept of European territoriality, as a common jurisdiction to investigate and prosecute, has been watered down in the proposal to a fragmented panoply of national jurisdictions.

The negotiations have just started and it remains to be seen if this proposal will proceed and which amendments will be introduced to the text.

Conclusion

Thanks to the increasing efforts of the international community to control transnational crime, MLA has become a pivotal issue of global governance and part of transnational criminal justice. This is clearly reflected in the evolution from the Vienna Convention towards UNTOC. Model laws and model bills have contributed to the standardization of national MLA legislative design and practice. Nevertheless, there are clearly loopholes and weaknesses

---

51 COM (2013) 534 final, available at http://eur-lex.europa.eu/LexUriServ/LexUriServ.do?uri=CO M:2013:0534:FIN:EN:PDF (accessed 15 January 2014).

52 See University of Luxembourg, Model Rules for the Procedure of the EPPO, http://www.eppo-project.eu/index.php/EU-model-rules (accessed 3 April 2014); K. Ligeti (ed.), *Toward a Prosecutor for the European Union: A Comparative Analysis*, Vol. 1, Oxford: Hart, 2012; K. Ligeti (ed.), *Toward a Prosecutor for the European Union. Draft Rules of Procedure*, Vol. 2, Oxford: Hart, 2014, forthcoming.

53 Draft Article 25(1).

54 See, for instance, Draft Article 18(6).

55 Draft Article 26(4).

that can be identified. Most of the efforts are linked up with the paradigm of drug trafficking, organized crime and terrorism and do not cover all forms of serious crimes for which MLA might be needed. Although the UN Conventions are global, the reach and effective implementation is certainly not as global as it could be. When it comes to the substance of the Conventions and the Model Law and Bills there are some striking features. Mutual legal assistance remains a model of sovereign state-to-state cooperation based on the executive model of central authorities. In some countries, these central authorities have delegated autonomous powers, but in many this is not the case. The MLATs are highly dominated by the interests of the executive and of the prosecutors. The grounds for refusal are mostly widely defined and reflect the same interest. This is the reason why in most cases they are optional, and thus depend on the discretionary power of the executive. Defense rights or fair trial rights, and human rights issues of flagrant denial of justice, do not seem to belong in the extant vocabulary of MLA and are not included as mandatory grounds of refusal in any case. When it comes to the MLA tools there is no clear substantive line of division between police cooperation, administrative assistance and MLA. It also deals with information exchange and can sometimes include assistance for administrative enforcement agencies. The MLA conventions remain very cautious when it comes to coercive measures and SITs and condition these upon stringent rules and procedures of the domestic law of the executing state. Application of *lex forum* provisions is sometimes submitted to conditions of conformity with domestic law; sometimes only to fundamental principles. Finally, the new digital techniques of investigation, such as digital surveillance or remote computer searches, are absent in MLA instruments, with the exception of the 2007 Model Law. The UN executive approach to MLA means also that the persons concerned (suspects and victims in particular) remain objects of MLA and cannot derive from the MLA scheme rights to gather evidence. If they have any rights it derives from applicable national law. It also remains unclear for the persons concerned if, and if so to what extent, they can derive rights from the UN human rights instruments in the area of MLA. In other words, there is a lot to be done at UN level in order to elaborate a modern MLA scheme that updates operational tools and includes human rights protection.

In the EU there has been a very substantive paradigm shift from MLA to MR. The emphasis is on direct cooperation between judicial authorities, and the grounds for refusal have been reduced. However, the lack of equivalent procedural investigative acts and related procedural safeguards in the Member States has led to distrust. The efforts under the Lisbon Treaty to harmonize basic fair trial rights through the directive on the right to translation and interpretation,[56] the directive on the right to information in criminal proceedings, and the directive on the right to access to a lawyer in criminal proceedings,[57] are only first steps. They do not resolve all the issues of fairness of the proceedings that might arise when executing MR evidence orders, such as access to the file/disclosure or remedies against the execution of the investigative act or against the transfer of the obtained evidence. The very recent second draft legislative package of the European Commission on procedural safeguards does not tackle these aspects at all.[58]

---

56 Directive of the European Parliament and of the Council on the right to interpretation and translation in criminal proceedings, 2010, OJ L 280/1.
57 Directive on the right of access to a lawyer in criminal proceedings and on the right to communicate upon arrest, 2013, OJ L 294/1.
58 Proposal for a Directive of the European Parliament and of the Council on the strengthening of certain aspects of the presumption of innocence and of the right to be present at trial in criminal proceedings, COM 2013 0821, available at http://eur-lex.europa.eu/LexUriServ/LexUriServ. do?uri=CELEX:52013PC0821:en:NOT (accessed 15 January 2014).

From the negotiations on the EEW and draft EIO we can conclude that the EU Member States are not aiming at a common approach in the AFSJ. They are trying as far as possible to limit the transnational gathering of evidence in their own territory, to place it under their own applicable law, and as far as possible to build requirements from their domestic legal orders into regional arrangements. The AFSJ remains to a large extent a patchwork of sovereign jurisdictions that have difficulty in accepting new tools for the gathering of criminal evidence in an integrated territory. When it comes to the supranational law enforcement agencies in the AFSJ (Eurojust and EPPO) it is quite clear that the existing law enforcement agencies and the future EPPO are neither designed as operational judicial authorities nor as competent MLA or MR authorities. They remain mostly mediators between national authorities and, to the extent that they get investigative powers, these are inserted into the applicable law of the domestic jurisdictions.

To wind up, in order to control transnational crime and to provide effective law enforcement that respects the rule of law and applicable human rights standards, there is a need for an innovative approach both at the UN and European regional level. At the global level instruments must be updated and have to take into account the digital dimension of our societies. The optional grounds for refusal linked to sovereignty should be reduced and mandatory grounds linked to human rights standards included. The MLA regimes should also take into account the interests of the defense as a legal subject with rights and remedies in the proceedings.

At the regional EU level there is a need for further harmonization of the investigative tools and procedural safeguards in the Member States, so that MR can function in the common territory of the AFSJ. The regional level should be able to deepen cooperation on MLA, integrate it with human rights protection, and make it less dependent upon national sovereignty.

9

Asset recovery

Charles Monteith and Pedro Gomes Pereira

Introduction

The increase of cross-border movements of persons, goods and capital in the second half of the twentieth century and the increasing international visibility of certain local criminal events has resulted in a response from the international community: transnational criminal law.[1] This increase in transnational crime shows that the traditional approach of reserving criminal law to the sovereignty of States is no longer sufficient to effectively prevent and combat criminal events. Sovereignty has become, in many instances, an aid to transnational criminals. Perpetrators structure their activities around legal and institutional ambiguities generated by conflicting legal systems and traditions. The interconnection between criminal law and sovereignty has therefore rendered the control of transnational crime solely at the local level insufficient.

In response, States have sought to enhance the cross-border co-ordination of their jurisdictions with regards to certain serious criminal offences such as corruption, terrorism and money laundering. The trans-nationalisation of criminal law has resulted in the establishment of rules on the co-ordination of jurisdiction and legal standing between sovereign States.[2] The effective co-ordination of different legal systems is paramount for the prevention and repression of these criminal offences, in order to avoid the superimposition of efforts of different States with jurisdiction over these criminal activities.

---

1 M.R. Machado, *Internacionalização do Direito Penal: A Gestão de Problemas Internacionais por meio do Crime e da Pena*, São Paulo: Editora 34, p. 18. See also N. Boister, *An Introduction to Transnational Criminal Law*, Oxford: Oxford University Press, 2012, pp. 13–23; R. Cryer, 'The Doctrinal Foundations of International Criminalization', in M.C. Bassiouni (ed.), *1 International Criminal Law: Sources, Subjects and Contents*, 3rd edn, Dordrecht: Nijhoff, 2008, p. 108; R.J. Currie, *International and Transnational Criminal Law*, Toronto: Irwin, 2010, p. 19.
2 Currie, *International and Transnational Criminal Law*, p. 20.

The approach taken by the international instruments[3] focuses on establishing minimum standards for certain criminal offences, while providing local law enforcement and prosecutors with the capacity to suppress the financial incentives of certain forms of criminality through the identification, seizure and confiscation of the proceeds of crime. They have allowed States to perceive their co-operation and co-ordination not solely as a mechanism of communication of official acts, but as a procedural relationship between their national procedures.

International instruments have furthermore expanded the focus of criminal proceedings to include not only investigating and prosecuting the perpetrators, but also pursuing their unlawful gains, whether through corruption or other forms of transnational crime. Depriving perpetrators of their unlawful gains is a more effective mechanism to combat these criminal offences, particularly in jurisdictions where penalties and sentences for corruption and fraud are low. Focusing on removing the profits of the criminal activity removes a major incentive for the perpetrators: criminals fear losing their lifestyles much more than serving two or three years in prison.

Enter the asset recovery process. It is succinctly understood as the process whereby jurisdictions identify, trace, restrain and confiscate proceeds of crime, whose true nature, origin and ownership have been disguised by the perpetrator of a criminal offence.[4]

This chapter discusses the main problems surrounding the asset recovery process at both the substantive and procedural levels. It then briefly discusses the main standard-setting provisions provided by international law and the various stages of the asset recovery process. Finally, it shows how some of the practical challenges facing asset recovery can be overcome through the adoption of an appropriate case strategy and through investigation planning.

Problems in asset recovery

Under traditional methods of combating crime, the identification, seizure and confiscation of the proceeds of crime are of secondary importance. The primary goal is to investigate, prosecute, convict and sentence the perpetrators. Only then are assets pursued, usually to compensate the victims of the offence, or to satisfy the related judicial costs of the proceedings. Confiscation to the State of all illegally obtained assets where there is no obvious victim is a relatively new phenomenon. Not all States have appropriate legislation to enable the seizure and confiscation of the proceeds of crime. Without it, proceedings tend to get entangled in legal arguments over establishing loss.

The proceeds of serious crime, however, are seldom found in one jurisdiction. The evidence that determines that the perpetrator has unlawfully obtained certain assets is therefore also to be found in multiple jurisdictions. As a result, orders for the production of

---

3   These include international and regional treaties including the United Nations Convention against Corruption (UNCAC) 31 October 2003, 2349 UNTS 41, in force 14 December 2005; the United Nations Convention against Transnational Organized Crime (UNTOC), 15 November 2000, 2225 UNTS 209, in force 29 September 2003; and the OECD Anti-Bribery Convention, 18 December 1997, 37 ILM 1, in force 15 February 1999. They also include soft law mechanisms such as the FATF Recommendations on Combating Money Laundering and the Financing of Terrorism and Proliferation, available at FATF, http://www.fatf-gafi.org/media/fatf/documents/recommendations/pdfs/FATF_Recommendations.pdf (accessed 25 February 2014).

4   International Centre for Asset Recovery (ICAR), *Development Assistance, Asset Recovery and Money Laundering: Making the Connection*, Basel: Basel Institute of Governance, 2011, p. 6, p. 9.

evidence and the execution of certain jurisdictional acts from one State have to be sought from the judicial authorities, and executed, in other States. Thus, while the repression of certain acts remains within the scope of local jurisdictions, their effects go beyond national borders.[5]

Boister defines transnational crime as any conduct having an actual or potential cross-border effect of national or international concern.[6] The result of this internationalisation of criminal law is twofold. It creates minimum standards in substantive criminal law with a view to facilitating co-ordination and co-operation, and it establishes procedures to co-ordinate jurisdictions through common rules on legal standing between sovereign and independent States, thus attempting to avoid their superimposition.

Standard provisions in asset recovery

International norms on asset recovery (treaties and soft law) deal, in general, with specific provisions States must undertake either in their substantive criminal law (jurisdiction) or in their criminal procedural law (legal standing). This subsection will focus upon two aspects of international standard setting in asset recovery: (i) jurisdiction and (ii) legal standing. While the former deals with matters closely linked to local substantive criminal law and sovereignty of States, the latter deals with local criminal procedural law in order to effect and co-ordinate international co-operation. Attention should be given to the fact that standard setting for the recovery of assets – the last stage of the asset recovery process – was only established at the international level through the United Nations Convention Against Corruption (UNCAC).[7]

The international treaties seek to standardise certain criminal offences. These standards of substantive criminal norms, such as corruption-related offences, money laundering, trans-national organised crime and trafficking in drugs, directly affect the jurisdiction of States. These States have, however, not ceded their sovereignty to a supranational body; rather, States have agreed to have a baseline definition for these criminal offences.

International standards furthermore determine the minimum standards for the application of the jurisdiction of a State in relation to the criminal offences they prescribe. In general, they require that the criminal offences established under it have territorial application. For the offence of money laundering, however, the international standards require States to apply their jurisdiction extra-territorially.

This is because the offence of money laundering requires the commission of a predicate offence.[8] In this case, the perpetrator will often attempt to disguise the true nature, origin and ownership of the proceeds of crime by utilising one or more different jurisdictions. Given that the predicate offence to money laundering may occur outside the jurisdiction that is investigating the money-laundering offence, and that it must be demonstrated in order to prove the money-laundering offence, extending the reach of the jurisdiction of the investigating State is necessary so that it may have jurisdiction over the predicate offence, even when it did not happen in the same jurisdiction where the money laundering took place.

---

5   N. Boister, 'Transnational Criminal Law?', *European Journal of International Law* 14, 2003, p. 955.
6   Ibid., p. 954.
7   31 October 2003, 2349 UNTS 41, in force 14 December 2005.
8   In money laundering, the perpetrator of the offence is seeking to disguise the true nature, origin and ownership of their unlawful gains, obtained through the commission of a predicate offence.

With regard to corruption-related offences, an important standard obliges States to criminalise the corruption of foreign public officials. This requires States to define what comprises a foreign public official in their criminal legislation. The added value of this standard is the fact that the jurisdictions involved are able to curb both the supply and the demand side of corruption, when the act of corruption has been carried out by a foreign company in the affected jurisdiction, or, conversely, where a public official has solicited a bribe from a foreign company.

At present, with regard to the corruption of foreign public officials, there are two main international standards: the UNCAC and the OECD Anti-Bribery Convention.[9] However, their approaches differ substantially: the former focuses on the asset recovery process and international co-operation, with a view to enforcing confiscation orders related to the proceeds of crime. The latter focuses on establishing penalties through settlements for the damages incurred by the unlawful activity. This could mean that once a settlement of a case in one jurisdiction has been obtained, the principle of *ne bis in idem* may apply, rendering ineffective the actions of the victim jurisdiction. Furthermore, once a settlement has been reached, there is less likelihood that the jurisdiction in which the settlement was reached would entertain a request for mutual legal assistance from the victim jurisdiction.[10]

Finally, attention should be given to the fact that not all treaty provisions are mandatory. The UNCAC itself provides for mandatory and non-mandatory offences, and leaves discretion for the States Parties on a number of issues.

The international conventions also set international standards pertaining to criminal procedural law that are touched upon below. These include the principle of dual criminality, and elements for the co-ordination of legal standing among jurisdictions. In relation to these, and relating to international co-operation, requests for international co-operation are generally to be executed in accordance with the procedural rules of the requested State. While the requesting State retains jurisdiction over the subject matter, it must respect the sovereignty of the requested State, which controls the execution of the request, and thus the request must observe the rules of procedure of the requested State. Notwithstanding, this rule allows exceptions, notably that the requests may be executed in accordance with the procedural rules of the requesting State, insofar as these rules do not clash with the fundamental and constitutional provisions of the requested State.

The asset recovery process

These international rules and standards have to be translated into the asset recovery process at an operational level. The international conventions prescribe, on the one hand, provisions for the criminalisation, in their domestic law, of certain offences;[11] on the other, they provide rules for application of jurisdiction and legal standing for the receipt, review, processing and execution of requests. Asset recovery is a four-phase process, comprising:[12]

---

9 OECD Anti-Bribery Convention, 18 December 1997, 37 ILM 1; in force 15 February 1999.
10 J.A. Oduor *et al.*, *Left Out of the Bargain: Settlements in Foreign Bribery Cases and Implications for Asset Recovery*, The World Bank, 2013, p. 57.
11 Boister, 'Transnational Criminal Law', p. 962.
12 International Centre for Asset Recovery (ICAR), *Development Assistance, Asset Recovery and Money Laundering: Making the Connection*, p. 6, p. 9.

1. The *intelligence-gathering phase*, during which law enforcement receives, analyses and verifies sources of information which may initiate an investigation.
2. The *investigative phase*, where the proceeds and instrumentalities of crime are identified and located, and evidence of the true nature, origin and ownership is collected. This phase involves substantiating the veracity of the intelligence and information collected in the previous stage and converting it into admissible evidence. The result of this investigation may result in the seizure of the proceeds and instrumentalities of crime.
3. The *judicial phase*, where a judgment against the perpetrator is obtained and, where applicable, a decision determining the confiscation of the proceeds and instrumentalities of crime is determined.
4. The *realisation phase*, where the property is actually confiscated and realised in accordance with the applicable law, taking into account international asset-sharing obligations, as well as compensation for victims and determination of what to do with the confiscated assets.

If States are to successfully capture illegally obtained assets, both the identification and the restraint of the proceeds and of crime have to be at the forefront of all investigations and prosecutions from the very beginning. Preventing the financial gains of the criminal activity from being quickly dissipated is the challenge. Securing them through the appropriate legal mechanisms, such as restraint of assets, is paramount, so that these may be subject to proceedings which will determine their nature, origin and ownership.

A first step is to ensure that each State has the appropriate domestic legal framework to restrain such assets. The next stage is to identify the proceeds of crime. Unlike traditional crimes, with investigators immediately responding to a crime scene complete with suspect, corruption and economic crime is usually not discovered until long after the crime has been committed. Therefore, investigators must gather and piece together information (often indirectly obtained) in order to form a cohesive picture of what happened and then trace this back to a suspect. Evaluation, analysis and dissemination are critical to their success.[13] The intelligence-gathering exercise allows law enforcement to arrive at new leads, which may not have been apparent at first.

An effective asset recovery system requires jurisdictions to have the capacity and sufficient resources (human, financial and otherwise) to collect voluminous amounts of information – in accordance with law and respecting the fundamental rights of the persons under investigation – distilling it down to relevant data and cross-pollinating it with other sources of intelligence, both local and international. Informed assessments arising from this exercise allow law enforcement to determine whether a certain activity may or not be lawful, and whether the resulting assets are the proceeds or instrumentalities of crime.

The leads stemming from intelligence gathering are the most common way to initiate an investigation[14] with relevant information helping to identify the nature, origin and ownership of assets. This data-gathering exercise is subject to the laws of each country and, for this

---

13 A. Bacarese, 'The Role of Intelligence in the Investigation and the Tracing of Stolen Assets in Complex Economic Crime and Corruption Cases', in ICAR, *Tracing Stolen Assets: A Practitioner's Handbook*, Basel: Basel Institute of Governance, 2009, p. 37.
14 While the asset recovery system focuses on intelligence gathering, it does not discard other forms of initiating a case, such as whistleblowers. Different forms of initiating an asset recovery case will be discussed in the course of this chapter.

reason, may not be easily shared both locally and internationally, given different international, regional and domestic rules on, for example, the access to financial information, data protection regulation, different levels of access to information within different governmental agencies, etc. Adding to this difficulty is the fact that the perpetrators seek to conceal the nature, origin and ownership of the assets. They utilise different legal mechanisms and corporate structures to achieve this goal. They take advantage of the discrepancies between legal systems in different jurisdictions.[15]

Numerous mechanisms have been set up in order to permit the sharing of information among investigators from different jurisdictions, but a common problem remains: the predicate offence to money laundering may not constitute an offence in the jurisdiction which has information supporting the investigation.[16] Given that perpetrators use all the tools at their disposal in order to mask the true origin, nature and ownership of the proceeds of crime, enforcers must do likewise, including information sharing and proactive mutual assistance across borders. In order to catch perpetrators and seize their ill-gotten gains, law enforcers have to start thinking like perpetrators, including trying to identify where the best place to conceal such assets might be.[17]

Once a case has been identified and the initial data-gathering exercise has determined the existence of potentially unlawful activity, a determination on which State has jurisdiction over the subject matter must be made. Determining jurisdiction over the subject matter of the case is necessary to ensure both that an investigation is initiated and that the State has the legitimacy to make requests to other States for the gathering of evidence to meet the requirements of its criminal process, or to restrain assets which may be located in another State.

Understanding jurisdiction requires first understanding sovereignty, which stems from the desire of the sovereign to gain political and territorial independence.[18]

The jurisdiction a State has over a determined territory is an expression of its sovereignty. Each State imposes principles and rules upon its exercise of sovereignty that internally limit and restrict its jurisdiction.[19] But sovereignty is also externally limited by international law.[20] The combination of limitations allows for States to reconcile their interests, recognising their plurality and, as a consequence, the realisation of foreign legal acts in each other's national territory.[21] In transnational crime, one or more States will normally have jurisdiction over the facts of the case, for similar or different criminal offences. It may also be that only one jurisdiction may have jurisdiction over the facts, but the evidence or the proceeds are in another jurisdiction, or spread across multiple other jurisdictions. This occurs as perpetrators utilise different legal systems and their legislation in an attempt to give an apparent legality to the proceeds of crime and to disguise their nature, origin and ownership. Nevertheless, the

---

15 An example of this is the challenge of identifying the true beneficial owners, which are often hidden by corporate structures and shell corporations. See J. Sharman, 'Shell Corporations and Asset Recovery: Piercing the Corporate Veil', in G. Fenner Zinkernagel, C. Monteith and P. Gomes Pereira, *Emerging Trends in Asset Recovery*, Berlin: Peter Lang, 2013, p. 67.
16 See Chapter 20 in this volume.
17 Issues relating to the principle of dual criminality will be examined in more detail below.
18 L. Ferrajoli, *A Soberania no Mundo Moderno: Nascimento e Crise do Estado Nacional*, São Paulo: Martins Fontes, 2002, p. 2; W. Goldschmidt, *Derecho Internacional Privado*, 9th edn, Buenos Aires: Depalma, 2002, p. 147; A.P. Madruga Filho, *A Renúncia à Imunidade de Jurisdição pelo Estado Brasileiro e o Novo Direito de Imunidade de Jurisdição*, Rio de Janeiro: Renovar, 2003, p. 24.
19 Ferrajoli, *A Soberania no Mundo Moderno*, p. 2.
20 Goldschmidt, *Derecho Internacional Privado*, p. 72.
21 O. Tenório, *Direito Internacional Privado*, 4th edn, Rio de Janeiro: Freitas Bastos, 1955, p. 433.

question posed is whether all of the involved jurisdictions, or only some, should apply their jurisdiction to the matter,[22] what their jurisdiction over the subject matter of the case is and, for those States applying their jurisdiction, whether they are competent to gather the required evidence and apply their jurisdiction to facts which will often have occurred outside their jurisdiction (extra-territorial application of the law). Ultimately, however, the jurisdiction in which the majority of the facts have taken place – and from where the proceeds of crime have originated – must take the necessary steps to initiate an investigation[23] over the facts and determine whether a criminal offence has occurred.[24]

The exercise of jurisdiction by a State cannot be done through force, and the legitimacy of exercising its jurisdiction resides in observance of due process requirements in both the requesting and requested States.[25] These are exercised through international co-operation[26] in criminal matters, an important component of the asset recovery process. International co-operation, however, is dependent on both jurisdiction and the right of the State to punish (substantive criminal law), and on the legal standing of both the requesting and requested States to assist one another in effecting the jurisdiction of the requesting State, through international co-operation (criminal procedural law). Legal process is one thing; human contact and communication in person is another. The need to establish trust through effective communication from the very beginning cannot be stressed sufficiently.

Thus, the facts of the case must be assessed. A determination must also be made as to whether the facts have violated a legal norm in one or more jurisdictions. Finally, if the facts demonstrate valid violations of legal norms in the affected jurisdictions, it has to be determined whether, and if so how, the rights, obligations, actions and exceptions of the affected parties (perpetrator and State) are engaged.[27] This relationship between fact and law must be verified in all affected States – that is, all States which have jurisdiction to investigate, prosecute and adjudicate.

Requests for mutual legal assistance must demonstrate these elements of existence, validity and effectiveness to the requested State, so that it may determine the execution of the request. The requesting jurisdiction does not have the legal standing to exercise its jurisdiction outside its territory, and must thus demonstrate to the requested State the feasibility of its request to

---

22 The application of jurisdiction over a case will depend on other factors such as resources (which are finite) and priorities (which are determined in public policies of each jurisdiction).

23 Office of the Attorney General of Switzerland, 'Arab Spring: Swiss Attorney General to request legal assistance from Egypt,' 31 January 2014, available at http://www.admin.ch/aktuell/00089/index.html?lang=en&msg-id=51874 (accessed 26 March 2014); Office of the Attorney General of Switzerland, 'La fille du président ouzbek dans la ligne de mire de la justice Suisse,' 12 March 2014, available at https://www.news.admin.ch/message/index.html?lang=fr&msg-id=52278 (accessed 26 March 2014).

24 In money-laundering cases, there must be the demonstration of the predicate offence, subject to the laws of the jurisdiction investigating the matter. Thus, if the investigation of money laundering occurs in a jurisdiction other than from where the predicate offence has taken place, the jurisdiction conducting the money-laundering investigation will require the active assistance of the other jurisdiction in order for it to collect the necessary evidence to demonstrate the occurrence of the predicate offence, in accordance with the legal thresholds established by the investigating jurisdiction.

25 Procedural requirements must be put in place or, at a minimum, reciprocity ensured among the States involved.

26 International co-operation is understood as extradition, mutual legal assistance and transfer of criminal proceedings or persons. The present chapter, however, will focus solely on mutual legal assistance, and will thus use both expressions interchangeably.

27 F.C. Pontes de Miranda, *Tratado das Ações*, vol. 1, Campinas: Bookseller, 1998, pp. 21–22.

the requested jurisdiction. Both the requesting and requested States must, however, establish the validity of the breach of the law in both jurisdictions (principle of dual criminality). While the requested State may not have jurisdiction over the subject matter of the case, it will continue to have legal standing over the requests it receives from the requesting State. Where the facts of the case do not indicate a valid breach of the law of the requested State, the request for mutual legal assistance – in particular when requesting compulsory measures – cannot be accepted, as doing so would equate to recognising facts that are not in violation of its substantive criminal law.

This principle of dual criminality[28] conveys that the offence under investigation in the requesting State must also correlate to an offence in the requested State. The offences in both the requesting and requested States do not have to be identical – if this were to be required, it would, in fact, greatly diminish the possibility of rendering assistance. Rather, the core elements of the offence in both States must be similar in nature. The principle of dual criminality is thus an expression of the interconnectedness between sovereignty and criminal law. Substantive criminal law attaches itself to the notion of jurisdiction, and can be applied based on the principle of territoriality (or extra-territorial application of the law).[29]

International co-operation will be used for the sharing of information, collection of evidence and the restraint of assets, all of which are to be found outside the jurisdiction conducting the investigation into the subject matter. Overcoming initial questions over jurisdiction and legal standing over the subject matter will lead to overcoming evidentiary thresholds and legal standards required in the requested State in order to collect the necessary evidence or to restrain the proceeds of crime, as well as the tools utilised to reach them.

The collection of evidence is fundamental for the substantiation of the facts of the case. However, given that these rely on the legal standing of each State to apply its internal procedural rules, this may result in different, and sometimes conflicting, thresholds to be met. While a less stringent standard may suffice for obtaining bank records in the requesting State, the requested State may in turn require a more demanding threshold to obtain such documents. Communication in these cases is key to ensure that both jurisdictions understand the other's legal requirements in order for these to be met.

Ultimately, the most important aspect of the asset recovery process is the ability to quickly restrain, from the outset, the proceeds of crime, so that these are not dissipated. All the previous steps mentioned refer to the identification and substantiation of evidence that will connect the proceeds of crime to its perpetrators (real beneficial owners), and these to the facts of the case and a criminal offence. Once these have been connected, and prior to the perpetrator gaining knowledge of the investigation, the assets must be restrained.

Restraining assets at the international level, however, can on occasion be a time-consuming exercise, for the reasons presented above. Due process must be ensured (given that assets will be restrained in the requested jurisdiction, but defence for the measure will normally require action in both the requesting and requested jurisdictions). The requested jurisdiction must have enabling legislation allowing it to restrain assets – which by its very definition is

---

28 Dual criminality is but one of the criteria establishing validity in the requested jurisdiction. The others include refusal to assist when the underlying subject matter deals with discriminatory issues of race, religion, sex and nationality of the perpetrator, or for humanitarian reasons.
29 M. Delmas Marty, *Três desafios por um direito mundial*, Rio de Janeiro: Lumen Juris, 2003, p. 286.

not an interlocutory decision – for a foreign jurisdiction, pending a final judgment of confiscation.[30]

Case strategy

Asset recovery is essentially a practical process, and there are significant examples of failed attempts to recover assets.[31] The following section outlines the steps required for an effective case strategy.[32]

Establishing the investigative strategy and tactics

Complex investigations involving economic crime or corruption have to sift through an alarming and ever-increasing volume of material and data. In the midst of such detail is it easy to lose the way. Added to this are the aggressive strategies and tactics used by proactive defence lawyers (challenging each and every move made), an uninterested public (where there does not appear to be an obvious victim), and the lapse of time before the corrupt activity is uncovered, all of which can put enforcement agencies on the back foot. It therefore becomes critical for such agencies to have their own strategy and tactics. A well-made, proactive investigation strategy is designed to provide and maintain some degree of essential control to enforcers. Establishing a clear methodology, strategy and investigative plan is crucial in assisting agencies to build upon initial allegations and conduct successful investigations.

Investigation strategy and plan

The investigative plan is intended to serve as a guide to the strategy: to assist in identifying the nature of the corrupt activity, to develop the evidence necessary to prove the corruption, and to evaluate the most effective use of investigative powers throughout the course of the investigation. It is a living document that should be revised throughout the life of the investigation. As an investigation proceeds, it is critical to revise and update the features of the investigative plan to ensure that it accurately reflects the evidence gathered at various stages, the developments in, and the understanding of the case.

The degree of information that an agency has during the early stages of the investigation is a critical factor in determining how an investigation will be conducted and helps inform the strategy. Information analysed in the intelligence phase of the investigation will form the heart of the subsequent plan.

---

30 *In Re: Any and All Funds or Other Assets in Brown Brothers Harriman & Co. Account # 8870792, et al., US v Opportunity Fund and Tiger Eye Investments*, – F.3d –, 2010 WL 2794281 (DC Cir. July 16, 2010), No. 09–5065, the Federal Court of Appeals for the District of Columbia circuit held that provisions under 28 USC § 2467(d)(3) (providing for enforcement of foreign judgments) were applicable only after a foreign judgment of forfeiture was entered. The law has since been changed allowing US prosecutors to restrain assets on behalf of foreign jurisdictions.

31 See the discussions of the tortuous attempts to recover Abacha's, Marco's and Montesino's stolen loot in M. Pieth (ed), *Recovering Stolen Assets*, Bern, Peter Lang, 2008.

32 See further ICAR, *Tracing Stolen Assets*; J.P. Brun, L. Gray, C. Scott and K.M. Stephenson, *Asset Recovery Handbook: A Guide for Practitioners*, Stolen Asset Recovery Initiative, World Bank/UNODC, 2011.

There are five essential features in investigation planning: a) the features of the corrupt activity; b) the proposed evidence-gathering strategy; c) use of investigation powers and tools; d) a media communication strategy; and e) evaluation.

Features of the corrupt activity

The features are who, what, when, where, why, how, etc.:

1. Who (subjects of the investigation): identify the businesses and individuals related to the corrupt activity and their relationship to each other (financial profiling of business associates and family is important).
2. What (types of corrupt agreement or arrangement): identify the events or actions.
3. Where (geographic area affected): identify locations where participants have held meetings and the geographic area affected to assess jurisdictional reach.
4. When (duration): identify all time factors related to the corrupt activity, assess statutory limitations.
5. Why (motive of the participants): identify causes for events or actions related to the corruption.
6. How (the way the corruption operates): identify the sequence of events and generation of the proceeds of crime (especially the use of intermediaries to move assets).

Determination of evidence required

Financial institutions collect a lot of information relating to customers in their due diligence and risk assessments, as well as through Suspicious Activity Reports (SARs), all of which should be routinely requested. In bribery cases the bribe is often disguised in the form of payments for children's school fees, or property, etc. given to children, parents or siblings, which may need substantiating. It is of particular importance to identify the proceeds generated by the corrupt activity, and to evidentially link assets back to the corrupt activity.

The start of the process involves an analysis of information obtained via the preliminary inquiry/intelligence sources, followed by a determination of the most effective strategy to turn this information into admissible evidence. Analysis of the evidence required to prove the offence allows the investigation team to identify any gaps in the evidence gathered to date and thus focus on acquiring any further relevant evidence from appropriate sources. Some agencies draft an outline of the evidence gathered ('evidence matrix'), setting out an evidence trail which is a useful reference throughout the course of the investigation to determine whether the evidence obtained would be admissible and likely to withstand judicial scrutiny.

Use of investigation powers and tools

The success of an investigation often largely depends on the choice of investigative tools and powers. Inappropriate choices and improper uses may lead to the investigation being ineffective and/or challenged. The choice of investigative tools should be re-evaluated as facts and evidence come to light during the course of the investigation.

Intelligence

Information on its own can be of little value, particularly where there is so much of it. A systematic method of collecting, assessing and prioritising information into effective intelligence (which, ideally, can then be turned into admissible evidence) is therefore paramount.

Intelligence-based techniques are particularly useful in tracing the proceeds of serious economic crime and corruption. The intelligence plan should cover:

Open source intelligence

Open source intelligence involves finding and selecting information from publically available sources and analysing it. There has been a huge growth of publically available personal and corporate information across the internet, such as social networking sites, databases of registries, government reports etc. In fact far too much of it; the best way to sift through it all is to use an effective search method that will extract and aggregate only relevant data. The International Centre for Asset Recovery (ICAR), for example, has developed an Asset Recovery Intelligence System (ARIS) as one such tool.[33]

Human intelligence

Many countries offer immunities and/or plea bargain arrangements in order to turn participating suspects into co-operating witnesses. They are particularly valuable because they can assist in identifying the target of the investigation and in prioritising the businesses, individuals and locations for investigation. They can also provide the best direct evidence of the corrupt offence. Even where they are not willing to become formal witnesses and testify against the main offenders, they are often able to offer valuable information throughout all stages of the investigation and are under a duty to co-operate fully throughout. With so much data to sift, they are of particular use in identifying where in the world crucial evidence lies, and thus play a vital role in focusing the investigation. Innocent informers and whistleblowers are another valuable source of vital information. They need to be encouraged to come forward through proactive outreach campaigns, and thereafter be properly protected and looked after.

Financial intelligence

When assets flow through the financial system, the transfer from one account to another usually leaves an audit trail record, which can be tracked and detected by financial investigators. But because the stolen assets are often distributed among different accounts and under different corporate names, investigators usually also need to refer to external information, such as financial documents and suspicious transfer reports filed in banks and with law enforcement agencies. Financial Intelligence Units (FIUs)[34] are now established in most countries in the world. They receive, analyse and disclose information provided by financial institutions relating to suspicious or unusual financial transactions. They also build up profiles of individuals and money-laundering techniques. Critically, they exchange information with their foreign counterparts.

Investigator analysts should build up a financial profile of the suspects together with tracing their assets. It cannot be stressed enough that it is of critical importance to connect assets back to the corrupt activity that generated these assets, otherwise it will not be possible to recover any of them as proceeds of crime. This is often overlooked and becomes a frequent issue when making mutual legal assistance (MLA) or information requests in relation to assets held abroad.

33 See the ICAR website, http://www.baselgovernance.org/icar (accessed 12 April 2014).
34 See Chapter 20 in this volume.

Using anti-money-laundering (AML) laws proactively to obtain information

Requesting countries often face difficulties in extracting financial information from other countries, which cannot provide that information without a solid legal basis for doing so. This has proved to be a particular problem in connection with sanctioned individuals where there may have been no suspicious activities to report up and until they are placed on the sanctioned list (and some may argue that this fact alone is still not enough).

This problem can be overcome by persuading the requested country to open its own investigation under its own money-laundering laws (this may have to be achieved through an initial letter of request). Thus the requested country makes its own request for further information back to the requesting country and in doing so supplies the originally requested information or evidence. Moreover, based upon its own investigation, the requested country would then generate SARs relating to the suspect's assets, which it would then pass to the requesting country's FIU.

Freezing assets

The need to act quickly to secure assets generated by crime before they can be dissipated is of paramount importance. Using the AML laws is a practical and convenient way to do this, particularly with assets held abroad. Engaging the foreign agency in freezing the assets under its own powers is often the quickest and most effective way. Usually the foreign agency can agree (on behalf of the Treasury in its country) that sums recovered or confiscated will be returned to the home country, with deduction of its reasonable costs. Best practice is to include this in the Memorandum of Understanding between the respective agencies. Again the connecting link from the assets back to the corrupt activity must be established.

Co-operating with foreign enforcement agencies

Co-operation can involve co-ordination of simultaneous searches, raids or inspections; exchange of information; or gathering information and interviewing witnesses on behalf of another agency. The co-ordination of surprise inspections across relevant jurisdictions, particularly in the early stages of a full-scale investigation, is a particularly effective way to minimise the potential destruction of evidence. Co-operation also plays an important role even in cases where parallel investigations are not being conducted in other jurisdictions. Other counterpart agencies may provide assistance by sharing information that may be located outside the investigating agency's territorial borders. In such cases, it can be useful to secure co-operation from an agency in the jurisdiction in which potentially relevant evidence may be located.

An increasing number of agencies have established international agreements, or Memoranda of Understanding, which may include State-to-State co-operation agreements, inter-agency co-operation agreements and mutual legal assistance agreements, as well as bilateral agreements.

The investigative plan should consider any timeframe issues for joint operations envisaged with other agencies, and other factors relevant to co-ordination.

Time constraints

Effective planning is important to ensure that all aspects of the investigation are accomplished within the prescribed statutory period. The investigative plan should include a basic schedule that identifies tasks, assigns responsibilities and sets deadlines and timeframes for completion. Such a schedule ensures that time constraints (such as statutes of limitations) are taken into account appropriately.

Prioritising and tasking

Some agencies create case agendas, task lists and timetables. These tools will become more important as staffing resources grow. In some cases, more than one method may be useful; in all cases, the investigation schedule should cover tasks to be accomplished, prioritising the most critical items. Agencies may also use software packages that assist with the creation of case agenda.

Covert actions

Agencies will often conduct their investigations in a covert manner before taking public investigative action such as dawn raids or searches. Conducting an investigation covertly ensures that the suspects are not alerted to the investigation before the public searches begin, which reduces the opportunity for evidence to be hidden or destroyed. Accordingly, in the covert investigatory phase, with the exception of co-operating suspects, agencies usually do not communicate with individuals or corporations that may be implicated in the alleged violation.

Electronic surveillance is a practical investigative tool if the agency has sufficient information about the details of the suspects' operations. It can provide valuable and powerful evidence of corrupt activity and may be a viable option where an agency has secured insider co-operation to assist with the use of hidden recording devices. Infiltration as an investigative tool may involve an agency sending an undercover agent inside a business for a period of time to obtain evidence.

Searching and seizing

Searches can be a very effective method of gathering evidence. They minimise the opportunity for document destruction and concealment, and can avoid deliberate or inadvertent failure to produce documents following an agency request. But the problem usually lies in the amount of material gathered, which is why an informer, or (where there is little risk of destruction) a compulsory disclosure order helps to focus on the relevant material

Compulsory requests for information

Compulsory information requests can result in the production of valuable information. Agencies should first identify the parties to which it is appropriate to issue a request for information and should then draft the request accordingly. They should not be sent where there is a risk of destruction or interference. Unnecessarily broad requests for information may cause investigational delays because of the time required to respond. Agencies should take special care to keep compulsory requests for information as specific and targeted as possible. Often a succinctly drafted document-production order with minimal instructions and definitions and a very limited number of requests can encourage a prompt response.

Outcomes

Investigators should never lose sight of the desired outcome, in terms both of imprisonment and of the proceeds of crime recovered. There are also civil remedies and civil actions to be considered alongside or as alternatives to the criminal penalties. If a settlement or civil action is preferred, then the stronger the investigation the greater the chances of recovering most of the assets.

Media communications

The public frequently do not understand and have unrealistic expectations about the legal processes that have to be gone through before any assets can be recovered. It is best to stress at the beginning of an investigation that the recovery of illegally obtained assets has to follow the due process of law (and court decisions) both in the country where the corruption occurred and in the country where the assets lie, which takes time.

Evaluation

Throughout the course of the investigation it is good practice to revise and adapt the investigation plan and strategy to reflect the evidence as it is obtained, evaluate the relevant issues, consider emerging issues, assess evidence-gathering strategies, and redistribute administrative tasks. Periodic team meetings are an effective way to ensure that the investigative plan is kept up to date and incorporates all relevant issues. In particular, the investigation team should discuss the investigative plan at key stages of the investigation, such as prior to conducting dawn raids or inspections, or interviewing parties, or following evidence evaluations. In addition to team meetings, agencies often hold more formal internal meetings periodically to update senior staff and decision-makers on the progress of the investigation at critical stages when decisions need to be made. Agency staff may prepare papers setting out updates, proof issues and case agendas for presentation and distribution at such meetings.

Civil recovery

Introduction

One important case strategy is to consider using civil recovery as an alternative (or in some cases in addition) to a prosecution. England and Wales, for example, use a form of non-conviction-based asset forfeiture, which allows for the recovery in civil proceedings before the High Court of property that is, or represents, property obtained through unlawful conduct.[35] Civil recovery is just one way of recovering proceeds of crime. Other ways include recovering them post-conviction for criminal matters, or taking action in the civil courts for a breach of contract or tort, among others. Only authorised enforcers can apply for an order, which is not a conviction or a sentence. Importantly, the proceedings are against the property itself (*in rem*) rather than against an individual (*in personam*). On the face of it, the absence of the need to have a suspect or defendant should make the recovery process easier, as the person in possession of the property need not be the person who carried out the unlawful conduct. These proceedings are civil and thus the civil standard of proof (the balance of probabilities) applies. The court, however, will still require cogent evidence in order to be satisfied that property is likely to be the proceeds of unlawful conduct.

Requirements

To prove that property was obtained through unlawful conduct, it is not necessary to prove the commission of a particular criminal offence by a particular person on a particular occasion. It is sufficient to prove that the property was obtained through offence(s) of a particular

---

35 Under Part 5 of the Proceeds of Crime Act, 2002 (UK).

type (drug trafficking, fraud, bribery, etc.), which cannot be done solely on the basis that the person holding the property has no identifiable lawful income to warrant their lifestyle. However, the absence of any evidence from the person to explain their lifestyle, or the giving of a false explanation, allows the court to infer that the source of the income was unlawful.

Relevant agencies and results

Within the UK, the agency that is most active against individuals is the National Crime Agency (previously SOCA – Serious and Organised Crime Agency). In the UK the highest recoveries have been made by enforcement agencies such as the Serious Fraud Office (SFO), which thus far has used civil recovery by consent and mainly against corporations. Since 2008 (when civil recovery orders became law in Britain) the following major orders have been granted:

- Balfour Beatty plc: £2.25 million (October 2008);[36]
- Macmillan Publishers: £11.3 million (July 2011);[37]
- DePuy: £4.829 million (April 2011);[38]
- M.W. Kellogg: £7 million (February 2011);[39]
- Mabey Engineering (Holdings): £130,000 (January 2012);[40]
- J. Oxford Publishing Limited (OPL): £1,895,435 (July 2012);[41] and
- BAE Systems plc: £500,000 fine[42]/£30 million *ex gratia* payment (December 2010).[43]

The M.W. Kellogg case is interesting in that it concerned an innocent parent company that was about to be paid tainted dividends by a US company which had engaged in the unlawful conduct. So far, SFO orders have concerned property that is, or is about to be, in the United Kingdom, and recovered from UK incorporated companies. The message for investors is to beware where they place their investments, and to try to ensure that there are appropriate anti-corruption measures in place.

Conclusion

The effective combating of transnational crime requires co-ordination of the competencies of States so these may be able to both validly and effectively ensure the rule of law and application of their national standards. Co-ordination, however, implies a multi-layered approach

---

36 H. Garlick and I. Trumper, *Deterring and Punishing Corporate Bribery: An Evaluation of UK Corporate Plea Agreements and Civil Recovery in Overseas Bribery Cases*, London: Transparency International UK, 2012, p. 54.
37 Ibid., p 61.
38 Ibid., p. 59.
39 Ibid., p. 58.
40 Available on the SFO Website, at http://www.sfo.gov.uk/press-room/latest-press-releases/press-releases-2012/shareholder-agrees-civil-recovery-by-sfo-in-mabey--johnson.aspx (accessed 26 March 2014).
41 Available on the SFO website, at http://www.sfo.gov.uk/press-room/latest-press-releases/press-releases-2012/oxford-publishing-ltd-to-pay-almost-19-million-as-settlement-after-admitting-unlawful-conduct-in-its-east-african-operations.aspx (accessed on 26 March 2014).
42 Garlick and Trumper, *Deterring and Punishing Corporate Bribery*, p. 36.
43 Ibid., p. 38.

encompassing not only permissive regulation, but also the ability of investigators and prosecution to communicate and interact with their counterparts at the local and international levels. Co-ordination also requires a proactive stance among the jurisdictions involved. They must communicate and share – to the limits imposed in law by each jurisdiction – information amongst themselves in order to determine the commission of criminal offences and take corrective action. Where more than one jurisdiction is involved, efforts should be made, as early on as possible, to develop case strategies, designate a lead authority, and communicate the relevant aspects of the case strategy to the involved jurisdictions.

Investigation of cases of corruption no longer appears to routinely fail because of capacity issues as has happened in the recent past. Much time and effort has gone into building the skills and experiences of enforcers around the world. More, though, needs to be done at the strategic level, as successful cross-border cases by definition must have good co-operation, co-ordination and sharing, none of which is achievable without planning and mutual trust. Trust can only be established through personal contacts, respect for each other's systems and ways of working, and, ultimately, through all being part of a wider strategy to obtain justice for victims and recover stolen assets.

10

Extradition of transnational criminals

Joanna Harrington

Introduction

Rather than creating new processes to facilitate cross-border cooperation, the effort to suppress transnational crimes relies largely upon various pre-existing extradition arrangements, with extradition being one of the oldest forms of inter-state cooperation in the criminal law field.[1] Its continuing availability, with or without the 'extradition' label,[2] reflects the fact that: 'As movement about the world becomes easier and crime takes on a larger international dimension, it is increasingly in the interests of all nations that suspected offenders who flee abroad should be brought to justice.'[3] It is also accepted that 'the establishment of safe havens for fugitives would . . . result in danger for the State obliged to harbour the protected person[.]'[4]

The term 'extradition' refers to a 'procedure of request and consent, regulated by certain general principles'[5] that aims to secure, upon request, the surrender from one state to another of an alleged criminal offender wanted for trial or for the execution of a sentence. At its core, therefore, extradition is a bilateral act of mutual legal assistance between a requesting (or receiving) state and a requested (or sending) state, valued for the very purpose of securing the individual's presence, with or without his or her consent, in the requesting state. While

---

1 See further C.L. Blakesley, 'The Practice of Extradition from Antiquity to Modern France and the United States: A Brief History', *Boston College International and Comparative Law Review*, 1981, vol. 4, pp. 39–60.

2 The European arrest warrant scheme, for example, qualifies as a procedure of request and consent designed to secure the surrender of criminal offenders wanted for trial or sentence, as does the 1966 scheme relating to the rendition of fugitive offenders within the Commonwealth.

3 *Soering v United Kingdom*, ECHR 1989, para. 89; *Öcalan v Turkey*, ECHR (Grand Chamber) 2005, para. 88.

4 Ibid. States within the UN General Assembly have expressed similar views: see United Nations Convention Against Transnational Organized Crime, UN Doc. A/RES/55/25 (2000), preamb. para. 9.

5 J. Crawford, *Brownlie's Principles of Public International Law*, 8th edn, Oxford: Oxford University Press, 2012, p. 482 (referring to the general principles that have been generated by a 'significant corpus of conventional law').

international law (in contrast with some domestic legal systems) imposes no bar on states granting a surrender request as a matter of discretion, courtesy or goodwill, many states prefer a treaty basis for their extradition relations, if only to ensure future reciprocity.

A typical extradition treaty will stipulate the conditions for and the exceptions to an agreed 'obligation to extradite', with the grounds for refusing an otherwise valid extradition request reflecting some desire on the part of sending states to ensure that certain safeguards are in place. However, these exceptions to extradition, accompanied by the challenges posed by greater recognition for a state's domestic and international human rights obligations,[6] have also made the extradition of transnational criminals a fraught process often hampered by delays despite efforts at law reform. The efforts to carve out certain 'exceptions to the exception' as a means to simplify the extradition process will be examined in this chapter, with the prospects for success being largely dependent on whether trust exists in another state's criminal justice system. I also examine, within a historical context, the efforts to replace, and in the alternative, supplement the traditional bilateral approach to extradition with a broader multilateral regime, only to see that effort return, since the 1990s, to an emphasis on the bilateral relationship, save for a recent European Union development that looks to the judiciary to provide the assistance.

The obligation to extradite with exceptions

Much of the content and form of today's extradition treaties, whether bilateral or regional in scope, dates back to the nineteenth century, when improvements in transportation gave fugitives a greater capacity to flee.[7] France, in particular, is credited with developing an influential set of rules for the conduct of extradition proceedings,[8] and its treaty-making activities helped spread many of the extradition principles that still have resonance today. These efforts have resulted in a network of treaties that impose upon their parties an obligation to extradite subject to certain terms, with those terms embracing certain exceptions, or grounds for refusing extradition. One of the earliest exceptions to be developed was that distinguishing between ordinary criminal offences and offences committed for political purposes, with the political offence exception to extradition first formalized in an 1834 Franco-Belgian treaty.[9] The treaties of the nineteenth century also embraced certain principles now considered central to extradition law, including the principle of double (or dual) criminality (requiring the conduct forming the basis of the extradition request to be criminal under the law of both the requesting and requested states), the principle of speciality (limiting the prosecution or punishment in the requesting state to the offence for which extradition was granted), and the nationality exception (a source of some frustration but which nevertheless permits a requested

---

6   See further R.J. Currie, Chapter 2 in this collection. See also J. Harrington, 'The Absent Dialogue: Extradition and the International Covenant on Civil and Political Rights,' *Queen's Law Journal*, 2006, vol. 32, no. 1, pp. 82–134.

7   'Extradition,' *American Journal of International Law Supplement*, 1935, vol. 29, pp. 15–434 at pp. 35–42; I.A. Shearer, *Extradition in International Law*, Manchester: Manchester University Press, 1971, pp. 5–11.

8   See the reference to the *Circulaire du Ministre de la Justice du 5 avril 1841 relatant les Principes de la Matière de l'Extradition* in 'Extradition' (ibid.), p. 41.

9   Shearer, *Extradition in International Law*, p. 18; C. van den Wijngaert, *The Political Offence Exception to Extradition: The Delicate Problem of Balancing the Rights of the Individual and the International Public Order*, Deventer: Kluwer, 1980, pp. 12–13.

state to decline to extradite its own nationals).[10] In providing for these exceptions and principles, the negotiated content of the extradition treaty enables states to balance their desire for inter-state cooperation with the maintenance of a sovereign ability to grant asylum or refuge when felt appropriate.

By the early twentieth century, several efforts were underway to encourage the development of a multilateral extradition convention to supplement, and eventually replace, the network of bilateral treaties that had arisen, complete with gaps and inconsistencies. Proposals were made in 1912 by the International Commission of American Jurists,[11] in 1928 by the International Law Association,[12] and in 1931 by the International Penal and Prison Commission.[13] Each of these proposed conventions embraced the 'obligation with exceptions' approach, albeit with additional details, and, in some cases, with certain specified offences (such as anarchy and the assassination of a head of state) to be made exempt from the exceptions. The prospect of a general extradition convention also interested the League of Nations. However, after studying a report on the subject prepared by Professors J.L. Brierly and Charles De Visscher, the League's Committee of Experts for the Progressive Codification of International Law concluded that 'although their solution by international agreement appeared very desirable, the difficulties in the way were too great for such solution to be realizable in the near future'.[14] A regional option was, however, considered a possibility, particularly for Latin American states with their shared legal traditions.[15]

In 1935, a group of eminent American academics published an extensive and comprehensive study of extradition law, under the auspices of the Research in International Law programme at Harvard University, as well as a draft convention of intended universal application that became known as the Harvard Draft.[16] While the content of the Harvard Draft embraced what had by then become an accepted list of exceptions for political offences, military offences, and offences covered by the *non bis in idem* principle, as well as exceptions for nationality and lapse of time, because of the difficulties identified by Brierly and de Visscher, the Harvard drafters opted to embrace the use of reservations on any point where there was a sharp divergence of views so as to encourage greater overall participation in the proposed scheme. On matters where there was this sharp divergence of views, such as on the extradition of nationals, the drafters made a deliberate choice to incorporate into the treaty text the 'better rule, from the point of view of the community of nations as a whole'.[17] This approach allowed the Harvard Draft to serve as a model of ideal form; however, it was a model that was never adopted by states, with attention diverted by World War II.

---

10 Shearer, *Extradition in International* Law, pp. 14–18; van den Wijngaert, *The Political Offence Exception*, p. 13.
11 Reprinted in 'Extradition,' *American Journal of International Law Supplement*, 1935, vol. 29, pp. 301–304.
12 International Law Association, *Report of the Thirty-fifth Conference held at Warsaw, 9–16 August 1928*, London: Sweet & Maxwell, 1929, pp. 19–43 and pp. 319–335, reprinted in 'Extradition' (ibid.), pp. 324–329.
13 Published in *Recueil de Documents en Matière Pénale et Penitentiaire*, 1931, vol. 1 and reprinted in 'Extradition' (ibid.), pp. 309–315.
14 See the Report on Extradition adopted by the Committee of Experts at its Second Session, held in January 1926, reprinted in *American Journal of International Law Supplement*, 1926, vol. 20, pp. 242–251.
15 See Montevideo Convention on Extradition, 26 December 1933, 165 LNTS 45, in force 26 December 1934.
16 'Extradition,' *American Journal of International Law Supplement*, 1935, vol. 29, pp. 21–31.
17 Ibid., p. 50.

The European Convention on Extradition

After World War II, it was the Council of Europe that took up the task of establishing an effective regional extradition treaty regime. After determining whether there were any extradition practices that would be acceptable to all member states, and after weighing the advantages and disadvantages of a bilateral approach, the Legal Committee of the Council's Consultative Assembly opted for a multilateral approach,[18] drawing some inspiration from the Harvard Draft.[19] The final text of the 'European Convention on Extradition' was adopted in 1957.[20] It remains in force today as the extradition regime of widest application, attracting adherence from all 47 Council of Europe states, plus three non-member states (Israel since 1967, South Africa since 2003 and South Korea since 2011).[21]

The primary aim of any extradition arrangement is to impose upon its parties an 'obligation to extradite' upon request provided certain terms are met. The most immediate of these terms concerns the nature of the offence underlying the request, which must be a crime of sufficient gravity in both the requesting and requested states. Gravity, however, need not be met by a listing of offences, with the Europeans abandoning an enumerative or 'list approach' for a standard expressed in terms of the sentence imposed. This 'no-list' approach also increases the number of extraditable offences as between the treaty parties,[22] and allows for the easier inclusion of new offences into the scheme, including transnational crimes. The Europeans also abandoned any requirement for the offence to have been committed within the requesting state, recognizing that states can and do exercise criminal jurisdiction over crimes committed abroad.[23]

In addition to the prerequisite of double criminality, the European extradition regime also provides for several exceptions to extradition, some mandatory in nature while others are optional. Like the Harvard Draft, the mandatory exceptions are those concerned with political offences,[24] military offences,[25] offences covered by the *non bis in idem* principle[26] and offences rendered stale by lapse of time.[27] The European Convention was also the first multilateral extradition regime to embrace a 'discrimination clause' requiring the refusal of extradition where there are 'substantial grounds for believing that a request . . . has been made for

---

18 Most European states welcomed the idea of a multilateral extradition convention, although the United Kingdom expressed the view that extradition should be based on bilateral treaties: Geoffrey de Freitas MP, 'A European Extradition Convention,' *Transactions of the Grotius Society*, 1955, vol. 44, p. 27.

19 Council of Europe, Consultative Assembly, Document 234, *Report on the Conclusion of a European Convention on Extradition* (18 May 1954). See also *Explanatory Report on the European Convention on Extradition*, Strasbourg: Council of Europe, 1969, pp. 5–9 and *Report of the European Committee on Crime Problems* in *Council of Europe Activities in the Field of Crime Problems 1956–1976*, Strasbourg: Council of Europe, 1977, pp. 15–16.

20 13 December 1957, 359 UNTS 273, ETS No. 24, in force 18 April 1960.

21 Article 30 of the convention expressly permits the accession of non-member states; a provision that enabled several European states to become convention parties before they became members of the Council of Europe.

22 I. Stanbrook and C. Stanbrook, *Extradition Law and Practice*, 2nd edn, Oxford: Oxford University Press, 2000, para. 1.22.

23 This point was expressly recognized by the Assembly's Legal Committee in its Document 234, *Report on the Conclusion of a European Convention on Extradition* (18 May 1954), p. 451.

24 European Convention on Extradition, Art. 3.

25 Ibid., Art. 4.

26 Ibid., Art. 9.

27 Ibid., Art. 10.

the purpose of prosecuting or punishing a person on account of his or her race, religion, nationality or political opinion'.[28]

As for the optional grounds, these included the nationality of the person sought,[29] although many European states lodged reservations to make this exception mandatory. There was, however, an innovation of note, with the European Convention introducing a consequential duty to submit a refused case to a requested state's own authorities for prosecution. Another optional exception embraced by the European regime, and which was made mandatory by reservation,[30] was that developed for states that had abolished the death penalty, leading to the demand for assurances that the death penalty would not be carried out in the requesting state. Some European states also chose to extend, by reservation, the application of this exception to other forms of punishment, including corporal punishment (Switzerland) and life imprisonment (Portugal). The European extradition regime also proved itself capable of accommodating certain grounds of a compassionate or humanitarian nature, with Sweden being the first to establish by reservation a bar on extradition by reason of a fugitive's youth, advanced age or ill health.

The presence of concerns about the trial standards in other states was also acknowledged through the use of reservations, with many states creating a bar on extradition if the person sought was to be tried before a special, *ad hoc* or extraordinary tribunal. Again, the Nordic states led the way, with Sweden first making this reservation in 1960, followed by Denmark in 1962. Several states also provided, by reservation, a more generally worded 'fair trial' exception to extradition so as to permit the refusal of an extradition request where there is a perceived lack of protections for the rights of the defence in the requesting state. A 1978 amendment to the treaty later added specific exceptions for extradition requests relating to judgments rendered *in absentia* and offences subject to an amnesty.[31]

As for the evidentiary basis for an extradition request, the European Convention departed from the approach taken in some bilateral extradition treaties by avoiding the imposition of a 'sufficient evidence' or '*prima facie* case' clause. Such clauses enable a requested state to refuse an extradition request when it considers the evidence justifying the requested individual's committal for trial to be insufficient according to its laws, rather than the laws of the requesting state. Many common law countries, as well as the Nordic states, had required such protections for extradition to take place, but the drafters of the European scheme saw this as a matter of regulating the procedure for extradition within a state, as well as a cause for delay, and being satisfied that there were safeguards in place within European states, the drafters thought it best to leave such matters to be determined by the law of each requested state.[32] This change did not sit well with the United Kingdom, which remained outside the Council of Europe's extradition scheme until 1991, and the development of greater trust in the legal systems of other states.[33]

---

28 European Convention on Extradition, Art. 3(2).

29 Ibid., Art. 6.

30 Italy was the first to do so, declaring in 1963 that 'it will not, under any circumstances, grant extradition in respect of offences punishable by death under the law of the requesting Party'.

31 Second Additional Protocol to the European Convention on Extradition, 17 March 1978, 1496 UNTS 328, ETS No. 98, in force 5 June 1983.

32 See de Freitas, 'A European Extradition Convention', pp. 41–44.

33 A. Harding, 'Treaty-making in the Field of International Co-operation', in A. Eser and O. Lagodny (eds), *Principles and Procedures for a New Transnational Criminal Law*, Freiburg im Breisgau: Max Planck Institute, 1992, p. 240. See also *European Convention on Extradition Order 2001*, SI 2001/962, para. 3 (removing the requirement to produce evidence of the commission of the offence in respect of which extradition was sought). In support of the *prima facie* case requirement, see Shearer, *Extradition in International Law*, ch. 6. See also G. Gilbert, *Responding to International Crime*, Leiden: Martinus Nijhoff, 2006, pp. 114–121.

For many European states, the development of a regional extradition regime was an important step forward for enhancing cross-border cooperation. The convention provided a means to close the gaps that inevitably arise within a network of overlapping bilateral treaties, while also encouraging some degree of uniformity in extradition law and practice. The convention also encouraged the development of new extradition rules within Europe, such as the contingent use of the nationality exception with a corollary duty to prosecute. Procedurally, however, the convention regime did retain the role of the executive, thus retaining space for national interests and political motivations to have an influence on extradition decisions, while also retaining the potential for delay. In addition, an absolute uniformity of terms would never be achieved given the acceptance of reservations, albeit that some reservations aim to restrict extradition where an individual's rights are perceived to be at risk in the requesting state.

Carving out exceptions to the exception

Interpreted broadly, exceptions to extradition can easily become obstacles to fruitful extradition relations, with the political offence exception being a prime example. As a result, a number of 'exceptions to the exception' have been developed to ensure that certain criminal offences, whatever the motive for their commission, are extraditable crimes. An early example of such efforts to exempt or 'depoliticize' certain crimes is the Belgian *attentat* clause concerning attacks on heads of state, which was first developed in the 1850s after the Belgian courts refused the extradition to France of those who had tried to kill the French Emperor Napoleon III.[34] In the late 1940s, a similar 'exception to the exception' was developed for international crimes, such as genocide and war crimes,[35] with the European extradition regime of 1957 later referencing the extradition obligations found in 'any other international convention of a multilateral character'[36] so as to bolster the bar on considering these offences to be non-extraditable crimes.[37]

Prompted by the increase in indiscriminate acts of terrorism from the 1960s on, a number of UN-sponsored multilateral crime suppression conventions have been adopted to ensure that certain prescribed offences are not considered exempt from extradition. Inspired by the European extradition convention, these treaties also impose a corollary obligation to submit for prosecution in the requested state an offender who cannot be extradited. The 1970 (Hague) Convention for the Suppression of Unlawful Seizure of Aircraft[38] provides a leading example, wherein Article 8 provides for the hijacking offence to be 'deemed to be included as an extraditable

---

34 This 'depoliticization' is first found codified in the Belgian Act of 22 March 1856, as discussed in van den Wijngaert, *The Political Offence Exception*, pp. 135–136. See also European Convention on Extradition, Art. 3(3).

35 See further Convention on the Prevention and Punishment of the Crime of Genocide, 9 December 1948, 78 UNTS 277, in force 12 January 1951, Art. VII. States are also required to extradite or submit for prosecution those suspected of grave breaches of the four Geneva Conventions: Geneva Convention for the Amelioration of the Condition of the Wounded and Sick in Armed Forces in the Field, 12 August 1949, 75 UNTS 31, Art. 49; Geneva Convention for the Amelioration of the Condition of the Wounded, Sick and Shipwrecked Members of Armed Forces at Sea, 12 August 1949, 75 UNTS 85, Art. 50; Geneva Convention Relative to the Treatment of Prisoners of War, 12 August 1949, 75 UNTS 135, Art. 129; Geneva Convention Relative to the Protection of Civilian Persons in Time of War, 12 August 1949, 75 UNTS 287, Art. 146; all in force 21 October 1950.

36 European Convention on Extradition, Art. 3(4).

37 See also Additional Protocol to the European Convention on Extradition, 15 October 1975, 1161 UNTS 450, ETS No. 86, in force 20 August 1979.

38 16 December 1970, 860 UNTS 105, in force 14 October 1971.

offence in any extradition treaty existing between Contracting States', while Article 4(2) requires each Contracting State to 'take such measures as may be necessary to establish its jurisdiction over the offence in the case where the alleged offender is present in its territory and it does not extradite him pursuant to Article 8 . . .'. In this way, the 'Hague formula' aims to facilitate both extradition and prosecution, ensuring double criminality by establishing the transnational offence as an extraditable crime while not making extradition automatic or mandatory, and thus permitting states to maintain the conditions they each impose on extradition. For states that cannot extradite in the absence of a treaty, further facilitation is provided by a provision that permits a state to treat the Hague Convention as the legal basis for extradition.

Similarly worded 'deeming' provisions, accompanied by an 'extradite or prosecute' obligation, as well as provisions to treat the convention as a sufficient legal basis for extradition when desired, can be found in a number of other crime suppression conventions, including those addressing violent acts against civil aviation,[39] attacks against internationally protected persons,[40] hostage-taking,[41] the theft of nuclear material[42] and maritime terrorism.[43] These conventions also oblige their parties to include the proscribed offences as extraditable crimes in all future extradition treaties. Some multilateral human rights treaties also contain provisions deeming a particular offence (such as torture) to be extraditable,[44] as well as an extradite or prosecute obligation,[45] while several of the second generation of crime suppression treaties (adopted from the late 1990s on) bolster the purpose of the deeming provisions by also abolishing the political offence exception.[46] No mention is made, however, of the political offence exception in the organized crime convention, which also expressly retains the discrimination and nationality exceptions to extradition, with only the latter triggering an obligation to prosecute.[47] Efforts to include a new, simplified, extradition process within the treaty itself

---

39 (Montreal) Convention for the Suppression of Unlawful Acts against the Safety of Civil Aviation, 23 September 1971, 974 UNTS 177, in force 26 January 1973, Arts 5, 7 and 8.

40 Convention on the Prevention and Punishment of Crimes Against Internationally Protected Persons, including Diplomatic Agents, 14 December 1973, 1035 UNTS 167, in force 20 February 1977, Arts 3(2), 7 and 8. See also Convention on the Safety of United Nations and Associated Personnel, 9 December 1994, 2051 UNTS 363, in force 15 January 1999, Arts 10(4), 14 and 15.

41 International Convention Against the Taking of Hostages, 13 April 2005, 2445 UNTS 89, in force 7 July 2007, Arts 5(2), 8 and 10.

42 Convention on the Physical Protection of Nuclear Material, 3 March 1980, 1456 UNTS 101, in force 8 February 1987, Arts 8, 10 and 11.

43 Convention for the Suppression of Unlawful Acts against the Safety of Maritime Navigation, 10 March 1988, 1678 UNTS 221, in force 1 March 1992, Arts 6, 10 and 11. See also Protocol for the Suppression of Unlawful Acts against the Safety of Fixed Platforms Located on the Continental Shelf, 10 March 1988, 1678 UNTS 304, in force 1 March 1992, Arts 1 and 3(4).

44 Convention Against Torture and Other Cruel, Inhuman or Degrading Treatment or Punishment, 10 December 1984, 1465 UNTS 85, in force 26 June 1987, Art. 8.

45 Ibid., Art. 7. See also *Questions relating to the Obligation to Prosecute or Extradite* (Belgium v. Senegal), ICJ 2012.

46 International Convention for the Suppression of Terrorist Bombings, 15 December 1997, 2149 UNTS 256, in force 23 May 2001, Art. 11; International Convention for the Suppression of the Financing of Terrorism, 9 December 1999, 2178 UNTS 197, in force 10 April 2002, Art. 14; International Convention for the Suppression of Acts of Nuclear Terrorism, 13 April 2005, 2445 UNTS 89, in force 7 July 2007, Art. 15. See also International Convention for the Protection of All Persons from Enforced Disappearance, UN Doc. A/61/488 (2006), Art. 13(1).

47 United Nations Convention Against Transnational Organized Crime (UNCTOC), 15 November 2000, 2225 UNTS 209, in force 29 September 2003, Art. 16(7), (10) and (14). The Office of the UN High Commissioner for Refugees had pushed for express retention of the political offence exception: UN Doc. A/AC.254/L.10 (22 January 1999).

were also unsuccessful, with the organized crime convention, along with the conventions on drug trafficking and corruption, only obliging states parties to 'endeavour to expedite extradition procedures and to simplify evidentiary requirements' and to 'seek to conclude bilateral and multilateral agreements . . . to enhance the effectiveness of extradition'.[48]

Regional suppression efforts within Europe

Similar efforts to modify all existing and future extradition arrangements to the extent of any incompatibility with a crime suppression treaty designating a proscribed offence as extraditable were also tried at the regional level, but without success. In 1977, a European Convention on the Suppression of Terrorism[49] was adopted with the aim of requiring its states parties to either extradite or submit for prosecution those accused of committing terroristic acts. Article 1 of that convention also specified expressly that certain offences were not to be regarded as political offences, with the listing going beyond the scope of the UN-sponsored conventions by including offences involving 'the use of a bomb, grenade, rocket, automatic firearm or letter or parcel bomb if this use endangers persons'. Sensing the ever-present desire for safeguards, the drafters of the 1977 Convention restricted the treaty's adherence to Council of Europe states,[50] with the rationale being that the 'the climate of mutual confidence among the like-minded member states . . . their democratic nature and their respect for human rights'[51] justified the imposition of an obligation to disregard, for the purposes of extradition, the political nature of certain odious crimes. Nevertheless, certain bars on extradition were retained, including the provision for refusing extradition when a request 'has been made for the purpose of prosecuting or punishing a person on account of his race, religion, nationality or political opinion' (Article 5). The 1977 Convention also retained the bar on extraditing nationals, as its use was not considered incompatible with the principle of 'extradite or prosecute'.

Yet, despite these safeguards, many European states were reluctant to ratify the 1977 Convention, and of those that did, many took advantage of a reservation provision that allowed the state to avoid the obligation to consider the proscribed offences as non-political provided the state gave due consideration to the 'particularly serious aspects of the offence' (Article 13). As noted by Lowe and Young: 'the breadth of the reservation allowed is remarkable; [and] there can be little doubt that were such reservations not expressly permitted they would be held impermissible as contrary to the nature and purpose of the convention.'[52] In practice, the reservations gutted the convention of all effect, with the Council of Europe's Parliamentary Assembly later referring to the convention as an 'optical gesture'[53] in the fight against terrorism.

---

48 UNCTOC, Art. 16(8) and (17); United Nations Convention against Illicit Traffic in Narcotic Drugs and Psychotropic Substances, 20 December 1988, 1582 UNTS 95, in force 11 November 1990, Art. 6(7) and (11); United Nations Convention against Corruption, 31 October 2003, 2349 UNTS 41, in force 14 December 2005, Art. 44(9) and (18).

49 27 January 1977, 1137 UNTS 93, CETS 90, in force 4 August 1978. See further A.V. Lowe and J.R. Young, 'Suppressing Terrorism under the European Convention: A British Perspective,' *Netherlands International Law Review*, 1978, vol. 25, no. 3, pp. 305–333 and M.C. Wood, 'The European Convention on the Suppression of Terrorism,' *Yearbook of European Law*, 1981, vol. 1, no. 1, pp. 307–331. See also *Explanatory Report on the European Convention on the Suppression of Terrorism*, Strasbourg: Council of Europe, 1977.

50 European Convention on the Suppression of Terrorism, Art. 15.

51 *Explanatory Report on the European Convention on the Suppression of Terrorism*, para. 12.

52 Lowe and Young, 'Suppressing Terrorism under the European Convention,' p. 318.

53 Council of Europe, Parliamentary Assembly, Document 6445, *Report on Strengthening the European Convention on the Suppression of Terrorism* (13 May 1991), p. 5.

The devastating attacks of 11 September 2001 later provided the catalyst for reform, leading to the adoption of a Protocol amending the European Convention on the Suppression of Terrorism[54] that currently awaits ratification. This Protocol, when in force, will further 'depoliticize' for the purposes of extradition all offences identified as terroristic by treaties adopted under the aegis of the UN, adding these offences to those listed in Article 1 of the 1977 Convention. It will also expand the 1977 Convention's discrimination clause in order to confirm that nothing in the revised treaty shall be interpreted so as to impose an obligation to extradite where there is a risk of torture, the death penalty or life imprisonment without parole (Article 4). A more rigorous regime for reservations will also be introduced, imposing time limits on their duration and an obligation to give reasons for their use (Article 12), and establishing an expert group to subject all reservations to scrutiny and discussion (Article 13).

Also in force at the regional level is a 2005 Council of Europe Convention on the Prevention of Terrorism,[55] which, despite its generic title, aims to criminalize, and make extraditable, the offences of public provocation to commit terrorism, recruitment for terrorism, and training for terrorism (Articles 5 to 7). This convention also aims to enhance international cooperation by modifying existing extradition arrangements as between contracting states so as to ensure that the above offences are recognized as extraditable crimes (Article 19). It also expressly 'depoliticizes' these crimes with respect to the application of the political offence exception (Article 20), although here again, states may lodge reservations for a specified period of time.[56] An obligation to submit a case for prosecution is also triggered when extradition is refused (Article 18). As for safeguards, Article 21 of the 2005 Convention expressly provides that nothing in the convention shall impose an obligation to extradite where there is a risk of discrimination on the grounds of race, religion, nationality, ethnic origin or political opinion, or where there is a risk of torture, inhuman or degrading treatment, the death penalty or life imprisonment without parole; codifying what have now become described by Council of Europe states as the 'important traditional grounds for refusal of cooperation'[57] (with US adherence to a rule of non-inquiry into conditions in the requesting state being a notable exception).

Regional cooperation in the Americas

Since World War II, a number of regional extradition arrangements have been developed, with the success of the European scheme inspiring members of the Organization of American States (OAS) to rekindle efforts to develop a regional extradition regime for the Americas.[58] Under the auspices of an advisory body of jurists known as the Inter-American Juridical Committee, four draft conventions were prepared over a 20-year period,[59] leading eventually to the adoption of

---

54 15 May 2003, ETS No. 190, not in force.

55 15 May 2005, ETS No. 196, in force 1 June 2007.

56 Denmark, the Netherlands and Sweden currently have reservations in place until 2016.

57 *Explanatory Report to the Council of Europe Convention on the Prevention of Terrorism*, Strasbourg: Council of Europe, 2005, para. 38.

58 Regional extradition conventions have also been prepared under the auspices of the League of Arab States, the African and Malagasy Common Organization, and the Economic Community of West African States.

59 Mention is made in the Convention's preamble of the four draft conventions prepared in 1955, 1957, 1973 and 1977, with the 1973 draft reproduced in *International Legal Materials*, 1973, vol. 12, pp. 537–549.

an 'Inter-American Convention on Extradition' in 1981.[60] However, unlike the European convention, which was designed to supersede all existing extradition arrangements[61] (and is itself now superseded in part by the European Union developments discussed below), the Inter-American Convention embraces a different model, having been designed only to supplement any pre-existing arrangements.[62] It has also attracted only six ratifications within the Americas.[63]

Like earlier models, the inter-American extradition regime embraces the 'obligation then exception' approach. The obligation to extradite is triggered when the requesting state has the necessary jurisdiction to try the offence underlying the extradition request,[64] and when the offence itself is an extraditable crime, defined in the inter-American context as an offence punishable by at least two years imprisonment, or for convicted fugitives, when six months of a sentence are remaining.[65] It lists six grounds for denying an extradition request, extending obligatory exceptions to time-barred prosecutions, political offences, and offences for which an amnesty, pardon, grace or acquittal has been granted, as well as exceptions to extradition for when a person may be persecuted or prejudiced for reasons of race, religion or nationality.[66] Exceptions to extradition are also recognized for persons who will be tried before extraordinary or *ad hoc* tribunals, and somewhat uniquely, for when an offence 'cannot be prosecuted unless a complaint or charge has been made by a party having a legitimate interest'.[67] Certain specified punishments also serve to bar extradition within the inter-American regime, most notably when the offence underlying the extradition request is punished 'by the death penalty, by life imprisonment, or by degrading punishment',[68] with many Latin American states viewing a life sentence to be as cruel and inhumane as a death sentence and contrary to the goal of prisoner rehabilitation.[69] The inter-American regime also embraces the rule of speciality[70] and makes specific mention of the right of asylum.[71] It also provides for a temporary exemption from extradition 'when the surrender of the person sought, would for reasons of health, endanger his life'[72] – to last until the person's health improves.

The inter-American scheme also permits the refusal of extradition when the domestic laws of a requested state prohibit the extradition of its nationals, with this exception accompanied by a discretion (rather than an obligation) to refer a refused case for prosecution.[73] The

60 25 February 1981, 1752 UNTS 191, OASTS No. 60, in force 28 March 1992.
61 European Convention on Extradition, Art. 28(1).
62 Inter-American Convention on Extradition, Art. 33. The convention's effect on existing extradition treaties was a significant issue of contention during the negotiations, as evidenced by the five proposed formulas to preserve their status found in an appendix to the 1973 draft.
63 The states parties are Antigua and Barbuda, Costa Rica, Ecuador, Panama, St Lucia and Venezuela.
64 Inter-American Convention on Extradition, Art. 2.
65 Ibid., Art. 3.
66 Ibid., Art. 4.
67 Ibid., Art. 4(6).
68 Ibid., Art. 9.
69 See further R. Labardini, 'Life Imprisonment and Extradition: Historical Development, International Context, and the Current Situation in Mexico and the United States,' *Southwestern Journal of Law and Trade in the Americas*, 2005, vol. 11, pp. 1–108.
70 Inter-American Convention on Extradition, Art. 13.
71 Ibid., Art. 6.
72 Ibid., Art. 20(2).
73 Other inter-American treaties can, however, make this referral mandatory: Inter-American Convention to Prevent and Punish Torture, 9 December 1985, OASTS No. 67, in force 28 February 1987, Art. 14; Inter-American Convention on Forced Disappearances, 6 December 1994, OASTS No. A–60, in force 28 March 1996, Art. VI; Inter-American Convention Against Corruption, 29 March 1996, OASTS No. B–58, in force 6 March 1997 Art. XIII(6).

inclusion of a nationality exception within the inter-American extradition regime was to be expected, given the civil law tradition of many Latin American states and their experience in the 1980s and 1990s with the United States seeking the extradition of many suspected drug-traffickers. For many Latin American countries, however, fundamental constitutional change is required in order to permit the extradition of a state's nationals.[74]

No prospects for a UN extradition treaty

Although there are several crime suppression conventions containing provisions supportive of extradition, there is no extradition treaty of universal application, and nor is there likely to be one given the political and cultural obstacles. Efforts within the UN have instead focused on the development of a template or 'Model Treaty on Extradition'[75] to guide the negotiation of future bilateral treaties, although the provisions are adaptable to a multilateral setting. Uniformity, however, remains an elusive goal for extradition law and practice, with the standards found in the Model Treaty of 1990, and in the revised version adopted in 1997,[76] providing for a degree of flexibility, or *à la carte* application, with footnotes being used to indicate where states may choose to assume greater or less extensive extradition obligations.

As is now standard, the Model Treaty begins with the imposition of a general 'obligation to extradite' provided the offence underlying the extradition request is punishable in both states and serious enough to warrant extradition. As with many modern extradition treaties, seriousness is measured by reference to the term of imprisonment attached to the crime and not by any listing of specific offences. The Model Treaty then provides for several exceptions to the obligation to extradite, seven of which are termed 'mandatory grounds for refusal', while eight are considered optional, with additional suggestions found in the template's footnotes. Building upon prior examples, the Model Treaty recommends the refusal of extradition when discrimination is suspected, improving upon earlier efforts by extending the grounds of prohibited discrimination to include 'ethnic origin, sex or status' as well as race, religion, nationality and political opinion.[77] The Model Treaty also recommends refusing an extradition request when there is risk of cruel, inhuman or degrading treatment or punishment in the requesting state or a risk that the fugitive will not receive the minimum guarantees in criminal proceedings.[78] It also contains an optional humanitarian clause to refuse extradition on account of a fugitive's 'age, health or other personal circumstances',[79] as well as a mandatory prosecution-in-lieu clause requiring a requested state to prosecute when extradition is refused on nationality grounds.[80]

74　The extradition of Columbian nationals to the United States was, for example, placed on hold until a 1998 amendment to the Columbian constitution removed the nationality exception.

75　Model Treaty on Extradition, UN Doc. A/RES/45/116 (1990).

76　International Cooperation in Criminal Matters, UN Doc. A/RES/52/88 (1997), with the Annex to this resolution entitled 'Complementary Provisions for the Model Treaty on Extradition'. Manuals offering further assistance, as well as a model national law, have also been prepared by the United Nations Office on Drugs and Crime (UNODC).

77　Model Treaty on Extradition, Art. 3(b).

78　Ibid., Art. 3(f).

79　Ibid., Art. 4(h).

80　Ibid., Art. 4(a). The Complementary Provisions for the Model Treaty on Extradition, adopted in 1997, build upon this by suggesting, alternatively, the temporary transfer of the national for trial and then return for sentence.

As for other exceptions to extradition, the Model Treaty lists several, including a pending prosecution clause,[81] a death penalty clause,[82] and an extraordinary and *ad hoc* tribunals clause, with this last to be invoked if it is likely that the accused has not received or will not receive a fair trial.[83] A footnote further suggests that the optional restriction on extradition to face the death penalty could also be applied to 'the imposition of a life, or indeterminate, sentence'.[84] The Model Treaty further suggests that extradition may be barred if the offence was committed within the territory of the requested state,[85] or committed outside the territory of either state,[86] or if the requested state, having jurisdiction over the offence, has decided to refrain from prosecuting the alleged perpetrator.[87] A mere footnote suggests that 'some countries may wish to add' an exemption for offences where an obligation to 'extradite or prosecute' has been assumed by treaty, or where a treaty specifically states that an offence is not political for the purposes of extradition, with the template's political offence exception being surprisingly bereft of limitation.

Following the adoption of a UN General Assembly declaration encouraging states 'when concluding or applying extradition agreements, not to regard as political offences . . . offences connected with terrorism which endanger or represent a physical threat to the safety and security of persons, whatever the motive which may be invoked to justify them',[88] the UN Model Treaty on Extradition was revised, and the footnote on 'extradite or prosecute' was moved into the main text.[89] However, there remains no expressly mandated 'exception to the exception' for certain terroristic offences, including those covered by the crime suppression conventions discussed above. The UN Security Council has since called upon all states to 'ensure, in conformity with international law, . . . that claims of political motivation are not recognized as grounds for refusing requests for the extradition of alleged terrorists';[90] a call that was reiterated by the UN General Assembly in 2005.[91]

A simplified regime for the European Union

The perceived complexities and potential for delay within the now standard extradition regime, stemming in part from the role granted to a state's executive branch, has prompted the member states of the European Union (EU) to develop a modified regime as between

---

81 Model Treaty an Extradition, Art. 4(c).
82 Ibid., Art. 4(d). The Complementary Provisions for the Model Treaty on Extradition, adopted in 1997, add an 'extradite or take prosecutorial action' obligation where extradition is refused by reason of the death penalty.
83 Model Treaty an Extradition, Art. 4(g).
84 Ibid., footnote 12.
85 Ibid., Art. 4(f).
86 Ibid., Art. 4(e).
87 Ibid., Art. 4(b).
88 Declaration to Supplement the Declaration on Measures to Eliminate International Terrorism, UN Doc. A/RES/51/210 (1996), Annex, para. 6.
89 Complementary Provisions for the Model Treaty on Extradition, para. 1.
90 UN Doc. S/RES/1373 (2001), para. 3(g).
91 Human Rights and Terrorism, UN Doc. A/RES/59/195 (2005), para. 10.

themselves,[92] leading to the adoption of a new simplified system of surrender that relies upon direct cooperation between judicial rather than executive authorities. In 2002, a Framework Decision was adopted by the Council of the European Union to end the application of all existing extradition arrangements as between EU states and instead make use of a fast-track process reliant on a common 'European arrest warrant'.[93] The operation of the European arrest warrant is based on the principle of mutual recognition of judicial decisions, presupposing a high level of confidence in the criminal justice systems of each EU state. The new procedure eliminates the executive aspect of extradition law, as between the EU states, and makes the surrender of offenders a matter of judicial action, with the judiciary making the final decision.

Similar to the 'backing of warrants' system used between neighbouring states such as Australia and New Zealand (and previously Ireland and the United Kingdom), a common arrest warrant is signed by one judicial authority for direct presentation to another for endorsement, thus speeding up the extradition process, while ostensibly removing the scope for political pressures to hold sway. The European arrest warrant procedure is also faster because it is simpler, with even the long-standing requirement for double criminality being modified (or partly eliminated) so as to be assumed to exist for some thirty-two listed offences, provided the related prison sentence is of at least three years' duration.[94] Verification of the double criminality of the act is therefore not required for a number of transnational crimes, including terrorism, human trafficking and corruption. Otherwise, verification of double criminality remains a requirement for surrender within the EU, with the common warrant procedure being made applicable to all criminal offences that meet a one-year imprisonment threshold.[95] With a speedy process being a desired goal, tight time frames have also been introduced.[96]

The Framework Decision also limits the grounds for refusing a European arrest warrant request, with only the passage of a final judgment, an amnesty and the age of criminal responsibility being listed as the accepted mandatory grounds for refusal.[97] In a bold move, the political offence exception and the rule of speciality have both been abolished, while only a few optional exceptions remain to address additional double jeopardy concerns, statute-barred proceedings and offences committed on the territory of the requested state.[98] The Framework Decision also intended to abolish the nationality exception to extradition as between EU states, but the Decision's required transposal into national law has led to some

---

92 A 'Convention on Simplified Extradition Procedure between the Member States of the European Union,' [1995] OJ C78/01, was adopted with the goal of providing for an accelerated extradition process as between EU states that bypassed the usual extradition formalities when the individual concerned consents to surrender. A year later, a second 'Convention relating to extradition between the Member States of the European Union,' [1996] OJ C313/02, was adopted with the aim of removing some of the exceptions to extradition as between EU states. The Council of Europe has also made available simplified and less formal procedures for those who consent to their surrender: Third Additional Protocol to the European Convention on Extradition, 10 November 2010, CETS No. 209, in force 1 May 2012.

93 Council Framework Decision 2002/584/JHA, [2002] OJ L190/01, reproduced in *Assange v Swedish Prosecution Authority*, [2012] UKSC 22, pp. 33–48. Introduced by the Treaty of Amsterdam, framework decisions are binding on EU member states as to the result to be achieved, but leave to the national authorities the choice of form and method.

94 Council Framework Decision 2002, Art. 2(2).

95 Ibid., Art. 2(1).

96 Ibid., Art. 17.

97 Ibid., Art. 3.

98 Ibid., Art. 4.

problematic attempts to reintroduce exceptions.[99] The Framework Decision also allows for the use of state-provided assurances, or 'guarantees',[100] that can be insisted upon by EU states to address concerns about judgments rendered *in absentia*, custodial life sentences, and the need for prison transfers to facilitate the reintegration of nationals. Article 26 of the Framework Decision also requires a deduction for time served in prison while awaiting surrender.

The linchpin for securing such efficiency in extradition has been the Union's and its members' professed respect for human rights and trust in each other's legal systems. From the beginning, the European Commission has tried to placate concerns about the criminal justice systems of other states by indicating that surrender under the new procedure would be '[s]ubject, of course, to the general rules for the protection of fundamental rights'.[101] Recitals have also been included within the Framework Decision containing express prohibitions on surrender where there is a serious risk to the fugitive of 'the death penalty, torture or other inhuman or degrading treatment or punishment' in the requesting state and to confirm that surrender can still be refused where a warrant has been issued to prosecute or punish a person 'on the grounds of his or her sex, race, religion, ethnic origin, nationality, language, political opinions or sexual orientation'.[102] It is further stipulated that nothing in the Framework Decision prevents an EU state from applying 'its constitutional rules relating to due process',[103] with a 2009 amendment drawing further attention to the procedural rights of the alleged offender.[104]

Conclusions

Viewed within a historical context, and with reference to illustrative developments in both Europe and the Americas, the extradition of transnational criminals continues to be guided by principles long established through the bilateral practice of states, with footnotes, reservations and discretionary variations preventing the development of a unified approach. A range of grounds to justify the refusal of cooperation continues to exist in many extradition arrangements, and their invocation for the benefit of the wanted offender can challenge the effectiveness and speed of extradition as a means to secure assistance in the suppression of transnational crime. Neither the development of a template treaty to guide future practice, nor the adoption of a series of treaties engendering a consensus that serious transnational crimes are extraditable, has brought a universal extradition scheme within reach, with the lingering sense of distrust in another state's criminal justice system (even among closely integrated allies) being a powerful obstacle to reform.

---

99 Upon the Framework Decision's coming into force in 2004, courts in Cyprus, Poland and Germany challenged the compatibility of this aspect with national constitutions. See further, M. Fichera, *The Implementation of the European Arrest Warrant in the European Union: Law, Policy and Practice*, Antwerp: Intersentia, 2011, pp. 128–135.

100 Council Framework Decision 2002, Art. 5(1).

101 Commission of the European Communities, *Proposal for a Council Framework Decision on the European arrest warrant and the surrender procedures between the Member States*, COM(2001) 522 final/2, [2001] OJ C332E/305, pp. 15–16.

102 Council Framework Decision 2002, Recital 13.

103 Ibid., Recital 12.

104 Council Framework Decision 2009/299/JHA, [2009] OJ L081/24.

Part III
Substantive crimes

A Migration and exploitation crimes

11

Human trafficking

Tom Obokata

Introduction

Trafficking of human beings has been widely accepted as a serious problem of the contemporary world. It has been estimated that around 27 million men, women and children are trafficking victims at any time globally,[1] and the annual profit generated from human trafficking and forced labour amounts to $31.6 billion.[2] Once trafficked, these victims are exploited in sex and other industries such as agriculture, fishery, construction and garment production. The transnational nature of human trafficking requires a concerted effort at national, regional and international levels, and an important step was taken when the United Nations adopted the Convention against Transnational Organized Crime (Organized Crime Convention)[3] and its Protocol to Prevent, Suppress and Punish Trafficking in Persons, Especially Women and Children (Trafficking Protocol) in 2000.[4] These instruments constitute the core international legal framework to address human trafficking. In particular, they are clear examples of transnational criminal law as their main aim is to promote indirect control of human trafficking at the national level.[5]

This chapter provides an overview of international law relating to human trafficking. After a brief historical development, a detailed analysis of the Organized Crime Convention and the Trafficking Protocol will be provided. In so doing, the chapter places particular focus on so-called 3P obligations: obligations to prohibit/prosecute trafficking, protect victims and prevent the practice. It will also explore the question of whether prohibition of trafficking, separate from prohibition of slavery, is emerging as a customary norm. The main conclusion is that, although transnational criminal law as represented by these key international treaties has made important progress to augment the action against human trafficking,

---

1   US Department of State, *Trafficking in Persons Report 2013*, p. 7.
2   United Nations Office of Drugs and Crime, *Global Report on Trafficking in Persons* (2012), p. 68, citing a figure released by the International Labour Office.
3   15 November 2000, 2225 UNTS 209, in force 29 September 2003.
4   15 November 2000, 2237 UNTS 319, in force 25 December 2003.
5   N. Boister, 'Transnational Criminal Law?' *European Journal of International Law*, 2003, vol. 14, p. 953.

it simultaneously displays a number of shortcomings, particularly from a human rights perspective. Consequently, transnational criminal law must be supplemented by other branches of international law such as human rights law.

Historical development

International law on human trafficking has gradually developed since the early twentieth century. One early legal instrument was the International Agreement for the Suppression of the White Slave Traffic 1904,[6] adopted as a response to the growing sale of white women into prostitution in Europe, which was partially facilitated by the stagnant economic climate at that time.[7] There are some important aspects to be mentioned in relation to this Agreement. First, it applied only to 'white women'. This meant that women of other ethnic backgrounds, as well as men, were excluded. Second, it was designed to regulate procurement of women or girls for immoral purposes abroad. Therefore, its emphasis was upon sexual exploitation of white women and girls and their trafficking outside of their States of origin. Finally, this Agreement lacked strong crime prevention provisions as it did not oblige States to prosecute and punish the white slave traffic at the national level and facilitate mutual legal assistance in criminal matters. Consequently, this legal instrument was not really effective in suppressing this practice.[8]

This led to the adoption of another treaty, the International Convention for the Suppression of the White Slave Traffic 1910 (the 1911 Convention).[9] Although the focus was still placed upon trafficking of white women and girls for sexual exploitation abroad, Articles 1 through 3 clearly obliged State Parties to prohibit the practice at the national level, thereby displaying some characteristics of transnational criminal law for the first time. It is also worth noting that, unlike the 1904 Agreement, the 1911 Convention facilitated a degree of international co-operation. For instance, it obliged States to communicate with each other about national legislation and records of conviction, and to make trafficking an extraditable offence.[10] In terms of content, the instrument applied to both consensual and non-consensual (i.e. through the use of coercion, violence or threats) white slave trafficking. However, the scope of application was limited for the same reason as the 1904 Agreement (non-applicability to women of other ethnicities and men/boys). It was also not designed to address the end purpose of trafficking, prostitution, as this was regarded as a matter of domestic jurisdiction.[11] For this reason, this instrument was also criticised as being ineffective.[12]

The League of Nations, which recognised the seriousness of trafficking, adopted two more treaties after World War I. The first was the International Convention for the Suppression of the Traffic in Women and Children 1921 (the 1921 Convention).[13] This treaty incorporated

---

6 18 May 1904, 1 LNTS 83, in force 18 July 1905.

7 N. Demleitner, 'Forced Prostitution: Naming an International Offence,' *Fordham International Law Journal*, 2000, vol. 18, p. 163, p. 167.

8 Ibid., 168.

9 4 May 1910, 8 LNTS 278, in force 5 July 1920.

10 Articles 4 to 6.

11 T. Obokata, *Trafficking of Human Beings from a Human Rights Perspective: Towards a Holistic Approach*, Leiden: Martinus Nijhoff, 2006, p. 15.

12 J. Chuang, 'Redirecting the Debate over Trafficking in Women: Definitions, Paradigms and Contexts,' *Harvard Human Rights Journal*, 1998, vol. 11, p. 65, pp. 74–75.

13 30 September 1921, 9 LNTS 415, in force 15 June 1922.

the description of trafficking under the 1910 Convention,[14] once again emphasising prostitution and sexual exploitation. The main difference, however, was that the 1921 Convention applied to women of all ethnicities as well as both male and female children. From the point of view of transnational criminal law, there were other noticeable differences. For instance, it provided for prohibition of so-called inchoate offences in addition to the act of trafficking itself.[15] Article 4 also made it clear that States were to extradite those who commit the offence specified in the Convention. The second treaty adopted by the League of Nations was the International Convention for the Suppression of the Traffic in Women of Full Age 1933.[16] This treaty was quite similar to its predecessors in terms of its nature and scope of application, except that it applied to adult women. Once again, the major issue with these two treaties was that they did not address the end purpose of trafficking, prostitution.

The final treaty on trafficking adopted prior to the Trafficking Protocol was the Convention for the Suppression of the Traffic in Persons and of the Exploitation of the Prostitution of Others 1949 (the 1949 Convention),[17] developed under the auspices of the United Nations. It consolidated the earlier treaties, but differed from its predecessors in some important respects. To begin with, the 1949 Convention referred specifically to exploitation of prostitution. It was also neutral in gender and was applicable to men and boys who were also exploited in prostitution, and applied to both internal and international trafficking. However, this treaty was criticised, *inter alia*, for not obliging States to criminalise prostitution itself while criminalising acts associated with prostitution such as running or keeping brothels.[18] One reason for this was that the drafters of the Convention feared that 'prohibition would drive prostitution underground, and that laws designed to punish both clients and prostitutes, in practice, would be selectively enforced only against prostitutes'.[19] Further, it did not take other forms of sexual exploitation, such as sex tourism, into consideration.[20] Finally, the 1949 Convention did not expand upon the provisions for mutual assistance in legal matters. Because of these and other reasons, the effectiveness of the 1949 Convention was also called into question.

In summary, the earlier treaties were concerned with addressing trafficking of mainly women and girls for prostitution. From the point of view of transnational criminal law, these instruments went as far as obliging States to prohibit trafficking itself, including inchoate offences, but left the issue of prostitution to each State to decide. This was understandable given that the legal position of prostitution varied (and still varies) among State Parties. Also, these instruments were not capable of addressing trafficking for other forms of exploitation such as forced labour. This was unfortunate as it left an impression that only trafficking for prostitution deserved the attention of the international community while ignoring trafficking for non-sexual purposes. In addition, the five treaties did not provide a solid legal basis for facilitating effective mutual assistance in criminal matters. This is revealing because, while States acknowledged the transnational dimension of human trafficking, they were still reluctant to implement proactive measures for international co-operation to suppress it. It is therefore apparent that the principle of State sovereignty was a dominant force in relation to

---

14 The 1910 Convention, Art. 1.
15 The 1921 Convention, Art. 3.
16 11 October 1933, 150 LNTS 431, in force 24 August 1934.
17 21 March 1950, 96 UNTS 271, in force 25 July 1951.
18 The 1949 Convention, Art. 2.
19 Demleitner, 'Forced Prostitution', p. 177.
20 Report of the Special Rapporteur on Violence against Women (Trafficking in Women, Women's Migration and Violence against Women), E/CN.4/2000/68, 22 and 23.

human trafficking throughout the twentieth century. This, however, changed to some extent at the turn of the twenty-first century with the adoption of the Organized Crime Convention and its Trafficking Protocol in 2000. An analysis of these instruments now follows.

The current international legal framework on human trafficking

International definition of human trafficking

One of the important contributions which the Trafficking Protocol has made so far is the adoption of a definition of human trafficking:

> Trafficking in persons shall mean the recruitment, transportation, transfer, harbouring or receipt of persons, by means of the threat or use of force or other forms of coercion, of abduction, of fraud, of deception, of the abuse of power or of a position of vulnerability or of the giving or receiving of payments or benefits to achieve the consent of a person having control over another person, for the purpose of exploitation.[21]

There are three key elements in this definition: i) act, ii) means and iii) purpose. The first element refers to the main conduct of trafficking, that is, recruitment, transportation, transfer, harbouring or receipt of trafficked people. The second element explains how these victims are transported. Traffickers use coercion and/or deception to traffic people from one place to another. This suggests that there is no genuine consent on the part of victims. The second element is closely interlinked with the first as they both constitute the *actus reus* of trafficking. Finally, the third 'purpose' element refers to the reasons as to why people are trafficked. Traffickers transport victims for them to be exploited in sex and non-sex industries.

It is important to highlight here that it is not necessary that victims actually be exploited for an act to be classified as trafficking. This is so because the purpose element relates to *mens rea*, and ulterior intention in particular, rather than *actus reus*.[22] A good analogy is the offence of burglary in the United Kingdom. This offence is complete as soon as one enters into premises as a trespasser with intention to steal, even when one does not actually steal anything.[23] An important consideration here is what one is thinking at the time of entry. By analogy, the above definition suggests that trafficking is established when a trafficker moves people from one place to another with the intention to exploit them later or with the full knowledge that they will be exploited by others at their destination. When trafficked victims are actually exploited, that would technically be regarded as a separate offence of slavery or forced labour, or alternatively as an aggravating factor which would increase the level of punishment, although this depends on how trafficking is defined by national legislation.

In any event, it is immediately clear that the Trafficking Protocol does not focus solely on trafficking for prostitution or other sexual exploitation. In this regard, Article 3(a) further provides:

---

21 Trafficking Protocol, Art. 3(a).
22 This is of course in addition to direct intention to traffic people.
23 Theft Act 1968, Sec. 9.

> Exploitation shall include, at a minimum, the exploitation of the prostitution of others or other forms of sexual exploitation, forced labour or services, slavery or practices similar to slavery, servitude or the removal of organs.[24]

This is broad enough to cover a wide range of exploitation experienced by victims, and it is clear that the international community has at last acknowledged that trafficking does not take place just for sexual exploitation. Finally, the Trafficking Protocol has also acknowledged that men and boys can also become the victims of this crime, and therefore its terms are gender-neutral. It is evident that the Trafficking Protocol is a welcome improvement on the earlier instruments.

The 3P obligations

The key aim of the Protocol is stipulated under Article 2:

(a) To prevent and combat trafficking in persons, paying particular attention to women and children;
(b) To protect and assist the victims of such trafficking, with full respect for their human rights; and
(c) To promote cooperation among State Parties in order to meet those objectives.

It is often said that international law on human trafficking imposes three key obligations (aka the 3P obligations). They are obligations to 1) prohibit/prosecute trafficking, 2) protect victims and 3) prevent trafficking. It is evident that Article 2 reflects these obligations, and this chapter now provides an analysis as to how the current international legal framework adequately establishes these obligations.

Obligation to prohibit/prosecute

In relation to the first obligation, Article 5 of the Trafficking Protocol explicitly provides that State Parties are to criminalise human trafficking. This obligation should be read in the light of other relevant obligations established by the Organized Crime Convention itself. For instance, under the Organized Crime Convention States must prohibit so-called inchoate offences such as attempt and conspiracy to commit organised crime, including human trafficking and joint criminal enterprise, as well as secondary participation (e.g. aiding and abetting).[25] Other related offences such as money laundering,[26] corruption[27] and obstruction of justice[28] are also to be criminalised under the Organized Crime Convention. In looking at these provisions, it is apparent that transnational criminal law as represented by the Trafficking Protocol and the Organized Crime Convention sufficiently encourages States to strengthen substantive criminal law at the national level.

---

24 Trafficking Protocol, Art. 3(a).
25 Articles 5(1)(a)(i), 5(1)(a)(ii) and 5(1)(b).
26 Article 7.
27 Article 8.
28 Article 23.

Given the sophisticated nature of human trafficking, often facilitated by organised criminal groups and syndicates, the law enforcement community must be equipped with appropriate investigative powers, in addition to regular powers to stop, search and seize, so that it can facilitate proactive intelligence-led law enforcement. Article 20 of the Organized Crime Convention is important in this regard as it provides for the use of special investigative techniques such as surveillance and undercover operations. It further encourages States to facilitate these measures through international co-operation, an example of which is the Schengen *acquis* under European Union law,[29] which allows EU Member States to facilitate cross-border surveillance.[30] This international co-operation element is further complemented by Article 19, which provides for establishment of joint investigation bodies or teams.

As these special investigative techniques are implemented covertly, States must ensure that there are enough safeguards to prevent their abuse and protect the human rights of suspects as well as the general public. While human rights protection in transnational criminal law is discussed in Chapter 2 of this book, an often discussed issue in this particular context is the right to privacy. The Human Rights Committee, which monitors the implementation of the International Covenant on Civil and Political Rights 1966 (ICCPR),[31] has made it clear in the past that any interference with the right to privacy requires a clear legal basis, and that relevant legislation must provide a detailed account of when such interference would be permitted.[32] In other words, the principle of legality must be fully observed by each State. The European Court of Human Rights has gone further to articulate that, in addition to a legal basis, the use of surveillance must have a legitimate aim and be proportionate.[33] Another important issue is the right to a fair trial. It has been recognised, for instance, that undercover operations could amount to entrapment if a crime was instigated by law enforcement agencies, and that this would undermine the right to a fair trial.[34] The use of improperly obtained evidence in court also raises an issue, particularly when it is the sole evidence relied upon and/or the accused does not have an opportunity to challenge its authenticity.[35] It is therefore essential that all States abide by the relevant human rights norms and principles to ensure the legitimacy of covert law enforcement operations in combating human trafficking.

Another important obligation related to prohibition/prosecution is the establishment of criminal jurisdiction over human trafficking. The transnational nature of trafficking means that the offence can be tried by multiple jurisdictions. The Organized Crime Convention provides clearer guidance on this. In accordance with Article 15(1), which also reflects the general principles of international law,[36] the territorial principle is regarded as the most important form of jurisdiction to prosecute human trafficking. Article 14(2) provides for

---

29 Convention implementing the Schengen Agreement of 14 June 1985 between the Governments of the States of the Benelux Economic Union, the Federal Republic of Germany and the French Republic on the gradual abolition of checks at their common borders, OJ L 239/19.

30 Ibid., Art. 40.

31 16 December 1966, 999 UNTS 171, in force 23 March 1976.

32 General Comment No. 16 (Right to Privacy) (1988), A/43/40 (29 September 1988).

33 *Malone v United Kingdom* (1984), Application no. 8691/79; and *Kruslin v France* (1990), Application No. 11801/85.

34 See for instance, *Teixeira de Castro v Portugal* (1998), Application No. 25829/94; and *Ludi v Switzerland* (1992), Application No. 12433/86.

35 *Schenk v Switzerland* (1988), Application No. 10862/84, 46–48. See also *Khan v United Kingdom* (2000), Application No. 35394/97.

36 *SS Lotus* (Permanent Court of International Justice), 45, 1927 PCIJ (ser. A), No. 10; and *Banković v Belgium* (European Court of Human Rights), 59, 4 ILM 57.

optional grounds under which State Parties *may* establish criminal jurisdiction: the nationality, passive personality and effects principles.[37] This is once again an improvement on the previous instruments on human trafficking, which did not contain useful guidance to address jurisdictional conflicts.

In addition, mutual assistance is an essential aspect of the obligation to prohibit/prosecute. The Organized Crime Convention in particular has strengthened this aspect. These include, but are not limited to, extradition,[38] broad mutual legal assistance (taking evidence, effecting judicial/legal documents, and executing searches, seizures and freezing assets)[39] and transfer of criminal proceedings,[40] in addition to other measures noted elsewhere in this chapter. As a multilateral treaty, the Organized Crime Convention can serve as a solid legal basis for State Parties. Inclusion of these provisions perhaps indicates the recognition by States that human trafficking cannot be addressed by the effort of a single State, and that rigid adherence to the principle of State sovereignty may not lead to effective suppression. In summary, it seems reasonable to argue that transnational criminal law as represented by the Trafficking Protocol and the Organized Crime Convention sufficiently establishes the obligation to prohibit and prosecute human trafficking.

Obligation to protect victims

Given that human trafficking is a gross violation of the rights of trafficked victims, their protection should be at the centre of any action against this crime. As noted, Article 2 of the Trafficking Protocol also lists the obligation to protect as one of the aims, and the Protocol provides for some measures of victim protection. Article 6 touches upon protection of a victim's privacy, assistance during criminal proceedings, and protection of physical and mental well-being of victims through, among others, provision of accommodation, medical/psychological assistance and compensation. This provision is based upon proposals submitted by the United States of America and Argentina.[41] Article 7 further provides for the possibility of issuing temporary or permanent residence arrangements. These are necessary so that victims can recover from their ordeals and decide whether or not to co-operate with law enforcement authorities to prosecute and punish traffickers. It is therefore clear that the obligation to protect victims is closely interlinked to the first obligation to prohibit trafficking.

While this list of protection measures looks reasonable in theory and surely demonstrates a sign of improvement compared to the previous treaties on human trafficking, it is unfortunate that the obligation to protect is very weak in practice. Articles 6 and 7 contain phrases such as 'to the extent possible', 'shall consider implementing measures' and 'shall endeavour to provide'. This in effect means that States will not be generally held accountable under international law if they cannot or do not take action, as long as they try to implement or think about implementing protection measures. During the drafting stage, international organisations such as the Office of the High Commissioner for Human Rights, the International Labour Organization and the United Nations Children's Fund called for a more robust provision to protect victims by adopting stronger language and other measures such as

---

37 The last principle, however, relates to participation in criminal groups and money laundering.
38 Article 16.
39 Article 18.
40 Article 20.
41 *Travaux Préparatoires* of the Negotiations for the Elaboration of the United Nations Convention against Transnational Organised Crime and the Protocols Thereto, UN, 2006, pp. 366–367.

access to embassies and protection against reprisal.[42] The retention of the weak language indicates that States generally were reluctant to be bound by hard obligations. This was even more so for developing States, some of which expressed concerns that they might not have enough resources to provide sufficient protection.[43] The only hard obligation ('shall ensure') relates to assistance during criminal investigation and proceedings. This enhances the perception that victims are used as tools for criminal justice and undermines the key aim of the Trafficking Protocol stipulated in Article 2.

This often raised issue of lack of resources is not a good justification for not providing sufficient protection to victims. States should be able to make more active use of criminal proceeds generated as a result of human trafficking, instead of using their own resources. As noted above, traffickers make large sums of money from trafficking operations, and effective confiscation of these proceeds should allow States to provide more than a sufficient level of protection. In order for this to happen, however, they must establish robust mechanisms for confiscation of criminal proceeds and asset recovery, and the Organized Crime Convention establishes a clear obligation in this regard, including international co-operation.[44] This obligation should be read in conjunction with Articles 6 and 7 of the same Convention relating to money laundering as it is essential that States are able to confiscate proceeds before they become difficult to trace. In addition to protection measures, the criminal proceeds should also be used to strengthen various victim compensation schemes which exist among State Parties. All of these will enable States to create a hostile environment for criminals to operate in and send a strong message that they will not be able to profit from human trafficking and exploitation.

What becomes apparent in looking at the protection provisions is that transnational criminal law is not adequate in relation to protection of victims. It might be argued that the main aim of transnational criminal law is to bring criminals to justice and therefore that protection of victims does not need to be part of this branch of international law. This, however, represents a narrow view of the role to be played by transnational criminal law and does not reflect the reality that protection of victims of crimes has been recognised as equally important under international law. The Declaration of Basic Principles of Justice for Victims of Crime and Abuse of Power 1985[45] adopted by the United Nations is a good example. It states that victims should be treated with compassion and respect for their dignity, and that they should have access to redress, stressing the importance of their protection. This is augmented by the human rights regime, where it has been held that the obligations of States go beyond prosecution and punishment of human rights crimes committed by non-State actors, to include provision of appropriate protection and assistance.[46] These developments make us realise that justice does not necessarily end when criminals are prosecuted and punished, and that there are other stakeholders who need to be taken into consideration along the way.

It is encouraging to note, however, that there is an instrument other than the Trafficking Protocol that clearly recognises the importance of protection: the Council of Europe Convention on Action against Trafficking of Human Beings 2005.[47] Unlike other

---

42 Ibid., *Travaux Préparatoires*.
43 Ibid.
44 Organized Crime Convention, Arts 12 and 13.
45 A/RES/40/34, (29 November 1985).
46 *Velasquez Rodriguez v Honduras* (Inter-American Court of Human Rights), Judgment of 29 July 1988, Ser. A, No. 4.
47 16 May 2005, ETS No. 197, in force 1 February 2008.

instruments, which only briefly mention victim protection[48] or contain soft obligations, the Council of Europe Convention has extensive provisions on protection of victims, ranging from provision of accommodation to medical/psychological assistance, in addition to penal provisions.[49] The fact that the protection provisions come before the penal provisions within the Convention also suggests that protection of victims is regarded as a priority. In any event, the existence of this treaty demonstrates that obligations to prohibit/prosecute trafficking and protect victims can co-exist in one instrument. In fact, these obligations reinforce each other. Prosecution of traffickers will reduce the risk of people being trafficked or re-trafficked in the future, and protection of victims can facilitate more effective investigations and prosecutions as they are likely to co-operate more willingly when their human rights are respected and protected. Unfortunately, the scope of application of this particular treaty is limited to Europe, and therefore an important question is how other States can be held accountable when they fail to provide sufficient protection.

It is submitted that international human rights law can fill this gap. To begin with, some human rights instruments contain provisions on protection of victims of trafficking. They are the Optional Protocol on the Sale of Children, Child Prostitution and Child Pornography 2000 to the Convention on the Rights of the Child 1989[50] and the Inter-American Convention on International Traffic in Minors 1994.[51] This obligation can also be implied from Article 16(2) of the Convention on the Protection of the Rights of Migrant Workers and Members of their Families 1990:

> Migrant workers and members of their families shall be entitled to effective protection by the State against violence, physical injury, threats and intimidation, whether by public officials or by private individuals, groups or institutions.[52]

In relation to other human rights treaties, this obligation to protect derives from a general duty to secure, ensure or restore rights and to provide remedies. The ICCPR in this regard obliges States to 'ensure that any person whose rights or freedoms as herein recognized are violated shall have an effective remedy, notwithstanding that the violation has been committed by persons acting in an official capacity'.[53] It is worth noting that the UN Human Rights Council explicitly acknowledged that Article 2(3) applies to the victims of trafficking.[54] The Special Rapporteur on Trafficking of Human Beings also emphasised that the right to an effective remedy is a fundamental human right of all persons, including the victims of trafficking.[55]

---

48 Inter-American Convention on Traffic in Minors 1994, 18 March 1994, OAS Treaty Series No. 79, in force 15 August 1997.
49 Chapter 3.
50 A/RES/54/263 (25 May 2000), in force 18 January 2002, Arts 8–10.
51 Articles 6 and 16.
52 Convention on the Protection of the Rights of Migrant Workers and Members of their Families, 1990, 18 December 1990, A/RES/45/158, in force 1 July 2003.
53 ICCPR, Art. 2.
54 Resolution 20/1, Trafficking in Persons, Especially Women and Children: Access to Effective Remedies for Trafficked Persons and Their Right to an Effective Remedy for Human Rights Violations, A/HRC/20/L1 (29 June 2012).
55 Trafficking in Persons, Especially Women and Children: A Note by the Secretary General, A/66/238 (9 August 2011), p. 12.

The obligation to protect has also increasingly been recognised by the human rights bodies at the international level. Treaty bodies including the Human Rights Committee,[56] the Committee on the Elimination of Discrimination against Women,[57] the Committee on the Rights of the Child,[58] the Committee on Migrant Workers[59] and the Committee against Torture[60] have urged/recommended States to provide greater assistance to victims. Of particular importance is the recognition by the Committee on the Elimination of Discrimination against Women that full realisation of Article 6, which touches upon suppression of trafficking, requires protection of victims.[61] In addition to these treaty bodies, the Special Rapporteurs on Trafficking of Human Beings,[62] Sale of Children[63] and Contemporary Forms of Slavery[64] are all in agreement that sufficient protection must be afforded to victims. Regionally, the European Court of Human Rights in *Rantsev v Cyprus and Russia* held that Article 4, the prohibition on slavery and forced labour, may require a State to take operational measures to protect victims, or potential victims of trafficking.[65] Once again, the link between the obligation to prohibit/prosecute and to protect is recognised. In view of these developments, it is clear that the obligation to protect under transnational criminal law can be greatly enhanced by international human rights norms and principles.

Obligation to prevent trafficking

The nature and extent of this obligation depend on whether a State is the origin or destination. In relation to States of origin, the core obligation is prevention of people being trafficked. In other words, they have to address 'push factors' of this crime such as poverty, gender/racial discrimination and humanitarian crises. As to States of destination, they have to deal with so-called 'pull factors' which attract trafficked victims, including the demand for trafficked people. A key provision in relation to prevention is Article 9 of the Trafficking Protocol. It begins by obliging States to establish comprehensive policies and programmes for prevention.[66] Article 9(3) is also important as States have to co-operate with the non-governmental/civil society sector. This recognises valuable contributions made by relevant NGOs. In addition, States are obliged to strengthen measures to alleviate major causes of

---

56 Concluding Observations: Poland, CCPR/C/POL/CO/6 (15 November 2010); and Concluding Observations: Belgium, CCPR/C/BEL/CO/5 (16 November 2010).
57 Concluding Observations: Denmark, CEDAW/C/DEN/CO/7 (7 August 2009).
58 Concluding Observations: Gabon, CRC/C/15/Add.171 (3 April 2002); Concluding Observations: Canada, CRC/C/15/Add.215 (27 October 2003); Concluding Observations: France, CRC/C/15/Add.240 (30 June 2004); and Concluding Observations: Malawi, CRC/C/MWI/CO/2 (27 March 2009).
59 Concluding Observations: Colombia, CMW/C/COL/CO/1 (22 May 2009).
60 Concluding Observations: Costa Rica, CAT/C/CRI/CO/2 (7 July 2008); and Concluding Observations: Madagascar, CAT/C/MDG/CO/1 (21 December 2011).
61 Concluding Observations: South Africa, CEDAW/C/ZAF/CO/4 (5 April 2011).
62 Trafficking in Persons, Especially Women and Children: A Note by the Secretary General, A/64/290 (12 August 2009).
63 Report Submitted by the Special Rapporteur on the Sale of Children, Child Prostitution and Child Pornography, A/HRC/7/8 (9 January 2008).
64 Report of the Special Rapporteur on Contemporary Forms of Slavery, A/HRC/24/43 (1 July 2013).
65 Application No. 25965/04, 7 January 2010, 286.
66 Trafficking Protocol, Art. 9(1).

trafficking such as poverty and underdevelopment.[67] While this obligation is mainly relevant to States of origin as noted above, Article 9(4) makes it clear that this is done through bilateral or multilateral co-operation, thereby recognising the contributions to be made by other States and the international community as a whole. Further, under Article 9(5), States must implement measures to reduce the demand for trafficked people. In relation to the Organized Crime Convention, Article 31 establishes a general obligation to prevent organised crime.

While these look fine on paper, there are several shortcomings in these prevention provisions. For instance, the phrase 'shall endeavour' is used throughout Article 31 of the Organized Crime Convention. This is also reflected in Article 9(2), which merely obliges States to 'endeavour to undertake' measures relating to research, information and media campaigns and social/economic initiatives to prevent trafficking. Although the Special Rapporteur on Violence against Women argued during the drafting stage that this language should be strengthened,[68] ultimately this was not accepted. A lack of comprehensive research into trafficking will prevent law enforcement authorities from facilitating intelligence-led enforcement, and the supply-and-demand chain for trafficked people in sex and other industries will remain unaffected without effective information and an awareness-raising campaign. Another problem is that Article 9 does not provide detailed guidance for the preventive measures that ought to be implemented in both States of origin and destination. While it is impossible for a single treaty to provide an exhaustive list of measures to be taken, clearer guidance can facilitate a degree of uniformity in prevention. Once again, the Council of Europe Convention may be regarded as an example of good practice as it provides more concrete examples such as gender mainstreaming, facilitation of legal migration and human rights education.[69]

Aside from legal issues for the Trafficking Protocol, some concerns were expressed about the actual implementation of prevention measures by States. For instance, it was reported that structural adjustment programmes initiated by international financial institutions have actually made things worse, particularly for women, because they have resulted in reduced opportunities for certain industries where the workforces have traditionally been dominated by women, such as the garment industry and agriculture.[70] Restrictive immigration policies in States of destination have also been recognised as counter-productive, as they have encouraged people to turn to traffickers who can facilitate illegal transportation.[71] In relation to the demand for trafficked people, while recognising the importance of targeting clients who continue to seek goods and services provided by trafficked victims, the Special Rapporteur on Trafficking has also stressed that labour sectors likely to be occupied by trafficked victims should be properly regulated so that these workers are granted more rights and freedoms.[72] These causal factors should not be considered in isolation as it is often the case that a combination of several factors facilitates the trafficking process. This requires States to take a comprehensive approach capable of addressing the major causes simultaneously.[73]

---

67 Trafficking Protocol, Art. 9(4).
68 *Travaux Préparatoires*, p. 393.
69 The Council of Europe Convention, Chapter II.
70 Trafficking in Persons, Especially Women and Children: A Note by the Secretary General, A/65/288 (9 August 2010), p. 23.
71 Ibid., p. 24.
72 Ibid., p. 38.
73 Ibid., p. 26.

Once again, the predominant focus on criminal justice within transnational criminal law as represented by the Trafficking Protocol and the Organized Crime Convention means that this branch of international law alone is not capable of facilitating effective prevention of trafficking. This can be ameliorated to some extent by international human rights law as it provides further guidance on what States must do to prevent trafficking. For instance, it has been argued elsewhere that the relevant instruments such as the International Covenant on Economic, Social and Cultural Rights 1966 (ICESCR),[74] the Convention on the Elimination of All Forms of Discrimination against Women 1979 (CEDAW)[75] and the Convention on the Rights of the Child 1989 (CRC)[76] impose various obligations such as poverty reduction, elimination of discrimination, and education of those who may be at risk of being trafficked, such as children,[77] so that 'push factors' in States of origin can be dealt with more effectively.

In relation to addressing the demand for goods and services provided/produced by trafficked victims, a duty to prohibit slavery and forced labour has long been established in international human rights law.[78] This duty constitutes customary international law, *jus cogens*, as well as an *erga omnes* obligation,[79] thereby enjoying a higher status in international law. Prohibition of slavery and forced labour is further strengthened by a general obligation to prevent non-State actors from breaching the human rights of others.[80] All of these would certainly be relevant to pimps and brothel owners who exploit the prostitution of women, as well as business owners in relevant sectors such as shellfish, agriculture and construction industries, which rely on cheap/forced labour. In relation to clients who purchase goods and services provided by victims of trafficking, the nature and extent of obligations is not straightforward as they do not necessarily engage in direct exploitation of victims. This is the case, for example, when consumers buy cheap goods produced by them. Nevertheless, States should at least implement proactive awareness-raising and education campaigns, as provided for under the Optional Protocol to the CRC on the Sale of Children,[81] and recognised by the Special Rapporteurs on Trafficking of Human Beings,[82] Sale of Children[83] and Contemporary Forms of Slavery[84] as well as the Committee on Economic, Social and Cultural Rights.[85] In

---

74 16 December 1966, 993 UNTS 3, in force 3 January 1976.

75 18 December 1979, 1249 UNTS 13, in force 3 September 1981.

76 20 November 1989, 1577 UNTS 3, in force 2 September 1990.

77 Obokata, *Trafficking of Human Beings*, pp. 161–164.

78 Article 8 of the ICCPR; Art. 4 of the ECHR; Art. 6 of the American Convention on Human Rights, OAS Treaty Series No. 36; and Art. 5 of the African Charter on Human and Peoples' Rights 1981, 21 ILM 58 (1982).

79 *Prosecutor v Kunarac*, IT-96-23-T & IT-96-32-1T (22 February 2001), 520; *Barcelona Traction Case (Second Phrase)*, ICJ Report 1970, p. 33; *Restatement (Third), Foreign Relations Law of the United States*, § 702; and M.C. Bassiouni, 'International Crimes: "Jus Cogens" and "Obligation Erga Omnes" ', *Law and Contemporary Problems*, 1996, vol. 59, p. 68.

80 *Velasquez Rodriguez v Honduras, supra*. In relation to economic and social rights, an obligation to 'protect' also requires States to prevent third parties from abusing the human rights of others. See Maastricht Guidelines on Violations of Economic, Social and Cultural Rights, 6, reprinted in *Human Rights Quarterly* 1998, vol. 20, p. 691.

81 Optional Protocol to the CRC on the Sale of Children Art. 9(2).

82 Reports of the Special Rapporteur on Trafficking in Persons, Especially Women and Children, A/HRC/23/48 (18 March 2013), and E/CN.4/2006/62 (20 February 2006).

83 Report of the Special Rapporteur on the Sale of Children, Child Prostitution and Child Pornography, E/CN.4/2006/67 (12 January 2006), p. 130.

84 Report of the Special Rapporteur on Contemporary Forms of Slavery, A/HRC/21/41 (10 July 2012), p. 98.

85 General Comment No. 13 (Right to Education) (1999), 55, E/C.12/1999/10 (8 December 1999).

view of the above, it seems reasonable to conclude that the effectiveness of transnational criminal law in promoting 3P obligations can be strengthened by international human rights law.

Customary status of prohibition on trafficking of human beings?

It has been clearly demonstrated that the main source of international law relating to human trafficking is treaty law. One major difficulty with treaty law is that it binds only those States which become Parties, creating an accountability gap for those which do not sign up. This also makes international co-operation more difficult in cases where there are no pre-existing bilateral arrangements. These are not desirable outcomes as they undermine the implementation of effective action against human trafficking. This raises a question as to whether there is a possibility of recognising the prohibition on human trafficking as a customary norm which would bind all States, regardless of whether or not they have ratified the Trafficking Protocol. The prohibition on slavery has been established as customary international law, as noted above. However, given that trafficking does not necessarily amount to slavery, a separate analysis of the customary status of its prohibition is required.

In order for a norm to be elevated to customary international law, it is well established that two elements must be proven: 1) State practice and 2) *opinio iuris*.[86] There is no clear dividing line between these two elements; in many cases as they can overlap. With this in mind, there are clear examples which constitute State practice and/or *opinio iuris* in relation to the prohibition on human trafficking. Adoption of national legislation is the case in point. Currently there are 193 Member States within the United Nations, and 139 States have adopted or amended laws on human trafficking in line with the Trafficking Protocol.[87] The national legislation of eight States is being amended at the time of writing.[88] In other States, while there are no specific laws on human trafficking, the crime is regulated through criminal, labour and other relevant laws. In addition to legislation, establishment of dedicated units or task forces within the law enforcement agencies and other government departments, as well as the adoption of national action plans, are evidence of State practice in relation to human trafficking. At the time of writing, 147 Member States of the UN have drafted and/or adopted national action plans and 130 States have established dedicated bodies to address human trafficking. It is worth noting that, of those States which did not previously have specific laws on human trafficking, more than half of them have adopted national action plans and/or established dedicated governmental bodies.[89] These examples of State practice may be regarded as the evidence of *opinio iuris* simultaneously, as States would not have taken positive steps to enact legislation, adopt action plans or establish dedicated governmental bodies if they did not feel obliged to do so.

---

86 *North Sea Continental Shelf Cases*, ICJ Report 1969 3, p. 77.
87 Based on the author's own analysis of national legislation. The sources consulted include *Trafficking in Persons Report 2013* (US Department of State); Legislationline (OSCE) at http://legislationline. org/topics/topic/14 (accessed 1 April 2014) and International Anti-Trafficking Legislation (Protection Project) at http://www.protectionproject.org/resources/law-library/international-anti-trafficking (accessed 1 April 2014).
88 They are Botswana, Burundi, Chad, Papua New Guinea, St Vincent, Samoa, San Marino and Togo.
89 They include Angola, Central African Republic, Japan, Maldives, Syria, Tunisia and Yemen.

Other examples of State practice and/or *opinio iuris* can be seen in 'multilateral forums'[90] in the sense of States taking actions through regional and international organisations. As of October 2013, 157 States were Parties to the Trafficking Protocol, and the number of ratifications had gone up to 178 for the Organized Crime Convention.[91] The resolutions of the UN General Assembly on human trafficking have called upon all Member States to criminalise trafficking in all its forms,[92] or have recognised an obligation to prosecute and punish it.[93] The same is true for the Human Rights Council (47 Member States),[94] the Economic and Social Council (54 Member States)[95] and the Security Council (15 Member States).[96] These resolutions may be regarded as being declaratory of a clear legal obligation to prohibit human trafficking. Further, the need to prohibit and combat trafficking has been explicitly recognised through a series of legally binding and non-binding instruments by regional organisations such as the Organisation of Islamic Cooperation (57 Member States),[97] the Council of Europe (47 Member States),[98] the European Union (28 Member States),[99] the Organization for Security and Cooperation in Europe (57 Participating States),[100] the North Atlantic Treaty Organization (28 Member States),[101] the Organization of American States (34 Member States),[102] the South Eastern Association for Regional Co-operation (8 Member States),[103] the

---

90 J. Charney, 'Universal International Law'. *American Journal of International Law*, 1993, vol. 87, p. 529.

91 See Status of Ratification at http://www.unodc.org/unodc/en/treaties/CTOC/signatures.html (accessed 1 April 2014).

92 A/RES/67/190 (Improving the Co-ordination of Efforts against Trafficking in Persons), 20 December 2012.

93 A/RES/67/145 (Trafficking in Women and Girls), 20 December 2012; and A/RES/65/190 (Trafficking in Women and Girls), 21 December 2010.

94 A/HRC/23/L.8 (Trafficking in Persons, Especially Women and Children), 6 June 2013; A/HRC/20/L.1 (Trafficking in Persons, Especially Women and Children), 29 June 2012; and A/HRC/14/L4 (Trafficking in Persons, Especially Women and Children) 11 June 2010.

95 ECOSOC Resolution 2006/27 (Strengthening International Co-operation in Preventing and Combating Trafficking in Persons and Protecting Victims of Such Trafficking), 27 July 2006.

96 Statement by the President of the Security Council (Threat to International Peace and Security: Illicit Cross-Border Movement and Trafficking), S/PRST/2012/16 (25 April 2012). See also Security Council Resolution 1674 (Protection of Civilians in Armed Conflicts), S/RES/1674, 28 April 2006 (though limited to armed conflicts).

97 Article 1 of the Charter of the Organisation of Islamic Cooperation.

98 Council of Europe Convention, *supra*.

99 Council Directive on 2011/36/EU on preventing and combating trafficking in human beings and protecting its victims, OJ L 1011/1, 15 April 2011; and Article 5(3) of the Charter of Fundamental Rights of the European Union 2007, which provides that 'trafficking in human beings is prohibited'. OJ C 301/1, 14 December 2007.

100 Decision No. 557, OSCE Plan of Action to Combat Trafficking in Human Beings, PC.DEC/557, 24 July 2003.

101 NATO Policy against Human Trafficking, 29 June 2004, at http://www.nato.int/docu/comm/2004/06-istanbul/docu-traffic.htm (accessed 1 April 2014).

102 Declaration on San Salvador on Citizen Security in the Americas 2011, AG/DEC.66 (XLI-O/11), 7 June 2011; Inter-American Convention on Traffic in Minors 1994; General Assembly Resolutions AG/RES.2707 (Prevention and Eradication of Commercial Sexual Exploitation, Smuggling and Trafficking in Minors) 4 June 2012; and AG/RES.2686 (Prevention and Eradication of Commercial Sexual Exploitation and Smuggling and Trafficking in Children), 7 June 2011.

103 SAARC Convention on Preventing and Combating Trafficking in Women and Children for Prostitution 2002.

Association of South East Asian Nations (10 Member States),[104] the Economic Community of West African States (15 Member States)[105] and the African Union (54 Member States).[106] A lack of explicit objections to these instruments on the part of States suggests that they are generally in support of the prohibition of human trafficking. In looking at these, it may be argued that State practice and *opinio iuris* relating to the prohibition on human trafficking are generally consistent and widespread in line with the reasoning of the International Court of Justice in the *Nicaragua* case.[107]

One hurdle for recognising the prohibition on trafficking as a customary norm is the length of time involved. While there were early treaties on the subject, as noted above, the modern understanding of this crime as stipulated in Article 3 of the Trafficking Protocol should be the starting point because previously there was no agreement as to what constituted human trafficking. It has been a little over ten years since the Trafficking Protocol was adopted, and a question here is whether this time period is sufficient for 'prohibition on trafficking' to be accepted as a customary norm. On this point, the International Court of Justice has held that a passage of a short period of time was not a bar to the formation of custom.[108] However, it was noted simultaneously that 'an indispensable requirement would be that within the period in question, short though it might be, State practice . . . should have been both extensive and virtually uniform'.[109] The notion of 'virtual uniformity' does not necessary require that every single State should behave in exactly the same way. In this regard, the International Court of Justice noted that State practice did not have to be in absolute rigorous conformity with the rule.[110] Applying this reasoning to the prohibition of trafficking, while the above examples demonstrate that State practice is becoming widespread, there still remains some inconsistency as a number of States have not enacted legislation in line with the Trafficking Protocol, adopted national action plans or established dedicated entities on human trafficking. This in turn casts some doubt upon the clear and uncontested existence of *opinio iuris*. A reasonable conclusion, then, is that the prohibition on human trafficking, separate from prohibition on slavery, has not yet crystallised into a customary norm. However, it seems reasonable to argue simultaneously that the customary norm is developing, and it may be only a matter of time before the prohibition on human trafficking is widely accepted as being part of customary international law.

Conclusion

This chapter has examined the international legal framework relating to human trafficking. While transnational criminal law, as represented by the Trafficking Protocol and the Organized Crime Convention, displays a number of improvements compared to earlier instruments and has become an important tool to address this crime, it is simultaneously evident that it cannot, on its own, facilitate effective action against this crime. In particular,

---

104 ASEAN Declaration against Trafficking in Persons, Particularly Women and Children 2004.
105 ECOWAS Declaration on the Fight against Trafficking in Persons 2001.
106 Ouagadougou Plan of Action on Trafficking in Human Beings Especially Women and Children 2006, adopted with the EU Member States.
107 *Military and Paramilitary Activities in and against Nicaragua*, ICJ Report 1986 vol. 14, p. 186.
108 *North Sea Continental Shelf Cases, supra*, p. 71, p. 73 and p. 74. See also Bin Cheng, 'United Nations Resolutions on Outer Space: "Instant" International Customary Law?' *Indian Journal of International Law* 1965, vol. 5, p. 23.
109 *North Sea Continental Shelf Cases, supra*, p. 74.
110 *Nicaragua case, supra*, p. 186.

it is not well equipped to address the human rights of the victims of trafficking as well as those of traffickers. Further, its capability to deal with the causes and consequences of trafficking is uncertain. A truly legitimate and effective response requires States to take these into consideration more seriously, and it has been demonstrated that international human rights law can fill this gap by imposing additional obligations. Another important development is the emergence of the prohibition of human trafficking as a customary norm. This seems to be a natural progression given the widespread recognition that trafficking is a serious crime, a violation of human rights as well as a contemporary form of slavery.

What is important, moreover, is to ask ourselves how the current international legal framework is interpreted and applied by States in practice. To begin with, effective implementation of international law on human trafficking requires that law and policy makers obtain a full understanding of the nature and extent of obligations. It is then their job to enact legislation that reflects the international standards, including the 3P obligations as well as protection and promotion of human rights. This will assist law enforcement agencies to execute these obligations on the ground. The role of the judiciary must also be emphasised here, as judges can impose appropriate penalties to punish traffickers for future deterrence, freeze and confiscate criminal proceeds, and ensure protection of victims during and after criminal proceedings, including the award of compensation. It is therefore clear that all organs of a State must work together to implement international law on human trafficking. Beyond this, it is essential that States co-operate with the civil society sector, other States, and regional and international organisations with expertise on the subject. When the responses to human trafficking are effectively co-ordinated at national, regional and international levels, this will reduce the ineffective use of resources and duplication of efforts, allowing the true potential of international law on trafficking to be realised sooner rather than later.

12

Migrant smuggling

Anne T. Gallagher

Introduction

The term 'migrant smuggling' refers to the unauthorized movement of individuals across national borders for the financial or other benefit of the smuggler. While aspects of illegally facilitated migration are established criminal offences in many countries, migrant smuggling itself was not the subject of international legal regulation until very recently. The origins of this shift can be traced back to the late 1980s and early 1990s when the imposition of tighter immigration controls to the preferred destinations, at a time when demand for such migration was rising rapidly, led to the increased involvement of third party facilitators. A focus on those facilitators of irregular migration, rather than just the migrants themselves, was widely viewed as a critical element in any effective response to irregular migration. The development of an international legal regime around transnational organized crime provided concerned States with the opportunity to internationalize the 'problem' of migrant smuggling, thereby encouraging the international cooperation that was considered essential to its effective resolution. The new specialist legal framework to emerge from that process comprises the Protocol against the Smuggling of Migrants by Land, Sea and Air[1] (Migrant Smuggling Protocol) and its parent instrument the United Nations Convention against Transnational Organized Crime[2] (UNTOC). In addition to defining smuggling, the Protocol and Convention detail a wide range of obligations on States: from criminalizing migrant smuggling and related offences to cooperating in the exchange of information, evidence and intelligence.

The novelty of the issue contributed to a general perception that this new specialist regime was a complete or self-contained one. However, the relevant international legal framework around migrant smuggling is older and considerably broader, comprising a dense web of rights, obligations and responsibilities drawn not just from the Protocol and Convention but

---

1 Protocol against the Smuggling of Migrants by Land, Sea and Air, supplementing the United Nations Convention against Transnational Organized Crime, 2241 UNTS 507, done 15 November 2000, entered into force 28 January 2004 (Migrant Smuggling Protocol).
2 United Nations Convention against Transnational Organized Crime, 2225 UNTS 209, done 15 November 2000, entered into force 29 September 2003 (Organized Crime Convention).

also from the law of the sea, human rights law and refugee law. Regional and bilateral migration control treaties are another important source of both rights and obligations in this area. Long-standing norms around sovereignty and jurisdiction dictate the capacity of States to act against migrant smuggling. Equally distinguished principles place a range of limitations on that capacity. The secondary rules of international law are also vital: most particularly in attributing responsibility for internationally wrongful acts associated with migrant smuggling itself as well as with State responses to migrant smuggling.

It is not possible, within the confines of the present chapter, to explore this dense and complex network of rules in any detail, and readers are referred to a recent, in-depth study that provides a full analysis of the relevant legal framework.[3] The scope of the chapter is accordingly a much narrower one. The first part covers the development of specialized rules around migrant smuggling, focusing particularly on examining the origins of the Migrant Smuggling Protocol and its core provisions. The second part of the chapter seeks to provide some insight into how the broader legal framework applies to several migrant smuggling issues of high contemporary significance. The areas selected for analysis are interception and rescue at sea (with specific reference to international maritime law) and protection and return of smuggled migrants (with specific reference to international human rights law).

While the focus of this chapter is firmly on the legal framework, it would be misguided to consider that framework in isolation from the broader political and social forces that have impacted on its development and continue to shape the way in which migrant smuggling is identified and responded to. Irregular migration is a source of long-standing anxiety for States, most particularly for the relatively wealthier countries of destination. The involvement of facilitators, with its implication of increased efficiency in approaching and evading fortified borders, is widely viewed as presenting an additional and serious threat. Criminalization of irregular migration is a common response but may have limited impact and brings with it certain political and legal risks, particularly for liberal democracies.[4] Criminalization of the facilitation of such migration can be seen and sold quite differently: less an attack on individual migrants than on those who are profiting from their vulnerability and desperation. By emphasizing the connection with transnational organized crime, States are more easily able to characterize migrant smuggling as a threat to public order and national security. This in turn helps to both justify and explain the growing externalization of border controls and the increased militarization of all aspects of border control – from surveillance to deterrence.[5]

---

3 A.T. Gallagher and F. David, *The International Law of Migrant Smuggling*, Cambridge: Cambridge University Press, forthcoming 2014.

4 Generally on criminalization of migration and migrants see C. Dauvergne, *Making People Illegal: What Globalization Means for Migration and Law*, Cambridge: Cambridge University Press, 2008. See also Council of Europe, Commissioner for Human Rights, *Criminalisation of Migration in Europe: Human Rights Implications*, 2010; L. Hales and L. Gelsthorpe, *The Criminalisation of Migrant Women*, Institute of Criminology, University of Cambridge, United Kingdom, 2012; B. Story, *Politics as Usual: The Criminalization of Asylum Seekers in the United States*, University of Oxford Refugee Studies Centre Working Paper No. 26, September 2005.

5 Generally on trends in the externalization of border controls and associated legal implications see B. Ryan and V. Mitsilegas (eds), *Extraterritorial Immigration Control: Legal Challenges*, The Hague: Martinus Nijhoff, 2010; M. den Heijer, *Europe and Extraterritorial Asylum*, Oxford, Hart, 2012; T. Gammeltoft-Hansen, *Access to Asylum: International Refugee Law and the Globalisation of Migration Control*, Cambridge: Cambridge University Press, 2011. On the increasing militarization attached to this trend see Migreurop, *The Externalisation of Migration Controls: 2010–2011 Report*, October 2011.

The politics of migrant smuggling are also very much the politics of asylum. In every part of the world, increasing numbers of asylum seekers, including those with genuine claims to refugee status, are being transported by smugglers. In the words of one refugee law scholar: 'human smugglers play a critical role in assisting refugees to reach safety.'[6] Efforts to characterize migrant smuggling as a form of transnational organized crime and to encourage its criminalization have been largely driven by this reality and the fear of States that facilitated movement of asylum seekers will lead to greatly increased movements from ever-distant points of origin.[7]

Migrant smuggling in transnational criminal law

History and context

The issue of migrant smuggling was not the subject of official discussions within international and regional organizations prior to the early 1990s. At that time several high-profile incidents highlighted the growing phenomenon of organized movement of migrants from China,[8] feeding unease amongst affected States, who quickly began pushing for greater international legal cooperation on the issue.[9] These efforts very rapidly found a receptive audience among the destination countries of western and central Europe, North America and elsewhere that had experienced a significant increase in the number of 'unauthorized arrivals', apparently facilitated by criminal groups that were organized and sophisticated enough to exploit legislative, policy and law enforcement weaknesses.[10]

Deficiencies in international law were seen as particularly acute and detrimental: as summarized by advocates of a new treaty on the subject, there was no agreed definition of smuggling, no domestic obligation to criminalize smuggling, and no obligation to extradite or prosecute perpetrators,[11] resulting in a 'legal lacuna under international law [that] is

---

6 J.C. Hathaway, 'Why Human Smuggling Is Vital', *National Post* (Canada), 13 September 2010.
7 See, for example, H. de Haas, *The Myth of Invasion: Irregular Migration from West Africa to the Maghreb and the European Union*, International Migration Institute Research Report, October 2007, esp. pp. 56–60; D. Kyle and R. Koslowski (eds), *Global Human Smuggling: Comparative Perspectives* Baltimore: Johns Hopkins University Press, 2nd edn, 2011, esp. chapter 10 (K. Koser, 'The Smuggling of Refugees').
8 The most prominent of these was the *Golden Venture* incident, in which a Chinese vessel, carrying 286 migrants, was deliberately run aground off the coast of New York. The migrants, who had each paid up to US $30,000 for a place on the vessel, were advised to jump into the sea and swim to shore. Ten died of drowning or hypothermia, and most of the survivors were deported back to China. The incident prompted significant legislative and policy changes in the United States on the issue of migrant smuggling. See A.J. Sein, 'The Prosecution of Chinese Organized Crime Groups: The Sister Ping Case and its Lessons', *Trends in Organized Crime*, 2008, vol. 11, no. 2, p. 157, p. 163.
9 D. McClean, *Transnational Organized Crime: A Commentary on the UN Convention and its Protocols*, Oxford: Oxford University Press, 2007, pp. 21–24; D. Vlassis, 'The Global Situation of Transnational Organized Crime, the Decision of the International Community to Develop an International Convention and the Negotiation Process', in United Nations Asia and Far East Institute for the Prevention of Crime and the Treatment of Offenders, *Annual Report for 2000 and Resource Materials*, Series No. 59 475 (2002) (hereafter: Vlassis, 'The Global Situation of Transnational Organized Crime').
10 See 'Measures to Combat Alien Smuggling: Report of the Secretary-General', UN Doc. A/49/350, 30 August 1994.
11 Letter dated 16 September, 1997 from the Permanent Representative of Austria to the United Nations addressed to the Secretary-General, UN Doc. A/52/357, 17 September 1997, at paras 2–3 (transmitting a draft of the proposed convention).

increasingly perceived as an obstacle to the efforts of the international community to cope in an efficient manner with the phenomenon of smuggling of illegal migrants for criminal purposes'.[12] The major destination countries were quick to understand that the default position – a purely national approach to sanctioning those who facilitated such migration, supplemented by *ad hoc* and largely ineffective bilateral cooperation – played directly into the hands of smugglers and traffickers.[13]

Attention initially focused on the International Maritime Organization (IMO) as a vehicle for promoting and supporting cooperation among States in suppressing 'unsafe practices associated with alien smuggling by ships'.[14] States also sought to simultaneously engage the United Nations and in December 1993 the UN General Assembly adopted a resolution on 'prevention of the smuggling of aliens'.[15] The resolution provided the multilateral hook essential for justifying the elevation of migrant smuggling as an issue of common concern, by affirming that these practices have 'transnational consequences' such that there is a 'need for States to cooperate urgently at the bilateral and multilateral levels, as appropriate, to thwart these activities'.[16] It called on States to take a set of actions to prevent 'the practice of smuggling aliens'.[17]

Parallel developments in Europe fed into and strengthened these early international efforts[18] and interest in developing an international regulatory framework around migrant smuggling quickly gained momentum. In 1997 the Government of Austria formally proposed the development of a new legal instrument to deal with the smuggling of migrants, focusing specifically on creation of a new criminal offence as well as measures related to investigation, prosecution and extradition.[19] In its proposal, the Austrian Government noted that this practice posed 'a growing threat to the international community as a whole' and, given that it constituted a 'very special form of transnational crime', required a special convention.[20] After

---

12 Ibid.
13 See generally Vlassis, 'The Global Situation of Transnational Organized Crime'. See also A. Kirchener and L. Schiano di Pepe, 'International Attempts to Conclude a Convention to Combat Illegal Migration,' *International Journal of Refugee Law*, 1998, vol. 10, p. 662. See also the observation of the United States Government in the 1994 UN report on alien smuggling ('Measures to Combat Alien Smuggling: Report of the Secretary-General,' UN Doc. A/49/350, 30 Aug. 1994), at paragraph 79, that '[c]ontrol of alien-smuggling is made more difficult in the United States by the fact that in a number of Central American countries, alien smuggling is not illegal and smugglers are often able to operate openly'.
14 International Maritime Organization, Assembly, *Enhancement of Safety of Life at Sea by the Prevention and Suppression of Unsafe Practices Associated with Alien Smuggling by Ships*, IMO Resolution A.773(18), 4 November 1993.
15 UN General Assembly, 'Prevention of the smuggling of aliens', GA Res. 48/102, UN GAOR, 48th session, Agenda Item 10, UN Doc. A/RES/48/102, 8 Mar. 1994, adopted 20 December 1993.
16 Ibid.
17 Ibid. at para. 2.
18 See for example Council of Europe, 'Texts adopted at the European Conference on Uncontrolled Migration (Budapest, 15–16 February 1993)', Fifth Conference of European Ministers responsible for migration affairs (Athens, 18–19 November 1993), Doc. MMG–5 (93) 5, 19 October 1993, p. 3.
19 Letter dated 16 September, 1997 from the Permanent Representative of Austria to the United Nations addressed to the Secretary-General, UN Doc. A/52/357, 17 Sept. 1997. See further Kirchener and Schiano di Pepe, 'International Attempts to Conclude a Convention to Combat Illegal Migration,' p. 670.
20 Letter dated 16 September, 1997 from the Permanent Representative of Austria to the United Nations addressed to the Secretary-General, UN Doc. A/52/357, 17 Sept. 1997, at introductory para. and para. 4. See also R.A. Pedrozo, 'International Initiatives to Combat Trafficking of Migrants by Sea', in J.N. Moore and M.H. Nordquist (eds), *Current Maritime Issues and the International Maritime Organization*, The Hague: Martinus Nijhoff, 1999, p. 53, pp. 62–63.

initially approaching the IMO with its own proposal, Italy decided to join forces with Austria in pushing for the development of a legal instrument against migrant smuggling within the context of the UN Commission on Crime Prevention and Criminal Justice's work against transnational organized crime.[21] This goal was secured in late 1998 when the Ad Hoc Committee, established to develop a convention on transnational organized crime, was mandated to also discuss the elaboration of an international instrument on 'illegal trafficking in and transportation of migrants, including by sea'.[22]

The Migrant Smuggling Protocol, the principal international treaty dealing with the smuggling of migrants and a central plank of the relevant international legal framework, was adopted by the General Assembly in 2000 alongside its parent instrument, UNTOC. The Protocol entered into force on 28 January 2004 and as at 1 January 2014 had 138 States Parties. The Protocol's stated purpose is to prevent and combat migrant smuggling, to promote international cooperation to that end, and to protect the rights of smuggled migrants.[23]

Definition of migrant smuggling

When the international community first came together to take concerted action against what is now known as migrant smuggling, there was still considerable confusion – and indeed overlap – between this concept and what is presently referred to as human trafficking. The differences nevertheless firmed up very quickly, with States agreeing to remove any 'exploitation' element from the concept of migrant smuggling, thereby shifting the focus of the definition onto the *action* of migrant smuggling, rather than its *impact* on those who are smuggled.

The Migrant Smuggling Protocol defines 'smuggling of migrants' as 'the procurement, in order to obtain, directly or indirectly, a financial or other material benefit, of the illegal entry of a person into a State Party of which the person is not a national or a permanent resident'.[24] While the term 'financial or other material benefit' is not defined in the Protocol, it is clear from a similar provision in UNTOC that the reference is intended to go beyond mere payment of money.[25] The reference to 'financial or other benefit' was included as an element of the definition in order to ensure that the activities of those who provide support to migrants on humanitarian grounds or on the basis of close family ties do not come within the scope of the Protocol.[26] The focus of the definition is firmly on those who procure or otherwise

---

21 Vlassis, 'The Global Situation of Transnational Organized Crime', p. 493.

22 UN General Assembly, 'Transnational organized crime', GA Res. 53/111, UN GAOR, 53rd sess, Agenda Item 101, UN Doc. A/RES/53/111, 20 Jan. 1999, at para. 10.

23 Migrant Smuggling Protocol, Art. 2.

24 Ibid., Art. 3(a).

25 See United Nations Office on Drugs and Crime, *Legislative Guides for the Implementation of the United Nations Convention against Transnational Organized Crime and the Protocols Thereto*, UN Sales No. E.05.V.2 (United Nations, 2004), p. 13 (paras 25–26) and p. 334 (para. 20) (hereafter: UNODC, *Legislative Guide*).

26 United Nations Office on Drugs and Crime, Travaux Préparatoires *of the Negotiations for the Elaboration of the United Nations Convention against Transnational Organized Crime and the Protocols Thereto*, UN Sales No. E.06.V.5 (United Nations, 2006) (hereafter: Travaux Préparatoires *for the Organized Crime Convention and Protocols*), at p. 469. The relevant Interpretative Note (ibid.) adds that '[i]t was not the intention of the protocol criminalize the activities of family members or support groups such as religious or non–governmental organizations'.

facilitate the smuggling of migrants. The Protocol does not address mere illegal entry and takes a neutral position on whether those who migrate illegally should be the subject of any offences.[27]

Criminalization obligations

Criminalization is at the heart of the Migrant Smuggling Protocol, 'serving not only to provide for the deterrence and punishment of the smuggling of migrants, but as the basis for the numerous forms of prevention, international cooperation, technical assistance and other measures'.[28] The core obligation is to criminalize the smuggling of migrants when committed intentionally.[29] States Parties are further required to criminalize certain constituent or related elements of the crime of migrant smuggling, including the production of fraudulent travel or identity documents for the purpose of enabling migrant smuggling;[30] procuring, providing or possessing[31] such a document for the purpose of enabling migrant smuggling; and enabling a person to remain unlawfully within the State concerned[32] – including the procurement of legal residence by some illegal means, 'even if the actual entry that preceded it was legal'.[33]

States Parties are also obliged to criminalize attempting to commit such offences;[34] participating as an accomplice in such offences;[35] and organizing or directing others to commit such an offence.[36] They are further required to recognize as aggravated smuggling offences those that involve danger to the lives of migrants or that entail degrading or inhuman treatment, including exploitation,[37] presumably through the imposition of relatively harsher penalties.[38] The Protocol is otherwise silent on the issue of penalties and the basic

---

27 Migrant Smuggling Protocol, Art. 5. See also UNODC, *Legislative Guide*, p. 340, p. 347. But see Article 6(4) of the Protocol, which provides that nothing in the Protocol limits the existing rights of States Parties to take action against those whose conduct constitutes an offence under national law.

28 UNODC, *Legislative Guide*, p. 349 (para. 55).

29 Migrant Smuggling Protocol, Art. 6(1)(a). In accordance with Art. 34(2) of the Organized Crime Convention, the co-requisites of transnationality and involvement of an organized criminal group do not apply to the obligation of criminalization except, as noted by the *Legislative Guide*, where the language of the criminalization requirement specifically incorporates one of these elements. UNODC, *Legislative Guide*, pp. 333–334 (para. 20).

30 Ibid., Art. 6(1)(b).

31 Ibid. An Interpretative Note attached to Art. 6 makes clear that the reference to 'possession' does not extend to possession of a fraudulent travel or identity document by a migrant for purposes of enabling his or her smuggling. Travaux Préparatoires *for the Organized Crime Convention and Protocols*, p. 489. See also UNODC, *Legislative Guide*, p. 349 (para. 54).

32 Migrant Smuggling Protocol, Art. 6(1)(b), 6(1)(c).

33 UNODC, *Legislative Guide*, p. 341, note 9.

34 'Subject to the basic concepts' of the legal system of the State: Migrant Smuggling Protocol, at Art. 6(2)(a). The UNODC *Legislative Guide*, p. 271 (para. 41), notes that this caveat was introduced to accommodate legal systems which do not recognize the criminal concept of 'attempt'.

35 Migrant Smuggling Protocol, Art. 6(2)(b).

36 Ibid., Art. 6(2)(c).

37 Ibid., Art. 6(3). See further UNODC, *Legislative Guide*, pp. 346–347; United Nations Office on Drugs and Crime, *Model Law against the Smuggling of Migrants* (United Nations, 2010) (hereafter: UNODC Model Law on Migrant Smuggling), pp. 40–45.

38 UNODC, *Legislative Guide*, p. 346 (para. 46). See also UNODC Model Law on Migrant Smuggling, pp. 41–42.

requirement of the Convention, that sanctions should take into account the gravity of the offence, will apply.[39]

The relationship between the Convention and the Protocol creates other obligations on States Parties to take certain measures with respect to offences established under the Protocol. For example, through the Convention, States Parties are required to criminalize the laundering of the proceeds of migrant smuggling;[40] ensure legal persons can be held liable for migrant smuggling offences;[41] ensure migrant smuggling offences are given broad jurisdictional application;[42] cooperate with other States Parties in the investigation, prosecution and judicial proceedings for migrant smuggling offences, through joint investigations,[43] mutual legal assistance[44] and extradition;[45] and provide for channels of communication and police-to-police cooperation in relation to the investigation of migrant smuggling offences.[46]

Migrant smuggling by sea

The Migrant Smuggling Protocol includes a detailed section on preventing and suppressing the smuggling of migrants by sea. Critically, it does not seek to provide a new legal regime around smuggling by sea. Rather, its relevant provisions affirm the following core principles of the international law of the sea codified in the United Nations Convention on the Law of the Sea (UNCLOS):[47] that coastal States have extensive jurisdiction over national waters, subject only to certain exceptions such as innocent passage; that ships have the nationality of the flag they are entitled to fly; that a flag State has a duty to exercise its jurisdiction and control over ships flying its flag; that ships are subject to the exclusive jurisdiction of the flag State on the high seas;[48] and that there exists a universal right of visit over vessels without nationality, and a heavily circumscribed right of approach and visit in other situations. This reinforcement of existing rules is carried through to the key obligation contained in Article 7 of the Protocol: for States Parties to cooperate in preventing and suppressing migrant smuggling by sea, 'in accordance with the international law of the sea'.[49] It also underlines Article 8, which establishes a cooperation regime intended to facilitate law enforcement action in relation to the smuggling of migrants involving the vessels of other States Parties.[50]

---

39 UNODC, *Legislative Guide*, p. 351 (para. 59) (referring to Article 11(1) of the Convention). See also Organized Crime Convention, Art. 10(4) (sanctions for legal persons to be effective, proportionate and dissuasive); United Nations Office on Drugs and Crime, *Model Legislative Provisions against Organized Crime* (United Nations, 2012) (hereafter: UNODC, *Model Legislative Provisions against Organized Crime*), p. 47.

40 Organized Crime Convention, Art. 6.

41 Ibid., Art. 10. See further UNODC, *Model Legislative Provisions against Organized Crime*, p. 50.

42 Organized Crime Convention, Art. 15. See further UNODC, *Model Legislative Provisions against Organized Crime*, p. 25.

43 Organized Crime Convention, Art. 19.

44 Ibid., Art. 18.

45 Ibid., Art. 16.

46 Ibid., Art. 27.

47 1833 UNTS 3, done 10 December 1982, entered into force 16 November 1994.

48 Ibid., Art. 92(1).

49 The Interpretative Note attached to this Article confirms that: '[t]he international law of the sea includes the United Nations Convention on the Law of the Sea as well as other relevant international instruments': Travaux Préparatoires *for the Organized Crime Convention and Protocols*, p. 494.

50 UNODC Model Law on Migrant Smuggling, p. 83.

The novelty and principal impact of the Migrant Smuggling Protocol relates to situations where a State Party other than the flag State encounters a vessel suspected of being engaged in migrant smuggling that either (i) has the nationality of another State Party, or (ii) is without nationality. However, even in this area, the Protocol does not really break new ground, rather extending and potentially rendering more effective actions that are already well within the law of the sea. The relevant provisions can be summarized as follows:

- A State Party may request the assistance[51] of other States Parties in suppressing the use of a vessel suspected of engaging in migrant smuggling (where the vessel is flying that State's flag or claiming its registry or, while not flying that State's flag but in reality of the nationality of that State).[52] States Parties so requested are required to render such assistance 'to the extent possible within their means'.[53]
- A State Party may further notify another State Party that a vessel exercising its freedom of navigation rights[54] and flying the other State Party's flag, or apparently registered to that other State Party, is reasonably suspected of engaging in migrant smuggling and may request confirmation of registry.[55] The Requested State must respond expeditiously to such a request.[56] Each State is required to designate an authority to receive and respond to such requests and that designation is to be notified to all States Parties within one month via the UN Secretary-General.[57] If registry is confirmed, the notifying State Party may request authorization from the flag State to *take appropriate measures* with regard to that vessel.[58]
- Amongst other things, 'appropriate measures' that may be authorized by the flag State include authority to board and search the vessel.[59] If evidence of migrant smuggling is found, the flag State may further authorize the Requesting State to 'take appropriate measures with respect to the vessel and persons and cargo on board'.[60] No additional measures can be taken without express authorization of the flag State except on the basis of relevant agreements or 'to relieve imminent danger to the lives of persons'.[61] The flag State is further entitled to impose conditions on the measures to be taken,[62] and to be informed of the results of such measures.[63]

---

51 The nature and extent of 'assistance' that may be requested or provided is not specified.
52 Migrant Smuggling Protocol, Art. 8(1).
53 Ibid.
54 I.e. on the high seas or in the exclusive economic zone of another State that is not otherwise part of that State's territorial sea. UNCLOS, Arts 58(1), 87(1)(a), 90.
55 Migrant Smuggling Protocol, Art. 8(2).
56 Ibid., Art. 8(4).
57 Ibid., Art. 8(6). See further UNODC Model Law on Migrant Smuggling, pp. 86–87.
58 Ibid.
59 'Appropriate measures' are not specified. Mallia cites a provision of the Council of Europe Agreement on Illicit Traffic at Sea as an example of the nature and extent of measures that could be considered 'appropriate' in the context of Article 8 of the Protocol. P. Mallia, *Migrant Smuggling by Sea: Combating a Current Threat to Maritime Security through the Creation of a Cooperative Framework*, The Hague: Martinus Nijhoff, 2009 (hereafter: Mallia, *Migrant Smuggling by Sea*), pp. 123–125.
60 Migrant Smuggling Protocol, Art. 8(2)(c).
61 Ibid., Art. 8(5). See also Mallia, *Migrant Smuggling by Sea*, pp. 123–125. Note that the original wording of this provision referred to imminent danger 'to the lives or safety of persons': Travaux Préparatoires *for the Organized Crime Convention and Protocols*, pp. 501, 503.
62 Migrant Smuggling Protocol, Art. 8(5).
63 Ibid., Art. 8(3).

- A State Party that has reasonable grounds to suspect that a vessel without nationality on the high seas is engaged in the smuggling of migrants by sea is entitled to board and search that vessel.[64] If evidence of migrant smuggling is found, the State Party is required to take 'appropriate measures in accordance with relevant domestic and international law'.[65]

Article 9 of the Migrant Smuggling Protocol reflects the very real humanitarian, operational and commercial risks that may be involved in stopping, searching and boarding vessels in the maritime environment, by subjecting measures taken by a State Party against smuggling of migrants at sea to detailed safeguards. Most critically, when carrying out such measures, States Parties are *required to ensure* the safety and humane treatment of all persons on board.[66] If suspicions about the vessel's involvement in migrant smuggling prove to be unfounded, then the State Party is required to compensate the vessel for any loss or damage.[67]

Prevention and cooperation

Article 31 of UNTOC contains a list of measures to be taken by States to prevent, *inter alia*, the smuggling of migrants.[68] The Migrant Smuggling Protocol additionally requires the adoption of general measures to prevent migrant smuggling with a particular focus on prevention through improved law enforcement. States Parties are required to strengthen border controls to the extent possible and necessary to prevent and detect migrant smuggling.[69] They are also encouraged to establish and maintain direct channels of communication between each other as a way of intensifying cooperation among border control agencies.[70] States Parties are to take steps to ensure both the quality and the security of travel documents issued on their behalf and to cooperate in preventing their fraudulent use.[71] Specialized training aimed at preventing, combating and eradicating migrant smuggling is to be provided or strengthened for immigration and other officials.[72] States Parties are further required to adopt appropriate legal and administrative measures to ensure the vigilance of commercial carriers and their liability in the event of complicity or negligence.[73]

Little attention is given to prevention through addressing the factors that encourage or compel people to seek out the services of migrant smugglers. States Parties are instead subject to a vague obligation of promoting or strengthening 'development programmes and cooperation . . . in order to combat the root socio-economic causes of the smuggling of migrants, such as poverty and underdevelopment'.[74] A key preventative element is seen to be the

---

64 Ibid., Art. 8(7).
65 Ibid.
66 Ibid., Art. 9(1) (emphasis added). As noted in the UNODC *Legislative Guide*, this obligation is of great practical importance, given the poor condition of vessels typically used by smugglers and the likelihood that boarding will take place far away from safe harbour conditions (p. 365 (para. 70)). See also UNODC Model Law on Migrant Smuggling, pp. 91–96.
67 Migrant Smuggling Protocol, Art. 9(2). This provision reflects Article 110(3) of UNCLOS.
68 See generally, UNODC, *Model Legislative Provisions against Organized Crime*, pp. 1–18.
69 Migrant Smuggling Protocol, Art. 11(1).
70 Ibid., Art. 11(6).
71 Migrant Smuggling Protocol, Arts 12–13.
72 Ibid., Art. 14.
73 Ibid., Art. 11(2)–11(4).
74 Ibid., Art. 15(3).

dissemination of negative information aimed at discouraging potential migrants.[75] States Parties are required to 'increase public awareness of the fact that [migrant smuggling] . . . is a criminal activity frequently perpetrated by organized criminal groups for profit and that it poses serious risks to the migrants concerned'.[76]

Improved cooperation between countries on the issue of migrant smuggling is the *raison d'être* of the Migrant Smuggling Protocol,[77] and the obligation of cooperation is accordingly integrated into a range of provisions, including those related to the sharing of information[78] and the return of smuggled migrants.[79] Cross-border cooperation is also envisaged with respect to the strengthening of border controls and general law enforcement against migrant smuggling.[80] States Parties are encouraged to develop bilateral and regional agreements to further the purposes of the Protocol.[81] These specific provisions are supplemented by the Convention, which, as noted above, constructs a detailed model of mutual legal and other assistance to facilitate cooperation between States in the prevention and suppression of transnational organized crime.

Assistance to and protection of smuggled migrants

A review of the drafting history of the Migrant Smuggling Protocol confirms that questions of assistance and protection for smuggled migrants were regularly raised throughout the drafting process, including in initial discussions.[82] However, while some States and regional groupings expressed a view that such matters should receive attention in the Protocol, most did not appear to consider this as a priority issue.[83] In its final version the Protocol includes a number of provisions aimed at protecting the basic rights of smuggled migrants and preventing

---

75 Ibid., Art. 15(1)–(2). The Article cross-references Article 31 of the Organized Crime Convention that, *inter alia*, requires States Parties to 'endeavour to promote public awareness regarding the existence, causes and gravity of and the threat posed by transnational organized crime'.
76 Migrant Smuggling Protocol, Art. 15(1).
77 Ibid., Preamble.
78 Ibid., Art. 10.
79 Ibid., Art. 18. Further, on the Protocol's provisions with respect to return, see *infra*.
80 Ibid., Arts 8, 11, 13–14.
81 Ibid., Art. 17.
82 The initial draft of the Migrant Smuggling Protocol submitted by Austria and Italy referred to 'illegal trafficking and transport of migrants' as 'a particularly heinous form of transnational exploitation of individuals in distress' in the Preamble: 'Draft elements for an international legal instrument against illegal trafficking and transport of migrants (Proposal submitted by Austria and Italy)', UN Doc. A/AC.254/4/Add.1, 15 Dec. 1998. Other discussions of the need to address the protection of smuggled migrants are noted in the *travaux préparatoires* with regard to the Preamble, the statement of purpose, the scope of application, the introduction of the aggravated offences, training, and the development of the specific 'protection' article: Travaux Préparatoires *for the Organized Crime Convention and Protocols*, pp. 453, 459, 461, 471–472, 486, 509, 520, 531–532, 537–540.
83 This was picked up by the UN High Commissioner for Human Rights, who was active in calling for greater attention to human rights in the Protocol. 'Informal note by the United Nations High Commissioner for Human Rights,' UN Doc. A/AC.254/16, 1 June 1999. See also 'Note by the Office of the United Nations High Commissioner for Human Rights, the Office of the United Nations High Commissioner for Refugees, the United Nations Children's Fund and the International Organization for Migration on the draft protocols concerning migrant smuggling and trafficking in persons,' UN Doc. A/AC.254/27, 8 Feb. 2000 (and UN Doc. A.AC.254/27/Corr.1, 22 Feb. 2000, correcting the title of that document).

the worst forms of exploitation that often accompany the smuggling process.[84] However, it is relevant to note the substantial differences between the carefully circumscribed provisions applicable to smuggled migrants and the entitlements provided for trafficked persons under the Protocol to Prevent, Suppress and Punish Trafficking in Persons, Especially Women and Children.[85] This is in keeping with the general consensus secured during the drafting process that smuggled migrants are not 'victims' in the same way that this term can be applied to those who have been trafficked.[86]

The limited protections granted to smuggled migrants are nevertheless significant. Most critically, migrants themselves are not to become liable to criminal prosecution under the Migrant Smuggling Protocol for the fact of having being smuggled.[87] The aggravated offences provision noted above represents further recognition of the human rights dimensions of migrant smuggling. Several additional provisions[88] reiterate and expand on the obligation to preserve and protect the rights of smuggled migrants.

The Migrant Smuggling Protocol also contains a broad savings clause to the effect that nothing in that instrument is to affect existing rights, obligations and responsibilities of States under international law, including international humanitarian law, international human rights law and, in particular, refugee law and the principle of *non-refoulement*.[89] The savings clause further requires the Protocol to be interpreted and applied in a way that is not discriminatory to smuggled migrants and that is 'consistent with internationally recognized principles of non-discrimination'.[90] The clause was hard won and secured virtually at the last minute.[91] Its significance – both symbolic and substantive – should not be underestimated. While a collision of norms could still occur (for example, between the obligation to act against smuggling of migrants and the obligation to ensure the rights of refugees and asylum seekers), the correct outcome has been clearly articulated: a State that acts against the letter or spirit of international law, including international refugee law, in implementing its obligations under the Migrant Smuggling Protocol is in violation of one of its central provisions.

---

84 Specific references to 'protecting' the rights of smuggled migrants are found in the Preamble ('Convinced of the need to provide migrants with humane treatment and full protection of their rights'), Article 2 ('The purpose of this Protocol is to prevent and combat the smuggling of migrants, as well as to promote cooperation among States Parties to that end, while protecting the rights of smuggled migrants'), Article 4 ('This Protocol shall apply . . . as well as to the protection of the rights of persons who have been the object of such offences'), Article 14(2) ('. . . Such training shall include . . . (e) The humane treatment of migrants and the protection of their rights as set forth in this Protocol'), and Article 16, titled, 'Prevention and assistance measures'.

85 Protocol to Prevent, Suppress and Punish Trafficking in Persons, Especially Women and Children, supplementing the United Nations Convention against Transnational Organized Crime, 2237 UNTS 319, done 15 November 2000, entered into force 25 December 2003.

86 Further, on the agreement secured during the drafting process to replace the term 'victim of smuggling' with 'smuggled migrant', and the legal implications of this change, see Gallagher and David, *The International Law of Migrant Smuggling*, Chapter 1.

87 Migrant Smuggling Protocol, Art. 5.

88 See *infra*.

89 Ibid., Art. 19(1). An Interpretative Note confirms that the Protocol does not cover the status of refugees. Travaux Préparatoires *for the Organized Crime Convention and Protocols*, p. 555.

90 Migrant Smuggling Protocol, Art. 19(2).

91 See further, A.T. Gallagher, 'Human Rights and Human Trafficking: Quagmire or Firm Ground? A Response to James Hathaway', *Virginia Journal of International Law*, 2009, vol. 49, no. 4, p. 789, pp. 840–841.

Key issues and overlaps

Introduction

As noted previously, the regime established under transnational criminal law to address the phenomenon of migrant smuggling represents only one part of the applicable legal framework. This section seeks to illustrate and expand on that point by examining the constellation of rules that govern several critical issues around State responses to migrant smuggling.

Maritime law: interdiction and rescue at sea

Migrants, including asylum seekers and refugees, have long turned to the sea to escape brutal regimes, humanitarian crises, hunger, poverty and unemployment. Smuggling by sea will often be the cheapest, or even the only option available to individuals who are forced or wish to move. It may also be just one part of a multi-stage journey that includes smuggling by air and across land borders. Sea travel for smuggled migrants is often dangerous, typically involving lengthy journeys on board overcrowded and barely functional vessels. While the data around smuggling-related fatalities is incomplete, available information appears to confirm that smuggling by sea carries with it a particularly high risk of death through drowning, suffocation, dehydration, starvation or violence. Smuggling by sea also places considerable strain on the search and rescue services of affected coastal States.[92]

Responses to migrant smuggling at sea take place against a complex legal landscape, comprised of cumulative rules and obligations imposed principally under the law of the sea as reinforced and occasionally supplemented by transnational criminal law, but also reflecting rules of international human rights law and refugee law. The core of many legal complexities in this area is jurisdiction. The oceans of the world are divided up into different areas, to which are attached different rights and responsibilities. Deciding which State has the capacity to act in a particular migrant-smuggling situation at sea, and establishing the correct limits on that capacity, is often very difficult. The allocation of responsibilities – toward smuggled refugees, for example, or toward smuggled migrants in distress – is similarly fraught, especially when two or more States are involved in a migrant smuggling response at sea or where the response is conducted under the banner of an international organization.

There are two ways in which States respond to migrant smuggling at sea. First, consistent with State sovereignty and the prerogative of border control, coastal States are *entitled* under certain circumstances to intercept or interdict vessels engaged in migrant smuggling at sea in order to prevent unauthorized migrants from entering their territory. Such law enforcement actions must take place in accordance with the law of the sea and other rules of international law, and within the bounds of any multilateral or bilateral agreement for interdiction of migrant smuggling at sea. Second, independently of interdiction, the law of the sea also *obliges* shipmasters and States to render assistance/rescue to any persons in distress at sea, including to smuggled migrants and migrant smugglers. The obligations of assistance under the law of the sea, including obligations of search and rescue, are motivated purely by humanitarian considerations and apply at all times in respect of any persons in distress at sea.

---

92 For detailed references see Gallagher and David, *The International Law of Migrant Smuggling*, Chapter 6.

Interdiction

Interdiction of vessels carrying smuggled migrants has become a central plank of the anti-smuggling response of many frontline coastal States. Sometimes interdiction is limited to the boarding, inspection and searching of a ship at sea suspected of being engaged in migrant smuggling. However, enforcement measures can extend further. For example, an interdiction could involve taking control of the vessel and either towing it to another regulatory zone (for example, from the territorial waters of the coastal State to the high seas), or returning it to the point of embarkation. A critical legal question that has occupied States, courts and scholars in recent years is if and when these so called 'push backs' constitute a legitimate form of law enforcement action. There is no clear answer to be found in the Migrant Smuggling Protocol or under the laws of the sea. The rules to be applied will depend on a wide range of factors including where the interdiction takes place; the status of the vessel; the status of the inter-dicting authority; and, of course, the conduct and outcome of the interdiction itself.

The rules governing enforcement action over vessels engaged in migrant smuggling gener-ally grant coastal States a wide degree of latitude to take law enforcement action in their national waters against foreign vessels engaged in migrant smuggling to or from that State. For example, a coastal State will usually be able to take law enforcement action within both its territorial sea and its contiguous zone against foreign-flagged vessels and vessels without nationality where this is necessary to prevent breaches of that State's immigration laws.[93] Action may also be taken against a foreign vessel by a coastal State in its territorial sea or contiguous zone through the exercise of the right of hot pursuit,[94] where suspected breaches of national law are involved.[95] In respect of flagged vessels, the consent of the flag State is not required in these situations. However, the capacity of States to unilaterally exercise law enforcement jurisdiction against flagged vessels in international waters is far more limited as such vessels are, with only narrow exceptions, subject to the exclusive jurisdiction of the flag State.[96]

These jurisdictional rules may be modified by consent, and considerable bilateral and multilateral efforts to address migrant smuggling have been directed to that end. For example, under the ship-rider model that has become a familiar feature of United States and European migration control, a State of origin/embarkation (State A) may conclude an agreement with a State of destination (State B) to permit an official of State A to be placed aboard an official vessel of State B. The official from State A is able to authorize an interdiction of a migrant smuggling vessel within the territorial waters of State A, enforcing State A's laws. A coastal or flag State may also permit another State to directly engage in interdictions in areas where that State has jurisdiction, for example agreeing to an official vessel from another State entering its territorial waters and interdicting vessels seeking to smuggle migrants through that maritime zone. International law permits States to give consent to other States to assume or share enforcement jurisdiction over a migrant smuggling vessel to the extent that the consenting State possesses the enforcement jurisdiction it grants to another. However, a State that consents to another State assuming or sharing enforcement jurisdiction over a migrant smuggling vessel

93 UNCLOS, Arts 19(2)(g), 21, 25, 33(1).
94 A right of hot pursuit effectively permits a coastal State to extend its sovereignty beyond a zone of existing enforcement jurisdiction by commencing and maintaining an uninterrupted pursuit of a fleeing vessel.
95 UNCLOS, Arts 33, 111.
96 Ibid., Art. 92.

may nevertheless be held responsible for unlawful acts that result from the exercise of enforcement jurisdiction. In relation to the examples given above, the involved States would be individually and jointly responsible for internationally wrongful acts that occur during or as the result of such interdiction.[97]

The vast majority of maritime vessels used to smuggle migrants are unregistered or improperly registered.[98] In relation to vessels without nationality suspected of carrying smuggled migrants, the Migrant Smuggling Protocol's requirements go beyond those set out in the law of the sea. As noted previously, States Parties that have reasonable grounds to suspect that a vessel without nationality is engaged in the smuggling of migrants by sea are empowered to board and search that vessel even if it is on the high seas and, if evidence of migrant smuggling is found, are required to take 'appropriate measures in accordance with relevant domestic and international law'.[99] The failure to specify what measures may be 'appropriate' means that the scope of enforcement jurisdiction that may be exercised in respect of a stateless vessel carrying smuggled migrants remains unclear.

Irrespective of the jurisdictional grounds for an interception and the maritime zone within which the interdiction takes place, international law requires that the use of force must be avoided as far as possible. When force is used it must be proportionate. Proportionality implies elements of both reasonableness and necessity.[100] Critically, as the Law of the Sea Tribunal has affirmed, '[c]onsiderations of humanity must apply in the law of the sea, as they do in other areas of international law.'[101] Applying these principles to the matter at hand, it becomes clear that States have a duty, when intercepting or otherwise dealing with a migrant smuggling vessel, its passengers and crew, to avoid using force that causes any unnecessary harm. Examples of unlawful use of force under this standard may include towing a boatload of distressed migrants in an overcrowded vessel back to the point of embarkation; or using weapons to move unwilling migrants from one vessel to another.

Human rights law provides an important, additional constraint on the use of force in responding to smuggling by sea. Recent developments appear to confirm that interdicting States will generally be held responsible under international law for violations of human rights that occur in relation to vessels or persons that are in some way or another under their authority or control, even if the relevant action or omission occurs outside the territorial jurisdiction of that State.[102] International rules relating to right to life, arbitrary detention, inhumane and degrading treatment and collective expulsion are particularly relevant to situations of interdiction and will bind all States engaged in interdiction irrespective of the purpose, circumstances or location of the interdiction.[103]

---

97 Further on State responsibility for joint operations see Gallagher and David, *The International Law of Migrant Smuggling*, Chapter 4.4.

98 See UN General Assembly, 'Oceans and the law of the sea: Report of the Secretary-General', UN Doc. A/53/456, 5 October 1998, at para. 135; and European Commission, Staff Working Document, 'Study on the International Law Instruments in Relation to Illegal Immigration by Sea', SEC(2007) 691, 15 May 2007, at para. 1.5.

99 Migrant Smuggling Protocol, Art. 8(7).

100 See generally D. Guilfoyle, *Shipping Interdiction and the Law of the Sea*, Cambridge: Cambridge University Press, 2009, pp. 280–282.

101 *M/V Saiga (No. 2) (St Vincent and the Grenadines v Guinea)*, International Tribunal for the Law of the Sea List of Cases: No. 2, 1 July 1999, [1999] ITLOS Rep 10, at para. 155.

102 For a detailed examination of these developments see Gallagher and David, *The International Law of Migrant Smuggling*, Chapter 6.3.

103 Ibid.

While interception of smuggled migrants on the high seas does not, of itself, violate the refugee law prohibition on *refoulement*, it is reasonable to assert that such actions may not result in asylum seekers and refugees being denied access to international protection, or result in persons in need of international protection being returned to a situation in which they are at risk of persecution or serious violations of human rights. However, the question of whether the obligation of *non-refoulement* automatically applies to interceptions that take place outside the territory of an intercepting State has not been settled. While the United Nations High Commissioner for Refugees (UNHCR) and many scholars have affirmed the extraterritorial application of the obligation of *non-refoulement*,[104] State practice in this area is ambiguous. In short, there is not yet strong evidence for State consent to an understanding of the obligation that extends to asylum seekers who are not at the borders or physically within the territory of the State.

Rescue at sea

In the context of migrant smuggling the lines between search and rescue and interdiction are often blurred, and rescue operations may coincide with or transform into operations to interdict or otherwise divert migrant smuggling vessels. However, the relevant rules are very different: the legal framework that governs rescue at sea does not apply to interception operations that have no search and rescue component.[105] At the same time, the right of States to regulate migration, including through interdiction, in no way displaces the duty of States and shipmasters to provide assistance to persons in distress at sea.[106]

International law has long required States and their shipmasters to render assistance to any person or vessel in distress at sea. This obligation, which applies to all States through a combination of customary and treaty law,[107] operates at all times and in all maritime zones. It extends to all persons and vessels regardless of nationality, legal status or any other difference. The obligation is subject to practical contingencies of safety and reasonableness, and the scope of required assistance should be commensurate with the nature and severity of the distress.

The obligation on shipmasters to render assistance and rescue at sea is supplemented by requirements on coastal and port States regarding search and rescue. The relevant legal

---

104 UN High Commissioner for Refugees, *Advisory Opinion on the Extraterritorial Application of Non-Refoulement Obligations under the 1951 Convention Relating to the Status of Refugees and its 1967 Protocol* (26 January 2007).

105 UN High Commissioner for Refugees, 'Expert Meeting on Refugees and Asylum-Seekers in Distress at Sea – How Best to Respond? Djibouti, 8–10 November 2011', *International Journal of Refugee Law*, 2012, vol. 24, no. 2, p. 485.

106 R. Barnes, 'The International Law of the Sea and Migration Control', in B. Ryan and V. Mitsilegas (eds), *Extraterritorial Immigration Control: Legal Challenges*, The Hague: Martinus Nijhoff, 2010, p. 103, p. 134.

107 UNCLOS, at Art. 98; Convention on the High Seas, 450 UNTS 11, done 29 April 1958, entered into force 30 September 1962, Art. 12. On the customary basis of the obligation see, generally, M. Pallis, 'Obligations of States towards Asylum Seekers at Sea: Interactions and Conflicts between Legal Regimes', *International Journal of Refugee Law*, 2002, vol. 14, p. 329, pp. 333–334; and B.H. Oxman, 'Human Rights and the United Nations Convention on the Law of the Sea', *Columbia Journal of Transnational Law*, 1998, vol. 36, p. 399. Fife argues that the obligation reflects 'elementary considerations of humanity' as a general principle of law and therefore as a source of law in its own right: R.E. Fife, 'The Duty to Render Assistance at Sea: Some Reflections after Tampa', in J. Petman and J. Klabbers (eds), *Nordic Cosmopolitanism: Essays in International law for Martti Koskenniemi*, The Hague: Martinus Nijhoff, 2003, p. 469, pp. 470–471, 482.

framework around maritime rescue of persons or vessels in distress comprises UNCLOS and two widely ratified treaties: the much-amended 1974 International Convention for the Safety of Life at Sea[108] and the 1979 International Convention on Maritime Search and Rescue.[109] Port and coastal States are required to establish search and rescue services aimed at coordinating the rescue of persons in distress at sea around their coasts.[110] Amendments to the key instruments that entered into force in 2004 following the *Tampa* incident[111] affirmed a number of additional obligations on port and coastal States, including a duty to ensure that masters of ships providing assistance to persons in distress at sea are relieved from their responsibilities as soon as practicable and that the involved States cooperate with the ship's master in delivering persons rescued at sea to a place of safety. The amendments further clarified that the State in whose Search and Rescue Region[112] the assistance is rendered is to take primary responsibility for ensuring such coordination and cooperation occurs, so that survivors assisted are disembarked from the assisting ship and delivered to a place of safety. While adding a measure of substance to the relevant obligations, the amendments have not resolved problems related to dysfunctional search and rescue zones and uncertainty and disagreement around whether and when coastal States may deny disembarkation of rescued smuggled migrants.

Human rights: protection and return

Human rights are central to the issue of migrant smuggling: first because they impose important limitations on how States may respond to smuggling, but also because human rights law confers certain legal entitlements on all persons, including smuggled migrants, that States and

---

108 International Convention for the Safety of Life at Sea, 1974, as amended, 1184 UNTS 278, done 1 November 1974, entered into force 25 May 1980.

109 International Convention on Maritime Search and Rescue, 1979, with annexes, 1405 UNTS 97, done 27 April 1979, entered into force 22 June 1985 (SAR Convention). The SAR Convention was amended in 1998 by IMO Resolution MSC.70(69) ('Amendments to the International Convention on Maritime Search and Rescue, 1979'), and again in 2004 by IMO Resolution MSC.155(78) ('Adoption of Amendments to the International Convention on Maritime Search and Rescue, 1979, as amended'). References to the SAR Convention are to the consolidated text.

110 UNCLOS, Art. 98.

111 This incident involved a Norwegian registered tanker, the *MV Tampa*, travelling from Western Australia towards Singapore, which, following a request by Australian authorities, rescued 438 smuggled asylum seekers from a vessel in distress. After pressure from the rescued migrants, the master of the vessel changed course for Australia. The vessel was instructed by Australian authorities to stop before it entered the Australian territorial sea and the master was threatened with prosecution for 'people smuggling' offences if he did not comply. Requests for medical and other assistance were not met for two days until a formal distress call was issued. The master then entered Australian territorial waters without permission, stating that his vessel was unseaworthy for travel to Indonesia and that some passengers were in extreme medical distress. Australian military personnel boarded the vessel and denied disembarkation to the rescued passengers. Further on the facts of this case and its impact on rules around search and rescue see Gallagher and David, *The International Law of Migrant Smuggling*, Introduction and Chapter 6.

112 The 1979 SAR Convention was developed with the aim of establishing an internationally agreed search and rescue plan that would cover the world's oceans. The Convention foreshadowed the establishment of Search and Rescue Regions by agreement as well as the establishment of national Rescue Coordination Centers that would be responsible for search and rescue operations within these zones (SAR Convention, at Annex, Rule 2.1.4). After its entry into force, the world's oceans were divided into thirteen such regions. The location of the rescue operation determines which State's Rescue Coordination Center is responsible for coordination of the rescue operation including delivery of any persons in distress to a 'place of safety'.

others are obliged to protect and respect. In relation to particular fundamental rights, such as the right to life and the prohibition on torture and inhumane treatment, the relevant entitlements are owed to all smuggled migrants (and indeed to all migrant smugglers), without distinction on any grounds including race, nationality or immigration status. Other rights may attach to a smuggled migrant by virtue of that person's particular status – for example as a child, a woman, a refugee, a person with disability, a victim of trafficking, or indeed a victim of crime or of human rights violations.

Protection of smuggled migrants

Persons who have been or are being smuggled are highly vulnerable to ill-treatment, violence, exploitation and life-threatening situations. For some persons, the act of smuggling may operate to enhance existing vulnerabilities. Children, particularly those who are unaccompanied, face risks of exploitation and abuse, and smuggled women migrants are at risk of violence, including sexual violence. For all smuggled migrants, the clandestine nature of their journey, the often unscrupulous and corrupt conduct of their facilitators and collaborators, and the extent to which some States will go to prevent their departure, transit or arrival, all operate to create or exacerbate serious risks to personal security and well-being.

Despite these grim realities, the status of 'smuggled migrant' has not been elevated to a legal category to which any special or additional rights are attached. In other words, a State will not necessarily owe different or extra obligations to a person merely because they are being, or have been, smuggled. The question of whether a positive obligation of protection and assistance exists toward smuggled migrants requires a consideration of general rules and instruments of international and regional human rights law, as well as of instruments dealing particularly with migrant smuggling and related issues, such as irregular migration and border management.

As noted previously, human rights protections under the Migrant Smuggling Protocol are equivocal and carefully circumscribed, a reflection of the fundamental tension that underlies its potentially conflicting purposes of addressing smuggling and protecting migrants. By withholding 'victim' status from smuggled migrants who have not otherwise been subject to abuse or exploitation, those persons are *prima facie* excluded from the special protections afforded to victims of crime and human rights violations under international law including transnational criminal law.

However, a number of important protections have been preserved. Most critically, migrants themselves are not to become liable to criminal prosecution under the Protocol for the fact of having being smuggled:[113] a direct and welcome affirmation that the purpose of the Migrant Smuggling Protocol is not to punish irregular migration or smuggled migrants. Of course, as noted previously, this concession does not provide blanket immunity to those who have been smuggled. While States may not use the Protocol to criminalize smuggled migrants, they retain full capacity to prosecute such persons under their national law for any acts that may be criminalized, such as illegal entry, illegal stay and the possession of fraudulent travel documents.[114]

---

113 Migrant Smuggling Protocol, Art. 5. The non-criminalization of smuggled migrants was raised even in the earliest stages of drafting: the original draft text of the Protocol submitted by Austria and Italy refers to 'Establishing a principle of penal sanctions against the perpetrators but not the victims', Letter dated 16 September, 1997 from the Permanent Representative of Austria to the United Nations addressed to the Secretary-General, UN Doc. A/52/357, 17 Sept. 1997, at para. 3.
114 UNODC, *Legislative Guide*, p. 340 (paras 27–28).

The main protection and assistance provisions of the Migrant Smuggling Protocol are set out in a provision which is 'intended to set an appropriate standard of conduct for officials who deal with smuggled migrants and illegal residents and to deter conduct on the part of offenders that involves danger or degradation to the migrants'.[115] Article 16 subjects its various obligations to the umbrella requirement that States Parties take into account the special needs of women and children.[116] Fortunately, the existing legal framework around the rights of children provides important guidance on ascertaining 'the special needs of children' and determining how those rights can be integrated into all aspects of a smuggled child's experience; from the provision of protection and assistance to the question of detention and return.[117] The situation is less clear in respect of smuggled women migrants, and there is very little useful guidance available on how this particular obligation could be met, or indeed how its implementation could be effectively judged.[118]

The first part of Article 16 of the Migrant Smuggling Protocol deals with the responsibility of States Parties, when implementing the Protocol, to preserve and protect the rights of smuggled migrants under international law. Specific reference is made to a number of pre-existing human rights (the right to life and to freedom from torture and other inhuman or degrading treatment or punishment) and their continued applicability to smuggled migrants.[119] The obligation to preserve the rights of smuggled migrants when implementing the Protocol is reinforced by a requirement that specialized training in combating migrant smuggling is to focus on humane treatment of smuggled migrants and protection of their Protocol rights.[120]

Article 16 sets out three additional obligations of protection and assistance: States Parties are required to:

- take appropriate measures to protect smuggled migrants from smuggling-related violence 'whether by individuals or groups';[121]
- provide assistance to migrants whose lives or safety are endangered through smuggling;[122] and
- in respect of detained smuggled migrants, ensure their right to be informed of consular access.[123]

---

115 Ibid., p. 364 (para. 69).
116 Migrant Smuggling Protocol, Art. 16(4).
117 Further on the protection and assistance of smuggled children see Gallagher and David, *The International Law of Migrant Smuggling*, Chapters 8.2.1 (protection), 9.4.3 (detention) and 10.5.2 (return).
118 The drafting history of the Protocol does not provide insight and the UNODC *Legislative Guide* is silent on the point of how States may implement this provision.
119 Migrant Smuggling Protocol, Art. 16(1). The *Travaux Préparatoires* confirm that: '[t]he intention in listing certain rights in this paragraph was to emphasize the need to protect those rights in the case of smuggled migrants, but the provision should not be interpreted as excluding or derogating from any other rights not listed. Travaux Préparatoires *for the Organized Crime Convention and Protocols*, p. 541. However, the limits of the provision are also clearly noted with a confirmation that it: 'should not be understood as imposing any new or additional obligations on States parties to this protocol beyond those contained in existing international instruments and customary international law'. Ibid.
120 Migrant Smuggling Protocol, Arts 14(1), 14(2)(e).
121 Ibid., Art. 16(2).
122 Ibid., Art 16(3). Note that States Parties are required to make smuggling offences that involve danger to the lives of migrants or that entail degrading treatment or exploitation into aggravating circumstances: ibid., Art. 6(3).
123 Ibid., Art. 16(5).

The Migrant Smuggling Protocol's savings clause has been previously noted but deserves to be flagged again at this point. Its intention and effect is to preserve existing rights, obligations and responsibilities of States Parties under international law, including international humanitarian law, international human rights law and, in particular, refugee law and the principle of *non-refoulement*.[124] The savings clause also requires the Protocol to be interpreted and applied in a way that is not discriminatory to smuggled migrants and that is 'consistent with internationally recognized principles of non-discrimination'.[125] This provision would operate to prohibit, for example, discriminatory treatment with a negative intent or outcome between different groups of smuggled migrants on the basis of, for instance, their national or ethnic origin or indeed their status as asylum seekers or refugees. It could arguably also extend to prohibit discriminatory treatment of different groups of smuggled migrants, reflecting their different modes of arrival. For example, some countries have established dual systems whereby those who arrive by air are subject to different procedures than those who arrive by sea, with potentially discriminatory results.[126]

Regional law and policy also affirms obligations of protection in relation to smuggled migrants. A useful example is the 2011 Fundamental Rights Strategy of Frontex: the European Border Agency.[127] The Strategy contains a detailed set of rights-based commitments to protection and assistance and sets out a number of measures to promote a rights-based approach to the work of the Agency. However, while identifying groups at particular risk (including unaccompanied children, women and trafficked persons), the Strategy follows the lead of the Migrant Smuggling Protocol in avoiding articulation of any protection or assistance obligations with respect to smuggled migrants who have been or are at risk of abuse or exploitation.[128]

Finally, it is important to note the specialist instruments of international human rights law as a separate and substantive source of legal obligation with respect to obligations of protection and assistance owed to all smuggled migrants. These instruments will often be of most immediate relevance to smuggled migrants who are in danger or who experience violence and exploitation. For example, the right to life[129] will require States to take positive steps to protect smuggled migrants from xenophobic violence, or from situations of extreme danger such as a threatened sinking of their vessel. Human rights instruments will also be of direct

---

124 Ibid., Art. 19(1). An Interpretative Note confirms that the Protocol does not cover the status of refugees. Travaux Préparatoires *for the Organized Crime Convention and Protocols*, p. 555.

125 Migrant Smuggling Protocol, Art. 19(2).

126 See for example, the discussion on children held by Australia in immigration detention on mainland Australia, and on those sent to Pacific Islands, with this decision resting solely on how they arrived in Australia in Australian Human Rights Commission, 'A last resort? The National Inquiry into Children in Immigration Detention', May 2004, available at www.humanrights.gov.au/publications/last-resort (accessed 13 December 2013), 7.8.3.

127 European Agency for the Management of Operational Cooperation at the External Borders of the Member States of the European Union, *Frontex Fundamental Rights Strategy* (2011).

128 For a useful insight into risks and shortcomings that have not been fully addressed by the Frontex Fundamental Rights Strategy, see Council of Europe, Parliamentary Assembly, Resolution 1932 (2013) Final version 'Frontex: human rights responsibilities,' adopted 25 April 2013, esp. at paras 8–10.

129 The right to life is enshrined in the Universal Declaration of Human Rights, adopted by GA Res. 217A (III), UN GAOR, 3rd sess., 183rd plen. mtg, UN Doc. A/810, at 71, 10 Dec. 1948 (UDHR) (Article 3); protected as a non-derogable right through International Covenant on Civil and Political Rights, 999 UNTS 171, done 16 December 1996, entered into force 23 March 1976 (ICCPR) (Article 6(1)), and all major regional human rights instruments.

relevance with respect to particular categories of smuggled migrants such as children. However, human rights instruments are not just relevant in these limited situations: they provide important guidance for the treatment of all smuggled migrants who come within the jurisdiction of the State. For example, the prohibition on cruel, inhuman or degrading treatment or punishment[130] will constrain the way in which States treat smuggled migrants who have been rescued, apprehended or detained and the way in which decisions are taken about their return (as discussed further below). The rights to food and shelter will further dictate the way in which the basic needs of smuggled migrants are assessed and met by the State.[131] The right to an adequate standard of health will require States to ensure that smuggled migrants, particularly those in need of emergency assistance, are able to access medical care and treatment.[132]

Return of smuggled migrants

The core obligation of the Migrant Smuggling Protocol does not *require* return but is rather directed at States Parties of origin, which are to facilitate and accept, without delay, the return of their smuggled nationals and those who have a right of permanent abode within their territories.[133] To that end States Parties may request each other to verify the nationality or right of permanent residence of a smuggled migrant, and the Requested State is required to provide such verification without undue or unreasonable delay.[134] A State Party so requested is also required to issue any travel documents or authorizations required for the smuggled migrant to enter its territory.[135] States Parties carrying out return of smuggled migrants are required to 'take all appropriate measures to carry out the return in an orderly manner and with due regard for the safety and dignity of the person'.[136]

Of course the rules around return of smuggled migrants are much more complex and nuanced than those set out in the Migrant Smuggling Protocol. Certainly international law preserves the right of States to return/expel irregular migrants, including those who have been smuggled. However, such return must be in conformity with certain legal obligations that are principally derived from rules of human rights and refugee law. Failure to observe those obligations renders the return of a smuggled migrant to his or her country of origin, or to a third country, an internationally wrongful act.

---

130 The prohibition of torture is recognized as a fundamental rule of international law from which there may be no derogation. It is enshrined in the Convention against Torture and Other Cruel, Inhuman or Degrading Treatment or Punishment, 1465 UNTS 85, done 10 December 1984, entered into force 26 June 1987 (Convention against Torture), as well as all major regional human rights instruments.

131 For a useful and detailed overview of how these rights operate in the context of asylum seekers and refugees (a category to which many smuggled migrants belong) see J.C. Hathaway, *The Rights of Refugees under International Law*, Cambridge: Cambridge University Press, 2005, pp. 471–507.

132 Ibid., pp. 507–514. The link between the right to life and access to life-saving medical care is noted in the UNODC Model Law on Migrant Smuggling, pp. 65–67.

133 Migrant Smuggling Protocol, Art. 18(1).

134 Ibid., Art. 18(3). The *travaux préparatoires* indicate that 'return under this article shall not be undertaken before the nationality or right of permanent residence of the person whose return is sought has been duly verified': Travaux Préparatoires *for the Organized Crime Convention and Protocols*, p. 552.

135 Migrant Smuggling Protocol, Art. 18(4).

136 Ibid., Art. 18(5).

Arbitrary expulsion

International law prohibits the *arbitrary expulsion* of persons who are 'lawfully present' within the country.[137] Smuggled migrants are, by definition, present without authorization in the country of arrival and it will therefore only be in relation to smuggled asylum seekers that the status of 'lawful presence' will have any chance of being established. Presuming lawful presence can be established (and it is not universally accepted that persons who have entered a country without authorization for purposes of claiming asylum are 'lawfully present'), the expulsion of such persons will be characterized as 'arbitrary' and therefore unlawful if the expulsion decision is not made in accordance with national law and with relevant international rules.

Collective expulsion

International law also prohibits measures compelling non-nationals, as a group or groups, to leave a State or the territory of a State except where such measures are taken on the basis of a reasonable and objective examination of the particular case of *each individual member* of the group.[138] This rule applies to asylum seekers even if the collective expulsion does not result in a violation of the rule of *non-refoulement*.[139] Interceptions and turn-backs at sea without individualized assessment can be characterized as violating the prohibition on collective expulsion even when undertaken outside the territory of the State (for example, on the high seas).

The obligation of non-refoulement

With only limited exceptions, no person, including a smuggled migrant, may be expelled or returned 'in any manner whatsoever to the frontiers of territories where his life or freedom would be threatened on account of his race, religion, nationality, membership of a particular social group or political opinion'.[140] Further, international human rights law prohibits the

---

137 See, for example, ICCPR, Art. 13.

138 UN Human Rights Committee, 'General Comment No. 15: The Position of Aliens under the Covenant', UN Doc. HRI/GEN.1/Rev.7, at 140, 12 May 2004, adopted 11 April 1986 (hereafter: HRC General Comment No. 15), at para. 9. See further Gallagher and David, *The International Law of Migrant Smuggling*, Chapter 10.

139 See, for example, Protocol No. 4 to the Convention of 4 November 1950 for the Protection of Human Rights and Fundamental Freedoms, 1496 UNTS 263, done 16 September 1963, entered into force 2 May 1968, Art. 4 ('Collective expulsion of aliens is prohibited'); American Convention on Human Rights, 1144 UNTS 123, 22 November 1969, entered into force 18 July 1978, Art. 22(9) ('The collective expulsion of aliens is prohibited'); African Charter on Human and Peoples' Rights, 1520 UNTS 217, done 27 June 1981, entered into force 21 October 1986, Art. 12(5) ('The mass expulsion of non-nationals shall be prohibited' and '[m]ass expulsion shall be that which is aimed at national, racial, ethnic or religious groups'). Note that while the ICCPR does not refer specifically to collective expulsion, the Human Rights Committee has interpreted Article 13 of that instrument as prohibiting such expulsion. HRC General Comment No. 15, at para. 10.

140 A recognized refugee who constitutes a threat to national security or public order; or in relation to whom there are reasonable grounds for regarding them as a danger to security; or who, having been convicted of a serious crime, constitutes a danger to the community, may not benefit from the Refugee Convention protections against expulsion and *non-refoulement*. Convention Relating to the Status of Refugees, 189 UNTS 137, done 28 July 1951, entered into force 22 April 1954, as amended by the Protocol relating to the Status of Refugees, 606 UNTS 267, done 31 January 1967, entered into force 4 October 1967, Arts 32 and 33.

return of any person, including a smuggled migrant, to a situation where he or she faces a real risk of torture or other serious violations of human rights.[141] It is important to recognize that many anti-smuggling measures, from interdiction at sea, to the creation of special zones at airports, to 'safe third country' arrangements, have practical implications for the obligation of *non-refoulement*. There is growing recognition that the obligation of *non-refoulement* applies in any area or space where the State exercises effective control.[142] In relation to arrangements with other countries, the test will generally be whether a return exposes the person concerned to the risk of subsequent *refoulement*.

Obligation to accept and facilitate return

International law protects the right of all persons to return home,[143] and smuggled migrants are entitled to exercise that right. This right imposes a corresponding obligation on States of origin (affirmed in the Migrant Smuggling Protocol) to accept returning nationals and to facilitate such return without undue delay. To that end they should cooperate with the returning State in relation to both identification and the issuing of necessary travel documents. These general obligations may be extended or modified by bilateral or regional readmission agreements. However, all such agreements are subject to the obligation of *non-refoulement* and related protections.

An otherwise lawful return may be rendered unlawful by the manner in which it is carried out. Smuggled migrants may be entitled to certain due process rights, including the right to challenge the decision related to return. Where such entitlement exists, these procedural rights must be recognized and granted. Any pre-return detention must not be punitive and must be in conformity with established rules, including the prohibitions on discrimination and on torture and cruel or inhuman treatment. The conduct of the return itself must also not violate established rules, including those same prohibitions. The use of excessive force in compelling a return is prohibited.[144]

International law also provides certain status-based entitlements that may be relevant to decisions about the return of smuggled migrants. For example, smuggled children and smuggled migrants who have been trafficked are entitled to special and additional rights that may preclude an otherwise lawful return or modify the way in which a return decision is taken or implemented.

---

141 Convention against Torture, Art. 3(1). Regional human rights instruments provide similar protections. See, for example, Charter of Fundamental Rights of the European Union, OJ C 364/1, 18 December 2000, done 7 December 2000, entered into force 1 December 2009, Art. 19(2) ('No one may be removed, expelled or extradited to a State where there is a serious risk that he or she would be subjected to the death penalty, torture or other inhuman or degrading treatment or punishment'). Note that smuggled migrants who are refused refugee status or excluded from the benefit of the refugee law prohibition on *refoulement* on one of the grounds stipulated in the previous note are still entitled to this protection.
142 For a detailed examination of the extraterritorial application of the obligation of *non-refoulement* see Gallagher and David, *The International Law of Migrant Smuggling*, Chapter 3.4.4.
143 The right of return is established in the UDHR (Article 13(2)) and is affirmed in the ICCPR (Article 12(4)).
144 For a detailed consideration of each of these points see Gallagher and David, *The International Law of Migrant Smuggling*, Chapter 10.4.

Conclusion

In December 2000, the international community confirmed migrant smuggling as an issue of common concern and as a legitimate focus for legal and operational cooperation between States. New legal instruments developed within the field of transnational criminal law imposed highly specific obligations on States to criminalize migrant smuggling within their domestic legal orders and to ensure that structures and processes are in place to enable inter-state cooperation. Of course, those rules did not emerge and do not operate in a vacuum. Other areas of international law, including the law of the sea, human rights and refugee law, and general rules around jurisdiction and responsibility, provide additional substance to the specialist obligations and dictate the parameters of State capacity to act against migrant smuggling. The key tasks of the international lawyer – understanding what States must and may not do in the name of addressing 'migrant smuggling'; identifying practices that are unlawful; confirming specific rights that attach to persons who have been smuggled; and calling States to account for violation of established rules – all require consideration of the full range of applicable norms. That process – ascertaining the relevant rules and ensuring they are applied correctly – is important because international law is ultimately a tool for change. As a collective expression of how things ought to be, it seeks to positively influence the behaviour of States. Practitioners of international law 'have power over the law, the only thing that can have power over the government.'[145]

It remains to repeat the observation made in the introduction to this chapter: international law may be central but it is ultimately just one part of the migrant-smuggling mosaic. In this area, as in all others, the relevant legal framework cannot be considered in isolation from broader political, social and economic forces that gave rise to and shaped its development, and that will ultimately determine its future. A nuanced understanding of those forces is essential to an appreciation of both the possibilities and limitations of the relevant international rules as well as to identifying opportunities for much needed change.

---

145 P. Allott, 'State Responsibility and the Unmaking of International Law', *Harvard International Law Journal*, 1988, vol. 291, p. 25.

13

Child sex tourism

*Lindsay Buckingham**

Introduction

The exploitation of children by travelling child sex offenders – child sex tourism – is a crime type that fits squarely within the wider body of transnational criminal law. Yet the key international obligations requiring states to implement criminal justice responses to child sex tourism are contained in human rights treaties – the Convention on the Rights of the Child[1] (CRC) and its Optional Protocol on the Sale of Children, Child Prostitution and Child Pornography[2] (Optional Protocol) – which define the measures required to build a strong legal and law enforcement response to child sex tourism. Notwithstanding the importance of human rights-based approaches to child protection in this context, the grave nature of criminal conduct associated with child sex tourism, the cross-border element of the crime, and the global drive to ensure perpetrators are brought to justice mean that international approaches must also focus on promoting effective and coordinated criminal justice responses.

There are clear links between child sex tourism and other forms of child exploitation and abuse. In particular, trafficking in children and the worst forms of child labour, when carried out for the purpose of sexual exploitation, can intersect with child sex tourism. The development in the 1990s of the Protocol to Prevent, Suppress and Punish Trafficking in Persons, Especially Women and Children (Trafficking Protocol)[3] and the International Labour

---

★   Principal Legal Officer with the Transnational Crime and Corruption Branch, Australian Government Attorney-General's Department. She has previously worked as a consultant on child sex tourism, trafficking in persons and migrant smuggling projects with the UNODC, Regional Centre for East Asia and the Pacific. The views expressed in this chapter are entirely those of the author, and should not be taken to reflect the views of the Australian Government or the United Nations.
1   Convention on the Rights of the Child, opened for signature 20 November 1989, 1577 UNTS 3; in force 2 September 1990 (CRC).
2   Optional Protocol to the Convention on the Rights of the Child on the Sale of Children, Child Prostitution and Child Pornography, opened for signature 25 May 2000, 2171 UNTS 227; in force 18 January 2002 (Optional Protocol).
3   Protocol to Prevent, Suppress and Punish Trafficking in Persons, Especially Women and Children, supplementing the United Nations Convention against Transnational Organized Crime, opened for signature 15 November 2000, 2237 UNTS 319; in force 25 December 2003 (Trafficking Protocol).

Organization's Convention Concerning the Prohibition and Immediate Action for the Elimination of the Worst Forms of Child Labour (1999) (ILO Convention 182),[4] timed almost in unison with the drafting of the Optional Protocol to the CRC, reflected the broader global movement at that time towards eradicating all forms of child sexual exploitation. Like many transnational crimes, including trafficking in persons, child sex tourism often involves a cross-border element, but this does not always occur and movement across borders is not a required element of the crime. Indeed, we know that some travelling child sex offenders seek to exploit children within their own home country. However, it is the cross-border element that poses some of the greatest challenges to achieving effective implementation of the international obligations. With this transnational feature, unified law enforcement networks and harmonized laws become essential tools for combating child sex tourism. Where there are gaps in law enforcement capability or legal frameworks, offenders will seek to exploit these gaps and will escape with impunity. Measures that seek to proactively address these gaps are critical to ensure children are protected, and offenders are brought to justice.

What is child sex tourism?

There is currently no internationally agreed legal definition of child sex tourism,[5] and understanding the true nature and scope of the crime can be challenging. Recent research undertaken by the United Nations Special Rapporteur on the Sale of Children, Child Prostitution and Child Pornography indicates an absence of robust data on both victims and perpetrators of child sex tourism.[6] As part of the Special Rapporteur's study, all UN member states were asked to complete a questionnaire on child sex tourism. Thirty-five states responded to the questionnaire, representing a wide cross-section of cultures and geographical regions.[7] However, only four were able to share data specifically on the prosecution of travelling child sex offenders.[8] The Special Rapporteur observed that there appeared to be a lack of understanding, and some misperceptions, about child sex tourism, which may have contributed to the limitations on available data and research material.[9] This observation reflects the views of the NGO ECPAT International,[10] which has also noted that confusion on the issue can result in incorrect classification of child sex tourism cases as other types of child abuse or exploitation.[11] The reluctance of some authorities to acknowledge the existence and extent of child sex tourism, potentially arising from concern that highlighting the problem could negatively impact the local tourism industry, was also noted by ECPAT International.[12] The limited capacity of criminal justice authorities in many countries where child sex tourism is known to

---

4 Convention Concerning the Prohibition and Immediate Action for the Elimination of the Worst Forms of Child Labour, opened for signature 17 June 1999, 2007 ATS 38; in force 19 November 2000 (ILO Convention 182).

5 ChildWise, *Travelling Child Sex Offenders in South East Asia: A Regional Review* (2008), p. 3.

6 N.M. M'jid, Report of the Special Rapporteur on the sale of children, child prostitution and child pornography, UN Doc. A/HRC/22/54, 24 December 2012, p. 6. See also: ECPAT International, *Combating Child Sex Tourism: Questions and Answers*, Bangkok, 2008, p. 7.

7 M'jid, Report of the Special Rapporteur, p. 4.

8 Ibid., p.6.

9 Ibid.

10 ECPAT International is a global network aiming to end child prostitution, child pornography and the trafficking of children for sexual purposes.

11 ECPAT International, *Combating Child Sex Tourism*, p. 7.

12 Ibid.

thrive is also a relevant factor. Without sufficient resources or technical expertise, law enforcement and prosecuting agencies cannot monitor and report thoroughly on the true nature and extent of child sex tourism, and struggle to keep pace with this constantly evolving crime.

There is a growing cohort of states, international organizations and non-governmental organizations (NGOs) dedicated to overcoming these challenges. The recent development of international standards requiring the domestic criminalization of child sex tourism is part of this global project. In light of the lack of a legal definition, this section provides a brief overview of child sex tourism – including some common definitions and known features of the crime – to facilitate the understanding of its nature and its relevance to transnational criminal law.

How is child sex tourism defined?

In simple terms, 'child sex tourism' refers to the sexual exploitation or sexual abuse of children by travelling child sex offenders (individuals who offend in locations away from their usual place of residence). Although there is currently no internationally settled definition, key institutions have provided their interpretations of the term. For example, the United Nations Special Rapporteur recently stated:

> The commercial sexual exploitation of children in travel and tourism (child sex tourism, CST) is the exploitation of children for sexual purposes by people who travel locally or internationally to engage in sexual activities with children. CST often involves the use of travel agencies, transport, accommodation and other tourism-related services that facilitate contact with children.[13]

The Special Rapporteur describes child sex tourism as being a specific form of the commercial sexual exploitation of children, and notes its close links with other forms of exploitation of children including trafficking, prostitution and pornography.[14] This interpretation is consistent with the links drawn between child sex tourism and the sale of children, child prostitution and child pornography in the Preamble to the Optional Protocol to the CRC.

An early definition developed by ECPAT International describes child sex tourism as:

> the sexual exploitation of children by a person or persons who travel from their home district, home geographical region, or home country in order to have sexual contact with children. Child sex tourists can be domestic travellers or they can be international tourists. [Child sex tourism] often involves the use of accommodation, transportation and other tourism-related services that facilitate contact with children and enable the perpetrator to remain fairly inconspicuous in the surrounding population and environment.[15]

Like the Special Rapporteur's definition, ECPAT International's definition is broad and descriptive. Both identify travel – either domestically or across international borders – as a key element. They also draw a direct link between the act of travelling and an active intention to have sexual contact with children – either travelling *to engage in* sexual activities with children (UN Special Rapporteur) or travelling *in order to* have sexual contact with children

---

13 M'jid, Report of the Special Rapporteur, p. 5.
14 Ibid.
15 ECPAT International, *Combating Child Sex Tourism*, p. 6.

(ECPAT International). This element is problematic, as it assumes that offenders always travel with the intention of having sexual contact with children. These descriptions cover only offenders who plan their abuse of children, and fail to recognize that the majority of offenders take advantage of an opportunity to sexually exploit a child, but do not plan for it in advance (often referred to as 'situational offenders').[16]

As global awareness of child sex tourism evolves, it is important that the definitions used by international organizations reflect our modern understanding. It is clear that neither the Special Rapporteur nor ECPAT International intended to exclude situational offenders – both refer to this type of conduct in their reports.[17] More recently ECPAT International has published a revised definition of child sex tourism which clearly includes situational offenders:

> Child sex tourism occurs when an individual travels, either within their own country or internationally, and engages in sexual acts with a child. Child sex tourists may be preferential abusers, who deliberately seek out children for sex, or may be situational abusers, who engage in sexual acts with children out of experimentation often fuelled by opportunity or a feeling of anonymity as a result of being away from their home. The rapid and global growth of low cost air travel, for example, has made airfares comparatively more accessible and so new and emerging destinations are within reach of a high number of tourists, including potential perpetrators of child sex crimes.[18]

The crafting of these different definitions reflects broader challenges associated with clearly defining child sex tourism. It also highlights the importance of developing a clear understanding of the term for the purpose of developing appropriate legal and policy responses to child sex tourism. For example, if domestic law reflected the Special Rapporteur's description of child sex tourism and required, as an element of an offence, to establish that a person travelled with the specific purpose of having sexual contact with children, the majority of offenders could never be prosecuted.

The debate around terminology is alive and well. Some organizations prefer not to use the term 'child sex tourism', noting that use of the term 'tourism' can be misleading – either because it connotes activities that may be acceptable or condoned, or suggests that the sexual exploitation of children by travelling child sex offenders occurs within the tourism sector alone.[19] Alternative terms, used in particular by NGOs, include 'sexual exploitation in travel and tourism'. Without making any comment on the appropriateness of particular terminology, this chapter uses the term 'child sex tourism' for consistency with the terminology contained in the Optional Protocol and used by the UN Special Rapporteur. The term 'travelling child sex offender' is used to describe offenders who engage in child sex tourism. Likewise, it is worth noting that some organizations favour terms such as 'child abuse material' instead of 'child pornography', on the basis that the term 'pornography' may imply that the material is acceptable. Again, for consistency with the UN terminology, 'child pornography' is used in this chapter.

---

16 K. Fredette, 'International Legislative Efforts to Combat Child Sex Tourism: Evaluating the Council of Europe Convention on Combating Commercial Child Sexual Exploitation', *Boston College International and Comparative Law Review*, 2009, vol. 32, p. 8.
17 ECPAT International, *Combating Child Sex Tourism*, p. 6; M'jid, Report of the Special Rapporteur, p. 7.
18 ECPAT International, *FAQs*, available at http://www.ecpat.net/faqs (accessed 4 November 2013).
19 See for example D. Ireland-Piper, 'Extraterritoriality and the Sexual Conduct of Australians Overseas', *Bond Law Review*, 2011, vol. 22, p. 2.

Who are the offenders?

There are many myths about the profile of travelling child sex offenders. The image of a middle-aged western man, who travels to a developing country and preys on vulnerable children, is a common stereotype. While some offenders may fit this profile, the true profile of offenders covers a wider demographic.[20] Research shows that most offenders are male – but they may also be female.[21] Child sex tourism may involve offenders from western countries, but often also involves local offenders. For example, some research suggests that Asian travellers represent the majority of travelling child sex offenders in the Asia region.[22] Further, travelling child sex offenders are not always foreigners. Offenders may also move within the borders of their own country.[23]

An offender can be any age. Research published in 2013 by the UK's Child Exploitation and Online Protection Centre shows that while middle-aged or older men comprise the majority of known travelling child sex offenders originating from the UK and United States,[24] younger people – as young as 18 and 19 – have also been identified as offenders.[25] Finally, travelling child sex offenders may not be known to law enforcement authorities in their home country. The UK research also found that registered sex offenders represented only a small minority of British nationals reported to have committed sex offences against children overseas.[26]

Understanding the behaviour of travelling child sex offenders – commonly categorized as either 'situational' or 'preferential' – is useful to inform legal and law enforcement responses. Situational offenders are those who take advantage of a situation in which a child becomes available to them, but do not typically have a sexual preference for children or travel with the intention of abusing a child.[27] Most travelling child sex offenders meet the situational profile;[28] however, very few are detected by law enforcement authorities and prosecuted.[29] In contrast, preferential offenders plan their abuse. They generally have a sexual preference for children and travel for the purpose of sexually abusing children.[30] Some organizations also distinguish these categories from paedophiles, described as having an exclusive preference for pre-pubescent children.[31] Other descriptions that may be used to describe behaviour include 'transient' offending (generally perpetrated for a short time, and not typically the result of a grooming process) and 'embedded' offending (repeatedly perpetrated against the same victim

20 M'jid, Report of the Special Rapporteur, p. 7.
21 Ibid.; ECPAT International, Combating Child Sex Tourism, p. 6.
22 UNICEF, Commercial Sexual Exploitation of Children, available at http://www.unicef.org/eapro/activities_3757.html (accessed 4 November 2013). See also UNODC, Child Sexual Exploitation in Travel and Tourism: An Analysis of Domestic Legal Frameworks, publication forthcoming.
23 UNODC, Child Sexual Exploitation in Travel and Tourism.
24 Child Exploitation and Online Protection Centre, Threat Assessment of Child Sexual Exploitation and Abuse, 2013, p. 15.
25 Ibid.; ECPAT International, Combating Child Sex Tourism, p. 6.
26 Child Exploitation and Online Protection Centre, Threat Assessment of Child Sexual Exploitation and Abuse, p. 14.
27 ECPAT International, Combating Child Sex Tourism, p. 6; M'jid, Report of the Special Rapporteur, p. 7.
28 ECPAT International, Combating Child Sex Tourism, p. 12.
29 Ibid., p. 13.
30 M'jid, Report of the Special Rapporteur, p. 7.
31 ECPAT International, Combating Child Sex Tourism, p. 12.

or victims as the result of an extended grooming process).[32] It is important, however, to note the limits of these profiles, and that offenders may not always fit neatly into a particular category. Researchers understand sexual offending to involve a process or continuum rather than just an independent act,[33] and the distinctions between different profiles can often be blurred.[34]

Where does child sex tourism occur?

No country is immune to child sex tourism.[35] Destinations that are attractive to travelling child sex offenders are constantly evolving.[36] Based on the data available, offending appears to be most prevalent in less developed countries where children may be more vulnerable to exploitation and where criminal justice responses to child exploitation and abuse are not robust. In general, victims of child sex tourism (including boys and girls of all ages) come from social or economic disadvantage, or are part of a minority group within their community.[37] In some cases, simply living in an area where there are significant differences between the wealth of locals and the wealth of travelling visitors may create an environment where a child is vulnerable to sexual exploitation.[38] These conditions, prevalent in many popular travel destinations around the world, allow child sex tourism to thrive.

Travelling child sex offenders may be particularly drawn to locations where their activities can be easily concealed, or will go unnoticed, and where their motives will be unsuspected.[39] Offenders are also drawn to locations where the risk of detection by law enforcement is limited.[40] For example, reviews of internet forums where offenders illegally share information to facilitate sexual exploitation of children show that strengthened law enforcement efforts to combat the sexual exploitation and abuse of children in the Philippines and Thailand have had a deterrent effect on potential offenders.[41] However, where law enforcement efforts strengthen in one area, gaps are exploited in another. In South East Asia, offenders are moving towards alternative locations, including Vietnam and Lao PDR, to take advantage of weaker legal frameworks.[42]

Developed countries are also not immune. The UK Child Exploitation and Online Protection Centre has identified that during the reporting period for its 2013 Threat Assessment of Child Sexual Exploitation and Abuse, 31 per cent of the data collected on child sex offences committed by British nationals abroad related to less developed countries, while 68 per cent of cases related to offences in more developed countries in North and

---

32 Child Exploitation and Online Protection Centre, *Threat Assessment of Child Sexual Exploitation and Abuse*, p. 14.
33 Ibid; V.M. Kendall and T.M. Funk, *Child Exploitation and Trafficking: Examining the Global Challenges and US Responses*, Maryland: Rowman & Littlefield, 2012, p. 17.
34 Kendall and Funk, *Child Exploitation and Trafficking*, p. 26.
35 Ibid., p. 17; M'jid, Report of the Special Rapporteur, p.7; ECPAT International, *Combating Child Sex Tourism*, p. 6.
36 M'jid, Report of the Special Rapporteur, p. 7.
37 Ibid., p. 15.
38 Ibid. See also: World Vision Australia, *Child Safe Tourism: The Tourist Perspective*, 2012, p. 6.
39 M'jid, Report of the Special Rapporteur, p. 6.
40 Ibid.
41 Child Exploitation and Online Protection Centre, *Threat Assessment of Child Sexual Exploitation and Abuse*, p. 16.
42 Ibid.

West Europe, North America and Australasia.[43] The higher proportion of cases in this second category could, in part, be explained by stronger law enforcement responses in those countries,[44] meaning greater rates of detection and reporting of cases. Based on this assumption, the report identifies that there is likely to be more prevalent offending by British nationals in the less developed countries than that reflected in the 31 per cent statistic, given that those countries typically have more limited law enforcement capability and greater child vulnerability.[45]

International legal frameworks

The primary international legal instruments which set standards for criminal justice responses to child sex tourism are the CRC and its Optional Protocol. This section focuses on the key obligations under these instruments. Other international instruments containing broader obligations include the United Nations Convention against Transnational Organized Crime (UNTOC)[46] and its Trafficking Protocol, ILO Convention 182, and the Council of Europe Convention on the Protection of Children Against Sexual Exploitation and Sexual Abuse.[47] Each has high levels of ratification and reflects widely agreed standards for the protection of children against sexual abuse and exploitation.[48]

This international legal architecture blurs traditional boundaries between legal disciplines, with standards traversing international law on crime, human rights and labour rights.[49] In particular, it is unusual to find comprehensive criminal justice obligations, as contained in the Optional Protocol, within a human rights treaty. While both international criminal justice and human rights norms play important roles in addressing child sex tourism, it is rare for detailed obligations on a transnational crime issue to be so heavily represented in an instrument focused squarely on human rights and developed through international human rights bodies. The specific and comprehensive nature of criminal justice obligations under the Optional Protocol are particularly unique in this context. By contrast, while ILO Convention 182 calls on states to take measures to secure the prohibition and elimination of the worst forms of child labour,[50] including through criminal or other sanctions,[51] these obligations are crafted in broad terms and do not detail the specific criminal justice measures to be implemented by states.

The positioning of transnational criminal law obligations within a human rights framework is largely explained in commentary on the development of the CRC and Optional

43 Ibid., p. 15.
44 Ibid.
45 Ibid., p. 17.
46 United Nations Convention against Transnational Organized Crime, opened for signature 15 November 2000, 2225 UNTS 209; in force 29 September 2003 (UNTOC).
47 Convention on the Protection of Children Against Sexual Exploitation and Sexual Abuse, opened for signature 12 July 2007, CETS 201; in force 1 July 2010.
48 Other international instruments also contain broad obligations, including the International Covenant on Civil and Political Rights (1966), the Convention on the Elimination of All Forms of Discrimination against Women (1979) and International Labour Organization Conventions 29, 105 and 138.
49 UNODC, *Child Sexual Exploitation in Travel and Tourism*.
50 ILO Convention 182, Article 1. Under Article 3, 'the worst forms of child labour' include the use, procuring or offering of a child for prostitution, for the production of pornography or for pornographic performances and the sale and trafficking of children.
51 Ibid., Article 7(1).

Protocol. As understanding of child sexual exploitation evolved, so did recognition of the need for global action to promote strong law enforcement measures. The CRC and Optional Protocol provided a platform to advance these objectives at a time when child exploitation issues were at the forefront of the international agenda. In particular, drafting of the Optional Protocol took place in parallel with drafting of the Trafficking Protocol and ILO Convention 182 and was closely informed by meetings of the World Congress against Commercial Sexual Exploitation of Children (in 1996 and 2001). As a result, incorporating child sexual abuse and exploitation into the CRC Optional Protocol meant that these issues have received almost universal acknowledgement; with the exception of just two states,[52] all other countries in the world have ratified the CRC. Likewise, with 166 states parties[53] the Optional Protocol has achieved wide recognition and acceptance.

From a criminal justice perspective, it is unfortunate that oversight mechanisms for the criminal justice obligations under the Optional Protocol are formally limited to human rights bodies – in particular, the Committee on the Rights of the Child, the Human Rights Council and the UN Special Rapporteur on the Sale of Children, Child Prostitution and Child Pornography. These bodies play important roles in the monitoring of states' implementation of child rights, but have limited responsibility for and expertise in criminal justice issues. In contrast, the United Nations institutions responsible for overseeing the implementation of transnational crime instruments cover a wide range of global crime and justice issues and focus on the domestic implementation of criminal justice obligations – for example, the Commission on Narcotic Drugs, which oversees implementation of the drug control conventions;[54] the Conference of the Parties to the United Nations Convention against Transnational Organized Crime (UNTOC COP), which works to improve the capacity of states to combat transnational organized crime and promotes and reviews states' implementation of the Convention and its Protocols;[55] and the Commission on Crime Prevention and Criminal Justice (CCPCJ), which guides UN activities across a wide range of crime prevention and criminal justice issues. Broader issues relating to the sexual exploitation of children are given consideration through mechanisms such as the CCPCJ and UNTOC COP, but any focus on child sex tourism is typically framed within the boundaries of child trafficking.[56] The limited

---

52 There are 193 states parties to the CRC. The United States and Somalia are the only two countries that have not ratified the convention. Available at http://treaties.un.org/Pages/ViewDetails.aspx?src=TREATY&mtdsg_no=IV–11&chapter=4&lang=en (accessed 2 November 2013).

53 United Nations Treaty Collection. Available at http://treaties.un.org/Pages/ViewDetails.aspx?src=TREATY&mtdsg_no=IV–11-c&chapter=4&lang=en (accessed 2 November 2013). Although the United States is not a state party to the CRC, it is party to the Optional Protocol through Article 13(1), which allows for states not party to the CRC to ratify the Optional Protocol if they have signed the CRC. For further information see UNICEF, *The State of the World's Children: Celebrating 20 Years of the Convention on the Rights of the Child*, p. 7, available at http://www.unicef.org/publications/files/SOWC_Spec._Ed._CRC_Main_Report_EN_090409.pdf (accessed 2 November 2013).

54 UNODC, *The Commission on Narcotic Drugs*. available at http://www.unodc.org/unodc/commissions/CND (accessed 2 November 2013).

55 UNODC, *Conference of the Parties to the United Nations Convention against Transnational Organized Crime and the Protocols Thereto*, available at https://www.unodc.org/unodc/en/treaties/CTOC/CTOC-COP.html (accessed 2 November 2013).

56 See for example: UNODC Press Release, 'We must act together to fight exploitation and human trafficking in tourism, say United Nations and international partners', available at http://www.unodc.org/unodc/en/press/releases/2012/April/we-must-act-together-to-fight-exploitation-and-human-trafficking-in-tourism-say-united-nations-and-international-partners.html (accessed 22 October 2013).

scope for rigorous analysis of states' implementation of the Optional Protocol's criminal justice obligations through multilateral fora means that states' implementation measures are not closely monitored, and limited support is available to assist states with building strong legal frameworks through technical assistance initiatives.

While there is value in assessing national and global approaches to child sex tourism in the context of UNTOC and the Trafficking Protocol, as well as from the human rights perspective, there is a risk that the current frameworks dilute global efforts to address child sex tourism from a law enforcement perspective and that there are limited opportunities to promote critical criminal justice initiatives to combat child sex tourism through the UN system. The positioning of criminal justice obligations to counter child sex tourism within the framework of the global human rights agenda is likely to remain unchanged. There were strong reasons for this positioning when the obligations under the Optional Protocol were drafted. However, a greater focus on, and closer coordination with, existing transnational criminal law institutions would be beneficial to maximize the successful implementation of the CRC and Optional Protocol obligations relevant to child sex tourism.[57]

Convention on the Rights of the Child

In accordance with its Article 3, the CRC provides a human rights framework requiring the best interests of the child be a primary consideration in actions undertaken by states concerning children. The CRC, together with its Optional Protocol, provides the basis for obligations requiring states to implement criminal justice responses to combat child sex tourism. The CRC sets broad legal standards relevant to child sex tourism, requiring states to take all appropriate national, bilateral and multilateral measures to protect children from all forms of sexual exploitation and sexual abuse (Article 34) – including inducement or coercion to engage in unlawful sexual activity, and the exploitative use of children in prostitution and pornography – and from abduction, sale or trafficking for any purpose or in any form (Article 35).

Although existing instruments provided broad protections for children, at the time the CRC entered into force Articles 34 and 35 were the first treaty provisions requiring states parties to implement domestic responses to specifically combat the sexual exploitation and abuse of children.[58] While the language of these articles is broad, it places emphasis on prohibiting sexual exploitation.[59] This reflects the intentions of the drafters, who were concerned with the growing prevalence of the sexual abuse and exploitation of children, particularly through means facilitated by advancements in communications and travel, and through the prevalence of transnational crime.[60] The drafters also recognized the close linkage between

---

57 UNODC is leading this approach through Project Childhood, a joint programme with Interpol and World Vision that works with partner governments to strengthen the capacity of criminal justice authorities to identify, investigate and prosecute travelling child sex offenders, and works with communities, governments and business to build effective prevention mechanisms. Project Childhood is a good example of how rights- and justice-based approaches to child sex tourism can be complementary. For information, see http://aid.dfat.gov.au/countries/eastasia/regional/Pages/initiative-project-childhood.aspx and http://www.unodc.org/southeastasiaandpacific/en/Projects/2010_08/project_childhood.html (both accessed 2 November 2013).

58 2V. Muntarbhorn, 'Article 34: Sexual Exploitation and Sexual Abuse of Children', in A. Alen, J. Van de Lanotte, E. Verhellen, F. Ang, E. Berghmans and M. Verheyde (eds), *A Commentary on the United Nations Convention on the Rights of the Child*, Leiden: Martinus Nijhoff, 2007, p. 5.

59 Ibid., p. 2.

60 Ibid.

child trafficking and the sexual exploitation of children, debating whether to combine or separate the two issues. Ultimately, the trafficking and exploitation of children were deliberately separated into two distinct articles, in recognition of the key differences between the crime types – in particular, that while some trafficking may include sexual exploitation, not all exploitation will constitute trafficking.[61]

The specific relevance of child sex tourism to the obligations under Article 34 is highlighted in supporting material to the CRC. States are required to report to the Committee on the Rights of the Child within two years of the entry into force of the CRC for that state party, and every five years thereafter,[62] and in 1996 the Committee issued Guidelines to assist states in preparing these reports. Reports outline the measures that have been implemented domestically to give effect to the rights and obligations under the CRC, and may also include information on progress made towards implementation and any challenges faced by the state in fulfilling its obligations under the CRC.[63] The Guidelines also refer to child sex tourism, requiring states to report on 'whether the principle of extraterritoriality has been incorporated in the legislation to criminalize the sexual exploitation of children by nationals and residents of the State party when committed in other countries'.[64] Although the CRC itself does not mention child sex tourism, this guideline highlights the relevance of the obligations under the CRC to the evolution of the legal concept of child sex tourism, which is expanded upon further under the Optional Protocol.

While Articles 34 and 35 are the most relevant to child sex tourism, the Convention is drafted to be read as a whole, and these Articles should be considered in the broader context of the CRC's general principles – including in particular, under Article 12, the opportunity to be heard in any judicial or administrative proceedings affecting that child, either directly or through a representative or appropriate body.[65] This obligation is expanded under the Optional Protocol which, as outlined below, requires specific protections to be implemented to support child victims participating in the criminal justice process. Other relevant obligations under the CRC include protection from all forms of violence including exploitation and sexual abuse (Article 19), protection from economic exploitation and hazardous work (Article 32); and promotion of the recovery and social reintegration of a child victim of any form of neglect, exploitation, or abuse (Article 39).

Optional Protocol on the Sale of Children, Child Prostitution and Child Pornography

The Optional Protocol entered into force in 2002, having evolved as a result of international pressure to develop a specific instrument to directly address the sexual exploitation of

---

61 S. Detrick, *A Commentary on the United Nations Convention on the Rights of the Child*, The Hague: Kluwer Law International, 1999, p. 589.
62 CRC, Article 44(1)(b).
63 Committee on the Rights of the Child, General guidelines for periodic reports, UN Doc. CRC/C/58 (1996), paragraph 1.
64 Ibid., paragraph 159.
65 See also UNICEF, *Implementation Handbook for the Convention on the Rights of the Child*, Geneva, 2007, p. 530.

children. This movement gained traction within multilateral institutions in the 1990s through steps such as the appointment by the UN Commission on Human Rights[66] of the first Special Rapporteur on the Sale of Children, Child Prostitution and Child Pornography in 1990,[67] and the decision of the Commission in 1994 to establish an open-ended working group to prepare guidelines for a draft Optional Protocol and consider the basic measures required to prevent and eradicate the sale of children, child prostitution and child pornography.[68] Outside the UN system, the first and second World Congresses against Commercial Sexual Exploitation of Children (Stockholm, 1996 and Yokohama, 2001) promoted the development of a global agenda to combat the commercial sexual exploitation of children,[69] based on obligations under the CRC. Non-binding instruments developed through the World Congresses – the Stockholm Declaration and Agenda for Action (1996) and Yokohama Global Commitment (2001) – set benchmarks for domestic responses (including through criminal laws that apply extraterritorial jurisdiction) to child sex tourism and the commercial sexual exploitation of children more broadly. And in 1999, member states of the UN World Tourism Organization agreed to the Global Code of Ethics (1999), which condemned the sexual exploitation of children and called on states to create domestic criminal offences (again, including legislation with extraterritorial reach).

There was some resistance to developing an Optional Protocol. In particular, the UN Committee on the Rights of the Child (together with some NGOs) raised concerns about the potential overlap of obligations being considered for the Optional Protocol and those contained in existing instruments, or instruments that were developing simultaneously (in particular, the Trafficking Protocol and ILO Convention 182), and argued for strengthening the implementation of existing obligations rather than creating a new instrument.[70] The working group pursued the development of comprehensive obligations, driven by a desire to directly address the sexual exploitation of children – including a particular focus on legal and law enforcement responses to child sex tourism.[71] The Optional Protocol was adopted by the UN General Assembly and opened for signature, ratification and accession on 25 May 2000.[72]

Criminalization

The Optional Protocol expands on the broad obligations under Articles 34 and 35 of the CRC and outlines comprehensive measures required to criminalize conduct, extend wide-reaching jurisdiction over offences, and provide protections for children involved in the criminal justice process. Under Article 1 of the Optional Protocol, states parties are obliged to implement measures to prohibit the sale of children, child prostitution and child pornography. Recognition of the close links between these forms

---

66 The Commission on Human Rights was replaced in April 2006 by the Human Rights Council. See UNICEF, *Implementation Handbook*, p. 681; OHCHR, *Background Information on the Human Rights Council*, available at http://www.ohchr.org/EN/HRBodies/HRC/Pages/AboutCouncil.aspx (accessed 2 November 2013).

67 UNICEF, *Implementation Handbook*, p. 515.

68 Ibid., p. 514.

69 Ibid., p. 516.

70 Ibid., pp. 514, 669–670; Committee on the Rights of the Child, *Report of the Twentieth Session*, UN Doc. CRC/C/84 (1999), paragraph 217.

71 UNICEF, *Implementation Handbook*, p. 669.

72 United Nations General Assembly, Resolution adopted by the General Assembly, UN Doc. GA Res A/RES/54/263 (2000).

of exploitation and child sex tourism is made in the Preamble, which notes that states parties are:

deeply concerned at the widespread and continuing practice of sex tourism, to which children are especially vulnerable, as it directly promotes the sale of children, child prostitution and child pornography.

Although most of the substantive provisions of the Optional Protocol do not directly refer to child sex tourism (the exception being Article 10, which refers to it in the context of international cooperation), the acknowledgement of child sex tourism in the Preamble and the broad definitions of the sale of children, child prostitution and child pornography under Article 2 encompass a wide range of conduct, including that typically engaged in by travelling child sex offenders:

For the purpose of the present Protocol:

(a) Sale of children means any act or transaction whereby a child is transferred by any person or group of persons to another for remuneration or any other consideration;
(b) Child prostitution means the use of a child in sexual activities for remuneration or any other form of consideration;
(c) Child pornography means any representation, by whatever means, of a child engaged in real or simulated explicit sexual activities or any representation of the sexual parts of a child for primarily sexual purposes.

Under Article 3 of the Optional Protocol, states parties are required to implement comprehensive criminal offences for conduct relating to the sale of children, child prostitution and child pornography. Criminalization, including penalties that take into account the grave nature of the offences,[73] must include offences relating to:

• offering, delivering or accepting, by whatever means, a child for the purpose of sexual exploitation of the child and engagement of the child in forced labour;
• offering, obtaining, procuring or providing a child for child prostitution;
• producing, distributing, disseminating, importing, exporting, offering, selling child pornography, or possessing child pornography for these purposes; and
• attempting to commit any of the acts listed above, and complicity or participation in any of these acts.[74]

Also in accordance with Article 3, conduct constituting offences relating to the sale of children, child prostitution and child pornography must be criminalized regardless of whether it is committed by an individual or on an organized basis, or committed domestically or transnationally.

---

73 Optional Protocol, Article 3(3).
74 Ibid., Article 3(1)–(2). Other obligations under Article 3 relate to criminalization of the transfer of organs and unlawful adoption, which do not relate directly to child sex tourism.

Jurisdiction

The obligation to assert wide-reaching jurisdiction over offences is a key feature of the Optional Protocol under Article 4. States are required to exercise basic jurisdiction when offences occur within the territory of the state (or on a ship or aircraft registered to that state).[75] In addition, the Optional Protocol provides states with the discretion to consider exercising extraterritorial jurisdiction. States may establish jurisdiction over offences that do not occur within their territory, if the alleged offender is a national (or has habitual residence in that state) or the victim is a national of that state.[76] This element of the Optional Protocol is particularly relevant to child sex tourism, which often involves offenders travelling across national borders, and has been implemented by some states parties as a basis for prosecuting their own nationals or permanent residents who are travelling child sex offenders.[77]

States are also required to assert jurisdiction, and refer the matter to their domestic prosecuting authority, if the state would refuse to extradite a person to face prosecution for offences under the Optional Protocol, on the basis of that person's nationality.[78] This obligation to extradite or prosecute (*aut dedere aut judicare*) is fundamental to effective cross-border law enforcement outcomes, and is aimed at ensuring that there are no safe havens so offenders cannot escape prosecution simply because of the existence of international borders.

Obligations under Articles 6 and 7 require states parties to provide a wide measure of assistance to facilitate investigations, prosecutions and extradition proceedings,[79] and to take action for the seizure and confiscation of materials, assets and the proceeds of those offences.[80] Key elements of these obligations include ensuring that offences are extraditable and that extradition arrangements may be made regardless of whether a treaty relationship is in place,[81] and carrying out obligations relating to the sharing of evidence in conformity with any existing mutual legal assistance treaties in place between the parties.[82] The Optional Protocol also places emphasis on the importance of wider forms of international cooperation, and in this context includes the only direct reference to child sex tourism contained in the substance of the treaty. Under Article 10(1):

> States Parties shall take all necessary steps to strengthen international cooperation by multilateral, regional and bilateral arrangements for the prevention, detection, investigation, prosecution and punishment of those responsible for acts involving the sale of children, child prostitution, child pornography and child sex tourism. States Parties shall also promote international cooperation and coordination between their authorities, national and international non-governmental organizations and international organizations.

Further discussion on the application of extraterritorial jurisdiction and the importance of international cooperation between states to promote criminal justice objectives is included below.

---

75 Optional Protocol, Article 4(1).
76 Ibid., Article 4(2).
77 UNODC, *Child Sexual Exploitation in Travel and Tourism*.
78 Optional Protocol, Article 4(3); Article 5(5).
79 Optional Protocol, Article 6.
80 Ibid., Article 7.
81 Ibid., Article 5.
82 Ibid., Article 6(2).

Protection

The obligation to uphold the rights and interests of child victims in the criminal justice process under Article 8 is an important element of the Optional Protocol. States are required to adopt appropriate measures to ensure that the best interests of the child are a primary consideration in the treatment of child victims in the criminal justice system.[83] The protection measures to be adopted by states include:

- recognizing the vulnerability of child victims and adapting procedures to recognize their special needs, including as witnesses;
- informing child victims of their rights, their role and the scope, timing and progress of the proceedings and of the disposition of their cases;
- allowing the views, needs and concerns of child victims to be presented and considered in proceedings;
- providing appropriate support services to child victims through the legal process;
- protecting the privacy and identity of child victims and taking measures to avoid inappropriate dissemination of identifying information;
- providing for the safety of child victims (and their families and witnesses) from intimidation and retaliation; and
- avoiding unnecessary delay in the disposition of cases and the execution of orders or decrees granting compensation to child victims.[84]

Special measures that support child victims' participation in the criminal justice process are essential: they assist states in guaranteeing the protection of children's rights and interests and, by facilitating safe participation by children in the criminal justice process, assist law enforcement agencies in using the evidence of child victims to compile robust briefs and increase the chances of successful prosecution.[85] The criminal justice system, including evidentiary interviews and trial proceedings, can be traumatic for children who have experienced any form of sexual abuse. The process can be confusing and intimidating, and without appropriate support some children are at risk of re-victimization through the process of recounting their experience to police, prosecutors and courts.[86] Strong evidence from victims is often essential to successful prosecution of sexual abuse cases, but the limited consistency and reliability of evidence provided by children can pose a challenge to law enforcement authorities.[87] Robust measures that respect and support children through the criminal justice process can contribute significantly to achieving successful outcomes.

Implementing international standards: key challenges

The wide reach of child sex tourism across the globe requires criminal justice responses that are consistent, robust and coordinated across jurisdictions – to ensure that offenders cannot

---

83 Ibid., Article 8(3).
84 Ibid., Article 8(1). See also UNODC, *Child Sexual Exploitation in Travel and Tourism.*
85 UNODC, *Child Sexual Exploitation in Travel and Tourism.*
86 F. David, 'Child Sex Tourism', in *Trends and Issues in Crime and Criminal Justice*, Australian Institute of Criminology: Canberra, 2000, p. 3.
87 Ibid.; Fredette, 'International Legislative Efforts to Combat Child Sex Tourism', pp. 24–26; For a similar argument in the context of trafficking in persons cases see A. Gallagher and P. Holmes, 'Developing an Effective Criminal Justice Response to Human Trafficking: Lessons from the Front Line', *International Criminal Justice Review*, 2008, vol. 18, p. 332.

escape justice by exploiting loopholes in legal systems or by simply moving to another location. Global law enforcement trends, monitored by Interpol, show that the number of travelling child sex offenders has increased in recent years. According to Interpol, the lack of relevant legislation in destination countries (or lack of effective implementation of legislation) is a key feature of this trend.[88] We know that offenders are more likely to move their activities to countries where law enforcement capacity and legal frameworks are weak and, as ECPAT International has noted, 'Weak legal frameworks are among the factors that increase children's vulnerability to sexual exploitation and encourage demand.'[89] This simply means that children in nations where legislation and justice institutions may still be advancing are at greater risk of exploitation by travelling child sex offenders – despite strong examples of some countries that are taking a proactive approach to strengthen their criminal justice responses.[90]

Effective domestic laws, which comprehensively criminalize sexual exploitation, are the first front line against travelling child sex offenders. Unfortunately, in many countries there are either significant gaps in the existing legal frameworks or impediments to the effective implementation of the relevant laws,[91] for example due to limited technical capacity and resources. While specific child sex tourism laws are not necessarily required, legislation that comprehensively covers all of the key obligations under the Optional Protocol is essential to ensure that all forms of relevant conduct are criminalized. Most countries do not have specific child sex tourism legislation but do criminalize relevant conduct, including sexual exploitation.[92] While the legislation need not strictly refer to 'child sex tourism', the offence provisions should include clear elements that cover travelling and engaging in sexual activities with a child.[93] For some countries, dedicated child sex tourism legislation may be helpful to emphasize the focus of the criminal offences and avoid any confusion with other existing legislation (for example, child trafficking or ordinary criminal law offences for rape and sexual abuse).

Harmonized legal frameworks can also be a powerful tool against child sex tourism. Legislation across different countries that reflects the same key international obligations minimizes loopholes – it helps to fill any legislative gaps that may be exploited by offenders simply by moving across international boundaries, and can facilitate cross-border cooperation between states (through informal police-to-police networks and through formal extradition and mutual legal assistance processes). Using the Optional Protocol as a benchmark for developing domestic legislation is the most effective way to achieve harmonized laws.

The exercise of extraterritorial jurisdiction can also assist law enforcement and prosecution authorities to secure convictions against offenders in circumstances where the offender would otherwise escape with impunity – for example, if the country in which the offender committed the offences is unable or unwilling to prosecute. Investigation and prosecution are typically more effective when they occur in the same territory in which the offences have occurred.[94]

---

88 Interpol, *Sex Offenders*, available at http://www.interpol.int/Crime-areas/Crimes-against-children/Sex-offenders (accessed 1 October 2013).

89 C. Beaulieu, 'Extraterritorial Laws: Why they are not really working and how they can be strengthened', in ECPAT International, *Creating a United Front against the Sexual Exploitation of Children in Travel and Tourism*, Bangkok, 2009, p. 6.

90 Fredette, 'International Legislative Efforts to Combat Child Sex Tourism', pp. 16–17; UNODC, *Child Sexual Exploitation in Travel and Tourism*.

91 Fredette, 'International Legislative Efforts to Combat Child Sex Tourism', pp. 13–14.

92 M'jid, Report of the Special Rapporteur, p. 11.

93 Ibid., pp. 11–12.

94 Fredette, 'International Legislative Efforts to Combat Child Sex Tourism', p. 13.

Key reasons for this include the increased likelihood of offences being detected, accessibility of physical evidence and witnesses, limited red tape involved when dealing in just one jurisdiction and the absence of language or cultural barriers.[95] As a general rule, legal and law enforcement responses to child sex tourism are best placed to achieve successful outcomes if they are aligned with the locations in which offences occur.[96] However, where this is not possible, extraterritorial jurisdiction can provide a useful alternative mechanism. In recognition of the seriousness of the sexual exploitation of children some states have created extraterritorial jurisdiction to enable the prosecution of travelling child sex offenders in their home states.[97] States typically considered 'sending' states have been particularly willing to exercise this form of jurisdiction.

Nevertheless, extraterritorial jurisdiction should never replace (or undermine) other cooperation frameworks, which are important not only for tackling child sex tourism but also more broadly for successful international cooperation across the full spectrum of crime types. Successfully prosecuting sex crimes is notoriously challenging even when the crime occurred within the territory of the prosecuting state. Successful prosecution of crimes that occurred entirely within the territory of another state is even more difficult, and statistics on the number of successful prosecutions under extraterritorial legislation are notoriously low.[98]

Targeted mechanisms to support states parties in their efforts to implement the criminal justice obligations under the CRC and Optional Protocol are also essential. The positioning of the criminal justice obligations relating to child sex tourism within human rights instruments means that the UN mechanisms charged with monitoring and supporting states in their implementation of the CRC and Optional Protocol will always view implementation efforts through a human rights lens. Given that these oversight bodies have mandates that do not prioritize crime and justice and have limited expertise in transnational crime issues, and there being no formal forum for states to consult on implementation challenges and good practices, there is an opportunity for the UN's human rights and criminal justice institutions to look at options to work more closely together to strengthen legal and law enforcement responses to child sex tourism. Ultimately, greater cooperation between human rights and criminal justice institutions, at both the international and domestic levels, is the key to achieving full, effective implementation of the international standards under CRC and the Optional Protocol to combat child sex tourism.

95 Ibid.
96 Ibid.
97 Beaulieu, 'Extraterritorial Laws', p. 7.
98 Ibid., p. 21.

B   Commodity crimes

14

Drug trafficking

Bernard Leroy

The building of the international norms[1]

Effects of unregulated trade pre drug control: China, Europe, United States

A confluence of interests led to the international regulation of drugs. China discontinued opium imports from India in the early part of the twentieth century and as a result cheap opium flooded Europe. Simultaneously, an unregulated market was developing in pharmaceutical preparations. In the United States, around 90 per cent of narcotic drugs were used for non-medical purposes.[2] Colonial interests in Great Britain combined with assertions of national sovereignty and rejection of imperialism in China to develop international regulation. Domestic interests in international regulation in Europe and the United States arose out of drug abuse problems and domestic lobbying against the opium trade, while commercial interests, having shifted to the developing pharmaceutical industry, sought to regulate other sources of drugs.

Narcotics control prior to the League of Nations

In 1909, representatives from thirteen nations met in the Shanghai International Opium Commission[3] to discuss the international consequences of the Chinese opium problem. They placed opium production under international control. It was agreed that drug smuggling, despite the fact that the opium trade was not illegal, 'should be subject to strict laws designed to prevent it'. That led to the conclusion of the first international narcotics convention, the

---

1 See generally United Nations Office on Drugs and Crime (UNODC), *A Century of International Drug Control*, Vienna: UNODC, 2008, available at http://www.unodc.org/documents/data-and-analysis/Studies/100_Years_of_Drug_Control.pdf (accessed 12 November 2013).
2 See L. Lewin, *Phantastica: L'histoire des drogues et de leur usage*, Paris: J. Lyon, 1996.
3 See H. Wright, 'The International Opium Commission', *American Journal of International Law*, 1909, vol. 3, p. 648, p. 823.

1912 Hague International Opium Convention.[4] It established international cooperation in the control of narcotic drugs. The control measures were extended to coca production. In 1919, the Treaty of Versailles provided that ratification of the Peace Treaty implied the ratification of the Hague International Opium Convention. As a consequence, all States involved in the First World War automatically became parties, and promptly enacted implementing legislation.

Narcotics control under the League of Nations

The international treaties that followed gradually established a legal framework of elaborate mechanisms tending indirectly towards prohibition. The mechanisms were strengthened as time went on: opium-smoking dens were closed; the possession of opium by minors and the sale of opium to minors were both forbidden. In 1925, at Geneva, States signed the International Opium Convention[5] aimed at controlling the manufacture of drugs. Governments were required to submit annual statistics concerning production of opium and coca leaves, manufacture, consumption and stocks of narcotic drugs to the newly created Permanent Central Opium Board. The next significant step was the adoption of the Geneva Convention for Limiting the Manufacture and Regulating the Distribution of Narcotic Drugs of 1931,[6] which established the principle of limiting narcotic drug manufacture to medical requirements and scientific needs. A system of international legislation was created under which new narcotic drugs could be added by decision of an international organ, which would be binding upon all signatory States. The Convention for the Suppression of the Illicit Traffic in Dangerous Drugs, signed in Geneva in 1936,[7] promoted international cooperation to combat trafficking and called upon States to establish a central office for the national and international coordination of law enforcement efforts. Specific measures were enacted to prevent offenders from escaping prosecution for technical reasons and to facilitate extradition for drug offences.

Narcotics control under the United Nations

The Lake Success Protocol signed on 11 December 1946[8] transferred the functions previously exercised by the League of Nations under the various narcotics treaties concluded before the Second World War to the United Nations. The Commission on Narcotic Drugs (CND) was created. In 1948 the Paris Protocol[9] extended the system of international control to new synthetic substances with effects comparable to those of opium. It authorized the

---

4   23 January 1912, 8 LNTS 187; in force in 23 January 1922.
5   81 LNTS 317; in force September 1923.
6   139 LNTS 301; in force 9 July 1933.
7   198 LNTS 300; in force 26 October 1939.
8   The Lake Success Protocol amending the Agreements, Conventions and Protocols on Narcotic Drugs concluded at the Hague on 23 January 1912, at Geneva on 11 February 1925 and 19 February 1925, and 13 July 1931, at Bangkok on 27 November 1931 and at Geneva on 26 June 1936, signed at Lake Success, New York, 11 December 1946, 12 UNTS 179. The Protocol came into force in 1948.
9   The Paris Protocol Bringing under International Control Drugs Outside the Scope of the Convention of 13 July 1931 for Limiting the Manufacture and Regulating the Distribution of Narcotic Drugs, as Amended by the Protocol signed at Lake Success, New York, on 11 December, 1946, signed at Paris on 19 November 1948, 44 UNTS 277; in force 1 December 1949.

World Health Organization (WHO) to place under full international control any new drug which was addictive or convertible into an addiction-producing drug. The 1953 New York Protocol[10] was adopted to limit the use of opium and its international trade to the quantities needed for medical and scientific purposes. The CND was entitled to allocate quotas to the various opium-producing countries and to put in place a system of international inspection to avoid legal overproduction and to limit the stocks of the drugs in the possession of individual States.

After 1960, a general ban on drugs used for other than therapeutic or scientific purposes was established by three conventions drawn up under the auspices of the United Nations. The 1961 Single Convention on Narcotic Drugs[11] unified codification of the existing multilateral drug control treaties, with the exception of some of the provisions of the 1936 Convention. It placed the burden of responsibility predominantly on producers of organic plants and to a lesser extent on manufacturing countries. It extended the existing control systems to the cultivation of plants that were grown as the raw material of narcotic drugs and prohibited traditional consumption such as opium smoking, opium eating, coca leaf chewing, cannabis resin smoking and the non-medical use of cannabis. It also tackled the new trends in drug abuse, in connection with the discovery of cannabis and LSD. The 1972 Geneva Protocol[12] simplified the international control machinery and merged the Permanent Central Opium Board and the Drug Supervisory Body into a single unit, the International Narcotics Control Board (INCB). It also established new provisions to prevent illicit production of, traffic in and use of narcotics and promoted the access of drug abusers to treatment and rehabilitation. The Protocol opened the possibility for judges to order treatment, education, after-care, rehabilitation and social reintegration instead of or in addition to imprisonment in penal cases involving abusers. It expanded the role of the INCB to include preventing illicit drug cultivation, production, manufacture, traffic and use and ensuring a better balance between the supply of and demand for narcotic drugs for medical and scientific purposes. The 1971 UN Convention on Psychotropic Substances[13] was adopted to address emerging abuse of hallucinogens, benzodiazepine, amphetamines, barbiturates, the over-prescription of sedatives and the increase in the diversion of new synthetic medicines to the illicit markets. In contrast to the 1961 Convention, which prohibited narcotic drugs produced in developing countries, the 1971 Convention dealt with synthetic drugs produced in industrialized countries. It contained compromises regarding scheduling criteria and procedures and scope of control, with new emphasis on public health and social problems. It depended for implementation less on law enforcement than on adequate regulation of the pharmaceutical industry and the integrity of public health systems.

---

10 The Protocol signed in New York on 23 June 1953 for Limiting and Regulating the Cultivation of the Poppy Plant, the Production of, International and Wholesale Trade in, and Use of, Opium, 456 UNTS 3; in force 8 March 1963.

11 30 March 1961, 520 UNTS 151; in force 13 December 1964. See Commentary on the Single Convention on Narcotic Drugs, UN Doc. No. E73.XI.1, New York: United Nations, 1973.

12 25 March 1972, 976 UNTS 3; in force 8 August 1975. See Commentary on the Protocol amending the Single Convention on Narcotic Drugs, UN Doc. No. E76.XI.6, New York: United Nations, 1976.

13 21 February 1971, 1019 UNTS 175; in force 16 August 1976. See Commentary on the Convention on Psychotropic Substances, UN Doc. No. E76.XI.5, New York: United Nations, 1976.

The 1988 Convention against Illicit Traffic in Narcotic Drugs and Psychotropic Substances[14] was a response to the trend away from the diversion of drugs to their illicit manufacture and traffic, a situation the earlier treaties were not adequate to deal with. It aims to:

- harmonize the definition and scope of drug offences at the global level;
- improve and strengthen international cooperation and coordination among state authorities; and
- provide States with the legal means effectively to interdict international trafficking.

The 1988 Convention facilitates the implementation of concrete measures against trafficking in and abuse of drugs including judicial cooperation, extradition of traffickers, controlled deliveries and anti-money-laundering measures. It sets up a system for the control and monitoring of some precursors, chemicals and solvents frequently used in illicit manufacture. Finally, it provides for communication between governments to identify suspicious transactions and develop large-scale mutual legal assistance in the suppression of illicit drug activity.

The permanent aims of the drug control conventions

Since the first Drug Control Convention in 1912, the common objective of the international community has always been:

- to ensure the availability of useful narcotic drugs and psychotropic substances for medical/scientific purposes[15] and prevent diversions from licit to illicit purposes; and
- to limit supply and use of drugs exclusively to medical and scientific purposes, thereby eliminating all non-medical use, with the objective of a society free of non-medical drug use.

The drug control conventions are adopted to codify universally applicable control, but also to oblige Parties to address the following issues:

- to take efforts to prevent drug abuse;
- to provide services for treatment and rehabilitation of drug abusers;[16]
- to establish effective measures to reduce the adverse health and social consequences of drug abuse.

Parties to the conventions are thus obliged to limit certain activities to 'medical and scientific purposes', although this expression is not defined, and it is left, subject to the international law on the interpretation of treaties, to the Parties to determine its outer limits. The term 'medical purposes' has, however, not been uniformly interpreted by Parties. Some have prohibited the consumption of controlled drugs by all addicts, excepting only when necessary to alleviate

---

14 20 December 1988, 1582 UNTS 95; in force 11 November 1990. See Commentary on the United Nations Convention against Illicit Traffic in Narcotic Drugs and Psychotropic Substances, UN Doc. No. E98.XI.5, New York: United Nations, 1998.
15 1961 Convention, Articles 2 and 4; 1971 Convention, Article 5.
16 1961 Convention, Article 38; 1971 Convention, Article 20; 1988 Convention, Article 14.

suffering during withdrawal treatment. Others have permitted consumption by addicts whose dependency has proved to be incurable, in the minimum quantities required to prevent painful withdrawal symptoms or to enable them to lead as normal a life as possible.

International law requires Parties to the conventions to perform their obligations in good faith according to the principle *pacta sunt servanda*.[17] It also requires them to interpret the language of the conventions in good faith, in accordance with the ordinary meaning given to those terms in their context, and in the light of the objects and purposes of the relevant conventions.[18] Accordingly, Parties cannot permit, ostensibly, for medical and scientific purposes, what is effectively the 'recreational' use of drugs, e.g. the organized commercial distribution of cocaine and heroin for retail sale, on the same basis as alcohol or tobacco.

The institutional infrastructure for international drug control

It is primarily the prerogative of the Parties to decide on their own interpretation of the terms of the conventions. However, the international drug control regime has developed in line with inter-Party practice and related discussions in policy-making organs. The 1961, 1971 and 1988 Conventions put in place international control organs and defined their functioning.

Commission on Narcotic Drugs (CND)

The CND was established by the Economic and Social Council in its Resolution 9(I) of 16 February 1946 as the central policy-making body within the United Nations system dealing with drug-related matters.[19] It consists of 53 states, serving four-year terms: eleven African; eleven Asian; ten Latin American and Caribbean; seven Eastern European; and fourteen Western European and other. One seat rotates between the Asian, and the Latin American and Caribbean States every four years. The CND is entitled to consider all matters pertaining to the aims of the conventions and see to their implementation, pursuant to the provisions of the conventions. It has the power to decide, upon the recommendation of the International Narcotics Control Board (INCB) or the World Health Organization (WHO), to place narcotic drugs and psychotropic substances within the schedules of the 1961 and 1971 Conventions (or to transfer them between these schedules). It enjoys the same power in regard to the precursor chemicals identified in Tables I or II of the 1988 Convention.

International Narcotics Control Board (INCB)

Established in 1968 in accordance with the terms of the 1961 Single Convention,[20] the INCB is the independent and quasi-judicial body which monitors the implementation of the United Nations international drug control conventions. Thirteen members are elected by the UN

---

17 Vienna Convention on the Law of Treaties, 1969, Article 26.
18 Vienna Convention on the Law of Treaties, 1969, Article 31(1).
19 The legal basis of its functioning includes the Single Convention on Narcotic Drugs, 1961, Article 8; the Convention on Psychotropic Substances of 1971, Article 17; and the United Nations Convention against Illicit Traffic in Narcotic Drugs and Psychotropic Substances of 1988, Article 21.
20 The legal bases are the Single Convention on Narcotic Drugs, 1961, Article 14; the Convention on Psychotropic Substances of 1971, Article 19; and the United Nations Convention against Illicit Traffic in Narcotic Drugs and Psychotropic Substances of 1988, Article 22.

Economic and Social Council (ECOSOC); three with medical, pharmacological or pharmaceutical experience are elected from a list of persons nominated by the WHO, and ten are elected from a list of persons nominated by governments. The INCB reviews on a regular basis the drug control situation in various countries and governments' overall compliance with the provisions of the international drug control treaties. The review covers various aspects of drug control, including the functioning of national drug control administrations, the adequacy of national drug control legislation and policy, national measures taken to combat drug trafficking and abuse, and States' fulfillment of their reporting obligations under the drug conventions. Article 14 of the 1961 Convention (as amended by the 1972 Protocol) and Article 19 of the 1971 Convention set out measures that the INCB may take to ensure the execution of the provisions of those conventions. Such measures, which consist of increasingly severe steps, are taken into consideration when the INCB has reason to believe that the aims of the conventions are being seriously endangered by the failure of a State to carry out their provisions. The States concerned are not named until the INCB decides to bring the situation to the attention of the Parties, the ECOSOC and the CND.

United Nations Office on Drugs and Crime (UNODC)

The UNODC was established by General Assembly Resolution 45/179 of 21 December 1990, to assist the UN in better implementing a coordinated, comprehensive response to the interrelated issues of illicit trafficking in and abuse of drugs, crime prevention and criminal justice, international terrorism and corruption, and to help Member States in their fight against illicit drugs, crime and terrorism. It is headed by an Executive Director, who is appointed by the Secretary-General. The three pillars of the UNODC work programme are:

- research and analytical work to increase knowledge and understanding of drugs and crime issues and expand the evidence base for policy and operational decisions;
- normative work to assist States in the ratification and implementation of the international treaties, the development of domestic legislation on drugs, crime and terrorism, and the provision of secretariat and substantive services to the treaty-based and governing bodies; and
- field-based technical cooperation projects to enhance the capacity of Member States to counteract illicit drugs, crime and terrorism.[21]

World Health Organization (WHO)

The WHO is the specialized agency designated for the evaluation of the medical, scientific and public health aspects of psychoactive substances under the 1961 Single Convention (as amended by the 1972 Protocol) and the 1971 Convention.[22] The WHO Expert Committee

---

21 See the UNODC's website at www.unodc.org.
22 The legal bases are: Article 3 of the 1961 Convention as amended by the 1972 Protocol amending the Single Convention on Narcotic Drugs 1961; Article 9 of the 1961 Convention (stipulating that three members of the INCB with medical, pharmacological or pharmaceutical experience are elected from a list of persons nominated by the WHO; Article 2 of the 1971 Convention (concerning whether or not to recommend international control of substances, as well as the assessment of exempted preparations under Article 3 of the 1971 Convention); and Article 14 of the 1988 Convention (concerning recommendations).

on Drug Dependence undertakes medical and scientific evaluations of the dependence-producing properties of substances to enable the CND to make decisions on their control status. This has led to a steady increase in the number of substances subject to control.

The institutional infrastructure for domestic drug control

States Parties must apply the conventions under their own legal systems. However, the definition of offences is a matter solely within the powers of a state. The challenge here may be a gap of intention between the aims of the conventions (international law) and the aims of national law. The conventions require Parties to create some specific institutions to coordinate their activities aimed at combating illicit drug trafficking and abuse, and to introduce into their domestic laws the required preventive, law enforcement and treatment provisions designed to restrict the use of the plants and substances in question to medical or scientific purposes. In order to carry out their obligations, Parties may have to develop national institutions to, *inter alia*, enable inter-ministerial coordination on drug control; regulate licit drugs[23] and chemical precursors;[24] suppress the illicit drug traffic through effective coordination of the activities of the police, customs and all other authorities involved in drug law enforcement action; enable international cooperation[25] in the transmitting and receiving of mutual legal assistance requests; authorize controlled delivery; and authorize high-seas interception.

Classification and licit control

The three conventions oblige Parties to:

- place under rigorous control the narcotic drugs, psychotropic substances and precursors listed in the schedules or tables annexed to them and authorize every State to place any other drugs under supervision;[26] and
- classify each controlled drug and chemical under domestic law to ensure the minimum required Convention controls apply.[27]

All substances classified by the conventions have to be incorporated and a differentiation has to be made between:

- prohibited drugs not used in medicine or for scientific experiment (for example heroin, cocaine, LSD, cannabis, etc.);
- dangerous drugs having a medicinal value (for example morphine, amphetamines);
- less dangerous drugs (for example benzodiazepines) frequently used in medicine; and
- chemical precursors useful to process illicit drugs.

All activities relating to the drugs in the first category must be prohibited. The production or manufacture of, trade in, use in industry, and supply to individuals of drugs in the second

---

23 1961 Convention, Article 17; 1971 Convention, Article 6.
24 1988 Convention, Article 12.
25 1988 Convention, Article 7.
26 1961 Convention, Articles 2 and 4; 1971 Convention, Article 2; 1988 Convention, Article 12.
27 1961 Convention, Articles 2 and 4; 1971 Convention, Article 2; 1988 Convention, Article 12.

category must be subject to very strict regulation and control; drugs in the third category and precursors must be subject to a more flexible system.

Regulation of trade in controlled drugs for licit use and in controlled chemicals

In order to limit the licit use of drugs to medical and scientific purposes,[28] Parties are obliged to regulate licit activities involving controlled drugs and chemicals. They must create specific provisions in respect of the cultivation, production, manufacture,[29] wholesale distribution of, wholesale trade and international trade in,[30] and use in industry, of plants, substances and preparations of highly dangerous drugs and dangerous drugs used in medicine. They must limit stocks, limit manufacture, and apply special provisions to international trade, commercial transport and postal consignments.

Control of cultivation

The 1961 Convention urges States to phase out the production of opium, coca and cannabis. States which authorize such production must entrust the monopoly for it to a government agency responsible for designating the areas and plots of land where cultivation is permitted, for authorizing and supervising the cultivators, and for purchasing their entire crops promptly after harvesting.

Measures relating to the dispensing of drugs to individuals

The 1961 and 1971 Conventions require that narcotic drugs and psychotropic substances, as well as medicines containing them, other than harmless preparations, be supplied to individuals by duly authorized persons only and on medical prescription only. In contrast, the 1988 Convention lays down no restrictions on the sale to individuals of products containing precursors.

Trafficking

Criminal offences

The 1961 and 1971 Conventions require Parties to treat as offences any intentional breach of their provisions and to lay down adequate punishments for serious offences, in particular imprisonment or other penalties of deprivation of liberty.[31] At the end of the 1980s, the international community expressed the need to increase the effectiveness of international efforts, and to strengthen the provisions of the international legal framework. The needs were threefold:

---

28 1961 Convention, Articles 2 and 4; 1971 Convention, Articles 5 and 7.
29 1961 Convention, Articles 4, 21, 21 bis, 24, 25, 27, 29, 30; 1971 Convention, Articles 2, 3, 7, 8; 1988 Convention, Article 12.
30 1961 Convention, Articles 4, 21, 23, 24, 25, 31, 32; 1971 Convention, Articles 2, 3, 4, 7, 8, 12, 13, 14; 1988 Convention, Article 12.
31 1961 Convention, Article 36; 1971 Convention, Article 22.

- to develop new and innovative approaches to the fight against drug trafficking, when old methods did not prove to be as successful as in the past;
- to ensure the harmonization of the definition of drug-related offences in order to enable prosecution of drug offences on universally recognized grounds; and
- to strengthen international cooperation in drug matters.

The 1988 Convention was adopted to strengthen measures to suppress illicit trafficking. It obliges Parties to suppress trafficking in narcotic drugs in all its forms. The law should accordingly establish as indictable offences – and fix the main penalties for – at least the following activities:[32]

- production and manufacture;
- international trafficking;
- trafficking (in all the forms provided for in Article 3 of the 1988 Convention); and
- organization, promotion or financing of drug trafficking.[33]

Penalties and aggravating circumstances

The 1988 Convention requires that the domestically enacted offences be subject to penalties that take into account the grave nature of these offences, and then suggests imprisonment and other forms of deprivation of liberty, pecuniary sanctions and confiscation.[34] The 1988 Convention also obliges Parties to take into account eight aggravating circumstances in their implementing legislation.[35] These include: the involvement of an organized criminal group; the use of violence; the fact that the offender holds a public office with which the offence is connected; the victimization or use of minors; and the fact that the offence is committed in a penal institution or a social service facility or in places to which schoolchildren and students resort for educational, sports or social activities. States are also obliged to take foreign convictions into account for the purpose of establishing recidivism.

Jurisdiction

The international nature of these offences calls for punishment of violators irrespective of their nationality, or the place of their crime, even if only part of the offence occurred within a Party's jurisdiction. Finally, the Party in whose territory an offender is found must either extradite them or establish its jurisdiction to enable it to prosecute them before its own courts.[36]

Treatment and rehabilitation

Treatment, education, after-care, rehabilitation and social reintegration may be provided for only as additional measures. In the case of minor offences, however, education, rehabilitation

---

32 1988 Convention, Article 3(1)(a).
33 Article 3(1)(a)(v).
34 1988 Convention Article 3(4)(a).
35 1988 Convention, Article 3(5).
36 1988 Convention, Article 4(2).

or social reintegration may be provided for as the principal measure and as an alternative to conviction and punishment; measures such as treatment or after-care may be provided if the offender is a drug abuser.[37]

Money laundering

The 1988 Convention also introduces the offence of drug money laundering. By distinguishing between conversion, disguise and use of property, it follows the conventional classification of the three stages of laundering: placement, layering and integration.[38] Property, as defined in the 1988 Convention, means assets of every kind, whether corporeal or incorporeal, movable or immovable, tangible or intangible, and legal documents or instruments evidencing title to, or interest in, such assets.[39]

Confiscation

Combating drug money presumes the power to seize it. To achieve this, the 1988 Convention set up a comprehensive mechanism of international mutual assistance in the area of confiscation, aimed at smoothing away the difficulties resulting from the fact that the property in which traffickers invest their profits is not always located in the country where the person involved carries on their activities, where they are resident, or even where they are arrested.[40] The 1988 Convention establishes measures to enable the tracing, freezing, seizing and ultimate confiscation of the proceeds of drug-related crime, notwithstanding bank secrecy laws. The treaty suggests, for those States constitutionally able to do so, introducing into legislation a reversal of the onus of proof by requiring the owner of the seized or frozen assets to show proof of their legitimate source.

Extradition

As regards drug offences, the 1988 Convention serves as a mutual legal assistance and extradition treaty between all Parties.[41] However, execution of a request can be postponed if it interferes with ongoing investigations, prosecution or judicial proceedings. It can be refused if the measures are contrary to the domestic law of the requested State or likely to prejudice its sovereignty, security, public order or other essential interests.

Mutual legal assistance

States are also required to afford one another the widest measure of mutual legal assistance and are prohibited from declining to do so on grounds of bank secrecy.[42] The possibilities of cooperation are very broad: taking evidence or statements from persons; effecting service of judicial documents; executing searches and seizures; examining objects and sites; providing

---

37 1988 Convention, Article 3(4).
38 1988 Convention, Article 3(1)(b)(i) and (ii) and Article 3(1)(c)(i).
39 1988 Convention, Article 1(q).
40 1988 Convention, Articles 3, 5.
41 1988 Convention, Article 6. See also the 1961 Convention, Article 36; 1971 Convention, Article 22.
42 1988 Convention, Article 7.

information and evidentiary items; providing originals or copies of documents; identifying or tracing proceeds, property, instrumentalities or other things for evidentiary purposes. Any other form of legal assistance is possible, subject to the domestic law of the requested party. Assistance is not limited to judicial procedures but extends to all kinds of police or justice investigations. The grounds for refusal are restrictively listed, and any refusal must be duly justified.

Law enforcement cooperation

For such purposes, governments are required to exchange information on the identity and activities of criminals, to set up, whenever necessary, teams of investigators composed of officials from several countries, and to allow for the use of controlled delivery at the international level, with a view to identifying and prosecuting traffickers.[43]

Special investigation techniques

The 1988 Convention also provides guidelines for controlled delivery[44] to identify and arrest persons organizing illicit drug shipments. The appropriate authority allows illicit consignments of drugs or precursors to circulate in the territory of the country when this appears to be the surest means of successfully identifying and arresting the persons dispatching the consignment, the carriers and the addressees. In the case of international carriage, that decision is made on the basis of agreements concluded with the other interested States. The 1988 Convention also authorizes States to perform searches of mail.[45] This can be combined with controlled deliveries in order to trace illicit consignments of drugs or precursors. Finally, the Convention empowers[46] law enforcement services to take action on the high seas where the vessel is exercising freedom of navigation according to international law. With the authorization of the Flag State, law enforcement authorities can board and search vessels, and take any appropriate action if evidence of involvement in trafficking is found.

Abuse

A punishable offence

Under the conventions, States have to establish possession, purchase or cultivation of drugs for illicit personal consumption as a criminal offence. Treatment or rehabilitation may be provided as alternatives to conviction and punishment for possession offences as well as for trafficking offences, 'in appropriate cases of a minor nature'.[47] Article 4, paragraph (c) is the main provision explicitly referring to use of drugs in the 1961 Convention. It obliges Parties to 'limit exclusively to medical and scientific purposes . . . the . . . use and possession of drugs'. Two other provisions deal with possession. Article 33 provides that 'the Parties shall not permit the possession of drugs except under legal authority'. Article 36, paragraph 1 requires that each Party,

43 1988 Convention, Article 9.
44 1988 Convention, Article 11.
45 1988 Convention, Article 19.
46 1988 Convention, Article 17.
47 1961 Convention, Articles 2, 4, 36; 1971 Convention, Articles 3, 5, 22; 1988 Convention, Article 3(2).

subject to its constitutional limitations . . . shall adopt such measures as will ensure that cultivation, production, manufacture . . . possession, offering, offering for sale . . . of drugs contrary to the provisions of this Convention . . . be punishable offences when committed intentionally, and that serious offences shall be liable to adequate punishment particularly by imprisonment or other penalties of deprivation of liberty.

Some States took the view that possession in Article 36 referred to possession for the purposes of supply or sale, whereas other States understood that possession should constitute an offence irrespective of whether it would be for personal or for commercial purposes. In reaction to the ambiguity of these provisions, the intention of the drafters of the 1988 Convention was to reach a text that clearly forbids and incriminates the non-medical use of drugs. Article 3(2) provides:

> Subject to its constitutional principles and the basic concepts of its legal system, each Party shall adopt such measures as may be necessary to establish as a criminal offence under its domestic law, when committed intentionally, the possession, purchase or cultivation of narcotic drugs or psychotropic substances for personal consumption contrary to the provisions of the 1961 Convention, the 1961 Convention as amended or the 1971 Convention.

'Safeguard clause': constitutional principles and basic concepts of the legal system

The purpose of the *chapeau* to Article 3(2) was not to exempt some Parties from its obligation to criminalize because their constitution includes provision on personal freedom to do what citizens want with themselves – as claimed by some supporters of the legalization of drug use[48] – but simply to take into account national specificity in the classification of crimes (misdemeanours or more serious crime) and rules for adoption (by law or administrative decree).[49] Contrary to what is sometimes said, the 1988 Convention does not offer considerable latitude to Parties concerning the criminalization or not of non-medical use.[50] The obligation to criminalize in Article 3 is explicit and unambiguous. If some latitude exists, it is not in the freedom to decide whether non-medical use is a crime or not. The latitude is, once the offence has been established, in the possibility for the prosecutor and the Court to be flexible in the answer: sanction, mitigation or alternative treatment. Parties may choose to apply punitive sanctions or therapeutic measures; they are at liberty to provide for compulsory treatment that is additional or alternative to punishment.

48 See, for example, K. Krawjeski, 'How Flexible are the United Nations Drug Conventions?', *The International Journal of Drug Policy*, 1999, vol. 10, p. 329, p. 335 *et seq.*

49 The author was present during the preparatory work and during the discussions for the adoption of the Convention, and no delegation affirmed that it would be unconstitutional in their country to prosecute possession for personal use based on specific provisions regarding personal freedom including the right to take drugs. It was only pointed out by academics as a theoretical risk to have to face such a situation in the future.

50 See, for example Krawjeski, 'How Flexible are the United Nations Drug Conventions', p. 333 *et seq.*

Treatment

Articles 33, 36 and 38 of the 1961 Convention, Articles 20 and 22 of the 1971 Convention, and Article 3 of the 1988 Convention oblige Parties to take all practicable measures for the prevention of drug abuse and for the early identification, treatment, education, after-care, rehabilitation and social reintegration of drug addicts. Compliance will necessarily depend on the interpretation by the Parties of these concepts, which are not defined by the treaties. State practice has shown that such interpretation may vary greatly from country to country and with it their understanding of how best to handle their respective drug-abuse-related problems, while complying with their treaty-based obligations.

Implementation challenges

Administrative instead of criminal sanctions[51]

For many, stigmatizing drug consumers with criminal sanctions, even where imprisonment is not the first option, is not a proportionate response, and may be seen as leading to their social marginalization. Resort may be had to administrative sanctions for conduct not serious enough to reach the threshold required for the intervention of the criminal justice system. Administrative sanctions offer a lesser degree of burden of proof and speedier procedures, coupled with reduced moral stigma, while retaining a dissuasive function. Fines, community services, travel restrictions or suspension of driving licences may in some countries be seen as being dissuasive, without leaving criminal records that can pose challenges to social rehabilitation. The recognition of different degrees of sanction for offences of different degrees of severity, in application of the principle of proportionality, indicates that administrative sanctions could be used at least for minor offences. Doing so may fall among the possibilities available under Article 3(2), as long as States concerned invoke the 'safeguard clause' and keep in perspective the implementation of the aims of the 1961 and 1971 Conventions: to limit use and possession to medical and scientific purposes.

Making treatment and rehabilitation measures available

The three UN conventions devote only two of their 116 articles and one paragraph of a third article to the treatment and reintegration of addicts. The divergent views of States regarding the attitude to be adopted in regard to drug abusers, the absence of any specific treatment for drug dependence, and the continual developments in and complexity of drug addict care dissuaded the drafters of the conventions from proposing treatment methods that might be immediately challenged or quickly overtaken and unsuited to the needs or resources of some countries. The 1961 and 1971 Conventions simply call upon governments to take all possible measures for the prevention of drug abuse and for the early identification, treatment, education, after-care, rehabilitation and social reintegration of addicts, while Article 3(4) of the 1988 Convention has only slightly more specific wording.

---

51 See generally the European Monitoring Centre for Drugs and Drug Addiction, *Illicit Drug Use in the EU: Legislative Approaches*, Lisbon, 2005, at www.emcdda.europa.eu/attachements.cfm/att_10080_ EN_EMCDDATP_01.pdf (accessed 14 March 2014).

Harm reduction measures

The 1961 and 1971 Conventions were drawn up before HIV and the hepatitis C virus were known, and the 1988 Convention before any correlation was made between injected drug use and HIV. In the 1998 Declaration on the Guiding Principles of Drug Demand Reduction the UN General Assembly recognized that '[a] rapidly changing social and economic climate coupled with increased availability and promotion of drugs and the demand for them have contributed to the increasing magnitude of the global drug abuse problem'.[52] The treaties, in their preambles, express concern for the health and welfare of mankind and for the health and social problems resulting from drug abuse. This might be construed as clear intent on the part of the treaties to combat drug abuse out of concern for its health and welfare consequences. Proponents of harm reduction may view this, in combination with the provisions of Article 14, paragraph 4 of the 1988 Convention, as express consent to alleviate the human suffering associated with drug abuse through harm-reduction policies. And on this basis, several States have developed specific programmes such as:

- syringe and needle exchange programmes, regarded as decreasing the number of injections, reducing infections and limiting the discarding of syringes;
- introduction of so-called 'low-threshold' care, said to improve the health of users by altering their behaviour and encouraging them to make contact with care facilities;
- organization of 'testing' in places where use occurs in a party context, although effectiveness remains unproven; and
- risk reduction programmes in prisons (syringe exchange), already being implemented in prisons in Europe, it is claimed, with positive results.[53]

Drug injection rooms, in contrast, facilitate the abuse of drugs by providing officially sanctioned places where illicit drugs can be used with impunity. This is not treatment and there is no evidence to date that injecting rooms are reducing drug abuse in the areas where they have been established. According to the INCB, official establishment or tolerance of drug injection rooms is contrary to the conventions.[54]

Cannabis problems

Cannabis is the most prevalent drug of abuse and its link to young people is at odds with the apparent permissiveness towards it under many national legal systems. Many developing countries that struggle to eliminate cannabis cultivation are discouraged by the apparent tolerance shown by their developed neighbours. Parties to the conventions are under the obligation:

- to prohibit the cultivation of the cannabis plant, if in the country or territory of the Party, 'the prevailing conditions . . . render the prohibition of the cannabis plant the most

---

52 Available on the UNODC website, http://www.unodc.org/pdf/report_1999-01-01_1.pdf (accessed 12 November 2013), p. 7.
53 K. Dolan, S. Rutter and A.D. Wodak, 'Prison-based Syringe Exchange Programmes: A Review of International Research and Development', *Addiction*, 2003, vol. 98, pp. 153–158.
54 INCB, *Report of the Interntional Narcotics Control Board for 1999*, UN Doc E/INCB,1991/1, pp. 176–177.

suitable measure in its opinion for protecting the public health and welfare and preventing the diversion of drugs into the illicit traffic;'[55]

- to take appropriate measures to prevent illicit cannabis cultivation and to eradicate cannabis plants cultivated illicitly;[56]
- to establish illicit cannabis plant cultivation as a serious criminal offence, 'liable to sanctions which take into account the grave nature' of the offence;[57] but, 'in appropriate cases of a minor nature' and in cases of possession, purchase or cultivation for personal use, education, rehabilitation, social reintegration, treatment and after-care measures may be taken in addition to or as an alternative to conviction and punishment;[58] and
- to seize and destroy any cannabis plants illicitly cultivated.[59]

Some States have made punishable by administrative fine the cultivation, purchase or possession for personal use of quantities of the drug below a statutory minimum limit (e.g. Italy, Spain, Austria, and some internal states of federal States such as the United States and Australia). More serious prosecution options usually remain open at the discretion of the authorities. Other States have taken advantage of the 1988 Convention provisions enabling 'appropriate minor' cultivation offences and/or possession purchase or cultivation for personal use offences to be addressed by non-penal alternatives rather than criminal justice sanctions of conviction and punishment.[60] These may include education, referral to a drug abuse help agency, or administrative caution, among other measures. Enforcement of obligations in regard to illicit cultivation can be lax in some developed States, because of the high proportion of illicit use in the population and the perception that cannabis products are not 'harmful enough' to justify expending scarce criminal justice resources. In developing countries, illicit cultivation penalties and sanctions are typically higher, but prosecutions are often not brought because of unwillingness to prosecute rural farmers, or the danger involved, or the lack of flexible criminal procedures and options to deal with cannabis cases except by full trial. Many law enforcement agencies prioritize prosecution of personal use because of ease of proof and convictions, and hence attractive statistical success rates. But this diverts resources from the more important and difficult cases (e.g. organized cultivation prosecutions and asset forfeiture cases), and tends to overload the criminal justice and penitentiary systems.

Recent developments in the United States, a party to all of the conventions (without reservation in regard to cannabis), are worthy of comment. In 1989, the CND authorized the medical use of cannabis, but only as pills under prescription. The United States followed suit, and the US Food and Drug Administration (FDA) issued advice against smoked medical cannabis. Marijuana remains illegal under federal law, but around twenty states have allowed the use of medical marijuana under prescription. In 2012, Colorado and Washington states undertook referendums regarding the legalization of non-medical use of cannabis. The Federal Government then took the position that it would leave states free to experiment with legalization. Colorado took the lead, enacting new laws permitting personal cultivation and

---

55 1961 Convention, Article 22(1).
56 1988 Convention, Article 14(2).
57 1988 Convention, Article 3, para. (1)(a)(ii) and para. (4)(a); see also 1961 Convention, Article 36(1)(a).
58 1988 Convention, Article 3(4) (c) and (d).
59 1961 Convention, Article 22(2).
60 1988 Convention, Articles 3(4)(c) and (d).

recreational use.[61] Under Article 4(c) of the 1961 Convention, States have 'to limit exclusively to medical and scientific purposes the production, manufacture, export, import, distribution of, trade in, use and possession of drugs'. That Convention includes provisions defining the way for governments to denounce their ratification or to initiate a revision process. The United States has not done so and is exposed, at least theoretically, to retaliation measures from the INCB under Article 14 of the 1961 Convention. Similar steps in Uruguay led to the INCB calling upon its authorities to carefully consider all possible repercussions.[62]

The legalization debate

Anti-prohibitionists proclaim the failure of prohibition and that many of the economic and social problems encountered are the fault of the conventions and the international control system and that therefore they must be dismantled.[63] Solutions envisaged range from liberalization, which would retain prohibition but not apply sanctions, to non-criminal prohibition where penal sanctions are replaced by civil or administrative measures, to decriminalization, where the possession and use of drugs would no longer be prohibited or subject to legal control, and to legalization, which can either be a synonym for decriminalization or mean not prohibiting drugs but organizing activities associated with drug production and marketing legally. Legalization involves a number of options. The production and use of all kinds of drugs could be freed of any legal restrictions. This idea, not applied in any country at present, is based on the assumption that deregulation of drugs would reduce drug prices drastically and therefore ruin the traffickers. Another option based on the same assumption would be to organize the drug trade under state monopoly in order to satisfy demand while avoiding the undesirable effects of the present trade thanks to the absence of competition and publicity. Controlled distribution would enable registered drug users to obtain their supplies with medical prescriptions.

Many of the proposals that legalization advocates make have been used in the past.[64] The total legalization of production, trade and use is actually the situation that existed at the beginning of the twentieth century. Opium was widely available in China, Europe and the United States. Morphine, heroin and cocaine all followed. Experiments with drug prohibition in China in 1906 and in the Philippines in 1909 showed that prohibition could be the right response to the abuse problem. Drug abuse declined progressively worldwide after the organization of international controls under the 1912 Convention and the subsequent national laws restricting production and trade to medical needs.

After the enactment in the United States of the Harrison Act of 1914 implementing the 1912 Convention, medical practitioners began to distribute, on medical prescription, heroin to drug addicts. This experiment of maintenance programmes, similar to those that Switzerland now wants experiment with, was stopped under pressure by the American Medical Association in 1923. It did not prove to have any impact as a treatment, because the access to drugs was easy, and addicts did not have any incentive to reduce their use. In the United Kingdom in the 1960s medical doctors were allowed to prescribe heroin to drug

---

61 Article 18(16) of the State Constitution.
62 See 'Lawmakers in Uruguay Vote to Legalize Marijuana', *New York Times*, 31 July 2013.
63 See S. Rolles, *After the War on Drugs: Blue Print for Regulation*, Transform Drug Policy Foundation, 2009.
64 See, N. Bejerot, 'Drug Abuse and Drug Policy', *Acta Psychiatrica Scandinavica*, Suppl. 1975, no. 256, pp. 3–277.

addicts. The system worked for a few years but, because of unscrupulous practitioners, prescribed drugs became readily available on the streets, adding to the existing drug problem. Defenders of what became known as 'the British system' acknowledged that many of the registered addicts attended clinics only when they could not afford their habit on the street, or when heroin was scarce, but would not stay in treatment. A similar experiment in Sweden, involving distribution of drugs on medical prescription was also tried between 1965 and 1967, leading to the same conclusions. According to Swedish authorities, many of the patients supplied a parallel market of prescribed drugs, and crime of all types by patients increased during the experience. A study undertaken among arrested drugs users during the period of changes in policy (1965 to 1970) showed an expansion of use and an increase in intravenous abuse.[65] This fell during the 'extra-restrictive policy' period that followed, which must be seen as a result of the reduced availability of drugs.

The most important ongoing European legalization experiment concerns the Netherlands, where cannabis use and retail trade is tolerated and de facto legalized, but production and wholesale trade is still unlawful.[66] The underlying policy is to establish clear lines between 'soft drugs' and 'hard drugs', to avoid the involvement of youngsters who would like to take cannabis in drug networks. Dutch authorities claim that the prevalence of cannabis (and heroin) use is lower than in other European countries, which is documented by surveys. Two side effects have resulted. First, very potent cannabis was developed and became readily available. Second, trafficking, not only in cannabis but in all sorts of prohibited drugs, increased. The INCB, in its report for 1994, stated about the Dutch experience that it was

> questionable whether the theory of separation of markets has ever demonstrated its practicability. Places where cannabis distribution is tolerated have attracted traffickers of other drugs and abusers, as well as potential abusers; thus all types of drugs seem to be readily available at such places. That situation might have influenced the attitude of advocates of legalization. The emphasis is no longer on separating the use of cannabis from the use of other drugs; instead, it is on mitigating or reducing the harmful consequences of drug abuse, as opposed to preventing drug abuse, because in their opinion the non-medical use of all drugs should be accepted by society. That philosophy does not differentiate any more between so-called 'soft' and 'hard' drugs; the aim is the acceptance of the use of drugs in general in European society.[67]

In 1995, the INCB reported with concern that the Netherlands was continuing 'the failed policy' of 'separation of markets'.[68] The pressure of the international community led the Dutch Government to review its policy.[69] While continuing to argue for the policy of separation of markets, they decided to close half of the existing coffee shops, to limit to five grams the maximum quantity of cannabis tolerated per person, and more generally to contain the nuisance drug use causes to society.

---

65 Ibid.
66 See E. Leuw and I.H. Marshall (eds), *Between Prohibition and Legalization: The Dutch Experiment in Drug Policy*, Amsterdam: Kugler, 1994.
67 INCB, *Report of the International Narcotics Control Board for 1994*, Vienna: UN, 1995, p. 56, para. 213.
68 INCB, *Report of the International Narcotics Control Board for 1995*, Vienna: UN, 1996, p. lxxiii, para. 9.
69 See T. Boekhout von Solinge, 'Dutch Drug Policy in a European Context', *Journal of Drug Issues*, 1999, vol. 29, no. 3, pp. 511–528.

The Bolivian denunciation/re-accession process

According to Article 49 of the 1961 Convention, coca leaf chewing had to be abolished. The article allowed countries only a temporary exemption, and coca chewing had to be phased out in any case within 25 years, which meant by 1989. Bolivia was a party to the Convention. In 2010, Bolivian President Evo Morales, who was previously the head of Bolivia's coca growing union, campaigned to get the UN to reverse what he called a 'historic wrong' and lift its long-standing ban on the chewing of coca leaves. In 2011, Bolivia decided to develop a new strategy to legalize the coca leaf and proposed an amendment to Article 49, deleting the above-mentioned obligation. Eighteen governments submitted objections to the proposal and the process was blocked. The Bolivian government then decided to withdraw from the 1961 Convention, and that was done by presenting to the UN General Secretary in New York a formal notification of denunciation. Bolivia subsequently re-acceded with a reservation! The other Parties were entitled to reject this strategy, a strategy not anticipated by the authors of the Convention. They were also entitled to delay the ongoing process by deciding to consult together with a view to the settlement of the dispute by negotiation, investigation, mediation, conciliation, arbitration, recourse to regional bodies and judicial process, including referring to the International Court of Justice for a decision. But nothing happened. The Bolivian House of Representatives then approved the law on 22 June 2011, and the Senate ratified the decision on 28 June.[70] The Bolivian denunciation/re-accession introduced a double problem. It created a precedent for States to change their mind at any time in regard to a treaty, endangering the whole regime of treaties. More specifically, the Parties had the possibility to react but they did not reach the required minimum of sixty States to stop the process. A gap emerged between their internal opposition to this step and their (absence of) expression, and the credibility of the UN drug conventions is now seriously in question.

70 See 'Bolivia: Morales Wins Victory as U.N. Agrees to Define Some Coca Use as Legal', *New York Times*, 11 January 2013.

15

Weapons smuggling

Catherine E. Drummond and Anthony E. Cassimatis*

Introduction

The international community has recently built upon international legal regulation of transfers of conventional weapons, including the suppression of weapons smuggling, which has been developed since the end of the Cold War.[1] For example, 2013 saw the negotiation of the Arms Trade Treaty,[2] which complements the 2001 Protocol against the Illicit Manufacturing of and Trafficking in Firearms, Their Parts and Components and Ammunition, Supplementing the United Nations Convention against Transnational Organized Crime (Firearms Protocol).[3] Developments in 2013 also enhanced and supplemented the operation of two important soft law instruments. In the same year as the UN General Assembly adopted the text of the Firearms Protocol, the international community also adopted the Programme of Action to Prevent, Combat and Eradicate the Illicit Trade in Small Arms and Light Weapons in All Its Aspects, 2001 (Programme of Action).[4] In 2005, members of the UN adopted the International Instrument to Enable States to Identify and Trace, in a Timely and Reliable Manner, Illicit

*   The authors wish to thank Nathalie Weizmann of the International Committee of the Red Cross and Cynthia L. Ebbs, Alison Mellon and Claire Mortimer of the ATT Legal Response Network for providing access to documents related to the negotiation of the Arms Trade Treaty. The authors remain entirely responsible, however, for any shortcomings in this chapter.

1   See, for example, Z. Yihdego, *The Arms Trade and International Law*, Oxford: Hart Publishing, 2007; A.E. Cassimatis and K. Greenwood, 'Arms, Traffic in', in R. Wolfrum *et al.* (eds), *The Max Planck Encyclopedia of Public International Law*, Volume I, Oxford: Oxford University Press, 2012, p. 646; M. Brehm, 'The Arms Trade and States' Duty to Ensure Respect for Humanitarian and Human Rights Law', *Journal of Conflict & Security Law*, 2008, vol. 12, p. 359; D.L. Rothe and J.I. Ross, 'The State and Transnational Organized Crime: The Case of Small Arms Trafficking', in F. Allum and S. Gilmour (eds), *Routledge Handbook of Transnational Organized Crime*, Abingdon: Routledge, 2012, p. 391.
2   2 April 2013; not yet in force.
3   31 May 2001, 2326 UNTS 208, in force 3 June 2005.
4   Report of the United Nations Conference on the Illicit Trade in Small Arms and Light Weapons in All Its Aspects New York, 9–20 July 2001, UN Doc A/CONF.192/15.

Small Arms and Light Weapons, 2005 (International Tracing Instrument).[5] This latter soft law instrument built upon the former soft law Programme of Action, providing more detailed standards to reduce the risk of illicit diversion of conventional weapons.[6] These global instruments have also been supported by arrangements developed specifically by arms-exporting States[7] and regional initiatives.[8]

The most significant development in 2013 was the General Assembly's adoption of the text of the Arms Trade Treaty.[9] Unlike the Firearms Protocol and the Programme of Action, which are principally focused on illicit transfers of weapons, the Arms Trade Treaty imposes legal obligations on States Parties in relation to lawful transfers of conventional weapons. There is, however, a link between the regulation of lawful transfers and the suppression of illicit transfers, such as weapons smuggling. The preamble to the Arms Trade Treaty, for example, underlines the treaty's potential to address, through its effective regulation of lawful transfers, the 'need to prevent and eradicate the illicit trade in conventional arms and to prevent their diversion to the illicit market, or for unauthorized end use and end users, including in the commission of terrorist acts'.[10]

As at 30 March 2014, the Arms Trade Treaty had been signed by 118 States, including significant arms-exporting States such as the United States, Germany, France, the United Kingdom, Spain and Italy.[11] This compares favourably with the Firearms Protocol, which had 109 States Parties as at 30 March 2014. If all major arms-exporting States become parties to the Arms Trade Treaty then it will also have a significant impact on the capacity of non-parties to the treaty to access arms in circumstances where the Arms Trade Treaty requires States Parties to prohibit transfers.

Another important development in 2013 was the adoption by the UN Security Council of Resolution 2117 (26 September 2013) on illicit transfers of small arms and light weapons. The significance of this resolution lies in the manner in which it formally links, under the authority of the Security Council (and with the support of the five permanent members of

---

5 See General Assembly Resolution 60/81 of 8 December 2005 and the Report of the Open-ended Working Group to Negotiate an International Instrument to Enable States to Identify and Trace, in a Timely and Reliable Manner, Illicit Small Arms and Light Weapons, UN Doc A/60/88, 27 June 2005.

6 Note other relevant soft law instruments including the International Ammunition Technical Guidelines (IATG) developed under the UN SaferGuard programme and the International Small Arms Control Standards (ISACS) – in arms and ammunition stockpile management practices – these are referred to in United Nations Secretary-General, Small Arms, Report of the Secretary-General, UN Doc S/2013/503, 22 August 2013.

7 The most important arrangement of this kind is the Wassenaar Arrangement on Export Controls for Conventional Arms and Dual-Use Goods and Technologies. As of January 2013, the 41 Participating States of the Wassenaar Arrangement included France, Germany, Italy, Japan, the Russian Federation, South Africa, Spain, Sweden, Switzerland, Ukraine, the United Kingdom and the United States. See http://www.wassenaar.org (accessed 17 April 2014).

8 Important regional initiatives have been taken by African States – see, for example, http://www.poa-iss.org/RegionalOrganizations/RegionalOrganizations.aspx (accessed 17 April 2014). The EU has also adopted important measures; see for example http://www.poa-iss.org/RegionalOrganizations/10.aspx (accessed 17 April 2014).

9 Annexed to General Assembly Resolution 67/234 B of 2 April 2013.

10 The fourth preambular paragraph of the Arms Trade Treaty.

11 These six states were all ranked in the top ten arms-exporting States for the period 2008–2012 – Stockholm International Peace Research Institute, SIPRI Yearbook 2013, Summary, 10, available at http://www.sipri.org/yearbook/2013/files/SIPRIYB13Summary.pdf (accessed 17 April 2014).

the Council[12]), the Firearms Protocol, the Programme of Action, the International Tracing Instrument and the Arms Trade Treaty. The close link between enhanced regulation of lawful arms transfers and the eradication of illicit transfers is also recognised, as is the need for enhanced cooperation between States and institutions such as Interpol and the importance of capacity-building measures.

In the second part of this chapter, we will examine the global and regional responses to *illicit* transfers of small arms and light weapons[13] and other forms of conventional weapons. In the third part we will review international standards that have been developed in relation to lawful transfers of such weapons. Recent significant events such as the General Assembly's adoption of the Arms Trade Treaty will be assessed. These developments, imposing, for example, obligations on States Parties to establish export control systems for arms, ammunition and components, reduce the risks of diversion of lawfully transferred weapons to illicit markets for such weapons. The legal obligations imposed on States by the Firearms Protocol and the Arms Trade Treaty supplement other international legal obligations imposed on States in relation to arms transfers. The chapter will then consider, in the fourth section, individual criminal responsibility for illicit transfers of arms, both directly under international law and under municipal law. The principal focus of the fourth part will be on the potential criminal liability of arms brokers. This focus on brokers is warranted in light of the significant role that arms brokers have played in weapons smuggling. The effective suppression of weapons smuggling appears impossible without the employment of a combination of intergovernmental and municipal regulatory and enforcement measures. Ensuring the coherent and consistent application of these international and national measures poses distinct regulatory challenges.

International instruments on the suppression of illicit transfers of firearms and other small arms and light weapons

Security Council resolutions

Security Council Resolution 2117 indentifies the threat that weapons smuggling poses to the taking of Chapter VII enforcement action by the Security Council. Security Council resolutions imposing arms embargoes directly bind States. States that transfer arms contrary to such resolutions violate their international legal obligations under the UN Charter.[14] The Security Council has also sought to address non-State actors that seek to smuggle arms in violation of Security Council resolutions.[15] Resolutions have emphasised the obligation on States to prohibit non-State actors within their jurisdiction from transferring arms in violation of UN

---

12 The Russian Federation abstained but explained that its abstention related to the resolution not including a strong prohibition of illicit transfers of small arms and light weapons to non-State actors – see Security Council, 7036th meeting, Thursday, 26 September 2013, UN Doc S/PV.7036, pp. 4–5.

13 The International Tracing Instrument offers a definition of 'small arms' and 'light weapons' in Art. 4.

14 Under Art. 25 of the UN Charter. According to Art. 103 of the Charter these obligations prevail over other international obligations.

15 See J.M. Farrall, *United Nations Sanctions and the Rule of Law*, Cambridge: Cambridge University Press, 2007, pp. 110–116.

sanctions.[16] National (and regional) enforcement of Security Council sanctions can, however, be problematic.[17]

Practical measures to ensure greater efficacy of Security Council resolutions imposing arms embargoes have included ensuring that panels of experts advising the Security Council's sanctions committees include experts in arms transfers.[18] The potential role of UN peacekeeping and peacebuilding missions, through their formal mandates[19] and through capacity building of local police forces and other authorities,[20] to take concrete steps to reduce the potential for weapons smuggling in violation of resolutions has also been considered. Such UN missions can also assist, for example, through capacity building in the context of tracing and the development of national inventories and marking of weaponry to minimise the risk of diversion of arms in violation of UN sanctions.[21]

The Firearms Protocol

Various treaties and soft law instruments have been negotiated to address illicit transfers. States Parties to the Firearms Protocol are required to criminalise within their national legal systems 'illicit trafficking in firearms, their parts and components and ammunition'.[22] The Firearms Protocol generally excludes from its application State-to-State transfers of firearms.[23] The *travaux préparatoires* of the Protocol do, however, indicate that it applies to commercial transfers of firearms 'between entities owned or operated by governments, such as State-owned arms manufacturers'.[24] Subject to that limited exception, however, the Firearms Protocol focuses on non-State transfers.

The Firearms Protocol applies to small arms and to a limited class of light weapons.[25] It also applies to certain parts and components of firearms and to ammunition.[26] States Parties are required to 'establish and maintain an effective system of export and import licensing or authorization, as well as of measures on international transit, for the transfer of firearms, their parts and components and ammunition'.[27] In order to facilitate tracing, the Firearms Protocol imposes obligations on States Parties to require distinct and identifiable markings to be applied to firearms manufactured in, or imported into, their territory.[28] States Parties that have not already established a system regulating firearm brokers and brokering are also required under Article 15 of the Firearms Protocol to 'consider establishing a system for regulating the activities of those who engage in brokering'. The absence of a legal obligation on States that do not currently regulate brokering to do more than 'consider' regulating

---

16 See, for example, UN Security Council Resolution 1970 (2011) adopted on 26 February 2011, para. 9.
17 See, for example, *Nada v Switzerland* [2012] ECHR 1691; and *Kadi and Al Barakaat v Council of the European Union* (2008) 47 ILM 923.
18 See, for example, Report of the Secretary-General.
19 Ibid., para. 35.
20 Ibid., paras 52–53.
21 Ibid., paras 46–48.
22 Art. 5 of the Firearms Protocol.
23 Art. 4 of the Firearms Protocol.
24 UNODC, *Travaux Préparatoires of the Negotiations for the Elaboration of the United Nations Convention against Transnational Organized Crime and the Protocols thereto*, New York, 2006, p. 627.
25 See Art. 3 of the Firearms Protocol.
26 See Arts 3(b) and (c) and 4(1) of the Firearms Protocol.
27 Art. 10 of the Firearms Protocol.
28 Art. 8 of the Firearms Protocol.

brokering is a major weakness of the Firearms Protocol, which, in this regard, goes no further than the relevant soft law instruments.[29]

Regional instruments

A regional treaty, the 1997 Inter-American Convention against the Illicit Manufacturing of and Trafficking in Firearms, Ammunition, Explosives and Other Related Materials,[30] which was negotiated under the auspices of the Organization of American States (OAS), contains provisions similar to those of the Firearms Protocol. The Inter-American Convention also potentially applies to State transfers (in cases where firearms are transferred to or across a State Party's territory without its authorisation) but the treaty does not address brokering. Brokering is, however, the subject of model legislation prepared under the auspices of the OAS.[31]

Regional and sub-regional initiatives have also been taken by developing States in the African region. These initiatives include three treaties, which impose international obligations on States Parties regarding traffic in small arms and light weapons.[32] The treaties require States Parties to enact and maintain national laws; criminalising illicit trafficking; imposing licensing and authorisation procedures for transfers (including brokering); and on tracing mechanisms. One of these treaties, the 2006 ECOWAS Convention on Small Arms and Light Weapons, Their Ammunition and Other Related Materials, negotiated under the auspices of the Economic Community of West African States (ECOWAS), requires collective authorisation (on the basis of consensus) by ECOWAS Member States before certain transfers are permitted under the treaty.[33] The allocation of sufficient human and financial resources is critical to ensuring compliance with the obligations established under these instruments. Inadequacies in institutional capacity have been a significant issue in past failures to address illicit transfers of arms within the African region.[34]

International rules and instruments regulating lawful transfers of small arms and light weapons

Customary international law

In the absence of treaty obligations to the contrary, States are generally free to manufacture and acquire conventional weapons. This general position under customary international law was recognised in *Military and Paramilitary Activities in and against Nicaragua (Nicaragua*

---

29 See para. 14 of the Programme of Action.
30 14 November 1997, 37 ILM 143 (1998); in force 1 July 1998.
31 See the OAS Department of Public Security website, http://www.oas.org/dsp/english/cpo_armas_claves.asp (accessed 17 April 2014).
32 The Protocol on Control of Firearms, Ammunition and Other Related Materials in the Southern African Development Community Region, 2001; the Nairobi Protocol for the Prevention, Control and Reduction of Small Arms and Light Weapons in the Great Lakes Region and the Horn of Africa, 2004; and the ECOWAS Convention on Small Arms and Light Weapons, Their Ammunition and Other Related Materials, 2006 – see http://www.poa-iss.org/RegionalOrganizations/RegionalOrganizations.aspx (accessed 17 April 2014).
33 Art. 6 of the ECOWAS convention sets out circumstances in which transfers will not be authorised.
34 See, for example, Cassimatis and Greenwood, 'Arms, Traffic in', p. 650.

v United States of America) (Merits),[35] where the International Court of Justice (ICJ) observed that:

> in international law there are no rules, other than such rules as may be accepted by the State concerned, by treaty or otherwise, whereby the level of armaments of a sovereign State can be limited, and this principle is valid for all States without exception.[36]

As recognised by the Court, States may assume obligations by treaty in relation to the transfer of arms. The Arms Trade Treaty is a recent and important example of such an instrument. Notwithstanding the apparently unqualified terms in which the ICJ expressed itself in the *Nicaragua case* regarding limitations on levels of armaments, States are also under customary obligations not to permit the transfer of arms in particular circumstances. For example, in the *Nicaragua case* itself, the Court recognised that a State may violate obligations under customary international law to respect, and ensure respect for, the rules of international humanitarian law if the State, by the transfer of arms, seeks 'to encourage persons or groups' engaged in armed conflict 'to act in violation of' the rules of customary international law that are reflected in Article 3 common to the four Geneva Conventions of 1949.[37]

States also appear to be under a due diligence obligation, which derives from their customary duty to prevent genocide, to restrict transfers of arms in cases where there is a 'serious risk' or 'serious danger' that genocide will be committed. This was suggested by the ICJ when it considered related obligations arising under the Convention on the Prevention and Punishment of the Crime of Genocide 1948 (Genocide Convention), in its 2007 merits judgment in the *Case Concerning the Application of the Convention on the Prevention and Punishment of the Crime of Genocide (Bosnia and Herzegovina v Serbia and Montenegro)*.[38]

In addition to these primary obligations under international law requiring States to restrict what would otherwise be lawful transfers of arms, there also appear to be secondary obligations requiring restrictions on transfers of arms. The International Law Commission (ILC) has recognised the possibility of derivative responsibility of a State that knowingly transfers arms that provide aid or assistance to a recipient State in the commission of an internationally wrongful act by the recipient State in Article 16 of the Articles on the Responsibility of States for Internationally Wrongful Acts (Articles on State Responsibility). While the ILC's commentary to Article 16 refers to the existence of an intention to facilitate the commission of the wrongful act on the part of the aiding or assisting State, the actual terms of Article 16 do not refer to such an intention. According to the express terms of Article 16, for a State to be responsible for aiding or assisting under Article 16, it must have 'knowledge of the circumstances of the internationally wrongful act'. Notwithstanding views to the contrary,[39] the Arms Trade Treaty confirms, in Article 6(3) (discussed further below), that a State will be responsible for aiding or assisting in the commission of an international wrongful act if the State providing the aid or assistance knows of the circumstances

---

35 ICJ Rep 1986, p. 14 (*Nicaragua case*).
36 Ibid., para. 269.
37 Ibid., para. 220.
38 ICJ Reports 2007, 43, paras 429–432 (*Bosnia Genocide case*).
39 See, in particular, H.P. Aust, *Complicity and the Law of State Responsibility*, Cambridge: Cambridge University Press, 2011.

surrounding the internationally wrongful act, whether or not an intention to facilitate that wrongful act can be independently demonstrated.[40]

Finally under customary international law, if a State has committed a serious breach of a peremptory norm, all other States appear to be under an international legal obligation not to render aid or assistance that would allow the State receiving such aid or assistance to maintain the situation created by the serious breach.[41] In the context of arms transfers, this would include violations of the peremptory prohibitions on the commission of genocide, war crimes and crimes against humanity. A transfer of arms in those circumstances would potentially give rise to State responsibility for the transferring State.

The above obligations are all framed in terms of State-to-State transfers of arms. The same principles, however, appear to apply to transfers of arms by non-State actors in one State to non-State actors in another. This conclusion is supported by: (a) the ICJ's finding in the *Bosnia Genocide case* that Serbia was responsible for violation of its duty to prevent genocide by virtue of its relationship with non-State actors, namely Bosnian Serb forces; (b) the due diligence nature of the obligation to prevent genocide recognised in the *Bosnia Genocide case* which must, logically and in principle, require a State to refuse to permit a non-State actor to transfer arms from its territory where the State has the requisite knowledge of the use to which those arms will be put by the intended recipient of those arms; and (c) the context in which the ICJ in the *Nicaragua case* framed the due diligence obligation to ensure respect for international humanitarian law. That case also involved transfers of arms to non-State actors, namely the Contra rebels.

The Arms Trade Treaty

The Arms Trade Treaty expressly addresses the obligations imposed on States by Security Council resolutions,[42] by treaties (for example, suppressing illicit trafficking of conventional arms)[43] and by relevant rules of customary international law. The statement of principles in the opening section of the Arms Trade Treaty implicitly encompasses customary obligations to restrict arms transfers.[44] In addition, Article 6(3) of the Arms Trade Treaty provides that:

---

40 The 26 July 2012 draft text of the Arms Trade Treaty, UN Doc A/CONF.217/CRP.1, provided in Art. 3(3) that '[a] State Party shall not authorise a transfer of conventional arms . . . for the purpose of facilitating the commission of genocide, crimes against humanity, war crimes constituting grave breaches of the Geneva Conventions, or serious violations of common article 3 of the Geneva Conventions.'

41 See the articles on State Responsibility, Arts 40 and 41 and commentaries.

42 See Art. 6(1) and (2) of the Arms Trade Treaty.

43 Such treaty obligations would also include the duty to prevent genocide set out in Art. 1 of the Genocide Convention.

44 The fifth principle of the Arms Trade Treaty is expressed in the following terms:

   The States Parties to this Treaty . . . [d]etermined to act in accordance with the following principles . . . [r]especting and ensuring respect for international humanitarian law in accordance with, *inter alia*, the Geneva Conventions of 1949, and respecting and ensuring respect for human rights, in accordance with, *inter alia*, the Charter of the United Nations and the Universal Declaration of Human Rights.

   The customary law study published by the International Committee of the Red Cross in 2005 and the inclusive character of the above principle, reflected in the use of '*inter alia*', make it clear that the above principle was intended to encompass customary obligations.

[a] State Party shall not authorize any transfer of conventional arms covered . . . [by the Arms Trade Treaty] if it has knowledge at the time of authorization that the arms or items would be used in the commission of genocide, crimes against humanity, grave breaches of the Geneva Conventions of 1949, attacks directed against civilian objects or civilians protected as such, or other war crimes as defined by international agreements to which it is a Party.

As foreshadowed above, this provision and the circumstances surrounding its adoption[45] have crystallised the position under customary international law: State responsibility for aid or assistance will arise where aid or assistance is given with knowledge that it will be used to commit internationally wrongful acts. There can now be no additional requirement to demonstrate that the authorising State intended to facilitate the commission of the internationally wrongful act.

Under Article 5(2) of the Arms Trade Treaty, States Parties 'shall establish and maintain a national control system[s]' for transfers[46] of conventional arms, ammunition and components. These obligations were intended, *inter alia*, to reduce the risks of diversion of lawfully transferred weapons to illicit markets for such weapons. As part of such a national control system, a State Party must establish a system of export assessment. Pursuant to Articles 7(1)(b) and 7(3) of the Arms Trade Treaty a State Party is obliged to refuse to authorise exports where the State determines that there is 'an overriding risk' that the exports could be used to:

i.   commit or facilitate a serious violation of international humanitarian law;
ii. commit or facilitate a serious violation of international human rights law; [or]
. . .
iv. commit or facilitate an act constituting an offence under international conventions or protocols relating to transnational organized crime to which the exporting State is a Party.

Under Article 7(4) of the Arms Trade Treaty, in making such an assessment, a State Party 'shall take into account the risk of the conventional arms . . . [ammunition or components covered by the treaty] being used to commit or facilitate serious acts of gender based violence or serious acts of violence against women and children'. The reference in Article 7(3) to 'an overriding risk' raises difficult questions and stands in sharp contrast to the terms 'serious risk' and 'serious danger' used by the ICJ in the *Bosnia Genocide case*, which are suggestive of a lower threshold.

The Arms Trade Treaty also imposes record-keeping obligations in relation to conventional arms[47] although it imposes more limited record-keeping obligations regarding ammunition and components.[48] The minimum period for which records are to be kept (10 years)[49] follows the Firearms Protocol[50] but is considerably shorter than the soft law standard set out in the International Tracing Instrument.[51]

---

45 See Art. 3(3) of the 2012 draft Arms Trade Treaty text.
46 In Art. 2(2) of the Arms Trade Treaty, 'transfer' is taken to encompass 'brokering'.
47 See Art. 12 of the Arms Trade Treaty.
48 Art. 12 (Record Keeping) of the Arms Trade Treaty does not refer to Arts 3 and 4, which address ammunition/munitions and parts and components.
49 Art. 12(4) of the Arms Trade Treaty.
50 Art. 7 of the Firearms Protocol.
51 Art. 12 of the International Tracing Instrument.

Article 10 of the Arms Trade Treaty obliges a State Party 'to regulate brokering taking place under its jurisdiction for conventional arms covered [by the Arms Trade Treaty]'. This obligation appears to be seriously undermined, however, by the next sentence of the Article, which is cast in permissive terms and which provides that '[s]uch measures may include requiring brokers to register or obtain written authorization before engaging in brokering'. In this regard, the Arms Trade Treaty appears to exhibit similar weaknesses in relation to brokering as those exhibited by the Firearms Protocol.[52]

Article 11 of the Arms Trade Treaty imposes obligations on States Parties to 'take measures to prevent . . . diversion' of conventional arms. These measures include national regulation, international cooperation and information sharing. In this regard, the Arms Trade Treaty formalises standards set out in the International Tracing Instrument.

Weapons smuggling and individual criminal responsibility – under municipal law and directly under international law

Arms brokers and individual responsibility

Arms brokers – individuals (or entities) who act as intermediaries in bringing together relevant parties and arranging or facilitating a potential transaction of arms in return for some form of benefit, whether financial or otherwise[53] – play a key role in the provision of arms that are used to commit gross violations of human rights and international humanitarian law. Whether such brokering activities are illicit is determined according to the national laws and regulations of the State in which the broker is operating, that State's international obligations and any international obligations imposed directly on the arms broker by international criminal law.

Unfortunately, illicit arms brokers carry on their business largely with impunity. As already noted, the Arms Trade Treaty and the Firearms Protocol impose limited obligations in relation to State regulation of brokering. The international arms trade is characteristically difficult to regulate because of the ready availability of small arms and light weapons; their easy portability, concealment and their relative inexpensiveness; the notorious dexterity of brokers' exploitation of legal loopholes; production of free use or fake end-user certificates; evasion of airport controls, customs and radar tracking; the overlap between black market illicit transfers and grey market government-complicit transactions; and the related lack of States' political will to implement and monitor tighter regulations and build concerted networks of international cooperation.[54] While there have been a number of domestic prosecutions of arms brokers, there have been no prosecutions by international criminal courts or tribunals. The closest international law has come is the 2012 conviction by the Special Court for Sierra Leone (SCSL) of the former Liberian President, Charles Taylor, for, *inter alia*, his supply of weapons to the RUF rebel group operating in the Sierra Leonean civil war.[55] This

---

52 Art. 15 of the Firearms Protocol.
53 Report of the Group of Governmental Experts established pursuant to General Assembly Resolution 60/81, UN Doc A/62/163 (30.08.2007), [8].
54 K. Orlovsky, 'International Criminal Law: Towards New Solutions In the Fight Against Illegal Arms Brokers', *Hastings International & Comparative Law Review*, 2006, vol. 29, p. 343, pp. 345–347; International Commission of Inquiry (Rwanda) (ICIR), Third Report, UN Doc S/1997/1010 (24 December 1997), paras 90–91.
55 *Prosecutor v Charles Taylor*, SCSL, Trial Judgment, 18 May 2012. Taylor was sentenced to 50 years' imprisonment.

is the first modern international criminal prosecution of a person completely external to a conflict for their culpable involvement in supplying arms and, in this respect, is an important precedent for arms brokers operating from transit or supplier States. This part of the chapter explores the current ways in which those involved in the direct supply of weapons are held accountable under international criminal law and assesses the strength of using such avenues for the prosecution of arms brokers and dealers. It also examines the ways in which individuals are held accountable under municipal law and comments on some synergies between international criminal and municipal prosecutions of arms brokers.

Individual criminal responsibility for arms transfers at international law

The framework for international criminal responsibility

Although illicit arms brokering is a type of illegal activity that takes place on an international stage, arms brokering is not an international crime. International criminal law imposes individual criminal responsibility on persons for their culpable involvement in the commission of core international crimes: genocide, war crimes and crimes against humanity.[56] If individuals, including arms brokers, supply weapons, they can be held responsible under international criminal law where those weapons are used in the commission or attempted commission[57] of one or more of these core international crimes.

Although international criminal law has only, thus far, been used to prosecute persons who have directly supplied weapons to the actors who physically perpetrate the international crimes (which may but does not necessarily capture arms brokers), there is no logical reason why the relevant crimes and modes of criminal liability under customary international law and the treaty-based regime of the International Criminal Court (ICC) cannot impose liability on the dealers and brokers who supplied the arms to intermediaries which were eventually distributed and used in the commission of these crimes. In this respect, aiding and abetting, complicity in genocide and common purpose liability will be explored below, as will some pragmatic factors inhibiting the recourse to international criminal law in prosecuting arms brokers.

Aiding and abetting (or otherwise assisting)

Customary international law imposes individual criminal responsibility on persons who aid and abet international crimes through the provision of weapons.[58] The customary requirements are that the

> aider and abettor carries out acts . . . [that] assist, encourage or lend moral support to the perpetration of a certain specific crime . . . and this support has a substantial effect upon the perpetration of the crime . . . [T]he requisite mental element is knowledge that the

---

56 This section will not address the crime of aggression.
57 Note that involvement in attempted commission can only be prosecuted at the ICC: Rome Statute, Art. 25(3)(f).
58 *The Zyklon B Case, Law Reports of Trials of War Criminals* (London, 1947) Vol. 1, p. 93, p. 102; *Prosecutor v Tadić*, International Criminal Tribunal for the former Yugoslavia (ICTY), Trial Judgment, 7 May 1997, paras 666, 667, 680, 684; Arts 7(1) and 6(1) of the ICTY and International Criminal Tribunal for Rwanda (ICTR) Statutes, respectively.

acts performed by the aider and abettor assist the commission of a specific crime by the principal.[59]

The provision of arms, being the means through which international crimes are committed, certainly assists and has a substantial effect upon their perpetration. For instance, in *Semanza*, a former *bourgmestre* (mayor) was found guilty by the ICTR of aiding and abetting a serious violation of Common Article 3 and Additional Protocol II for distributing weapons to the paramilitary organisation Interahamwe, 'the very instruments that assured the commission of the genocidal massacre that was unfolding on Mwulire Hill'.[60]

The most difficult element to satisfy in respect of arms brokers would be the knowledge that the weapons would be used in the commission of international crimes. Brokers who are not geographically proximate to the commission of crimes could plausibly deny knowledge of their end use, as did South African arms broker Willem Ehlers, who met with Colonel Bagosora, a high-ranking officer in the Rwandan Government during the 1994 genocide, and sold him two arms shipments that were ultimately used to perpetrate the genocide. Ehlers subsequently denied knowing Bagosora's true identity, or the final destination or end use of the weapons.[61] International criminal law permits knowledge to be inferred from surrounding circumstances,[62] which could include the imposition of an arms embargo against a particular State and the expectation that such an embargo would come to the broker's attention through the ordinary course of their trade transactions.[63] However, challenges in proving that the brokers possessed the required knowledge remain.

A recent development may make it even harder to prosecute arms brokers under customary international criminal law. In 2013, the Appeals Chamber of the ad hoc tribunals in *Perišić*[64] held that a customary *actus reus* requirement of aiding and abetting was that the assistance must be 'specifically directed' to assist the commission of the crimes, as opposed to constituting general support for an organisation that engaged in both lawful and unlawful activities. The Appeals Chamber held that this specific direction requirement establishes the culpable link between the assistance provided by the accused and the commission of the international crimes[65] but that, where an accused was geographically proximate or physically present during the commission of the crimes, the specific direction requirement could be implied.[66] This development was heavily criticised by the Appeals Chamber of the SCSL in the *Taylor* appeal as introducing a new element not required by customary international law.[67] The SCSL confirmed that the culpable connection between the assistance and the crimes is satisfied by the causal threshold requirement that the contribution 'substantially' contribute to the

---

59 *Prosecutor v Tadić*, ICTY, Appeal Judgment, 15 July 1999, para. 229.
60 *Prosecutor v Semanza*, ICTR, Trial Judgment, 15 May 2003, paras 225, 431–435, 531, 535.
61 ICIR, Third Report, para. 28.
62 *Tadić* Trial Judgment, paras 676–677; *Prosecutor v Kvoćka*, ICTY, Trial Judgment, 2 November 2001, para. 324 (*Kvoćka* Trial Judgment).
63 Orlovsky, 'Towards New Solutions', p. 349.
64 *Prosecutor v Perišić*, ICTY, Appeal Judgment, 28 February 2013, paras 17, 25–36. Followed in *Prosecutor v Stanišić*, ICTY, Trial Judgment, 30 May 2013.
65 *Perišić* Appeal Judgment, para. 37.
66 *Perišić* Appeal Judgment, para. 38. According to the Appeals Chamber, this explained why prior jurisprudence of the *ad hoc* tribunals had not focused explicitly on proving the specific direction requirement.
67 *Prosecutor v Taylor*, SCSL, Appeal Judgment, 26.9.2013, paras 471–481.

commission of the crimes.[68] If specific direction operated as a mental element (as is more consonant with domestic criminal law inquiries into the purpose for which conduct is undertaken), this would operate to transform the knowledge requirement into an intent standard, making it significantly more difficult to prosecute arms brokers for aiding and abetting international crimes.

The position under Article 25(3)(c), the aiding and abetting provision,[69] of the Rome Statute of the International Criminal Court (Rome Statute) also poses its own challenges. This provision requires largely the same elements as at customary international law,[70] with one key exception: the aider must intend to facilitate the commission of the crime. Article 30 of the Rome Statute provides that a person has intent (in respect of conduct) where they mean to engage in the conduct and (in respect of an outcome) they are aware that a circumstance *will* occur in the ordinary course of events. This would appear to capture arms brokers who deliberately provide arms and who are aware that crimes will occur in the ordinary course of events. However, the Pre-Trial Chamber has held that use of the term 'will' in Article 30 denotes a high standard of virtual or practical certainty,[71] which is a higher *mens rea* standard than that required at customary international law[72] and which will make ICC prosecution of arms brokers under this provision difficult.[73]

Complicity in genocide

Individual criminal responsibility for complicity in genocide derives from Article III(e) of the Genocide Convention and appears in both the ICTY and ICTR Statutes.[74] It exists only at customary international law and does not appear in the Rome Statute.[75] Unlike aiding and abetting, complicity is not a mode of liability through which a specific international crime is committed, but rather is itself an international crime; a variant of the crime of genocide. In the large majority of cases, there is no material distinction between aiding and abetting

---

68 *Taylor* Appeal Judgment, para. 475.
69 Art. 25(3)(c) provides that 'a person shall be criminally responsible and liable for punishment for a crime within the jurisdiction of the Court if that person . . . [f]or the purpose of facilitating the commission of such a crime, aids, abets or otherwise assists in its commission or its attempted commission, including providing the means for its commission'.
70 Some authors suggest that there is no causal contribution required by Art. 25(3)(c), in that the aid does not have to have a substantial effect on the commission of the crime: A. Boivin, 'Complicity and Beyond', *International Review of the Red Cross*, 2005, vol. 87, no. 859, p. 467, p. 483; K. Ambos, 'Article 25', in O. Triffterer (ed.), *Commentary on the Rome Statute of the International Criminal Court*, Oxford: Hart, 1999, p. 483. However, the Pre-Trial Chamber in *Mbarushimana* clearly stated that a substantial contribution is required: *Prosecutor v Mbarushimana*, ICC, Decision on the Confirmation of Charges, 16 December 2011, para. 285. Cf. liability for aiding and abetting the attempted commission of a crime under the ICC Statute as compared to derivative responsibility at customary international law.
71 *Prosecutor v Bemba Gombo*, ICC, Decision Pursuant to Arts 61(7)(a) and (b) of the Rome Statute, 15 June 2009, para. 362.
72 *Mbarushimana*, Confirmation of Charges, para. 281.
73 However, some authors contend that the ICC has accepted the lower *mens rea* requirements contained in the elements of the crimes: Cryer *et al.*, *An Introduction to International Criminal Law and Procedure*, 2nd edn, Cambridge: Cambridge University Press, 2010, p. 386.
74 Art. 4(3)(e) of the ICTY Statute and Art. 2(3)(e) of the ICTR Statute provide that the 'following acts shall be punishable . . . Complicity in genocide'.
75 Acts constituting complicity in genocide are likely to be caught by other liability provisions of the ICC Statute, such as Art. 25(3)(c) and Art. 25(3)(d).

genocide and complicity in genocide.[76] However, there is scope for complicity in genocide to prohibit acts broader than aiding and abetting, and in such cases it has been suggested that the specific genocidal intent to destroy, in whole or in part, a national, ethnical, racial or religious group is required.[77] It is widely accepted that complicity in genocide includes procuring means, such as weapons, used to commit genocide.[78] Semanza was found guilty by the ICTR of being complicit in genocide for supplying weapons, with genocidal intent, to the Interahamwe.[79] As regards a potential avenue for the prosecution of arms brokers, where their acts fall outside the scope of aiding and abetting,[80] if a higher genocidal intent is required, it will make such a task particularly difficult.

Contributing to the commission of a crime by a group acting with a common purpose[81]

Article 25(3)(d) of the Rome Statute provides a 'residual form of accessory liability which makes it possible to criminalize those contributions to a crime which cannot be characterized as . . . aiding or abetting'.[82] It requires an accused to make a significant[83] contribution to the commission or attempted commission of a crime within the jurisdiction of the ICC by a group of persons acting with a common purpose, where the accused means to engage in the conduct that contributes to the crime and is at least aware that his or her conduct contributes to the activities of the group.[84] This sets a lower threshold than aiding and abetting in Article 25(3)(c) of the Statute as it requires knowledge, not intent, and only a significant, not a substantial, contribution.[85] In the *Situation in Darfur*, the Pre-Trial Chamber held that there

---

76 *Semanza* Trial Judgment, paras 394–395; *Prosecutor v Krstić*, ICTY, Appeal Judgment, 19 April 2004, para. 138.

77 *Krstić* Appeal Judgment, para. 142; *Prosecutor v Ntakirutimana*, ICTR, Appeal Judgment, 13 December 2004, paras 500–501; W. Schabas, *Genocide in International Law*, Cambridge: Cambridge University Press, 2000, p. 300; H. Olásolo, *The Criminal Responsibility of Senior Political and Military Leaders as Principals to International Crimes*, Oxford: Hart, 2010, fn. 511. Cf. *Prosecutor v Milosević*, ICTY, Decision on Motion for Judgment of Acquittal, 16 June 2004, paras 295–297.

78 *Prosecutor v Akayesu*, ICTR, Trial Judgment, 12 September 1998, [473], paras 533, 536 and 537; *Prosecutor v Musema*, ICTR, Trial Judgment, 27 January 2000, para. 179.

79 *Semanza* Trial Judgment, para. 225, paras 431–433.

80 Where conduct could be characterised as either aiding or abetting or complicity in genocide, the ICTY has held, subsequent to the *Semanza* trial, that an accused's responsibility is better characterised as aiding and abetting genocide: *Krstić* Appeal Judgment, paras 138–139.

81 There are two other forms of common-purpose liability, joint criminal enterprise and control of the crime, which were developed by the *ad hoc* tribunals and the ICC respectively and which provide liability for individuals who supply weapons used in the commission (or attempted commission) of international crimes. See, for example, *Prosecutor v Simba*, ICTR, Trial Judgment, 13 December 2005, paras 398, 400, 401, 403, 406, 418–419 and 426; and *Prosecutor v Karemera and Ngirumpatse*, ICTR, Trial Judgment, 2 February 2012, paras 1450, 1453, 1458, 1460 and 1616–1617 in respect of joint criminal enterprise (JCE) through the provision of weapons; and *Prosecutor v Hussein*, ICC, Decision on the Prosecutor's Application Under Article 58, 1 March 2012, [21], [25], [29] and [39] in respect of control of the crime (indirect co-perpetration) through, *inter alia*, the provision of ammunition.

82 *Prosecutor v Lubanga*, ICC, Decision on the Confirmation of Charges, 29 January 2007, para. 337.

83 *Mbarushimana*, Confirmation of Charges, para. 285.

84 *Mbarushimana*, Confirmation of Charges, paras 270–289.

85 'Significant' is a lower threshold than 'substantial': *Prosecutor v Brdanin*, ICTY, Appeal Judgment, 3 April 2007, para. 430; *Prosecutor v Krajisnik*, ICTY, Appeal Judgment, 17 March 2009, para. 215.

were reasonable grounds to believe that Kushayb and Harun were criminally responsible under Article 25(3)(d) for, *inter alia*, promising to deliver and in fact delivering arms to the Janjaweed, a group that shared a common criminal purpose to persecute civilians they associated with rebels, primarily from the Fur, Zaghawa and Masalit tribes, through indiscriminate attacks against the civilian population.[86] Further, the Pre-Trial Chamber has explicitly considered that 'arms dealers' can satisfy all the requirements of Article 25(3)(d).[87] Given the lower *mens rea* threshold and the explicit recognition of applicability to 'arms dealers', Article 25(3)(d) appears to be the strongest avenue through which to prosecute arms brokers under international criminal law.

Individual criminal responsibility for arms transfers under municipal law

The international instruments, both soft and hard, regulating the illicit trade in small arms and light weapons explored earlier in this chapter are suppression instruments. They encourage or oblige States Parties to take domestic legislative and executive action to criminalise and enforce prohibitions on, *inter alia*, illicit brokering and trafficking in arms. The three main instruments that impose such obligations or encourage such measures are the Arms Trade Treaty, the Firearms Protocol and the Programme of Action.[88]

As noted above, the Arms Trade Treaty imposes obligations on States Parties to establish export control systems for arms, ammunition and components, which includes the regulation of brokering and the taking of appropriate measures to 'enforce' national laws and regulations implementing the provisions of the treaty.[89] It appears to leave, however, a significant margin of discretion to States regarding the precise manner in which they are able to implement their general obligations and does not specify that criminalisation is required. By contrast, the Firearms Protocol in Article 5 specifically requires States Parties to criminalise certain conduct under their municipal laws.[90]

The absence of criminalisation requirements in the Arms Trade Treaty and their presence in the Firearms Protocol means there is a gap in the weapons that are caught by mandatory criminalisation obligations. While the Firearms Protocol covers all small arms, its definition of light weapons is more limited than that recognised by the Arms Trade Treaty, and covers only light weapons that use cartridge-based ammunition which can be moved or carried by one person.[91] Illicit brokering and trafficking in other forms of light weapons not covered by the Firearms Protocol may not, therefore, be caught by States' municipal criminalisation implementing their obligations under these instruments. The non-binding Programme of Action calls upon States to, *inter alia*,

86 *Prosecutor v Ahmad Harun and Ali Kushayb*, ICC, Decision on the Prosecution Application Under Article 58(7) of the Statute, 27 April 2007, paras 85, 88, 89, 105, 106, 107 and 178.
87 *Mbarushimana*, Confirmation of Charges, fn. 681.
88 While the tracing instrument is relevant, it only imposes a very general obligation to implement laws to ensure the effective implementation of the instrument, which could include dealing in arms that did not comply with marking requirements, but States have a very large discretion in this respect. See International Tracing Instrument, para. 24.
89 Arms Trade Treaty, Arts 3–5, 10, 14.
90 See also the Legislative Guides for the Implementation of the United Nations Convention Against Transnational Organized Crime and the Protocol Thereto, pp. 465–494.
91 Small Arms Survey, 'The Arms Trade Treaty: A Step Forward in Small Arms Control?' (Research Notes, No. 30, June 2013), p. 1.

adopt and implement . . . the necessary legislative or other measures to establish as criminal offences under their domestic law the illegal manufacture, possession, stockpiling and trade of small arms and light weapons within their areas of jurisdiction, in order to ensure that those engaged in such activities can be prosecuted under appropriate national penal codes.[92]

It also encourages States to

develop adequate national legislation or administrative procedures regulating the activities of those who engage in small arms and light weapons brokering. This legislation or procedures should include measures such as registration of brokers, licensing or authorization of brokering *transactions as well as the appropriate penalties for all illicit brokering activities* performed within the State's jurisdiction and control.[93]

and to

take appropriate measures, including all *legal* or administrative means, against any activity that violates a United Nations Security Council arms embargo in accordance with the Charter of the United Nations.[94]

The UN convenes voluntary periodic reviews of the progress made by States in implementing the Programme of Action's recommendations.[95] However, the Programme of Action contains no definition of small arms and light weapons, creating uncertainty as to whether the criminalisation provisions cover ammunition, parts and components, as the Firearms Protocol and Arms Trade Treaty clearly do.[96] This could lead to incomplete criminalisation that leaves loopholes ripe for exploitation. The 2012 Review Conference report noted that implementation of national laws has been 'uneven' and highlighted the need for international assistance and cooperation.[97] The last published national implementation report in 2010 noted that many States who voluntarily reported had not criminalised illicit arms transfers and smuggling.[98]

Other regional arrangements, such as the OAS Model Regulations for the Control of the International Movement of Firearms, their Parts and Components, and Ammunition – Broker Regulations[99] and the Wassenaar Arrangement[100] encourage criminalisation of illicit

---

92 Programme of Action, II, para. 3.

93 Programme of Action, II, para. 14 (emphasis added).

94 Programme of Action, II, para. 15 (emphasis added).

95 Programme of Action, II, para. 33.

96 Small Arms Survey, 'The Arms Trade Treaty', p. 1.

97 Report of the United Nations Conference to Review Progress Made in the Implementation of the Programme of Action to Prevent, Combat and Eradicate the Illicit Trade in Small Arms and Light Weapons in All its Aspects, UN Doc A/CONF.192/2012/RC/4, 18 September 2012, para. 9.

98 S. Parker, *National Implementation of the United Nations Small Arms Programme of Action and the International Tracing Instrument: An Analysis of Reporting in 2009–2010*, June 2010, p. 36.

99 Model Regulations for the Control of the International Movement of Firearms, their Parts and Components, and Ammunition – Broker Regulations, Arts 5–7. The OAS Model Regulations include criminal liability for corporations / entities: see Art. 7.

100 Wassenaar Arrangement, Elements for Export Controls of Man-Portable Air Defense Systems (MANPADS), para. 4; Elements for Effective Legislation on Arms Brokering, para. 3; Best Practices for Effective Enforcement, para. 14.

brokering and arms trafficking. In implementing their obligations under these instruments, States criminalise and prosecute weapons smuggling and illicit brokering in different ways. Some States criminalise certain conduct through their criminal codes, through specific brokering legislation, through import and export legislation, through firearms legislation which sets out the overall regulatory framework and licensing requirements for those possessing weapons which might subsequently be the subject of smuggling, through legislation under which States make regulations requiring compliance with Security Council arms embargoes or through defence-related legislation.[101] Some States, such as the United States, have chosen to prosecute arms trafficking and weapons smuggling under broader provisions than those that specifically criminalise illicit arms transfers. This occurs largely where connections to US territorial or personal jurisdiction, within which the trafficking and smuggling criminalisation provisions operate, are tenuous. For example, the United States has prosecuted notorious arms dealers and brokers under the 'conspiracy to commit terrorism' provisions of the US Code.[102] The 'dangerous and powerful international arms trafficker' Viktor Bout was convicted in April 2012 for conspiracy and conspiring to provide material support to the terrorist organisation FARC.[103] Patrick Nayyar was convicted in 2012 for conspiracy and providing material support to a terrorist organisation for a plan to supply arms to Hezbollah.[104] Notorious drug trafficker Al Kassar was the subject of a decade-long sting operation by the American Drug Enforcement Administration in respect of crimes with no tangible connection to the United States soil, which culminated in his arrest and conviction for, *inter alia*, conspiracy to kill Americans, conspiracy to kill officers and employees of the United States, conspiracy to supply material support to terrorists, and conspiracy to acquire and use anti-aircraft missiles.[105] The inconsistency with which these suppression and criminalisation provisions are implemented into municipal law necessarily leaves gaps and creates loopholes that can be exploited by weapons smugglers. The emergence of arms trafficking safe-haven States with poor criminalisation is a real danger to the effective implementation of international obligations and the prosecution of weapons smugglers.

Synergies between international and municipal prosecutions of arms brokers

There are opportunities for synergies between domestic and international prosecutions. The Office of the Prosecutor of the ICC has indicated that financial transactions, for example, in purchasing of weapons, can be important evidence in proving the commission of international crimes.[106] National authorities can assist the ICC in acquiring evidence in relation to such illicit arms sales and, conversely, evidence procured by ICC investigations could be passed on to national authorities for the prosecution of brokers and dealers whom the ICC is not pursuing or whose conduct is characterised not as an international crime, but which contravenes national criminalisation of illegal brokerage and smuggling laws. It has also been argued that the international attention and threat of international prosecution by the ICC by

---

101 See, for example, Canada's suite of legislation that implements its international obligations including criminalisation outlined in R.J. Currie and J. Rikhof, *International and Transnational Criminal Law*, 2nd edn, Toronto: Irwin Law, 2013, pp. 357–360.

102 See, for instance, 18 USC § 1114, § 1117, § 2332(b), § 2332g and § 2339B.

103 *US v Bout* [2013] US App LEXIS 19868 (27 September 2013).

104 *US v Nayyar* [2013] US Dist LEXIS 79002 (4 June 2013).

105 *US v Al Kasser et al.* [2013] 660 F.3ed 108 (21 September 2011).

106 Office of the Prosecutor of the ICC, Policy Paper, September 2003, pp. 2–3.

the Prosecutor's opening up of *proprio motu* preliminary examinations can serve as a catalyst to overcome weak political will by States to prosecute domestically.[107]

Concluding observations

For the international community to effectively suppress weapons smuggling, the employment of a combination of intergovernmental and municipal regulatory and enforcement measures appears necessary. The eradication of weapons smuggling is unlikely to be achieved by a strategy that focuses solely on principles of State responsibility. Similarly, relying solely on individual criminal responsibility (under either international or national law) for weapons smuggling is unlikely to be effective in dealing with cross-border arms transfers.

An effective response to the pernicious effects of arms smuggling appears to require both international and national regulation of lawful and illicit arms transfers. It also appears to require the harmonisation and coherent and consistent application of international and national standards and measures. Integration of the regulation of lawful trade, measures designed to prevent diversion, and measures to suppress illicit transfers appear essential. Developments since 2001 have reflected increasing consensus regarding the general character of measures required to address weapons smuggling. Significant work remains to be done, however, in translating these general commitments into specific standards and enforcement action to suppress the movement of weapons, which has had such horrific consequences for the vulnerable in areas of conflict all around the world.

107 H. Olásolo, 'The Role of the International Criminal Court in Preventing Atrocity Crimes through Timely Intervention', Inaugural Lecture as Chair in International Criminal Law and International Criminal Procedure at Utrecht University, 18 November 2010, pp. 6–7.

16
Cultural property trafficking

Arianna Visconti

Introduction

National and international lawmakers are currently paying increasing attention to crimes against 'cultural heritage', and particularly trafficking in 'cultural property'. Both expressions, however – and particularly the former, which has in recent years become largely preferred over 'cultural property'[1] as more capable of conveying the true essence of this 'universal community's interest'[2] – appear to suffer from an unavoidable vagueness,[3] which poses some problems when such terminology is transferred to the field of criminal law with its requirements of clear and precise definition of offences.

Definitions of both 'cultural property' and 'cultural heritage', as included in relevant international documents,[4] use general terms intuitively understood as reflecting a culture which is

---

1   See, for instance, J. Blake, 'On Defining the Cultural Heritage', *International and Comparative Law Quarterly*, 2000, vol. 49, p. 61, pp. 65–67; M.F. Brown, 'Heritage Trouble: Recent Work on the Protection of Intangible Cultural Property', *International Journal of Cultural Property*, 2005, vol. 12, p. 40, pp. 41–42; C. Forrest, 'Cultural Heritage as the Common Heritage of Humankind: A Critical Re-evaluation', *The Comparative and International Law Journal of Southern Africa*, 2007, vol. 40, p. 124; F. Francioni, 'A Dynamic Evolution of Concept and Scope: From Cultural Property to Cultural Heritage', in A.A. Yusuf (ed.), *Standard Setting in UNESCO*, Vol. I, Paris: UNESCO, 2007, p. 221; M. Frigo, 'Cultural Property v. Cultural Heritage: A "Battle of Concepts" in International Law?', *International Review of the Red Cross*, 2004, vol. 86, p. 367; L. Prott and P.J. O'Keefe, 'Cultural Heritage or Cultural Property', *International Journal of Cultural Property*, 1992, vol. 1, p. 319; T. Scovazzi, 'La notion de patrimoine culturel de l'humanité dans les instruments internationaux', in J.A.R. Nafziger and T. Scovazzi (eds), *Le patrimoine culturel de l'humanité – The Cultural Heritage of Mankind*, Leiden: Martinus Nijhoff, 2008, pp. 3–144.
2   G. Ziccardi Capaldo, 'Editor's Introduction. A New Dimension of International Law: The Global Law', *The Global Community. Yearbook of International Law and Jurisprudence*, 2005, vol. 5, p. XVI.
3   Blake, 'On Defining', pp. 62–67; C. Forrest, *International Law and the Protection of Cultural Heritage*, New York: Routledge, 2011, pp. 1–3.
4   See for instance the Preamble to the 1968 UNESCO Recommendation Concerning the Preservation of Cultural Property Endangered by Public or Private Works, issued by the General Conference meeting in Paris from 15 October to 20 November 1968, and Art. 2(a) of the Framework Convention on the Value of Cultural Heritage for Society, Council of Europe, Faro, 27 October 2005, CETS No. 199.

inherited from the past,[5] and which possesses a universal value that transcends economic quantification, as well as specific national, ethnic or religious identities;[6] as such, cultural heritage is a man-made aspect of the environment that, just as the natural ones, is 'essential . . . to the enjoyment of basic human rights',[7] and which therefore 'need[s] to be preserved as part of the world heritage of mankind as a whole'.[8]

But both 'culture' and 'heritage' are largely polysemous words.[9] On the one hand, 'culture' is a term susceptible of encompassing various contents according to the different (through time, and/or through communities) societies to which it is referred; on the other hand, 'heritage' implies 'an active choice as to which elements of this broader "culture" are deemed worthy of preservation';[10] it can include a number of heterogeneous goods (movable and immovable properties of the greatest variety, including even particularly man-shaped, or man-venerated, landscapes or natural elements[11] as well as immaterial goods[12]); finally, it can be regarded either in its purely aesthetic value, or in its expressive capacity (particularly in relation to peoples' identities), or as historical evidence, or as an economic commodity, as well as, obviously, as a mix of all these facets.[13] In brief, cultural heritage includes a wide range of apparently contradictory meanings and values – both local and universal, both material and immaterial[14] – which, however, are all part of a complex value commonly considered relevant to humankind as well as to each individual, to present generations as well as to future ones, which have a right to its preservation.

The concept of cultural heritage, as important as it is to understanding the increasing international commitment to its protection, will remain, with all its complexity, in the background of our analysis: trafficking by definition impinges upon specific cultural objects, and particularly movable ones (which include, of course, objects which have been *made* movable – for instance, parts of monuments which have been removed from their original sites).

A lot of attention has been devoted to defining what constitutes 'movable cultural property' by international conventions and documents concerning the regulation of its import and export and related offences. We can take as representative the definition provided by Article 1 of the UNESCO Convention on the Means of Prohibiting and Preventing the Illicit Import, Export and Transfer of Ownership of Cultural Property (1970 UNESCO Convention),[15] according to which 'the term "cultural property" means property which, on religious or secular grounds, is specifically designated by each State as being of importance for archaeology, prehistory, history, literature, art or science and which belongs to' a long series of categories listed in detail in the same article. Other definitions are provided in further

---

5 Forrest, *International Law*, p. 2.
6 A. Vigorito, *Nuove tendenze della tutela internazionale dei beni culturali*, Naples: ESI, 2013, pp. 15–16.
7 Declaration of the United Nations Conference on the Human Environment, issued in the meeting held in Stockholm from 5 to 16 June 1972, 11 ILM 1416 (1972).
8 Preamble to the UNESCO Convention Concerning the Protection of the World Cultural and Natural Heritage, Paris, 16 November 1972, 1037 UNTS 151; in force 17 Dec. 1975 (1972 UNESCO World Heritage Convention).
9 Blake, 'On Defining', pp. 67–68; Forrest, *International Law*, pp. 2–3.
10 Blake, 'On Defining', p. 68.
11 See Art. 1 of the 1972 UNESCO World Heritage Convention.
12 Brown, 'Heritage Trouble', p. 41.
13 Forrest, *International Law*, pp. 3–13.
14 See also T. Loulanski, 'Revising the Concept for Cultural Heritage: The Argument for a Functional Approach', *International Journal of Cultural Property*, 2006, vol. 13, p. 209.
15 Paris, 14 November 1970, 823 UNTS 231; in force 24 April 1972.

conventions[16] and international documents,[17] but they all basically follow the outlined model: the range of application of the law needs to be circumscribed to precise, easily recognisable occurrences, thus obviating the intrinsic vagueness of concepts such as 'cultural heritage' or 'cultural property', without leaving unguarded objects of relevant value for a nation and/or a local community. The results are complex definitions, enumerating long series of typologies of objects deemed of potential cultural value, without any grading, and open to interpretation and adaptation by each State. Nonetheless, the effort to establish a common ground for the identification of movable cultural property subject to protection is especially needed in relation to criminal law, both for the delimitation of the relevant offences, and in view of predictable problems related to police and judicial cooperation, seizure and return/ restitution,[18] extradition, and other related issues, all of which often imply requirements of double criminality and/or law harmonization.

The empirical dimension of trafficking in cultural property

Any evaluation of the efficacy of national and international provisions aimed at the prevention and fighting of trafficking in cultural property, as well as of proposed criminal policy strategies, would not be possible without a previous knowledge of the main features and causes of this phenomenon.

In general, crimes against movable cultural property include a wide range of offences, as diverse as art thefts, looting of archaeological sites and pillaging, frauds and forgeries involving works of art, acts of vandalism or iconoclasm, and – what directly concerns us – illicit import and export of cultural objects, trafficking and smuggling, laundering of the proceeds of crime, etc.[19] As for these latter, increasing efforts have been made to try to assess the real extent of the

---

16 See for instance Art. 2 and Annex to the UNIDROIT Convention on Stolen or Illegally Exported Cultural Objects, Rome, 24 June 1995, 34 ILM 1322 (1995); in force 1 July 1998 (1995 UNIDROIT Convention). At regional level, see Arts 2 and Appendix 1 of the European Convention on Offences relating to Cultural Property, Delphi, 23 June 1985, ETS No 119, not yet in force (1985 European Convention); see also comparable definitions of 'cultural goods' provided respectively by Art. 1 and Annex I of the EU Council Regulation No. 116/2009 of 18 December 2008 on the export of cultural goods (codified version), and by Art. 1 and Annex of the EU Council Directive 93/7/EEC of 15 March 1993 on the return of cultural objects unlawfully removed from the territory of a Member State (now abrogated by Directive 2014/60/EU).

17 Namely Art. 1 of the UN Model Treaty for the Prevention of Crimes that infringe on the Cultural Heritage of Peoples in the Form of Movable Property, issued in the Eighth United Nations Congress on the Prevention of Crime and the Treatment of Offenders, Havana, 27 August–7 September 1990 (Model Treaty).

18 About the (not always uniform) use of the terms 'return' and 'restitution' in the 1995 UNIDROIT Convention and in other international documents see M.-A. Renold, 'International Tools: Return, Restitution, and Beyond', in S. Manacorda and A. Visconti (eds), Beni culturali e sistema penale, Milan: Vita e Pensiero, 2013, pp. 127–128.

19 For a general overview see C. Adler and K. Polk, 'Crime in the World of Art', in H.N. Pontell and G. Geis (eds), International Handbook of White-Collar and Corporate Crime, New York: Springer, 2007, p. 347; J.E. Conklin, Art Crime, Westport CT: Praeger, 1994; M. Durney and B. Proulx, 'Art Crime: A Brief Introduction', Crime Law and Social Change, 2011, vol. 56, p. 115, pp. 119–126; N. Passas and B. Bowman Proulx, 'Overview of Crimes and Antiques', in S. Manacorda and D. Chappell (eds), Crime in the Art and Antiquities World. Illegal Trafficking in Cultural Property, New York: Springer, 2011, p. 51, pp. 54–61.

illicit dealing in cultural property,[20] a task made quite difficult by a particularly large information gap. Currently 'there are no reliable statistics describing either the material volume or monetary value of the trade';[21] nor, therefore, do we have any factual basis for the (frequently heard) claim that trafficking in cultural property is the third or fourth most common form of trafficking.[22] This lack of actual knowledge reflects the structural traits of such traffic, and it is therefore intimately connected to problems of prevention and repression.

First, quite often cultural properties disappear from unregistered and/or unmonitored sites, their very existence unknown to the authorities. Second, the art and antiquities market is intrinsically opaque, so much so that we should think in terms of a 'grey market', with licit and illicit dealings closely interwoven.[23] The subculture of this market mainly follows the rule 'don't ask, don't tell',[24] where even subjects not actively involved in trafficking often turn a blind eye to suspicious goods, forgetting to ask questions about provenance and ownership. This situation not only increases the opportunities for illicit dealings, but provides potential and actual offenders with a range of very effective neutralizations.[25] The ever growing number of online transactions greatly increases these problems, and widens the international dimension intrinsic to this market. This latter feature poses, per se, great difficulties to national investigations and prosecutions, as well as to seizures, confiscations, returns, etc., of the illicitly trafficked objects.

Even the available partial data, however, show that trafficking represents a widespread phenomenon, and the overall conclusion reached by empirical studies is that a significant proportion of the antiquities currently traded on the market, or appearing in catalogues of museums, collections and the like, are of illicit or, at best, dubious provenance.[26]

20 See, amongst others, R. Fisman and S.J. Wei, *The Smuggling of Art and the Art of Smuggling: Uncovering the Illicit Trade in Cultural Property and Antiques*, Working Paper 13446, Cambridge MA: National Bureau of Economic Research, 2007; S. Mackenzie, *Going, Going, Gone: Regulating the Market in Illicit Antiquities*, Leicester: Institute of Art and Law, 2005, pp. 10–14; for a comprehensive and updated overview see N. Brodie, J. Dietzler and S. Mackenzie, 'Trafficking in Cultural Objects: An Empirical Overview', in Manacorda and Visconti, *Beni culturali*, p. 19.

21 N. Brodie, 'Congenial Bedfellows? The Academy and the Antiquities Trade', *Journal of Contemporary Criminal Justice*, 2001, vol. 27, p. 411.

22 S. Calvani, 'Frequency and Figures of Organized Crime in Art and Antiques', in S. Manacorda (ed.), *Organised Crime in Art and Antiquities*, Milan: ISPAC, 2009, pp. 29–30.

23 B.A. Bowman, 'Transnational Crimes Against Culture. Looting at Archaeological Sites and the "Grey" Market in Antiquities', *Journal of Contemporary Criminal Justice*, 2008, vol. 24, p. 225, pp. 226–228; Conklin, *Art Crime*, pp. 187–201; D.C. Lane *et al.*, 'Time Crime: The Transnational Organization of Art and Antiquities Theft', *Journal of Contemporary Criminal Justice*, 2008, vol. 24, p. 243, pp. 250–257; L. Massy, 'The Antiquity Art Market: Between Legality and Illegality', *International Journal of Social Economics*, 2008, vol. 35, p. 729; E.A.J.G. Tijhuis, 'The Trafficking Problem: A Criminological Perspective', in Manacorda and Chappell, *Crime in the Art and Antiquities World*, pp. 88–92.

24 G. Melillo, 'La cooperazione giudiziaria internazionale nei reati contro il patrimonio culturale', in Manacorda and Visconti, *Beni culturali*, p. 66.

25 The expression 'techniques of neutralization' is used by criminologists to define a set of strategies by which people who commit illicit or deviant acts temporarily neutralize those internal restraints which would normally prevent them from such actions. See G.M. Sykes and D. Matza, 'Techniques of Neutralization: A Theory of Delinquency', *American Sociological Review*, 1957, vol. 22, p. 664. For an empirical analysis of the techniques of neutralization most commonly used in the art and antiquities market see Mackenzie, *Going, Going, Gone*, pp. 205–226.

26 See for instance D.W.J. Gill and C. Chippindale, 'Material and Intellectual Consequences of Esteem for Cycladic Figures', *American Journal of Archaeology*, 1993, vol. 97, p. 601; D.W.J. Gill and C. Chippindale, 'Material Consequences of Contemporary Classical Collecting', *American Journal of Archaeology*, 2000, vol. 104, p. 463. For a comprehensive overview of like studies see Brodie, Dietzler and Mackenzie, 'Trafficking', pp. 23–25.

This peculiar opacity of the market, coupled with the aforementioned difficulties in discovering, investigating and prosecuting these offences, shows that crimes against cultural property share some significant traits with white-collar crime.[27] Not only because they (at least in the steps following the illicit appropriation) are generally 'committed by a person of respectability and high social status' in the course of their occupation,[28] that is by respectable businesspeople, dealers in antiquities and works of art, auctioneers, etc. (with all the related problems of 'double standards'[29] at both regulatory and enforcement level);[30] but also (or mainly) because they are often interwoven with many other typically 'white-collar' crimes, such as corruption[31] (for instance, to ease illicit export from countries of origin where sometimes corruption and bribery are endemic)[32] and money laundering.[33]

The connections with other serious crimes, and the knowledge that channels for transnational smuggling are largely used by organized crime for other trafficking (involving drugs, arms, human beings, etc.), have raised increasing concern about the possible spreading of trafficking in cultural property, and the possible involvement of traditional organized criminal groups[34] in an extremely profitable market. International organizations occasionally appear to take for granted the significant involvement of such criminal organizations in cultural property trafficking,[35] and this is one of the main reasons for the growing interest in the subject, as well as for a certain pressure for States to make increasing use of the UN Convention Against Transnational Organized Crime (UNTOC)[36] in this area.

A look at the available empirical knowledge should suggest, however, a slightly more cautious approach.[37] Presently, there is no way of determining the real penetration of

27 Adler and Polk, 'Crime in the World of Art', pp. 347–356; Mackenzie, *Going, Going, Gone*, pp. 193–226.

28 E.H. Sutherland, *White-Collar Crime. The Uncut Version*, New Haven: Yale University Press, 1983, p. 7.

29 See amongst others G. Forti and A. Visconti, 'Cesare Beccaria and White-Collar Crimes' Public Harm. A Study in Italian Systemic Corruption', in Pontell and Geis, *International Handbook*, p. 490, pp. 495–6; D. Nelken, 'White-Collar Crime', in M. Maguire, R. Morgan and R. Reiner (eds), *The Oxford Handbook of Criminology*, Oxford: Oxford University Press, 2002, p. 844, pp. 868–869; T.G. Poveda, *Rethinking White-Collar Crime*, Westport CT: Praeger, 1994, p. 45.

30 See for further details S. Mackenzie, 'Illicit Deals in Cultural Objects as Crimes of the Powerful', *Crime Law and Social Change*, 2011, vol. 56, p. 133.

31 Adler and Polk, 'Crime in the World of Art', p. 352; N. Brodie, J. Doole and P. Watson, *Stealing History: The Illicit Trade in Cultural Material*, Cambridge: The McDonald Institute for Archaeological Research, 2000, pp. 16–17; Lane *et al.*, 'Time Crime', p. 251.

32 Empirical studies have evidenced a correlation between (estimated) rates of illicit export of cultural properties and the level of corruption in the exporting country as measured by survey-based indexes: see Fisman and Wei, *The Smuggling of Art*, pp. 9–13.

33 Bowman, 'Transnational Crimes', pp. 231–232.

34 See Chapter 25 in this volume. With regard to organized crime and cultural property trafficking see also J. Dietzler, 'On "Organized Crime" in the Illicit Antiquities Trade: Moving Beyond the Definitional Debate', *Trends in Organized Crime*, 2013, vol. 16, p. 329, pp. 333–336.

35 See for instance ECOSOC Resolution 2004/34; ECOSOC Resolution 2008/23; ECOSOC Resolution 2010/19; ECOSOC Resolution 2011/42; and finally the Resolution adopted by the UN General Assembly at its 89th plenary meeting, on 19 December 2011 (A/RES/66/180), which all express alarm at 'the growing involvement of organized criminal groups in all aspects of trafficking in cultural property'.

36 Palermo, 12–15 December 2000, 2225 UNTS 209; in force 29 September 2003.

37 S. Manacorda and D. Chappell, 'Introduction', in *Crime in the Art and Antiquities World*, pp. 3–5.

organized crime into the art and antiquities market.[38] What appears certain enough is that trafficking generally requires the involvement of a plurality of subjects (thieves, smugglers, facilitators, sellers and buyers) and at least a minimum of organization,[39] and that it is a typically transnational phenomenon.[40] In this meaning, it generally meets the requirements of Article 2 UNTOC with its wide definition of 'organized criminal group'.[41] On the other hand, we lack reliable data about the actual involvement of 'traditional' (Mafia-like) organized criminal groups, and 'while there are many features that the illicit traffic in antiquities seems to share with other forms of organized crime, there are a number of features that immediately stamp this traffic as different': mainly the sufficiency of really minimal amounts of organization and the great asymmetry between the source and market sides of the trafficking (with the illegality, and occasional violence, almost entirely on the side of the former, and a largely legitimate trade on the side of the latter).[42] Thus, while trafficking in cultural property is usually 'organized' through 'networks whose task is to handle the numerous changes that take place from the time of the theft (or the clandestine excavation) to the time the objects reach the final users', this 'does not necessarily denote the involvement of "traditional" criminal associations and even less so the presence of a "Mafia" '.[43]

From a precautionary perspective, as Mackenzie notes, several factors contribute to make the antiquities market 'a high-risk market in terms of opportunities presented to organised criminals'[44] (be they traditional organized criminal groups, or networks constituted *ad hoc* for the purposes of exploiting a vulnerable cultural heritage). This preliminary evidence should certainly suggest an increase in national and international authorities' commitment to the prevention and repression of cultural property trafficking, including, when needed, through a more incisive use of criminal law. At the same time, this does not appear enough to support recurring invocations for 'emergency policies', with the ensuing troubling requests of over-criminalization and over-sanctioning, unrestrained recourse to special – and quite 'invasive' – investigative techniques, exceptions to usual standards of evidence (for instance, through reversals of the burden of proof) and the like. Requests such as these are hardly compatible with the respect for basic democratic principles such as *extrema ratio* and the presumption of innocence.[45]

38 Such were also the conclusions of the international conference on Organised Crime in Art and Antiquities held in Courmayeur (Italy) on 12–14 December 2008: see 'Conclusions', in Manacorda, *Organised Crime*, p. 246.
39 K. Polk, 'The Antiquities Trade Viewed as a Criminal Market', *Hong Kong Lawyer*, 2000, vol. 82, pp. 82–91.
40 Adler and Polk, *Crime in the World of Art*, pp. 351–54; Dietzler, 'On "Organized Crime" ', pp. 333–340.
41 In the same sense D. Chappell and K. Polk, 'Unraveling the "Cordata": Just How Organized is the International Traffic in Cultural Objects?', in Manacorda and Chappell, *Crime in the Art and Antiquities World*, p. 103.
42 Chappell and Polk, 'Unraveling the "Cordata" ', pp. 103–106 (quote at p. 104).
43 G. Nistri, 'The Experience of the Italian Cultural Heritage Protection Unit', in Manacorda and Chappell, *Crime in the Art and Antiquities World*, p. 184.
44 S. Mackenzie, 'The Market as Criminal and Criminals in the Market: Reducing Opportunities for Organised Crime in the International Antiquities Market', in Manacorda and Chappell, *Crime in the Art and Antiquities World*, pp. 76–80 (at p. 76).
45 S. Manacorda, 'Criminal Law Protection of Cultural Heritage: An International Perspective', in Manacorda and Chappell, *Crime in the Art and Antiquities World*, p. 23.

International law and cultural property protection

Even if cultural heritage attracts increasing interest and concern, and several conventions aimed at its protection have been adopted since the end of World War II, only a very limited number of their provisions pertain to criminal law. The corpus of relevant international law is, on one hand, extremely heterogeneous, and, on the other, basically reflects 'a sort of "penal minimalism" ',[46] with a marked prevalence of civil and administrative measures, even if, as we will see, current trends in international policies regarding cultural property trafficking appear more open to criminalization. For the sake of completeness some brief notes will be addressed to all the primary conventions forming this international juridical framework, regardless of their lack of criminal law provisions.

Protection in the event of armed conflict

The first serious attempt at an international protection of cultural heritage is represented by the Convention for the Protection of Cultural Property in the Event of Armed Conflict, signed at The Hague on 14 May 1954 (1954 Hague Convention),[47] and prompted by the then recent experience of massive looting and destruction perpetrated during World War II. It is debated whether the principles outlined by this Convention have become part of customary international law, even if this appears to be the predominant opinion amongst scholars.[48]

The 1954 Hague Convention provides grounds for individual criminal liability for crimes against cultural property perpetrated in case of declared war, national and international armed conflicts, or military invasion of a foreign country,[49] even if its scope is limited (with a formulation which has elicited some criticism for its vagueness[50]) to 'movable or immovable property of *great importance* to the cultural heritage of every people' (italics added). To this general protection, Chapter II adds a 'special protection' for 'a limited number of refuges intended to shelter movable cultural property in the event of armed conflict', and 'of centres containing monuments and other immovable cultural property of very great importance' listed in the 'International Register of Cultural Property under Special Protection'.[51] The 1954 Hague Convention binds each State to refrain from any use of cultural property for purposes likely to expose it to destruction or damage in the event of armed conflict, as well as from any act of hostility directed against it.[52] With specific regard to the risk of trafficking, States are bound to prohibit, prevent and stop 'any form of theft, pillage or misappropriation' and to 'refrain from requisitioning movable cultural property situated in the territory of another High Contracting Party'.[53]

---

46 Manacorda, 'Criminal Law Protection', pp. 24–25.
47 14 May 1954, 249 UNTS 240; in force 7 August 1956.
48 J.-M. Henckaerts, 'New Rules for the Protection of Cultural Property in Armed Conflicts', *International Review of the Red Cross*, 1999, vol. 81; see also A.M. Maugeri, *La tutela dei beni culturali nel diritto internazionale penale*, Milan: Giuffrè, 2008, p. 26. For an overview of the different positions expressed on this topic, see also Forrest, *International Law*, pp. 127–130.
49 Articles 18 and 19. See also Forrest, *International Law*, pp. 81–84.
50 Y. Dinstein, *The Protection of Cultural Property and Places of Worship in International Armed Conflicts*, in AA. VV., *Studi di diritto internazionale in onore di Gaetano Arangio-Ruiz*, vol. 3, Naples: ESI, 2004, p. 1913; Maugeri, *La tutela*, pp. 29–30.
51 See Art. 8 and annex *Regulations*.
52 See Art. 4(1).
53 See Art. 4(3)–(4).

The only norm that vaguely 'comes within the punitive province'[54] is Article 28, which requires State Parties to 'take, within the framework of their ordinary criminal jurisdiction, all necessary steps to prosecute and impose penal or disciplinary sanctions upon those persons, of whatever nationality, who commit or order to be committed a breach' of the 1954 Hague Convention. Evidently, such a provision is neither very demanding, nor potentially very effective.[55] The definition of the prohibited acts is imprecise, failing to enumerate and detail specific criminal offences; also, the obligation is in itself too general, and allows for the use of disciplinary sanctions as an alternative to criminal ones.

Contemporary with the 1954 Hague Convention is its First Protocol,[56] which requires each contracting State to 'prevent the exportation, from a territory occupied by it during an armed conflict, of cultural property',[57] 'to take into its custody cultural property imported into its territory either directly or indirectly from any occupied territory',[58] and to 'return, at the close of hostilities, to the competent authorities of the territory previously occupied, cultural property which is in its territory', if such property has been illicitly exported.[59] This Protocol, too, is not very demanding, in terms of criminalization, as States are only generally required to 'take all necessary measures to ensure [the] effective application' of the aforementioned norms,[60] so that they are given the largest liberty as to what kind of sanctions – if any – should be introduced to this effect.[61]

The framework of international humanitarian law concerned with protection of cultural property[62] includes other instruments, beginning with the First[63] and Second[64] Additional 1977 Protocols to the Geneva Conventions.[65] As they, like Article 8 of the subsequent 1998

---

54 Manacorda, 'Criminal Law Protection', p. 27.
55 N. Boister, *An Introduction to Transnational Criminal Law*, Oxford: Oxford University Press, 2012, p. 114; Manacorda, 'Criminal Law Protection', p. 27; Maugeri, *La tutela*, p. 40.
56 Protocol for the Protection of Cultural Property in the Event of Armed Conflict, The Hague, 14 May 1954.
57 Article I(1).
58 Article I(2).
59 Article I(3).
60 Article III(11).
61 See also Forrest, *International Law*, pp. 104–108.
62 For the inclusion of international rules aimed at protecting cultural heritage in the event of armed conflicts within the heading of 'humanitarian law' see F. Bugnion, 'The Origins and Development of the Legal Protection of Cultural Property in the Event of Armed Conflict', *International Review of the Red Cross*, 2004, vol. 854.
63 Protocol Additional to the Geneva Conventions of 12 August 1949, and relating to the Protection of Victims of International Armed Conflicts (Protocol I), 8 June 1977, 1125 UNTS 3; in force 7 December 1978 (First Protocol to the Geneva Conventions).
64 Protocol Additional to the Geneva Conventions of 12 August 1949, and relating to the Protection of Victims of Non-International Armed Conflicts (Protocol II), 8 June 1977, 1125 UNTS 609; in force 7 December 1978.
65 It is generally agreed amongst scholars that these provisions, too, are 'an expression of customary rules which, as such, apply to all belligerents, whether or not they are bound by the Additional Protocols'. Bugnion, 'The Origins'. See also Forrest, *International Law*, pp. 127–130; Maugeri, *La tutela*, p. 45; R. O'Keefe, *The Protection of Cultural Property in Armed Conflict*, Cambridge: Cambridge University Press, 2006, p. 202.

Rome Statute of the International Criminal Court,[66] basically deal with war crimes which impinge upon *immovable* cultural property – or have as their result the *destruction* or damage of cultural objects – we will not analyse their provisions here.[67] More relevant to the scope of this chapter is the Second Protocol added in 1999 to the 1954 Hague Convention, which contains more specific provisions for the criminalization of offences[68] against cultural heritage,[69] including the 'extensive destruction or *appropriation* of cultural property protected under the Convention and this Protocol'[70] (italics added) and the '*theft, pillage or misappropriation* of, or acts of vandalism directed against cultural property protected under the Convention'[71] (italics added). These actions, like all the others listed in Article 15 (which focus instead only on the risk of damage or destruction), are deemed 'serious violations' of the Protocol, and, differently from the 1954 Hague Convention, each State Party is compelled to 'adopt such measures as may be necessary to establish [them] as criminal offences under its domestic law . . . and to make such offences punishable by appropriate penalties'.[72] For the first of such serious violations, States are also obligated to introduce a universal penal jurisdiction,[73] as well as to set provisions for extradition[74] according to the principle *aut dedere aut judicare*.[75]

Article 15(2) also binds State Parties to 'comply with general principles of law and international law, including the rules extending individual criminal responsibility to persons other than those who directly commit the act'. This provision, coupled with the explicit statement in Article 16 that the Protocol 'does not preclude the incurring of individual criminal responsibility or the exercise of jurisdiction under national and international law that may be applicable, or affect the exercise of jurisdiction under customary international law', has led to debate whether this responsibility might extend to every form of participation, including so-called command responsibility,[76] the norm apparently referring (also) to Articles 86 and 87 of the First Protocol to the Geneva Conventions, as well as to Article 28 of the Rome Statute.

However, for provisions different from those of Article 15, far less demanding obligations are set: Article 21 requires State Parties to 'suppress', when 'committed intentionally', any 'illicit export, other removal or transfer of ownership of cultural property from occupied territory in violation of the Convention or this Protocol', but also leaves to each national authority the choice between 'such legislative, administrative or disciplinary measures as may be necessary'.

---

66 Statute of the International Criminal Court, done at Rome on 17 July 1998, 2187 UNTS 90; in force 1 July 2002 (Rome Statute). For a detailed analysis of Art. 8 see Maugeri, *La tutela*, pp. 245–336. For a reform proposal concerning the Rome Statute in this respect, see Y. Gottlieb, 'Criminalizing Destruction of Cultural Property: A Proposal for Defining New Crimes under the Rome Statute of the ICC', *Penn State International Law Review*, 2005, vol. 23, p. 857.

67 For a detailed analysis see Forrest, *International Law*, pp. 108–110; Manacorda, 'Criminal Law Protection', pp. 27–28; Maugeri, *La tutela*, pp. 45–57.

68 It is voluntary in nature; see Art. 15(1).

69 See Forrest, *International Law*, pp. 122–126; Manacorda, 'Criminal Law Protection', pp. 28–29; Maugeri, *La tutela*, pp. 61–62.

70 Article 15(1)(c).

71 Article 15(1)(e).

72 Article 15(2).

73 Article 16(1)(c). See also Forrest, *International Law*, pp. 125–126; Manacorda, 'Criminal Law Protection', p. 29; Maugeri, *La tutela*, p. 64; O'Keefe, *The Protection*, p. 274.

74 Articles 18 and 20.

75 Article 17(1).

76 Forrest, *International Law*, p. 125; Manacorda, 'Criminal Law Protection', pp. 29–30; Maugeri, *La tutela*, pp. 67–8; O'Keefe, *The Protection*, pp. 281–282.

International regulation of cultural property circulation

After a first phase mainly focused on the risks of destruction and dispersion posed to cultural heritage by armed conflicts, more general problems posed by the circulation of cultural objects on the market (namely the always present risk of illicit export, import and trafficking) have elicited international concern. However, as anticipated, barring some regional and/or sectoral instruments (which will be discussed below), the possible criminalization of such acts has received little or no consideration in the major conventions dealing with these issues, which will now be briefly reviewed.

The 1970 UNESCO Convention: a limited opening for criminal law

The UNESCO Convention on the Means of Prohibiting and Preventing the Illicit Import, Export, and Transfer of Ownership of Cultural Property (the UNESCO Convention)[77] has many valuable features. This includes the above-mentioned attempt at providing a precise and comprehensive definition of (movable) 'cultural property' in Article 1. It also includes the many articles which commit State Parties to adopt administrative,[78] civil,[79] economic,[80] social and educational[81] measures aimed at protecting cultural heritage against 'the illicit import, export and transfer of ownership' – deemed 'one of the main causes of the impoverishment of the cultural heritage of the countries of origin'[82] – as well as to establish international cooperation to facilitate this.[83]

'Illicit' is defined as any act of 'import, export or transfer of ownership of cultural property effected contrary to the provisions adopted under [the] Convention',[84] which sets an obligation of prohibiting exportation of cultural objects 'unless accompanied by the . . . export certificate' provided for in Article 6(a).[85] States are also required 'to prohibit the import of cultural property stolen from a museum or a religious or secular public monument or similar institution in another State Party . . . provided that such property is documented as appertaining to the inventory of that institution';[86] export restrictions are more stringent than limitations to importing.[87] Finally, States are also required to 'oblige antique dealers . . . to maintain a register recording the origin of each item of cultural property, names and addresses of the supplier, description and price of each item sold and to inform the purchaser . . . of the export prohibition to which [it] may be subject'.[88] Each of these prohibitions and obligations

---

77 Paris, 14 November 1970, 823 UNTS 231; in force 24 April 1972. About which see also R.D. Abramson and S.B. Huttler, 'The Legal Response to the Illicit Movement of Cultural Heritage', *Law and Policy in International Business*, 1973, vol. 5, p. 948; Boister, *An Introduction*, pp. 114–115; Forrest, *International Law*, pp. 166–196; Manacorda, 'Criminal Law Protection', pp. 30–34.
78 Articles 5 and 6(a), which bind State Parties to introduce an export certificate.
79 Article 13(c).
80 See, for instance, Art. 14.
81 See Arts 5(f), 6(c), and particularly 10(b).
82 Article 2.
83 See Arts 7(b)(ii), 9, and 13(b) and (d).
84 Article 3.
85 Article 6(b).
86 Article 7(b)(i).
87 While each exported object must be accompanied by the required certificate, forbidden importations only concern registered properties stolen from specific sites.
88 Article 10(a).

is required to be backed up by sanctions, but it is left to each Party's discretion to decide whether to use criminal or administrative ones.[89]

All in all, 'the fulcrum of the system controlling the illicit circulation of cultural assets lies . . . in instruments of an administrative or private law nature . . ., even when the transfer itself involved acts of penal significance, such as theft'.[90] Nonetheless, market countries, concerned about the protection of the interests of bona fide purchasers, have ratified this Convention only in recent years,[91] and occasionally with significant reservations (as happened with Australia and the United States); moreover, few of the signatory States have actually enacted the requested legislation.[92]

The 1995 UNIDROIT Convention: the prevalence of the private law

The UNIDROIT Convention on the International Return of Stolen or Illegally Exported Cultural Objects (UNIDROIT Convention),[93] developed by the International Institute for the Unification of Private Law, is not concerned at all with issues of criminalization.[94] Instead, it provides a set of private international law rules for the recovery and restitution of stolen or illicitly exported cultural objects,[95] including some exceptions to common private law principles, on account of the importance of such items, at the same time introducing a 'fair and reasonable compensation' for good faith possessors.[96] As lucidly outlined in the Preamble, this Convention, albeit certainly contributing 'to the fight against illicit trade in cultural objects by taking the important step of establishing common, minimal legal rules for the restitution and return of cultural objects', cannot 'by itself provide a solution to the problems raised by illicit trade', but can only 'enhance international cultural co-operation'.

Regional and sectoral instruments

More robust obligations of criminalization have been provided in the two conventions briefly addressed below, though each is either geographically or sectorally limited in the scope of its application.

---

89 Articles 8 and 10(a). That Art. 8 applies only to sub-paragraph (i) of Art. 7(b), contrary to its literal formulation, is self-evident interpretation, as its provisions could not be extended to acts pertaining to States. Manacorda, 'Criminal Law Protection', p. 33.
90 Manacorda, 'Criminal Law Protection', p. 32.
91 Japan and United Kingdom in 2002, Switzerland and Sweden in 2003, Germany and Norway in 2007, Belgium and the Netherlands in 2009.
92 Forrest, *International Law*, pp. 191–194.
93 Rome, 24 June 1995, 34 ILM 1322 (1995); in force 1 July 1998.
94 See Forrest, *International Law*, pp. 196–223; P. Lalive, 'A Disturbing International Convention: Unidroit', *Art Antiquity and Law*, 1999, vol. 4, no. 3; Manacorda, 'Criminal Law Protection', pp. 34–36; L.V. Prott, *Commentary on the UNIDROIT Convention*, London: Institute of Art and Law, 1997; L.V. Prott, 'The UNIDROIT Convention on Stolen or Illegally Exported Cultural Objects. Ten Years On', *Uniform Law Review*, 2009, p. 215.
95 Defined in Art. 2 and Annex.
96 In particular Arts 4 and 6.

The 2001 UNESCO Convention

The UNESCO Convention on the Protection of the Underwater Cultural Heritage, adopted in Paris on 2 November 2001 (2001 Underwater Cultural Heritage Convention),[97] as declared by its heading, only deals with one particular area of cultural heritage, albeit something it deems 'an integral part' of it 'and a particularly important element in the history of peoples'. It is – quite reasonably – considered both subject to specific risks, and in need, for its 'survey, excavation and protection', of 'the availability and application of special scientific methods . . . all of which indicate a need for uniform governing criteria'.[98]

After having defined and circumscribed its object in Article 1, the 2001 Underwater Cultural Heritage Convention mainly focuses on aspects of the international maritime law which might affect the protection of underwater cultural heritage, as well as on measures to enhance international cooperation, reporting of findings, conservation *in situ*, and public awareness and concern for it.[99]

In relation to trafficking, Article 14 commits contracting Parties to 'take measures to prevent the entry into their territory, the dealing in, or the possession of, underwater cultural heritage illicitly exported and/or recovered, where recovery was contrary' to the Convention itself. Such measures shall be enforced through sanctions 'adequate in severity to be effective in securing compliance . . . and to discourage violations wherever they occur'; national legislation must also work to 'deprive offenders of the benefit deriving from their illegal activities'.[100] This article offers an opening for – but does not compel – the use *also* of criminal sanctions to prevent and repress illicit trafficking in cultural properties retrieved from the sea. It further commits States to provide for the seizure not only of illicitly dealt goods,[101] but also of any other proceeds of such activities. However, again, there is no obligation to use deprivation measures penal in their nature, civil or administrative ones being sufficient to satisfy the requirements of the Convention.

The 1985 European Convention on Offences Relating to Cultural Property

The 1985 European Convention on Offences Relating to Cultural Property[102] is currently the only international convention specifically and organically aimed at the criminalization of acts that impinge upon cultural property[103] (of which it gives a complex and comprehensive definition);[104] possibly for this reason, it has never come into force, even though it requires[105] only three ratifications.[106]

---

97   41 ILM 40 (2002); in force 2 January 2009.
98   Preamble.
99   For further details see G. Camarda and T. Scovazzi (eds), *The Protection of the Underwater Cultural Heritage: Legal Aspects*, Milan: Giuffrè, 2002; Forrest, *International Law*, pp. 331–361.
100 Article 17.
101 About which see also Art. 18.
102 Delphi, 23 June 1985, ETS No 119, not yet in force.
103 About this convention see also Boister, *An Introduction*, p. 115; Manacorda, 'Criminal Law Protection', pp. 37–38; J.A.R. Nafziger, 'International Penal Aspects of Protecting Cultural Property', *The International Lawyer* 19, 1985, pp. 840–841.
104 Article 2 states that the Convention shall automatically apply to the cultural property listed in Appendix II, paragraph 1 (which largely matches the definition adopted in the 1970 UNESCO Convention), but also offers to Contracting States the possibility of declaring 'cultural property' a far wider range of movable or immovable objects.
105 Article 21.
106 Presently, only six Member States of the Council of Europe have signed the Convention (none of which is a primary market country), but no ratification has yet been issued.

According to Article 3 and Appendix III, a first group of offences against cultural property – namely theft, appropriation through violence or menace, and receiving of the two previous offences' objects – are subject to an obligation of criminalization. A second group of offences (also possible steps in the trafficking chain) – mainly including other acts of illicit appropriation and dispersion – are allowed to be made into criminal offences, so that other contracting Parties could not object. Finally, State Parties may at any time declare to deem offences against cultural property any other harmful act or omission not listed within the 1985 European Convention. Article 12 commits contracting States to 'take the necessary measures for adequate sanctioning' (leaving an open choice, in relation to criminal offences, amongst custodial and non-custodial sanctions, including fines, bans and disqualifications), while further articles contain detailed provisions about jurisdiction, plurality of proceedings, application of the *ne bis in idem* principle, letters rogatory and restitution of cultural property.[107]

Future perspectives on international criminal law and cultural heritage protection

Limited efficacy

As Nafziger observes,

> the efficacy of this comprehensive legal framework is debatable. Its primary effect thus far has not been so much to punish individuals, but rather to facilitate the restitution, return, or forfeiture of cultural property, and to raise public consciousness and respect for the integrity of cultural provenance and property ownership, whether public or private.[108]

All are deserving purposes, of course, as indeed no criminal policy could hope for effectiveness without preceding and combining criminal law provisions with a comprehensive set of social, cultural and non-criminal legal measures.[109] It cannot be denied, however, that the international community has not yet managed to converge upon shared criminal policy lines with regard to cultural property trafficking, mainly because of the great divergences, both of interests and of normative frameworks, between source and market countries.[110] The former, in effect, have a strong interest in increasing both regulation and criminalization (though in some cases they lack the resources to effectively pursue their criminal policies), as well as in enhancing international cooperation for both investigative and judicial purposes, and with a view to the return of and restitution for illicitly trafficked goods. These States also often already possess more restrictive rules for export and trade in cultural properties, and more strict criminal legislation. The latter, instead, are generally in favour of the greatest possible

---

107 See Arts 6–19.
108 Nafziger, 'International Penal Aspects', p. 846.
109 For a development of this idea, see A. Visconti, 'Le prospettive internazionali di tutela penale: strategie sanzionatorie e politico-criminali', in Manacorda and Visconti, *Beni culturali*, pp. 139–159.
110 See Mackenzie, *Going, Going, Gone*, pp. 62–88; E.A. Posner, 'The International Protection of Cultural Property: Some Skeptical Observations', *Chicago Journal of International Law*, 2007, vol. 8, pp. 220–221; L.V. Prott and P.J. O'Keefe, *National Legal Control of Illicit Traffic in Cultural Property*, Paris: UNESCO, 1983.

liberalization,[111] of minimal import barriers, of extended protection of 'good faith' possessors' rights, and of short limitation periods, as they are against specific criminalization of offences against cultural heritage, which they generally deem sufficiently sanctioned through ordinary criminal law provisions, when applicable.

Nonetheless, recent years have seen an increasing commitment from the Commission on Crime Prevention and Criminal Justice, ECOSOC and UNODC to the development of international cooperation and possibly of new international instruments for the prevention of and fight against cultural property trafficking.[112] These efforts are currently pursuing three main directions.

Development and implementation of the UN Model Treaty

Adopted at the Eighth United Nations Congress on the Prevention of Crime (Havana, 1990), this Model Treaty,[113] unlike other contemporary ones, has never been converted into a Resolution by the General Assembly, so that it currently has no binding force; it simply represents an example, or draft, which might be used by States to enhance cooperation in this area. It includes provisions for the prohibition – backed up by 'appropriate and effective administrative and penal sanctions'[114] – of importing (which is one of its most innovative features) and exporting of 'movable cultural property (i) which has been stolen . . . or (ii) which has been illicitly exported',[115] as well as of the acquisition of, and dealing with, illicitly imported cultural property.[116] Its formulation also allows for specific provisions against trafficking undertaken in an associated or organized form,[117] and for the introduction of corporate liability.[118] Although something less than even a soft law tool, the Model Treaty might offer a starting point for the discussion and introduction of new international instruments. On more than one occasion, ECOSOC has directed the UNODC to explore ways of making it more effective,[119] as well as encouraging Member States to take it into account when concluding relevant bilateral or multilateral agreements[120] and to keep submitting comments made with a view to its improvement.[121] Similar recommendations have come from the Expert Group on

111 For a summary of this position see Posner, 'The International Protection', pp. 221–231; for a summary of the opposite position see T. Scovazzi, 'La dimensione internazionale della tutela. Principi etici e norme giuridiche in materia di restituzione dei beni culturali', in Manacorda and Visconti, *Beni culturali*, pp. 95–126.

112 See also C. Castañeda de la Mora, 'The Work of the United Nations Office on Drugs and Crime in the Area of Illicit Trafficking in Cultural Property', in Manacorda and Visconti, *Beni culturali*, pp. 3–18.

113 About which see also S. Mackenzie, *Protection against Trafficking in Cultural Property*, background paper for the meeting of the expert group on protection against trafficking in cultural property held in Vienna on 24–26 November 2009, UNODC/CCPCJ/EG.1/2009/CRP.1, pp. 10–4; Manacorda, 'Criminal Law Protection', pp. 36–37.

114 Preamble. See also Art. 3(a).

115 Article 2(a).

116 Articles 2(b) and 3(b).

117 Articles 2(c) and 3(c).

118 As Art. 3 refers to the responsibility of 'persons *or institutions*' (italics added).

119 See ECOSOC Resolution 2004/34 and ECOSOC Resolution 2008/23.

120 See ECOSOC Resolution 2003/29.

121 See ECOSOC Resolution 2010/19 and ECOSOC Resolution 2011/42, now adopted by the General Assembly as Resolution 66/180, United Nations A/RES/66/180.

protection against trafficking in cultural property convened pursuant to ECOSOC Resolution 2008/23.[122]

Use of the UN Convention against Transnational Organized Crime (UNTOC)

Far stronger recommendations have been made regarding the widely ratified[123] UNTOC, which does not specifically include trafficking in cultural property but is increasingly seen as a useful tool to strengthen international cooperation in this area. Also valued is the potential for State Parties to make use of its provisions concerning (*inter alia*) criminalization and other measures against laundering of proceeds of crime, seizure and confiscation, extradition, special investigative techniques, and measures to enhance legal testimonies and cooperation with legal enforcement authorities.[124] To this effect, the Conference of the Parties to the UNTOC, in its Resolution 5/7 of 2010,[125] encouraged contracting States to employ it to tackle criminal offences against cultural property, and particularly invited them to consider such offences as 'serious crimes' according to Article 2(b), in order to bring them within the range of application of this Convention. Similar recommendations were included in UN General Assembly Resolution 66/180 of 19 December 2011 and in several other international documents.[126]

This approach, understandable because of UNTOC's relative ease of use, should nonetheless be regarded with some caution: while UNTOC can certainly be a viable instrument in combating the most serious offences related to trafficking in cultural property, a basic respect for harm and proportionality principles should suggest that Parties avoid making every such offence into serious crimes as defined in Article 2 (and therefore punishable 'by a maximum deprivation of liberty of at least four years or a more serious penalty'), simply in order to bring them within the scope of application of this Convention. This is even more so because of the lack of uniformity amongst national legislation about which offences should fall under the (currently rather vague) label of 'cultural property trafficking', the term potentially encompassing all stages of the illicit dispersion of cultural property, thus including also purely instrumental offences, as well as any kind of facilitation, any risk-enhancing activity, etc.

Development of specific 'Guidelines'

Following a recommendation by the Expert Group on protection against trafficking in cultural property,[127] the Commission on Crime Prevention and Criminal Justice (CCPCJ)

---

122 See the Report on the Meeting of the Expert Group on Protection against Trafficking in Cultural Property held in Vienna from 24 to 26 November 2009, UNODC/CCPCJ/EG.1/2009/2; see also the Report on the Meeting of the Expert Group on Protection against Trafficking in Cultural Property held in Vienna from 27 to 29 June 2012, UNODC/CCPCJ/EG.1/2012/4.
123 Since its adoption in 2000 the Convention has been ratified by 179 Parties, including all the major market countries for cultural property.
124 See Arts 6 and 7, 12–14, 16, 20 and 23–26.
125 Conference of the Parties to the United Nations Convention against Transnational Organized Crime, Report of the Conference of the Parties to the United Nations Convention against Transnational Organized Crime on its fifth session, held in Vienna from 18 to 22 October 2010, CTOC/COP/2010/17.
126 See UNODC/CCPCJ/EG.1/2009/2 and UNODC/CCPCJ/EG.1/2012/4.
127 See UNODC/CCPCJ/EG.1/2009/2.

requested the UNODC to develop a set of Guidelines on Crime Prevention and Criminal Justice Responses with respect to Trafficking in Cultural Property,[128] which as a result were drafted,[129] and then discussed in a further meeting of the Expert Group.[130] On the occasion of the CCPCJ's twenty-second meeting, in April 2013,[131] a Draft Resolution was adopted, to be submitted to the General Assembly, in order to provide for a further review and final adoption of the Guidelines. Whatever their fate through such a complex procedure, these Guidelines could be, as the Model Treaty is, an instrument useful to the improvement of national laws and their harmonization (including, if possible, the uniform definition of what constitutes 'cultural property trafficking'[132]), or at least to the development of further bilateral or multilateral agreements, particularly with regard to police and judicial cooperation.[133] Unlike the former instrument, however, the Guidelines, on the one hand, are not shaped as a draft convention, and, on the other, encompass a far larger range of potential measures, roughly listed as 'prevention strategies' (Chapter I), 'criminal justice policies' (Chapter II) and provisions pertaining to 'cooperation' (Chapter III), and covering both issues of criminalization (with a detailed list of possible offences, sanctions, and investigative and judicial measures), and other, wider, criminal policy strategies.

Conclusions

The issue of trafficking in cultural property still lacks a comprehensive, uniform and effective international juridical framework; in this complex and scattered landscape, the largest gaps are possibly those related to the specific criminalization of acts – thefts, lootings, illicit exports and imports, illicit dealing, etc. – which appear both widespread and seriously harmful to the cultural heritage of humankind. Pervasive and long-lasting conflicts of interest and legislation between source and market countries make an imminent and substantial evolution quite unlikely. Yet, hints of a possible, albeit slow and probably roundabout, change can be observed in the renewed and energetic commitment of several international organizations to combat these offences. Only time will tell how much the international balance of power will switch towards source countries, some of which are developing increasing awareness and influence, and which international instruments (if any) will arise in this field.

128 CCPCJ, Report on the Twentieth Session (3 December 2010 and 11–15 April 2011), E/2011/30 – E/CN.15/2011/21.

129 See Guidelines on Crime Prevention and Criminal Justice Responses with respect to Trafficking and Other Illicit Behaviours in Cultural Property, advanced unedited version.

130 See UNODC/CCPCJ/EG.1/2012/4.

131 See CCPCJ, Report on the Twenty-second Session (7 December 2012 and 22–26 April 2013), E/2013/30 – E/CN.15/2013/27.

132 See in particular Guideline 16.

133 See in particular Chapter III.

17

Environmental theft and trafficking

Rob White

Introduction

This chapter examines a selection of prominent transnational environmental crimes that involve theft and/or trafficking of vulnerable resources including illegal, unregulated and unauthorised fishing, illegal logging and the traffic in protected species. It begins by discussing the definitions and nature of transnational environmental crime, and the ways in which these are reflected in various international legal instruments. This is followed by discussion of environmental law enforcement as this pertains to these types of transnational crimes, and the varied organisations and agencies involved in translating legal prescription and proscription into grounded practice. The final section reviews issues relating to environmental crime and courts, and the potential for new legal concepts that might inform the prosecution of transnational environmental crime in the future.

Transnational crime and the environment

The notion of transnational crime evokes at least two different conceptual concerns. First, the crime must involve the movement of people, objects or decisions *across borders*. Second, the harm must be *recognised internationally* as a crime. There are limitations with each of these considerations. For example, the core international crime of genocide is universally acknowledged as an evil (even if there are disputes in practice as to whether or not genocide is in fact occurring), but it may occur within a particular country's borders. In addition, transnational harms may happen (such as disposal and congregation of plastic waste in the ocean, or the migration of toxic substances from producer countries to formerly pristine wilderness areas, thereby affecting humans and animals in the latter even though they have no connection whatsoever with the former), but these may not be considered 'crimes' in international law. The study of transnational harm or crime always involves contested definitions (restrictive or expansive, depending upon the place of formal legality in the definition) and complexities related to scale (since it may manifest in specific local or regional contexts, as well as across regions). The same applies to transnational environmental crime.

What is transnational environmental crime?

To speak of *environmental crime* or *eco-crime* is to acknowledge some kind of specificity in the act or omission that makes it distinctly relevant to environmental considerations. Yet, as with crime generally, there is much dispute over what gets defined as environmentally harmful and what ends up with the legal status as 'crime' per se.

Transnational environmental crime, as defined in conventional legal terms, refers to:

- unauthorised acts or omissions that are *against the law* and therefore subject to criminal prosecution and criminal sanctions;
- crimes that involve some kind of *cross-border transference* and an international or *global dimension*; and
- crimes related to *pollution* (of air, water and land) and *crimes against wildlife* (including illegal trade in ivory as well as live animals).

These are the key foci of national and international laws relating to environmental matters, and are the main task areas in regard to environmental crime agencies such as Interpol.

In its more expansive definition, as used by green criminologists for example, transnational environmental crime also extends to *harm*.[1] It therefore includes:

- transgressions that are *harmful to humans, environments and non-human animals*, regardless of legality per se; and
- environmental harms that are facilitated by *the state*, as well as *corporations and other powerful actors*, insofar as these institutions have the capacity to shape official definitions of environmental crime in ways that allow or condone environmentally harmful practices.

The definition of transnational environmental crime depends upon who is defining the harm, and what criteria are used in assessing the nature of the activities so described (for example legal versus ecological, criminal justice versus environmental justice).[2]

The post World War II period has seen major growth in the conclusion of treaties, agreements, protocols and conventions in relation to environmental protection and with respect to the securing of environmental resources. Nation-states have in recent years been more interested in taking governmental action on environmental matters, since much of this pertains to national economic interests. Moreover, the transboundary nature of environmental harm is evident in a variety of international protocols and conventions that deal with such matters as the illegal trade in ozone-depleting substances, the dumping and illegal transport of hazardous waste, illegal trade in chemicals such as persistent organic pollutants, and illegal dumping of oil and other wastes in oceans.[3] In technical legal terms, transnational environmental crime has been defined as follows:

1   R. White, *Transnational Environmental Crime: Toward an Eco-Global Criminology*, London: Routledge, 2011.

2   Y. Situ and D. Emmons, *Environmental Crime: The Criminal Justice System's Role in Protecting the Environment*, Thousand Oaks: Sage, 2000; P. Beirne and N. South (eds), *Issues in Green Criminology: Confronting Harms against Environments, Humanity and other Animals*, Devon: Willan, 2007; R. White, *Crimes Against Nature: Environmental Criminology and Ecological Justice*, Devon: Willan, 2008.

3   G. Hayman and D. Brack, *International Environmental Crime: The Nature and Control of Environmental Black Markets*, London: Sustainable Development Programme, Royal Institute of International Affairs, 2002.

transnational environmental crime involves the trading and smuggling of plants, animals, resources and pollutants in violation of prohibition or regulation regimes established by multilateral environmental agreements and/or in contravention of domestic law.[4]

This definition embodies huge complexities of scale, scope and content. For example, the legal framework governing environmental matters in international law is defined by over 270 multilateral environmental agreements and related instruments.[5] The laws and rules guiding action on environmental crime vary greatly at the local, regional and national levels, and there are overarching conventions and laws that likewise have different legal purchase depending upon how they are translated into action in each specific local jurisdiction. In part, differences in law-in-practice and conceptions of what is an environmental crime stem from the shifting nature of what is deemed harmful or not.

According to the Australian Crime Commission,[6] the most common environmental crimes fall into four categories:

- *biodiversity crime* – such as illegal trade in endangered species of flora and fauna;
- *natural resources-related crime* – such as illegal fishing or logging;
- *illegal movement and disposal of hazardous wastes* – such as illegal movement of nuclear waste or dumping of oil; and
- *banned substances crime* – such as illegal trade in ozone-depleting substances.

The main concern of this chapter is with the former two types of environmental crime, namely those relating to biodiversity and natural resources rather than pollution-related crimes.[7]

International legal instruments

Each area of environmental concern is reflected in domestic law according to its specific nature. There may not be any domestic legislation in place even after an international obligation has been agreed to, as the pace of introduction and implementation, and the content of domestic laws, will vary greatly. In countries such as Australia, for instance, there is sometimes convergence between specific domestic and international laws, as in the case of the Antarctic Marine Living Resources Act 1980, which directly connects with the Convention on the Conservation of Antarctic Marine Living Resources (1980).[8] Other domestic legislation, such as the Environmental Protection and Biodiversity Conservation Act 1999, has relevance in regard to several different international instruments, including the Convention on Biological Diversity (1992), the Convention on the Conservation of Migratory Species (1979) (Bonn Convention), the Convention on Wetlands of International Importance Especially as Waterfowl Habitat (1971) (Ramsar Convention), and the International Convention for the Regulation of Whaling (1946) (International Whaling Convention).[9]

---

4 O. Forni, 'Mapping Environmental Crimes', *Freedom From Fear Magazine*, 2010, March, p.34.
5 Ibid.
6 Australian Crime Commission, *Environmental Crime*, 2013, https://www.crimecommission.gov.au/publications/intelligence-products/crime-profile-fact-sheets/environmental-crime (accessed 16 June 2014).
7 The latter two types are dealt with in Chapter 18 of this volume.
8 See n. 15 below.
9 See n. 19 references below.

Many different international instruments speak to matters pertaining to the protection of biodiversity (see Table 17.1).

Table 17.1 Selected international agreements protecting species

---

International Convention for the Protection of Birds (1950) protects birds in their wild state, considering that in the interests of science, the protection of nature and the economy of each nation, all birds should as a matter of principle be protected.[10]

Convention on Wetlands of International Importance Especially as Waterfowl Habitat (1971), also known as the Ramsar Convention, brings together the protection of birds and the preservation of wetlands. States party to the agreement must designate at least one wetland within their territory that they agree to safeguard from human encroachment.[11]

Convention on International Trade in Endangered Species of Wild Fauna and Flora (CITES) (1973) focuses on protecting endangered species through limiting trade, since it is often demand in one part of the world that impacts conservation status in another part of the world.[12]

Agreement of the Conservation of Polar Bears (1973) achieves protection of the polar bear as a significant resource of the Arctic region through further conservation and management measures.[13]

Convention on the Conservation of Migratory Species (1979), also known as CMS or the Bonn Convention, aims to conserve terrestrial, marine and avian migratory species throughout their range. It is differentiated from CITES by its focus on naturally migrating species rather than species moved internationally by human trade.[14]

Convention on the Conservation of Antarctic Marine Living Resources (1980), CCAMLR, has as its goal to ensure that the marine resources of the Antarctic are used sustainably so that they can continue to be harvested indefinitely.[15]

Convention on Biological Diversity (CBD) (1992) focuses on the whole of biodiversity conservation, the idea that it is the diversity of species and genetic material that must be protected rather than specific species or locations.[16]

The Cartagena Protocol on Biosafety (2000) focuses on avoidance of possible harms from genetic modification of organisms and the export of living modified organisms.[17]

The Convention on Fishing and Conservation of Living Resources of the High Seas (short title Marine Life Conservation Convention) (1958) encourages international cooperation to solve the problems involved in the conservation of living resources of the high seas, considering that because of the development of modern technology some of these resources are in danger of being overexploited.[18]

The International Convention for the Regulation of Whaling (1946) protects all species of whales from overhunting; to establish a system of international regulation for the whale fisheries to ensure proper conservation and development of whale stocks; and to safeguard for future generations the great natural resources represented by whale stocks.[19]

---

10 International Convention for the Protection of Birds, Paris 18 October 1950; in force 17 January 1963.
11 Ramsar Convention on Wetlands, Ramsar 2 February 1971; in force 21 December 1975.
12 CITES, Washington 3 March 1973; in force 1 July 1975.
13 Agreement on the Conservation of Polar Bears, Oslo 15 November 1973; in force 26 May 1976.
14 CMS, Bonn 23 June 1979; in force 1 November 1983.
15 CCAMLR, Canberra 20 May 1980; in force 7 April 1982.
16 CBD, Rio de Janeiro 5 June 1992; in force 29 December 1993.
17 Cartagena Protocol, Montreal 29 January 2000; in force 11 September 2003.
18 Marine Life Conservation Convention, Geneva 29 April 1958; in force 20 March 1966.
19 IWC, Washington, 2 December 1946; in force 10 October 1948.

A key international instrument of relevance to wildlife protection is the CITES Convention, which has the aim of ensuring that international trade in specimens of wild animals and plants does not threaten their survival. The CITES Convention works by subjecting international trade in specimens of listed species to certain controls, based upon where the roughly 6,000 species of animals and 30,000 species of plants are situated in the three Appendices to the Convention that reflect the extent of the threat to the species, and the controls that apply to the trade. As with most of the international agreements cited in Table 17.1, there are no set or overt penal provisions in the Convention itself. For example, the system of control in CITES is backed up by limited provision for penal sanction in Article 8(1) which provides:

> 1. The Parties shall take appropriate measures to enforce the provisions of the present Convention and to prohibit trade in specimens in violation thereof. These shall include measures:

> (a) to penalize trade in, or possession of, such specimens, or both; and
> (b) to provide for the confiscation or return to the State of export of such specimens.

There is thus little in the way of actual 'crimes' within the treaties. These conventions and agreements are in the main regulatory instruments, with few substantive provisions requiring states to actually enact crimes and/or describing those crimes. Nor is there provision for procedural cooperation like mutual legal assistance and extradition. This is in stark contrast to conventions which do make provision for substantive criminalisation and procedural cooperation, such as the UN Convention against Transnational Organized Crime (UNTOC).[20]

Another area of environmental concern is illegal logging and trafficking in illegal timber. The International Tropical Timber Agreement (ITTA, 2006) aims to promote the conservation and sustainable management, use and trade of tropical forest resources through the forum of the International Tropical Timber Organization (ITTO).[21] As with other international environmental agreements, there are no criminal sanctions provided for in the ITTA instrument, and little is mentioned beyond a general objective: 'Strengthening the capacity of members to improve forest law enforcement and governance, and address illegal logging and related trade in tropical lumber.'[22] Thus it is specific legislation passed at the domestic level that is most relevant to regulation and prosecution of illegal logging and trafficking. For example, the 2008 amendments to the US Lacey Act constituted the first ban on the trading of illegally sourced wood products.[23] The Lacey Act is a 1900 US law that bans trafficking in illegal wildlife. In 2008, it was amended to include plants and plant products such as timber and paper. The 2008 amendments also included a requirement that wood products importers make a declaration describing their product(s), including the scientific names of all tree species included in the product, the country of origin, the volume and the value. Also related to this development is the passing of Australia's Illegal Logging Prohibition Act (ILPA) in November 2012, and the entering into force of the European Union Timber Regulation (EUTR)[24] on 3 March 2013 in the 27 EU member states.

---

20 Palermo 15 November 2000; in force 29 September 2003 (UNTOC Convention).
21 ITTA, Geneva 27 January 2006; in force 7 December 2011.
22 ITTA, Article 1(n).
23 R. Nogueron and A. Middleton, *Tuning In: Tracking Wood from Honduran Forests to U.S. Guitars*, Issue Brief, World Resources Institute, Washington DC, 2013.
24 Regulation 995/2020, 20 October 2010.

Types of transnational environmental crime

Similar to the category differentiations described earlier, the UNODC categorises environmental crimes as one of two forms: 'natural resources crimes' and 'pollution crimes'.[25] A major example of the former is IUU fishing – illegal, unreported or unregulated fishing. Ambiguity surrounds the precise nature of the 'crime', however, as illustrated in the following observation.

> Many fishing vessels engaged in IUU fishing do so by avoiding conservation and management rules and regulations, but they do not necessarily operate in contravention of them. In other words, the term 'IUU fishing' includes conduct that is not necessarily illegal. The concept of IUU fishing is moreover potentially problematic because its focus is largely on the activities of fishing vessels. From a crime perspective this focus may become too narrow since criminal activities may also arise in the context of for instance aquaculture. Moreover, the definition does not seem to include criminal activities up- and downstream of the illegal fishing activities such as money laundering, corruption, document fraud or handling of stolen goods.[26]

For these reasons, there is a stated preference to refer to criminal conduct that may impact negatively on the marine living environment as 'marine living resources crimes'.[27]

In recent years, criminologists have begun to give concerted and detailed attention to environmental crime, especially around questions relating to animal and plant life. This work has been motivated by either a concern with species justice or an interest in conventional environmental crimes such as illegal fishing. For instance, study over the past decade has been carried out in respect of:

- genetically modified organisms (GMOs) and the abrogation of human rights and United Nations agreements in attempts to impose GMO crops on reluctant nation-states;[28]
- deforestation and the devastation to plant, animal and human welfare and rights that has accompanied this process;[29]
- the illegal theft and trade of reptiles in South Africa;[30]
- fishing-related crimes, including the poaching of abalone and of lobster;[31]
- animal abuse that involves both systemic uses of animals such as factory farming and one-on-one abuses of animals;[32]

25 UNODC, *Transnational Organized Crime in the Fishing Industry*, Vienna: United Nations, 2011.
26 Ibid., p. 96.
27 Ibid.
28 R. Walters, 'Crime, Bio-Agriculture and the Exploitation of Hunger', *British Journal of Criminology*, 2005, vol. 46, no. 1, p. 26.
29 T. Boekhout van Solinge, 'Equatorial deforestation as a harmful practice and a criminological issue', in R. White (ed.), *Global Environmental Harm: Criminological Perspectives*, Devon: Willan, 2010, p. 20.
30 J. Herbig, 'The illegal reptile trade as a form of conservation crime: a South African criminological investigation', in R. White (ed.), *Global Environmental Harm: Criminological Perspectives*, Devon: Willan Publishing, 2010, p. 110.
31 J. McMullan and D. Perrier, 'Lobster Poaching and the Ironies of Law Enforcement', *Law & Society Review*, 2002, vol. 36, no. 4, p. 679.
32 P. Beirne, *Confronting Animal Abuse: Law, Criminology, and Human–Animal Relationships*, New York: Rowman & Littlefield Publishers, 2009.

- crime prevention and the illicit trade in endangered species involving many different kinds of animals;[33] and
- the illegal wildlife market in Africa, and in particular the trade in elephant ivory.[34]

The transnational nature of environmental crime is well established in and through such studies. Recent work has generally involved engagement with activities and circumstances that span many parts of the globe. In part, this is because the producers and consumers, the markets and the institutions of world trade (both legal and illegal) are linked together in complex chains of transference which can involve quite sophisticated relationships.

The illegal harvest, shipment and sale of protected animals and plants has been estimated to trail behind only the illicit drug and arms trades in overall commercial value. In the specific area of illegal wildlife trade, it has been noted that the extent of exploitation is driving many species to the brink of extinction.[35] There is lots of money to be made, but the consequences are devastating from the point of view of biodiversity and overall ecological resilience on a world scale.

It has been observed that every year some ten million hectares of forest are destroyed, that industrial timber exports total around US$150 billion per year, and that estimates are that illegal logging accounts for about 25 per cent of removals worldwide.[36] Much of the illegal logging necessarily involves corrupt government officials, including law enforcement officers, as well as banks and financial backers, and business people who import timber or wood-based products. Bribery and 'goodwill' payments, smuggling, illicit trafficking, money laundering and forging of documents are all part of the illegal logging industry.[37]

Deforestation is not only the result of logging, however. Land clearance is also due to agricultural exploitation, cattle farming, mining, oil and gas installations, and hydroelectric dams. There is also the phenomenon of 'conflict timber', associated with West Africa, for example, in which deforestation is linked to the funding of civil wars and armed conflicts.[38]

The ecological impact of logging and land clearance is thus something that transcends the legal–illegal divide insofar as vast amounts of forest are subject to destruction in many different locations – from Peru and Brazil, and from Liberia and Sierra Leone, to Indonesia and Australia. The purposes and motivations may vary, depending upon the social context and industry interests, but the result is further depletion of many different kinds of trees and varieties of forests.

Recent information about transnational environmental crime provides a snapshot of the cost, and damage, caused by illegal trade and trafficking, as seen in Table 17.2.

33 J. Schneider, 'Reducing the Illicit Trade in Endangered Wildlife: The Market Reduction Approach', *Journal of Contemporary Criminal Justice*, 2008, vol. 24, no. 3, p. 274.
34 A. Lemieux and R. Clarke, 'The International Ban on Ivory Sales and its Effects on Elephant Poaching in Africa', *The British Journal of Criminology*, 2009, vol. 49, no. 4, p. 451.
35 See for example the websites for Traffic, the International Fund for Animal Welfare, WWF, Humane Society International and similar organisations.
36 B. Setiono, 'Fighting Illegal Logging and Forest-related Financial Crimes: The Anti-money Laundering Approach', in L. Elliot (ed.), *Transnational Environmental Crime in the Asia-Pacific: A Workshop Report.* Canberra: Australian National University, 2007, p. 97.
37 Ibid.
38 T. Boekhout van Solinge, 'Crime, Conflicts and Ecology in Africa', in R. Sollund (ed.), *Global Harms: Ecological Crime and Speciesism*, New York: Nova Science Publishers, 2008, p. 13; T. Boekhout van Solinge, 'The Land of the Orangutan and the Bird of Paradise under Threat', in R. Sollund (ed.), *Global Harms: Ecological Crime and Speciesism*, New York: Nova Science Publishers, 2008, p. 51.

Table 17.2 Cost of environmental crime – selected commodities[39]

Wildlife crime
US$15–20 billion annually
Examples: birds, ivory and rhino horn, reptiles and insects, tigers, wild game

Illegal, unreported and unregulated fishing
US$10–23.5 billion annually
Estimated 20 per cent of world catches
Examples: abalone, caviar, shark fin, sturgeon

Illegal logging
US$30–100 billion annually
Accounts for 15–30 per cent of the overall global trade
Examples: timber production, land clearing, crop substitution

---

Resource extraction of this kind is obviously financially lucrative, and has a major impact economically, ecologically and socially. Again, this is reflected in specific studies and analyses of things such as wildlife poaching and theft.

- Trafficking in birds and other animals (alive or dead) constitutes one of the world's largest illegal trade with an estimated value of 18 to 26 billion euros per year.[40]
- Birds and other animals are traded for medicine, gourmet foods, clothing, ornamentation, exotic pets, sport and trophies.[41]
- The number of rhinoceros poached in South Africa has increased every year from 2007 until 2012, with the total in 2012 almost a 50 per cent increase on the 2011 figure: given the current rates of decline the probable date for total extinction of wild rhinos in Africa is estimated to be 2025.[42]
- Many of the species involved in the international illegal trade are endangered, both by the trade itself and by other threats to their habitat.[43]

In 2008, it was observed that the combined global value of *legally* traded commodities derived from wild plants and animals was approximately US$24.5 billion.[44] By contrast, the *illegal gains* are estimated, just in the East Asia and Pacific regions alone, to be:

39 United Nations Environmental Programme, 'Theft of natural resources is a new challenge', UNEP, *One World South Asia*, 7 November 2013, available at http://southasia.oneworld.net/news/theft-of-natural-resources-is-a-new-challenge-unep (accessed 2 January 2014).
40 J. Ayling, 'Harnessing Third Parties for Transnational Environmental Crime Prevention', *Transnational Environmental Law*, 2013, vol. 2, no. 2, p. 339.
41 R. Sollund, 'Causes for Speciesism: Difference, Distance and Denial', in R. Sollund (ed.), *Global Harms: Ecological Crime and Speciesism*, New York: Nova Science Publishers, 2008, p. 109.
42 J. Ayling, 'What Sustains Wildlife Crime? Rhino Horn Trading and the Resilience of Criminal Networks', *Journal of International Wildlife Law and Policy*, 2013, vol. 16, no. 1, p. 57.
43 Boekhout van Solinge, 'Crime, Conflicts and Ecology in Africa' and 'Equatorial Deforestation'.
44 UNODC, *Transnational Organized Crime in East Asia and the Pacific: A Threat Assessment*, Vienna: UNODC, 2013, p. 77.

- *Illegal wildlife trade in East Asia and the Pacific* (China, Vietnam, Cambodia, Myanmar, Lao PDR, Thailand, Malaysia, Soloman Islands, Papua New Guinea, Indonesia, the Philippines): US $2.5bn (this excludes illegal timber and off-shore fishing);[45]
- *Illicit trade in wood-based products from the region to the world*: US $17bn (second only to counterfeit goods sent to Europe and the US) (30–40 per cent of the total quantity and export value of wood-based products exported from the region in 2010 was derived from illegal sources).[46]

Various laws and agreements are in place to prevent the illegal trade in endangered species. Ironically, the focus on protection can in some situations make the threatened species even more attractive to criminal syndicates or private collectors, since it confirms the scarcity (and thus 'value') of the species in question.

Illegal trade is not the only threat to particular 'wild' animal species. The intense competition for food worldwide is also evident in the ways in which commercial fishing takes place. The issue here is not only that of biodiversity, but of wholesale destruction of major breeding grounds and fishing beds.

The greatest negative impact to the long-term sustainable management of global fisheries is a combination of illegal, unreported and unregulated fishing.[47] This IUU fishing may involve huge factory ships that operate on the high seas, and which process thousands of tons of fish at any one time. Alternatively, it may be organised around dozens of smaller vessels, each of which is contracted to provide a catch that ultimately brings reward to the originating contractor. In other words, such production can be organised according to the economies of scale (e.g. factory ships) or the economies of scope (e.g. small independent fishers). In each case, however, there is a link to legitimate markets (e.g. for abalone, for lobsters, for Patagonian toothfish) for the value of the commodity to be realised in dollar terms.

In each case, as well, the damage is manifest in phenomena such as over-fishing and destruction of habitat that, in turn, affect subsequent market prices for the commodity in question. Scarcity is a major motivator for illegal as well as legal forays into particular kinds of harvesting and production activity.

Transnational crime and environmental law enforcement

Responding to transnational environmental crime requires not only the right kinds of laws and regulatory mechanisms, but the right kinds of environmental law enforcement practices and procedures.

Cross-border dynamics

According to the Division of Environmental Law and Conventions (DELC), United Nations Environment Programme,[48] the transnational nature of illegal environmental activity makes it distinctive and difficult to combat:

---

45 Ibid., p. 86.
46 Ibid., p. 96.
47 See R. Wilson and K. Tomkins, 'The Australian Approach to Combating Illegal Foreign Fishing', in L. Elliot (ed.), *Transnational Environmental Crime in the Asia-Pacific: A Workshop Report*, Canberra: Australian National University, 2007, p. 76.
48 UNEP Division of Environmental Law and Conventions, 2013, http://www.unep.org/delc/ Environmental Crime/tabid/54407/Default.aspx (accessed 2 January 2014).

> Transnational criminal activities are a central problem for the effective implementation, compliance with and enforcement of environmental laws, including MEAs [Multilateral Environment Agreements]. The implementation of international environment law requires that international legal mechanisms are established and enforced at national level through appropriate legal regimes. Illegal activities challenge enforcement and undermine implementation of environmental law, including MEAs. Often these illegal activities have transnational elements and need to be combated through internationally coordinated efforts.[49]

Accordingly, a large part of the role of the DELC is to help build capacity among member states in fighting environmental crime and in defining international environmental norms. This involves activities intended to enhance environmental laws at all levels and increase understanding of the inter-linkages between human rights and the environment, strengthening institutions and laws which protect natural resources in the global commons, and developing strategies that help to build a sustainable green economy. In the specific area of transnational environmental crime, the DELC works with partners towards:

- a better understanding of the global problems of and existing gaps in transnational or cross-border environmental crime;
- common approaches to more efficiently and effectively tackling the problem of transnational environmental crime from a legal standpoint;
- strengthening and reinforcing current international and national legal and institutional arrangements and law enforcement mechanisms to combat transnational environmental crime;
- strengthening and reinforcing national environmental laws to counter environmental crime;
- fostering and enhancing cross-border cooperation in the field of environmental crime; and
- strengthening and developing partnerships, coordination and cooperation between stakeholders.[50]

These activities build upon existing partnerships and initiatives such as the Green Customs Initiative[51] and the DELC capacity-building programme for judges[52] that aims to better equip legal practitioners, judges and jurists in their roles in interpreting and applying environmental laws.

Criminal network dynamics

The United Nations Interregional Crime and Justice Research Institute has recently observed that there has been a considerable expansion of transnational environmental crimes in recent years due to the involvement of organised criminal groups acting across borders:

---

49 Ibid.
50 Ibid.
51 See generally Green Customs, http://www.greencustoms.org (accessed 28 January 2014).
52 A UNEP Division of Environmental Law and Conventions sponsored programme, www.unep. org/delc/judgesprogramme/tabid/78617/Default.aspx (accessed 28 January 2014).

Led by vast financial gains and facilitated by a low risk of detection and scarce conviction rates, criminal networks and organized criminal groups are becoming increasingly interested in such illicit transnational activities. These phenomena fuel corruption and money-laundering, and undermine the rule of law, ultimately affecting the public twice: first, by putting at risk citizens' health and safety; and second, by diverting resources that would otherwise be allocated to services other than crime. The level of organization needed for these crimes indicates a link with other serious offences, including theft, fraud, corruption, drugs and human trafficking, counterfeiting, firearms smuggling, and money laundering, several of which have been substantiated by investigations.[53]

It is not only traditional criminal networks and syndicates that are implicated in transnational environmental crimes. There are also links between terrorist groups and engagement in particular types of environmental crime. It was recently reported, for example, that:

The recent terror attack on the popular Westgate shopping mall in Nairobi, Kenya, has placed environmental crimes like the ivory and rhino horn trade under increased scrutiny. Al-Shabab, the Islamist militant group that has taken credit for the attack, is widely believed to fund as much as 40 percent of its activities from elephant poaching, or the 'blood ivory' trade.[54]

Responding to these kinds of players demands robust action across the various dimensions of the enforcement chain.

Not surprisingly, greater attention has been given by those with an interest in environmental law enforcement issues to the UNTOC Convention, since this offers the promise of concerted action and harsher penalties against environmental criminals. The link to the UNTOC Convention, however, depends upon whether the conduct in question meets the definition of transnational organised crime including the requirement that the crime is 'serious' (an offence punishable by a maximum deprivation of liberty of at least four years or a more serious penalty). Yet, the majority of states that are party to CITES do not impose this level of penalty on wildlife criminals.[55]

In recent years, addressing shortfalls or technical difficulties in environmental crime prevention and law enforcement has led to a range of collaborations between international bodies, government and non-government organisations, and national governments.[56]

International environmental law enforcement initiatives

The nature of environmental crime poses a number of challenges for effective policing and hence prosecution. Environmental crimes may have local, national, regional and global

53 UNICRI, *Environmental Crimes*, 2013, http://www.unicri.it/topics/environmental (accessed 13 June 2014).
54 IRIN, 'Environmental crimes increasingly linked to violence, insecurity', 3 October 2013, http://www.irinnews.org/printreport.aspx?reportid=98872 (accessed 2 January 2014).
55 G. Wright, 'Conceptualising and Combating Transnational Environmental Crime', *Trends in Organised Crime*, 2011, vol. 14, p. 332.
56 See R. White, 'Environmental Law Enforcement: the Importance of Global Networks and Collaborative Practices', *Australasian Policing: A Journal of Professional Practice and Research*, 2011, vol. 3, no. 1, p. 2; R. White, 'NGO Engagement in Environmental Law Enforcement: Critical Reflections', *Australasian Policing: A Journal of Professional Practice and Research*, 2012, vol. 4, no. 1, p. 7.

dimensions. They may be difficult to detect (as in the case of some forms of toxic pollution undetectable to human senses). They may demand intensive cross-jurisdictional negotiation, and even disagreement between nation-states, in regard to specific events or crime patterns. Some crimes may be highly organised and involve criminal syndicates, such as illegal fishing. Others may include a wide range of criminal actors, ranging from the individual collector of endangered species to the systematic disposal of toxic waste via third parties.

A range of international collaborations have emerged around specific types of commodity, and in relation to specific enforcement and regulatory bodies. For example, the International Consortium Combating Wildlife Crime (ICCWC),[57] which supports national and regional law enforcement in this regard, is comprised of five inter-governmental organisations: CITES, Interpol, UNODC, the World Bank and the World Customs Organization. More broadly, the International Network for Environmental Compliance and Enforcement (INECE) brings together approximately 4,000 individual members from more than 150 countries with a view to improving policy and practice in this area. There are also various Multilateral Environment Agreement (MEA) secretariats that coordinate the work and efforts of their member countries, and cover particular themes and commodities (e.g. whaling, migratory birds and the Antarctic).

The World Customs Organisation (WCO), among others, is involved in the Green Customs Initiative. The objective of this initiative is to enhance the capacity of customs and other relevant enforcement personnel to monitor and facilitate the legal trade and to detect and prevent illegal trade in environmentally sensitive commodities covered by the relevant conventions and MEAs. The initiative provides coordinated training, a green customs guide, workshops and relevant website and materials.

Agencies such as Interpol are also central players in global environmental law enforcement. In 2010, at the 79th Interpol General Assembly, the Chiefs of Police from 188 countries adopted an Environment Enforcement Resolution. This resolution acknowledges that:

> Environmental law enforcement is not always the responsibility of one national agency, but rather, is multi-disciplinary in nature due to the complexity and diversity of the crime type which can encompass disciplines such as wildlife, pollution, fisheries, forestry, natural resources and climate change, with reaching effect into other areas of crime.[58]

Reflecting concern over environmental issues, a summit of International Chiefs of Environmental Compliance and Enforcement was held in March 2012. A summary of the event pointed out that:

> Particular concern was expressed from [*sic*] many delegates on the scale of environmental crime and the connection with organized transnational crime, including issues of smuggling, corruption, fraud, tax evasion, money laundering, and murder:
>
> - The interconnectivity of environmental crime with other forms of criminal activity requires cooperation and collaboration across all levels of law enforcement in order to combat and prevent the illegal activities;

---

57 See generally ICCWC Information Note 2011, http://www.cites.org/eng/prog/iccwc.php (accessed 28 January 2014).
58 Interpol and United Nations Environment Programme, *Summit Report: International Chiefs of Environmental Compliance and Enforcement*, Lyon, France: Interpol and UNEP, 2012, p. 2.

- The current scale of environmental crime involves very similar approaches, means and severity as other forms of crime, but is aggravated and exacerbated further by the direct serious implications it has on the development goals of many countries;
- Particular concern is raised on the sheer scale of environmental crime including, but not limited to, illegal logging and deforestation, illegal fisheries and smuggling of toxic waste, and the severe implications of this not only on the environment, but also on human security and economic development.[59]

It is not only issues that have been highlighted at such summits, but operational policies and practices as well. This is reflected in efforts to link up agencies and personnel across jurisdictions and across substantive enforcement areas.[60]

Project Leaf (Law Enforcement Assistance for Forests), for example, is an Interpol and United Nations Environment Programme (UNEP) climate initiative consortium that is directed against illegal logging and related crimes. The objectives of this project are to:

- form National Environmental Security Task Forces (NESTs) to ensure institutionalised cooperation between national agencies, Interpol NCBs (National Central Bureaus) and international partners;
- conduct operations to suppress criminality, disrupt trafficking routes, and ensure the enforcement of international and national legislations on sustainable forestry; and
- expand the project through awareness raising, making a real contribution to global emissions goals, the protection of biodiversity, and preventing environmental destruction.

Similar initiatives dealing with other environmental crimes include *Project Scale*, designed to detect, suppress and combat fisheries crime; *Project Predator*, which targets the illegal poaching and trade in Asian 'big cats'; and *Project Wisdom*, which supports and enhances the governance and law enforcement capacity for the conservation of elephants and rhinoceros.

Environmental law enforcement also includes a wide range of NGOs that operate in various official and unofficial capacities. For instance, animal welfare may be deemed to be the official responsibility of organisations such as the Royal Society for the Prevention of Cruelty to Animals (RSPCA), who then investigate and prosecute cases of animal abuse. Other NGOs, such as Greenpeace Amazon, may not have an 'official' role per se, but nonetheless gather evidence of activities such as illegal logging, which can then be passed on to relevant police and judicial authorities.

Agencies such as Interpol and organisations such as the International Network of Environmental Enforcement and Compliance provide forums for the exchange of information and knowledge transfer about 'best practice' and 'what works' in specific situations. Participation in common training programmes and attendance at conferences and workshops provides opportunities to enhance overall law enforcement capabilities as well as contributing to shared understandings and values in regards to specific types of criminal activity. At a practical level, a productive strategy for harmonisation of enforcement efforts is to focus on consistency in delivering regulatory and enforcement tasks, rather than focusing on uniform legislation as such.

---

59 Ibid.
60 See Interpol, *Environmental Crime*, http://www.interpol.int/Crime-areas/Environmental-crime/Environmental-crime (accessed 22 January 2014).

A 'joined-up' approach also means that links can be made between different forms of crime as well as between different agencies and different parts of the world. For instance, illegal fishing has been tied to trafficking of persons, smuggling of migrants and the illicit traffic in drugs. This is due to the influence of transnational organised crime in the fishing industry worldwide.[61] International cooperation is also necessitated by the sophistication and transnational nature of the crimes. In response, the International Monitoring, Control and Surveillance Network has been formed and is dedicated to preventing and deterring illegal, unreported and unregulated fishing.[62] It has participation from over 50 countries.

Transnational environmental crime and adjudication

Environmental crime has typically been assigned a low value by magistrates and judges, as reflected objectively in sentencing outcomes (i.e. sentencing patterns over time in relation to various environmental offences).[63] These kinds of issues are being addressed in various ways, most of which involve in one form or another specialist knowledge or the establishment of specialist courts.

The notion of 'special expertise' in dealing with environmental harms and crimes does not refer solely to the establishment of specific and separate environmental courts as such. Such developments are not always needed or desirable, particularly in jurisdictions which have experienced the recent consolidation of a wide range of criminal matters (including environmental) into generalist courts (as opposed to the development of crime-specific and client-specific specialist tribunals, courts and agencies). What *is* vital, however, is the development and growth of specific expertise in regard to environmental matters, incorporating elements pertaining to valuation of the harm, degrees of seriousness, extent and nature of victimisation, and remedies suited to the nature of the crime and its perpetrator(s). Interpol, for example, provides information to support the work of prosecutors of environmental crimes, while in England a substantial toolkit has been prepared to guide magistrates in assessing the seriousness of environmental offences, determining sentencing criteria for environmental offences, and working through specific types of cases.[64] The work of ecological economics is also essential in this regard. This kind of analysis provides multiple criteria by which to evaluate the value of natural resources, wilderness, animals, fish and other species. In the context of courts, both economic and non-market valuation is a vital part of deliberation over the nature of harm and potential damage claims against perpetrators.[65]

---

61 See UNODC, *Transnational Organized Crime in the Fishing Industry*, 2011.

62 See generally International Monitoring Control and Surveillance Network, http://www.imcsnet. org (accessed 28 January 2014).

63 See P. de Prez, 'Excuses, Excuses: the Ritual Trivialisation of Environmental Prosecutions', *Journal of Environmental Law*, 2000, vol. 12, no. 1, p. 65; P. de Prez, 'Beyond Judicial Sanctions: the Negative Impact of Conviction for Environmental Offences', *Environmental Law Review*, 2000, vol. 2, p. 11; White, *Transnational Environmental Crime*.

64 Interpol Pollution Crime Working Group, 'Arguments for Prosecutors of Environmental Crimes', *Advocacy Memorandum*, 5 June 2007; Magistrates' Association (UK), *Costing the Earth: Guidance for Sentencers*, London: Magistrates' Association, 2009.

65 L. Richardson and J. Loomis, 'The Total Economic Value of Threatened, Endangered and Rare Species: An Updated Meta-analysis', *Ecological Economics*, 2009, vol. 68, no. 5, p. 1535; J. Duffield, 'Nonmarket Valuation and the Courts: The Case of the *Exxon Valdez*', *Contemporary Economic Policy*, 1997, vol. 15, no. 4, p. 98.

From a legal perspective, the cost of environmental harm is linked to the seriousness of environmental offences, material environmental harm and level of nuisance.[66] Assessing the seriousness of environmental offences usually involves criteria such as the immediate and direct impact of the environmental crime; its wider effects in environmental, social and economic terms; human fatality, injury or ill health; the health of flora and fauna; the offence pattern, especially for serial offenders; and so on.[67]

Research into US legal systems has demonstrated that environmental criminal statutes and environmental sentencing guidelines represent two very different ways of defining and assessing the social harm addressed by environmental crimes.[68] Federal environmental crimes contained in legislation such as the Clean Water Act, Clean Air Act and Resource Conservation and Recovery Act tend to utilise criminal provisions mainly to punish failure to abide by these regulatory systems. The point of each regulatory system is to manage contact between a pollutant and the air, water or soil, not to prevent it. The net result is that the focus is not on environmental harm as such, but rather on unacceptable (or significant) environmental harm – as measured by predetermined technical and administrative thresholds.

By contrast, US federal environmental crime-sentencing guidelines focus more on matters of actual harm rather than risk-reduction concerns. There is evidence here of the importance of graduated punishments based on the seriousness of the social harm being addressed, and support for increased punishment for violators who actually harm the environment. Interestingly, in both sets of legal instruments there is little formal definition of 'environmental harm', and the lack of clarity gives rise to different interpretations of what this might refer to. There are also difficulties with conceptualisations of 'seriousness' and 'causality'.[69]

Greater consistency in approach and outcome can be achieved by specialist agencies that deal with environmental crimes, harms and issues on a regular basis. It is notable, therefore, that today there are over 350 environmental courts and tribunals (ECTs) authorised in some 41 countries, and the number is growing.[70] In part, the growth in the number of ECTs has mirrored the increasing importance of environmental matters in international forums and law. The impetus of specialist judicial forums stems from continual pressures worldwide for effective resolution of environmental conflicts and/or expanding recognition of the need for procedural and substantive justice *vis-à-vis* environmental matters.

Among the building blocks for an effective environmental court or tribunal are the mobilisation of scientific and technical expertise and the competence of judges and decision-makers. The establishment of courts with special expertise in environmental matters provides an institutional setting within which judicial training can find most purchase. For example, UNEP has put resources into judicial training on environmental law.[71] This initiative is underpinned by the idea that environmental crime needs to be taken seriously, and to do so

---

66 S. Bricknell, *Environmental Crime in Australia*, AIC Reports, Research and Public Policy Series no. 109, Australian Institute of Criminology, 2010, p. 13.
67 See Magistrates Association, *Costing the Earth*.
68 S. Mandiberg, 'Locating the Environmental Harm in Environmental Crimes', *Utah Law Review*, 2009, vol. 4, p. 1177.
69 Ibid.
70 G. Pring and C. Pring, *Greening Justice: Creating and Improving Environmental Courts and Tribunals*, The Access Initiative, 2009, p. 1.
71 UNEP, *Judicial Training Modules on Environmental Law: Application of Environmental Law by National Courts and Tribunals*, Nairobi: UNEP, 2007.

sanctions are needed that reflect the seriousness of the crime. However, a defined environment court reaffirms and concretises the importance of these ideas. It does so by providing a ready forum for the development of specialist expertise aided by the availability of technical experts within the court itself.[72] Moreover, such courts and tribunals provide a ready platform for the further extension of environmental jurisprudence and coherent sanctioning processes.

The multiple demands placed upon specific environmental protection agencies by different sections of government, business and communities, and the varied tasks they are required to juggle (e.g. compliance, education, enforcement), may lead to a dilution of their enforcement capacities and activities in both the national sphere and the international arena. The expense of fighting cases in higher courts is itself a deterrent for agencies that are cash-strapped yet have to assume the legal costs associated with prosecution. Special environmental courts and tribunals offer the hope of lower costs and an array of alternative dispute resolution procedures.[73] Accordingly, the establishment of such agencies may well have a positive ripple effect throughout the environmental law enforcement and prosecution landscape.

It may well be that an International Environment Court (or equivalent) with requisite United Nations support is required as well. This is especially so if we are to adequately deal with environmental matters such as, for example, those pertaining to the international spaces of our oceans (e.g. pollution, concentrations of plastic, illegal fishing, transference of toxic materials). Such a court could draw together transboundary expertise from the various environmental law enforcement networks to assess environmental crimes and harms that have international or global consequences.

There is also growing momentum behind the idea of embedding the crime of ecocide as one of the five 'Crimes against Peace'[74] and this, too, would lend itself to support for some sort of international court dealing with environment issues. Ecocide has been defined as 'the extensive damage, destruction to or loss of ecosystems of a given territory, whether by human agency or by other causes, to such an extent that peaceful enjoyment by the inhabitants of that territory has been severely diminished'.[75] Where this occurs as a result of human agency, then it is purported that a crime has occurred. There were major efforts to include ecocide among the crimes associated with the establishment of the International Criminal Court, although the final document refers only to war and damage to the natural environment.[76] Nonetheless,

---

72 See B. Preston, 'Operating an environment court: the experience of the Land and Environment Court of New South Wales and 12 benefits of judicial specialisation in environmental law', Keynote Address, Renewing Environmental Law: A Conference for Public Interest Environmental Law Practitioners, University of Victoria Environmental Law Centre, West Coast Environmental Law and Ecojustice, Vancouver: British Columbia, 2011.

73 Pring and Pring, *Greening Justice*.

74 See P. Higgins, *Eradicating Ecocide: Laws and Governance to Prevent the Destruction of our Planet*, London: Shepheard-Walwyn, 2010; P. Higgins, *Earth Is Our Business: Changing the Rules of the Game*, London: Shepheard-Walwyn, 2012.

75 Higgins, *Earth Is our Business*, p. 3.

76 See generally M.A. Drumbl, 'Waging War against the World: the Need to Move from War Crimes to Environmental Crimes', *Fordham International Law Journal*, 1998–9, vol. 22, p. 122. Article 8(2) (b)(iv) of the Rome Statute of the International Criminal Court, 17 July, 1998, UN Doc. A/CONF.183/9, prohibits '[i]ntentionally launching an attack in the knowledge that such attack will cause incidental loss of life or injury to civilians or damage to civilian objects or widespread, long-term and severe damage to the non-human environment which would be clearly excessive in relation to the concrete and direct overall military advantage anticipated'.

environmental activists and international lawyers have continued to call for the establishment of either a specific crime of 'ecocide' and/or the incorporation of ecocide into existing criminal laws and international instruments.

In addition to proposed legal developments, a range of penalty types, approaches and mechanisms have emerged in relation to environmental sanctions. These fall broadly into the categories of civil, administrative and criminal justice responses. The sanctioning process for environmental offences presently covers a broad range of strategies, with new possibilities on the horizon.[77] For example, UNEP's 'Global Judges Programme' includes reference to the imposition of deterrent fines based upon 'economic benefit of noncompliance' (EBN). This takes into account the value to the violator of deferred compliance, that is, the money that should have been spent on environmental improvements that was presumably invested elsewhere, earning a rate of return on an annual basis.[78] Financial sanctions with bite are at least on the agenda, if not yet fully realised in practice.

Conclusion

This chapter has provided a description and overview of those transnational environmental crimes related to biodiversity and the illegal exploitation of animals and plants. A myriad of laws and international instruments exist pertaining to environmental protection and environmental regulation. Yet the bottom line is that without adequate resources for detection, investigation and prosecution, and the development of specialist expertise in terms of adjudication and sanctioning processes, then such crimes will continue to flourish with few real checks. Nonetheless, considerable and growing efforts are being undertaken globally to construct transnational collaborative efforts that will better ensure the translation of law on the books into more effective law in practice. Through such efforts resource theft and trafficking can be curtailed in a more meaningful way. Recent research and grounded initiatives also acknowledge that social and economic circumstance ultimately underpin much of the illegal trade – thereby requiring substantial changes at system levels as well as legal institutions before ecological justice can be attained.

77 See S. Bell and D. McGillivray, *Environmental Law*, 7th edn, Oxford: Oxford University Press, 2008.
78 UNEP, *Judicial Training Modules on Environmental Law*.

18

Environmental degradation

The dumping of pollution as a transnational crime

Jay L. Batongbacal

Introduction

'Dumping' is one of those terms prone to confusion because it has ordinary and technical meanings. In layman's usage, dumping can mean 'throwing, discarding, disposing, depositing, or discharging,' which makes it easily correspond with pollution *per se*, itself basically an act of discharge. It is thus easy to think that 'dumping' might be synonymous with 'pollution,' if one were totally unfamiliar with the term. At the same time, 'dumping' has also been used to refer to very specific acts of pollution in recent international agreements such as the London Protocol,[1] which uses the term particularly to refer *inter alia* to the disposal, storage, or abandonment of wastes and other matter into the sea by ships, aircraft, and offshore platforms.[2] These activities, however, are entirely different from that involved in 'dumping' in international trade parlance, which uses the term to refer to the practice of an exporting State of under-pricing its goods in order to unfairly compete with similar goods of the importing State.[3] Yet, 'dumping' has also sometimes been used to refer to the trans-boundary shipment of wastes, including toxic or hazardous materials, so that one State can export its pollution to another State.[4]

To prevent confusion, this chapter uses the term 'dumping of pollution,' which directly implies an intentional act of transferring pollution away from one State's jurisdiction and into

---

1 1996 Protocol to the London Convention on the Prevention of Marine Pollution by Dumping of Wastes and Other Matter amended in 2006, 7 November 1996, 36 ILM 1 (1997), in force 24 March 2006. Available from International Maritime Organisation at http://www.imo.org/blast/blastData.asp?doc_id=13203&filename=PROTOCOL%20Amended%202006.doc (accessed 13 September 2013) (hereinafter the London Protocol).
2 Ibid., Article 1(4).
3 See J. Viner, 'Dumping as a Method of Competition in International Trade', *The University Journal of Business*, 1922, vol. 1, no. 1, p. 34; World Trade Organization, 'Technical Information on Anti-Dumping', available at http://www.wto.org/english/tratop_e/adp_e/adp_info_e.htm (accessed 6 February 2014).
4 UNEP and Secretariat of the Basel Convention, *The Basel Convention at a Glance*, Geneva: Secretariat of the Basel Convention, 2001.

another's, or into areas beyond national jurisdiction. This nuance is significant, as intentionality denotes the idea of knowingly acting in a wrongful manner in order to transfer the object, which in turn implies a purposeful and directed movement of the pollution discharged, whether in the form of matter (solid, liquid, or gaseous substances) or energy (heat, radioactivity). The terminology also avoids the confusion that may arise from the multiple meanings of the term 'dumping' alone. The key element that distinguishes 'dumping of pollution' from pollution *per se* is therefore made clearer: human decision and direction across national jurisdictional borders of what would otherwise probably be an indiscriminate and undirected discharge. This element tends to highlight the difference between acts committed with criminal intent, and acts arising from pure negligence. Although negligence that results in a transfer of pollution is possible and may also be considered criminal in nature, the intentional dumping of pollution is expected to be treated more seriously and with higher penalties. It may be noted, however, that intentionally criminal acts and merely negligent acts are not very clearly distinguished in international law; it is up to States to clarify any such distinctions in accordance with their own legal systems. Finally, the requirement that the transfer be from one jurisdiction to another jurisdiction highlights the transnational and trans-boundary character of the act, to distinguish it from purely domestic acts that can be addressed by domestic legislation.

International action against dumping of pollution

Law enforcement agencies have recognized the dumping of pollution as among the diverse kinds of transnational crimes that emerged with recent developments in the international legal order. Just as globalization brought nations closer through networks of political and economic relations regulated by States at the formal level, so have *sub rosa* criminal networks emerged to take advantage of gaps and opportunities presented by greater and more liberal civilian access to foreign lands and peoples. These criminal networks are believed to have begun with more traditional criminal activities such as maritime piracy, smuggling, illegal drugs trading, and slave trading, but gradually extended and branched out to more sophisticated activities such as money laundering, intellectual property piracy, and many others. It was inevitable for transnational criminal activities to diversify as much as transnational economic activities, as crime frequently reflects the 'dark side' of legitimate, accepted, and regulated behavior in society.[5]

The United Nations Interregional Crime and Justice Research Institute (UNICRI) had examined environmental crimes as early as 1991,[6] and Interpol formed an Environmental Crimes Committee to study the emerging patterns in environmental law enforcement in 1993.[7] By 2005, it was noted that environmental crimes had evolved into organized criminal

---

5 For an early examination of the nature and origins of transnational crime, see P. Williams and D. Vlassis (eds), *Combating Transnational Crime: Concepts, Activities and Responses*, London and Portland, OR: Frank Cass, 2001.

6 V.L. Cortemigilia, 'Combating Transnational Trafficking of Waste: The Case of Italy', presented at Environmental Crime – Current Trends and Emerging Threats, Rome, 29 October, 2012, available at http://www.unicri.it/topics/environmental/conference/Expert_Group_III_-_Vittoria_Luda. pdf (accessed 23 November 2013).

7 Interpol, 'Environmental Compliance and Enforcement Committee', available at http://www. interpol.int/Crime-areas/Environmental-crime/Environmental-Compliance-and-Enforcement-Committee (accessed 23 November 2013).

activities on an international scale.[8] Five years later, the illegal trade in environmental resources was included in the threat assessments of the UN Office of Drugs and Crime (UNODC),[9] the lead agency in implementing the United Nations Convention Against Transnational Organized Crime.[10] In March 2012, Interpol and UNEP convened the first International Chiefs of Environmental Compliance and Enforcement Summit,[11] where delegates expressed concern about the existence and operation of transnational criminal networks engaged in environmental crime.[12] These criminal operations were identified initially as specialized smuggling activities dealing with timber and CITES-protected species, but were expanded to include black markets in ozone-depleting substances (ODS) and other prohibited chemicals, illicit trans-boundary movement of toxic or hazardous wastes, and even illegal, unregulated, and unreported fishing.[13] Typically, all such crimes are in violation of both multi-lateral environmental agreements and the domestic legislation that implements them.[14]

More recent works denominate this set of criminal activities as 'transnational environmental crimes.'[15] However, it is clear that the dumping of pollution, all of which is created artificially by human industry, forms a category of activities distinct from the others, which in contrast may be seen as forms of illegal trafficking of natural resources. While illegal trafficking of natural resources consumes and diminishes the living components of such environment, dumping of pollution additionally inserts unwanted, non-natural, and destabilizing inputs into a local natural environment, rendering it inhospitable to life. At present, Interpol appreciates this distinction by operationally addressing dumping by pollution through the Pollution Crimes Working Group under the Environmental Compliance and Enforcement Committee that held its first meeting in Nairobi, Kenya on 7–8 November 2013.[16] Concerted international law enforcement action on a large scale against dumping of pollution may thus be described as a fairly recent phenomenon that has practically only just begun.

Legal origins

The degradation of the environment has been a major area of concern for all States ever since the United Nations Conference on the Human Environment[17] affirmed a 'fundamental right to freedom, equality and adequate conditions of life, in an environment of a quality that permits a life of dignity and well-being.'[18] The Stockholm Declaration reflects a formal consensus of the international community that expressly recognizes the pollution of the land,

---

8 L. Elliott, 'Fighting Transnational Environmental Crime', *Journal of International Affairs*, 2012, vol. 66, no. 1, p. 87, at p. 87.

9 Ibid.

10 15 November 2000, 2225 UNTS 209, in force 29 September 2003.

11 Interpol, 'Environmental Compliance and Enforcement Committee'.

12 Elliott, 'Fighting Transnational Environmental Crime', p. 87.

13 Ibid., p. 89; M. Martini, *Environmental Crime and Corruption*, U4 Expert Answer 326, Transparency International, 2012, p. 1.

14 L. Elliott, 'Combating Transnational Environmental Crime: "Joined Up" Thinking about Transnational Networks', in K. Kangaspunta and I.H. Marshall (eds), *Eco-Crime and Justice: Essays on Environmental Crime*, Turin: UNICRI, n.d., p. 55, p. 59.

15 Ibid.

16 Interpol, 'Environmental Compliance and Enforcement Committee'.

17 UN Doc A/Conf.48/14/Rev. 1(1973); 11 ILM 1416 (1972) (Stockholm Declaration).

18 Ibid., Principle 1.

water, and air as among the main causes of harm to the environment,[19] and establishes common principles specifically addressing pollution. It provides the basis for a common, albeit broad definition of 'pollution' as '[t]he discharge of toxic substances or of other substances and the release of heat, in such quantities or concentrations as to exceed the capacity of the environment to render them harmless,' and which all States have an obligation to prevent.[20] Having been negotiated against a background of prominent oil spill incidents, and convening the same year as the opening of the Third United Nations Conference on the Law of the Sea, Stockholm also calls on States to take action to prevent marine pollution specifically.[21]

More importantly, Stockholm recognizes the responsibility of States 'to ensure that activities within their jurisdiction or control do not cause damage to the environment of other States or of areas beyond the limits of national jurisdiction.'[22] This implicitly includes a duty to regulate pollution within their borders so as to prevent it from affecting neighboring States: a modern restatement in international law of the ancient Roman axiom *sic utere tuo ut alienum non laedas* insofar as State-to-State relations are concerned,[23] and arguably evidence of an *erga omnes* obligation in the international commons.

This duty to prevent, contain, and abate pollution was reiterated 20 years later by the Rio Declaration,[24] which added more specific obligations to enact 'effective environmental legislation'[25] including domestic and international legal regimes for liability and compensation for those adversely affected by 'pollution and other environmental damage,'[26] as well as measures to prevent the displacement of such damaging activities or substances from one State to another.[27] These pollution-specific principles are a major pillar of the principles of sustainable development that the Stockholm and Rio principles represent. Although both instruments were crafted originally as non-binding soft-law instruments, their substantive content has undoubtedly had normative influence. The number of international environmental treaties opened for signature and the explosion of national environmental legislation in the aftermath of these declarations are undeniable evidence of their impact on national and international law.

Dumping of pollution as a transnational environmental crime

Stockholm and Rio spurred international law-making activity leading, among other things, to multi-lateral anti-pollution treaties. Most of these subsequent agreements require States to directly regulate their nationals and their activities in order to control and prevent pollution within their own jurisdictions. But some specifically address trans-boundary pollution activities, signifying a convergence of international opinion that certain acts should be regarded as

---

19 Stockholm Declaration, preambular paragraph 3.
20 Ibid., Principle 6.
21 Ibid., Principle 7.
22 Ibid., Principle 21.
23 The rule that 'one should not use her/his property in a way that injures another's property' is recognized to have been elevated into international status by the *Trail Smelter Case (United States/Canada)*, III Reports of International Arbitral Awards 1905–82. See also J.E. Read, 'The Trail Smelter Dispute', *Canadian Yearbook of International Law*, 1963, vol. 1, pp. 213–229.
24 UN Doc. A/CONF.151/26 (vol. I); 31 ILM 874 (1992) (Rio Declaration).
25 Ibid., Principle 11.
26 Ibid., Principle 13.
27 Ibid., Principle 14.

internationally prohibited activities. That such activities are unauthorized acts or omissions in violation of law, subjecting the violator to criminal prosecution and penalties, properly leads to their classification as crimes *per se*, while the additional harm they cause to not only people's physical health or safety but also to the environment itself highlights their nature as environmental crimes particularly.[28] State practice in the implementation of these agreements through national legislation, particularly those that penalize such prohibited acts, demonstrates an emergent international opinion that these prohibited acts should be considered as transnational environmental crimes. This applies particularly to acts that constitute dumping of pollution.

Marine pollution

Marine pollution has been an area of particularly intensive regulatory activity since the late 1960s because of the high visibility of marine pollution incidents that provided political momentum, as well as the existence of an international organization that provided a continuing venue for negotiations. The International Maritime Organization (IMO) has been at the center of unbroken diplomatic activity resulting in at least 17 conventions directly concerned with marine pollution prevention, abatement, and compensation.[29] These IMO conventions oblige accepting States to make them part of national law and implement them as such.[30] Of these, the International Convention for the Prevention of Pollution from Ships and its subsequent Protocols (MARPOL),[31] the London Convention,[32] and the London Protocol that amends the latter, stand out.

The MARPOL Conventions are keystone efforts against marine pollution globally, comprising agreements governing operational vessel-source pollution.[33] Among the many obligations of member States are those in which they promise to prohibit and penalize violations, wherever committed, of prescribed anti-pollution technical standards, equipment requirements, and operating procedures for ships.[34] Sanctions are expressly required to be of

---

28 See Y. Situ and D. Emmons, *Environmental Crime: The Criminal Justice System's Role in Protecting the Environment*, Thousand Oaks, CA: Sage Publications, 2000, pp. 3–4.

29 International Maritime Organization, 'List of IMO Conventions', available at http://www.imo.org/About/Conventions/ListOfConventions/Pages/Default.aspx (accessed 13 November 2013).

30 International Maritime Organization, 'Implementation, Control and Coordination', available at http://www.imo.org/OurWork/Safety/Implementation/Pages/Default.aspx (accessed 2 February 2014).

31 International Convention for the Prevention of Pollution from Ships, 2 November 193, 1340 UNTS 184, 12 ILM 1319 (1973); Protocol relating to the International Convention for the Prevention of Pollution from Ships, 17 February 1978, 1340 UNTS 61, 17 ILM 546 (1978) (MARPOL Conventions); both in force 2 October 1983.

32 Convention on the Prevention of Marine Pollution by the Dumping of Wastes and Other Matter, 29 December 1972, 1046 UNTS 120; 11 ILM 1294 (1972) in force 30 August 1975 (London Convention).

33 To date six annexes have been appended to the original MARPOL 73/78 Conventions. Each annex is addressed toward a particular kind of vessel-source pollution: Annex I for oil pollution, Annex II for noxious liquid substances, Annex III for harmful substances in packaged form, Annex IV for sewage, Annex V for garbage, and Annex VI for air pollution from ships. For general information, see International Maritime Organization, 'Pollution Prevention', available at http://www.imo.org/OurWork/Environment/PollutionPrevention/Pages/Default.aspx, (accessed 24 November 2013).

34 MARPOL Convention, Art. 4(1).

'adequate severity' under the law of the member States,[35] which may take action against the offending vessel either directly or through the flag State.[36] In the latter case, the flag State is obliged promptly to inform the complaining State of the action taken.[37] In addition, MARPOL takes a step further by also obliging the Parties to co-operate in the detection of violations and enforcement of the Convention, inspection of ships and investigation of violations, and exchange of information on violations.[38]

Implementation of the MARPOL Conventions by flag States is undertaken not only by direct regulation by the flag-State but also through private-sector-driven activities such as ship surveys and classification processes that operate in diverse ways, and may not necessarily be reflected in government legislation and regulations. Thus, it would take far more time and space than is available in this chapter to review national implementation of each MARPOL Convention by each flag State. However, attention may be focused on a related IMO convention, the London Convention as amended by the London Protocol.

The London Convention and Protocol specifically prohibit the disposal into the sea of 'any wastes or other matter in whatever form or condition'.[39] The London Protocol is intended to replace the original Convention, but the present status of ratifications of the two differ: the London Convention has been ratified by 87 States while the London Protocol has been ratified by only 42 States.[40] This results in a variance in approaches to the common objective of regulating waste disposal into the sea. While the London Convention takes a 'black-listing' or 'grey-listing' regulatory approach whereby listed wastes cannot be disposed of into the sea,[41] the London Protocol takes a more stringent 'reverse-listing' approach whereby the disposal of all wastes or other matter is prohibited, except for those listed in the annexes that can be disposed of only under certain conditions and with a corresponding permit issued by the State's regulatory agency.[42] The London Protocol additionally prohibits waste incineration at sea[43] and the export of wastes to other countries purposely for dumping or incineration at sea.[44]

Despite the regulatory differences, States Parties are obliged to take appropriate measures 'to prevent and if necessary punish acts' that contravene their provisions, and to co-operate in the development of procedures to effectively apply the London Convention in areas beyond national jurisdiction.[45] It also encourages them to enhance co-operation through regional agreements[46]

---

35 Ibid., Art. 4(4).
36 Ibid., Art. 4(2).
37 Ibid., Art. 4(3).
38 Ibid., Art. 6.
39 London Convention, Art. IV(1); London Protocol, Art. 4(1).
40 International Maritime Organization, 'London Convention and Protocol', available at http://www.imo.org/OurWork/Environment/LCLP/Pages/default.aspx (accessed 23 November 2013).
41 London Convention, Art. IV(1) and IV(2) and Annex I to III.
42 London Protocol, Art. 4(1) and 4(2) and Annex 1 and 2. The reverse list in Annex I includes dredged material, sewage sludge, fish waste or by-products of industrial fish processing, vessels and platforms or other man-made structures at sea, inert or inorganic geological material, organic materials of natural origin, and bulky items made of durable substances for which the concern is physical impact and if they cannot be disposed of on land. However, if any such materials contain certain levels of radioactivity, they still cannot be disposed of sea.
43 Ibid., Art. 5.
44 Ibid., Art. 6.
45 London Convention, Art. VII, para. 2 and 3; London Protocol, Art 10, para. 2 and 3.
46 London Convention, Art. VIII; London Protocol, Art. 12.

and competent international organizations.[47] Ratifications of the London Convention and Protocol have yet to be universal, and are unevenly split between them. But among those that have ratified there is an approximate balance between developed and developing States, so the Convention is regarded as one of the more successful treaties of the 1970s.[48]

Norway's legislation is a leading example of national implementation. As one of the traditional maritime States, it ranks twelfth in the top 20 flag registries with 1.46 percent of world gross tonnage, has actively participated in the IMO, and implements the Convention through its Pollution Control Act[49] and regulations.[50] Geographically, the Act applies to the full extent of the Norwegian continental shelf, as well as to all Norwegian flag vessels wherever located.[51] On the strength of the Act, general regulations ban dumping[52] and establish the permit system for the select types of wastes that may be disposed of at sea.[53] These exceptions are limited to dredged silt, fish waste, and materials whose disposal on land would result in unacceptable danger or damage,[54] though in such cases the government is required to conduct an impact assessment and cost–benefit analysis.[55] The regulations absolutely prohibit waste incineration at sea.[56] All violations of the Norwegian Pollution Control Act are punished with coercive fines[57] and imprisonment.[58]

The United States uses a different kind of law, its Marine Protection, Research, and Sanctuaries Act,[59] implemented through Ocean Dumping Regulations[60] to comply with the Convention and Protocol. The Act prohibits the transportation from the United States or

---

47 London Convention, Art. XII; London Protocol, Art. 17.
48 P. Birnie, A. Boyle and C. Redgwell, *International Law and the Environment*, 3rd edn, Oxford: Oxford University Press, 2009, p. 472.
49 Lovomvern mot forurensningerog om avfall (Forurensningsloven), 13 March 1981 No. 6 (Pollution Control Act).
50 Forskriftombegrensningavforurensning (forurensningsforskriften), 1 June 2004 (last updated 22 July 2013) (Pollution Regulations).
51 Norwegian Pollution Control Act, s. 9–1, and Norwegian Pollution Regulations, s. 22–1.
52 Norwegian Pollution Regulations, s. 22–4: 'Dumping is prohibited. It may still be authorized pursuant to s. 22–6 for dumping of: a) silt soil, sediments, and rocks; b) ships with metal hulls up to 31 December 1998; c) other ships up to 31 December 2004; d) fish waste from fish processing/processing on land; e) other waste/material in special situations where disposal on land entails unacceptable danger or damage.' Additionally, s. 22–5 states that '[it] is prohibited to place material in the sea or rivers for a different purpose than it was originally built or designed, except where permission is granted pursuant to s. 22–6.'
53 Ibid., s. 22–6. Generally, permits for disposal of silt, ships, and fish waste are issued by the County Governor, but cases falling under 'special situations' and all other cases must be permitted by Norway's Environment Directorate.
54 Ibid., s. 22–4.
55 Section 22–6 particularly requires that the application for dredging, dumping, or placing of materials 'shall contain the information necessary to assess whether permission should be granted and the conditions to be set, including information on the waste/material to be dumped/placed and on the seabed of the dredge and/or dump site,' and that the decision should give 'the pollution disadvantages of the measure along with the advantages and disadvantages that the measure will entail.'
56 Ibid., s. 21–2: 'The incineration of waste or other material on board ships and offshore units is banned in Norway. Within the remit of international law, this also applies to incineration in the Norwegian Economic Zone and on the Norwegian Continental Shelf. The ban includes incineration on board Norwegian ships in all waters.'
57 Norwegian Pollution Control Act, s. 73, and Pollution Regulations, s. 41–6.
58 Norwegian Pollution Control Act, ss. 78–79.
59 33 USC s. 1401–1445 (MPRSA).
60 40 CFR s. 220–238.

from any location any material for the purpose of dumping it into ocean waters, as well as the dumping into the US territorial sea and contiguous zone of any material from a location outside the United States, unless authorized by a government permit.[61] The US Environmental Protection Agency is required to conduct environmental impact assessments before issuing permits for dumping, and to allow dumping only in designated sites.[62] However, emergency dumping of industrial wastes is allowed under certain conditions if there is no other alternative and to protect public health and safety.[63] Dumping of dredged material is also allowed if it will not have unreasonably detrimental impacts on the marine environment, human health, or economic potentials.[64] Those who violate the Act's restrictions on dumping are liable for civil penalties[65] and criminal penalties of a fine and/or imprisonment.[66] They are also liable for private civil suits[67] and subject to injunctive relief.[68] Vessels used in committing the offence may be subject to proceedings *in rem*,[69] as well as seizure and forfeiture.[70]

Australia fulfills its obligations under the London Convention and Protocol through the Sea Dumping Act[71] and its regulations.[72] It takes a slightly different approach by focusing on the means of transportation of the polluting material,[73] and prohibits, unless in accordance with a government permit, the dumping of any wastes or other matter within the meaning of the London Convention and Protocol;[74] incineration of controlled material

---

61 MPRSA, s. 1411:

> (a) Except as may be authorized by a permit issued pursuant to section 1412 or section 1413 of this title, and subject to regulations issued pursuant to section 1418 of this title, (1) no person shall transport from the United States, and (2) in the case of a vessel or aircraft registered in the United States or flying the United States flag or in the case of a United States department, agency, or instrumentality, no person shall transport from any location any material for the purpose of dumping it into ocean waters. (b) Except as may be authorized by a permit issued pursuant to section 1412 of this title, and subject to regulations issued pursuant to section 1418 of this title, no person shall dump any material transported from a location outside the United States (1) into the territorial sea of the United States, or (2) into a zone contiguous to the territorial sea of the United States, extending to a line twelve nautical miles seaward from the baseline from which the breadth of the territorial sea is measured, to the extent that it may affect the territorial sea or the territory of the United States.

62 MPRSA, s. 1412. The system for issuance of permits is detailed in the Ocean Dumping Regulations.
63 Ibid., s. 1412a.
64 Ibid., s. 1413.
65 Ibid., s. 1415(a).
66 Ibid., s. 1415(b).
67 Ibid., s. 1415(d) and (g).
68 Ibid., s. 1415(d).
69 Ibid., s. 1415(e).
70 Ibid., s. 1415(i).
71 Act 101, 1981 as amended. Environment Protection (Sea Dumping) Act (Sea Dumping Act).
72 Statutory Rules 1983 No. 8 as amended. Environment Protection (Sea Dumping) Regulations 1983.
73 Sea Dumping Act, s. 10A to 10C.
74 Ibid., s. 10A provides that:

> [a] person is guilty of an offence against this section if, otherwise than in accordance with a permit, the person: (a) dumps controlled material into Australian waters from any vessel, aircraft or platform; or (b) dumps controlled material into any part of the sea from any Australian vessel or Australian aircraft, or (c) dumps a vessel, aircraft, or platform into Australian waters; or (d) dumps an Australian vessel or Australian aircraft into any part of the sea.

at sea;[75] and even mere loading of materials or export for the purpose of dumping or incineration.[76] Offenders are punished upon conviction by imprisonment and/or fine,[77] and made liable for the costs and expenses of the suit.[78]

Terrestrial pollution

The more stringent regulation of pollution by States since the 1970s had the unintended effect of creating an illegal market for trade in wastes and pollution as affected industries attempted to comply by shipping their pollution to willing receivers elsewhere.[79] Trade in wastes shifted to developing states in Africa, Latin America, and the Caribbean as developed countries closed landfills, restricted waste incineration, and experienced escalating disposal costs.[80] In the late 1980s, the burgeoning trade was enough of a concern to prompt the international community to act against the displacement of pollution through adoption of the Basel Convention[81] in 1989.[82] Since entering into force in 1992 it has gained universal acceptance by the international community[83] and undergone numerous developments.[84] The Basel Convention is also one of three major multi-lateral treaties addressing international trade in toxic substances, the others being the Rotterdam Convention on Prior Informed Consent[85] and the Stockholm Convention on Persistent Organic Pollutants.[86]

The Basel Convention recognizes the sovereignty of the State to determine acceptable environmental impacts on its territory,[87] including the right to prohibit the importation of hazardous wastes or other wastes for disposal.[88] It obliges them to prohibit or disallow the

---

75 Ibid., s. 10B states that:

> [a] person is guilty of an offence against this section if, otherwise than in accordance with a permit, the person incinerates controlled material at sea: (a) on a vessel or platform in Australian waters; or . . . (c) on an Australian vessel in any part of the sea.

76 Ibid., s. 10C and 10D.
77 Ibid., s. 10A, para. 2; 10B, para. 2; 10C, para. 2; 10D, para. 2.
78 Ibid., s. 17.
79 Illegal markets emerge as a result of attempts to protect society from market forces for certain goods and services through regulation. See P. Arlacchi, 'The Dynamics of Illegal Markets', in P. Williams and D. Vlassis (eds), *Combating Transnational Crime: Concepts, Activities and Responses*, London: Frank Cass, 2001, p. 7 at pp. 7–8.
80 Birnie, Boyle and Redgwell, *International Law and the Environment*, p. 444.
81 Basel Convention on the Control of Transboundary Movements of Hazardous Wastes and their Disposal, 22 March 1989, 1673 UNTS 57; 28 ILM 657 (1989); in force 5 May 1992 (Basel Convention).
82 UNEP and Secretariat of the Basel Convention, *The Basel Convention at a Glance . . .*, Geneva: Secretariat of the Basel Convention, 2001, p. 1.
83 UNEP Basel Convention Secretariat, 'Parties to the Basel Convention', available at http://www. basel.int/Countries/StatusofRatifications/PartiesSignatories/tabid/1290/Default.aspx (accessed 24 November 2013).
84 See Basel Convention Secretariat, *Basel Convention: Text and Annexes*, Switzerland: United Nations Environment Programme, 2011, pp. 5–10 available at http://www.basel.int/Portals/4/Basel%20 Convention/docs/text/BaselConventionText-e.pdf (accessed 24 November 2013).
85 10 September 1998, 2244 UNTS 337; 38 ILM (1999) 1; in force 24 February 2004.
86 23 May 2001, 2256 UNTS 119; 40 ILM (2001) 532; in force 17 May 2004.
87 Birnie, Boyle and Redgwell, *International Law and the Environment*, p. 473.
88 Basel Convention, Art 4.1(a). 'Disposal' is broadly defined in Art. 2.4 and Annex IV, while wastes are 'hazardous' if listed in Annexes I, III, XIII, and IX, or defined as such by national law and notified to the Basel Secretariat under Art. 1.1(b).

export of such wastes to those States that exercise that right.[89] In cases where the State does not prohibit importation of waste, written consent to the specific import is required; prior informed consent of the States of transit is also necessary.[90] All Parties also expressly 'consider that illegal traffic in hazardous wastes or other wastes is criminal,'[91] and are obliged to take legal, administrative and other measures for implementation and enforcement, 'including measures to prevent and punish conduct in contravention of the convention.'[92] The Basel Convention takes the additional steps of obliging all parties to not permit the export of hazardous wastes and other wastes to non-parties,[93] and to not allow any exports for disposal within the area south of 60 degrees south latitude.[94] Examples of national implementation through legislation are even more abundant with respect to this treaty.

The Philippines was among the first countries to enact legislation implementing Basel, through the Toxic Substances and Hazardous and Nuclear Wastes Control Act of 1990.[95] Although the Act itself does not mention the Basel Convention, it establishes the legal foundation and administrative framework for direct implementation of a broad scope of measures to control the movement, whether within the Philippines or across its borders, of all chemical substances, mixtures, and wastes. The government established a chemical substances inventory,[96] and controls or restricts the import and manufacture of substances not included in the inventory through chemical control orders.[97] Imports and exports of hazardous wastes are restricted and subject to prior written approval by the government,[98] and transit through Philippine jurisdiction is prohibited.[99] The transit prohibition also applies to nuclear wastes.[100] The Act penalizes the use of substances or mixtures acquired in violation of the Act or its regulations, failure to file periodic reports on the use of such substances or mixtures, failure to comply with requirements for manufacture or import, and the storage

---

89 Ibid., Art 4.1(b).
90 Ibid., Art. 4.1(c), 4.2(f), 6.1–6.2, 6.10, and 7.
91 Ibid., Art. 4.3. It should be noted that trade in wastes *per se* is not illegal, but rather unauthorized or unregulated trade. See Birnie, Boyle and Redgwell, *International Law and the Environment*, pp. 473–477.
92 Ibid., Art. 4.4.
93 Ibid., Art. 4.5.
94 Ibid., Art. 4.6.
95 Republic Act No. 6969, 26 October 1990. An Act to Control Toxic Substances and Hazardous and Nuclear Wastes, Providing Penalties for Violations Thereof, and For Other Purposes. [RA 6969] It was enacted in the year after the Philippines signed the treaty, and three years' prior formal ratification, on October 21, 1993.
96 DENR Administrative Order No. 29, s. 1992. Implementing Rules and Regulations of RA 6969, s. 14. The inventory includes all substances stored, imported, exported, used, processed, manufactured, or transported as of 31 December 1993. The government requires information on these substances to be reported periodically. Substances not included in the inventory and to be subsequently imported into or manufactured in the Philippines are considered as 'new chemical substances' and subject to pre-importation or pre-manufacture requirements.
97 Ibid., s. 20.
98 Ibid., s. 31, para. 1: 'Any person who wishes to import into the Philippines or export hazardous substances must seek and obtain prior written approval from the Department.'
99 Ibid., s. 24 para. 1: 'It shall be the policy of the Department to prohibit the entry even in transit of hazardous wastes and their disposal into the Philippine territorial limits for whatever purpose.'
100 Ibid., s. 32 para. 1: 'It shall be the policy of the Department to prohibit the entry, even in transit, of nuclear wastes and their storage or disposal into the Philippine territorial limits for whatever purpose.'

or transportation of any amount of hazardous or nuclear wastes.[101] Such violations are penalized by imprisonment and fine, dismissal and disqualification from public office in the case that the offender is a government employee, deportation and barring from entry in the case of foreigners, cancellation of licenses in the case of businesses, confiscation and forfeiture of all proceeds, tools, equipment, and vehicles used, and liability for expenses of returning the wastes back to their origin.[102] Administrative fines may also be imposed for any other violations of regulations issued under the Act.[103]

Panama, currently the top flag registry of the world with over 22 percent of world gross tonnage flying the Panamanian flag, is one of the strategic nodes of global shipping since a large proportion of world trade between the Pacific and Atlantic Ocean passes through the Panama Canal. Panama simply and absolutely prohibits the transportation of 'any' forms of toxic and hazardous waste through its territory.[104] Its strategic position undoubtedly discourages trans-boundary movement of toxic and hazardous wastes through the region. Violators are penalized with imprisonment and fines, in addition to damages and indemnification for expenses for returning the wastes to their country of origin.[105] These sanctions are expressly made applicable to activities covered by the Basel Convention,[106] even though the legislation itself contains only a very brief and general definition of what constitutes toxic or hazardous wastes.[107]

In contrast, Colombia implements the Basel Convention through Law 1252,[108] which is very detailed and encompasses a wide range of substances and activities that may be regulated or prohibited, closely following the terms and conditions of the Convention. The introduction, importation, trafficking, disposal, and reception of wastes, whether by natural

---

101 RA 6969, s. 13:

Prohibited Acts. – The following acts and omissions shall be considered unlawful:

a) Knowingly using a chemical substance or mixture which is imported, manufactured, processed or distributed in violation of this Act or implementing rules and regulations or orders;

b) Failure or refusal to submit reports, notices or other information, access to records, as required by this Act, or permit inspection of establishments where chemicals are manufactured, processed, stored or otherwise held;

c) Failure or refusal to comply with the pre-manufacture and pre-importation requirements; and

d) Cause, aid or facilitate, directly or indirectly, in the storage, importation, or bringing into Philippines territory, including its maritime economic zones, even in transit, either by means of land, air or sea transportation or otherwise keeping in storage any amount of hazardous and nuclear wastes in any part of the Philippines.

102 Ibid., s. 14.

103 Ibid., s. 15.

104 Ley No. 8 de 7 Junio 1991. The general prohibition is stated in Art. 1: 'The importation of any form of toxic wastes or pollutants into the territory of the Republic of Panama is prohibited.'

105 Ibid., Art. 3.

106 Ibid., Art. 4: 'The penalties provided in the preceding article are applicable to those incurred in the Basel Convention [and] qualified as illicit traffic.'

107 Ibid., Art. 2:

For the purposes of this Law, toxic or polluted wastes are all substances, radioactive or not, or elements with immediate or delayed effects, that cause disturbances to human health, any type of animal or plant life, or produces harmful effects to the ecological balance of the country.

108 Ley No. 1252 de 27 Noviembre 2008.

or juridical, public or private persons, are absolutely prohibited.[109] Any waste found being transported within Colombian territory is to be returned to its origin without prejudice to criminal and civil sanctions against those responsible.[110] The Minister of Environment is authorized to issue regulations,[111] as well as impose administrative, civil, or criminal penalties for violations.[112] Law 1252 provides for a wide range of penalties such as fines, suspension of license, closure of the business, demolition of the offender's facilities, and confiscation of the proceeds of the crime.[113] They also include preventive measures such as warnings, preventive confiscation, cease-and-desist orders, and assessment studies.[114]

It is also possible to implement the Basel Convention without special legislation, and to resort instead to special administrative regulations. In Mexico, the General Law on Integrated Waste Prevention and Management[115] and the General Act on Ecological Equilibrium and Environmental Protection[116] are the latest laws applicable to the control of all forms of wastes, including those considered toxic and hazardous. The Mexican Waste Prevention and Management Act specifically addresses solid wastes, and devotes an entire chapter to the strict regulation of the import and export of hazardous wastes,[117] emphasizing that it is subject to both domestic laws and international treaties.[118] Imports are permitted only for purposes of reuse and recycling, but in no case allowed if there are persistent organic compounds.[119] Exports shall be authorized only with the prior consent of the importing country.[120] All trade in hazardous wastes is to be tracked and recorded,[121] and wastes illegally entering Mexican territory are to be sent back to their origin.[122] The Ecological Equilibrium and Environmental Protection Act disallows the importation of wastes of all kinds into Mexican territory and jurisdictions for storage or disposal, and transit is permitted only upon prior consent of the State.[123] An entire chapter is likewise devoted to the regulation of imports and exports of toxic and hazardous wastes,[124] especially the issuance of permits and authorization. Both the general laws above are applicable to Mexico's obligations under the Basel Convention, as they

---

109 Ibid., Art. 4.
110 Ibid., Art. 5.
111 Ibid., Art. 6.
112 Ibid., Art. 17.
113 Ibid., Art. 17(1).
114 Ibid., Art. 17(2).
115 Ley General Para La Prevención y Gestión Integral de los Residuos, 8 de Octubre de 2003, as amended on 19 June 2007 (Waste Prevention & Mgmt Act).
116 Ley General del Equilibrio Ecológico y La Protección al Ambiente, 28 de Enero 1988, as amended on 16 May 2008 (Eco Equilibrium & Enviro Protection Act).
117 Waste Prevention & Mgmt Act, Chapter VII.
118 Ibid., Art. 85.
119 Ibid., Art. 86.
120 Ibid., Art. 87.
121 Ibid., Art. 88.
122 Ibid., Art. 92–93.
123 Eco Equilibrium & Enviro Protection Act, Art. 142:

Under no circumstances shall there be authorization for the importation of wastes for collection, deposit, containment, storage, incineration or any treatment for destruction or disposal in the country or in areas where the country has sovereignty or jurisdiction. The authorization for transit of non-hazardous wastes through the territory to another nation may be granted only when there is prior consent' [translation].

124 Ibid., Arts 150–153.

provide the Minister with sufficiently broad powers to issue administrative regulations to enforce the Acts through a very wide range of administrative sanctions.[125]

Atmospheric pollution

Widely regarded as the single most successful environmental agreement to date, the Montreal Protocol[126] seeks to arrest the decline of ozone levels in the Earth's upper atmosphere by regulating the usage of ozone-depleting chemical compounds. A follow-up to the framework set by the Vienna Convention,[127] Montreal is a highly technical agreement that sets specific targets and timetables for the reduction and eventual abolition of the use of listed ODS. The Protocol has been amended four times, and has been universally ratified or acceded to by all States.[128] In addition to requiring States Parties to steadily reduce and eliminate their own consumption of ODS, it seeks to control the trade in such substances by obliging parties to either ban or restrict the import and export of the listed substances from/to non-parties.[129] Such prohibitions or restrictions of trade are often implemented through customs laws and regulations that carry penal sanctions for violations. The import and export bans have also led to the emergence of a black market, as such substances continue to have industrial applications in developing countries.[130] Just like Basel, Montreal is amply supported by numerous instances of national implementation by States Parties, but more often through administrative regulations issued under general statutes instead of special legislation.

Canada used the Canadian Environmental Protection Act (CEPA)[131] as a basis for issuing a series of regulations to control ODS, culminating in its Ozone-depleting Substances Regulations (ODSR) 1998,[132] to meet the Montreal Protocol phase-out schedules. The regulations mainly restrict and prohibit the use of hydrochlorofluorocarbons (HCFCs), implement an HCFC reduction schedule, establish a permits system for products containing ODS, and prohibit the import of products containing ODS or of recycled ODS.[133] The ODSR 1998 has been amended five times to expand coverage of ODS, accelerate the schedule for elimination

125 Waste Prevention & Mgmt Act, Chap. V; Eco Equilibrium & Enviro Protection Act, Chap. IV.
126 1987 Montreal Protocol on Substances that Deplete the Ozone Layer, 16 September 1987, 152 UNTS 3; 26 ILM 1550 (1987); in force 1 January 1989 (Montreal Protocol).
127 1985 Vienna Convention for the Protection of the Ozone Layer, 151 UNTS 323; 26 ILM 1529 (1987).
128 UNEP Ozone Secretariat, 'Status of Ratification for the Montreal Protocol and the Vienna Convention.'
129 Montreal Protocol, Art. 4.
130 L. Coppens, 'The UNEP Approach to Combating Illegal Trade in Ozone Depleting Substances,' in *Transnational Environmental Crime in the Asia-Pacific: A Workshop Report*, Canberra: Australian National University, n.d., p. 51, pp. 52–53; Elliott, 'Fighting Transnational Environmental Crime', pp. 90–91.
131 1999, c. 33, assented to 14 September 1999. An Act respecting pollution prevention and the protection of the environment and human health in order to contribute to sustainable development [Canadian Environment Protection Act, CEPA], s. 166.
132 Environment Canada, 'Ozone-Depleting Substances Regulations, 1998', Canada Law Database, Justice Laws Website, available at http://laws-lois.justice.gc.ca/eng/regulations/SOR-99-7/index.html (accessed 6 February 2014) (ODSR1998).
133 Environment Canada, 'Ozone-Depleting Substances Regulations 1998 and Its Amendments', Canada Law Database, available at http://www.ec.gc.ca/ozone/default.asp?lang=En&n=CD92C144–1 (accessed 5 June 2013).

of some substances, and streamline reporting requirements.[134] It expressly prohibits ODS imports from and exports to non–State Parties to the Montreal Protocol.[135] Violations of CEPA or its regulations are a punishable offence[136] rendering the offender liable for a fine and/or imprisonment.[137]

Colombia's approach is explicitly based on the text of the international agreement. Trade in ODS is regulated by the Ministry of Environment and the Ministry of Commerce, Industry and Tourism through various joint ministerial resolutions using extant provisions of Colombia's environmental code.[138] The Ministry of Environment issued Resolution 304 under its general regulatory authority,[139] expressly to carry out the regulation and phasing out of CFCs.[140] Subsequently, numerous resolutions updated and tightened up the import/export restrictions, keeping in step with amendments to the Montreal Protocol.[141] Sanctions for violations are the same as those against violations of the Basel Convention, including fines, punitive and compensatory damages, suspension of license, cease-and-desist orders, demolition at the owner's expense, and confiscation of the materials.[142] Preventive measures may also be imposed, including warnings, preventive confiscation, suspension of activities, and performance of impact assessment studies.[143]

Mexico's compliance with the Montreal Protocol was laid out as early as 1993 with the issuance by the Department of Environment of regulations to determine and monitor ozone levels,[144] pursuant to the provisions of the Ecological Equilibrium and Environmental Protection Act. Subsequently, it initiated the phase-out of CFCs by setting technical standards for refrigeration and electrical equipment as part of its energy efficiency program.[145] A national CFC reduction program was established[146] to reduce CFC consumption to only 50 tons per annum from 2007, then down to zero by 2010.[147] Thus, Mexico at present totally bans all CFC imports.

134 Ibid.
135 ODSR 1998, s. 4.
136 CEPA, s. 272(1).
137 CEPA, s. 272(2).
138 Ley 99 de 22 Diciembre 1993.
139 Ley 99 de 22 Diciembre 1993, Art. 5(1).
140 Republica de Colombia, Ministerio del Medio Ambiente, Resolucion No. 304 de 16 Abril 2001, Art. 1.
141 See e.g. Republica de Colombia, Ministerio de Ambiente y Desarrollo Sostenible, y Ministerio de Comercio, Industria y Turismo, Resolucion 171 de 22 Febrero 2013; Resolucion No. 301 de 31 Enero 2008; Resolucion 1652 de 10 Septiembre 2007; Resolucion No. 901 / 902 de 23 May 2006; Resolucion No. 2188 de 28 Diciembre 2005; Decreto 423 de 21 Febrero 2005; Resolucion No. 734 de 22 Junio 2004.
142 Ley 99 de 22 Diciembre 1993, Art. 85.
143 Ibid., Art. 85(2).
144 Norma Oficial Mexicana NOM-036-ECOL-1993, Que establece los metodos de medicion para determinar la concentracion de ozono en el aire ambiente y los procedimientos para la calibracion de los equipos de medicion. 18 de Octubre de 1993.
145 Norma Oficial Mexicana NOM-022-ENER/SCRI/ECOL-2000, Efficiencia energética, requisitos de seguridad al usuario y eliminación de clorofluorocarbonos (CFCs) para aparatos de refrigeración comercial autocontenidos, Limites, métodos de prueba y etiquetado, 09 de Marzo de 2001.
146 Acuerdo mediante el cual se informa al publico el calendario de reduccion en el consumo y en los inventarios de clorofluorocarbonos en los Estados Unidos Mexicanos, 13 de Marzo de 2007.
147 Ibid., Art. 1.

Similarly, the Philippines used its general law, the Toxic Substances and Hazardous and Nuclear Wastes Control Act, to administratively carry out its obligations under the Montreal Protocol and achieve a total phase-out of CFCs in 2010.[148] The broad regulations[149] of the Act permitted the Department of Environment and Natural Resources to issue a series of chemical control orders[150] for ODS that closely followed the technical aspects of the Montreal Protocol's phase-out program.[151] The orders simply added new items to a list of substances subjected to monitoring and import controls. In addition to civil and criminal liability under the Act, violators are held liable administratively for fines and revocation of business and professional licenses.[152]

Observations and conclusion

There is little doubt that the simple, general principle expressed in the Stockholm Declaration that States ought to prevent pollution has steadily evolved into an elaborate international system of treaty rules binding not only upon States, but extending downward to govern the conduct of private parties and individual citizens as well. Though cursory, the above perusal of examples of national legislation implementing corresponding international agreements against the dumping of pollution demonstrates high degrees of parallelism, if not uniformity, in the practice of States across geographical regions and legal systems. Through either special laws or special regulations of general laws, States clearly consider the unauthorized disposal of wastes into the sea, the trans-boundary movement of toxic or hazardous wastes without prior permission of either origin or destination State, and international trade in ODS, to be prohibited acts under international and municipal law. Valid permission from the State is essential in order to be excluded from the prohibition, which extends beyond the operative act itself (i.e., the act of disposal or transport), and applies to acts and instruments merely associated with the operative act (e.g., the offender's business, ships used). Sanctions range from simple fines and imprisonment to more severe punishments like forfeiture of property and cessation of businesses. This wide scope shows how seriously States intend the prohibition to be enforced. A broader sampling of legislation will surely yield more variations of text, but these essential elements of the acts and the prohibitions will always be present: dumping of pollution is a criminal act everywhere in the world.

---

148 N. Corsino and GMA News TV, 'Philippines Finally Bans CFCs Beginning in 2010 – DENR', Online News, 19 December 2009, available at http://www.gmanetwork.com/news/story/179799/news/nation/philippines-finally-bans-cfcs-beginning-in-2010-denr (accessed 13 November 2013).
149 Department of Environment and Natural Resources Administrative Order No. 29, s. 1992: Implementing Rules and Regulations of Republic Act 6969.
150 Ibid., s. 20.
151 DENR Administrative Order No. 18, s. 2000: Chemical Control Order for Ozone Depleting Substances; DENR Administrative Order No. 8, s. 2004: Revised Chemical Control Order for Ozone Depleting Substances [CCO for ODS]; DENR Administrative Order No. 27, s. 2005: Revised Priority Chemical List.
152 CCO for ODS, s. 12.

19

Intellectual property offences

Henning Grosse Ruse-Khan

Transnational IP crimes

The history of labelling intellectual property infringements as piracy, plagiarism and theft

For several hundred years, unauthorized uses of someone else's intellectual works have received labels associating such actions – interferences with state-granted monopolies – with committing a crime: from plagiarism, via piracy and theft, to modern associations with organized crime and (financing) terrorism. Those who own and control the exclusivity which intellectual property (IP) confers have been quite creative in labelling unauthorized uses as an ethical and moral wrong. The term *plagiarism*, for example, originates from the Latin word *plagiarius*, meaning 'kidnapper, seducer, plunderer, one who kidnaps the child or slave of another',[1] and was pioneered by the poet Marcus Valerius Martialis (Martial), who worked and published in Rome in the first century AD.[2] Martial apparently complained that another poet had 'kidnapped' his verses to denote someone stealing his work, appropriating it without due recognition to him as author: a literary thief who kidnaps someone else's words. About 1,500 years later, in the seventeenth century, the term was used in this way in English by dramatist Ben Jonson, to describe as a 'plagiary' someone guilty of literary theft.[3]

At the same time, the term *piracy* became a synonym for acts such as unauthorized reprinting of books in England where, prior to the Statute of Anne (1710) as the first Copyright Act, members of the Stationers' Company enjoyed printing monopolies by royal prerogative. As Justin Hughes observes in his etymological study:

> It is worth noting that during this pre-Statute of Anne period, 'piracy' was widely used to describe unauthorized printing of books. Adrian Johns traces 'piracy' as a description

---

1 See *The Online Etymology Dictionary*, http://www.etymonline.com/index.php?term=plagiarism (accessed 4 January 2014).
2 B. Marsh, *Plagiarism: Alchemy and Remedy in Higher Education*, Albany: SUNY Press, 2007, p. 31.
3 First used in his satirical play *Poetaster*, 1602, Act IV, Scene III.

of unauthorized copying to John Fell, the Bishop of Oxford who resuscitated the fledgling Oxford University Press after the Restoration. According to Johns' exhaustive study of book publishing in England, *The Nature of the Book*, piracy had a 'technical meaning' in the seventeenth century: 'a pirate was someone who indulged in the unauthorized reprinting of a title recognized to belong to someone else by the formal conventions of the printing and bookselling community.' Beyond this technical meaning, piracy 'soon came to stand for a wide range of perceived transgressions of civility emanating from print's practitioners.[4]

Hughes explains the curious fact that the notion of piracy *precedes* a statutory concept of exclusive (property) rights by a common sense of belonging which – in cases of interferences – finds its legal, ethical or social expression in notions of 'piracy' or 'theft'. Piracy so understood, then, is primarily a rhetorical tool which advocates 'a normative agenda in favor of some kind of property or ownership' – especially in circumstances where the author has no or contested legal entitlements to property, but feels exposed to unauthorized takings of her or his intellectual output.[5]

The use of terms like piracy and theft by right holders seems to fulfil the very same functions today. In the 1980s, when the computer industry was fighting for the expansion of copyright protection to cover software, the UK-based Federation Against Software Theft (FAST) relied on the slogan 'Piracy is theft' in advertisements – designed as comic strips – primarily targeting teenagers and young adults.[6] In the same decade in the United States, the Motion Picture Association of America (MPAA), a trade association that represents the six big Hollywood film studios, felt so threatened by the popular use of video cassette recorders (VCRs) for home recording of movies that its then-president Jack Valenti drew a parallel between the threat of the VCR and that of the Boston Strangler, a serial murderer in the early 1960s.[7] With little success: the legal battle by the studios against Sony, a major producer of the new technology, for contributory copyright infringement ended in the US Supreme Court in 1984 when the court decided that home recording of copyright-protected TV content is a form of fair use and there was no copyright infringement in which the producers of VCRs participated.[8] But the fight over normative perceptions of, and moral associations with, unauthorized uses of another's intellectual output continued. Subsequent campaigns by the MPAA, for example, together with the Intellectual Property Office of Singapore (IPOS), involved 45-second trailers screened in cinemas around the world with the following message: 'You wouldn't steal a Car. You wouldn't steal a Handbag. You wouldn't steal a Mobile Phone.

4   J. Hughes, 'Copyright and Incomplete Historiographies: Of Piracy, Propertization, and Thomas Jefferson', *Southern California Law Review*, 2006, vol. 79, p. 993; Cardozo Legal Studies Research Paper No. 166, at p. 1009 (footnotes omitted). Available at SSRN: http://ssrn.com/abstract=934869 (accessed 13 November 2013).

5   Ibid., at p. 1010.

6   Federation Against Software Theft, 'Piracy is Theft' campaign, available at http://www.ntk.net/2002/11/29/elspa.gif (accessed 5 January 2014).

7   Hearings before the Subcommittee on Courts, Civil Liberties, and the Administration of Justice of the Committee on the Judiciary, House of Representatives, Ninety-seventh Congress, Second Session on Home Recording of Copyrighted Works, HR 4783, HR 4794, HR 4808, HR 5250, HR 5488 and HR 5705, 12–14 April, June, 11 August, 22–23 September 1982.

8   *Sony Corp. of America v Universal City Studios, Inc.*, 464 U.S. 417 (1984).

You wouldn't steal a Movie. Movie Piracy is Stealing. Stealing is Against the Law. Piracy. It's A Crime.'[9]

This campaign has triggered hundreds of parodies on YouTube and Facebook.[10] It shows that instead of successfully portraying unauthorized users of IP-protected content as criminals, the use of associations like piracy has at times proven counterproductive. The logo of the British music industry 1980s campaign against recording music on audiocassettes, a stark black and white pirate-flag image showing a stylized skull and crossbones made out of an audiotape, now features on the mainsail of The Pirate Bay, a well-known Swedish file-sharing website.[11] A related response comes in form of the Pirate Party, a political movement that initially formed itself in Sweden in opposition to attempts to criminalize internet users for up- and downloading copyright-infringing 'pirated' content and which is now active in more than forty countries. On its international website, the Pirate Party explains the use of the name 'Pirate' as a 're-appropriation of the title that was given to Internet users by the representatives of the music and film industries'.[12] Next to issues such as transparency and free access to information, digital rights, such as in a form of online privacy, and civil liberties, the political agenda of the Pirate Party is strongly related to a radical reform of copyright and patent protection.[13]

These examples suggest that the moral and ethical charges inherent in the 'pirate' label have not necessarily led to any social stigma upon or change in behaviour by those accused of piracy or theft in relation to IP rights. A different question, of course, is how law has dealt with the types of activities stigmatized as piracy, theft or even *counterfeiting*, another term that is used frequently in the context of international trade in illicit, dangerous and/or IP-infringing goods, from luxury items to pharmaceuticals. Before this is examined in more detail in the following sections, the transnational dimension of IP-infringing activity and the inherent difficulty in capturing this in legal terms needs to be discussed.

The transnational dimension

In the international context, the meaning of piracy and other terms discussed so far is particularly ambivalent and multi-faceted. The Organisation for Economic Cooperation and Development (OECD), for example, one of the main international organizations involved in the analysis of the transnational dimension of 'counterfeiting and piracy', explains these terms as describing 'a range of illicit activities linked to intellectual property rights (IPR) infringement', focusing 'on the infringement of IPRs described in the WTO Agreement on

---

9 Internet Archive of: Intellectual Property Office of Singapore (IPOS), 'Be HIP at the Movies', available at http://web.archive.org/web/20040804074635/http://www.ipos.gov.sg/main/news-room/media_rel/mediarelease1_270704.html> (accessed 5 January 2014).

10 See, for example, the Facebook group 'I wouldn't steal a car, But I'd download one if I could', available at https://www.facebook.com/pages/I-wouldnt-steal-a-car-But-id-download-one-if-i-could/183252739422 (accessed 5 January 2014).

11 F. Rohrer, 'Getting inside a downloader's head', *BBC News Magazine*, 18 June 2009, available at http://news.bbc.co.uk/2/hi/uk_news/magazine/8106805.stm (accessed 5 January 2014).

12 Pirate Parties International, 'About the PPI', available at http://www.pp-international.net/about (accessed 5 January 2014).

13 Pirate Party UK, 'Copyright and Patents', available at http://www.pirateparty.org.uk/Copyright (accessed 5 January 2014). The UK branch, for example, calls for a reduction of the duration of copyright protection to 10 years (instead of the international minimum term of 50 years after the death of the author).

Trade-Related Aspects of Intellectual Property Rights' (TRIPS),[14] which includes trademarks, copyrights, patents and industrial design rights.[15] The World Health Organization (WHO), whose work focuses on counterfeiting in the field of medical drugs, on the other hand acknowledges that counterfeit medicines are 'defined differently in different countries' and that 'the absence of a universally accepted definition not only makes information exchange between countries very difficult but it also limits the ability to understand the true extent of the problem at global level'.[16] In order to address this problem, the WHO uses the following definition:

> A counterfeit medicine is one which is deliberately and fraudulently mislabelled with respect to identity and/or source. Counterfeiting can apply to both branded and generic products and counterfeit products may include products with the correct ingredients or with the wrong ingredients, without active ingredients, with insufficient active ingredients or with fake packaging.[17]

Interpol on the other hand uses the terminology of 'trafficking in illicit goods' to describe all types of 'illicit trade', including 'counterfeiting (trademark infringements), piracy (copyright infringements), smuggling of legitimate products and tax evasion'.[18] It further explains:

> Selling fake or counterfeit products as the real thing is one aspect of this crime; so is selling genuine goods on the black market to avoid paying taxes. By avoiding regulatory controls the criminals behind these activities typically peddle often dangerous goods with a complete disregard for the health and safety of consumers. The phenomenon has grown to an unprecedented level, posing tremendous risks to society and the global economy.[19]

Not surprisingly in light of its mandate, Interpol is the main international organization which focuses on the role of organized crime in this context. It claims that there is a 'clear link' between the trafficking of illicit goods and transnational organized crime: the 'lucrative profits involved in trading counterfeit or fake goods' attract criminals involved on a regional and increasingly global scale where 'organized crime networks exploit new technology, differences among national regulatory regimes and links between the global economic, finance and transportation systems' and 'use the profits to fund other criminal activities such as drug trafficking, people smuggling and robbery'.[20] In a very similar fashion, the United Nations Office on Drugs and Crime (UNODC), in its January 2014 campaign 'Counterfeit: Don't buy into organized crime', aims to raise 'consumer awareness of links between

---

14 Marrakesh Agreement Establishing the World Trade Organization, Annex 1C, 15 April 1994, 1867 UNTS 3; in force 1 January 1995.
15 OECD, *The Economic Impact of Counterfeiting and Piracy*, 2007, p. 8, available at http://www.oecd.org/industry/ind/38707619.pdf (accessed 10 January 2014).
16 WHO, 'General information on counterfeit medicines', available at http://www.who.int/medicines/services/counterfeit/overview/en (accessed 10 January 2014).
17 Ibid.
18 Interpol, 'Trafficking in illicit goods and counterfeiting', available at http://www.interpol.int/Crime-areas/Trafficking-in-illicit-goods-and-counterfeiting (accessed 10 January 2014).
19 Ibid.
20 Ibid.

organized crime and $250 billion a year counterfeit business.'[21] In its press release, UNODC highlights 'the illicit trafficking and sale of counterfeit goods' as a 'significant source of income' for criminals and a tool for 'laundering other illicit proceeds', and goes on to emphasize the links between counterfeits and: (1) consumer safety due to dangerous and faulty character of the goods; (2) public health because of the high-volume sales of fraudulent medicines with no active ingredients or even deadly components; (3) ethical issues related to labour exploitation and migrant smuggling; as well as (4) environmental problems caused by unregulated waste disposal and pollution.[22] Without a specific reliance on questions of IP infringements, it seems that – although a concrete definition is missing – the notion of counterfeits here is primarily one based on the violation of health and safety standards.

This brief review highlights the diverse range of understandings of terms such as piracy and counterfeiting by the main international organizations involved. In essence, two principal approaches emerge which either (1) emphasize the IP (especially trademark and copyright) infringements involved, or (2) focus on the substandard quality, even health hazards that the 'illicit' goods involve. These distinct approaches point to the ambiguity that still underlies any use of the terms piracy, counterfeiting or equivalent expressions that relate to criminal activity in this context.

The territorial nature of IP rights

One of the key factors explaining the ambiguity described above is the *territorial nature of IP rights*. Despite an increasingly dense network of international treaties on IP, the rights which provide protection to authors, inventors and other right holders are granted by virtue of national laws and limited to the territory of the granting state. In other words, a patent granted by the US Patent and Trademark Office (USPTO) is valid only in the United States, and the very same invention can freely be used and commercialized in any other country – unless the patent owner has obtained a patent in other jurisdictions as well. This implies that the question of copyright or trademark infringements, one of the most common causes for considering a specified activity as piracy or counterfeiting, can be answered only in relation to the use of a brand, logo (or other potential trademark-protected sign) or creative work in the territory of a given country. It will always be the respective national law of that country which determines: who is the right holder; whether a specific conduct falls under the exclusive rights granted by the domestic law; if any defence applies in favour of the user; and what type of remedies, including criminal sanctions, are available.

This is not only a technical distinction for IP theorists – it has crucial consequences for examining (criminal) IP infringements. To the extent that they are understood in relation to IP violations, transnational IP crimes can only be judged against the domestic laws of the countries

---

21 See UNODC, 'Counterfeit: Don't buy into organized crime', available at http://www.unodc.org/counterfeit. In UNODC, *Focus on: The Illicit Trafficking of Counterfeit goods and Organized Crime*, UNODC, Vienna, no date, the UNODC emphasizes that 'with the combination of high profits and low penalties resulting from a greater social tolerance compared to other crimes, the illicit trafficking of counterfeit goods is an attractive money-making avenue for organized criminal groups.' See http://www.unodc.org/documents/counterfeit/FocusSheet/Counterfeit_focussheet_EN_HIRES.pdf (accessed 21 January 2014).

22 UNODC, Press Release, Vienna, 14 January 2014, available at http://www.unodc.org/documents/counterfeit/PressRelease/Press_Release_-_English_-_Counterfeit_Campaign_2014.pdf (accessed 21 January 2014).

where the alleged criminals have acted. Whether their action triggers criminal liability first and foremost depends on whether they have infringed IP rights locally. This in turn may well differ quite a lot from country to country: despite an increasing degree of international harmonization through IP treaties that prevent the discrimination of foreign right holders and impose a significant amount of minimum standards which countries are obliged to implement in their domestic IP laws, there is still room for important differences in national laws, in particular relating to what kind of IP infringements must be sanctioned by criminal statutes. In addition, the territorially limited nature of IP rights means that often protection for inventions and brands (and other subject matter that requires a formal grant of an IP right by a state authority) may exist in some countries, but not in others where the inventor or brand owner has not applied for protection. In the latter countries, the unauthorized use of the brand or invention does not amount to an IP infringement and hence certainly is not a criminal offence.

With this crucial aspect in mind, the remaining part of this chapter examines the attempts within international IP law to deal with activity that may be loosely framed under the term of transnational IP crimes. On the one hand, this relates to the type of IP-infringing conduct which, by virtue of international IP treaties, must be considered as a criminal offence in the national laws of all contracting parties. In particular, Article 61 of the TRIPS Agreement contains an obligation on WTO member states to impose criminal sanctions in cases of specific, grave types of IP infringements. The next section examines the scope of Article 61 of the TRIPS, a WTO dispute where a Panel had to judge on the consistency of China's criminal law with Article 61, and attempts to introduce more stringent obligations for criminal sanctions in the Anti-Counterfeiting Trade Agreement (ACTA). Aside from specific obligations to provide for criminal sanctions, international IP treaties deal with transnational trade in counterfeit trademark goods and pirated copyright goods by requiring countries to stop and seize infringing imports of such goods at their borders. Although not technically part of criminal law, these border measures can be viewed as a crucial tool in the fight against counterfeiting and piracy. As the example in the following section shows, these measures, however, also involve a danger of interfering with legitimate trade in products, such as generic medicines, that are not dangerous or of substandard quality and are not even IP-infringing other than in the country where they have been seized. In light of the focus on IP-related crimes, this chapter does not deal with other international instruments in the fight against counterfeits or piracy (understood more broadly to encompass any sort of substandard product), such as the UN Convention against Transnational Organized Crime (UNTOC) as a general platform for cooperation in tackling organized crime.[23]

Criminal sanctions for counterfeiting and piracy

Article 61 TRIPS and its flexible interpretation by WTO Panels

For much of their history of almost 150 years, multilateral IP treaties have been silent about the need to provide criminal law sanctions against certain forms of IP infringements in

---

23 UNODC, for example, proposes to use the Convention as a framework for states parties 'to adopt tougher laws in order to tackle the illicit trafficking of counterfeit goods, particularly in the case of public health and safety threats'. See UNODC, *Focus on: The Illicit Trafficking of Counterfeit goods and Organized Crime*, p. 7. For a proposal for a new international convention tackling counterfeit medicines see A. Attaran, R. Bate and M. Kendall, 'Why and How to Make an International Crime of Medicine Counterfeiting', *Journal of International Criminal Justice*, 2011, vol. 9, p. 1.

national laws. The main multilateral IP treaties from the late nineteenth century, the Paris Convention for the Protection of Industrial Property of 20 March 1883 (Paris Convention) and the Berne Convention for the Protection of Literary and Artistic Works of 9 September 1886 (Berne Convention), do not contain any explicit obligations to introduce criminal law sanctions against IP infringements. This changed with the entry into force of the TRIPS Agreement, Annex 1C of the Agreement Establishing the World Trade Organization. The first international IP treaty with a comprehensive set of provisions on the enforcement of IP rights, TRIPS in Article 61 obliges WTO member states to:

> provide for criminal procedures and penalties to be applied at least in cases of wilful trademark counterfeiting or copyright piracy on a commercial scale. Remedies available shall include imprisonment and/or monetary fines sufficient to provide a deterrent, consistently with the level of penalties applied for crimes of a corresponding gravity. In appropriate cases, remedies available shall also include the seizure, forfeiture and destruction of the infringing goods and of any materials and implements the predominant use of which has been in the commission of the offence. Members may provide for criminal procedures and penalties to be applied in other cases of infringement of intellectual property rights, in particular where they are committed wilfully and on a commercial scale.

Distinct from some earlier drafts which covered all forms of IP infringements,[24] the final version of Article 61 of TRIPS requires criminal sanctions only in 'cases of wilful trademark counterfeiting or copyright piracy on a commercial scale'. For other forms of IP infringements – even if committed wilfully and on a commercial scale – the last sentence of Article 61 of the TRIPS foresees only an (optional) right for WTO members to introduce criminal sanctions, but no obligation to do so. Article 61 further contains two sentences on the types of remedies mandated: WTO members can choose between 'imprisonment and/or monetary fines sufficient to provide a deterrent'. This choice must be made consistent 'with the level of penalties applied for crimes of a corresponding gravity'. Hence, while providing general benchmarks for choosing appropriate remedies, TRIPS does not mandate specific criminal law sanctions for IP infringements. Finally, the available remedies must 'also include the seizure, forfeiture and destruction of the infringing goods and of any materials and implements the predominant use of which has been in the commission of the offence'. However, this obligation is qualified by the chapeau phrase 'in appropriate cases' – which arguably leaves a lot of leeway to WTO member states to decide the circumstances in which these specific remedies apply.

It follows that the core international minimum standard is the TRIPS obligation to provide criminal sanctions 'in cases of wilful trademark counterfeiting or copyright piracy on a commercial scale'. Both 'trademark counterfeiting' and 'copyright piracy' are further defined in Footnote 14 to Article 51 of the TRIPS, which provides:

> For the purposes of this Agreement:
>
> (a) 'counterfeit trademark goods' shall mean any goods, including packaging, bearing without authorization a trademark which is identical to the trademark validly

---

24 Negotiating Group on Trade Related Aspects of Intellectual Property Rights (1990), Chairman's Report to the GNG – Status of Work in the Negotiating Group, MTN.GNG/NG11/W/76 23 July 1990, at para. 24.

registered in respect of such goods, or which cannot be distinguished in its essential aspects from such a trademark, and which thereby infringes the rights of the owner of the trademark in question under the law of the country of importation;

(a) 'pirated copyright goods' shall mean any goods which are copies made without the consent of the right holder or person duly authorized by the right holder in the country of production and which are made directly or indirectly from an article where the making of that copy would have constituted an infringement of a copyright or a related right under the law of the country of importation.

The obligation to impose criminal sanctions under TRIPS thus applies only to two specific types of trademark and copyright infringements – which will in any case have to be judged based on the national IP laws of the country where the allegedly infringing activity has taken place. For these defined cases, Article 61 of TRIPS contains two further qualifications. Next to the condition of 'wilfulness', WTO members are only obliged to introduce criminal sanctions for acts committed 'on a commercial scale'.[25]

This rather ambiguous phrase was at the heart of a dispute which the United States initiated in 2007 under the WTO Dispute Settlement Understanding (DSU) against China, *inter alia* claiming that the thresholds in Chinese law for criminal liability for IP infringements are inconsistent with China's obligations under Article 61 of the TRIPS Agreement.[26] The core issue for the United States was an interpretative rule by the Chinese Supreme Court whereby individuals could avoid criminal liability for IP infringements where they were caught with fewer than 500 IP-infringing copies – a high threshold that the United States considered to be arbitrary. In January 2009, a WTO Panel issued its report which concluded that the United States had '*not* established that the criminal thresholds are inconsistent with China's obligations under the first sentence of Article 61 of the TRIPS Agreement'.[27] In its report, the Panel acknowledges four limits to the obligation to provide for criminal sanctions against IP enforcement. First, 'the obligation applies to trademarks and copyright rather than to all intellectual property rights covered by the TRIPS Agreement.'[28] The second limitation is that the first sentence of Article 61 'applies to counterfeiting and piracy rather than to all infringements of trademarks and copyright'.[29] Subject to context-specific differences, the Panel considered that the definitions in Footnote 14 to Article 51 of TRIPS are relevant in understanding the terms used in Article 61.[30] The third limitation is indicated by the word 'wilful', which focuses on the infringer's intent and reflects the criminal nature of the enforcement procedures at issue. The Panel applies it to both trademark counterfeiting and copyright piracy and hence concludes that 'there is no obligation to make such penalties available with

25 C. Correa, *Trade Related Aspects of Intellectual Property Rights: A Commentary on the TRIPS Agreement*, Oxford: Oxford University Press, 2007, p. 41; H. Xue, 'An Anatomical Study of the United States versus China at the World Trade Organisation on Intellectual Property Enforcement', *European Intellectual Property Review*, 2009, no. 6, p. 295.

26 Panel Report, *China: Measures Affecting the Protection and Enforcement of Intellectual Property Rights (China – IPRs)* (WT/DS3262/R), 26 January 2009, at 7.396–7.479, 7.480–7.482.

27 Emphasis added. The Panel exercised judicial economy with respect to the further claims regarding China's criminal enforcement laws under the second sentence of Article 61 as well as Article 41(1) TRIPS; see *China – IPRs*, at 7.669, 7.681 and 8.1. Neither party has appealed the ruling, which was accepted by the WTO Dispute Settlement Body (DSB) on 20 March 2009.

28 Ibid., at 7.518.

29 Ibid., at 7.519.

30 Ibid., at 7.522.

respect to acts of infringement committed without the requisite intent'.[31] Finally, criminal sanctions need only be attached to actions that are conducted 'on a commercial scale'. Again, the Panel considers this qualification to apply to both trademark counterfeiting and copyright piracy.[32]

In light of the high threshold of 500 infringing copies for criminal liability in Chinese law, the appropriate interpretation of this fourth condition is at the centre of the further elaborations of the Panel. After a long, technical examination of the ordinary[33] and contextual meaning[34] of the phrase, and a full discussion of the arguments of the parties and third parties,[35] the Panel concludes that:

> a 'commercial scale' is the magnitude or extent of typical or usual commercial activity. Therefore, *counterfeiting or piracy 'on a commercial scale' refers to counterfeiting or piracy carried on at the magnitude or extent of typical or usual commercial activity with respect to a given product in a given market.* The magnitude or extent of typical or usual commercial activity with respect to a given product in a given market forms a benchmark by which to assess the obligation in the first sentence of Article 61. *It follows that what constitutes a commercial scale for counterfeiting or piracy of a particular product in a particular market will depend on the magnitude or extent that is typical or usual with respect to such a product in such a market, which may be small or large.*[36]

In essence, this relative, situation-specific interpretation of the term 'commercial scale' leaves considerable discretion to national legislators to set thresholds for criminal liability on the basis of products and markets. Indeed, the Panel observes that what is typical or usual in commerce is a flexible concept. Hence, determinations of commercial scale 'depend on circumstances, which vary according to the differing forms of commerce and of counterfeiting and piracy to which these obligations apply'.[37] Since the United States did not provide the Panel with sufficient evidence that the possession of and/or trade in any specific product on the Chinese market amounted to a commercial activity below the Chinese threshold of 500 copies, it lost the case. In essence, the 2009 Panel Report highlights the flexibility that WTO member states enjoy when implementing their obligation under Article 61 TRIPS to provide for criminal sanctions in their national laws. Countries with a strong IP-reliant industry, however, viewed that flexibility as a major threat to effective international enforcement of IP rights in the fight against transnational IP crimes which needed to be addressed.

Attempts towards further development of international IP norms: the Anti-Counterfeiting Trade Agreement

The response to the *China – IPRs* report came in the form of enhanced rules on criminal IP enforcement, embodied, for example, in the Anti-Counterfeiting Trade Agreement (ACTA).[38]

---

31 Ibid., at 7.523.
32 Ibid., at 7.524–7.525.
33 Ibid., at 7.533–7.538.
34 Ibid., at 7.539–7.545.
35 Ibid., at 7.546–7.576.
36 Ibid., at 7.577 (emphasis added).
37 Ibid., at 7.578.
38 Anti-Counterfeiting Trade Agreement (ACTA), Tokyo, 1 October 2011, 50 ILM 243 (2011).

By October 2007 the United States, Japan, South Korea, Mexico, New Zealand, Switzerland and the European Union (EU) had announced their intention to negotiate ACTA.[39] The expressed idea was to 'establish new international norms, helping to create a new global gold standard on IPR enforcement'.[40] However, ACTA has caused controversy not only because the treaty obligations it would create seemed to go significantly beyond the existing international standards in TRIPS, but also due to the almost complete absence of transparency in the negotiation process, for example concerning access to any draft negotiating texts.[41] After years of secrecy and various leaked draft texts, the negotiating parties concluded the agreement in 2011,[42] but ACTA has faced criticism ever since news about its negotiation became public. In particular NGOs, academics and officials from developing countries have voiced concerns regarding, *inter alia*, access to medicines, the protection of privacy, the free flow of information on the internet and criminal enforcement measures.[43] To alleviate these concerns, the European Commission, for example, emphasized in a press release that 'the overall objective of ACTA is to address large-scale infringements of intellectual property rights which have a significant economic impact', and stressed that 'ACTA will by no means lead to a limitation of civil liberties or to "harassment" of consumers'.[44] Nevertheless, in an unprecedented move, on 4 July 2012 the European Parliament rejected ACTA – after it had received a petition, signed by 2.8 million citizens worldwide, as well as interventions by thousands of EU citizens who called on the Parliament in street demonstrations, e-mails to MEPs and calls to their offices to prevent the ratification of ACTA in Europe.[45]

Although the final ACTA text was much less controversial than earlier leaked drafts and the half-truths bred by the secret negotiation process, it significantly expands IP enforcement rules beyond those contained in TRIPS. Regarding criminal enforcement, Articles 23 to 26 contain comprehensive provisions on 'Criminal Offences', 'Penalties', 'Seizure, Forfeiture and Destruction' and '*Ex Officio* Criminal Enforcement'. The general approach is to go beyond Article 61 of TRIPS by either (1) introducing additional definitions or interpretations of existing TRIPS obligations;[46] (2) otherwise strengthening existing

---

39 The number of parties negotiating ACTA has changed subsequently. Subsequently, Morocco, Singapore, Australia and Canada have joined the negotiations.

40 EU Commission (2007), 'European Commission seeks mandate to negotiate major new international anti-counterfeiting pact', press release of 23 October 2007 (IP/07/1573).

41 M. Geist, *ACTA Guide, Part Three: Transparency and ACTA Secrecy*, (2010), available at http://www.michaelgeist.ca/content/view/4737/125 (accessed 11 January 2014).

42 The Agreement was signed on 1 October 2011 in Tokyo by the representatives of eight of the negotiating parties (Australia, Canada, Japan, Republic of Korea, Morocco, New Zealand, Singapore and the United States) and on 26 January 2012 by the European Union and 22 of its member states. Due to concerns about the Agreement, Cyprus, Estonia, Germany, the Netherlands and Slovakia decided not to sign ACTA. Other member states of the EU which signed the Agreement, such as Poland, Czech Republic, Latvia, Austria, Bulgaria and Romania, later decided to freeze the ratification of ACTA.

43 See, for example, the Institut für Rechtsinformatik, *Opinion of European Academics on ACTA*, available at http://www.iri.uni-hannover.de/acta-1668.html (accessed 11 January 2014).

44 European Commission, Press Release, 'Anti-Counterfeiting Trade Agreement: European Commission welcomes release of negotiation documents', 21 April 2010, available at http://trade.ec.europa.eu/doclib/press/index.cfm?id=552 (accessed 17 January 2014).

45 It was the first time that Parliament exercised its Lisbon Treaty power to reject an international trade agreement which hence cannot become law in the EU: 478 MEPs voted against ACTA, 39 in favour and 165 abstained; see European Parliament, *News: European Parliament rejects ACTA*, available at http://www.europarl.europa.eu/news/en/news-room/content/20120220FCS38611/1/html/European-Parliament-rejects-ACTA (accessed 15 January 2014).

46 For example, by a proposed definition of the term 'commercial scale' in ACTA, Article 23(1).

obligations;[47] (3) removing existing flexibilities;[48] or (4) introducing completely new provisions on criminal enforcement.[49] In Article 23 dealing with 'Criminal Offences', Section 1 reiterates the core obligation under TRIPS: to 'provide for criminal procedures and penalties to be applied at least in cases of wilful trademark counterfeiting or copyright piracy on a commercial scale'. However, this is then further defined in Article 23 so as to include at least acts 'carried out as commercial activities for direct or indirect economic or commercial advantage'. A footnote also clarifies that ACTA parties must treat 'wilful importation or exportation of counterfeit trademark goods or pirated copyright goods on a commercial scale as unlawful activities subject to criminal penalties'.[50] These obligations are expanded under Article 23(2) to cover labels or packaging of counterfeit trademark goods.

Under Article 23(1), the acts carried out on a commercial scale 'include at least those carried out as commercial activities for direct or indirect economic or commercial advantage'. Compared to previous drafts, this definition focuses on both qualitative elements and intentions. It remains unclear whether the term 'as commercial activities' is an additional quantitative element requiring a certain minimum size or magnitude of the infringing activity or – qualitatively – whether it merely refers to the intention of the infringer to act for a commercial purpose. If requiring additional quantitative elements prevails in ACTA interpretation and implementation, it would be more in line with the approach of the WTO Panel described above. Nevertheless, the obligation to impose criminal sanctions against all wilful trademark counterfeiting or copyright piracy 'for direct or indirect economic or commercial advantage' appears much broader than the one in Article 61 of TRIPS. The notion of 'indirect economic or commercial advantage' might go as far as covering internet users downloading copyrighted files without right-holder authorization and so receiving an (indirect) economic advantage of not having to pay the retail price.

Leaving possible differing interpretations aside, the crucial point with the criminal enforcement rules in ACTA is that they are designed to go beyond TRIPS standards and to specifically override the 2009 Panel decision on commercial scale. A leaked document of the EU Commission explains that 'the ACTA wording defines the concept of TRIPS and redresses the doubts created by the recent WTO Panel against China, which introduced high quantitative thresh-holds – 500 fakes – for penal measures to kick in'.[51] This points to a particularly controversial aspect of norm-making in the field of international IP law. Those who are not satisfied with the existing, multilateral standards in the TRIPS Agreement try wherever possible to introduce stronger IP protection and enforcement rules either via regional or bilateral free trade agreements (FTAs) or by establishing a new 'gold standard' amongst like-minded countries that can be included in further agreements which countries otherwise opposed to higher IP enforcement standards accept as trade-offs against market access or other concessions. As early as 2006 another leaked text shows that the United States and Japan, the original initiators of ACTA, agreed that 'the *intent of the agreement is to address the IPR problems of third-nations* such as China, Russia, and Brazil, not to negotiate the different

---

47 For example, by requiring contracting parties to provide for both monetary fines and imprisonment; see Article 24.

48 For example, by including specific and comprehensive obligations on seizures, forfeiture and destruction; see Article 25.

49 For example, in relation to trafficking of counterfeit labels or recording motion pictures in movie theatres (unauthorized camcording); see Article 23(2), (3).

50 See ACTA, footnote 9 to Article 23.

51 EU Commission, Provisions of ACTA that provide value compared to existing international standards and in particular WTO/TRIPS, leaked document, November 2010, on file with author.

interests of like-minded countries'.[52] In that sense, ACTA is merely one example of the wider tendency in international IP rule-making in general and in international criminal IP enforcement in particular to continuously expand the protection offered to right holders. Whether or not that is a sensible approach to deal with piracy and counterfeiting as a wider socio-economic phenomenon is a contested issue which cannot be addressed here.[53] One should, however, be wary of the wider implications of a trend where ever more detailed rules are cast into the stone of international binding treaty obligations that are hard to adjust should a changing economic, technological or social environment demand new responses to counterfeiting and piracy.[54] The next section examines another area where increasingly detailed rules on a regional or bilateral level have superseded multilateral provisions to deal with counterfeiting and piracy and where this has caused problems for international trade in legitimate goods.

Stopping global trade in counterfeit and pirated goods

In particular with regard to the high volume of trade in 'counterfeit goods' (here understood as those potentially infringing IP rights), rights holders are ever more concerned about perceived insufficiencies in the enforcement of IP, especially in emerging markets like Brazil, India, China or Russia where technological advances allow widespread imitation and copying. While most of these emerging economies – and in particular China – have moved from imitation to innovation in key areas of technology,[55] the production, domestic distribution and exportation of IP-infringing goods remain an issue. In the fight against global trade in counterfeits, the ability to stop IP-infringing goods at the border – that is, before they leave the country of production, and especially before they reach the domestic market they are destined for – is a crucial tool. The TRIPS Agreement obliges WTO members to provide 'border measures' to tackle international trade in IP-infringing goods under Section 4 of Part III (Articles 51–60) of the agreement. In a nutshell, these provisions set out the minimum standards of IP enforcement at the border which rights holders shall be able to enjoy and

---

52 Cable 06TOKYO4025, PM KOIZUMI'S ADVISOR PROPOSES BILATERAL IPR AGENDA, 2006, at para. 6, available at http://wikileaks.ch/cable/2006/07/06TOKYO4025.html (accessed 12 January 2014).

53 See for example J. Karaganis (ed.), *Media Piracy in Emerging Economies*, Social Science Research Council, 2011, available at http://piracy.americanassembly.org/wp-content/uploads/2011/06/MPEE-PDF-1.0.4.pdf (accessed 20 June 2014). For a law and economics analysis on criminal enforcement see A. Wechsler, 'Criminal Enforcement of Intellectual Property Law – An Economic Approach', in C. Geiger (ed.), *Criminal Enforcement of Intellectual Property: A Handbook of Contemporary Research*, Edward Elgar, Cheltenham (UK), 2012, available at http://ssrn.com/abstract=1775686 (accessed 22 January 2014); and C. Buccafusco and J. Masur, 'Innovation and Incarceration: An Economic Analysis of Criminal Intellectual Property Law', *Southern California Law Review*, 2014, forthcoming; University of Chicago Public Law Working Paper No. 435, available at http://ssrn.com/abstract=2297488 (accessed 22 January 2014).

54 See H. Grosse Ruse-Khan *et al.*, *Principles for Intellectual Property Provisions in Bilateral and Regional Agreements*, available at http://www.ip.mpg.de/en/pub/news/fta_statement.cfm (accessed 13 January 2014).

55 For a review of China's innovative and technological capacity and its response via the IP system see for example A. Wechsler, *Intellectual Property Law in the P.R. China: A Powerful Economic Tool for Innovation and Development*, Max Planck Institute for Intellectual Property, Competition and Tax Law Research Paper No. 09-02, 12 November 2008, available at http://ssrn.com/abstract=1354546 (accessed 24 January 2014).

equally contain minimum safeguards for traders and the owners of goods so that border measures are not abused in a way that creates 'barriers to legitimate trade'.[56]

In terms of their scope, the TRIPS rules on global trade in IP-infringing products are limited in two significant aspects. First, TRIPS obligations on border measures apply only to 'counterfeit trademark' and 'pirated copyright goods'[57] (hence covering only certain forms of copyright and trademark infringements, while not covering infringements of other IP rights such as patents and rights related to copyright at all).[58] Second, Article 51 of TRIPS demands that WTO members implement border measures against the 'importation' of such types of infringing goods, but does not require measures against goods destined for exportation.[59] This second limitation had been another crucial issue in the *China – IPRs* dispute where the United States was also concerned about China's regime of border controls. Since almost all trade in counterfeit goods concerned exports out of China (rather than imports into China),[60] the Panel's conclusion that there is no obligation to apply the requirements of Articles 51 to 60 of TRIPS to goods destined for exportation[61] meant that the limited victory of the United States on legal grounds has been worth nothing in terms of economic and political relevance.

However, similarly to the dynamic norm development seen in the area of criminal sanctions, the international rules on border measures have been strengthened significantly in recent years. As TRIPS seems unable to accommodate the current IP enforcement wish list of rights holders, other forums and venues are pursued to strengthen border measures. Next to 'TRIPS-plus' provisions in various FTAs pursued by the United States and the EU as well as in ACTA,[62] the EU had since 2003 introduced considerably stricter rules aiming to prevent international trade in counterfeits and other forms of IP-infringing goods. The application of these rules, however, proved rather controversial, as the following scenario illustrates. Beginning in late 2008, Dutch authorities in particular have delayed and returned several shipments of generic drugs transiting EU ports en route to destinations in South America and Africa on account of suspected patent infringements.[63] The shipments predominantly originated in India and were all destined for developing countries such as Brazil, Venezuela, Colombia, Peru and Nigeria.[64]

---

56 See the general obligation in Article 41(1) TRIPS which applies to the specific provisions on border measures as well.

57 Footnote 14 to Article 51 TRIPS further defines these terms – see the discussion in the previous section on criminal sanctions.

58 See Correa, *Trade Related Aspects of Intellectual Property Rights*, pp. 439–440.

59 See Article 51 TRIPS, first and third sentences.

60 According to uncontested statistics prepared by China Customs, 99.85 per cent by value of infringing goods at stake in the dispute were destined for exportation. See *China – IPRs*, at 7.228.

61 Ibid.

62 For details see H. Grosse Ruse-Khan, 'China – Intellectual Property Rights: Implications for TRIPS-Plus Border Measures', *Journal of World Intellectual Property*, 2010, vol. 13, no. 5, p. 620.

63 See ICTSD, 'Dutch Seizure of Generic Drugs Sparks Controversy', *Bridges Weekly Trade Digest*, 28 January 2009, vol. 13, no. 3, available at http://ictsd.net/i/news/bridgesweekly/38841 (accessed 22 January 2014).

64 For example, a UNITAID-funded shipment consisting of 49 kilograms of abacavir sulfate tablets was confiscated at Amsterdam Schiphol Airport by Dutch customs authorities under the claim that it contained counterfeit goods. The medicines, manufactured by the Indian company Aurobindo, are used in second-line treatment of HIV/AIDS in Nigeria for a programme implemented by the Clinton Foundation on behalf of UNITAID. UNITAID protested sharply, insisting that the shipment did not involve any counterfeit drugs or any other infringement of IP rights, see T. Jaeger and H. Grosse Ruse-Khan, 'Policing Patents Worldwide? EC Border Measures against Transiting Generic Drugs under EC- and WTO Intellectual Property Regimes', *International Review of Intellectual Property and Competition Law*, 2009, vol. 40, no. 5, p. 502.

The measures taken against generic drugs in transit through the EU are based on the EC Border Measures Regulation (BMR),[65] enacted in 2003, which prescribes EU-wide uniform procedures for customs action against infringing goods. The drugs at issue were protected in the EU, but not in the countries of origin or destination. The EU practice of seizing goods in transit on account of a potential infringement of IP rights that exist merely at the place of stopover, but not at the places of origin or of destination, has come in for heavy criticism.[66] The World Health Organization (WHO) in particular has voiced concerns over the 'potential consequences for the supply of medicines in developing countries',[67] calling for an appropriate balancing of the interests of trade and health so as not to impede the flow of legitimate generic medicines. On 12 May 2010, India and Brazil initiated separate WTO dispute settlement proceedings against the EU and against the Netherlands by requesting consultations over the seizures of generic medicines in transit, arguing that these seizures amount to breaches of TRIPS obligations not to apply IP enforcement procedures in a way that creates barriers to legitimate trade, as well as of rules on the freedom of transit in the General Agreement on Tariffs and Trade (GATT).[68] About a year later, the Indian Government announced that it had reached an 'Understanding on [the] Issue of Seizure of Indian Generic Drugs in Transit' with the EU, whereby the EU undertakes to ensure that these seizures do not reoccur.[69]

Although these particular instances may have not had any statistical relevance in relation to the amount of 'true' counterfeit goods traded globally, they provide anecdotal evidence that the fight against 'counterfeit' goods is not always a straightforward matter. The continuous relevance of territorial rights granted in accordance with national laws makes it inherently difficult to deal with a global problem by means of international rules which nevertheless refer back to national, territorially limited rights for the preliminary question as to whether there is an IP infringement (and hence a counterfeit good) in the first place. It also shows that using the IP-infringing character of goods is not always a good proxy to judge whether these items are also of substandard quality or even dangerous. This in turn may open up new perspectives in the fight against the arguably more severe problems of counterfeits in the sense of dangerous and/or faulty products (such as medicines with no, not enough or the wrong active ingredients) sold especially to consumers in developing countries. The problem of course is that tools to detect such characteristics are much more difficult to develop and apply on a large scale so that IP infringements – rightly or wrongly – are likely to remain the main default mechanism by which the 'counterfeit' or 'pirated' nature of a product will be judged. If that is the case, one should refer to such cases primarily as problems of violating private

65 Council Regulation (EC) No. 1383/2003 of 22 July 2003 concerning customs action against goods suspected of infringing certain intellectual property rights and the measures to be taken against goods found to have infringed such rights (BMR), OJ 2003/L 196/7.

66 See F. Abbott, 'Worst Fears Realised; The Dutch Confiscation of Medicines Bound from India to Brazil', *Bridges Weekly Trade Digest*, March 2009, vol. 13, no.1, available at http://ictsd.net/i/news/bridges/44192 (accessed 22 January 2014).

67 WHO Statement of 13 March 2009, 'Access to medicines', available at http://www.who.int/media-centre/news/statements/2009/access-medicines-20090313/en/index.html (accessed 22 January 2014).

68 Request for Consultations by India, *European Union and a Member State–Seizure of Generic Drugs*, at 1, WT/DS408/1 (19 May 2010); and Request for Consultations by Brazil, European Union and a Member State – Seizure of Generic Drugs in Transit, WT/DS409/1 (19 May 2009).

69 Press information Bureau, Government of India, *India EU Reach an Understanding on Issue of Seizure of Indian Generic Drugs in Transit*, 28 July 2011, available at http://pib.nic.in/newsite/erelease.aspx?relid=73554 (accessed 22 January 2014).

rights – and not mix this with issues of health and safety unless there is a proven, concrete link between the two.

Quo vadis?

This chapter has attempted to map out the history and the current issues of dealing with IP-infringing activities that are regarded as criminal offences and where global trade in infringing goods is intercepted by border measures. It has shown that the dichotomy between national, territorially limited rights and transnational conduct cannot be fully addressed by international harmonization in international IP treaties such as the TRIPS Agreement. The alternative of a global, uniform IP protection system is, however, neither politically feasible nor socio-economically desirable: IP protection, with its primary aim to incentivize new innovations and creations, needs to be tailored to the relevant domestic environment. In other words, one size does not fit all. If that means that some obstacles remain in the fight against 'counterfeiting' and 'piracy' (however these terms are understood), then that is a side effect we have to live with. The current problems on the ground may often be less about the need for more and stricter international rules than about the effective implementation of existing ones in countries which lack sufficient enforcement resources. Here, ACTA, as well as programmes by the World Customs Organization (WCO), Interpol and the WHO try in different ways to build on the existing options for technical assistance and institutional cooperation under TRIPS. A key and not sufficiently resolved question is whether and when it is appropriate to use issues of IP infringement as a proxy for health and safety problems with the goods concerned.

In the future, one can expect further attempts to come up with international rules addressing IP infringements on the internet.[70] As the WTO TRIPS Agreement was concluded in 1994 it does not address this issue with specific rules. Subsequent bilateral and regional agreements, especially those negotiated by the EU and the United States, including ACTA, increasingly establish binding international standards on how IP infringements on the internet have to be countered. One crucial issue in this regard is the question of the liability of internet service providers (ISPs). As gatekeepers, ISPs are in a technologically unique position to take down infringing content, to block access to websites, to monitor the behaviour of their users and even to prevent individuals from accessing the internet. So far, countries such as France and the UK have experimented with the idea of introducing so-called 'three-strike' systems, whereby consecutive IP infringements by users lead to a 'graduated response' that eventually cuts off or significantly slows down the internet connection of a user. These scenarios point to new contestations over expanding the enforcement machinery against IP offences: as the case of the Pirate Bay website in front of the European Court of Human Rights (ECtHR) indicates,[71] users and website operators are increasingly turning to human rights such as freedom of information, the protection of personal data and privacy in order to oppose criminal sanctions for IP infringements. It remains to be seen how courts around the world will apply the stricter new standards of IP enforcement on the internet when balancing the interests of users and right holders.

---

70 See in this context Article 10(1) of the 2001 Council of Europe Convention on Cybercrime, which obliges parties to criminalize the wilful commercial scale use of a computer system *inter alia* to infringe copyright and thereby establishes a similar standard as in Article 61 TRIPS.

71 *Fredrik Neij and Sunde Kolmisoppi v Sweden*, Application no. 40397/12, ECtHR Judgment of 19 February 2013.

These expansionist trends online and the counter-reactions they provoke, especially amongst internet users, show that it is an open question whether criminal law and penal sanctions, and indeed the law as such, are appropriate tools to deal with changes in the way we use data, information and other content. Some right holders in the entertainment or music industry seem to cling to old-fashioned business models and try to uphold them by pushing for harder (criminal) sanctions against an ever expanding range of IP-infringing activities. Some law-makers seem ready to listen to their lobbying. This hardly appears to be a sensible and appropriate response to the technological and societal changes the internet and the digital environment have brought about in how we use, modify and create content. It is also unlikely to provide long-term relief to those who continue to rely on outdated business models. The essential question in the online, digital environment hence is how to rethink especially copyright law in a way that offers incentives for creators without prohibiting those uses – such as hyperlinking, online data searches and content generation and modification – which are at the core of the internet's communication and information functions. If we can introduce fresh approaches here – for example by significantly raising the bar of what content actually does receive copyright protection – then there will be much less infringement to worry about and criminal law will truly remain a measure of last resort.

C Facilitative and organizational crimes

20

Money laundering

William Gilmore

Introduction

Throughout the last quarter of the twentieth century those involved in the criminal justice area became increasingly aware of the challenges posed by the growth of transnational criminal activity. As Lord Griffiths said in 1990: 'Unfortunately in this century crime has ceased to be largely local in origin and effect. Crime is now established on an international scale and the common law must face this new reality.'[1] In response the members of the international community have demonstrated a growing acceptance of the need to intensify cooperation in criminal matters across national boundaries. At one level this has been reflected in a willingness both to strengthen and to extend the mechanisms of inter-state cooperation. This has been very much the case with the evolving treatment of the problem of money laundering.

As the European Union Committee of the House of Lords explained in 2009: 'Money laundering is the process by which the source and ownership of criminally derived wealth and property is changed to confer on it a perception of legitimacy.'[2] The term appears to have first been coined by American law enforcement officials and to have entered popular usage in the mid-1970s. Its emergence in the accepted vocabulary of diplomacy and legislative drafting is even more recent. Nonetheless, the concept is entirely rational in relation to financially motivated criminal conduct. As McClean has remarked:

> From the point of view of the criminal, it is no use making a large profit out of criminal activity if that profit cannot be put to use. . . . Putting the proceeds to use is not as simple as it may sound. Although a proportion of the proceeds of crime will be kept as capital for further criminal ventures, the sophisticated offender will wish to use the rest for other purposes. . . . If this is to be done without running an unacceptable risk of detection, the

---

1 *Liangsiriprasert v US Government* [1990] 2 All ER, p. 866, p. 878.
2 House of Lords, European Union Committee. *Money Laundering and the Financing of Terrorism*, HL Paper 132-I, 2008–09, p. 7.

money which represents the proceeds of the original crime must be 'laundered', put into a state in which it appears to have an entirely respectable provenance.[3]

Not all criminals will resort to elaborate schemes in order to create the perception of legitimacy of the source and ownership of wealth and property. Small-time criminals will rarely do so. Even in more substantial ventures the perception of the need to engage in laundering activity will differ widely from country to country. Here the judgement of those involved as to the effectiveness of the local criminal justice system and the associated level of risk of detection and prosecution will be central considerations.

While considerable variations exist, both between countries and among sectors of criminality, as to the scope, complexity and sophistication of the money-laundering schemes which are in fact resorted to, several factors have contributed to the internationalisation of the process. As Chaikin and Sharman have noted,

> with the rise of both cross-border crime and the growth in legitimate international finance and trade, money laundering has taken on an increasingly international character. To a greater and greater extent, criminals have faced the problem of returning 'dirty money' from foreign markets to their home country. But there are also increased opportunities for obscuring the true source of this money from national law enforcement authorities provided by the complexities of increasingly globalized banking and finance sectors. Those looking to escape the long arm of the law can gain advantage from the relative ease and speed of using the international financial system compared with the difficulties and delays associated with cooperation between different national police and judicial institutions.[4]

Global responses to money laundering: the UN Conventions

The 1988 Drugs Convention

Sustained international interest in money laundering first arose in the 1980s primarily in a drug-trafficking context. At that time the two central pillars of the global effort to address the complex issue of drug abuse were the 1961 UN Single Convention on Narcotic Drugs,[5] as amended by a 1972 protocol,[6] and the 1971 UN Convention on Psychotropic Substances.[7] Both had attracted substantial levels of endorsement by states. Although they were effective against drugs crime, it gradually became apparent to policy makers that they were not adequate to the task of addressing a range of complex issues raised by modern international drug trafficking.

The evolving policy discussion focused in part on the vast profits generated by drug trafficking. The resulting economic power wielded by criminal elements was considered to pose

---

3 J.D. McClean, *International Cooperation in Civil and Criminal Matters*, Oxford: Oxford University Press, 2002, p. 261.
4 D. Chaikin and J.C. Sharman, *Corruption and Money Laundering: A Symbiotic Relationship*, New York: Palgrave MacMillan, 2009, p. 15.
5 New York, 30 March 1961, 520 UNTS 151; in force 13 December 1964.
6 Protocol Amending the Single Convention on Narcotic Drugs, 1961, Geneva, 25 March 1972, 976 UNTS 3; in force 8 August 1975.
7 Vienna, 21 February 1971, 1019 UNTS 175; in force 16 August 1976.

a threat to, *inter alia*, good governance and the rule of law. Existing law enforcement strategies, both international and domestic, had failed to focus to any significant degree on this aspect of the trafficking phenomenon. As Nadelmann pointed out in an influential article in 1986, a number of rationales supported the view that 'going after the money' was a particularly appropriate law enforcement strategy:

> The most basic of these is that insofar as criminals . . . act as they do for the money, the best deterrent and punishment is to confiscate their incentive. A second rationale is that, while the higher level and more powerful criminals rarely come into contact with the illicit goods, such as drugs, from which they derive their profits, they do come into contact with the proceeds from the sale of those goods. That contact often provides a 'paper trail' or other evidence, which constitutes the only connection with a violation of the law.[8]

The need to integrate a policy of 'financial devastation' into efforts to combat the illegal drugs trade found reflection in the Comprehensive Multidisciplinary Outline of Future Activities in Drug Abuse Control adopted by the 1987 UN Conference on Drug Abuse and Illicit Trafficking.[9] This view also found a receptive audience at the UN Conference for the Adoption of a Convention against Illicit Traffic in Narcotic Drugs and Psychotropic Substances held in Vienna from 25 November to 20 December 1988. This important gathering, attended by representatives from 106 countries, succeeded in adopting, by consensus, a detailed Convention against Illicit Traffic in Narcotic Drugs and Psychotropic Substances (1988 Convention) consisting of 34 articles and one annex.[10] In force in 1990, as of January 2014 it had attracted some 188 parties; a remarkable geographical spread of participation which embraces the major producer, transit and consumer countries. As will be seen at a later stage, this instrument has had a major influence on subsequent initiatives of global reach.

The importance of the desire to target the financial dimension of the illicit drugs trade is underlined in paragraphs five and six of the preamble of the 1988 Convention.[11] The substantive treatment of money laundering and confiscation are, in turn, pivotal to the realisation of that goal.

Central to the attempt to provide an effective regime to counter the illicit traffic in drugs in the 1988 Convention was the need to define with care the specific activities that notion should encompass. The outcome of the deliberations at Vienna, Article 3(1),[12] is a detailed provision that serves as the cornerstone of the convention because the major obligations of cooperation articulated elsewhere are tied directly to it. By way of contrast, personal use offences are contained in Article 3(2) and fall outside that system of obligations.

Article 3(1)(a) imposes a strict obligation for each participating country to criminalise a fairly comprehensive list of activities concerning drug trafficking which have a major

---

8 E. Nadelmann, 'Unlaundering Dirty Money Abroad', *Inter-American Law Review*, 1986, vol. 18, p. 33, p. 34.
9 See *Report of the International Conference on Drug Abuse and Illicit Trafficking, Vienna, 17–26 June 1987*, New York, United Nations, 1987, pp. 60–63.
10 Vienna, 20 December 1988, 1582 UNTS 95; in force 11 November 1990.
11 See *Commentary on the United Nations Convention Against Illicit Traffic in Narcotic Drugs and Psychotropic Substances 1988*, New York: United Nations, 1998, pp. 17–18.
12 See ibid., pp. 50–78

international impact, including the financing of trafficking operations. The latter was believed to be a particularly important component of the effort to reach those involved at the highest levels of the drugs trade.[13] Subparagraph (b) then requires that drug-related money laundering be established as a criminal offence. The actual term was not (because of its then relative novelty and for translation reasons) used in the text. Rather the concept was expressed in these words:

> (i) the conversion or transfer of property, knowing that such property is derived from any offence or offences established in accordance with subparagraph (a) of this paragraph, or from an act of participation in such offence or offences, for the purpose of concealing or disguising the illicit origin of the property or of assisting any person who is involved in the commission of such an offence or offences to evade the legal consequences of his actions; (ii) the concealment or disguise of the true nature, source, location, disposition, movement, rights with respect to, or ownership of property, knowing that such property is derived from an offence or offences established in accordance with subparagraph (a) of this paragraph or from an act of participation in such an offence or offences.

Furthermore, the same article requires each party, to the extent that it is not contrary to its constitutional principles and the basic concepts of its legal system, to criminalise 'the acquisition, possession or use of property, knowing, at the time of receipt' that it was derived from drug trafficking[14] as well as conspiracy, aiding and abetting, and facilitating the commission of drug-trafficking offences including money laundering.[15] It is of importance to note that the term 'property' is broadly defined in Article 1(q). It means 'assets of every kind, whether corporeal or incorporeal, moveable or immoveable, tangible or intangible, and legal documents or instruments evidencing title to or an interest in such assets'. The issue of the appropriate burden of proof in relation to all such offences is addressed in Article 3(3), which provides that knowledge, intent or purpose 'may be inferred from objective factual circumstances'. Many of the remaining provisions of this complex article seek to ensure that money laundering and other trafficking offences are treated with appropriate seriousness by the judiciary and the prosecutorial authorities.

The significance of the approach adopted in Article 3 of the 1988 Convention to drug-related money laundering for the future of international cooperation should not be underestimated. By requiring its criminalisation and treating it as a serious offence in paragraph 1, the drafters have sought to ensure that cooperation in respect of confiscation, mutual legal assistance and extradition will be forthcoming. For example, it substantially reduces the potential for dual criminality problems to arise in this context. A further indication of the sensitivity of the drafters of this convention to the transnational dimension of the problem is to be seen in Article 3(10), which seeks to restrict the possibility that money launderers and others involved in the drugs trade could take advantage of two traditional restrictions on international cooperation: namely, the political offence and fiscal offence exceptions. The provision in question restricts, but does not entirely eliminate, the possibility of invoking such grounds.

---

13 See ibid., pp. 58–59.
14 1988 Convention, Article 3(1)(c)(i).
15 1988 Convention, Article 3(1)(c)(iv).

A second major feature of the approach adopted in the drafting relates to the subject of the confiscation of the proceeds derived from, and the instrumentalities used in, drug trafficking. This is treated in detail in Article 5 of the 1988 Convention, which addresses both the measures to be taken at the national level and the necessary mechanisms to give effect to international cooperation in this vital area.

The first three paragraphs of Article 5 treat the issue of confiscation at the level of domestic law and practice. They impose a series of broad obligations which are free from any limitations or safeguard clauses. Paragraph 1 reads:

> 1. Each Party shall adopt such measures as may be necessary to enable confiscation of: (a) Proceeds derived from offences established in accordance with article 3, paragraph 1, or property the value of which corresponds to that of such proceeds; (b) Narcotic drugs and psychotropic substances, materials and equipment or other instrumentalities used in or intended for use in any manner in offences established in accordance with article 3, paragraph 1.[16]

While framed in mandatory terms, this paragraph was deliberately worded so as to leave to each state a wide measure of discretion as how best to achieve the desired result. This emphasis on flexibility also permitted due account to be taken of the differing approaches to confiscation which had evolved in domestic legislation. In order to ensure the effectiveness of the confiscation procedure, paragraph 2 makes provision for necessary preliminary steps to be taken to 'identify, trace, and freeze or seize proceeds, property, instrumentalities or any other thing referred to in paragraph 1 . . .'.

The Vienna Conference also acted to ensure that the concept of bank secrecy did not needlessly hinder the search for and the eventual confiscation of the assets derived from this form of criminal activity. Article 5(3) requires that each State Party empower its courts or other relevant authorities to order that bank, financial or commercial records be made available. Most importantly it is specifically provided that 'A Party shall not decline to act under the provisions of this paragraph on the ground of bank secrecy'. The inclusion of this affirmative obligation has been widely characterised as a major breakthrough.[17]

While there is no doubt that the bank secrecy provision in Article 5(3) is of considerable significance to the effectiveness of confiscation, it has been argued that it does not go far enough. There has been a growing perception that the removal of such secrecy provides only an illusory benefit where additional layers of protection, such as anonymous trusts and shell companies, are available. In this context particular concern has been expressed about the range of services provided in some offshore financial centres.[18]

It was also accepted by the negotiators that action in the confiscation sphere when undertaken on a unilateral basis at the level of domestic law was unlikely to be fully effective in combating an activity, such as drug trafficking, which has conspicuous transnational features. As McClean pointed out: 'The facility with which assets, particularly in the form of financial credits of some sort, can be passed across national boundaries means that an order enforceable

---

16 The term 'proceeds' is afforded a broad definition in Article 1(p).
17 D.W. Sproule and P. Saint-Denis, 'The UN Drug Trafficking Convention: An Ambitious Step', *Canadian Yearbook of International Law*, 1989, p. 263, pp. 281–282.
18 See J.A. Blum, M. Levi, R.T. Naylor and P. Williams, *Report on Financial Havens, Banking Secrecy and Money Laundering*, New York: UN Office for Drug Control and Crime Prevention, 1998.

only in the country of origin may be of limited value.'[19] The need for effective international cooperation in this context was therefore viewed as being critical. It too is treated in Article 5 of the 1988 Convention.

A mandatory framework is provided in Article 5(4)(a), which, none the less, recognises the need for a substantial element of flexibility for national legislatures. Provision is also made to ensure that a requested party shall take effective provisional measures, including tracing and freezing proceeds and property, 'for the purpose of eventual confiscation to be ordered either by the requesting Party or, pursuant to a request under subparagraph (a) of this paragraph, by the requested Party'.[20]

Two further points deserve emphasis. First, although these actions take place according to the domestic laws and procedures of the requested state, the requested state's legal system must permit such assistance to be granted. Second, no further international action is required to perfect this obligation, although States Parties are encouraged to enter into detailed bilateral and multilateral agreements in order to make their confiscation arrangements as effective as possible. In the absence of such agreements, the parties to the 1988 Convention are obliged to regard it as sufficient.

Article 5 of the 1988 Convention goes on to treat the important issue of the final disposition of the proceeds and property which are eventually confiscated. The basic rule is that such matters are to be determined in accordance with the domestic law of the state which gives effect to the confiscation. In so far as confiscations resulting from international cooperation are concerned, paragraph 5(b) of Article 5 invites parties to give special consideration to contributing such funds to inter-governmental bodies specialising in efforts to counter trafficking or drug abuse or to concluding agreements for sharing the same with other states. 'Since 1988, practice has tended to focus on the latter.'[21]

Another provision particularly worthy of note in the context of money laundering is that contained in Article 5(6). This has as its focus the need to ensure that proceeds derived from and instrumentalities used in illegal trafficking could not escape forfeiture simply because their form had been changed or they had been commingled with other property. Here again the convention uses mandatory language.[22] Given the robust and intrusive nature of Article 5 as a whole, it was felt necessary to provide that its provisions 'shall not be construed as prejudicing the rights of bona fide third parties'.[23]

From the above, and necessarily partial, overview of this highly complex article it is easy to see why it attracted great praise from commentators. In the words of Sproule and Saint-Denis:

> The provisions now contained in this article are clear, specific, and in most cases, mandatory. They can be properly viewed as a major breakthrough in attacking the benefits derived from drug trafficking activities and are a forceful endorsement of the notion that attacking the profit motive is essential if the struggle against drug trafficking is to be effective.[24]

---

19 J.D. McClean, 'Seizing the Proceeds of Crime: The State of the Art', *International and Comparative Law Quarterly*, 1989, p. 334, p. 339.
20 Article 5(4)(b).
21 *Commentary on the United Nations Convention Against Illicit Traffic in Narcotic Drugs and Psychotropic Substances 1988*, p. 150.
22 Sproule and Saint-Denis, 'The UN Drug Trafficking Convention', p. 284.
23 1988 Convention, Article 5(8).
24 Sproule and Saint-Denis, 'The UN Drug Trafficking Convention', p. 281.

The precedents established by the 1988 UN Convention in the fields of money laundering and confiscation are supported by a range of other important mechanisms designed to promote international cooperation. Of these perhaps the most significant is its Article 7 dealing with the provision of mutual legal assistance in investigations, prosecutions and judicial proceedings relating to money laundering and other serious convention offences.

In contrast with confiscation, the drafters of the 1988 text were able to build upon an established and developing international practice in this area in relation to which the Council of Europe had played a major role. The Convention envisages the provision of assistance in a number of highly practical areas. A non-exhaustive list includes: the taking of evidence or statements; effecting service of judicial documents; executing searches and seizures; examining objects and sites; providing information and evidentiary items; providing relevant documents and records including bank, financial, corporate or business records; and identifying or tracing proceeds and instrumentalities for evidentiary purposes.

In the course of deliberations a number of delegations pressed for the specific inclusion of a statement to the effect that requests for assistance could not be refused on the ground of bank secrecy. Such concerns find reflection in the wording of Article 7(5) of the final text. The authorised grounds for the refusal of a request are set out in such a way as to ensure the protection of the essential interests of the requested state.

By embracing in such detail the concept of mutual legal assistance, the 1988 UN Convention made a major contribution towards increasing its availability in areas of the world, and within legal traditions, where it was, at the time, underdeveloped or unknown. In addition, it provided a critical level of support for those charged with prosecuting money-laundering offences containing a substantial international dimension.[25]

Subsequent UN Conventions

In the period since its conclusion the approach of the 1988 UN Convention to the criminalisation of money laundering and the provision of related international cooperation has had a major influence on other major initiatives in this sphere. By way of illustration, in drafting the influential 1990 Council of Europe Convention on Laundering, Search, Seizure and Confiscation of the Proceeds of Crime[26] those charged with the negotiations utilised the 1988 UN Convention's text as a primary point of reference.[27] Similarly, the 1988 UN Convention provided a precedent that was central to the early work of the Financial Action Task Force (FATF), aspects of the activities of which are outlined in a later section of this chapter. It will suffice for present purposes to recall that the FATF was created at the behest of the G7 (as it then was) in 1989. It is best known for its comprehensive package of countermeasures on money laundering and, since 2001, the financing of terrorism.[28] The first iteration of these

---

25 See, G. Kriz, 'International Cooperation to Combat Money Laundering: The Nature and Role of the Mutual Legal Assistance Treaties', *Commonwealth Law Bulletin*, 1992, p. 723.

26 8 November 1990, ETS No 141; in force 1 September 1993. For an overview of this treaty and its successor, the Convention on Laundering, Search, Seizure and Confiscation of the Proceeds from Crime and on the Financing of Terrorism (Warsaw Convention), 16 May 2005, CETS 198; in force 1 May 2008, see W.C. Gilmore, *Dirty Money: The Evolution of International Measures to Counter Money Laundering and the Financing of Terrorism*, Strasbourg: Council of Europe Publishing, 4th edn, 2011, pp. 175–195.

27 See W.C. Gilmore (ed.), *International Efforts to Combat Money Laundering*, Cambridge: Grotius Publications, 1992, p. 197.

28 See Gilmore, *Dirty Money*, chapters IV–VI.

standards took the form of 40 recommendations issued in 1990. These focused on three central areas: i) improvements to national legal systems, ii) the enhancement of the role of the financial system in the prevention of money laundering; and iii) the strengthening of international cooperation. While the approach adopted was more ambitious in scope than the 1998 UN Convention, the measures which it contained were regarded as critical. Consequently the very first of the 1990 FATF Recommendations was that 'Each country should, without further delay, take steps to fully implement the Vienna Convention [1988 Convention] and proceed to ratify it'. Particularly in the area of securing improvements to national criminal justice systems the FATF Recommendations explicitly called for consistency with the approach taken in the UN text.[29]

More than a decade later the authors of the UN Convention against Transnational Organized Crime (UNTOC) built on the 1988 Convention's precedent in regard to money laundering. It fully embraced the strategy of seeking to undermine and disrupt organised crime groups by focusing on their finances. The most interesting innovation in this context was the decision to include detailed treatment of measures to prevent money laundering, something that was not included in the 1988 Convention. The negotiations on this issue were somewhat controversial and, as a consequence, the resulting text represents something of a compromise. In particular, the generality and open-textured nature of the wording eventually adopted has attracted some adverse comment. That said, in certain key areas mandatory terminology is used. The approach adopted in this respect is well illustrated in Article 7(1)(a), which reads:

> 1. Each State Party: (a) Shall institute a comprehensive domestic regulatory and supervisory regime for banks and non-bank financial institutions and, where appropriate, other bodies particularly susceptible to money-laundering, within its competence, in order to deter and detect all forms of money-laundering, which regime shall emphasise requirements for customer identification, record-keeping and the reporting of suspicious transactions.

Article 7(3) then calls upon participating countries 'to use as a guideline' relevant international anti-money-laundering initiatives in establishing their domestic regulatory and supervisory regimes. While the best-known and most firmly established such guidance is contained in the 40 FATF Recommendations, there are no specific references to those standards in the text. However, the interpretative notes for the official record make it clear that the terminology used was 'understood in particular' to refer to the FATF Recommendations.

The issue of the criminalisation of money laundering is treated in Article 6. As with other criminal justice and international criminal cooperation issues, the influence of the 1988 instrument, as well as of the 1990 Council of Europe Convention and the FATF Recommendations, is clearly evident. Paragraph 1 of Article 6 provides the definition of the laundering of the proceeds of crime for the purposes of criminalisation. In so doing it draws heavily on the 1988 Convention's precedent.[30] Importantly, however, paragraph 2 has the effect of extending the obligation to criminalise this form of conduct well beyond the area of drug trafficking. It is worded thus:

---

29 See e.g. Recommendations 4, 6 and 8 reproduced in Gilmore, *International Efforts*, at pp. 15–16.
30 See J.D. McClean, *Transnational Organized Crime: A Commentary on the UN Convention and its Protocols*, Oxford: Oxford University Press, 2007, pp. 76–83.

2. For purposes of implementing or applying paragraph 1 of this article: (a) Each State Party shall seek to apply paragraph 1 of this article to the widest range of predicate offences; (b) Each State Party shall include as predicate offences all serious crime as defined in article 2 of this Convention and the offences established in accordance with article, 5, 8 and 23 of this Convention [participation in an organized criminal group; corruption; obstruction of justice]. In the case of States Parties whose legislation sets out a list of specific predicate offences, they shall, at a minimum, include in such list a comprehensive range of offences associated with organized criminal groups.

Among the other innovations contained in Article 6 as compared to the 1988 text are the explicit treatment afforded to extraterritorial predicate offences[31] and the criminalisation of 'self' or 'own funds' laundering.[32]

Two further features of the 2000 Convention are deserving of attention for present purposes. The first relates to the issue of corporate liability, a matter afforded some prominence by the FATF in its anti-money-laundering programme since 1990[33] but left untreated in 1988. Article 10 recognises the diversity of approaches which exist in this area within differing legal traditions. It does so by acknowledging that while liability of legal persons for participation in relevant offences (including money laundering) must be provided for in national legal systems, such liability 'may be criminal, civil or administrative'. However, the decision not to require common recourse to the concept of corporate criminal liability does have implications for the provision of international cooperation. This is particularly so in instances in which the state requesting assistance has given effect to criminal liability and the requested jurisdiction has used a civil or administrative option. The UNTOC seeks to minimise this potential barrier to cooperation. For instance, Article 18(2) provides that:

[M]utual legal assistance shall be afforded to the fullest extent possible . . . with respect to investigations, prosecutions and judicial proceedings in relation to the offences for which a legal person may be held liable in accordance with article 10 of this Convention in the requesting State Party.

While it thus emphasises the desirability of the provision of mutual assistance in such circumstances, it does not require it; a point highlighted in Article 18(9), which permits mutual assistance to be declined 'on the ground of absence of dual criminality'.

The second issue is that of the ultimate disposal of confiscated criminal proceeds. The 1988 Convention embraced the principle that the disposition of confiscated proceeds and property is to be determined by the jurisdiction in which such confiscation finally takes place, and only encouraged asset sharing. The extension of money-laundering and confiscation regimes to an ever broader range of predicate offences called into question the adequacy of this principle in international cases. Such concerns manifested themselves in the course of the elaboration of the UNTOC. The outcome of those negotiations, reflected in Article 14, saw

---

31 Article 6(2)(c).
32 Article 6(2)(e). See e.g. G. Stessens, *Money Laundering: A New International Law Enforcement Model*, Cambridge: Cambridge University Press, 2000, pp. 121–122.
33 See FATF Recommendation 7 (1990), Recommendation 6 of the 1996 revised text, and Recommendation 2 of the 2003 revised Task Force standards. See further N. Boister, *An Introduction to Transnational Criminal Law*, Oxford: Oxford University Press, 2012, p. 109.

some progress recorded in the direction of facilitating the return of property. Although the traditional basic rule is repeated in the first paragraph of the article, it is supplemented by the following provision:

> 2. When acting on the request made by another State Party in accordance with article 13 of this Convention, State Parties shall, to the extent permitted by domestic law and if so requested, give priority consideration to returning the confiscated proceeds of crime or property to the requesting State Party so that it can give compensation to the victims of the crime or return such proceeds of crime or property to their legitimate owners.

Asset sharing in such international cases remains, as with the 1988 Convention, optional in nature.

Significantly, the same issue was to become one of the central concerns when, shortly thereafter, the international community turned its attention to the negotiation of a global convention against corruption; a task completed when the UN Convention against Corruption (UNCAC)[34] was adopted and opened for signature in December 2003. It entered into force two years later and by November 2013 had some 170 parties.

The treatment of plundered state assets had been a source of concern for some time; this treatment owed much to highly publicised examples of the looting of national wealth by several rulers of developing countries. From an early stage it was apparent that securing progress on this matter would be both symbolically and substantively important for the process as a whole. As a result Chapter V of the UNCAC was devoted to the asset recovery issue; one described in the text as constituting a 'fundamental principle'.[35] Article 57 of the UNCAC, entitled 'Return and disposal of assets', is of special interest. While it commences with a restatement of the orthodox rule, participating states are required to take such steps as may be necessary to permit the return of confiscated property when requested so to do by another State Party, 'taking into account the rights of bona fide third parties'.[36] The exercise of this authority is governed by paragraph 3, which affords particularly favourable treatment to the return of embezzled public funds.

It was to be expected that a measure seeking to suppress corrupt practices would embrace the strategic focus on the profit motive. A full range of relevant provisions designed to strengthen domestic criminal justice systems and to promote international cooperation have found inclusion in the UNCAC. Some, such as Article 23 on the laundering of the proceeds of crime, draw heavily on the 1988 Convention and UNTOC. Others, such as Article 24 on the concealment or retention of tainted property, have a more innovative quality.

However, what distinguishes the UNCAC from earlier multilateral treaty initiatives at the global level is the extent to which it embraces a strategy to prevent acts of corruption in both the public and private sectors. That said, Article 14 on measures to prevent money laundering owes much to the approach adopted in Article 7 of the UNTOC. However, the two are not identical. In this regard, it should be noted that the negotiators of the 2003 Convention were in a position to take account of both the Special Recommendations of the FATF on the financing of terrorism, which had been formulated in October 2001, and the amendments to the 40 FATF Recommendations which were finalised in June 2003.

---

34 New York, 31 October 2003, 2349 UNTS 41, in force 14 December 2005.
35 Article 51.
36 Article 57(2).

For instance, the 2003 FATF amendments had an obvious impact on the formulation of Article 52 on the prevention and detection of transfers of proceeds of crime – a provision with no counterpart in the UNTOC. This has as its primary purpose the imposition on financial institutions of obligations of enhanced scrutiny in relation to the affairs 'of individuals who are, or have been, entrusted with prominent public functions and their family members and close associates'. The treatment of shell banks and correspondent banking relationships in Article 52(5) also echoes distinct concerns embodied in that amended version of the 40 FATF Recommendations.

No summary of global measures embracing the philosophy of financial devastation would be complete without some mention of the 1999 UN International Convention for the Suppression of the Financing of Terrorism.[37] Given the lengthy engagement of the United Nations with terrorist-related issues and the range of relevant multilateral instruments which had been concluded under its auspices, it is perhaps curious that the issue of terrorist finances had been largely ignored. However, in December 1998, the UN General Assembly decided in Resolution 53/108 that an ad hoc committee should elaborate a draft international convention for the suppression of terrorist financing to supplement related existing international instruments, and after surprisingly swift negotiations the final text was adopted in December 1999 and opened for signature the following month. Its principal focus is on activities which possess a transnational dimension. It entered into force in April 2002. It too has been widely ratified.

One of the keys to success was agreement on the critical issue of the definition of terrorism for the purposes of the convention.[38] In this regard the text of Article 2(1) is of particular importance. It is worded as follows:

> 1. Any person commits an offence within the meaning of this Convention if that person by any means, directly or indirectly, unlawfully and wilfully, provides or collects funds with the intention that they should be used or in the knowledge that they are to be used, in full or in part, in order to carry out: (a) An act which constitutes an offence within the scope of and as defined in one of the treaties listed in the annex; or (b) Any other act intended to cause death or serious bodily injury to a civilian, or to any other person not taking an active part in the hostilities in a situation of armed conflict, when the purpose of such act, by its nature or context, is to intimidate a population, or to compel a government or an international organisation to do or to abstain from doing any act.

The obligation for participating states to criminalise the provision or collection of funds[39] is thus triggered in two major ways. The obligation is first triggered by reference to acts specifically prohibited in one of the pre-existing counter-terrorism conventions of global reach. These are listed in the annex to the 1999 Convention and range from the unlawful seizure of aircraft to terrorist bombing. Second, and more innovatively, the prohibition is engaged by reference to what is, in effect, a free-standing mini-definition of terrorism. Contained in Article 2(1)(b), this is broad in scope.[40] The prohibition contained in Article 2

---

37 New York, 9 December, 1999, 2178 UNTS 197, in force 10 April 2002.
38 See A. Aust, 'Counter-Terrorism: A New Approach', *Max Planck UN Yearbook*, 2001, vol. 1, pp. 4–17.
39 A term broadly defined in Article 1(1) of the Suppression of the Financing of Terrorism Convention.
40 See *International Convention for the Suppression of the Financing of Terrorism: Message from the President of the United States*, 106th Congress, 2nd Session, Senate, Treaty Doc. 106–49, VII.

extends, among other things, to attempts to commit such offences as well as to their organisation. Importantly, however, 'for an act to constitute an offence set forth in paragraph 1, it shall not be necessary that the funds were actually used to carry out an offence referred to in paragraph 1, sub-paragraphs (a) or (b).'[41]

Several other provisions seek to ensure that adequate powers exist in national legal systems to address the issue of the funding of international terrorism. Of particular significance for present purposes is the requirement, contained in Article 5, to introduce (if necessary) criminal, civil or administrative liability for legal persons and, in Article 8, to take appropriate measures for the tracing, freezing and confiscation 'of any funds used or allocated for the purpose of committing the offences set forth in article 2 as well as the proceeds derived from such offences.' Curiously, however, there is no specific requirement to criminalise the laundering of such funds; a loophole subsequently closed, in effect, by the 2001 FATF Special Recommendations on the financing of terrorism.[42]

These and other obligations to enhance domestic legal powers are, as is common in UN treaty practice, supplemented by a range of provisions designed to facilitate international cooperation in the investigation and prosecution of relevant offences. Significantly, domestic measures of prevention and associated international cooperation are also set out in some detail. Of particular relevance for present purposes is that Article 18(1)(b) requires states to take steps, including:

> Measures requiring financial institutions and other professions involved in financial transactions to use the most efficient measures available for the identification of their usual or occasional customers, as well as customers in whose interest accounts are opened, and to pay special attention to unusual or suspicious transactions and report transactions suspected of stemming from a criminal activity.

The text then sets out several illustrations of steps to be considered in this context, the content of which has been clearly influenced by the package of FATF countermeasures (although that source, as with the UNTOC, Article 7, and the UNCAC, Articles 23 and 52, is not specifically acknowledged).

In these and other ways, the 1999 UN Convention provides, for the first time, an agreed global framework within which the international community can collaborate more effectively in seeking to 'tackle the difficult problem of financial "godfathers", without whom most terrorist crimes would not be possible'.[43]

Global responses to money laundering: the FATF

As previously noted, the Financial Action Task Force (FATF) was created on the initiative of the Paris summit of the G7 in 1989. It is, primarily, a standard-setting and policy-making body; though one of limited membership. It is located in but is not formally part of the Paris-based Organisation for Economic Cooperation and Development (OECD). Initially the FATF had a single-issue agenda; namely, to set standards and promote implementation of

---

41 Article 2(3) of the Suppression of the Financing of Terrorism Convention.
42 Special Recommendation II was worded thus: 'Each country should criminalise the financing of terrorism, terrorist acts and terrorist organisations. Countries should ensure that such offences are designated as money laundering predicate offences.'
43 Aust, 'Counter-Terrorism', p. 4.

legal, regulatory and operational measures to combat the laundering of the proceeds of crime. To this end it formulated, in 1990, a package of 40 recommendations.

Since its inception the FATF has expanded its membership, deepened its mandate and periodically revisited and amended its standards. It now consists of 34 OECD and strategically important countries plus two regional bodies.[44] It has also, over time, promoted the establishment of FATF-style regional bodies (FSRBs) the members of which are committed to the effective implementation of its recommendations. There are currently eight such regional bodies, of which the best known and most firmly established are those for the Caribbean (CFATF) and Europe (MONEYVAL). Largely as a consequence, in excess of 180 jurisdictions around the world have endorsed the FATF standards.[45]

As noted, the FATF has periodically revised and updated its standards in the light of experience. This it did in 1996 and again, but in more significant fashion, in 2003. Following the 9/11 attacks against the United States, the issue of the financing of terrorism was added to its mandate and nine specific recommendations were formulated to address this important issue. The recent 2012 revisions contain a range of changes of both form and substance.[46] They include, for the first time, treatment of the financing of the proliferation of weapons of mass destruction. In particular, a new Recommendation[47] is aimed at ensuring consistent and effective implementation of targeted financial sanctions in this sphere when these are mandated by the UN Security Council.

Through this process of periodic revision of its 'soft law' standards the FATF has remained at the cutting edge of policy making in the areas of concern reflected in its mandate.[48] This is well illustrated by the progressive expansion of the expectations in relation to the scope of the criminalisation of money laundering. It will be recalled that in 1990 Recommendation 4 called for the criminalisation of 'drug money laundering as set forth in the Vienna Convention', while Recommendation 5 encouraged countries to

> [c]onsider extending the offense of drug money laundering to any other crimes for which there is a link to narcotics; an alternative approach is to criminalize money laundering based on all serious offenses, and/or on all offenses that generate a significant amount of proceeds, or on certain serious offenses.

In each of the subsequent revision exercises the expectations of the FATF in this regard have been deepened. In the 2012 version this core issue is addressed in Recommendation 3, the associated Interpretive Note and relevant definitions contained in the Glossary. The text of Recommendation 3 is brief. It reads in full as follows:

> Countries should criminalize money laundering on the basis of the Vienna Convention and the Palermo Convention. Countries should apply the crime of money laundering to all serious offences, with a view to including the widest range of predicate offences.

---

44 The European Commission and the Gulf Cooperation Council.
45 See *Financial Action Task Force: Annual Report 2012–2013*, Paris: FATF, 2013, p. 10.
46 The nine Special Recommendations on terrorist financing have now been fully integrated into the FATF 40. See *International Standards on Combating Money Laundering and the Financing of Terrorism and Proliferation: The FATF Recommendations*, Paris: FATF, 2012, available at www.fatf-gafi.org (accessed 12 April 2014).
47 Recommendation 7.
48 See 'Financial Action Task Force Mandate (2012–2020), 20 April 2012, Washington, D.C.,' available at www.fatf-gafi.org (accessed 12 April 24014).

Importantly, by virtue of the Glossary 'the word *should* has the same meaning as *must.*'

Further detail is contained in the Interpretative Note to Recommendation 3. This acknowledges, for example, that the goal of extending money laundering to the widest range of predicate offences can be achieved in a number of different ways: on an all-crimes basis, through recourse to a 'threshold' of punishment system, by using a 'list' approach, or indeed through a combination of such devices. However, it is further stipulated that: 'Whichever approach is adopted, each country should, at a minimum, include a range of offences within each of the designated categories of offences.' These designated categories, some 21 in number, are listed in the Glossary. They range from 'insider dealing and market manipulation' to 'terrorism, including terrorist financing'. By virtue of the 2012 amendments the list now includes 'tax crimes (related to direct taxes and indirect taxes)'.

In addition to their standard-setting work, the FATF and the FSRBs have also pioneered an innovative and intrusive process known as mutual evaluation through which they monitor, on a country-specific basis, both formal compliance with and (increasingly) the effective implementation of the recommendations.[49] The FATF has completed three rounds of evaluation to date. Compliance by individual countries with the revised recommendations of February 2012 will be monitored through a new cycle of country-specific mutual evaluations. These will be conducted, according to an agreed methodology, by the FATF, the FSRBs, and on occasion by the IMF and the World Bank.

Significant changes have also been agreed in this area and are embodied in the new methodology of February 2013.[50] Under the new procedures two, inter-linked, evaluation reports will be produced for each jurisdiction subject to the process. First, there will be a technical compliance assessment. This will address formal compliance with the specific requirements of each recommendation. As in the past a rating will be allocated to each recommendation. These will range from 'compliant' ('there are no shortcomings') through to 'non-compliant' (there are 'major shortcomings'). Within the Task Force it is anticipated that the compliance assessment will be, in effect, a desk-based review which will be undertaken in advance of an on-site visit by the evaluation team.

The second element of the new process is an effectiveness assessment. This is the most significant innovation introduced for the fourth round of evaluations and will be the major focus of the evaluation team during its in-country visit. As has been noted elsewhere:

> Assessing effectiveness is based on a fundamentally different approach to assessing technical compliance with the Recommendations. It does not involve checking whether specific requirements are met, or that all elements of a given Recommendation are in place. Instead, it requires a judgment as to whether, or to what extent, defined outcomes are being achieved, i.e., whether the key objectives of an AML/CFT system . . . are being effectively met in practice.[51]

In this process the attention of the evaluation team is directed to 11 so-called immediate outcomes, each of which is said to represent one of the key goals which an effective

---

49 See, M. Levi and W. Gilmore, 'Terrorist Finance, Money Laundering and the Rise and Rise of Mutual Evaluation: A New Paradigm for Crime Control?', in M. Pieth (ed.), *Financing Terrorism*, Dordrecht: Kluwer Academic Publishers, 2002, pp. 87–114.

50 See Methodology for Assessing Compliance with the FATF Recommendations and the Effectiveness of AML/CFT Systems, Paris, FATF, 2013. Available at www.fatf-gafi.org (accessed 12 April 24014).

51 Ibid., p. 14.

anti-money-laundering system should achieve. To assist the evaluators, the new common methodology sets out, for each of the 11 immediate outcomes, the following: 1) the main relevant features; 2) the core issues to be considered; 3) examples of the types and sources of information that could support the conclusions on core issues; and 4) examples of the specific factors that could support the conclusions on core issues. Importantly in the present context, immediate outcome 7 is concerned with the investigation and prosecution of money-laundering offences while immediate outcome 8 has as its focus the confiscation of proceeds and instrumentalities.

This is a highly intrusive process which places a heavy burden on both the assessors and the evaluated country. The methodology explicitly places the onus on the country concerned to demonstrate the effectiveness of its system. In its words: 'if the evidence is not made available, assessors can only conclude that the system is not effective.'[52] As with the technical assessment, ratings are also allocated in this context, i.e. a methodology for each of the 11 immediate outcomes. They are:

a) 'High level of effectiveness' (the immediate outcome is achieved to a very large extent. Minor improvements needed);
b) 'Substantial level of effectiveness' (the immediate outcome is achieved to a large extent. Moderate improvements needed);
c) 'Moderate level of effectiveness' (the immediate outcome is achieved to some extent. Major improvements needed); and
d) 'Low level of effectiveness' (the immediate outcome is not achieved or achieved to a negligible extent. Fundamental improvements needed).

No overall effectiveness rating for the jurisdiction is, however, envisaged.

As yet no evaluations using the new procedures have been completed. Initial reports will be of great interest, not least for what they reveal about the structure and detail of the assessment texts and, importantly, the approach taken in practice to the allocation of effectiveness ratings. By that time it is also hoped that the FATF will have fully clarified the manner in which the outcome of fourth-round evaluations will impact on the process of identifying and taking measures against high risk and non-cooperative jurisdictions; the so-called International Co-operation Review Group (ICRG) process.

Conclusions

When, in the mid-1980s, states first started to discuss the potential of a strategy which targeted the proceeds of profit-generating criminal offences, the necessary legal framework was found to be lacking in most domestic legal systems and was totally absent at the international level. That situation has now been totally transformed.

At the global level this has been brought about primarily by a combination of global 'hard law' treaty instruments of ever greater scope and ambition, negotiated under the auspices of the United Nations, and 'soft law' standards elaborated within the confines of the FATF, an informal inter-governmental body of limited membership but considerable influence. As a consequence, the offence of money laundering and the procedures for the identification,

---

52 Ibid.

tracing, seizure and confiscation of proceeds of crime have become standard criminal justice tools at the national level. International cooperation in these spheres is now facilitated by an ever more intricate and extensive network of agreements and arrangements. Unprecedented obligations have been imposed on financial institutions and other private sector businesses and professions to ensure their active participation in efforts to detect and prevent money laundering. Increasingly, and particularly through the FATF-inspired growth of mutual evaluation, attention has turned to the monitoring of the effective national implementation of all of these elements of the anti-money-laundering strategy. These have been, by any measure, impressive (though on occasion controversial) achievements in the development of transnational criminal law and policy.[53]

---

53 See e.g. Boister, *An Introduction to Transnational Criminal Law*, pp. 110–111.

21

Criminalizing corruption

The global initiatives

John Hatchard

Introduction

The past 20 years have seen unprecedented global efforts aimed at combating corrupt practices. With particular reference to criminalizing corruption, this chapter explores some of these efforts in four sections. The first considers the development of the regional and other anti-corruption initiatives which culminated in the United Nations Convention against Corruption (UNCAC),[1] whilst the second explores the scope of the substantive criminal offences contained in these conventions. The third part discusses combating corruption offences involving the private sector and the liability of legal persons whilst the fourth reviews the monitoring procedures contained in the anti-corruption conventions. The chapter concludes with a short overview.

The development and scope of the anti-corruption initiatives

The Inter-American Convention Against Corruption (IACAC)

The IACAC is the first regional anti-corruption instrument, and was adopted by the Organization of American States (OAS) on 29 March 1996.[2] In its Preamble, Member States recognize that corruption has international dimensions which require effective coordinated action and highlight their 'deep concern' over 'the steadily increasing links between corruption and the proceeds generated by illicit narcotics trafficking which undermine and threaten legitimate commercial and financial activities, and society, at all levels'.[3]

The Convention adopts a holistic approach to addressing the problem, with State Parties being required to: i) take measures to prevent corruption; ii) criminalize 'acts of corruption';

---

1 New York, 31 October 2003, 2349 UNTS 41, in force 14 December 2005.
2 35 ILM 724; in force 6 March 1997. Barbados remains the only one of the 34 OAS member states that has not ratified the Convention.
3 Paragraph 8 of the Preamble.

iii) facilitate international cooperation; and iv) facilitate asset recovery. These anti-corruption 'pillars' are reflected in other regional anti-corruption instruments as well as the UNCAC.

The IACAC does not define 'corruption,' but rather requires State Parties to adopt legislative and other measures to establish as criminal offences a series of 'acts of corruption' including active and passive bribery involving public officials,[4] abuse of office by a public official and the 'fraudulent use or concealment of property' derived from such offences.[5] Provision is also made for a State Party to establish the offence of illicit enrichment 'insofar as its laws permit'.[6]

As regards international cooperation, Article XIV requires State Parties to

> afford one another the widest measure of mutual assistance by processing requests from authorities that, in conformity with their domestic laws, have the power to investigate or prosecute the acts of corruption described in the Convention, to obtain evidence and take other necessary action to facilitate legal proceedings and measures regarding the investigation or prosecution of acts of corruption.

State Parties also undertake to provide each other with the widest measure of mutual technical cooperation on the most effective ways and means of preventing, detecting, investigating, and punishing acts of corruption. To facilitate international cooperation, State Parties are required to maintain a Central Authority which is responsible for making and receiving requests for assistance and cooperation.[7]

The Convention itself does not include a monitoring mechanism, but in 2001 the Follow-up Mechanism for the Implementation of the Inter-American Convention against Corruption (MESICIC) was established by the OAS General Assembly (see below).

European initiatives

Both the Council of Europe (CoE) and the European Union (EU) have taken steps to combat corruption. The Council of Europe Criminal Law Convention on Corruption (the CoE Convention) was adopted by the Committee of Ministers of the Council of Europe on 27 January 1999.[8] In its Preamble, the Member States of the Council of Europe and other signatory states recognize the need to pursue a common criminal policy aimed at protecting society against corruption and that an effective fight against corruption requires increased, rapid and well-functioning international cooperation in criminal matters.

Like the IACAC, the CoE Convention does not define 'corruption' but rather requires State Parties to criminalize bribery, trading in influence, money laundering, and what are referred to as 'account offences'.[9] As regards bribery, a feature of the Convention is that active

---

4 Unlike later conventions, it does not specifically address corruption in the private sector.
5 Article VI. States also undertake to consider establishing a series of other corruption-related offences: see Article XI.
6 Article IX: see the discussion below.
7 IACAC Article XVIII.
8 ETS No 173; in force 1 July 2002. Note also the Council of Europe Civil Law Convention on Corruption, ETS No. 174, 4 November 1999, entered into force 1 November 2003, Article 1 of which requires State Parties to provide effective remedies for persons who have suffered damage as a result of acts of corruption. The Convention was adopted on 4 November 1999.
9 In other words, acts or omissions designed to commit, conceal or disguise the commission of any convention offence: see IACAC Art. 14.

and passive bribery are considered as separate offences with State Parties being required to criminalize, on the basis of a set of common elements, the bribery of domestic, foreign, and international public servants, members of legislatures, and judges, including prosecutors and holders of judicial office.[10] As regards the laundering of the proceeds of corruption, Article 13 requires State Parties to adopt legislative and other measures to establish as criminal offences the money-laundering offences referred to in Article 6(1) and (2) of the Council of Europe Convention on Laundering, Search, Seizure and Confiscation of the Proceeds from Crime[11] when the predicate offence consists of any of the convention offences.

Convention provisions are mandatory, although a state may, at the time of signature or when depositing its instrument of ratification, acceptance, approval, or accession, make a reservation as regards specific Convention provisions. This reflects the intention of its drafters that Parties assume obligations under the Convention only to the extent consistent with their constitution and the fundamental principles of their legal system.[12]

Chapter IV of the Convention addresses international cooperation issues. In particular, Article 25 provides that for the purposes of the investigation and prosecution of Convention offences, State Parties agree to cooperate with one another to the widest extent possible 'in accordance with the provisions of relevant international instruments on international cooperation in criminal matters' or other arrangements. In practice, there are a range of Council of Europe instruments already covering this area and therefore in essence the Chapter is a safety net designed to provide a basis for international cooperation in the absence of any other international treaty or agreement.[13] Monitoring the implementation of the Convention is the responsibility of the Group of States Against Corruption (GRECO) (see below).

The European Union has made the fight against corruption one of its priorities. Thus Article 29 of the Treaty on European Union lists the preventing and combating of corruption and fraud as an objective towards creating a European area of freedom, security, and justice through, amongst other things, the 'approximation' of criminal laws of the Member States in order to fight corruption. In support of this objective, the 1995 Convention on the Protection of the European Union's Financial Interests[14] requires Member States to criminalize fraud affecting the EU's financial interests whilst the First Protocol to the 1995 Convention specifically addresses corruption by or against national and Community officials 'which damages or is likely to damage the European Communities' financial interests'.[15] The 1997 Convention on the Fight against Corruption involving Officials of the European Communities or Officials of Member States of the European Union[16] also requires Member States to criminalize corrupt conduct involving officials of both the Community and Member States even if the conduct took place in its own territory or was instigated by one of their own nationals. There is currently no monitoring system in place.

---

10 IACAC Arts 2–11.

11 8 November 1990, ETS No. 141; in force 1 September 1993. This is subject to the extent the State Party has not made a reservation or declaration with respect to those offences.

12 Council of Europe Criminal Law Convention on Corruption, Explanatory Report, para. 27, available at http://conventions.coe.int/Treaty/en/Reports/Html/173.htm (accessed 4 April 2014).

13 In particular the CoE Convention on Mutual Assistance in Criminal Matters, ETS No. 30, and the CoE Convention on Extradition, ETS No 24.

14 OJ 1995, C316/49.

15 OJ 1996, C313.

16 OJ 1997 C195/2; in force 28 September 1998.

African initiatives[17]

The African Union Convention on Preventing and Combating Corruption (the AU Convention) was adopted by the Heads of State and Government of the African Union on 12 July 2003 and came into force on 5 August 2006.[18] As at 1 October 2013, it had been ratified by 31 of the 54 AU Member States. Its 28 articles also address the four anti-corruption 'pillars':

- effective corruption prevention measures;
- strategies to facilitate the investigation and criminalization of corruption and related offences;
- effective international cooperation in the investigation and prosecution of corruption and related offences; and
- strategies for recovering the proceeds and instrumentalities of corruption.

In particular, State Parties undertake to adopt the necessary legislative and other measures to establish as offences a series of 'acts of corruption and related offences'.[19] These include active and passive bribery in both the public and private sectors, misuse of public office, trading in influence, unlawful diversion of state assets by public officials and the laundering of the proceeds of corruption-related offences. Subject to the provisions of their domestic law, State Parties also undertake to establish the offence of illicit enrichment.

State Parties are required to 'provide each other with the greatest possible technical cooperation and assistance in dealing immediately with requests' for mutual legal assistance.[20] To facilitate this process, State Parties are required to establish independent national authorities[21] for the purpose of making and receiving requests for mutual legal assistance.[22]

A follow-up mechanism is provided for through the work of the Advisory Board on Corruption within the African Union which was established in 2009 (see below).

The Southern African Development Community Protocol against Corruption came into force on 6 July 2005 and thus pre-dates the AU Convention.[23] Whilst lacking in detail, its 22 articles again cover the four anti-corruption 'pillars'. State Parties are required to adopt the necessary legislative and other measures to establish as criminal offences a series of 'acts of corruption' that are, in essence, almost identical to those in the AU Convention.[24] State

---

17 For a detailed examination of the African anti-corruption initiatives see J. Hatchard, *Combating Corruption: Legal Approaches to Supporting Good Governance and Integrity in Africa*, Cheltenham: Edward Elgar, 2014.
18 11 July 2003, 43 ILM 5; in force 5 August 2006.
19 'Corruption' means 'the acts and practices including related offences proscribed in this Convention': see Article 1.
20 Article 18. The inclusion of the word 'immediately' is unique to this anti-corruption convention and, given the practical problems often associated with mutual legal assistance requests, a somewhat unrealistic requirement.
21 Widely referred to as 'Central Authorities'.
22 Article 20.
23 Adopted 14 August 2001. The Southern African Development Community (SADC) comprises 15 states: Angola, Botswana, Democratic Republic of Congo, Lesotho, Madagascar, Malawi, Mauritius, Mozambique, Namibia, Seychelles, South Africa, Swaziland, Tanzania, Zambia, and Zimbabwe.
24 The Economic Community of West African States (ECOWAS) Protocol on the Fight against Corruption of the Economic Community of West African States was signed in December 2001 but still awaits ratification.

Parties are required to report every two years to the Committee of State Parties on the progress made in the implementation of the Protocol.

Asia-Pacific initiatives

The Asia-Pacific has no binding regional anti-corruption instrument. However, 28 jurisdictions in the region have formally endorsed the Asia Development Bank/Organisation for Economic Cooperation and Development (OECD) Anti-Corruption Initiative for Asia-Pacific, which was launched in 2000.[25] The current strategic objective of the Initiative is to support its member countries in implementing the international anti-corruption standards as set forth in the UNCAC and the OECD Anti-bribery Convention (see below). Accordingly, in the Preamble to the Initiative, governments 'concur' in taking 'concrete and meaningful priority steps' to deter, prevent, and combat corruption at all levels. Developing regional cooperation and adopting a holistic and international approach are seen as critical strategies in this regard.

OECD instruments

The Convention on Combating Bribery of Foreign Public Officials in International Business Transactions (the OECD Anti-bribery Convention) entered into force on 15 February 1999 and as of 8 April 2014 had been ratified by 41 states worldwide.[26] Article 1 requires each State Party to establish the offence of the bribery of a foreign public official 'in order to obtain or retain business or other improper advantage in the conduct of international businesses'. On the face of it, the Convention is of limited scope in that it focuses solely on active bribery and related accounting offences. However, as Nicholls *et al.* point out, its importance lies in the fact that the State Parties to the Convention are home to just about all the major multinational/international companies. Thus the steps taken by them to counter the bribery of foreign public officials by companies based in their jurisdictions can have a direct effect on international trade generally and on good governance in specific trading partners in particular. In addition, they note that the OECD Convention has also influenced the wording of the UNCAC.[27] A key feature of the Convention is its effective and systematic monitoring programme undertaken by the Working Group on Bribery (see below).

UN Convention against Transnational Organized Crime (the Palermo Convention)[28]

The Palermo Convention is the first global instrument to address corruption. It came into force on 29 September 2003 and as at 1 October 2013 had been ratified by 178 State Parties. It contains several provisions directly relating to corruption. First, Article 8(1) requires State Parties to adopt the necessary legislative and other measures to establish bribery involving public officials as a criminal offence. State Parties are also to consider criminalizing other

---

25 See further http://www.oecd.org/site/adboecdanti-corruptioninitiative (accessed 18 October 2013).

26 See further http://www.oecd.org/daf/anti-bribery/WGBRatificationStatus_May2014.pdf (accessed 20 June 2014).

27 C. Nicholls, T. Daniel, A. Bacarese and J. Hatchard, *Corruption and Misuse of Public Office*, 2nd edn, Oxford: Oxford University Press, 2011, para. 13.22.

28 15 November 2000, 2225 UNTS 209, in force 29 September 2003.

forms of corruption, including the bribery of foreign public officials and of international civil servants.[29] Second, in recognition of the fact that organized criminal groups may use corrupt practices to facilitate their activities, Article 9(1) requires each State Party 'to the extent appropriate and consistent with its legal system, [to] adopt legislative, administrative or other effective measures to promote integrity and to prevent, detect and punish the corruption of public officials'.[30] In addition, each State Party is required to take measures 'to ensure effective action by its authorities in the prevention, detection and punishment of corruption of public officials, including providing authorities with adequate independence to deter the exertion of inappropriate influence on their actions'.[31]

The United Nations Convention Against Corruption

Whilst the Palermo Convention was a significant step forward, the desire for a global, comprehensive international legal instrument through which to combat corruption in both the public and private sectors led to the development of the UNCAC. This entered into force on 14 December 2005 and as at 1 October 2013 had been ratified by 167 State Parties.

The Convention seeks to build upon the earlier multilateral anti-corruption instruments, which it notes 'with appreciation'. In the Preamble, State Parties also highlight the 'links between corruption and other forms of crime, in particular organized crime and economic crime, including money laundering'. In structure, the UNCAC comprises four operative chapters which again reflect the four 'pillars' in the fight against corruption: i) prevention (Chapter II); ii) criminalization and law enforcement (Chapter III); iii) international cooperation (Chapter IV); and iv) asset recovery (Chapter V).[32]

The range of criminal offences contained in the UNCAC essentially mirrors those in the regional anti-corruption instruments and these are considered in the next section. A notable feature of the UNCAC is its extensive and detailed provisions relating to international cooperation in criminal matters. These are particularly significant in that law enforcement is strictly territorial in nature. Thus where a corruption or other criminal investigation or prosecution involves a transnational element, a state (the requesting state) must make a formal mutual legal assistance (MLA) request to another state (the requested state) for assistance in gathering evidence or information that is held in that state.[33] It is then up to the requested state to decide whether it is willing and/or able to provide the assistance requested. The need for effective MLA arrangements is a cornerstone of transnational cooperation in criminal matters and this is reflected in Article 46. This requires State Parties to 'afford one another the widest measure of mutual legal assistance in investigations, prosecutions and judicial proceedings' in relation to convention offences. Article 46 then goes on to set out detailed

---

29 Article 8(3) also requires each State Party to adopt such measures as may be necessary to establish as a criminal offence participation as an accomplice in an offence established in accordance with Article 8.

30 For the purposes of Article 9 and Article 8(1) a 'public official' means 'a public official or a person who provides a public service as defined in the domestic law and as applied in the criminal law of the State Party in which the person in question performs that function': Article 8(4).

31 Article 9(2).

32 Chapter I contains 'General Provisions' whilst Chapter VI addresses technical assistance and information exchange.

33 Strictly speaking a formal mutual legal assistance request is only required where the requested state is being asked to exercise a coercive power or obtain a court order: see further Hatchard, *Combating Corruption*, pp. 303–317.

provisions relating to the MLA arrangements that all State Parties are required to have in place. Further, State Parties must also 'cooperate closely with one another, consistent with their respective domestic legal and administrative systems, to enhance the effectiveness of law enforcement action to combat the [Convention] offences. . .'.[34]

Chapter VII sets out 'Mechanisms for Implementation' with Article 63 establishing a review process through the Conference of the State Parties to the Convention (see below).

The criminal law provisions in the anti-corruption conventions

Bribery offences

Elements

The bribery offences in the anti-corruption conventions cover much the same ground. For example, Article 15 of the UNCAC requires each State Party to adopt such legislative and other measures[35] as may be necessary to establish offences relating to the bribery of public officials. Article 15(a) deals with 'active bribery', i.e.:

> The promise, offering or giving, to a public official, directly or indirectly, of an undue advantage, for the official himself or herself or another person or entity, in order that the official act or refrain from acting in the exercise of his or her official duties.

Paragraph (b) deals with 'passive bribery', the elements of the offence being a 'mirror image' of paragraph (a).

Article 16(1) of the UNCAC also requires State Parties to criminalize the bribery of foreign public officials and officials of public international organizations. The elements of the offence essentially follow those in Article 15(a). As noted earlier, these key provisions largely reflect those in the OECD Anti-bribery Convention.

Public officials

Reflecting the approach in all the anti-corruption instruments, the term 'public official' in the UNCAC is widely defined and refers to any person holding a legislative, executive, administrative, or judicial office[36] of a State Party, whether appointed or elected, whether permanent or temporary, whether paid or unpaid, irrespective of that person's seniority.[37]

---

34 Article 48.
35 The reference to 'other' measures is not intended to require or permit criminalization without legislation. Such measures are additional to, and presuppose the existence of, legislation: UNODC Office for Treaty Affairs, *Legislative Guide for the Implementation of the United Nations Convention Against Corruption*, New York: UN, 2006, para. 15, available at https://www.unodc.org/pdf/corruption/CoC_LegislativeGuide.pdf (accessed 1 April 2014).
36 Paragraph 3 of the Interpretative Notes, *infra*, indicate that the term 'office' is understood to encompass offices at all levels and subdivisions of government from national to local. In states where subnational governmental units (for example, provincial, municipal and local) of a self-governing nature exist, including states where such bodies are not deemed to form a part of the state, 'office' may also be understood by the states concerned to encompass those levels.
37 Paragraph 4 of the Interpretative Notes, *infra*, indicates that each State Party shall determine who is a 'public official' for the purposes of this paragraph and how each of those categories is applied.

It also covers any other person who performs a public function, including for a public agency or public enterprise, or provides a public service, as defined in the domestic law of the State Party. Paragraph 2 of the Interpretative Notes for the official records of the negotiation of the United Nations Convention against Corruption (the interpretative notes)[38] indicate that the word 'executive' is understood to encompass the military branch, where appropriate.

A 'foreign public official' means 'any person holding a legislative, executive, administrative or judicial office of a foreign country, whether appointed or elected; and any person exercising a public function for a foreign country, including for a public agency or public enterprise'. The 'foreign country' need not be a State Party to the UNCAC. An 'official of a public international organization' means 'an international civil servant or any person who is authorized by such an organization to act on behalf of that organization'.[39] However, according to paragraph 23 of the Interpretative Notes this

> is not intended to affect any immunities that foreign public officials or officials of public international organizations may enjoy in accordance with international law. The States Parties noted the relevance of immunities in this context and encourage public international organizations to waive such immunities in appropriate cases.[40]

'Undue advantage'

The term 'undue advantage' appears in several anti-corruption instruments and both the Legislative Guide to the UNCAC and the CoE Explanatory Report on the Criminal Law Convention provide some assistance as to its meaning. The Legislative Guide indicates that an undue advantage may be something tangible or intangible, whether pecuniary or non-pecuniary, and that it does not have to be given immediately or directly to a public official of the state. However, the undue advantage or bribe must be linked to the official's duties. The CoE Explanatory Report also indicates that the undue advantage will generally be of an economic nature, the essence of the offence being that a person is, or would be, placed in a better position than that prior to the offence and that the public official was not entitled to the benefit. Such advantages might consist of, for example, holidays, loans, food and drink, or better career prospects.[41] The Explanatory Report also suggests that the word 'undue' should be interpreted as something that the recipient is not lawfully entitled to accept or receive. It adds that '[f]or the drafters of the Convention, the adjective "undue" aims at excluding advantages permitted by the law or administrative rules as well as minimum gifts, gifts of very low value or socially acceptable gifts'.[42]

---

38 Report of the Ad Hoc Committee for the Negotiation of a Convention against Corruption on the work of its first to seventh sessions, Addendum: Interpretative notes for the official records (travaux préparatoires) of the negotiation of the United Nations Convention against Corruption, UN Doc A/58/422/Add.1 (Interpretative Notes), available at <https://www.unodc.org/pdf/crime/convention_corruption/session_7/422add1.pdf> (accessed 1 April 2014).
39 Article 2.
40 Interpretative Notes, para. 23.
41 See para. 37.
42 See para. 38.

Intention

The offeror's intention must be not only to promise, offer, or give an undue advantage but also with the ulterior intent of influencing the conduct of the public official. In this context, intention may be inferred from objective factual circumstances.[43]

Depending on the factual situation, the promise or offering of a bribe may constitute an attempt to bribe. This is emphasized in Article 27 of the UNCAC where each State Party, in accordance with its domestic law, has an option to establish as a criminal offence any attempt to commit a Convention offence.

Embezzlement, misappropriation, or other diversion of property by a public official

The scope of the anti-corruption conventions is reflected in the fact that they require State Parties to criminalize the theft of state property by public officials,[44] which is conduct that is not necessarily regarded as constituting 'corruption'. For example Article 17 of the UNCAC provides:

> Each State Party shall adopt such legislative and other measures as may be necessary to establish as criminal offences, when committed intentionally, the embezzlement, misappropriation or other diversion by a public official for his or her benefit or for the benefit of another person or entity, of any property, public or private funds or securities or any other thing of value entrusted to the public official by virtue of his or her position.[45]

At least as regards common law jurisdictions, 'embezzlement, misappropriation or other diversion of property' is often covered by the single offence of theft by a public servant or fraud. However, paragraph 30 of the Interpretative Notes explains that 'the term "diversion" is understood in some countries as separate from "embezzlement" and "misappropriation", while in others "diversion" is intended to be covered by or is synonymous with those terms'.

Trading in influence

The elements of this offence are essentially the same as those of the bribery offences in Articles 15 and 16 of the UNCAC save for the fact that the offence involves the use of real or supposed influence in order to obtain an undue advantage for a third person from an administration or public authority of the State Party. The *mens rea* for the offence is intention. As paragraph 64 of the CoE Explanatory Report puts it:

> criminalizing trading in influence seeks to reach the close circle of the official or the political party to which s/he belongs and to tackle the corrupt behaviour of those persons who are in the neighbourhood of power and try to obtain advantages from their situation, contributing to the atmosphere of corruption.[46]

---

43 Article 28.
44 See, for example, the 'grand corruption' cases discussed in Nicholls *et al.*, *Corruption and Misuse of Public Office*, paras 8.118 *et seq.*
45 UNCAC, Article 17.
46 CoE Explanatory Report to the Criminal Law Convention.

Thus, unlike bribery, the influence peddlers are 'outsiders' who cannot take decisions themselves but misuse their real or alleged influence on other persons. The scope of the offence remains controversial in that there are concerns that it unduly limits the lobbying of public officials. However, paragraph 65 of the Explanatory Report stresses that 'the acknowledged forms of lobbying do not fall under the notion of "improper" influence which must contain a corrupt intent by the influence peddler'.

Abuse of functions

Article 19 of the UNCAC provides that:

> Each State Party shall consider adopting such legislative and other measures as may be necessary to establish as a criminal offence, when committed intentionally, the abuse of functions or position, that is, the performance of or failure to perform an act, in violation of laws, by a public official in the discharge of his or her functions, for the purpose of obtaining an undue advantage for himself or herself or for another person or entity.

In many common law countries, such conduct falls within the offence of 'misconduct in a public office'[47] and, as the Interpretative Notes to the UNCAC indicate, the Article 19 offence encompasses a range of conduct.[48] This includes, first, the abuse of public office in circumstances where this goes beyond the need for disciplinary action; for example, where a public official awards a lucrative government contract to a company of which s/he is a secret beneficiary or arranges for the sale of government land to a company owned or controlled by his/her family at a price far below the market value.[49]

Second, a single charge may reflect a course of conduct or address a situation where no financial reward is involved. For example, in *Sin Kam Wah v HKSAR*,[50] the accused, a senior police officer, was in command of a department responsible for investigating vice offences. He was convicted on three charges of misconduct in that on several occasions he had been provided with prostitutes by the owner of several nightclubs in return for protection from police investigation. Third, it can address the important contemporary problem of the improper disclosure by a public official of classified or privileged information.[51] A charge of conspiracy is also available against those seeking to cause public officials to abuse their powers.

Illicit enrichment

The offence of illicit enrichment applies where there is a 'significant increase in the assets of a public official that he or she cannot reasonably explain in relation to his or her income'.[52] Thus once the prosecution has proved that the accused is a public official and has enjoyed a

---

47 For a detailed analysis of this offence see J. Hatchard 'Combating Corruption: Some Reflections on the Use of the Offence and the Tort of Misconduct/misfeasance in a Public Office', *Denning Law Journal*, 2012, vol. 24, pp. 65–88.
48 UN Doc A/58/422/Add.1, para. 31.
49 See, for example the facts of *Marin & Coye v Attorney General of Belize* [2011] CCJ 9 (Caribbean Court of Justice).
50 [2005] 2 HKLRD 375.
51 See, for example *R v W* [2009] EWCA Crim 2219.
52 UNCAC, Art. 20.

'significant increase' in his or her assets, that person has the legal burden of providing a reasonable explanation to the court as to how the assets were acquired or faces conviction.

In *Attorney General v Hui Kin-hong*[53] the Court of Appeal of Hong Kong recognized the effectiveness of the illicit enrichment offence in the fight against corruption, especially in view of the 'notorious evidential difficulty' in proving that a public official had solicited or accepted a bribe, and the offence is found in the criminal laws of many states.[54] However, because of constitutional issues in some countries relating to the protection of the presumption of innocence this is not a mandatory provision.[55] Even so, evidence of 'illicit enrichment' may form the basis for prosecuting public officials for tax offences or failing to declare their assets (see below).

Accounting and other offences and prosecutorial policy

Whilst convictions on corruption or bribery charges make excellent headlines, in practice prosecutors often face significant difficulties in proving such allegations, particularly when the cases involve powerful political figures and/or corporate entities. Thus determining the appropriate charge in such cases is often the key to a successful prosecution: for example, a charge of illicit enrichment against a senior public official will remove the necessity for the prosecution to prove any specific instance of bribe-taking, although, as noted above, this may fall foul of constitutional right to fair trial provisions. Yet such payments almost inevitably involve the commission of a range of separate accounting and tax evasion offences as well as the offence of failing to declare assets.[56] This point is reflected in several anti-corruption conventions in which State Parties are required to establish a series of accounting offences relating to both the public and private sectors.[57] In addition, the threat of debarment following a conviction for a corruption-related offence may encourage corporations to do 'deals' by agreeing to plead guilty to accountancy and other related offences (see below).

Similarly, the effectiveness of the offence of the failure to declare assets is neatly illustrated by the case of Solomon Alamieyeseigha, Governor of Bayelsa State in Nigeria from 1999 to 2005. During this period he had acquired assets exceeding £10 million, largely through the theft of public funds or from bribes; in 2007 he pleaded guilty to six charges of making false declarations of assets and caused two of his offshore companies to plead guilty to money laundering.[58]

---

53 [1995] 1 HKCLR 227.
54 See generally L. Muzila, M. Morales, M. Mathias and T. Berger, *On the Take: Criminalizing Illicit Enrichment to Fight Corruption*, Washington DC: World Bank, 2012.
55 For example, Canada has an express understanding not to implement such a provision as 'the offence contemplated by Article IX [of IACAC] would be contrary to the presumption of innocence guaranteed by Canada's Constitution'. See http://www.oas.org/juridico/english/Sigs/b–58.html (accessed 1 October 2013).
56 A classic case is that of Frederick Chiluba, the former President of Zambia. In a highly charged trial that attracted international attention he was acquitted on several counts of theft by a public servant having given testimony that the money had been given to him by political well-wishers. Whatever the truth, the fact was that he admitted that he had not declared this income for tax purposes or included them as part of his asset and income declaration and this would have founded criminal liability without anything more: see *The People v Chiluba* (2009, unreported, copy in the possession of the author, especially page J237).
57 See, for example, UNCAC, Art. 12(3).
58 See *Federal Republic of Nigeria v Santolina Investment Corp and Others* [2007] EWHC 3053.

Money laundering

Corruption-related offences and money laundering are often inextricably interlinked. Indeed the importance of preventing those involved in corrupt practices from enjoying the proceeds of their crime is reflected in the fact that all the anti-corruption conventions require State Parties to establish a series of money-laundering offences.

Of particular significance is the fact that the commission of a money-laundering offence often includes a transnational element and thus encourages the prosecution of launderers and their 'allies' in other states. This is particularly relevant in seeking to combat the laundering of the proceeds of 'grand corruption' by public officials (often referred to as 'politically exposed persons' (PEPs)) in circumstances where a criminal prosecution in their home state is unlikely.[59] For example, seemingly due to considerable ongoing political support, James Ibori, the former Governor of Delta State in Nigeria, was not prosecuted successfully in Nigeria although there was considerable evidence of corrupt practices on his part. However, in 2012 he was convicted in a London court of conspiracy to defraud and money laundering involving sums totalling almost £50 million. The case is interesting in that it demonstrates that given the 'transnational political will' and effective international cooperation arrangements (particularly by way of mutual legal assistance), other states are able to prosecute foreign PEPs successfully and turn their perceived 'safe haven' for the laundering of the proceeds of corruption into a prison cell. It also highlights that, whilst PEPs may enjoy constitutional immunity[60] or political protection in their home state, with the exception of serving heads of state, such persons do not enjoy such immunity and therefore remain vulnerable to prosecution abroad, as do those who assist them.

Offences concerning the private sector and the liability of legal persons

The bribery of foreign public officials and the threat of debarment

Effective national and transnational efforts are needed to combat the bribery of foreign public officials and, as noted above, the OECD Anti-bribery Convention leads the way in this regard. The challenge of doing so is starkly illustrated by the *Siemens* case, in which the activities of the giant German-based engineering firm were described as being 'unprecedented in scale and geographic reach and which involved more than US$1.4 billion in bribes to government officials in Asia, Africa, Europe, the Middle East and the Americas'.[61] However, the issue is not restricted to the bribery of foreign public officials for, as the Transparency International *Bribe Payers Index 2011* indicates, bribery is just as prevalent between companies across different sectors as it is between firms and public officials.[62]

The impact of the OECD Convention is highlighted by the fact that all State Parties have introduced legislation outlawing the bribery of foreign public officials. In this regard the United States has taken the lead through the Foreign Corrupt Practices Act (FCPA), which

---

59 According to the Glossary to the Financial Action Task Force Recommendations 2012, PEPs are 'individuals who have been entrusted . . . with prominent public functions'.
60 Such as Nigerian state governors: see Constitution of Nigeria 1999, Article 308.
61 Department of Justice press release, 15 December 2008: available at http://www.justice.gov/opa/pr/2008/December/08-crm-1105.html (accessed 1 July 2013).
62 Transparency International, *Bribe Payers Index 2011* p. 12, available at http://bpi.transparency.org/bpi2011/in_detail accessed 1 July 2013.

criminalizes foreign bribery as well as containing a series of accounting provisions.[63] As well as this, the FCPA contains wide jurisdictional provisions which enable two US enforcement agencies, the Department of Justice (DOJ) and the Securities and Exchange Commission (SEC), to recommend to the court severe penalties on companies, some of which have only a minimal link with the United States. As a result, it is commonplace for prosecutors to reach an agreement whereby the defendant company pleads guilty to an FCPA accounting offence and agrees to pay a substantial fine so as to avoid a corruption conviction. For example, following its admission of involvement in bribery noted earlier, in 2008 Siemens agreed to plead guilty to a violation of the FCPA's accounting provisions,[64] to pay record fines in the United States, and to be monitored to ensure future compliance with anti-bribery laws.[65]

The case also highlights another key weapon in the fight against transnational bribery in the corporate sector, for the threat of debarment proceedings following a criminal conviction for a corruption offence may persuade companies – even the most powerful – to 'do a deal' with prosecutors. Debarment (also known as 'blacklisting' or 'exclusion') is the mechanism through which a company or individual is prevented from tendering for, or participating in, a project (or projects) for a specific reason, such as previous involvement in corrupt practices. In some cases, debarment is discretionary (for example the World Bank); in others (for example under the European Union Procurement Directives) a purchasing body must exclude from acceptance tenders from any company that has been convicted of corruption.[66] Debarment systems operate at the national level in several countries, including in the United States under the FCPA.

The liability of legal persons

All the anti-corruption instruments require State Parties to address the liability of legal persons. However, establishing the *criminal* liability of a legal person is potentially difficult. For many common law jurisdictions, corporate criminal liability is restricted to acts of the 'directing' or 'controlling' minds of the corporation who carry out the functions of management and speak and act as the 'company'.[67] For civil law jurisdictions, establishing corporate criminal liability at all has proved problematic and to do so would require a change in the entire basis of their domestic laws.[68] As a result, Article 26 of the UNCAC, for example, requires State Parties to 'adopt such measures as may be necessary, consistent with its legal principles, to establish the liability of legal persons' for convention offences and adds that 'the liability of legal persons may be criminal, civil or administrative'. However, whatever type of 'liability' is imposed, State Parties must ensure that legal persons are subject to 'effective, proportionate and dissuasive criminal or non-criminal sanctions, including monetary sanctions'.[69]

63 Indeed the FCPA pre-dates the OECD Anti-bribery Convention by many years: for a detailed account of the legislation see Nicholls *et al., Corruption and Misuse of Public Office*, Ch. 16.
64 Under the 'books and records' provisions set out in section 78m(b)(2)(B), 78m(b)(5), and 78ff(a) of Title 15 of the US Code. It also pleaded guilty to a violation of the FCPA's internal control provisions under section 78m(b)(2)(B), 78m(b)(5), and 78ff(a).
65 Siemens is listed on the New York Stock Exchange and accordingly it is subject to the FCPA.
66 See Directives 2004/17/EC and 2004/18/EC of the European Parliament and of the Council of 31 March 2004. See further J. Hatchard, 'Recent Developments in Combating the Bribery of Foreign Public Officials: A Cause for Optimism?', *University of Detroit-Mercy Law Review*, 2007, vol. 85, p. 1.
67 See *Tesco Supermarkets Ltd v Nattrass* [1971] 2 All ER 127.
68 Commentary 20 to the OECD Anti-bribery Convention states that 'in the event that, under the legal system of a Party, criminal responsibility is not applicable to legal persons, that Party shall not be required to establish such criminal responsibility'.
69 UNCAC, Art. 16(4).

The CoE Convention contains similar, albeit more detailed, provisions regarding legal persons. Article 18(1) requires State Parties to adopt such legislative and other measures as may be necessary to ensure that legal persons can be held liable for active bribery, trading in influence, and money laundering where those offences were committed for the corporation's benefit by a natural person with a 'leading position' within the legal person based on:

- a power of representation of the legal person; or
- an authority to take decisions on behalf of the legal person; or
- an authority to exercise control within the legal person;

as well as for involvement of such a natural person as perpetrator, accessory, or instigator in the above-mentioned offences. Again, this does not impose any obligation to establish criminal liability for legal persons.

However, Article 18(2) of the CoE Convention goes further and addresses liability for a *failure* to put in place corruption-preventive measures by legal persons. Thus State Parties are required to take the necessary steps to ensure that a legal person can be held liable 'where the lack of supervision or control by a natural person has made possible the commission of the corruption offences mentioned in [Article 18(1)] for the benefit of that legal person by a natural person under its authority'. This approach is reflected, for example, in section 7 of the Bribery Act 2010 (UK), which makes it an offence for a 'relevant commercial organization' to fail to prevent bribery by a 'person associated' with it.[70]

Monitoring procedures

A notable feature of several anti-corruption conventions is the provision for some form of a 'monitoring' system. Thus one the key strengths of the OECD Anti-bribery Convention is its programme of systematic monitoring by way of peer review of state compliance, which is undertaken by the Working Group on Bribery (WGB). This comprises a country visit by examiners from different OECD countries, whose task is to assess state compliance with particular aspects of the convention. Their report is presented to the WGB in plenary and the report and recommendations for action are then made public.[71] There is also provision for a follow-up process to assess state compliance with the recommendations. For example, the response of the WGB to the UK's decision not to proceed with an investigation into allegations of bribery concerning BAE Systems' acquisition of multi-billion-dollar arms contracts with Saudi Arabia was to publicly criticize its action and to conduct a detailed supplementary review of the UK's compliance with its convention obligations.[72]

Similarly, under the CoE Convention, the Group of States against Corruption (GRECO) was established by the Council of Ministers with the aim of improving 'the capacity of its

---

70 Bribery Act 2010 (UK), section 7(1). The offence only applies where the bribery has been committed with intent to obtain or retain business or a business advantage for the organization's benefit. It is an offence of strict liability, but is subject to the defence that the organization had adequate procedures in place to prevent persons associated with it from committing bribery: see further Nicholls *et al.*, *Corruption and Misuse of Public Office*, para. 4.88 *et seq.*

71 Reports can be found on the OECD's website: http://www.oecd.org/bribery (accessed 1 October 2013).

72 See the WGB Phase 2 *bis* report available at http://www.oecd.org/investment/anti-bribery/anti-briberyconvention/41515077.pdf (accessed 1 October 2013). The case is explored in detail in Nicholls *et al.*, *Corruption and Misuse of Public Office*, at para. 7.208 *et seq.*

members to fight corruption by following up, through a dynamic process of mutual evaluation and peer pressure, compliance with their undertakings' in the fight against corruption.[73] Again, a key feature of the process is the systematic verification of the action taken by each of the 49 CoE Member States as regards the implementation of the recommendations, including a requirement to submit a Situation Report on the measures taken to implement those recommendations.[74]

A less confrontational approach is adopted in the Follow-up Mechanism of the Inter-American Convention against Corruption (MESICIC), whose objective is to promote the implementation of the IACAC and facilitate harmonization of national anti-corruption legislation throughout the hemisphere. In addition, MESICIC also seeks to facilitate technical cooperation activities and the exchange of information, experiences, and best practices. A Committee of Experts, which comprises members designated by each State Party, reviews the implementation of the Convention by State Parties through a system of 'rounds', which appraise progress made on implementation of particular aspects of the Convention by State Parties. The reports of the Committee are readily available and are an invaluable source of information about individual state compliance with the Convention. Of course, whilst this may usefully indicate the progress being made in compliance, the danger is that such a process will be little more than self-serving and contain little critical analysis. Only time will tell as to whether this is the case.

The AU Convention provides for an Advisory Board on Corruption within the African Union[75] whose mandate is limited to promoting and encouraging the adoption of anti-corruption measures and the collection and dissemination of information amongst Member States.

As regards the UNCAC, a Conference of the States Parties to the Convention (CoSP) was established to improve the capacity of and cooperation between State Parties to achieve the objectives set forth in the Convention and to promote and review its implementation.[76] Through ratifying the Convention, each State Party agrees to take the necessary measures, including legislative and administrative measures, in accordance with the fundamental principles of its domestic law, to ensure the implementation of its obligations under the Convention.[77] Critically, the Mechanism is to be non-intrusive, producing no form of ranking, with each State Party merely being required to provide information to the Conference on its compliance and implementation of the Convention. Provision is made for a review of each State Party by two other State Parties with a report from the reviewers on good practice and challenges in Convention implementation being produced. Such reports are to remain confidential although executive summaries are made public.[78]

---

73 Statute of GRECO, Article 1.

74 See <http://www.coe.int/t/dghl/monitoring/greco/evaluations/> (accessed 1 October 2013).

75 African Union Convention on Preventing and Combating Corruption, Art. 22(1).

76 See Art. 63(1).

77 Article 65(1). The review mechanism was adopted by the CoSP in Resolution 3/1.

78 Full details of the work of the CoSP are available on the website of the UNODC: see http://www.unodc.org/unodc/en/corruption/index.html (accessed 1 October 2013). The executive summaries are available at http://www.unodc.org/unodc/en/treaties/CAC/country-profile/index.html (accessed 1 October 2013).

Overview

The adoption of the anti-corruption conventions represents a significant development in the fight against corruption at both the national and transnational levels. However, the discussion calls for some general comments and has highlighted several challenges:

i) Whilst the regional conventions and the UNCAC require State Parties to take a holistic approach to combating corruption, the majority of their substantive provisions focus on the criminalization and international cooperation pillars.

ii) The scope of 'corruption' goes well beyond the payment or receipt of bribes and the anti-corruption conventions require State Parties either to 'adopt' or to 'consider adopting' a wide range of criminal offences which can be best described as 'acts of corruption and other related offences'.

iii) There remains a considerable challenge in seeking to prove the bribery/corruption offence, especially in that this is often a 'victimless' crime.[79] It is therefore vital that in determining the appropriate charges, prosecutors consider using the whole range of 'corruption and other related offences'. Thus, for example, rather than seeking to prove a bribery offence involving senior public officials, a charge of illicit enrichment may be a viable alternative as this does not require proof of any specific bribe-taking. Where constitutional problems prevent the use of this offence, accounting and tax offences may offer the most realistic prospect of conviction. Prosecutorial policy, then, is key to making the criminal law provisions 'work' in practice.

iv) The need for the political will to combat corruption, and the fact that those called upon to make the necessary decisions to do so are often the very actors who benefit most from the status quo,[80] mean that taking action at the national level is often problematic. It follows that also addressing the issue from a transnational perspective is vital. This means that other State Parties must fulfil their convention obligations and take steps to prosecute those who seek to bribe foreign public officials. Similarly, states must display a willingness to prosecute all those involved in the laundering of the proceeds of corruption, including the financial institutions and 'gatekeepers'[81] who facilitate the process, as well as taking active steps to assist victim states recover the proceeds of corruption, no matter where in the world they are located.

v) The prospect of a legal person being debarred from involvement in lucrative contracts if convicted of a corruption offence means that the *threat* of a criminal prosecution for such an offence represents a powerful incentive for the doing of 'deals' with prosecutors in which there is an admission of liability for a 'non-corruption' offence in return for the dropping of the corruption charges. Whilst the transparency of such 'deals' is questionable, they ensure that the offending enterprise suffers financial and reputational damage whilst removing the often challenging task of mounting a successful bribery prosecution.

vi) In order to facilitate investigations, prosecutions, and the recovery of the proceeds of corruption, the anti-corruption conventions rightly emphasize the need for all states to have in place effective international cooperation mechanisms.

---

79 Of course, the victims are those who suffer direct or indirect harm as a result of the illegal bargain.
80 L. Lawson, 'The Politics of Anti-corruption Reform in Africa', *Journal of African Law*, 2009, vol. 47, no. 1, p. 73, p. 74.
81 Such as legal practitioners, real estate agents, and accountants.

vii) A striking feature of the UNCAC and OECD conventions in particular is the recognition that the private sector plays a key role in combating corruption. Yet the challenge of dealing with the *criminal* liability of legal persons remains. As regards many common law jurisdictions, this calls for a re-examination of the basis of corporate criminal liability itself. In addition, placing legal obligations on corporate entities and their senior management to take active steps to put in place effective corruption preventive measures is a promising development.

viii) The monitoring of state compliance with their convention obligations is a significant feature of the anti-corruption conventions. The question of how 'intrusive' such monitoring can be varies markedly and the remit of the CoSP, in particular, demonstrates the determination on the part of some states to avoid any kind of ranking or assessment of their compliance with those obligations.

ix) Above all, the transnational nature of many corruption-related offences emphasizes the need for states worldwide to implement fully their obligations under the anti-corruption conventions.

22

Piracy and suppression of unlawful acts against the safety of maritime navigation

Douglas Guilfoyle

Introduction

The high seas are an asset to all States, principally as a highway for international trade, a status preserved by the doctrine of freedom of navigation on the high seas and the exclusive jurisdiction of each flag State over its vessels on the high seas. Crimes of violence on the high seas may endanger both the safety of navigation of individual vessels and the general public good provided by freedom of navigation. The classic criminal actor on the high seas is the pirate and, rhetorically at least, the pirate is often invoked as the original international criminal. The conflation of piracy with much more serious international crimes tends to obscure the function served by the law of piracy – protecting freedom of navigation. Certain gaps in the law of piracy have, in part, been cured by later treaty law concerned with offences against the safety of navigation on the high seas more generally.

Piracy in the twenty-first century

Piracy has, at various times, been dismissed as of chiefly historical interest[1] only to become periodically the subject of renewed practical importance. In the Malacca Strait the 'prevalence of attacks on shipping (both in international and territorial waters) in the years 2000–4 led to the area being classified by . . . [insurers] as a "war risk" zone' in 2005 and 2006.[2] Cooperative regional arrangements and patrolling by Indonesia, Malaysia and Singapore subsequently saw attacks decline sharply after 2004.[3] Piracy in the Malacca Strait, however,

---

1 See E. Dickinson, 'Is the Crime of Piracy Obsolete?', *Harvard Law Review*, 1924–5, vol. 38, p. 334; 'Report of the Committee of Experts for the Progressive Codification of International Law', 13 June 1927, reproduced in 22 *American Journal of International Law Special Supplement*, 1928, vol. 22, p. 222 (*AJIL Spec Supp*); A. Rubin, *The Law of Piracy*, 2nd edn, New York: Transnational, 1997, pp. 331–335.

2 D. Guilfoyle, *Shipping Interdiction and the Law of the Sea*, Cambridge: Cambridge University Press, 2009, p. 55.

3 'Piracy attacks are down as new initiative bears fruit', *Lloyd's List*, 4 July 2007, 14; though see R. Balkin, 'The International Maritime Organization and Maritime Security', *Tulane Maritime Law Journal*, 2006, vol. 30, p. 11, n. 65 (the decline in attacks may be attributable to the 2004 tsunami).

largely comprised armed robbery committed against transiting vessels. Since 2006, the great piracy hot-spot has been the Indian Ocean off Somalia. Somali pirates, using 'mother ships' (often previously hijacked regional fishing vessels) to operate far out to sea, have typically attacked and boarded ships from speedboats in order to seize control of and ransom both vessels and crew. In 2011, for example, Somali pirates attacked 219 ships, captured 25 and took US $135 million in ransoms; at one point in 2011 Somali pirates held over 30 ships and 600 crew members, often subjecting the latter to terrible violence.[4] While claims have been made that illegal fishing and alleged toxic waste dumping in Somali waters have caused Somalis to turn to piracy, there is little evidence of such a link or, indeed, of maritime waste dumping.[5] Somali piracy is 'now considered a form of transnational organized crime, complete with ... well-organized and well-funded backing'.[6] The response to Somali piracy has involved multinational naval patrols, with the patrolling naval powers concluding agreements to transfer suspected pirates to regional States for prosecution; it has also involved increasing international engagement with national and regional authorities in Somalia. Efforts at sea and ashore appear to have reduced the incidence of pirate attacks significantly. In 2012 only five vessels were taken by pirates and by July 2013 only one vessel and 54 hostages remained held by Somali pirates.[7] Not all maritime violence, as discussed below, is covered by the definition of piracy. In the 1980s the Suppression of Unlawful Acts against the Safety of Maritime Navigation Convention was drafted in response to the *Achille Lauro* hijacking and in order to avoid some of the arbitrary limitations found in the definition of piracy.

An international crime or a rule of jurisdiction?

There is a divergence of opinion as to whether piracy is an international crime in the strict sense (i.e. a substantive and clearly defined crime which is directly punishable under international law) or simply a special rule of jurisdiction allowing States extra-territorial prescriptive and enforcement jurisdiction over events on the high seas which they would otherwise lack.[8] In particular, some point to the lack of any direct statement in treaty law that piracy is prohibited and punishable as an offence; or to the fact that it is not at present a crime within the jurisdiction of any international court.[9] These arguments may, however, seem rather formal. Perhaps the best argument for the jurisdiction thesis is the well-documented lack of uniformity in the definitions of piracy adopted under national law.[10]

---

4 House of Commons Foreign Affairs Committee (United Kingdom), *Piracy off the Coast of Somalia*, London: The Stationery Office, 2012, p. 15, p. 30, p. 39, p. 56.
5 'Report of the Secretary-General pursuant to Security Council Resolution 2020' (2011), UN Doc. S/2012/783, 22 October 2012, paras 64–66. On the social function of such allegations see A. Klein, 'The Moral Economy of Somali Piracy: Organised Criminal Business or Subsistence Activity?', *Global Policy*, 2013, vol. 4, p. 94.
6 United Nations Office on Drugs and Crime, 'Awash with money – organized crime and its financial links to Somali piracy', 25 May 2011, http://www.unodc.org/unodc/en/frontpage/2011/May/awash-with-money---organized-crime-and-its-financial-links-to-somali-piracy.html (accessed 3 September 2013).
7 See: EU Naval Force Somalia, 'Key Facts and Figures', http://eunavfor.eu/key-facts-and-figures (accessed 9 July 2013).
8 Harvard Research in International Law, 'Part IV: Piracy', *American Journal of International Law Supplement*, 1932, vol. 26, pp. 751–756 (hereafter 'Harvard Research').
9 R. Geiss and A. Petrig, *The Legal Framework for Counter-Piracy Operations in Somalia and the Gulf of Aden*, Oxford: Oxford University Press, 2011, pp. 140–141.
10 Harvard Research, p. 749.

Discussion of piracy tends to conflate two concepts: the pirate as the original international criminal, an enemy of all mankind; and piracy as the subject of a special jurisdictional rule because it occurs in an area *beyond* national jurisdiction. As Judge Moore of the Permanent Court of International Justice (PCIJ) put it in the *Lotus Case*:

> as the scene of the pirate's operations is the high seas, which it is not the right or duty of any nation to police, he is denied the protection of the flag which he may carry, and is treated as an outlaw, as the enemy of all mankind – *hostis humani generis* – whom any nation may in the interest of all capture and punish.[11]

From the point of view of the law of the sea the critical part of the law of piracy is that it is an exception to the otherwise exclusive jurisdiction of the flag State. That exclusive jurisdiction is, in effect, immunity from interference by foreign governments with a vessel on the high seas and the mechanism by which freedom of navigation on the high seas is upheld. The point is *not* that piracy has a specially heinous character comparable to war crimes (it often involves quite minor acts of violence);[12] rather, without such a jurisdictional rule pirates, precisely because they operate on the high seas, could readily evade those States otherwise having jurisdiction over their conduct, such as 'the flag state of their ship, or their national State'.[13] A good argument may thus be made that piracy is better seen as providing the prototypical *transnational* crime (as pirates cross the jurisdictional boundary between vessels on the high seas) rather than the prototypical *international* crime (being those of concern to the international community as a whole due to their unique moral gravity).[14]

This highlights a critical feature of jurisdiction over piracy. In most cases universal jurisdiction is merely prescriptive. It authorises States to enact laws criminalising extra-territorial conduct lacking a conventional nexus with the prosecuting State; it does not, however, authorise extra-territorial police action to suppress such crimes or apprehend criminals (enforcement jurisdiction). Uniquely, universal jurisdiction over piracy authorises both prescription in municipal law and extra-territorial enforcement action (albeit only in areas beyond any State's territorial jurisdiction).

Historical approaches

The history of piracy as a legal phenomenon is a confused one. For present purposes it is important to note that: there has been no single stable definition of piracy across time; in the Renaissance and later times the term was often used in contradistinction to State-licensed privateers; and national laws have varied considerably in terms of how they define piracy.[15]

---

11 *The Lotus Case (France v Turkey)*, PCIJ Series A No. 10, 70.
12 See cases discussed in M. Gardner, 'Piracy Prosecutions in National Courts', *Journal of International Criminal Justice*, 2012, vol. 10, p. 797.
13 V. Lowe and C. Staker, 'Jurisdiction', in M. Evans (ed.), *International Law*, 3rd edn, Oxford: Oxford University Press, 2010, p. 327.
14 N. Boister, *An Introduction to Transnational Criminal Law*, Oxford: Oxford University Press, 2012, p. 29.
15 See, generally, A. Rubin, 'The Law of Piracy', *Denver Journal of International Law and Policy*, 1986–7, vol. 15, pp. 173–174 but note pp. 191–193 ('piracy' and 'privateering' treated as synonymous in numerous historical contexts); and Harvard Research, p. 749, p. 764 (divergent municipal law definitions); pp. 777–778, 798–799, 801–803, 809, 864–865 (status of privateers); pp. 796, 804, 807 (use as term of invective, not art).

On the latter point, in some of the older national cases the term 'piracy' is used to cover both purely national offences (occurring within the prosecuting States' waters) and the international crime.[16] This led some to assert, wrongly, that 'piracy' extends to cover maritime attacks within territorial jurisdiction.

As to the supposedly ancient origins of the crime, Rubin has convincingly demonstrated that most of the ancient texts relied on for the proposition that pirates have been considered *hostis humani generis* since time immemorial either do not refer to 'piracy' as we would now understand it or rely on legal doctrines or assumptions quite distinct from universal jurisdiction. One should also note that the word 'piracy' in English 'was applied as a pejorative with political implications but no clear legal meaning' from the Renaissance onwards.[17] Some acts, denounced as piratical, such as exacting taxes on vessels using disputed sea-lanes, simply involved contested understandings of the law of the sea.[18]

The major international law publicists of the sixteenth century onwards continued to express a diversity of views as to the correct definition of piracy. A key touchstone, however, became the idea of pirates as being engaged in unsanctioned or unauthorised violence outside the State-based system of international law. Piracy thus constituted acts not either sanctioned by a State or otherwise allowed under the laws of war. This idea that the lawful character of violence on the high seas depended on State licence extends back to at least Gentili (writing in 1612), and was to have a significant influence on later thinking.[19]

On this point of the relationship between piracy and State sanction or the laws of war, an issue emerged in the nineteenth century around State practice regarding civil wars.[20] If an insurgency in a civil conflict took to the seas to attack the shipping of the government they sought to overthrow, such acts were generally not regarded as piracies by neutral States.[21] However, if such an insurgency attempted to exercise belligerent rights against neutral shipping (such as seizure of contraband or enforcement of a blockade), were such acts piratical? The question largely arose in relation to the wars of independence of the Spanish–American colonies of the early nineteenth century and later the US Civil War. In short, the general view was that insurgencies had no rights against the shipping of a neutral power unless their belligerency had been *recognised* by the State in question.[22] Otherwise, such acts against neutral shipping generally fell to be treated as piracies.[23] How to formulate a rule covering this relatively narrow exceptional case proved a major question for the

---

16 D.P. O'Connell, ed. I.A. Shearer, *The International Law of the Sea*, Oxford: Clarendon, 1984, vol. 2, pp. 966–967.

17 Rubin, 'The Law of Piracy', p. 209.

18 Ibid., pp. 189–190, p. 213.

19 Ibid., pp. 196–198 and p. 203.

20 See, for short treatments, Guilfoyle, *Shipping Interdiction*, pp. 32–42; and D. Kritsiotis, 'The Contingencies of Piracy', *California Western International Law Journal*, 2011, vol. 41, pp. 312–319.

21 Though during the US Civil War the Federal Government attempted to treat as piracy such acts by Confederate forces on the theory the rebels were criminals, not combatants. The US Supreme Court did not uphold this view: *Prize Cases* 67 US 635 (1862).

22 However, the correct application of doctrine of recognition of belligerency was highly contentious. See generally L. Moir, *The Law of Internal Armed Conflict*, Cambridge: Cambridge University Press, 2002, pp. 5–17; H. Lauterpacht, *Recognition in International Law*, Cambridge: Cambridge University Press, 1953, pp. 250–3.

23 E. Lauterpacht (ed.), *International Law: The Collected Papers of Hersch Lauterpacht*, vol. 5, Cambridge, Cambridge University Press, 2004, p. 669 citing *The Ambrose Light* 25 Fed 408 (SDNY 1885) and *The Three Friends* 166 US 1 (1897).

twentieth-century codification efforts (discussed below).[24] It is also important to note that this issue is now something of an anachronism, as the doctrine of recognition of belligerency has fallen into desuetude.[25]

The other key question in historical debate was whether piracy had to be committed with *intent to rob*. Lauterpacht, summarising the debate as at 1937, suggested that '[p]iracy in its original and strict meaning is every unauthorised act of violence committed by a private vessel on the open sea against another vessel with intent to plunder (*animo furandi*)'.[26] However, he noted the narrowness of this definition and that 'if unauthorised acts of violence, such as murder . . . are committed on the open sea without intent to plunder, such acts are in practice considered to be piratical'.[27] That *animo furandi* was irrelevant in practice was certainly the view of the Privy Council in 1934. In *Re Piracy Jure Gentium* it held that the definition of piracy 'nearest to accuracy' was 'any armed violence at sea which is not a lawful act of war'.[28] Indeed, it rather caustically dismissed the suggestion that murder on the high seas could never be piracy unless the attackers 'stole, say, an article worth sixpence'.[29]

Codification in the twentieth century

The idea that the crime of piracy is an ancient one in international law is further belied by the history of its codification in the twentieth century.[30] Codification efforts commenced with the (ultimately abandoned) work of the League of Nations Committee of Experts for the Progressive Codification of International Law in 1926 and were carried forward in the work of the Harvard Research in International Law project on piracy and its resultant draft convention and commentaries ('the Harvard Research'). As works of codification these projects both had their flaws, especially in terms of historical methodology.[31] Nonetheless, the Harvard Research had a decisive influence on the work of the International Law Commission (ILC) on the law of the sea,[32] and the ILC's draft articles on piracy were reproduced almost verbatim in both the 1958 Geneva High Seas Convention (HSC) and the 1982 UN Convention on the Law of the Sea (UNCLOS).[33] These various efforts will be discussed in turn.

The League of Nations Committee of Experts' attempt at codification was brief. It consisted essentially of a set of draft articles and memorandum on the subject produced by Ambassador Matsuda (who provided no scholarly references or detailed commentary), which provoked numerous responses from governments and a brief debate within the Committee of

---

24 E.g. Harvard Research, p. 857.
25 Y.M. Lootsteen, 'The Concept of Belligerency in International Law', *Military Law Review*, 2000, vol. 166, pp. 110–111, p. 125.
26 H. Lauterpacht, *Oppenheim's International Law*, 5th edn, London: Longmans, Green & Co, 1937, p. 486.
27 Ibid.
28 *In re Piracy Jure Gentium* [1934] AC 586, p. 598; cf. 'unauthorised warfare' in *US v The Ambrose Light*, 25 Fed. 408, 413 (SDNY 1885).
29 *In re Piracy Jure Gentium*, p. 594.
30 Indeed, piracy has not always had a strong pejorative sense in English: Rubin, *The Law of Piracy*, Chapter 1.
31 As acerbically analysed in Rubin, *The Law of Piracy*, pp. 331–372.
32 See *Yearbook of the International Law Commission*, 1955, vol. I, p. 40 ff.; and *Yearbook of the International Law Commission*, 1956, vol. II, p. 253, pp. 282–284.
33 Articles 14–22, Geneva Convention on the High Seas, 29 April 1958, 450 UNTS 82; entered into force 30 September 1962 ('HSC'); Articles 100–107, 110, United Nations Convention on the Law of the Sea, 10 December 1982, 1833 UNTS 3, entered into force 16 November 1994 ('UNCLOS').

Experts, before the topic was abandoned as being of insufficient practical interest.[34] Nonetheless, certain of Matsuda's drafting choices, such as the historically important formulation that piracy must be undertaken for 'private ends', had an obvious influence on the Harvard Research.[35]

For its part, much of the Harvard Research is an enormous compilation of loosely organised quotations from sources with additional commentary by the authors. This methodology (or lack of it) was perhaps in part a response to the difficulty of the subject matter. The Harvard codifiers[36] found themselves confronted by a 'paucity' of relevant case law and modern State practice on the important questions:

> Except for a few international . . . [and] municipal law cases, there are no official determinations which will help an investigator to cut a way through the jungle of expert opinion. Indeed the lack of adjudicated cases and of . . . state practice is the occasion for the *chaos of expert opinion*. Most of the municipal law cases on piracy are of little value . . . [as] the judicial opinions are colored by . . . national legislation [which is often at variance with international law].[37]

Imposing order on chaos required a number of decisions to be made and the result was far more in the nature of progressive development of the law than codification.

A principal problem was the status of insurgents who committed acts not authorised by the laws of war against foreign shipping on the high seas. To resolve this Matsuda introduced, and the Harvard Research subsequently adopted, the words 'for private ends' as being the relevant test. Nonetheless, the codification efforts diverged more sharply on this point than their relatively common wording might suggest. According to Matsuda, 'piracy consists in sailing the seas for private ends *without authorization from the Government of any State* with the object of committing depredations upon property or acts of violence against persons.'[38] He further took the view that in characterising piracy one should generally rely on 'the external character of the facts without entering too far into the often delicate question of motives'.[39] Thus he (and the League Committee of Experts) took the view that political insurgencies *could* commit piracy.[40] Nonetheless, he thought there should be a narrow exception for 'acts

---

34 See Rubin, *The Law of Piracy*, pp. 331–335; and materials reproduced in: *AJIL Spec Supp*, 1926, vol. 20, pp. 223–229; *AJIL Spec Supp*, 1928, vol. 22, p. 222; S. Rosenne, *League of Nations Committee of Experts for the Progressive Codification of International Law (1925–1928)*, Dobbs Ferry, NY: Oceana, 1972, vol. 1, pp. 124–126.

35 Matsuda appears to have taken the formulation from US textbook author Joel Prentiss Bishop (or his editors), who used them only as a synonym for *animo furandi*: D. Guilfoyle, 'Piracy and Terrorism', in P. Koutrakos and A. Skordas (eds), *The Law and Practice of Piracy at Sea: European and International Perspectives*, Oxford: Hart, 2014.

36 None actually came from Harvard. Most appear to have been chosen on the basis of proximity to the San Francisco Bay, the project's Reporter being based at Stanford.

37 Harvard Research, p. 764 (emphasis added).

38 League of Nations Document C.48.M.25.1926.V., Annex (emphasis added); reproduced in *AJIL Spec Supp*, 1926, vol. 20, p. 223.

39 Ibid., p. 224.

40 Minutes of the League of Nations Committee of Experts for the Progressive Codification of International Law, Second Session, 14th Meeting, 20 January 1926, reproduced in Rosenne, *League of Nations Committee of Experts*, vol. 1, p. 124 (uncontested view of the Committee President, summarising Matsuda's views).

committed with a purely political object'.[41] What was meant by 'purely political' was never defined, but from the Committee's debates it was clear that the intention was that this would be a narrow exception to the basic definition focusing on the unauthorised character of the violence.[42]

The Harvard codifiers acknowledged that there was case law supporting the proposition that States could 'treat as pirates unrecognized insurgents against a foreign government who have pretended to exercise belligerent rights on the sea against neutral commerce'.[43] Nonetheless, they felt this was an anomaly better explained by the idea that neutral States whose shipping was injured by such insurgents had a special jurisdiction to prosecute individuals involved.[44] The Harvard Research Draft Convention thus described piracy as being 'for private ends', which they intended to indicate a test of subjective motivation ordinarily excluding insurgents from being pirates. This approach contradicts much of the authority cited in the Harvard Research (which generally stresses the unauthorised character of the violence).[45] The Harvard codifiers reasoned that, after the abolition of privateering in 1856, there seemed 'no good reason why jurisdiction over' politically motivated

> wrongful attacks on persons or property . . . whether they are made on behalf of States, or of recognized belligerent organizations, or of unrecognized revolutionary bands . . . should not be confined to the injured State, the State or recognized government on whose behalf the forces were acting, and the States of nationality and domicile of the offender.[46]

Nonetheless, it is important to note the limited number of cases involved here: the attacks covered needed some connection with either a State or, under the laws of war, a recognised or unrecognised belligerent group.

The ILC Draft Articles on the Law of the Sea relied heavily on the Harvard Research and unsurprisingly added little to previous codification efforts. The ILC concurred with the Harvard Research and the League of Nations Committee of Experts on the other major controversies, holding that: piracy can only be committed seaward of the territorial sea of any State (or on *terra nullius* islands); coastal raiding involving 'pirates' descending from the high seas is not piracy in international law; mutiny of crew or passengers on the high seas is not of itself piracy (unless the mutineers go on to attack other vessels); and government vessels cannot commit piracy unless the crew first mutinies (unlawful acts by government vessels being otherwise a question of State responsibility).[47] The ILC Draft Articles were largely replicated in the HSC and UNCLOS provisions.

---

41 *AJIL Spec Supp*, 1926, vol. 20, pp. 228–229 (Article 1 of the Matsuda Draft).
42 See further Guilfoyle, 'Piracy and Terrorism'.
43 Harvard Research, p. 798.
44 Harvard Research, p. 746 (Article 16); commentary at p. 786 and p. 857 ff.
45 Ibid., pp. 798–802.
46 Ibid., p. 786. On the abolition of privateering see Art. 1, *Paris Declaration Respecting Maritime Law* 1856, 115 CTS 1.
47 *Yearbook of the International Law Commission*, 1955, vol. I, pp. 37–44 especially at p. 40, para. 32; *Yearbook of the International Law Commission*, 1956, vol. II, pp. 282–283.

Elements of the crime of piracy

It is now generally taken as settled that the definition of piracy found in the HSC and UNCLOS represents customary international law. While it may be problematic to argue that these definitions codified pre-existing custom (given the contradictory sources that confronted the codifiers),[48] the successive re-enactment of this definition from the HSC to UNCLOS and then in subsequent treaties, regional instruments and Security Council resolutions, evidences States' general acceptance of its customary status.[49] Article 15(1) of the HSC and Article 101(a) of UNCLOS define piracy as:

(1) 'any illegal acts of violence or detention, or any act of depredation';
(2) committed for private ends;
(3) on the high seas or in a place outside the jurisdiction of any State; and
(4) committed by the crew or passengers of a private craft (or aircraft), against another vessel or persons or property aboard.

Piracy also encompasses voluntary participation in a pirate vessel, with knowledge of the facts making it a pirate vessel.[50] Such vessels are defined to include those intended for use in piracy as well as those which have so been used, or vessels under the control of pirates.[51] Thus it is erroneous to say no piracy has been committed before an attack has taken place; 'cruising with piratical intent' is equally piracy (though proving it may prove difficult).[52] A person committing 'any act of inciting or of intentionally facilitating' is also guilty of piracy.[53]

These elements have raised a number of greater and lesser controversies. The reference to 'illegal acts' in (1) has been criticised as question-begging.[54] Under what system of law must the violence be illegal? The best answer is that, while infelicitously phrased, the drafting was clearly intended to capture the broadest possible range of conduct.[55] Further, as any prosecution for piracy must (currently at least) be before a national court, the question of which system of law will characterise the violence involved is likely moot. It will be that of the forum State. The phrase may also still usefully exclude lawful acts of self-defence.

---

48 Rubin, *The Law of Piracy*, pp. 331–372.
49 Article 101(b), UNCLOS; Art. 15(2), HSC; Art. 1(1), Regional Cooperation Agreement on Combating Piracy and Armed Robbery against Ships in Asia 2005, (2005) 44 ILM 829 (ReCAAP); Art. 1, Code of Conduct concerning the Repression of Piracy and Armed Robbery against Ships in the Western Indian Ocean and the Gulf of Aden (2009), http://www. imo.org/ourwork/security/piu/pages/dcoc.aspx (accessed 4 September 2013). Security Council resolutions on Somali piracy from 2008 have consistently held that UNCLOS 'sets out the legal framework applicable to combating piracy and armed robbery at sea': e.g. UN Sec Res 2077 (2012), preamble.
50 Article 101(b), UNCLOS; Art. 15(2), HSC.
51 Article 103, UNCLOS; Art. 17, HSC.
52 D. Guilfoyle, 'Prosecuting Somali Pirates: A Critical Evaluation of the Options', *Journal of International Criminal Justice*, 2010, vol. 10, p. 767.
53 Article 101(c), UNCLOS; Art. 15(3), HSC.
54 Rubin, *The Law of Piracy*, p. 344 and O'Connell, *The International Law of the Sea*, p. 969.
55 M. McDougal and W. Burke, *The Public Order of the Oceans*, New Haven: Yale University Press, 1962, pp. 811–812.

As foreshadowed, the words 'for private ends' have caused some controversy.[56] The conventional view is that this excludes politically motivated acts from being piracy. The view is, however, entirely ahistorical. The words 'for private ends' (found nowhere in the historic case law)[57] were introduced by the League of Nations and Harvard Research codification projects to deal solely with what would now be considered a narrow question of the laws of armed conflict. The better view is that any act of violence not sanctioned by State authority is one for 'private ends', the correct dichotomy being not 'private/political' but 'private/public'.[58] It is a view that has now been upheld in a number of national court cases concerning violent environmental protest at sea.[59] The question is then not one of the subjective motive of the pirate (be it *animus furandi* or some political cause), but whether the violence in question is State-sanctioned. Those who advocate the popular view that subjective motivation is the key test have yet to explain why international law should generally make violence between vessels on the high seas the subject of universal jurisdiction but then provide a complete defence to suspects who can establish that they acted with political motives.

The remaining points are less controversial and can be swiftly disposed of. As regards the geographical limitation in (3), it is not as restrictive as it might appear. While it is frequently noted that the creation of the 200-nautical-mile exclusive economic zone (EEZ) has had the effect of significantly diminishing the area of the high seas, this does not affect the law of piracy. Article 58(2) UNCLOS provides that 'Articles 88 to 115 and other pertinent rules of international law apply to the exclusive economic zone in so far as they are not incompatible with' the EEZ regime. The law of piracy thus applies beyond the 12-nautical-mile territorial sea. It also applies to 'place[s] outside the jurisdiction of any State'. This phrase was first intended to provide for the possibility of islands unclaimed as territory by any State (*terra nullius*),[60] but may now apply only to Antarctica.

The final element of the offence (or final prerequisite for jurisdiction, depending on one's view) is that it be committed by the crew or passengers of a private craft (or aircraft), against another vessel or persons or property aboard. This 'two-vessel' requirement excludes acts of mutiny by passengers or crew from being considered piracy. However, the drafting requires only that a private craft (or mutinied State vessel) attack *another* craft. Thus attacks from a private craft against a warship constitute piracy. Indeed, a number of hapless Somali pirates have attacked US and German military vessels.[61] Intriguingly, both the HSC and UNCLOS,

---

56 For arguments against the view adopted here, see: Boister, *An Introduction to Transnational Criminal Law*, p. 31; Y. Tanaka, *The International Law of the Sea*, Cambridge: Cambridge University Press, 2012, pp. 355–356; and R. Churchill, 'The Piracy Provisions of the UN Convention On the Law of the Sea – Fit for Purpose?' in P. Koutrakos and A. Skordas (eds), *The Law and Practice of Piracy at Sea: European and International Perspectives*, Oxford: Hart, 2014. The last makes a distinction based on the idea that piratical violence is indiscriminate (but for objections that such an approach is unworkable and unsupported in law see Brown J in *The Ambrose Light*, 25 F. 408 (1885), 423–424).

57 Guilfoyle, 'Piracy and Terrorism'.

58 Ibid., and Guilfoyle, *Shipping Interdiction*, pp. 32–42; Kritsiotis, 'The Contingencies of Piracy', pp. 312–319; Geiss and Petrig, *The Legal Framework for Counter-Piracy Operations in Somalia*, pp. 61–62.

59 *Castle John and Nederlandse Stichting Sirius v NV Mabeco and NV Parfin* (Belgian Court of Cassation, 1986), 77 ILR 537; *Institute of Cetacean Research v Sea Conservation Society*, United States Court of Appeals for the Ninth Circuit, No. 12-35266, 25 February 2013 (amended 24 May 2013).

60 *Yearbook of the International Law Commission*, 1956, vol. II, p. 282.

61 On US cases arising from attacks on the USS *Nichols* and USS *Ashland* see: Megan McKee, 'Federal judge sentences Somali pirate to 30 years', *Jurist* blog, 30 November 2010, http://jurist.org/paperchase/2010/11/federal-judge-sentences-somali-pirate-to-30-years.php (accessed 5 September 2013).

as a progressive development of international law, contemplate that the attacking pirate craft might be an aircraft and that the victim vessel might also be an aircraft so long as the latter is on the high seas (i.e. not in flight). This was apparently done to extend the application of the general principles of the law of piracy to new technology.[62] The reasons for not including within the definition of piracy attack by a private aircraft (while airborne) against another aircraft (also airborne) are less readily apparent.

In recent State practice some controversy has arisen regarding the extent of universal jurisdiction over persons committing 'any act of inciting or of intentionally facilitating' piracy.[63] The words as they appear in the treaty law are notably *not* expressly constrained by the references to the high seas or places beyond the jurisdiction of any State found in the definition of the core offences.[64] In the context of Somali piracy the issue has become particularly germane. In *US v Ali* the trial court initially dismissed charges of aiding and abetting piracy brought against a Somali defendant, alleged to have acted as a translator for Somali pirates, on the basis that only a trivial amount of his conduct occurred on the high seas.[65] This ruling was overturned, the appeal court holding that the treaty language creating offences of 'inciting' or 'facilitating' piracy were not constrained by geographical references and were to be given their plain meaning.[66] On this reasoning, universal jurisdiction exists over such ancillary offences even when committed on dry land. It is to be hoped the more expansive approach taken by the appeal court in *US v Ali* will be followed elsewhere given the importance of targeting not just 'front line' pirates but the kingpins and financiers behind them.[67]

Offences under the SUA Convention: 'terrorism' and piracy

Introduction: 'terrorism' conventions or 'suppression' conventions?

The Convention on the Suppression of Unlawful Acts against the Safety of Maritime Navigation (SUA Convention)[68] was famously inspired by the *Achille Lauro* incident, in which an Italian cruise ship was internally hijacked and a hostage aboard killed.[69] The sponsoring governments who first introduced the draft Convention at the International Maritime Organization (IMO) (Austria, Egypt and Italy) cited as part of their reason for doing so the

---

62 Although there is no precise explanation in the ILC proceedings: *Yearbook of the International Law Commission*, 1955, vol. I, pp. 54–55.

63 Article 101(c), UNCLOS; Art. 15(3), HSC.

64 United Nations Division for Ocean Affairs and the Law of the Sea, 'Piracy: elements of national legislation pursuant to the United Nations Convention on the Law of the Sea, 1982', IMO Doc. LEG 98/8/1 (18 February 2011), p. 4, n. 15.

65 *US v. Ali*, Criminal Case No. 11–0106, US District Court (District of Columbia), Memorandum Opinion of 13 July 2012.

66 *US v. Ali*, Case No. 12-3056, US Court of Appeals (District of Columbia), 11 June 2013, 12–15.

67 A point noted in numerous Security Council Resolutions, most recently UN Sec Res 2077 (2012), preamble and paras 5, 9, 18–19, 21–22, 24.

68 IMO Convention for the Suppression of Unlawful Acts Against the Safety of Maritime Navigation and the Protocol for the Suppression of Unlawful Acts Against the Safety of Fixed Platforms on the Continental Shelf, Rome, 10 March 1988, 1678 UNTS 201, in force 1 March 1992.

69 Members of the Palestinian Liberation Front infiltrated the vessel by posing as passengers before seizing control in international waters. They demanded that Israel release a large number of prisoners, and killed a US citizen (Mr Leon Klinghoffer) when that demand was not met. For a useful, concise account see L. McCullough, 'International and Domestic Criminal Law Issues in the *Achille Lauro* Incident: A Functional Analysis', *Naval Law Review*, 1986, vol. 36, p. 53.

inherent limitations of piracy as an offence: that it necessarily involved an act for private ends, and that the requirement of an attack by a private vessel against another excluded internal hijacking.[70] Another relevant inspiration for the Convention was General Assembly Resolution 40/61 (1985), calling upon the IMO to 'study the problem of terrorism aboard or against ships' (notably, there already existed treaties dealing with hijacking and sabotaging aeroplanes and these proved influential in drafting the subsequent treaty[71]). The SUA Convention is thus commonly called a 'terrorism suppression' convention. It is important to note, however, that the word 'terrorism' appears only in its preamble. A terrorist motive does *not* form any express element of the offences it creates and those offences may therefore apply to acts which are not politically motivated (the rest of this chapter will therefore use the less loaded term 'suppression convention').

It might be thought counter-intuitive that an instrument designed to respond to terrorism can apply to non-politically motivated crime. This, however, is simply a result of the history of the suppression conventions. Historically, the international community could not agree a definition of terrorism, largely due to debate about whether those struggling for self-determination should be excluded from the concept.[72] It was thus easier to agree on a case-by-case basis that certain acts or tactics associated with terrorism were always crimes, irrespective of who committed them or why. In this sense, the SUA Convention followed a series of earlier suppression conventions and drew heavily on those dealing with offences against the safety of aircraft.[73] Arguably, it was only with the 1999 Convention Against Terrorist Financing that the international community was able to agree a form of words which might constitute a 'general' definition of terrorism.[74] However, this definition (including a motive requirement) obviously cannot be read back into earlier instruments such as the SUA Convention, which deal only with prohibiting certain conduct, albeit conduct associated with terrorism.

Offences under the SUA Convention

Article 3 of the SUA Convention defines several crimes. Relevantly, Article 3(1)(a) states that '[a]ny person commits an offence if that person unlawfully and intentionally . . . seizes or exercises control over a ship by force or threat thereof'. There is no requirement that the seizure be internal or politically motivated. Thus any pirate seizure of a vessel off Somalia, for example, clearly falls within this definition. The following acts, if committed in a manner 'likely to endanger the safe navigation' of a ship, are also *inter alia* offences under Article 3(1):

---

70 IMO Doc. PCUA 1/3, 3 February 1987, Annex.
71 Convention for the Suppression of Unlawful Seizure of Aircraft, The Hague, 16 December 1970, 860 UNTS 105; Convention for the Suppression of Unlawful Acts against the Safety of Civil Aviation, Montreal, 23 September 1971, 974 UNTS 177.
72 K. Trapp, *State Responsibility for International Terrorism*, Oxford: Oxford University Press, 2011, pp. 14–19.
73 See note 71, *supra*.
74 2178 UNTS 197. Article 2(1)(b) covers, without exceptions:

> Any . . . act intended to cause death or serious bodily injury to a civilian, or to any other person not taking an active part in the hostilities in a situation of armed conflict, when the purpose of such act, by its nature or context, is to intimidate a population, or to compel a government or an international organization to do or to abstain from doing any act.

- performing an act of violence against a person on board a ship;
- destroying or causing damage to a ship (or damaging its cargo);
- placing (by any means) on a ship a device or substance which is likely to destroy or damage that ship (or damage its cargo); or
- knowingly communicating false information.

Killing or injuring anyone in connection with attempting to commit one of these crimes is also an SUA Convention offence,[75] as is attempting, abetting and threatening such an offence.[76] The only case in which the Convention does not apply to the covered acts when committed at sea is where the offence was committed solely within a single State's territorial sea and the vessel was not scheduled to navigate beyond that sea and the suspected offender was subsequently found within that State's territory.[77]

Jurisdiction under the SUA Convention

In contrast to the law of piracy, parties to the SUA Convention have an express obligation to investigate, and where appropriate, prosecute those suspected of offences under the Convention.[78] To this end they must have adequate national laws making the offences under the Convention punishable before their Courts.[79] States Parties *must* establish their jurisdiction over Article 3 offences carried out against or aboard one of their flag vessels, within their territorial jurisdiction (including the territorial sea), or by one of their nationals.[80] States Parties *may* also assert jurisdiction on a variety of other bases, notably including the passive personality principle.[81]

The SUA Convention contains a further obligation to either extradite a suspect or submit the case for potential prosecution. Where a State finds a suspect or offender within its territory (the territorial State) and another State Party or Parties have jurisdiction over the offence, then the territorial State 'shall . . . if it does not extradite him, be obliged . . . to submit the case without delay to its competent authorities for the purpose of prosecution', in accordance with national law.[82] To this end, each party must enact a law allowing it to prosecute 'in cases where the alleged offender is present in its territory and it does not extradite him' to any State Party having jurisdiction. Put simply, if a State Party has a suspect in their territory, and another State Party has jurisdiction over the offence, then the first State Party must either prosecute that suspect or extradite them to a State which will. This may be described as a limited form of universal jurisdiction (or 'quasi-universal jurisdiction') among the parties to the Convention, as it allows the prosecution of individuals lacking relevant 'links' to the prosecuting State. Notably, however, this jurisdiction may only be exercised among States Parties: each party effectively delegates to every other State Party a power which it could otherwise use itself.

---

75 Article 3(1).
76 Article 3(2).
77 Article 4.
78 Article 10, SUA Convention (subject to Art. 6). Quasi-universal jurisdiction under the Convention is discussed further below.
79 Article 5, SUA Convention.
80 Article 6, SUA Convention.
81 Ibid.
82 Article 10(1), SUA Convention.

The Convention further provides that a State finding a suspect on its territory is required to commence a preliminary investigation and, if necessary, take the suspect into custody pending a decision about extradition or prosecution.[83] That investigating State is also required to communicate with States having jurisdiction. Crucially, Article 7(5) provides that an investigating State Party 'shall promptly report its findings to [those] States and . . . indicate whether it intends to exercise jurisdiction'. It is occasionally suggested that an extradite or prosecute obligation is triggered *only* by an extradition request. However, the structure of Article 7 makes it plain that an SUA Convention party has an independent duty to take action if it becomes aware by any means that it has a suspect on its territory, and it may elect to prosecute irrespective of the wishes of any State seeking extradition. Thus a State has a free choice whether to extradite or prosecute and need not defer to another State's jurisdiction.

SUA Protocol 2005

The SUA Convention was extended by a Protocol of 2005[84] to cover a range of further offences, essentially dealing with the proliferation of weapons of mass destruction (WMD) and precursor technologies at sea and terrorist offences involving WMD attacks against or from a ship. The Article 3*bis* added to the SUA Convention by the 2005 Protocol thus creates offences of, *inter alia*:

- using on or against a ship or discharging from a ship 'any explosive, radioactive material or BCN [biological, chemical or nuclear] weapon in a manner that causes or is likely to cause death or serious injury or damage' when 'the purpose of the act, by its nature or context, is to intimidate a population, or to compel a government or an international organization to do or to abstain from doing any act'; or
- transporting aboard a ship a BCN weapon or precursor technology that could 'significantly contribute' to BCN weapon manufacture.

Article 8*bis* also includes a system by which a State Party to the Protocol ('the requesting State') may seek permission to board another State Party's flag vessel ('the flag State') on the high seas where that vessel is suspected 'on reasonable grounds' of involvement in an offence under the SUA Convention or 2005 Protocol.[85] The *express* consent (which may be subjected to conditions) of the flag State is necessary before the requesting State may conduct such a boarding. The only exception is if the flag State has opted into a system whereby either a requesting State is deemed to have consent to a boarding and search if the flag State has not responded to an *acknowledged* request for such permission within four hours; or where the flag State has simply granted comprehensive permission in advance to other States Parties to conduct such boarding and search operations against its vessels.[86]

The utility of the Protocol is open to doubt. For the 2005 SUA Protocol to be regarded as a success, two requirements must be met. First, it must be sufficiently widely ratified. Second,

---

83 Article 7, SUA Convention.
84 Protocol to the Convention for the Suppression of Unlawful Acts against the Safety of Maritime Navigation, 1 November 2005, IMO Doc. LEG/CONF.15/21 (SUA Protocol 2005); entered into force 28 July 2010. A consolidated text is found in A.V. Lowe and S.A.G. Talmon (eds), *Legal Order of the Oceans: Basic Documents on the Law of the Sea*, Oxford: Hart, 2009.
85 Article 8*bis*(5), SUA Protocol 2005.
86 Article 8*bis*(5)(d) and (e), SUA Protocol 2005.

it is ultimately reliant upon national legislation for its enforcement: the crimes it creates can only be prosecuted under national law.[87] Despite the diplomatic effort made by the United States, UK and like-minded States to secure its conclusion, as at 31 July 2013 the Protocol has gained only 24 ratifications. None of these are from the United States, UK or other G8 States. Certainly two of the world's three largest flag States by registered tonnage, Panama and the Marshall Islands, have ratified the Protocol and have relevant laws prohibiting BCN or WMD transfers.[88] While this might allow suspect cargoes aboard such vessels to be interdicted at sea by a third State under the Protocol, this could only occur if a significant naval power ratified it. None has.

Further, the requesting State would – if it intended to prosecute any offences discovered aboard a flag State vessel (and was permitted to do so by the flag State) – need an applicable national law. The UK, which has not ratified the Protocol, has no such law applicable to foreign vessels.[89] Relevant US law is broad enough to capture the acts of foreigners outside the United States conspiring to use WMD against a US citizen abroad or any person or property within the United States.[90] In addition, US law also criminalises transport of WMD materiel by 'any vessel . . . on the high seas' with knowledge it is intended for use in a terrorist offence 'transcending national boundaries'.[91] However, the US also has not yet ratified the Protocol.

Conclusions: the law of piracy and SUA Convention compared

There is potential overlap between the range of acts covered by the law of piracy and those covered by the SUA Convention. As noted, the historic failure by the international community to agree on a single comprehensive definition of terrorism left a fragmentary legal framework aimed at the 'suppression' of certain acts or tactics associated with terrorism, parts of which could apply to piracy. Thus, pirates could be prosecuted under a number of the suppression conventions, depending on the tactics which they adopt.[92] This is equally true of the SUA Convention. Its basic Article 3 offence of 'unlawfully and intentionally' seizing control of a ship by force is clearly something Somali pirates do. Conversely, acts of theft ('depredation') which did not endanger the safety of a vessel and were committed by one vessel against another would be piracy, but would not be an SUA Convention offence. Thus pirates in the Malacca Strait, who typically steal aboard vessels to make off with valuable property in a type of maritime smash–and–grab burglary, will generally *not* commit an SUA Convention offence. The SUA Convention, therefore, clearly does not cover piracy *in toto*, but some acts

---

87 See M.D. Fink, 'The Right of Visit for Warships: Some Challenges in Applying the Law of Maritime Interdiction on the High Seas', *Military Law and Law of War Review*, 2010, vol. 49, p. 19.

88 See relevant 1540 Committee Reports: UN Doc. S/AC.44/2004/(02)/82 (Marshall Islands, 10 December 2004); S/AC.44/2004/(02)/120/Add.1 (Panama, 8 March 2006).

89 See e.g. sections 44 and 47(7) of the Anti-terrorism, Crime and Security Act 2001, c. 24 (nuclear and biological weapons offences only extend extra-territorially to acts done by a 'United Kingdom person'). There have been no amendments to the Aviation and Maritime Security Act 1990 c. 31 implementing the SUA Convention.

90 See 18 USC § 2332a and b.

91 18 USC § 2283; however, the offence must *also* constitute a federal offence listed in 18 USC § 2332b(g)(5)(B).

92 For example, the Somali piracy model involves taking hostages to compel private actors to follow a certain course of action (pay a ransom). *Prima facie* this falls squarely within the offence defined in Art. 1, International Convention Against the Taking of Hostages 1979, 1316 UNTS 205.

constituting piracy under UNCLOS may also be SUA Convention offences. The result, that one course of conduct could be characterised as any one of several crimes, is scarcely unique to international law. It is sometimes suggested that if the law of piracy covered political offences, then the SUA Convention would not have been necessary. It is a view, however, of little merit. The essence of the *Achille Lauro* incident was that it was an internal hijacking: by definition an event not covered by the laws of piracy.

If there is potential overlap between the law of piracy and the SUA Convention (and there is), does the SUA Convention offer any advantages over the general law of piracy? The answer is that it does, in at least two respects. First, unlike the law of piracy, the SUA Convention creates an express obligation upon parties to enact national laws. Under Article 6, States Parties *must* make the offences in Article 3 a crime under national law when committed against or on board their flag vessels; within their territory or territorial sea; or by one of their nationals.[93] In addition, States Parties may establish criminal jurisdiction on certain other bases, including on the basis that the victim of the offence is their national.[94] No such express obligations are found in the law of piracy. Second, while the law of piracy contains a duty to cooperate in the suppression of piracy but only discretion to prosecute suspects, the SUA Convention places express obligations upon States Parties both to have adequate national laws in place and to either extradite or prosecute suspects found within their territory.

However, the law of piracy does have its advantages. Only the law of piracy provides an exception to the exclusive jurisdiction of the flag State that can justify the stopping, searching, arrest or seizure of suspect pirate vessels and persons aboard on the high seas. The SUA Convention does not provide any such automatic right of high seas interdiction (although the 2005 Protocol contains a mechanism for seeking the flag State's permission for such a boarding). While piracy is a crime of universal jurisdiction, the SUA Convention creates a more limited form of 'quasi-universal' jurisdiction between parties to the treaty.

In conclusion, the regulation of maritime violence under international law is often conceptualised as divided into the (somewhat arbitrary) categories of piracy and terrorism. The concept that a clear distinction exists has turned on the idea that piracy (an act for 'private ends') must be non-political and that political motivation must be an essential agreement of 'terrorism'. This involves a misreading of the law and history of both piracy (where the codifiers used the word 'private' *only* to exclude certain acts regulated by the laws of war) and the suppression conventions (which prior to 1999 prohibited certain acts essentially without reference to motives). However, even though these categories may overlap in some cases, that does not mean they coincide. The law applicable to crime at sea still suffers from serious fragmentation. This fragmentation is most apparent in the lack of a positive obligation to prosecute pirates or even a requirement that States have a law enabling the assertion of universal jurisdiction over their acts.

93 Article 6(1), SUA Convention.
94 Article 6(2), SUA Convention.

23
Cybercrime

Christopher Ram*

What is 'cybercrime'?

'Cybercrime' is not a legal or forensic term, nor does it define or describe a clear category of criminal offences. There is general agreement on a core list of specific computer abuses and offences, but beyond this there is no global consensus on what it means. This arises from the versatile and ubiquitous nature of computers and the dynamic evolution of technologies and the ways they are used since the late 1950s. Computers, networks and data are now found in so many different applications that they can be linked in some way to almost every form of crime and in almost any conceivable role. They have become instruments for both crime and the prevention and investigation of crime, they have created new motives and opportunities for crime, and they often alter the balance of risks and rewards for offenders. Depending on context, 'cybercrime' can refer to crimes committed by means of technologies or against technologies and their users as such, but also to many other scenarios in which they play a range of indirect or supporting roles.

Constant innovation over the past five decades has made the technologies and the legitimate and criminal activities they support a complex and rapidly moving target. Changes in crime have often outpaced the development of laws and law-enforcement capacity, and created asymmetries or discrepancies between one jurisdiction and another. They have also transformed some of the underlying concepts on which criminal law and law in general are based, in areas such as privacy, property and jurisdiction, especially as they have become interconnected into a global network. One result is uncertainty about whether existing crimes are 'cyber' or not. Another has been whether an increasing range of on-line activities are sufficiently harmful to require designation as 'crimes'. The market for computer devices and the Internet are both global, but their beneficial and negative effects often depend on

*   The author is at present employed as Legal Counsel, Canada Department of Justice and from 1999 to 2003 was a Crime Prevention Expert with the UN Office on Drugs and Crime, Vienna. Except where the contrary is specified, all positions attributed to Canada, other countries or the United Nations, past or present are solely the opinion of the author.

underlying factors such as the degree of technological or economic development, the style or model of government, and legal or social concepts of the rule of law and human rights. This has led to greater differences about what interests the criminal law should be used to protect, in areas ranging from intellectual property to privacy and national security.

Cybercrime can be seen from technological, legal and social perspectives, and all of these have introduced constantly evolving variables since the problem first arose. In technological terms, criminal activities that first arose with large stand-alone mainframe computers have been transformed by the development of the personal computer and the evolution of inter-connectedness from limited and dedicated links to a local and then world-wide web of networks and into the Internet as it now exists. The computer itself has become smaller, to the point where microchips that are clearly 'computers' are used in everything from household appliances to orbital communications satellites, and in networks that make it difficult to determine where one device ends and another begins.[1] The nature of value, property and the offences based on property have all been transformed, and the existence of digital documents and electronic transactions has had a similar effect on forgery and a range of identity-related crimes. The global nature of the Internet has also challenged traditional territorial models of criminal jurisdiction, and the use of the Internet as a means of communication and accessing stored data has transformed policies and laws that relate to privacy rights and investigative measures that infringe on those rights. This has led many experts to frame cybercrime offences in ways which are 'technology-neutral', focusing as much as possible on very fundamental descriptions of conduct and the reasons it is harmful, and as little as possible on details that will differ depending on what technology is used or targeted by offenders in each case.[2]

Legislatures and courts have wrestled with many legal challenges. 'Cybercrime' usually includes a core cluster of new crimes made possible by the technologies, and more traditional crimes that have been significantly changed as a result of new opportunities or the use of technologies as an instrument, but beyond this the waters become more clouded. Computers and networks can be essential or central to an offence; they may play a highly specialised role or only a minor or peripheral role, and this often depends as much on the *modus operandi* of individual offenders as it does on the type of crime committed. As a label, 'cybercrime' does not always conform to the conceptual frameworks on which traditional criminal offences are based, and as a result the extent to which cybercrime consists of old crimes using new technologies, or an entirely new sort of crime instead, has been an open issue since the 1970s.[3]

---

1 For early discussions of the meaning of 'computer' and other key terms see J.K. Taber, 'On Computer Crime', *Computer Law Journal*, 1978, vol. 1, p. 517; S. Nycum, 'Computer Crime Legislation in the United States', *Israeli Law Review*, 1986, vol. 24, p. 64. For a more recent review see J. Clough, *Principles of Cybercrime*, 3rd edn, Cambridge: Cambridge University Press, 2010, p. 52.

2 'Technology-neutral' rules support innovation because they do not favour one line or area of development over another. The advantages in criminal law lie in better international interoperability and offences and powers that do not become obsolete as technologies evolve. Reed describes the latter as 'future-proofing'. See B-J. Koops, 'Should ICT Regulation be Technology-Neutral', in B-J. Koops, M. Lips, C. Prins and M. Schellekens (eds), *Starting Points for ICT Regulation: Deconstructing Prevalent Policy One-liners*, The Hague: TMC Asser Press, 2006, p. 77; C. Reed, 'Taking Sides on Technology Neutrality', *SCRIPT-ed*, 2007, vol. 4, no. 3, p. 263, http://www.law.ed.ac.uk/ahrc/script-ed/vol4–3/reed.asp (accessed 18 June 2014).

3 See note 6, *infra*.

The first assessments saw traditional offences using new instruments, followed by a few crimes directed at the technologies, as the offenders, who were 'insiders', began to innovate. But as computers, networks and their uses have spread, it has become apparent that the technologies have not only transformed criminal offending, but also the underlying interests the criminal law seeks to protect. Theft, for example, consists of the *taking* or *appropriation* of *property* that belongs to someone else with some element of *dishonesty or fraud*, and the *intention to deprive* the owner of it, and all of these concepts have been affected by technologies. Property is no longer always tangible, and the nature of its value, and links between value and exclusivity of access or use, have all changed. An inexpensive storage device may hold high-value data, for example, which can be copied without depriving the owner of it, affecting not only economic value and interests but privacy as well.[4] Legislatures have developed offences based on harms which are roughly analogous to specific attributes of tangible property, such as the appropriation of the value of computer time, access or actual data, trespass to 'property' without physical location or dimension, damaging data in ways similar to criminal damage or mischief, and interfering with the access to or use of data by those entitled to it.[5] Apart from new definitions and concepts based on rapidly evolving technologies, there has been the question of whether to treat cybercrime as a new phenomenon or to attempt to apply, and if necessary to expand or adjust, existing crimes, or to create entirely new ones.[6]

The making of criminal law and the administration of criminal justice always involve balancing between coercive and punitive measures to regulate conduct on one hand, and the countervailing need for safeguards to protect human rights on the other. Here also the underlying interests have been transformed by the technologies. The technologies create new ways to commit crime and new ways to investigate it, which in turn has generated changes to procedural powers, but they have also created new or expanded interests in areas such as privacy and freedom of expression and proposals to create new cybercrime offences both to protect and to control the various new activities made possible. The global nature of cybercrime has also generated litigation based on transnational events and dual-criminality

---

4   On whether information or data can be 'property' and stolen, see *Oxford v Moss* (1979) 68 Cr App Rep 183, [1979] Crim LR 119 (UK), and *R v McLaughlin*, [1980] 2 SCR 331 and *R v Stewart*, [1988] 1 SCR 963 (Canada). *Moss* and *Stewart* pre-date digital technologies but apply to them. See also R.G. Hammond, 'Theft of Information', *Law Quarterly Review*, 1984, vol. 100, p. 252 (discussing *Stewart*); J.T. Cross, 'Protecting Confidential Information Under the Law of Theft', *Oxford Journal of Legal Studies*, 1991, vol. 11, p. 264; M.R. McGuire, *Technology, Crime and Justice: The Question Surrounding Technomia*, Abingdon: Routledge, 2012, p. 66.

5   For different approaches taken by various legislatures in Australia, Canada, New Zealand, the UK and the USA, see Clough, *Principles of Cybercrime*, chapters 3 (access offences), 4 (data impairment) and 8 (whether copyright infringement is 'theft' or not). For an earlier assessment of the same issues, see U. Sieber, *The International Handbook on Computer Crime*, New York: Wiley, 1986, Chapter IV.

6   Taber, 'On Computer Crime'; D. Ingraham, 'On Charging Computer Crime', *Computer Law Journal*, 1980, vol. 2, p. 429 (computer crimes as conventional crimes by new means); and D.B. Parker, 'Computer Abuse Research Update', *Computer Law Journal*, 1980 vol. 2, p. 329 (computer crime as a new criminal law problem). For more recent assessments, see M.E. O'Neill, 'Old Crimes in New Bottles: Sanctioning Cybercrime', *George Mason Law Review*, 2000, vol. 9, p. 237; S. Brenner, 'Cybercrime Metrics: Old Wine in New Bottles?' *Virginia Journal of Law and Technology*, 2004, vol. 9, no. 13, p. 1; McGuire, *Technology, Crime and Justice*, pp. 35–38, 66–73; Clough, *Principles of Cybercrime*, pp. 8–11.

requirements that have tested the meaning or scope of specific offences and generally exerted pressures for common approaches to the framing of criminal offences.[7]

In social terms, computer networks have also transformed many basic social, political and economic functions and activities, and the exact nature of these transformations varies significantly from one country to another depending on the pre-existing context in which it occurs. At the same time the global nature of the networks has bridged gaps that previously kept some distance between cultures and between potential offenders and victims, generating new pressures on the boundaries of the criminal law itself. Most countries maintain some degree of respect or protection for rights such as the freedoms of expression and association, for example, and also some exceptions in which the criminal law is used to suppress content or communications that the state regards as sufficiently harmful to individual interests, economic interests or state security interests, but there is no global consensus on what should be criminalised or where the line between protected access, use or expression and criminal conduct should be drawn.

Thus, outside of core 'cybercrime' activities, there is a much larger range of activities that some countries and experts would label as 'cybercrime', that others might be willing to regulate outside of the criminal law, and that some countries or experts would be unwilling or unable to regulate at all for reasons of fundamental law and the protection of human rights. Most countries agree that the trade in digital child pornography is harmful and should be suppressed, but other content that is protected as free expression in some countries is criminalised as religious blasphemy, hate propaganda or a threat to national security in others.[8] The

7　Regarding dual criminality in cybercrime cases see, for example, *King v USA* [2006] EWHC 3033 (Admin); *R v Bow Street Magistrates' Court and Allison, ex parte Government of the USA* [1999] 3 WLR 620; [1999] UKHL 31, and *Yarimak v Governor of HMP Brixton & Zezev v Government of USA* [2002] EWHC 589 (Admin). Early concerns involved gaps between countries that had cybercrime offences and those that had not yet enacted them, as transnational hacking and malware cases outstripped policy and legislative development. See D. Goldstone and B. Shave, 'International Dimensions of Crimes in Cyberspace' *Fordham International Law Journal*, 1998, vol. 22, p. 1924, pp. 1933–1934; M.D. Goodman and S.W. Brenner, 'The Emerging Consensus on Criminal Conduct in Cyberspace'. *International Journal of Law and Information* Technology, 2002, vol. 10, p. 139, pp. 139–141. More recently concerns have focused on areas where there is no consensus on criminalisation, such as intellectual property crime, and on the similarity of underlying or computer-related offences. Differences in the framing of offences, such as whether offences based on unlawful access or trespass are the same as those based on theft of computer time or services arise less often because in most countries dual criminality requirements are met if the actual conduct itself is a crime in both jurisdictions, but the absence of an essential element in one place or the other can still be problematic (*Allison, supra.*).

8　For historical reasons, France and Germany criminalise 'hate propaganda' and 'Nazi' or other extremist political content that in the United States are protected as free speech, leading to a series of judicial decisions in both countries when French interest groups attempted to obtain a French court order against Yahoo!, which was using file-servers in Delaware, USA to advertise Nazi memorabilia for sale. See W. Crane, 'World-Wide Jurisdiction: An Analysis of Over-Inclusive Internet Jurisdictional Law and an Attempt by Congress to Fix It', *De Paul Journal of Arts and Entertainment Law*, 2001, vol. 11, p. 267, pp. 303–305, and C. Dawson, 'Creating Borders on the Internet: Free Speech, the United States, and International Jurisdiction', *Virginia Journal of International Law*, 2004, vol. 44, p. 637, pp. 640–644. The United States, on the other hand, might suppress content in the 2011 'WikiLeaks' disclosures on national security grounds that it is protected by press-freedom laws in Sweden, where many of the WikiLeaks file-servers are located. See: D. Corneil, 'Harboring WikiLeaks: Comparing Swedish and American Press Freedom in the Internet Age', *California Western International Law Journal*, 2010–11, vol. 41, p. 477. Conduct such as the defacing or burning of the Qur'an or publication of cartoons depicting the Prophet Muhammad in a satirical light were legal in Denmark, but would have led to prosecutions – and did incite violence – in many Islamic countries. See L.B. Lidsky, 'Incendiary Speech and Social Media', *Texas Tech Law Review*, 2011–12, vol. 44, p. 147.

new and increased values associated with data have also generated pressures to use the criminal law to protect intellectual property.[9]

A number of different labels have been used since concerns first arose in the late 1950s as technologies and offending evolved and typologies developed, eventually arriving at 'cybercrime' as a general description, in part due to difficulties with attempts at more precise classification.[10] Specific terms used have included 'computer crime',[11] 'computer-related crime', 'high-technology crime',[12] 'cybercrime'[13] and, most recently, 'cyber-security'.[14] The earliest commentaries refer variously to 'telecommunications crime', 'computer crime' or 'high-tech crime', without much consideration of the exact meaning, but as cases began to accumulate, typologies emerged. During the 1990s, 'computer crime' and 'computer-related crime' were used to distinguish between entirely new offences made possible by computers and pre-existing offences being committed in new ways using computers and networks.[15] By the late 1990s, increasing concerns about the importance of networks as critical infrastructure that were threatened by some forms of cybercrime led to the use of 'cyber-security'.[16] Many

9   See S. Sardar and B. Shaw, 'Social Media, Censorship, and Control: Beyond SOPA, PIPA, and the Arab Spring', *U. of Pennsylvania Journal of Law and Social Change*, 2011–12, vol. 15, p. 577.

10 See e.g. M. Hildebrandt, 'Extraterritorial Jurisdiction to regulate Cyberspace: Bodin, Schmitt, Grotius in Cyberspace', *University of Toronto Law Journal*, 2013, vol. 63, no. 2, p. 196, pp. 198–201.

11 See Taber, 'On Computer Crime'; Parker, 'Computer Abuse Research Update'. See also OECD Committee on Information, Computer and Communications Policy (1983–85), Report No.10: *Computer-Related Crime: An Analysis of Legal Policy*, OECD Publications, Paris, 1986, No.43735; Sieber, *International Handbook on Computer Crime*, 1986. Prof. Sieber participated in the OECD study and describes computer crime as 'any illegal, unethical or unauthorized behaviour involving automatic data-processing or the transmission of data'. He later raises the problem of over-breadth that this represents and proposes an issue-by-issue or offence-by-offence approach for responses such as legislation and prosecution, based on problems as they arise. See pp. 2–3 and 27. See also U. Sieber, 'Legal Aspects of Computer-Related Crime in the Information Society', Study prepared for the European Commission, 1 January 1998, http://ec.europa.eu/archives/ISPO/legal/en/comcrime/ sieber.html (accessed 20 June 2014).

12 See e.g. Goodman and Brenner, 'The Emerging Consensus', pp. 144–146.

13 See Brenner, 'Cybercrime Metrics' pp. 2–6; S.D. Moitra, 'Developing Policies for Cybercrime: Some Empirical Issues', *European Journal of Criminal Law and Criminal Justice*, 2005, vol. 13, no. 3, p. 435; O'Neill, 'Old Crimes in New Bottles', pp. 256–264.

14 D. Satola and H.L. Judy, 'Towards a Dynamic Approach to Enhancing International Cooperation and Collaboration in Cybersecurity Legal Frameworks: Reflections on the Proceedings of the Workshop on Cybersecurity Legal Issues at the 2010 United Nations Internet Governance Forum', *William Mitchell Law Review*, 2011, vol. 37, p. 1745; S. Gosnell-Handler, 'New Cyber Face of Battle: Developing a Legal Approach to Accommodate Emerging Trends in Warfare', *Stanford Journal of International Law*, 2012, vol. 48, p. 209, pp. 211–212.

15 Goodman and Brenner, 'The Emerging Consensus', pp. 144–154. See also M.A. Sussmann, 'The Critical Challenges From International High-Tech and Computer-Related Crime at the Millennium', *Duke Journal of Comparative and International Law*, 1998–99, vol. 9, p. 451, p. 455; H. Kaspersen, 'Crimes Related to Computer Networks', Background Paper for the 10th UN Congress on the Prevention of Crime and Treatment of Offenders, UN Doc. A/CONF.187/10, 2000, para. 14. Some of these describe the differentiation as between scenarios where the computer is the 'subject' or 'object' of crime.

16 See E. Schmidt and J. Cohen, *The New Digital Age: Reshaping the Future of People, Nations and Business*, New York: Knopf, 2013, Chapter 3.

sources discuss specific forms of criminality without attempting to define them,[17] and legislatures have usually referred to terms such as 'computer system' or 'data' only as specific elements of either computer-specific or more general offences, or as offences specifically based on the use of computers or other technologies as instruments. Some countries have enacted specific offences of 'computer fraud', for example,[18] and a number have enacted offences of copying, damaging or impeding access to or use of 'data' because it is not covered by pre-existing offences based on tangible property.[19]

The terms 'cybercrime' and 'cyber-security' are sometimes used interchangeably, but the distinctions remain important. Generally, discussions of 'cyber-security' encompass elements such as natural threats to technologies that are beyond the scope of criminal law, and state-based conduct such as 'cyber-warfare', where the actors are beyond its grasp.[20] Many conventional cybercrimes do not raise any national security elements, and in many countries the investigation of conventional crimes and national security threats has a very different legal and institutional basis. 'Cyber-security' is also in some contention because there are underlying differences concerning governance and whether on-line activities constitute free expression or a security threat.

A brief history of cybercrime, 1965–2013

The first known electronic computer was developed in the UK as a means of decrypting enemy communications during the Second World War, although official secrecy would conceal this development and its inventors for more than three decades afterwards.[21] Computers did not become practical for lesser applications until the invention of the transistor in the early 1950s, and throughout the 1950s and 1960s they would remain large, expensive mainframe, stand-alone devices, found almost exclusively in government institutions, universities and a few large companies and financial institutions. The earliest known 'computer

17 See S. Charney and K. Alexander, 'Computer Crime', *Emory Law Journal*, 1996, vol. 45, p. 931; Goldstone and Shave, 'International Dimensions of Crimes in Cyberspace'; Sussmann, 'The Critical Challenges'; all discussing general problems to be addressed. Lists or descriptions of specific activities or offences can be found in Sieber, *International Handbook on Computer Crime;* Goodman and Brenner, 'The Emerging Consensus', p. 144 *et seq.*, and Brenner, 'Cybercrime Metrics', pp. 2–6.

18 See Council of Europe Convention on Cybercrime, Budapest, 23 November 2001, ETS No 185, in force 1 July 2004, Arts 8 (fraud) and 9 (forgery). Some States Parties have adopted specific offences to implement this, while others may rely on the interpretation of existing fraud offences. See also Clough, *Principles of Cybercrime*, Chapter 7.

19 Clough, *Principles of Cybercrime*, Chapter 4; *DPP v Lennon* (2006) [2006] EWHC 1201 (Admin); *Whiteley v The Queen* (1991) 93 Cr App R 25 (holding pre-existing offence of criminal damage to property applied to intangible damage).

20 See J. Hunker, 'U.S. International Policy for Cybersecurity: Five Issues That Won't Go Away', *Journal of National Security Law and Policy*, 2010, vol. 4, p. 197, for a discussion of the range of issues other than responding to cybercrime, that are included in discussions of cyber-security.

21 S. Singh, *The Code Book*, London: Fourth Estate Books, 1999, Chapters 4 and 6. Devices known as 'bombes' developed by Alan Turing were first used to electronically test and reverse German 'Enigma' encryption algorithms at Bletchley Park in 1942, and programmability was added by another Bletchley Park mathematician, Max Neumann, late in the war in a machine known as 'Colossus', designed to break a more difficult code. These preceded the first publicly known computer, the University of Pennsylvania's ENIAC, which began operations in 1945.

crime' occurrences emerged in the 1950s,[22] and most of the cases prior to the late 1970s involve forms of economic crimes on the part of the few 'insiders' who had access to the devices, software and data.[23] Attacks on computers and data also occurred on occasion, generally by dissatisfied employees, but as the practical and symbolic importance of computers began to increase they also became a target for political protestors.[24]

Many of the major issues of today first arose in the 1970s or early 1980s, including the effects of technologies on privacy interests, jurisdictional issues, the need for new evidence and investigative laws and techniques, and the first concerns about remote, unauthorised access all arose before the Internet became a significant factor in the early 1990s. The first remote access cases involved telephone connections with mainframe computers and the first automated banking machines in the 1970s,[25] and the first known computer virus infected and disrupted a small number of computers on the ARPANET in November 1988.[26]

As the value of data and the use of computers increased, they became the targets of offenders, and legislatures began to respond. The OECD, G–7 (later G–8), Council of Europe and United Nations all became engaged in work aimed at studying the problem and recommending legislative responses from the mid–1980s to the mid–1990s.[27] The first national legislative responses specific to cybercrime in the United States,[28] Canada,[29] the UK,[30] Japan,

22 D. Van Tassel, 'Computer Crime,' American Federation of Information Processing Societies, Fall proceedings, November 1970, p. 445, http://www.computer.org/csdl/proceedings/afips/1970/5076/00/50760445.pdf (accessed August 2013).

23 Sieber, *International Handbook on Cybercrime*; D.B. Parker, *Crime by Computer*, New York: Scribner's, 1976; and A. Bequai, *Computer Crime*, Lexington, MA: Lexington Books, 1978, Chapter 16.

24 Bequai, *Computer Crime*, p. 13. In 1969, a student occupation at Sir George Williams (now Concordia) University in Montreal, Canada, caused damage valued at $2 million in a matter of a few minutes, mostly in losses of data and equipment as a result of a fire and fire-fighting efforts. See http://archives.concordia.ca/computer-riot (accessed 18 June 2014) and *Re S (AC)* [1969] QJ no 22, 7 CRNS 42 (Quebec SC).

25 Sieber, *International Handbook on Cybercrime*, p. 9; Parker, *Crime by Computer*, p. 59.

26 *US v. Morris*, 928 F.2d 504, 506 (2d Cir. 1991), upholding the conviction of Robert Morris, author of the 'Morris worm' (then known as the 'Cornell Virus') and J. Castillo, B. Doyle and S. Dubney, 'Computer Crime', *American Criminal Law Review*, 1991–92, vol. 29, p. 221, pp. 228–230.

27 For a review of international developments in general in this period see Charney and Alexander, 'Computer Crime'; Goldstone and Shave, 'International Dimensions of Crimes in Cyberspace'; Sussmann, 'The Critical Challenges', pp. 451–489, R. Broadhurst, 'Developments in the Global Law Enforcement of Cyber-Crime', *Policing: International Journal of. Police Strategy and Management*, 2006, vol. 29, p. 408; *United Nations Manual on the Prevention and Control of Computer-related Crime, International Review of Criminal Policy*, Nos. 43 and 44, 1995 (United Nations publication, Sales No. E.94.IV.5), http://www.uncjin.org/Documents/irpc4344.pdf (accessed 18 June 2014).

28 Comprehensive Crime Control Act (1984), including the Counterfeit Access Device and Computer Fraud and Abuse Act, 18 USC § 1030 and Computer Fraud and Abuse Act (1986), 18 USC § 1030. Federal legislation was proposed as early as the late 1970s, but not enacted. See Bequai, *Computer Crime*, pp. 43–45; J. Becker, 'Trial of a Computer Crime', *Computer Law Journal*, 1980, vol. 2, p. 441.

29 An Act to amend the Criminal Code, S.C. 1985, c. 27, s. 45. See also D.K. Piragoff, 'Computers' (Comment on Canadian *Criminal Code* amendments), *Ottawa Law Review*, 1984, vol. 16, p. 306.

30 A series of UK enactments from 1980 to 1985 dealt with cybercrime-related issues, including the Forgery and Counterfeiting Act (1981), the Copyright (Computer Software) Amendment Act (1985), the Data Protection Acts (1984, 1998), the Police and Criminal Evidence Act (1984), the Computer Misuse Act, 1990 (offences) and the Regulation of Investigatory Powers Act, 2000 (lawful and unlawful interception of communications). See N. MacEwen, 'The Computer Misuse Act 1990: Lessons from its Past and Predictions for its Future', *Criminal Law Review*, 2008, vol. 12, p. 955.

Germany[31] and a number of other European countries date from the late 1970s to 1986 or 1987. In 1997, the Council of Europe convened a Committee of Experts (PC-CY) to consider questions of substantive and procedural law and international cooperation and mandated it to elaborate an international legal instrument, which eventually produced the Council of Europe Convention on Cybercrime (hereinafter the Budapest Convention) in late 2000.[32]

The period since 2000 has included the expansion and consolidation of early legislative responses in developed countries and the enactment of new offences in many developing countries, often driven by a combination of self-interested assistance from aid-donors seeking to defeat cybercrime at its source, to the extent possible, and the desire of recipient countries both to protect themselves from cybercrime displaced out of countries with stronger laws and better security measures and law enforcement capacities, and to support expanding high-technology development of their own. It has also seen significant convergence between the traditional forms of cybercrime that were the subject of the Budapest Convention and what many countries regard as the need to control the Internet for what they regard as essential national security interests. The fact that this cannot be done effectively at the national level has led to pressure from some countries for a global legal instrument that would allow them to apply limits on access and content in domestic law and seek at least some minimal international cooperation in their application and enforcement.

Two groups of countries have now engaged in a debate, with many other countries either undecided where their interests lie or awaiting a sense of direction from the primary antagonists. In general, countries with relatively closed political and governance structures seek a treaty that would afford them greater means of limiting information and controlling or suppressing dissent, and some developing countries seek a treaty as a legal basis for gaining greater access to technical assistance to protect themselves and support their own development. Developed countries with relatively open governance systems, on the other hand, argue that an unrestricted or unregulated Internet is essential for innovation and the exercise of basic human rights, and oppose the development of a comprehensive treaty in favour of a more *ad hoc* and practical approach. Proposals to start discussions on Internet governance in general at the UN have not made much progress.[33] Debate continues in other *fora*, notably the

---

31 Zweites Gesetz zur Bekämpfung der Wirtschaftskriminalität (Second Law for the Prevention of Economic Crimes), enacted 26 June 1986, *Bundesgesetzblatt*, part I, vol. 28, p. 271. See also Sieber, *International Handbook of Computer Crime*, p. 212 *et seq.* (English summary and commentary).

32 Council of Europe Convention on Cybercrime, Budapest, 8 November 2001, ETS No. 185; in force 1 July 2004. See Council of Europe, *Convention on Cybercrime: Explanatory Report*, http://conventions.coe.int/Treaty/en/Reports/Html/185.htm (accessed 18 June 2013).

33 General Assembly Resolutions 60/242 of 27 March 2006 and 65/141 of 20 December 2010. See also J. Waz and P. Weiser, 'Internet Governance: The Role of Multi-stakeholder Organizations', *Journal on Telecommunications and High-Tech Law*, 2012, vol. 10, p. 331, http://papers.ssrn.com/sol3/papers.cfm?abstract_id=2195167 (accessed 18 June 2014).

International Telecommunications Union (ITU)[34] and U.N. Commission on Crime Prevention and Criminal Justice.[35]

The substance of cybercrime: criminology and criminal offences

Early computers were stand-alone mainframe devices, most early crimes were economic offences committed by the insiders who had access to them, and many of the early discussions within and among countries started in the context of 'white-collar' or economic crime. Offenders were portrayed as non-violent, intelligent and motivated by altruistic or thrill-seeking challenges. Their advanced skills obscured criminal motives, a perception consistent with the general tendency to under-estimate the culpability of 'white-collar' criminals,[36] and a persistent source of frustration for law enforcement and prosecutors.[37] The nature and scope of the problem was transformed by a number of developments from the mid–1980s to the end of the millennium, including a reduction in the size and cost of computers, and dramatic increases in the speed, capacity and raw numbers of computers, the interconnectedness and geographic expansion of the Internet,[38] and by increasing reliance on the technologies for everything from social networking and casual communications to essential economic and national security functions.

---

34 See e.g. T. Maurer, 'Cyber Norm Emergence at the United Nations: An Analysis of the UN's Activities Regarding Cyber-security', 2011, Discussion Paper 2011–11, Cambridge, MA.: Belfer Center for Science and International Affairs, Harvard Kennedy School, September 2011, http://belfercenter.ksg.harvard.edu/files/maurer-cyber-norm-dp–2011–11-final.pdf; L. Kelion, 'US resists control of internet passing to UN agency', BBC News, 2 August 2012, http://www.bbc.co.uk/news/technology–19106420>; and US Department of State Fact Sheet on US positions in the 2012 World Conference on Information Technologies, http://www.state.gov/e/eb/rls/fs/2012/195921.htm (all accessed 18 June 2014).

35 In 2010, the UN Crime Congress held in Salvador, Brazil featured a debate and negotiation between the two factions that led to a compromise in which an open-ended intergovernmental expert group would be convened to conduct a comprehensive study of the problem of cybercrime. One group regards this as a first step in the direction of a treaty process and the other sees it as more likely to generate recommendations and results of a more practical nature. The author serves as the Rapporteur of this group and some of the content in this segment is based on personal notes and discussions. See also the Report of the Congress, General Assembly Resolution 65/230, Annex, paragraphs 39 and 41–42, and paragraph 9 of the resolution itself, under which the group was convened in January of 2011. As of late 2013, the process was still ongoing. The General Assembly sessions of 2012 and 2013 both included negotiations in which one faction maintained that it was essential to find consensus in the expert group process on next steps and the other was trying to alter the mandate to allow for a political debate on the treaty and other questions without a final outcome from the expert process itself. Political questions aside, the lack of resources to support the time-consuming and expensive intergovernmental expert process were a significant problem.

36 Parker, *Crime by Computer*, p. 45; Bequai, *Computer Crime*, pp. 1–5.

37 Charney and Alexander, 'Computer Crime', p. 954 *et seq.*

38 From 200 connected computers in 1981, the Internet had crossed the one billion threshold by 2014. The last available count, for January 2014, stood at 1,010,251,829 'internet hosts' on-line. See: Internet Systems Consortium (http://www.isc.org), *Internet Host Count History*, http://www.isc.org/solutions/survey/history. There is no accurate way to determine the number of users or websites, but the latter are now estimated at about 15 billion. See Cisco Systems white paper, 2012, *Cisco Visual Networking Index: Forecast and Methodology, 2011–2016*, http://www.cisco.com/en/US/solutions/collateral/ns341/ns525/ns537/ns705/ns827/white_paper_c11–481360.pdf (accessed 18 June 2014).

By the late 1980s, as data volumes, interconnectedness and reliance on technologies increased, the need for specific offences and law enforcement capacity became evident. While economic crimes remained a problem, the value of data and data-processing, and the non-economic interests affected, led to the development of crimes based on trespass or theft, consisting of unauthorised access to or use of computer systems, and the taking or copying of data.[39] The intentional and unintentional damage caused by 'hacking' also led to offences analogous to mischief, vandalism or damage to property.[40]

Rather more novel was the problem of 'malware', which caused damage indirectly as it spread from machine to machine.[41] A further category of legislative changes took the form of amendments to traditional offences as access to the technologies transformed criminal behaviours in ways which went beyond pre-existing laws, such as economic frauds, identity-related crimes,[42] and the production and trafficking in child pornography.[43] Not all of the effects of technologies take the form of new or modified offending. Organised crime has also moved on-line, making much the same use of networks for communications, coordination and security as does legitimate commerce, but the effects have been transformative nonetheless. Organised criminal groups have globalised and changed from hierarchical and territorial organisations to much more fluid, loosely organised and transnational criminal networks.[44]

Investigating cybercrime: the gap between traditional sovereignty and jurisdiction and non-traditional digital cross-border offending

The concept of territorial jurisdiction arises from the principles that each state has exclusive control of laws and their application to events in its territory, of the sovereign equality of

39 Hammond, 'Theft of Information'.
40 Castillo, Doyle, and Dubney, 'Computer Crime'; Goodman and Brenner, 'The Emerging Consensus; P. Grabosky, 'Computer Crime: A Criminological Overview', *Forum on Crime and Society*, 2001, vol. 1, p. 35; L. Lanza-Kaduce, 'The Process Of Criminalization: The Case Of Computer Crime Laws', *Criminology*, 1988, vol. 26, Part 1, p. 101; Kaspersen, 'Crimes Related to Computer Networks'; O'Neill, 'Old Crimes in New Bottles; Sieber, *International Handbook on Cybercrime*; Sussmann, 'The Critical Challenges', pp. 451–489.
41 The first known 'malware' incident, the 'Cornell Virus' or 'Morris Worm', occurred in November 1988. See Castillo, Doyle, and Dubney, 'Computer Crime', pp. 228–230 and *United States v Morris*, 928 F.2d 504, 506 (2d Cir. 1991).
42 J.J. Rusch, 'Don't Look Now', *George Mason Law Review*, 2000, vol. 9, p. 289; J.J. Rusch, 'Iago's Net: Notes for an International Legal Regime to Combat Identity-Related Crime', *Georgetown Journal of International Law*, 2011, vol. 42, p. 923. See also *Report of the Secretary General: Results of the Second Meeting of the Intergovernmental Expert Group to Prepare a Study on Fraud and the Criminal Misuse and Falsification of Identity*, UN Doc. no. E/CN.15/2007/8 and /8/Add.1-Add.3.
43 J. Bailey, 'Confronting Collective Harm: Technology's Transformative Impact on Child Pornography', *University of New Brunswick Law Journal*, 2007, vol. 56, p. 65. Increases in child-pornography crimes are probably a combination of real increases in opportunity and reduced risks, and increased visibility of the problem. See: M. Hamilton, 'The Child Pornography Crusade and its Net-Widening Effect', *Cardozo Law Review*, 2011–12, vol. 33, p. 1679.
44 K.R. Choo and R.G. Smith, 'Criminal Exploitation of Online Systems by Organised Crime Groups', *Asian Journal of Criminology*, 2008, vol. 3, p. 37; R. McCusker, 'Organised Cybercrime: Myth or Reality, Malignant or Benign?', in Annual Proceedings of the UN International Scientific and Professional Advisory Council (ISPAC), 2011, *Cybercriminality: Finding a Balance between Freedom and Security*, p. 107; and S. Brenner, 'Organized Cybercrime? How Cyberspace May Affect the Structure of Criminal Relationships', *North Carolina Journal of Law and Technology*, 2002, vol. 4, no. 1, p. 1.

states and of deference ('comity') and non-interference by one state in the internal affairs of another.[45] Its coercive nature makes criminal law a particularly sensitive matter. Early discussions of cybercrime as a new challenge sometimes treated 'cyberspace' as if it were a physical location and a new form of *terra nullius*, and proposed new forms of universal or international law-based jurisdiction,[46] but unlike international waters, outer space or Antarctica, every part of the Internet has a physical presence *somewhere* that is or could be made subject to local law,[47] and attempts to establish jurisdiction over 'cyberspace' *per se* or to create some new global jurisdictional construct would infringe the existing sovereignty of almost every country because Internet infrastructure is now everywhere.

That said, countries generally accept that foreign cybercrime offences, as exercises of prescriptive and adjudicative jurisdiction, may apply in their territories, provided that jurisdiction is asserted by another country that also has a sufficient justification for doing so. Many countries have enacted cybercrime offences, and in recent years early problems with inadequate offences or jurisdictional gaps have diminished. Extended or objective territorial jurisdiction is now often based on the occurrence of an element of an offence, its effects or some other significant link to or within a state's territory,[48] and the problem is more a question of determining which country is in the best position to prosecute the offenders based on factors such as the locations of the evidence or offenders themselves. Countries which do have

45 M. Akehurst, 'Jurisdiction in International Law', *British Yearbook of International Law*, 1972–73, vol. 46, p. 145; M.N. Shaw, *International Law*, 4th edn, Cambridge: Cambridge University Press, 1997, Chapter 12; B. Simma and A.T. Müller, 'Exercise and the Limits of Jurisdiction', in J. Crawford and M. Koskenniemi (eds), *The Cambridge Companion to International Law*, Cambridge: Cambridge University Press, 2012, p. 135. See also in this volume Clark, Chapter 6.

46 See S. Shackleford, 'Computer-Related Crime: An International Problem in Need of an International Solution', *Texas International Law Journal*, 1992, vol. 27, p. 479; B. McLachlin, 'Criminal Law: Towards an International Legal Order', *Hong Kong Law Journal*, 1999, vol. 29, p. 448: S. Schjolberg, 'Potential new Global Legal Mechanisms on Combatting Cybercrime and Global Cyberattacks', in S. Manacorda (ed.), *Cybercriminality: Finding a Balance between Freedom and Security*, ISPAC, 2011, p. 179. All of these discuss the merits of a new international tribunal with universal jurisdiction, but there has been no support for the idea among governments. Even if countries were willing to compromise on sovereignty, the sort of emerging juridical architecture established for the International Criminal Court is viable for the prosecution of small volumes of major crimes against international law, but a very different sort of institution would probably be needed to oversee the large volumes of cybercrime investigations now being encountered and to try the cases that resulted.

47 McGuire, *Technology, Crime and Justice*, p. 77. On the nature of 'cyberspace' and the policy, legal and jurisdictional implications, see Hildebrandt, 'Extraterritorial Jurisdictionce'. On the range of views and evolution of jurisdictional models see H.H. Perritt, 'The Internet at 20: Evolution of a Constitution for Cyberspace', *William and Mary Bill of Rights Law Journal*, 2013, vol. 20, p. 1115, pp. 1133–1137, and sources there cited.

48 For a summary of US jurisdictional law see R.W. Downing, 'Shoring Up the Weakest Link: What Lawmakers around the World Need to Consider in Developing Comprehensive Laws to Combat Cybercrime' *Columbia Journal of Transnational Law*, 2005, vol. 43, p. 705, pp. 736–738. In Canada, objective territorial jurisdiction is based on case law, primarily *Libman v The Queen*, [1985] 2 SCR 178. The Canadian *Libman* doctrine was based on a dissenting judgment of Diplock, LJ in *Treacy v DPP* [1971] AC 537, but UK law itself remained more narrowly focused on the location of either conduct or effects within the UK for some time. It has now evolved into a more general model similar to that of Canada. See *R. v Smith (Wallace Duncan) (No 4)* [2004] QB 1418, and G. Gilbert, 'Crimes *Sans Frontières*: Jurisdictional Problems in English Law', *British Yearbook of International Law*, 1992, vol. 63, p. 415, pp. 436–437.

jurisdictional or other objections can refuse to surrender accused offenders or to provide other cooperation on a case-by-case basis.

Enforcement jurisdiction is another matter. International law is clear that, while offences may be given extraterritorial application to protect essential interests, any form of extraterritorial investigation or enforcement requires the consent of any country on whose territory it takes place.[49] This includes any kind of investigative measures, especially if they entail significant intrusions on the rights or interests of a country's nationals or residents. Domestic laws usually limit measures such as search, seizure and communications interceptions to the state's own enforcement agencies and subject them to its legal safeguards, criminal offences and exceptions or justifications. All of those apply based on the state's own territorial jurisdiction, and without consent, foreign investigative measures would be fully subject to local criminal laws. Foreign intrusions would also usually be regarded as an infringement of sovereignty calling for some form of retaliatory action.[50]

Obtaining consent and the assistance of local law enforcement usually requires formal mutual legal assistance requests and the observance of domestic judicial or other safeguards, which takes time. It is the conflict between the time needed to meet domestic legal and human rights requirements and the high-speed nature of most transnational cybercrime offences and investigations that poses one of greatest challenges for cybercrime investigators. A number of proposals have been made for direct cross-border investigative processes, but these all entail unacceptable compromises of sovereignty.

An 'exigent circumstances' exception has been suggested,[51] but this would still infringe sovereignty and entail *ex post facto* judicial reviews which would be largely moot if any evidence seized or intercepted is already beyond the jurisdiction of the reviewing court and subject to foreign law. The idea was proposed in the negotiation of the Budapest Convention, but was eventually dropped for lack of consensus.[52] Article 32 of the Convention allows for a direct search only where the data are publicly accessible or where a person with lawful authority to do so consents to the search.[53] Another option raised has been so-called 'fast freeze, slow thaw' schemes in which domestic authorities are authorised to immediately

49 A. Aust, *Handbook of International Law*, 1st edn, Cambridge: Cambridge University Press, 2005, p. 49; Akehurst, 'Jurisdiction in International Law', p. 145, pp. 145–151, and Shaw, *International Law*, pp. 456–457, pp. 479–480 (arrest). See in this volume Clark, Chapter 6.

50 The most frequently cited example is the 2001 FBI 'sting' operation which induced two Russian suspects to download incriminating evidence from their own computers. See *United States v Gorshkov*, 2001 WL 1024026, summarised in J. Herrera-Flanagan, 'Cybercrime and Jurisdiction in the United States', in B-J. Koops and S. Brenner (eds), *Cybercrime and Jurisdiction: A Global Survey*, The Hague: Asser Press, 2006, p. 313, pp. 322–324.

51 Sussmann, 'The Critical Challenges', pp. 471–473.

52 W.K. Kaspersen, 'Jurisdiction in the Cybercrime Convention', in B-J. Koops and S. Brenner (eds), *Cybercrime and Jurisdiction: A Global Survey*, The Hague: Asser Press, 2006, p. 19.

53 In the *Gorshkov–Ivanov* investigation, the FBI persuaded the suspects to either download or allow for the downloading of the incriminating data from their own computers. In the US view, it was sufficient that this was done with the consent of the offenders, who had control of the data (software). The Russian government has argued that this was an infringement of Russian sovereignty for which the consent of the state itself was required. The US action was consistent with Article 32 of the Budapest Convention, which the Russian Federation now opposes for the same reason. Russian authorities have also charged the FBI investigators with Russian cybercrime offences.

freeze targeted data based on a foreign request, with eventual release dependent on formal requests and judicial and executive proceedings.[54] This does address sovereignty and some practical problems, but is still problematic in scenarios where even an expedited request is not fast enough or where quick access to the data is needed for further investigative steps, such as the tracing of a communication routed through a number of countries. Court orders compelling elements of companies within the jurisdiction (usually service providers) to retrieve data effectively make them agents of law enforcement and they are still seen as a sovereignty infringement in the searched country. They also have the potential to place companies with a choice between disobeying a court order in one country and committing privacy or cybercrime offences in another.[55]

Ultimately, the customary law foundations of jurisdiction are as much a matter of pragmatic diplomacy and international relations as matters of law. Positions of individual countries are also largely driven by domestic public opinion, which resists infringements on privacy even by domestic authorities accountable under domestic law. The strength of opposition to any form of direct investigation by foreign authorities was recently demonstrated by reactions to the June 2013 disclosures about foreign communications interceptions by US security contractor Edward Snowden. In the autumn of 2013, as successive media disclosures were published, popular sentiment in a number of affected countries, as well as within the United States itself, was strongly against the programmes revealed.[56] While the disclosures involved security intelligence more than criminal justice matters, a major area of concern was allegations that reciprocal surveillance and intelligence-sharing among allies was used as a means of circumventing national legal and constitutional constraints in each country. The governments of countries targeted by the surveillance cannot have been surprised to learn that their data and communications were being intercepted. Their reactions are better regarded as an expression of popular concern about foreign intrusions against the privacy

---

54 Sussmann, 'The Critical Challenges', pp. 469–470 (optimistically referring to 'quick freeze, quick thaw'). See also Budapest Convention Articles 16–18 and 29–31 (expedited preservation of data and partial release of 'traffic data') and 32 (direct seizure of data based on public access or lawful consent).

55 G. Hosein, 'International Cooperation: A Promise and a Threat', in B-J. Koops and S. Brenner (eds.), *Cybercrime and Jurisdiction: A Global Survey*, Information and Technology Law Series, The Hague: Asser Press, 2006, pp. 23–46. Hosein describes several varying examples. See also *US v. Bank of Nova Scotia* 691 F.2d 1384 (11th circ., 1982), cert. denied 462 US 1119 (1983). Canada and other countries faced with orders from US courts on companies doing business in both countries have adopted blocking legislation compelling domestic elements not to comply. See e.g. Canada's Foreign Extraterritorial Measures Act, RSC, 1985, c. F–29.

56 T. McKelvey, 'US spies on the entire globe', BBC News online, 25 October 2013, http://www.bbc.co.uk/news/magazine–24627187; D. Roberts, S. Ackerman and A. Travis, 'NSA surveillance: anger mounts in Congress at "spying on Americans"', *The Guardian*, 12 June 2013, http://www.theguardian.com/world/2013/jun/12/anger-mounts-congress-telephone-surveillance-programmes; N. Bryant, 'The Snowden effect on US diplomacy', BBC News online, 24 October 2013, http://www.bbc.co.uk/news/world-us-canada–24664045; A.J. Rubin, 'French Condemn Surveillance by N.S.A.', *New York Times*, 21 October 2013, http://www.nytimes.com/2013/10/22/world/europe/new-report-of-nsa-spying-angers-france.html; and *Der Speigel*, 'German Trust in the United States Plummets', 8 November, 2013, http://www.spiegel.de/international/germany/nsa-spying-fallout-majority-of-germans-mistrust-united-states-a–932492.html (all accessed 19 June 2014). As this book was going into production the *Bank of Nova Scotia* issue were renewed in respect of cybercrime, when a US District Court judge issued an order compelling Microsoft to obtain and produce email data held on one of its servers in Dublin, Ireland, for use in US criminal proceedings. See Order of the US District Court (SDNY) No 13 Mag 2814, 25 April 2014.

interests of the individuals involved, and of the widespread fear that anyone who uses the technologies could be a target.[57]

Pragmatists and law enforcement interests continue to search for some form of practical path between the rock of national sovereignty and legal frameworks and the hard place of fast-paced transnational cybercrime. At the present time, however, the best view of domestic and international law is that there are no exceptions to the principle that extraterritorial investigative measures require consent, and this seems unlikely to change in the near future.[58] In general, the more intrusive the action, the more likely it will be resisted as an infringement of sovereignty, and it will usually be the opinion of the affronted country that matters most.

Conclusion: the future of cybercrime

The evolution of cybercrime has been driven by so many complex and interacting influences that predicting the future is a daunting challenge. The evolution of any type of crime must be assessed to a large degree in contextual terms, because crime patterns are determined by the dynamic interactions of both offenders and victims, as well as of legislators, law enforcement and other key players, and of the broader social, economic and technical environments in which crimes are committed. This is also true of cybercrime, but the uncertainties are much greater because of the speed with which technologies continue to evolve and expand, and the scope of the transformative effects they have on communications, commerce and almost every type of social and political activity. Each new development creates a range of new legitimate possibilities, but it also creates new opportunities for offenders, and new opportunities and challenges for the prevention and investigation of crime. Technologies have supported globalisation in general and crime is no exception: offences can be committed against many victims and across global distances, and new innovations by the most creative offenders spread quickly across into other jurisdictions and down into the hands of less innovative offenders.

It seems inevitable that the constant increase in the speed and capacity of computers and networks of the past decades will eventually reach a natural limit, but predictions of limits on

---

57 J. Marcus, 'NSA spying allegations: Are US allies really shocked?', BBC News online, 26 October 2013, http://www.bbc.co.uk/news/world-europe-24676392; E. Nakashima, '[U.S.] Officials alert foreign services that Snowden has documents on their cooperation with U.S.', Washington Post (online), 24 October 2013, http://www.washingtonpost.com/world/national-security/officials-alert-foreign-services-that-snowden-has-documents-on-their-cooperation-with-us/2013/10/24/930ea85c–3b3e–11e3-a94f-b58017bfee6c_story.html (both accessed 19 June 2014); Rubin, 'French Condemn Surveillance by N.S.A'; McKelvey, 'US spies on the entire globe'.

58 See J.L. Goldsmith, 'The Internet and the Legitimacy of Remote Cross-Border Searches', University of Chicago Legal Forum, 2001, p. 103, arguing that for practical reasons jurisdiction should be based on the location of the searchers, not the data. P.L. Bellia, 'Chasing Bits across Borders', University of Chicago Legal Forum, 2001, p. 35, rejects Goldsmith's position and argues that unilateral cross-border searches infringe the sovereignty of the searched country and that such searches are equally inconsistent with customary international law whether the incursion is physical or electronic. N. Seitz, 'Transborder Search: A New Perspective In Law Enforcement?', Yale Journal of Law and Technology, 2004–05, vol. 7, p. 24, argues that no exceptions exist given the present state of international law. In extreme cases, it could probably be argued that a state's inherent right to actual or anticipatory self-defence under the United Nations Charter might be invoked, but the facts needed to justify this would make the case one of national security and not a criminal investigation in most countries (see Bellia, 'Chasing Bits across Borders', pp. 100–101).

'Moore's Law'[59] have been confounded before. Even if the capacities of technologies approach limits, no such end is in sight for human innovation and the uses – both legitimate and illicit – to which the technologies may be put. Innovation by offenders is likely to continue both as a dynamic force in itself and in reaction to developments that create criminal opportunities and new security measures that must be circumvented. The global proliferation of technologies can also be expected to continue, as access becomes cheaper and developing countries and their populations come on-line, and this will continue to generate new patterns in offending. As more reliance is placed on technologies, the convergence between conventional or traditional forms of cybercrime and broader cyber-security issues also seems likely to continue, but the responses of the various players is difficult to predict. Some countries and much of the private sector can be expected to continue to seek a single, global, unregulated Internet, but the influence of manufacturers and service providers who serve or reflect the views of countries that do not share this vision will increase. Many of those countries see themselves in a struggle which pits their perceptions of governance as a closed and centrally managed affair against the chaos generated by the open traffic in information, ideas and social, economic and political discourse of a free and open Internet. Whether they ultimately transform the Internet, it transforms them, or some combination of both, remains to be seen.

---

59 Moore's Law' is a suggestion emanating from the technology field that the processing speed of computers will double every two years. See J. Clark, 'Microsoft "Catapults" geriatric Moore's Law from CERTAIN DEATH', *The Register*, 16 June 2014, http://www.theregister.co.uk/2014/06/16/microsoft_catapult_fpgas (accessed 20 June 2014).

24

Terrorism as a transnational crime

Ben Saul

Introduction: origins of transnational criminal cooperation on terrorism

Transnational legal efforts to confront terrorism originated in national extradition law. In nineteenth-century Europe, violence was used by political rebels against monarchical or authoritarian regimes, ethnic separatists against imperial powers, socialist revolutionaries against capitalist states, or anarchists against governments of all stripes, and such actors often fled across national borders to escape local punishment. Foreign states then faced requests from victim states to hand over the suspects. Governments and the courts had to develop legal criteria to decide whether a suspect should be returned, or their extradition refused.

Initially, some European courts refused to extradite 'political' offenders,[1] namely those who sought to overthrow the government of a foreign state, or who committed related political offences. One rationale was that the state of refuge should not interfere in domestic political struggles in a foreign state, by assisting the foreign government to repress its opponents. Another rationale was that individuals should be protected from return to political persecution, unfair trials, or summary punishment. A refusal of extradition was thus closely bound up with decisions by the state of refuge to grant political asylum.

This approach, however, created a risk of impunity for egregious offenders. Few states at that time extended extraterritorial criminal jurisdiction over violence committed by foreign nationals abroad, so prosecution in the state of refuge was seldom possible. The result was that assassins or 'terrorists' would walk free in a country of refuge. Some states and their courts responded by narrowing the scope of the political offence exception. Certain kinds of political violence, such as attacks on heads of states or government and their families, came to be viewed as beyond the pale, because they were considered both barbarous and damaging to the stability of international relations.

---

1 See G. Gilbert, *Transnational Fugitive Offenders in International Law: Extradition and Other Mechanisms*, Dordrecht: Martinus Nijhoff, 1998; C. Van den Wijngaert, *The Political Offence Exception to Extradition*, Boston: Kluwer, 1980; M.C. Bassiouni, *International Extradition and World Public Order*, Leiden: A.W. Sijthoff, 1974, pp. 370–428.

Over time, further types of violence came to be treated as non-political and thus extraditable. Tests developed by different courts to determine whether an offence is political or non-political for extradition purposes included whether violent acts are indiscriminate or atrocious,[2] or too remote from, or disproportionate to, a political end.[3] Courts later applied similar factors in interpreting the meaning of serious non-political crimes in modern refugee law.[4] Terrorist acts often failed these tests for being disproportionate, remote, barbarous and so forth. More recently, some courts have preferred to use the term 'terrorism' to depoliticise offences on the basis that it is more precise than those other, more subjective tests.[5]

The depoliticisation of some political violence, however, accentuated the risk that offenders could be returned to political persecution or unfair trials. As a result, two developments occurred. First, separate, more targeted safeguards arose in some national extradition laws to protect suspects from being returned to face discrimination, an unfair trial, torture, or the death penalty. Second, where extradition was not possible for any of these reasons, it sometimes became possible to prosecute offenders in a state of refuge where that state had extended extraterritorial criminal jurisdiction over such offences, thus preventing impunity.

The central difficulty remained that extradition laws were largely a matter of national law and varied widely. Efforts in national laws to grapple with transnational political offenders eventually stimulated greater transnational criminal cooperation. As early as 1937, states in the League of Nations negotiated a treaty to criminalise terrorism and another to establish an international criminal court to prosecute it.[6] The treaties were a response to an international terrorist incident in France in 1934, in which Balkan separatists assassinated King Alexander of Yugoslavia and the French Foreign Minister, almost precipitating war. Neither treaty ever entered into force, largely because of the advent of the Second World War.

But this initiative signalled a concerted attempt by the international community to standardise rules in this area. It was a precursor to efforts with a similar goal made since the Second World War. This chapter considers how the international community has pursued transnational criminal cooperation against terrorism through a variety of legal means: numerous 'sectoral' treaties; efforts to draft a comprehensive international treaty; regional conventions; UN Security Council measures; war crimes liabilities; and debate about an emerging customary law crime. It discusses these developments in the light of: the purposes of criminalising terrorism and cooperating transnationally to repress it; the effectiveness of current measures; and the costs of those measures in terms of respect for human rights and political freedoms.

---

2   See e.g. *Ellis v O'Dea*, Record No. 441 SS/1990 (30 July 1990), transcript, 36; *Della Savia*, Swiss Federal Tribunal (26 November 1969) 95 ATF I, 469; *Morlacci*, Swiss Federal Tribunal (12 December 1975), 101 ATF Ia, 605; *Re Atta (Mahmoud Abed)* (1989) 706 F Supp 1032, approved (1990) 910 F 2d 1063.

3   See e.g. *McGlinchey v Wren* [1983] Irish L Rep Monthly 169; *Shannon v Fanning* [1984] IR 548; *Folkerts v Public Prosecutor* (1978) 74 ILR 498.

4   Under Art. 1F(b) of the 1951 Convention relating to the Status of Refugees, 28 July 1951, 189 UNTS 150; entered into force 22 April 1954; see e.g. *T v Home Secretary* [1996] 2 All ER 865; *McMullen v INS* (1986) 788 F 2d 591; *Minister for Immigration v Singh* [2002] HCA 7; *Zrig v Canada (Minister of Citizenship and Immigration)* (CA) [2003] 3 FC 761.

5   *T v Home Secretary* [1996] 2 All ER 865 (Lord Mustill).

6   The Convention for the Punishment and Prevention of Terrorism, Geneva, 16 November 1937, 7 Hudson 862, never in force (only India ratified); The Convention for the Creation of an International Criminal Court, Geneva, 16 November 1937, 7 Hudson 878, never in force (no ratifications).

International counter-terrorism treaties

Renewed interest in transnational criminal cooperation against terrorism came in the 1960s, in reaction to spectacular attacks (such as hijacking and hostage taking) against international civil aviation, particularly by certain national liberation movements. The international community reacted pragmatically by, from the 1960s onward, adopting more than a dozen 'sectoral' treaties[7] to suppress particular kinds of violence commonly used by terrorists, often by way of ad hoc responses to graphic incidents.

Some of the treaties prohibit violent or dangerous criminal acts against especially vulnerable, or politically or economically significant targets (such as international aircraft, airports, ships, fixed platforms, and internationally protected persons).[8] Some target particular methods or means (such as hijacking or hostage taking).[9] Others prohibit the use of particular weapons (such as plastic explosives, nuclear material, and bombs).[10] One recent treaty prohibits the financing of terrorism.[11] Most of the treaties also contain a number of ancillary offences.[12]

All of the treaties require a transnational element to their offences and do not apply to purely domestic acts.[13] Thus the treaties typically do not apply where an offence is committed in a single state, the offender and victims are nationals of that state, the offender is found in the state's territory, and no other state has jurisdiction under those treaties.[14]

---

7 See e.g. Convention on Offences and Certain Other Acts Committed on Board Aircraft, 14 September 1963, in force 4 December 1969, 704 UNTS 219; Convention for the Suppression of Unlawful Seizure of Aircraft, 16 December 1970, 860 UNTS 105; in force 14 October 1971; Convention on the Prevention and Punishment of Crimes against Internationally Protected Persons, including Diplomatic Agents, 14 December 1973, 1035 UNTS 167; in force 20 February 1977; International Convention against the Taking of Hostages, 17 December 1979, 1316 UNTS 205; in force 3 June 1983; Convention for the Suppression of Unlawful Acts against the Safety of Maritime Navigation, 10 March 1988, 1678 UNTS 221; in force 1 March 1992; Protocol for the Suppression of Unlawful Acts against the Safety of Fixed Platforms Located on the Continental Shelf, 10 March 1988, 1678 UNTS 403; in force 1 March 1992; Protocol on the Suppression of Unlawful Acts of Violence at Airports Serving International Civil Aviation, 24 February 1988, 974 UNTS 177; in force 6 August 1989; Convention on the Marking of Plastic Explosives for the Purpose of Detection, 1 March 1991, in force 21 June 1998; International Convention for the Suppression of Terrorist Bombings, 15 December 1997, 2149 UNTS 256; in force 23 May 2001; International Convention for the Suppression of the Financing of Terrorism, 9 December 1999, 2178 UNTS 229; in force 10 April 2002; International Convention for the Suppression of Acts of Nuclear Terrorism, 13 April 2005, in force 7 July 2007.
8 See e.g. 1970 Hague Convention; 1971 Montreal Convention and 1988 Montreal Protocol; 1973 Protected Persons Convention; 1994 UN Personnel Convention; 1988 Rome Convention; 1988 Rome Protocol.
9 See e.g. 1970 Hague Convention; 1971 Montreal Convention; 1979 Hostages Convention.
10 See e.g. 1980 Vienna Convention; 1991 Montreal Convention; 1997 Terrorist Bombings Convention; 2005 Nuclear Terrorism Convention.
11 1999 Terrorist Financing Convention; see A. Aust, 'Counter-terrorism: A New Approach – The International Convention for the Suppression of the Financing of Terrorism', *Max Planck Yearbook of United Nations Law*, 2001, p. 287.
12 Such as attempt, threats, complicity, abetting, organising or directing, or intentionally contributing to the commission of an offence by a group of persons acting with a common purpose: see e.g. 1970 Hague Convention, Art. 1; 1971 Montreal Convention, Art. 1.
13 1963 Tokyo Convention, Art. 1(3); 1970 Hague Convention, Art. 3(4)–(5); 1971 Montreal Convention, Art. 4(2)–(4); 1988 Rome Convention, Art. 4(1)–(2); 1973 Protected Persons Convention, Art. 1(a)–(b); 1979 Hostages Convention, Art. 13; 1980 Vienna Convention, Art. 2(1)–(2); 1991 Montreal Convention, Arts 2–3.
14 1997 Terrorist Bombings Convention, 1999 Terrorist Financing Convention, and 2005 Nuclear Terrorism Convention, common Art. 3.

The treaties do not give rise to direct individual criminal responsibility under international law but instead rely on domestic prosecutions, facilitated by transnational judicial cooperation. Most of the treaties follow a similar pattern. They define certain conduct as offences which must be criminalised in domestic law. They then provide for the establishment of state criminal jurisdiction over such offences, though the bases of jurisdiction vary between the treaties. Commonly they specify certain mandatory bases of criminal jurisdiction (based on the territoriality and nationality principles), and give states the option to widen extraterritorial jurisdiction on further grounds (such as the passive personality and protective principles).[15] The treaties do not, however, establish priority of jurisdiction.

A core obligation in most of the treaties is the 'prosecute or extradite' principle (*aut dedere aut judicare*). States are required to either extradite an alleged offender to a state which requests extradition and which has jurisdiction over the alleged offence, or submit the case for prosecution by its own competent authorities. The latter option is thus a duty to genuinely consider prosecution, not to actually proceed with prosecution in all cases, such as where the evidence would be insufficient to secure a conviction. The treaties do not specify whether prosecution or extradition takes priority; the choice is left to the custodial state.

Extradition may be refused, for instance, largely in accordance with the usual grounds in a particular state's national law, including: that the state does not extradite its own nationals; where principles of 'dual criminality' (the conduct must be an offence in both states) or 'specialty' (the suspect must only be prosecuted for the requested offence) are not satisfied; if a person would be returned to discrimination, persecution, torture, the death penalty, or an unfair trial; or if the offence is regarded as 'political'.

In relation to the latter, only the two most recent sectoral treaties expressly exclude the political offence exception to extradition;[16] it remains available under the earlier treaties. The treaties themselves are intended to provide a basis for ensuring the dual criminality rule is satisfied. Some of the treaties also explicitly require extradition or cooperation to be refused where it is for the purpose of discriminatory punishment or prosecution.[17] Under general international law, there are also treaty and customary law prohibitions against return to persecution (unless the offence is a serious non-political one),[18] or torture, or cruel, inhuman, or degrading treatment.[19] Many states have also agreed not to return a person to the death penalty.[20]

It is striking that most of the treaties do not mention 'terrorism' or establish 'terrorist' offences (with the exception of the more recent Terrorist Bombings, Terrorist Financing, and

---

15 See e.g. 1997 Terrorist Bombings Convention, Art. 6. The jurisdiction provisions in the other treaties are: 1970 Hague Convention, Arts 4–5; 1971 Montreal Convention, Arts 1, 3, 5; 1973 Protected Persons Convention, Art. 3; 1979 Hostages Convention, Art. 5; 1980 Vienna Convention, Art. 8; 1988 Rome Convention, Art. 6; 1988 Rome Protocol, Art. 3; 1999 Terrorist Financing Convention, Art. 7; 2005 Nuclear Terrorism Convention, Art. 9.

16 1997 Terrorist Bombings Convention, Art. 11; 1999 Terrorist Financing Convention, Art. 14.

17 See e.g. 1997 Terrorist Bombings Convention, Art. 12.

18 1951 Refugee Convention, Art. 33.

19 International Covenant on Civil and Political Rights (adopted 16 December 1966, 999 UNTS 171, entered into force 23 March 1976), Art. 7; Convention against Torture and Other Cruel, Inhuman or Degrading Treatment or Punishment (adopted 10 December 1984, 1465 UNTS 85, entered into force 26 June 1987), Art. 3.

20 Second Optional Protocol to the ICCPR aiming at the destruction of the death penalty, 15 December 1989, 1642 UNTS 414; in force 11 July 1991.

Nuclear Terrorism Conventions). Instead, most treaties simply require states to prohibit and punish in domestic law certain physical acts without recognising specifically 'terrorist' elements in the definition of offences, such as proof of a political, religious, or ideological motive,[21] or an intention to coerce, intimidate, or terrorise civilians or governments.

This pragmatic, functional approach enabled the repression of common terrorist methods while side-stepping the irresolvable problem of defining 'terrorism', especially during the Cold War when states were unable to agree on the legitimacy of violence by self-determination movements or state forces. Ever since the 1970s, states in the United Nations General Assembly have been unable to agree on an international legal definition of terrorism, despite frequent political condemnation of it.

The pragmatic approach was necessary because it was the only achievable one at the time. It is not, however, an entirely satisfactory means of regulating the criminal aspects of terrorism. In the first place, because the sectoral treaties were adopted in an ad hoc and reactive fashion, they do not comprehensively suppress all possible terrorist methods, or even the most commonly used ones. Thus, terrorist attacks by small arms or light weapons (such as semi-automatic weapons, machine guns, or even hand-held weapons such as machetes or knives) are not criminalised, nor is the use of poisons or toxins against civilian populations, nor even sabotage of public transport or electronic networks, and so on. The present treaties criminalise violence by terrorists only in specific contexts or by particular methods, and thus fail to prohibit the terrorist killings of civilians by *any* means or method. There is accordingly still a need to comprehensively plug the gaps in the transnational repression of terrorist violence.

In addition, the focus of the treaties on physical methods of terrorism arguably fails to capture the conceptual essence of what is considered *wrongful* about terrorism by the international community. In the practice of the international community, concentrated through the United Nations organs and regional organisations, consensus has emerged that transnational terrorism is wrongful because it: (1) seriously threatens or destroys basic human rights and freedoms; (2) jeopardises the state and stable, peaceful politics; and (3) can threaten international peace and security.[22] While those explanations are not entirely convincing,[23] they suggest that simply prohibiting terrorism as common physical crime does not satisfactorily target what the world believes is wrongful about terrorism.

Largely for these two reasons, ever since the 1930s the international community has sought to define 'terrorism' in a more general way, beyond mere reference to physical acts of violence. Doing so enables 'terrorism' *as such* to be specifically condemned and stigmatised, as part of the denunciatory and deterrence functions of the criminal law. The question then becomes what are the indispensable elements of 'terrorism' which differentiate it from other crimes and express the international community's concerns about it.

For some, the ulterior motive (or 'specific intent') behind terrorism is what distinguishes it from ordinary crime or private violence. In 1994, for example, the UN General Assembly adopted a Declaration on Measures against International Terrorism which defines terrorism as '[c]riminal acts intended or calculated to provoke a state of terror in the general public, a

---

21 J. Lambert, *Terrorism and Hostages in International Law: A Commentary on the Hostages Convention 1979*, Cambridge: Grotius, 1990, p. 49.

22 See B. Saul, *Defining Terrorism in International Law*, Oxford: Oxford University Press, 2006, Chapter 1.

23 Ibid.

group of persons or particular persons *for political purposes*' (emphasis added).[24] In national law, various common law states have defined terrorism by reference to a political, religious, or ideological cause, purpose, objective, or motive.

For others, terrorism is the instrumental use of violence to coerce or intimidate. Thus, the Terrorist Financing Convention prohibits the financing of harmful acts whose purpose 'is to *intimidate* a population or to *compel* a government or an international organization to do or to abstain from doing any act' (emphasis added).[25] This approach has been endorsed by various United Nations bodies and in the law of some regional organisations. It is also the foundation of ongoing efforts in the General Assembly since 2000 to negotiate a comprehensive terrorism treaty.

The Draft UN Comprehensive Terrorism Convention

In 1994 Algeria proposed to the General Assembly a modest new terrorism convention to consolidate existing sectoral treaty offences.[26] More ambitiously, in 1996 India proposed a comprehensive convention to more generally define terrorism offences.[27] The terrorist attacks on US embassies in Kenya and Tanzania in 1998 encouraged many states to support the initiative. India submitted a revised draft text to a UN Ad Hoc Committee on terrorism in 2000 and negotiations commenced. The attacks of 9/11 stimulated rapid progress on the drafting and agreement was reached on most of the 27 articles by 2002.[28] At this point, negotiations stalled over a few key outstanding issues, namely its scope of application to certain non-state and state violence. Little headway was made between 2003 and the time of writing (late 2013), despite the urgings of high-level UN reports and world leaders' meetings.[29]

Perhaps surprisingly, agreement was fairly readily reached on the core definition of terrorist offences, although human rights concerns have been raised in this respect.[30] Draft Article 2(1) proposes an offence if a person 'unlawfully and intentionally' causes: '[d]eath or serious bodily injury to any person'; '[s]erious damage to public or private property'; or '[d]amage to property, places, facilities, or systems . . . resulting or likely to result in major economic loss'.[31] The purpose of any such conduct, 'by its nature or context', must be 'to intimidate a population, or to compel a Government or an international organization to do or abstain from doing any act'.[32] There is no further requirement of a political, religious, or ideological purpose.

---

24 UN General Assembly Resolution 49/60 (9 December 1994): Declaration on Measures to Eliminate International Terrorism, para. 3.

25 1999 Terrorist Financing Convention, Art. 2(1)(b).

26 Report of the UN Secretary-General, UN Doc. A/49/257 (25 July 1994).

27 UN Doc. A/C.6/51/6 (11 November 1996).

28 See UNGA (57th Session) (6th Committee), Measures to Eliminate International Terrorism: Working Group Report, 16 October 2002, A/C.6/57/L.9, annex II, 7–8.

29 United Nations High-Level Panel on Threats, Challenges and Change, *A More Secure World: Our Shared Responsibility*, 2004; United Nations Secretary-General, *In Larger Freedom: towards Development, Security and Human Rights for All*, UNGA (59th Sess), 21 March 2005, UN Doc. A/59/2005; 2005 World Summit Outcome, paras 83–84.

30 Amnesty International and Human Rights Watch, 'Comprehensive Convention against International Terrorism', Joint Letter to Ambassadors, 28 January 2002.

31 UNGA (56th Session) (6th Committee), Measures to Eliminate International Terrorism: Working Group Report, 29 October 2001, UN Doc. A/C.6/56/L.9, annex I, 16 (informal Coordinator texts).

32 Ancillary offences are found in the Draft Comprehensive Convention, Art. 2(2), (3) and (4) (a)–(c).

However, the key unresolved controversies concern limitations on the Convention's scope of application, or, to put it another way, on the scope of exceptions to terrorist offences. Depending on how one sees the problem, this is really another way of saying that the apparent agreement on the definition of terrorism is still subject to disagreement. The ongoing controversy is surprising given that the earlier sectoral treaties had managed to reach a consensus on the scope of exceptions. In particular, some earlier treaties exclude the 'activities of armed forces during an armed conflict' (whether state or non-state), as well as the activities of state military forces exercising their official duties 'inasmuch as they are governed by other rules of international law'.[33] Other treaties exclude acts against persons taking an active part in hostilities in armed conflict,[34] or against military ships or aircraft.[35]

During the drafting of the comprehensive convention, controversy was reignited by the Organisation of Islamic Cooperation, supported by the League of Arab States, who sought to exclude any '[p]eople's struggle including armed struggle against foreign occupation, aggression, colonialism, and hegemony, aimed at liberation and self-determination'.[36] This proposed exception was based on that in the Organisation of Islamic Cooperation's (OIC) regional convention. By contrast, Western and other states thought that terrorism was terrorism regardless of its motivation. In addition, they argued that self-determination conflicts are already governed by international humanitarian law (IHL). There is no such exclusion in the prior sectoral treaties, and many states objected[37] to Pakistan's reservation to this effect in the Terrorist Bombings Convention.

The drafting of the comprehensive convention thus remains at an impasse over the language of draft Article 18. One dispute is whether the convention should exclude the activities of the 'parties' – rather than the 'armed forces' – during armed conflict. Reference to the 'parties' aims to exempt members of organisations such as the PLO, Hamas, Islamic Jihad and Hezbollah.[38] It could preclude civilians taking part in hostilities from being treated as 'terrorists'.[39] The International Committee of the Red Cross (ICRC) observes that 'armed forces' should be interpreted to cover both government forces and organised non-state armed groups.[40] The term does not, however, encompass all violence by anyone associated with a liberation movement (i.e. those who are not members of organised armed groups), as the OIC's mention of the 'parties' intends.

---

33 2005 Nuclear Terrorism Convention, Art. 4; 1997 Terrorist Bombings Convention, Art. 19(2); 1980 Vienna Convention, Art. 2(4)(b).

34 1999 Terrorist Financing Convention, Art. 2(1)(b).

35 1963 Tokyo Convention, Art. 1(4); 1970 Hague Convention, Art. 3(2); 1971 Montreal Convention, Art. 4(1); 1988 Rome Convention, Art. 2.

36 S. Subedi, 'The UN Response to International Terrorism', *International Law Forum*, 2002, vol. 4, p. 159, p. 163.

37 Austria, Australia, Canada, Denmark, Finland, France, Germany, India, Israel, Italy, Japan, Netherlands, New Zealand, Norway, Spain, Sweden, UK and United States.

38 S. von Schorlemer, 'Human Rights: Substantive and Institutional Implications of the War on Terror', *European Journal of International Law*, 2003, vol. 14, p. 265, p. 272; C. Walter, 'Defining Terrorism in National and International Law', in C. Walter, S. Vöneky, V. Röben and F. Schorkopf (eds), *Terrorism as a Challenge for National and International Law*, Heidelberg: Springer, 2003, p. 23, pp. 39–40.

39 UNGA Sixth Committee, Report of the Working Group on Measures to Eliminate International Terrorism (8 October 2004), UN Doc. A/C.6/59/L.10.

40 ICRC Report, 'Terrorism and International Law: Challenges and Responses: The Complementary Nature of Human Rights Law, International Humanitarian Law and Refugee Law', Geneva, 2002, p. 5.

A second disagreement is whether 'foreign occupation' should also be excluded.[41] This is intended to cover situations where there are no actual hostilities. Politically, it is aimed at excluding non-state violence against Israel in the Palestinian Occupied Territories and India in Kashmir.[42] This disagreement is more political than legal, since occupation is already classified as international 'armed conflict' under IHL. The activities of (state or non-state) armed forces during occupation are accordingly already excluded.

A third disagreement is whether state military forces exercising their official duties (whether in war or peace) are excluded if they are merely 'governed' by international law or required to be 'in conformity' with it. The OIC proposes that military forces would be liable for terrorism if they were not 'in conformity' with international law, so as to cover 'state terrorism' in or outside armed conflict. As discussed below, acts of terror against civilians in armed conflict are already war crimes, so the OIC proposal adds little in that context; it merely criminalises what is already criminal. Yet it may also have the negative effect of criminalising state conduct which is prohibited (but not criminalised) by IHL, thus interfering in IHL's delicate balancing of the interests of military necessity and humanitarian protection.

On the other hand, in peacetime situations the OIC proposal has the virtue of criminalising state military action which attacks civilian targets outside armed conflict – and thus terrorises victims in a manner morally comparable to that perpetrated by terrorist groups. State military personnel currently do not bear international criminal responsibility in these circumstances, where the attack does not rise to the level of a crime against humanity. Negotiations on the comprehensive convention are set to continue in 2014[43] – a drafting process of over a decade.

Regional counter-terrorism treaties

In the absence of international agreement on a criminal definition of terrorism, greater progress has been made at the regional level. The regional conventions fall into a number of categories. First, some conventions follow the limited approach of the sectoral treaties by proscribing certain acts or protecting certain targets.[44] Second, some conventions declare that terrorism offences should not be regarded as political offences in extradition law, or that states must cooperate, but do not explicitly require states to criminalise the offences.[45] Third, some

41 OIC proposal, in UN General Assembly Ad Hoc Committee on Terrorism, Report (2002), annex IV, p. 17.
42 N. Rostow, 'Before and After: The Changed UN Response to Terrorism since September 11th', *Cornell International Law Journal*, 2002, vol. 35, p. 475, pp. 488–489.
43 For details of the drafting, see the annual reports of the UN Ad Hoc Committee established by General Assembly resolution 51/210 of 17 December 1996: Measures to Eliminate International Terrorism, available at http://www.un.org/law/terrorism (accessed 13 April 2014).
44 Organization of American States (OAS) Convention to Prevent and Punish Acts of Terrorism Taking the Form of Crimes against Persons and Related Extortion that are of International Significance, 2 February 1971, 1438 UNTS 194; in force 16 October 1973; Inter-American Convention against Terrorism, 3 June 2002.
45 Council of Europe Convention on the Suppression of Terrorism, 27 January 1977, ETS No. 90; in force 4 August 1978; Protocol amending the European Convention on the Suppression of Terrorism, 15 May 2003, ETS No. 190; South Asian Association for Regional Cooperation (SAARC) Regional Convention on Suppression of Terrorism, 4 November 1987, in force 22 August 1998; Treaty on Cooperation among the States Members of the Commonwealth of Independent States (CIS) in Combating Terrorism, 4 June 1999, in force 4 June 1999; African Union Protocol of 2004 to the Organisation of African Unity Convention on the Prevention and Combating of Terrorism 1999, 8 July 2004.

regional conventions define terrorism by reference to other treaties and then create preparatory or inchoate offences which states are required to criminalise.[46]

Fourth, and more controversially, some regional conventions define terrorism generally
and require states to criminalise those terrorist offences in domestic law. Examples include
the Arab Convention on the Suppression of Terrorism of 1998,[47] the OIC Convention on
Combating International Terrorism of 1999, and the Shanghai Cooperation Organisation
Convention on Combating Terrorism, Separatism and Extremism of 2001.[48] While not a
treaty as such, also relevant is the European Union Framework Decision on Combating
Terrorism of 2002,[49] which requires approximation of terrorist offences in the domestic law
of EU member states.

Some of the definitions of terrorism in this category of treaties are drafted very loosely.
Some of the conventions reclassify as terrorism ordinary crimes, public order offences,[50] or
insurrection.[51] Some criminalise conduct infringing diffuse values such as the 'stability, territorial integrity, political unity or sovereignty' of states,[52] or imperilling the 'honour' or
'freedoms' of individuals.[53] Some safeguard objects in ambiguous language, such as protecting
against jeopardy to a 'national resource'[54] or damage to 'environmental or cultural heritage'.[55]
One intermingles terrorism with 'separatism' or 'extremism'.[56] Another includes an ill-
defined element of 'seriously destabilising or destroying the fundamental political, constitutional, economic or social structures of a country or an international organization'.[57]

The elimination of the political offence exception in the context of such wide definitions
of terrorism is especially problematic, since it curtails the freedom of populations to resist
violent, oppressive governments. Under such conventions, other states in the region are
legally obliged to aid in the criminal suppression of resistance movements, often even where
such movements limit their violence to discriminate and proportionate attacks on military
objectives. At the other extreme, three regional conventions (OIC, Arab League, and African
Union) 'carve out' acts by liberation movements in pursuit of self-determination, implying
that any means – however indiscriminate – may be justified in pursuit of a just cause.

UN Security Council obligation to criminalise terrorism

After 9/11 the UN Security Council assumed a more active role in responding to the threat
of international terrorism. Among other things, Resolution 1373 of 2001, adopted under

---

46 Council of Europe Convention on the Prevention of Terrorism of 2005, 16 May 2005, ETS
No. 196, Art. 5(2) (not yet in force); SAARC Additional Protocol of 2004, 6 January 2004.
47 Arab Convention on the Suppression of Terrorism, 22 April 1998; in force 7 May 1999.
48 Shanghai Cooperation Organisation Convention on Combating Terrorism, Separatism and
Extremism, 15 June 2001, in force 29 March 2003.
49 EU Framework Decision on Combating Terrorism (2002/475/JHA), 13 June 2002, OJ L164/3,
22 June 2002, entered into force 22 June 2002.
50 Arab Convention, Art. 1(2); Organisation of the Islamic Conference Convention on Combating
International Terrorism, 1 July 1999, annexed to res. 59/26-P, Art. 1(2).
51 Organisation of African Unity (OAU) Convention on the Prevention and Combating of Terrorism,
14 July 1999; in force 6 December 2003, Art. 1(3).
52 OIC Convention, Art. 1(2).
53 Ibid.
54 Arab Convention, Art. 1(2); OIC Convention, Art. 1(2).
55 OAU Convention, Art. 1(3).
56 Shanghai Cooperation Organization Convention, Art. 1.
57 EU Framework Decision, Art. 1(1).

Chapter VII of the UN Charter, required all states to domestically criminalise terrorist acts as well as certain conduct preparatory to it. Paragraph 2(e) provides that states shall:

> Ensure that any person who participates in the financing, planning, preparation or perpetration of terrorist acts or in supporting terrorist acts is brought to justice and ensure that, in addition to any other measures against them, such terrorist acts are established as serious criminal offences in domestic laws and regulations and that the punishment duly reflects the seriousness of such terrorist acts.

In adopting this Resolution, the UN Security Council circumvented the protracted international debates about defining terrorism, as well the contemporaneous deadlock in the General Assembly over the drafting of the comprehensive convention. It was able to do so in part because it refrained from dictating to states any common definition of terrorism. Instead, it permitted states discretion in the implementation of their obligation to criminalise terrorist acts. States could thus enact their own unilateral criminal definitions and offences of terrorism, under the imprimatur of Security Council authorisation. The Council's own exercise of 'quasi-legislative' powers in this manner was also controversial for other legal reasons.[58]

The decentralised criminalisation of terrorism had a number of consequences. It shifted the hitherto widespread attitude at the national level that it was sufficient to prosecute terrorism as ordinary crime rather than as a special offence. It thus signalled a new preparedness by the international community to explicitly demarcate 'terrorism' as a form of universal deviance to be condemned and stigmatised in the strongest way by domestic criminal laws.

However, the absence of a universal definition of terrorism in Resolution 1373 produced a wide range of disparate definitions of terrorism offences in national legal systems. This in turn was problematic for at least two reasons. From the standpoint of the effectiveness of counter-terrorism efforts, it impeded optimal transnational cooperation. This is because many states are unable to extradite suspects or cooperate in foreign investigations where the underlying crimes are defined differently (due to the double criminality rule). In addition, excessive or abusive foreign terrorist laws may prevent a requested state from cooperating because of the protections imposed by the latter state's human rights or constitutional laws.

From a human rights perspective then, quite a few national laws have defined terrorist offences inconsistently with international human rights law. Some laws are excessively vague, while others bring risks of discrimination against minorities. Some states defined terrorism to suit their own political purposes, to camouflage assaults on fundamental civil and political rights (including peaceful opposition through expression, assembly, and association), or to deviate from ordinary fair trial protections.[59]

The UN Human Rights Committee has especially criticised the vagueness of national terrorism laws in monitoring compliance with the ICCPR.[60] The prohibition on

---

58 See e.g. S. Talmon, 'The Security Council as World Legislature', *American Journal of International Law*, 2005, vol. 99, p. 175; P. Szasz, 'The Security Council Starts Legislating', *American Journal of International Law*, 2002, vol. 96, p. 901.

59 See generally UN High Commissioner for Human Rights, *Report on the Protection of Human Rights and Fundamental Freedoms while Countering Terrorism* (A/HRC/8/13), paras 20–23.

60 See Concluding Observations of the UN Human Rights Committee: USA, CCPR/C/USA/CO/3 (15 September 2006), para. 11; Algeria, CCPR/C/79/Add.95, 18 August 1998, para. 11; Egypt, CCPR/C/79/Add.23, 9 August 1993, para. 8; Democratic Peoples' Republic of Korea, CCPR/CO/72/PRK, 27 August 2001, para. 14; Portugal (Macao), CCPR/C/79/Add.115, 4 November 1999, para. 12; Peru, CCPR /C/79/Add.67, 25 July 1996, para. 12.

retrospective punishment (for instance, under Article 15 of the International Covenant on Civil and Political Rights 1966) encompasses the principle of legality, which requires that an offence be sufficiently certain to enable a person to prospectively know the scope of their legal liabilities.[61] The problem of vagueness extends to the preparatory offences many states have enacted in response to Resolution 1373, including those based on various forms of involvement with terrorist groups (embracing sometimes innocent associations), speech-related offences, financing offences which lower fault requirements, and blunt or sweeping crimes such as 'material support for terrorism'.

The UN Security Council's Counter-Terrorism Committee paid little attention to national definitions of terrorism during the early phases of its monitoring process, thus encouraging states with rights–violating definitions.[62] Faced with an increasingly vociferous backlash from human rights bodies and civil society, the UN Security Council eventually signalled its own conception of terrorism in Resolution 1566 (2004), where it:

> *Recalls* that criminal acts, including against civilians, committed with the intent to cause death or serious bodily injury, or taking of hostages, with the purpose to provoke a state of terror in the general public or in a group of persons or particular persons, intimidate a population or compel a government or an international organization to do or to abstain from doing any act, which constitute offences within the scope of and as defined in the international conventions and protocols relating to terrorism, are under no circumstances justifiable by considerations of a political, philosophical, ideological, racial, ethnic, religious or other similar nature, and *calls upon* all States to prevent such acts and, if not prevented, to ensure that such acts are punished by penalties consistent with their grave nature . . .[63]

The definition is only a working one which does not require states to conform their laws to it. Indeed, there is little evidence thus far that the resolution has influenced state practice at all, given that it was not framed as a mandatory obligation on states under Chapter VII of the UN Charter. Nonetheless, it provides useful guidance to states on how to define terrorism in a manner which is more respectful of human rights. Its relatively narrow scope complements efforts by the UN human rights bodies[64] to wind back excessive national criminal laws, helping to re-balance security and human rights given the disequilibrium after 9/11.

Its cumulative elements define conduct as terrorism only: (a) when it is committed to harm people; (b) with the purpose to provoke a state of terror, or to intimidate a population, or to compel a government or an international organisation; and (c) and where such conduct *also* constitutes an offence under the existing sectoral anti-terrorism treaties. Thus it would not criminalise any conduct which is not already criminal under existing sectoral treaties. Rather, it reclassifies as 'terrorism' existing criminal wrongs where they are designed to terrorise,

---

61 See e.g. *Kokkinakis v Greece* (1993) 17 EHRR 397, para. 52; see also *Castillo Petruzzi et al v Peru* [1999] IACHR 6 (30 May 1999), para. 121.

62 Report of the Special Rapporteur (Martin Scheinin) on the promotion and protection of human rights and fundamental freedoms while countering terrorism, E/CN.4/2006/98, 28 December 2005, para. 62.

63 UNSC Resolution 1566 (8 October 2004), para. 3 (emphasis in original).

64 Including the UN Human Rights Committee, various Special Rapporteurs on terrorism and human rights, the Human Rights Council, and the Office of the UN High Commissioner for Human Rights.

intimate, or compel. There is no further requirement of a political, religious, or ideological purpose, thus avoiding concerns about the discriminatory targeting of religious or political beliefs.[65] The lack of a motive element does, however, dilute the special character of 'terrorism' as an offence against human rights and the political process.

The war crime of spreading terror in armed conflict

Most terrorist-type conduct committed in any type of armed conflict is already criminalised as various war crimes, including various types of attacks on civilians.[66] In addition, IHL specially prohibits terrorism. Article 33(1) of the Fourth Geneva Convention 1949 prohibits 'collective penalties and likewise all measures of intimidation or of terrorism' against protected persons 'in the hands of a Party' (as in detention or occupied territory) to an international conflict.[67] All civilians in international conflict (including those not 'in the hands of' a party) are protected by Article 51(2) of Protocol I of 1977, which prohibits 'acts or threats of violence the primary purpose of which is to spread terror among the civilian population'. The same acts are prohibited in non-international conflict by Article 13(2) of Protocol II. Both provisions are part of wider prohibitions on attacking civilians.[68] Article 4(2)(d) of Protocol II further prohibits 'acts of terrorism' in non-international conflicts.

In the *Galic* case, the International Criminal Tribunal for the former Yugoslavia found that a violation of Article 51(2) of Protocol I attracts individual criminal responsibility,[69] despite the article not being a 'grave breach' provision. The war crime of spreading terror against a civilian population was committed by a campaign of sniping and shelling of civilians in the besieged city of Sarajevo, by deliberately targeting the routines of everyday life and thereby intending to put civilians in 'extreme fear'.[70] The crime requires that the perpetrator possess the primary purpose to spread terror, but the infliction of actual terror is not required. While all civilians caught in a conflict are likely to be incidentally afraid, the prohibition on spreading terror targets the special intention (*dolus specialis*) to spread terror.

The war crime of terror is not, however, the same as the peacetime legal conceptions of terrorism discussed earlier, namely violence committed to compel a government to do or refrain from doing something, or to advance a political, religious, or ideological cause. The meaning of terrorism in IHL is thus more limited than definitions outside of armed conflict. Partly for this reason, the purported law of war offence of providing 'material support for

---

65 Such concerns may, however, be misplaced: see B. Saul, 'The Curious Element of Motive in Definitions of Terrorism: Essential Ingredient or Criminalising Thought?', in A. Lynch, E. MacDonald and G. Williams (eds.), *Law and Liberty in the War on Terror*, Sydney: Federation Press, 2007, p. 28.

66 See H. Gasser, 'Acts of Terror, "Terrorism" and International Humanitarian Law', *International Review of the Red Cross*, 2002, vol. 84, p. 547.

67 Geneva Convention Relative to the Protection of Civilian Persons in Time of War (Fourth) [1949] 75 UNTS 287, Art 4.

68 Protocol Additional to the Geneva Conventions of 12 August 1949, and relating to the Protection of Victims of International Armed Conflicts, 8 June 1977, 1125 UNTS 3; in force 7 December 1978, Art. 51(2), and Protocol Additional to the Geneva Conventions of 12 August 1949, and relating to the Protection of Victims of Non-International Armed Conflicts, 8 June 1977, 1125 UNTS 609; in force 7 December 1978, Art. 13(2).

69 *Prosecutor v Galic*, ICTY–98–29-T, 5 December 2003, paras 65–66; affirmed in *Prosecutor v Galic (Appeals Chamber Judgment)*, IT–98–29-A, 30 November 2006, paras 87–90.

70 *Prosecutor v Galic*, ibid., para. 137.

terrorism',[71] prosecuted by the United States in military commissions at Guantanamo Bay, was found to be unknown to international and US law and thus unlawfully retrospective.[72]

The war crime of terrorism is significant for a number of reasons. War crimes attract universal criminal jurisdiction, as well as a 'prosecute or extradite' obligation, thus addressing the risk of impunity. There is no defence of superior orders. Extended modes of criminal liability apply, including command responsibility. Finally, unlike terrorism, war crimes come within the complementary jurisdiction of international criminal tribunals, where national legal orders are unable or unwilling to genuinely prosecute.

Peacetime terrorism as a customary international law crime

In 2011 the UN Security Council's Special Tribunal for Lebanon, established to prosecute terrorist bombings against Lebanese democracy in 2005, found that there exists a customary international law crime of transnational terrorism in peacetime[73] (when interpreting the scope of domestic terrorism offences under Lebanese law). The elements of the crime were:

(i)   the perpetration of a criminal act (such as murder, kidnapping, hostage taking, arson, and so on), or threatening such an act;
(ii) the intent to spread fear among the population (which would generally entail the creation of public danger) or directly or indirectly coerce a national or international authority to take some action, or to refrain from taking it;
(iii) when the act involves a transnational element.

The finding was significant because the ambit of the purported international crime was wider than that of the Lebanese offences read in isolation. The Lebanese offences were limited to certain enumerated acts of violence (in this respect following the approach of the sectoral treaties), and the more general international crime could be perpetrated by any method. The Tribunal's assessment of customary law is, however, highly controversial and has been heavily criticised by scholars.[74] Close analysis of the sources relied upon by the Appeals Chamber[75] demonstrates that its conclusion was mistaken: there is no customary international crime of transnational terrorism.[76] Thus far the Tribunal's conclusion has been largely of theoretical rather than practical legal consequence. None of the suspects before the Special Tribunal has been charged with acts coming within the wider ambit of the purported international crime.

71 Military Commission Act 2006 (US), s. 950v(25)(A); see also Military Commission Manual (2007), Part IV–18–19 (pp. 261–262).
72 *Hamdan v United States*, US Court of Appeals (DC Circuit), 16 October 2012. The case is subject to appeal.
73 UN Special Tribunal for Lebanon (Appeals Chamber), *Interlocutory Decision on the Applicable Law: Terrorism, Conspiracy, Homicide, Perpetration, Cumulative Charging*, STL–11–01/I, 16 February 2011, para. 85.
74 B. Saul, 'Legislating from a Radical Hague: The UN Special Tribunal for Lebanon Invents an International Crime of Transnational Terrorism', *Leiden Journal of International Law*, 2011, vol. 24, p. 677; K. Ambos, 'Judicial Creativity at the Special Tribunal for Lebanon: Is There a Crime of Terrorism under International Law?' *Leiden Journal of International Law*, 2011, vol. 24, p. 655.
75 Including regional anti-terrorism treaties, General Assembly resolutions, UN Security Council Resolution 1566 (2004), the UN Draft Comprehensive Anti-Terrorism Convention, the 1999 Terrorist Financing Convention, 37 national laws, and nine national judicial decisions.
76 See Saul, 'Legislating from A Radical Hague' generally.

Instead, they have only faced charges falling squarely within the orthodox scope of the Lebanese domestic offences. The Decision has nonetheless influenced at least one foreign domestic court.[77] It has not otherwise been endorsed or embraced by states, or stimulated the resolution of the impasse in the negotiations over the UN draft comprehensive convention.

Conclusion

The transnational criminal repression of terrorism aims to safeguard important international values, including the protection of human life and human rights, peaceful and stable political systems, and international peace and security. However, as the legal roots of the problem (i.e. early extradition and asylum law) indicate, the definition and repression of terrorism is not a straightforward matter of protecting civilians from violence. It also involves difficult, and often damaging, social and political judgements about who is entitled to use violence, against whom, and for what purposes. State violence enjoys a privileged place in international law, and states wish to preserve their monopoly on force by characterising much non-state violence as terrorist crime. This is perhaps understandable where democracies are safeguarding their citizens and institutions from indiscriminate violent attack. The logic breaks down where citizens rebel against violent, authoritarian, or genocidal rulers.

This largely accounts for the great difficulty in securing international agreement on the transnational repression of terrorism between states of widely differing political persuasions. A democracy should not extradite Hitler's assassin back to Nazi Germany, or even prosecute the offender. Depending on the scope of the international definitions of terrorism and any exceptions to them, the criminalisation of terrorism risks empowering the state – including autocratic ones – at the expense of other (legitimate) political claims to violence. Terrorism may often jeopardise the human rights of civilians; but if terrorism is defined more widely as any violence against the state, then the criminalisation of terrorism itself strips away the human freedom to resist oppressive or authoritarian regimes. Criminalising terrorism may serve to safeguard the stability of the state and its political order; but those political orders which systematically violate human rights may warrant destabilisation and subversion. Protecting democracy from terrorism is one thing, but protecting all states is different matter.

The gradual adoption and accumulation of the many sectoral counter-terrorism treaties proceeded fairly cautiously in expanding transnational cooperation against terrorism. Offences were limited to widely abhorred forms of attack on civilians, conduct in armed conflict was excluded, the political offence exception was largely preserved, and other protections (such as against return to discrimination) were provided. After 9/11, much of this principled caution was abandoned in the decentralised rush by states to criminalise terrorism as directed by the UN Security Council and, in the enthusiasm of the Lebanon Tribunal, to invent a customary crime of terrorism. Human rights protections have been stripped away, or ignored. The prior delicate balancing of interests has been overridden. States have arrogated more power to protect themselves. It is less clear whether civilians are safer, or the price is worth it. The draft comprehensive convention is an opportunity to reorder things and bring

---

77 *R v Mohammed Gul*, Court of Appeal (Criminal Division), 22 February 2012, [2012] EWCA Crim 280.

back a vestige of the earlier cautious and consensual approach to law-making. The process is currently mired in ideological disagreement, some of it principled, some of it less so. It may, however, be too late for the convention to make a difference. The legislative window has already closed for most states, content with what the UN Security Council gifted them after 9/11.

25

Transnational organised crime

Andreas Schloenhardt

Introduction

Labelled as 'one of the most important developments in international criminal law',[1] the United Nations (UN) Convention against Transnational Organized Crime marks a significant milestone in the global fight against criminal organisations, 'closing the gap that existed in international cooperation in an area generally regarded as one of the top priorities of the international community in the 21st century'.[2]

The Convention – often referred to by the acronym UNTOC – was approved by the UN General Assembly on 15 November 2000,[3] and made available for governments to sign at a high-level conference in Palermo, the heartland of the Italian Mafia, on 12–15 December 2000, hence also the name Palermo Convention. One hundred and thirty two of the UN's 191 member nations signed the Convention in Palermo.[4] The Convention entered into force on 29 September 2003.[5] Today, the Convention has 179 Parties and 147 Signatories.[6]

The Convention is supplemented by three protocols: the Protocol against the Smuggling of Migrants by Land, Air, and Sea,[7] the Protocol to Prevent, Suppress, and Punish Trafficking in Persons, especially Women and Children,[8] and the Protocol against the Illicit Manufacturing

---

1 G. Kemp, 'The United Nations Convention against Transnational Organized Crime: A Milestone in International Criminal Law', *South African Journal of Criminal Justice*, 2001, vol. 14, p. 152, p. 166.
2 D. Vlassis, 'The United Nations Convention against Transnational Organized Crime and its Protocols: A New Era in International Cooperation', in *The Changing Face of International Criminal Law*, Vancouver, BC: International Centre for Criminal Law Reform and Criminal Justice, 2002, p. 75.
3 UN General Assembly, *Report of the Ad Hoc Committee on the Elaboration of a Convention against Transnational Organized Crime*, UN Doc. A/55/383, 2 November 2000.
4 See ibid., Annex I for the full text of the Convention in its final form. The text has also been reprinted in (2001) 40 ILM 335; 2225 UNTS 209.
5 Article 38, Convention against Transnational Organized Crime.
6 UNODC, *Signatories to the United Nations Convention against Transnational Crime and its Protocols*, http://www.unodc.org/unodc/en/treaties/CTOC/signatures.html (accessed 20 July 2013).
7 2241 UNTS 507.
8 2237 UNTS 319.

of and Trafficking in Firearms, their Parts and Components, and Ammunition.[9] The UNTOC Convention is frequently referred to as the 'parent convention' as it is intended to set out general rules about organised crime that also impact on the application and interpretation of the three protocols, a 'system which can easily be supplemented by additional protocols in the future which then may focus on other specific, maybe new, upcoming areas of transnational organised crime'.[10]

The Convention has two main goals.[11] One is to eliminate differences among national legal systems. The second is to set standards for domestic laws so that they can effectively combat transnational organised crime. The Convention is intended to encourage countries that do not have provisions against organised crime to adopt comprehensive counter-measures, and to provide these nations with some guidance in approaching the legislative and policy questions involved. It also seeks to eliminate safe havens for criminal organisations by providing greater standardisation and coordination of national legislative, administrative, and enforcement measures relating to transnational organised crime, and to ensure a more efficient and effective global effort to prevent and suppress it.

This chapter explores the evolution of UNTOC, outlines its main provisions, their scope and application, and analyses at some length the centrepiece of the Convention: the offence criminalising participation in an organised criminal group. Drawing on the available academic literature, scholarly commentary, and the interpretative tools and implementation frameworks developed by the United Nations Office on Drugs and Crime (UNODC), the 'guardian' of the Convention and its Protocol,[12] this chapter offers an assessment of the Convention and reflects on its principal strengths and weaknesses.

Evolution

Towards an international instrument against organised crime

Among the first advocates for an international treaty against transnational organised crime was the Italian Judge Giovanni Falcone, who was involved in the prosecution and conviction of many leaders of the Italian Mafia. Just two months before his death in 1992, he attended the inaugural session of the UN Commission on Crime Prevention and Criminal Justice, where he advocated closer international cooperation against organised crime and suggested a high-level international conference to initiate work in this field.[13] Mr Falcone, his wife, and three police officers escorting them, were assassinated by the Mafia on 23 May 1992 near

---

9 UN Doc. A/55/255, 31 May 2001.
10 M. Kilchling, 'Substantive Aspects of the UN Convention against Transnational Organised Crime', in H. Albrecht and C. Fijnaut (eds), *The Containment of Transnational Organised Crime: Comments on the UN Convention of December 2000*, Freiburg: Edition Isucrim, 2002, p. 83, p. 87.
11 See further, A. Schloenhardt, 'Transnational Organised Crime and International Law: The Palermo Convention' *Criminal Law Journal*, 2005, vol. 29, p. 350; A. Schloenhardt, 'Transnational Organized Crime and International Criminal Law', *Waseda Proceedings of Comparative Law*, 2008, vol. 10, p. 311.
12 See further, UN Secretariat, Organization of the United Nations Office on Drugs and Crime, UN Doc. ST/SGB/2004/6, 15 March 2004.
13 Vlassis, 'The United Nations Convention against Transnational Organized Crime and its Protocols', pp. 77–78; D. Vlassis, 'Challenges in the Development of International Criminal Law', in M.C. Bassiouni (ed.), *International Criminal Law, Volume I*, Leiden: Martinus Nijhoff, 3rd edn, 2008, p. 907, pp. 909–10.

Capaci, Sicily, on their way to Palermo airport. This assassination occurred within weeks of the killing of Judge Paolo Bosselini who, like Falcone, was responsible for convicting a number of key Mafia leaders.[14]

Following Falcone's assassination, the Italian Government strengthened its commitment to fight organised crime and submitted proposals for international cooperation against transnational organised crime to the UN. In 1993, the UN Commission on Crime Prevention and Criminal Justice, followed by the UN General Assembly, endorsed the idea of a first international conference on organised transnational crime, to be hosted by Italy in 1994.[15] The specific objective of this international conference was 'to consider whether it would be feasible to elaborate international instruments, including conventions, against organised transnational crime'.[16]

The World Ministerial Conference on Organised Transnational Crime met on 21–23 November 1994 in Naples, Italy. The principal features of the conference were the recognition of the global growth of organised transnational crime[17] and the development of appropriate countermeasures.[18] The conference called, *inter alia*, for the universal criminalisation of participation in criminal organisations, measures for confiscation and forfeiture of assets, and enhanced efforts to combat money laundering and corruption.[19] The conference concluded with the signing of the Naples Political Declaration and Global Action Plan against Organized Transnational Crime (hereinafter the Naples Declaration),[20] which provides a first set of elements for an international convention against organised crime. In December 1994, the UN General Assembly endorsed the Naples Declaration,[21] thus opening the way for the elaboration of an international convention against transnational organised crime under the auspices of the UN.[22]

14 T. Blickman, 'The Rothschilds of the Mafia on Aruba', *Transnational Organized Crime*, 1997, vol. 3, no. 2, p. 50, p. 55.

15 UN General Assembly, Crime Prevention and Criminal Justice, UN Doc. A/RES/48/103, 20 December 1993. See further P. Gastrow, 'The Origin of the Convention', in H. Albrecht and C. Fijnaut (eds), *The Containment of Transnational Organised Crime: Comments on the UN Convention of December 2000*, Freiburg: Edition Isucrim, 2002, p. 19, pp. 24–27.

16 UN Economic and Social Council (ECOSOC), World Ministerial Conference on Organized Transnational Crime, UN Doc. E/RES/1993/29, 27 July 1993, at para. 1(e).

17 See UN ECOSOC, World Ministerial Conference against Organized Transnational Crime, Problems and Dangers Posed by Organized Transnational Crime in the Various Regions of the World, UN Doc. E/CONF.88/2, 18 August 1994.

18 The background papers to the conference (UN Docs E/CONF.88/1–6) have also been reprinted in M.C Bassiouni and E. Vetere (eds), *Organized Crime: A Compilation of UN Documents 1975–1998*, Ardsley, NY: Transnational Publishers, 1998, p. 450, and also in P. Williams and E. Savona, *The United Nations and Transnational Organized Crime*, Portland, OR: Frank Cass, 1996, p. 1.

19 See Convention against Transnational Organized Crime 40 ILM 353 at para. 5 (2001); and UN ECOSOC, World Ministerial Conference against Organized Transnational Crime, 'National Legislation and its Adequacy to Deal with the Various Forms of Organized Transnational Crime', UN Doc. E/CONF.88/3, 25 August 1994, and UN Office at Vienna, 'The World Ministerial Conference on Organized Transnational Crime', *UN Crime Prevention and Criminal Justice Newsletter*, 26/27, 1995, pp. 7–8.

20 Reprinted in UN General Assembly, Crime Prevention and Criminal Justice: Report of the World Ministerial Conference on Organized Transnational Crime, UN Doc. A/RES/49/748 Annex, 2 December 1994.

21 UN General Assembly, Naples Political Declaration and Global Action Plan against Organized Transnational Crime, UN Doc. A/RES/49/159, 23 December 1994, para. 3.

22 See further D. McClean, *Transnational Organized Crime*, Oxford: Oxford University Press, 2007, pp. 6–8; Vlassis, 'Challenges in the Development of International Criminal Law', pp. 912–914; Gastrow, 'The Origin of the Convention', pp. 27–29.

Development of the Palermo Convention

On 12 December 1996, the Government of Poland submitted a first draft UN framework convention against transnational organised crime.[23] This document was further discussed at an Informal Meeting on the Question of the Elaboration of an International Convention, held in Palermo, from 6 to 8 April 1997.[24] Pursuant to the recommendations of this meeting, the UN Economic and Social Council, followed by the UN Secretary-General, decided to establish an inter-sessional open-ended intergovernmental group of experts to prepare a preliminary draft convention.[25] The expert group met in Warsaw from 2 to 6 February 1998[26] and presented its report together with an outline of options for contents of a convention to the UN Commission on Crime Prevention and Criminal Justice at its Seventh Session in April 1998.[27] The Commission then decided to establish an in-sessional working group to implement the Naples Declaration and further discuss the draft convention. This working group met in Buenos Aires from 31 August to 4 September 1998 and produced a new consolidated draft to serve as a basis for future formal consultations.[28] The findings of the Buenos Aires meeting were then presented to the Commission on Crime Prevention and Criminal Justice and subsequently to the UN General Assembly.

On 9 December 1998, the UN General Assembly decided to establish an open-ended intergovernmental ad hoc committee to draft the main text of:

(a) a new comprehensive international convention against transnational organised crime, and
(b) three additional international legal instruments on:

    i.   trafficking in women and children;
   ii.   illicit manufacturing and trafficking in firearms, their parts and components, and
  iii.   illegal trafficking in and transporting of migrants, including by sea.[29]

Between January 1999 and October 2000, the Ad Hoc Committee held eleven sessions in Vienna to discuss and finalise the text of the Convention and the three supplementing

---

23 UN Doc. A/C.3/51/7, reprinted in UN ECOSOC, Follow-up to the Naples Political Declaration and Global Action Plan against Organized Transnational Crime, UN Doc. E/RES/1997/22, 21 July 1997, Annex III. See further Vlassis, 'The United Nations Convention against Transnational Organized Crime and its Protocols', at pp. 80–82; McClean, *Transnational Organized Crime*, pp. 6–7; Vlassis, 'Challenges in the Development of International Criminal Law', pp. 914–915.
24 See further McClean, *Transnational Organized Crime*, pp. 7–8.
25 UN ECOSOC, Follow-up to the Naples Political Declaration and Global Action Plan against Organized Transnational Crime, UN Doc. E/RES/1997/22, 21 July 1997, para. 14; UN General Assembly, Follow-up to the Naples Political Declaration and Global action Plan against Organized Transnational Crime, UN Doc. A/RES/52/85, 30 January 1998, para. 14. See further McClean, *Transnational Organized Crime*, pp. 8–9.
26 See further Vlassis, 'Challenges in the Development of International Criminal Law', pp. 917–18.
27 UN Commission on Crime Prevention and Criminal Justice, Implementation of the Naples Political Declaration and Global Plan of Action against Organized Transnational Crime: Question of the elaboration of an International Convention against organized transnational crime and other international instruments, UN Doc. E/CN.15/1998/5, 18 February 1998.
28 Vlassis, 'The United Nations Convention against Transnational Organized Crime and its Protocols', pp. 82–85.
29 UN General Assembly, Transnational Organized Crime, UN Doc. A/RES/53/111, 20 January 1999, para. 10; UN General Assembly, Strengthening the United Nations Crime Prevention and Criminal Justice Programme, in Particular its Technical Cooperation Capacity, UN Doc. A/RES/53/114, 20 January 1999, para. 13.

protocols. Consultations about the main Convention and the trafficking in persons and migrant smuggling protocols finished at the eleventh session in October 2000. An additional twelfth session to conclude the Firearms Protocol was held in March 2001.[30] In retrospect – and in comparison to other international treaties – the development of UNTOC and its protocols took only a short time, which, in the view of one commentator, 'reflects the urgency of the needs faced by all States, developed and developing alike, for new tools to prevent and control transnational organised crime'.[31]

Outline of the Convention

UNTOC can be divided into four parts: criminalisation, international cooperation, technical cooperation, and implementation. Of particular interest to this chapter are those parts of the Convention that deal with the criminalisation of organised crime. To that end, the Convention introduces four offences: participation in an organised criminal group (Article 5), money laundering (Article 6),[32] corruption (Article 8),[33] and obstruction of justice (Article 23). The Legislative Guides for the Implementation of the United Nations Convention against Transnational Organized Crime and the Protocols thereto stress that:

> The activities covered by these offences are vital to the success of sophisticated criminal operations and to the ability of offenders to operate efficiently, to generate substantial profits and to protect themselves as well as their illicit gains from law enforcement authorities. They constitute, therefore, the cornerstone of a global and coordinated effort to counter serious and well-organised criminal markets, enterprises, and activities.[34]

Criminal liability for each offence also extends to particpants and accomplices. Article 10 of the Convention further extends the four offences to legal persons (i.e. corporations), but leaves it to States Parties to decide whether to make such liability criminal, civil, or administrative.

Articles 12 to 14 set out a range of measures pertaining to confiscation and seizure of assets and international cooperation for purposes of confiscation. In Articles 16–21 and 27, the Convention sets out a broad range of other international cooperation measures, which, as mentioned earlier, were at the heart of the original idea to develop an international treaty against organised crime. These measures include extradition, transfer of sentenced persons, mutual legal assistance, joint investigations, the use of special investigative techniques, transfer of criminal proceedings, and law enforcement cooperation. The protection of witnesses, a crucial element to succeed in prosecuting organised crime, is covered by Articles 24 and 25

---

30 See UN General Assembly, Report of the Ad Hoc Committee on the Elaboration of a Convention against Transnational Organized Crime, UN Doc. A/55/383, 2 November 2000, paras 77, 102, 108, 120. See further Vlassis, 'The United Nations Convention against Transnational Organized Crime and its Protocols', pp. 87–88; McClean, *Transnational Organized Crime*, pp. 9–13.

31 Vlassis, 'The United Nations Convention against Transnational Organized Crime and its Protocols', p. 76, p. 88; Vlassis, 'Challenges in the Development of International Criminal Law', pp. 920–925.

32 See further R.S. Clark, 'The United Nations Convention against Transnational Organized Crime', *Wayne Law Review*, 2004, vol. 50, p. 161, pp. 174–175; A. Schloenhardt, 'Transnational Organized Crime and International Criminal Law', in M.C. Bassiouni (ed.), *International Criminal Law, Volume I*, Leiden: Martinus Nijhoff, 3rd edn, 2008, p. 939, pp. 954–956.

33 Clark, 'The United Nations Convention against Transnational Organized Crime', pp. 175–176.

34 UNODC, *Legislative Guides for the Implementation of the United Nations Convention against Transnational Organized Crime and the Protocols Thereto*, New York: United Nations, 2004 (hereinafter *Legislative Guides*), p. 17.

of the Convention. In addition, Article 26 sets out a range of measures to encourage former participants of criminal organisations to cooperate with law enforcement agencies. The remaining substantive Articles of the Convention, 28 to 31, deal with information exchange, training and technical assistance, economic development, and prevention.

Definition of organised criminal group

Article 2(a) of the Convention defines 'organised criminal group' as

> [a] structured group of three or more persons, existing for a period of time and acting in concert with the aim of committing one or more serious crimes or offences established in accordance with this Convention, in order to obtain, directly or indirectly, a financial or other material benefit.[35]

This definition of an organised criminal group combines elements relating to the structure of criminal organisations with elements relating to the objectives of the group.[36]

Structured group of three or more persons

The definition in Article 2(a) focuses specifically on sophisticated criminal organisations and on the people that constitute that organisation, rather than focusing on the activities in which the organisation and its members engage. For this reason, only 'structured groups' of three or more persons can be the subject of the measures under the Convention. The term 'structured group' is further defined in Article 2(c) to exclude from the definition of 'organised criminal group' randomly formed associations for the immediate commission of an offence without any prior existence, as well as associations that do not need to have formally defined roles for members, continuity of membership or a developed structure.[37] Acts committed by individuals or fewer than three persons,[38] or acts done by three persons not 'acting in concert', also fall outside the scope of the Convention.[39] States Parties to the Convention are, however, free to raise or lower the number of members required by this definition.[40]

---

35 For more on the development and history of this definition see McClean, *Transnational Organized Crime*, pp. 38–40.

36 See also McClean, *Transnational Organized Crime*, pp. 41–42; Schloenhardt, 'Transnational Organized Crime and International Criminal Law', pp. 950–952.

37 Article 2(c), Convention against Transnational Organized Crime: 'structured group'. See further A. Orlova and J. Moore, ' "Umbrellas" or "Building Blocks"?: Defining International Terrorism and Transnational Organised Crime in International Law', *Houston Journal of International Law*, 2005, vol. 27, no. 2, p. 267, p. 282; McClean, *Transnational Organized Crime*, p. 43.

38 It is noteworthy that the requirement of three members is higher than the two persons required for a conspiracy. See also M.C. Bassiouni, 'Organized Crime and Terrorist Criminal Activities', *Emory International Law Review*, 1990, vol. 4, no. 1, p. 9, p. 10.

39 McClean, *Transnational Organized Crime*, p. 41, suggests that it is not necessary that 'all members must join the activity' but 'that this must be a group activity, not merely the simultaneous acts of some of its members, each acting on his or her own account'.

40 UN General Assembly, Interpretative notes for the official records (Travaux Préparatoires) of the negotiations of the United Nations Convention against Transnational Organized Crime and the Protocols Thereto, UN Doc. A/55/383/Add.1 (hereinafter *Travaux Préparatoires*), para. 2.

The concept of an organised criminal group under the Convention recognises the structural and managerial features of sophisticated criminal enterprises. On the one hand, the definition under Article 2(a) and (c) is wide enough to encompass a great variety of structural models. This is also confirmed in the *Travaux Préparatoires*, which indicate that

> the term 'structured group' is to be used in a broad sense so as to include both groups with hierarchical or other elaborate structures and non-hierarchical groups where the role of members of the group need not be formally defined.[41]

On the other hand, the definition is limited to formal, developed organisations, thus avoiding criminalisation of informal and random associations such as youth groups and one-off criminal enterprises.[42]

Existence for some period of time

The definition further requires that the organised criminal group 'exists for a period of time', thus excluding single, ad hoc operations from the definition. The Convention recognises that the ongoing existence of criminal organisations is generally independent from individual criminal activities; organised crime is characterised by criminal activities that are carried out on a sustained, repeated basis. Furthermore, the continued existence of large criminal organisations is often independent from individual members; their operations generally continue after individuals are arrested, die, or otherwise leave the organisation.[43] The Convention offers no specific guidance about the 'period of time', whether it is of short or long duration, for which a group ought to exist before it qualifies as an organised criminal group. In UNODC's Model Legislative Provisions against Organized Crime it is noted that:

> As a practical matter, some States may want or need to be more specific about some elements of this definition, such as the definition of the 'period of time' for which a group has to exist. In this regard it may be clearer to refer simply to 'any period of time'.[44]

Aim to commit serious crime

Only structured associations that 'act in concert with the aim of committing one or more serious crimes or offences established in accordance with this Convention' qualify as organised criminal groups under UNTOC. Accordingly, the group must have one of two aims: either (1) to commit one or more of the Convention offences in Articles 5, 6, 8, or 23, such as corruption and money laundering; or (2) to commit one or more serious crimes.

Under Article 2(b) ' "serious crime" shall mean conduct constituting an offence punishable by a maximum deprivation of liberty of at least four years of imprisonment or a

---

41 *Travaux Préparatoires*, para. 4. Cf. Orlova and Moore, ' "Umbrellas" or "Building Blocks"?', p. 282; McClean, *Transnational Organized Crime*, p. 43.
42 *Legislative Guides*, p. 14.
43 Cf. Bassiouni, 'Organized Crime and Terrorist Criminal Activities', p. 11; McClean, *Transnational Organized Crime*, p. 41.
44 UNODC, *Model Legislative Provisions against Organized Crime*, Vienna: UNODC, 2012, p. 8.

more serious penalty.[45] Seriousness is thus determined by reference to the criminal penalty associated with the crime, not by reference to any type of conduct, the gravity of any harm or damage caused, or the motivation of the perpetrator.[46] The definition is tied to determination by domestic legislators, which allows for a degree of flexibility and for national adjustments to be made. The Conference of States Parties to the Convention against Transnational Organized Crime recognises that:

> This more flexible approach means that there is no exhaustive or indicative list of offences that would provide for a uniform approach among States Parties. Depending on the penalty, an offence may be considered a serious crime in one State and not in others.[47]

UNTOC leaves the decision of what crimes fall within and outside the scope of the Convention to national authorities that can raise penalties to bring offences within the ambit of 'serious crimes', or lower them to keep them out in order to avoid Convention obligations.[48] Vincenzo Militello notes that this approach 'ends up . . . embracing groups of subjects involved in highly differentiated criminal activities that vary according to the countries in which they operate'.[49] Critical of this approach, Roger Clark refers to this matter as the 'specific-content-free definition of serious crime' and remarks that '[t]he scope of the Convention's application turns ultimately on the seriousness of the particular activities (judged in a rough and ready way by the penalty) rather than on substantive content'.[50]

The definition of 'serious crime' is seen as one of the main weaknesses of the concept of organised crime under the Convention as it enables, and perhaps encourages, discrepancies between States Parties. Leaving the decision of what does and does not amount to 'serious crime' to national legislators means that even if an organised criminal group engages in exceptionally violent, heinous, or detrimental conduct, the group will not fall within the definition of the Convention unless such conduct attracts a penalty of four year's imprisonment or more. David Freedman similarly notes that:

> Ultimately, countries themselves define the activities that fall within the rubric of serious crime, given that the definition is linked to punishment rather than a list of predicate offences specifically enumerated. However, since offences and their punishment vary

---

45 Cf. UN Ad Hoc Committee on the Elaboration of a Convention against Transnational Organised Crime, Analytical study on serious crime, UN Doc. A/AC.254/22, 30 November 1999; McClean, *Transnational Organized Crime*, p. 42.

46 UN Conference of the Parties to the United Nations Convention against Transnational Organized Crime, The notion of serious crime in the United Nations Convention against Transnational Organized Crime, UN Doc. CTOC/COP/2012/CRP.4, 20 September 2012, p. 2, para. 3.

47 UN Conference of the Parties to the United Nations Convention against Transnational Organized Crime, The notion of serious crime in the United Nations Convention against Transnational Organized Crime, UN Doc. CTOC/COP/2012/CRP.4, 20 September 2012, p. 2, para. 3; see pp. 4–5, paras 18–22 of the same document for a 'summary of the negotiating history of the notion of serious crime'.

48 Cf. *Legislative Guides*, p. 14.

49 V. Militello, 'Participation in an Organised Criminal Group as International Offence', in H. Albrecht and C. Fijnaut (eds), *The Containment of Transnational Organised Crime: Comments on the UN Convention of December 2000*, Freiburg: Edition Isucrim, 2002, p. 97, p. 102.

50 Clark, 'The United Nations Convention against Transnational Organized Crime', p. 169.

from country to country, the four-year threshold has the potential to raise doubt about which offences should be prosecuted as organised criminal activity.[51]

'Because domestic laws, and not international standards, determine this aspect of the definition, some states may change the penalties in their domestic criminal statutes to remove crimes from the scope of the Convention',[52] notes Jennifer Smith. Carrie-Lyn Donigan Guymon suggests that 'this provision would be more meaningful if there were a more definitive list of what constitutes serious crime',[53] a point also supported by Militello.[54]

Such criticism fails to recognise that attempts to include a list of offences remained unsuccessful during the negotiations of the Convention because 'consensus could not be reached on which offences would have needed to be included in such a list'.[55] The Conference of States Parties also recently justified the definition of 'serious crime' in Article 2(b) of the Convention by noting that this concept

> enables the application of the Convention to a broad range of offences in a flexible manner. Moreover, new forms and dimensions of transnational organized crime fall under the scope of the Convention, considerably enhancing the use of the Convention, in particular for purposes of international cooperation.[56]

Concerns have also been expressed about the fact that the definition also extends to criminal groups aiming to commit only a single serious crime. Alexandra Orlova and James Moore ask whether 'the commission of just one crime (unless the crime is ongoing), no matter how grave, [is] enough to view an entity as part of organised crime'.[57]

Financial or material benefit

The definition under Article 2(a) requires that the purpose of the group's activity is 'to obtain, directly or indirectly, a financial or other material benefit'. Here, the Convention recognises the profit motive that characterises organised crime. The *Travaux Préparatoires* further explain that 'other material benefit' may also include non-material gratification such as sexual services.[58] The Legislative Guides add that '[t]his is to ensure that organisations trafficking in human beings or child pornography for sexual and not monetary reasons are not excluded'.[59]

---

51 D. Freedman, 'The New Law on Criminal Organizations in Canada', *Canadian Bar Review*, 2007, vol. 85, p. 171, p. 196. See also Orlova and Moore, ' "Umbrellas" or "Building Blocks"?', p. 284.
52 J. Smith, 'An International Hit Job: Prosecuting Organised Crime Acts as Crimes against Humanity', *Georgetown Law Journal*, 2009, vol. 97, p. 1111, p. 1119.
53 C.D. Guymon, 'International Legal Mechanisms for Combating Transnational Organised Crime', *Berkeley Journal of International Law*, 2000, vol. 18, p. 53, p. 95.
54 Militello, 'Participation in an Organised Criminal Group as International Offence', p. 102.
55 UN Conference of the Parties to the United Nations Convention against Transnational Organized Crime, The notion of serious crime in the United Nations Convention against Transnational Organized Crime, UN Doc. CTOC/COP/2012/CRP.4, 20 September 2012, p. 5, paras 21–22.
56 Ibid., p. 8, para. 34.
57 Orlova and Moore, ' "Umbrellas" or "Building Blocks"?', p. 283. See also McClean, *Transnational Organized Crime*, p. 41.
58 *Travaux Préparatoires*, para. 3.
59 *Legislative Guides*, p. 13 (with reference to the *Travaux Préparatoires*).

Since the definition is limited to 'material benefit', concerns that the 'term has [the] potential of being interpreted very broadly to include non-economically motivated crimes such as environmental or politically motivated offences'[60] seem unwarranted. Indeed, the Legislative Guides note that the definition is intended to exclude groups with purely political or social motives:

> This would not, in principle, include groups such as some terrorist or insurgent groups, provided that their goals were purely non-material. However, the Convention may still apply to crimes committed by those groups in the event that they commit crimes covered by the Convention (for example, by committing robbery in order to raise financial or material benefits).[61]

Importantly, the 'financial or material benefit' element also effectively excludes terrorism from the definition of organised crime, so long as it does not serve financial or material gain (for example fund-raising activities or other ways of financing terrorism). During the drafting of UNTOC, several countries fought hard to include terrorism within the scope of the Convention and later expressed regret that the scope was not extended in this way.[62]

Despite some criticsm of individual elements and aspects, the definition of organised criminal group under UNTOC features most of the established characteristics of criminal organisations while allowing some flexibility to target a diverse range of associations and structures. Others, however, see the definition in Article 2 as no more than the lowest common denominator, 'referring to almost every kind of formation, thus rendering it almost meaningless'.[63] Orlova and Moore have described the definition as 'a conceptually weak compromise definition that is, at once, overly broad and under inclusive'.[64] Smith commented that:

> The United Nations (UN) Convention against Transnational Organized Crime will not be a completely effective mechanism to counter organised crime either, because it lacks international standards to define organised crime and an international mechanism to enforce and punish organised crime.[65]

Donigan Guymon remarks that:

> Perhaps one of the most significant failures of the drafters of the UN Convention thus far has been the removal from the draft of any attempt to describe or define the activities of international organised crime, a key element of an effective international convention addressing transnational organised crime.[66]

---

60 Orlova and Moore, ' "Umbrellas" or "Building Blocks"?', p. 283.
61 *Legislative Guides*, p. 13.
62 McClean, *Transnational Organized Crime*, p. 40.
63 Orlova and Moore, ' "Umbrellas" or "Building Blocks"?', p. 283.
64 Ibid., p 304. See also Militello, 'Participation in an Organised Criminal Group as International Offence', p. 103.
65 Smith, 'An International Hit Job: Prosecuting Organised Crime Acts as Crimes against Humanity', p. 1115.
66 Guymon, 'International Legal Mechanisms for Combating Transnational Organised Crime', p. 93.

Participation in an organised criminal group, Article 5(1)(A)

The criminalisation of participation in an organised crime group is generally seen as one of the most important elements of UNTOC and was one of the main motivators to develop an international treaty in this field. Early discussions about this point, however, also recognised that it would be difficult to find consensus on the design and elements of such an offence.[67]

Development

The original draft of the Convention presented at the first session of the Ad Hoc Committee in January 1999 included a basic model to serve as the starting point for discussion and seeking to build a bridge between civil and common law systems:[68]

Article 3 Participation in a criminal organisation

1. Each State Party shall undertake in accordance with the fundamental principles of its domestic legal system, to make punishable one or both of the following types of conduct:

   (a) Conduct by any person consisting of an agreement with one or more persons that an activity should be pursued which, if carried out, would amount to the commission of a crime or offences that are punishable by imprisonment or other deprivation of liberty of at least . . . years; or

   (b) Conduct by any person who participates in a criminal organisation, where such participation is intentional and is either with the aim of furthering the general criminal activity or criminal purpose of the group or made in the knowledge of the intention of the group to commit offences.

2. Nothing contained in this article shall affect the principle that the description of offences to which it refers and of legal defences thereto is reserved to the domestic law of a State Party and that such offences shall be prosecuted and punished in conformity with that law.[69]

This draft, created only for the purpose of discussion, nonetheless set out two separate criminalisation models which survive in the final version of the Convention: Draft Article 3(1)(a) attaches criminal liability to an agreement to commit criminal offences; Draft Article 3(1)(b), on the other hand, creates liability for participation in a criminal organisation. These two approaches are reflective of common and civil law influences respectively and the draft (as well as the final Convention) envisaged that States Parties would choose 'one or both' models when they implemented this criminal offence into domestic law.

---

67 See further, McClean, *Transnational Organized Crime*, p. 60.
68 UN Ad Hoc Committee on the Elaboration of a Convention against Transnational Organized Crime, Draft United Nations Convention against Transnational Organized Crime, UN Doc. A/AC.254/4, 15 December 1998, Article 3, fn. 12.
69 Ibid., Article 3.

A new, more advanced text for Draft Article 3 was proposed by the United Kingdom during the first session of the Ad Hoc Committee[70] and was further discussed at the second session in March 1999. It reads:

1. Each State Party shall establish as criminal offences the following conduct:

    (a) Organizing, directing, aiding, abetting, facilitating or counselling the commission of serious crime involving an organized criminal group; and
    (b) Either or both of the following as criminal offences distinct from those involving the attempt or completion of the criminal activity:

        (i) Agreeing with one or more other persons to commit a serious crime for any purpose relating directly or indirectly to the obtaining of a financial or other material benefit and, where required by domestic law, involving an act undertaken by one of the participants in furtherance of the agreement;
        (ii) Conduct by a person who intentionally, and with knowledge of either the aim and general criminal activity of an organized criminal group or its intention to commit the crimes in question, takes active part in:

            a. Activities of an organized criminal group referred to in article 2 *bis* of this Convention;
            b. Other activities of the group in the knowledge that the person's participation will contribute to the achievement of the above-described criminal aim.

2. The knowledge, intent, aim, purpose or agreement referred to in paragraph 1 of this article may be inferred from objective factual circumstances.[71]

The offences set out in Article 3(1)(b)(i) and (ii) of this draft are the basis of the offences contained in Article 5(1)(a) of the final version of the Convention. Changes to the British proposal were relatively minor and the final text of the participation offence was largely settled during the seventh session of the Ad Hoc Committee in January 2000.[72]

Current concept

Under Article 5(1)(a) of the Convention against Transnational Organized Crime

[e]ach State Party shall adopt such legislative and other measures as may be necessary to establish as criminal offences, when committed intentionally:

(a) Either or both of the following as criminal offences distinct from those involving the attempt or completion of the criminal activity:

---

70 UN Ad Hoc Committee on the Elaboration of a Convention against Transnational Organized Crime, Proposals and contributions received from Governments on the draft United Nations Convention against Transnational Organized Crime, UN Doc. A/AC.254/L.4, 20 January 1999.

71 UN Ad Hoc Committee on the Elaboration of a Convention against Transnational Organized Crime, Revised draft United Nations Convention against Transnational Organized Crime, UN Doc. A/AC.254/4/Rev.1, 10 February 1999, Article 3, option 2.

72 UN Ad Hoc Committee on the Elaboration of a Convention against Transnational Organized Crime, Revised draft United Nations Convention against Transnational Organized Crime, UN Doc. A/AC.254/4/Rev.6, 24 Dec 1999, Article 3. See also, McClean, *Transnational Organized Crime*, p. 61.

(i) Agreeing with one or more other persons to commit a serious crime for a purpose relating directly or indirectly to the obtaining of a financial or other material benefit and, where required by domestic law, involving an act undertaken by one of the participants in furtherance of the agreement or involving an organized criminal group;

(ii) Conduct by a person who, with knowledge of either the aim and general criminal activity of an organized criminal group or its intention to commit the crimes in question, takes an active part in:

    a. Criminal activities of the organized criminal group;

    b. Other activities of the organized criminal group in the knowledge that his or her participation will contribute to the achievement of the above-described criminal aim.

Article 5 applies 'to the prevention, investigation and prosecution' of 'serious crime' 'where the offence is transnational in nature and involves an organized criminal group', as defined in Article 3(1).[73] The application of the offences under Article 5 is limited to 'transnational organized crime', i.e. to offences that occur across international borders, as defined in Article 3(2).[74] Article 34, however, stresses that the criminalisation of participation in an organized criminal group in domestic laws should not require the conduct to be transnational in nature.[75]

As an international treaty that needs to be adaptable to the systems, traditions, and needs of individual States Parties, the Convention does not determine set penalties for the offence under Article 5 (and any of the other offences). To offer guidance and ensure that States Parties recognise the seriousness of organised crime, Article 11(1) provides that penalties for Convention offences should take into account the gravity of the offence. Article 26(2) and (3) also encourage States Parties to consider mitigating sentences, exercising leniency, or granting immunity from persecution for persons who cooperate with the authorities in the investigation and/or prosecution of organised crime.[76]

As mentioned earlier, Article 5(1)(a) of UNTOC offers States Parties a choice between two different organised crime offences:

(i) a conspiracy offence, and
(ii) an offence for participating in an organised criminal group.

The two different offences recognise different traditions and developments in civil and common law jurisdictions and allow States Parties to choose the offence[s] best suited to their domestic legal system. The offence contained in paragraph (i) builds on the offence of conspiracy that is recognised across most common law jurisdictions, while the participation

73 UN Conference of the Parties to the United Nations Convention against Transnational Organized Crime, The notion of serious crime in the United Nations Convention against Transnational Organized Crime, UN Doc. CTOC/COP/2012/CRP.4, 20 September 2012, p. 3, para. 11; see further McClean, *Transnational Organized Crime*, pp. 51–52.
74 See further McClean, *Transnational Organized Crime*, pp. 52–56.
75 UN Conference of the Parties to the United Nations Convention against Transnational Organized Crime, The notion of serious crime in the United Nations Convention against Transnational Organized Crime, UN Doc. CTOC/COP/2012/CRP.4, 20 September 2012, p. 3, para. 12.
76 See further, UNODC, *Model Legislative Provisions against Organized Crime*, Article 11, pp. 47–49.

offence under (ii) – also sometimes referred to by its French name, *association des malfaiteurs* – may be more palatable for civil law countries, many of which do not permit the criminalisation of mere planning and agreement without any physical activity pursuant to the ageement.[77] The two models are not mutually exclusive and several States Parties have implemented both models concurrently.

Article 5(1)(a)(i): the conspiracy model

Liability for the offence in Article 5(1)(a)(i) of the Convention is based on an agreement to commit serious crime. The design of this offence is, for the most part, identical with conspiracy offences found in most common law jurisdictions, where the concept of conspiracy can be traced back to the early seventeenth century (though the Convention does not use the term conspiracy).

Rationale

Put simply, conspiracy criminalises agreements between two or more persons to commit an unlawful act where there is an intention to commit that unlawful act. The rationale of conspiracy is based on the view that if one person agrees with another about the commission of a crime, this is 'increasing the direct risk to the community of criminal activity in two ways. First, it increases the likelihood of success of the crime. Secondly, it makes the commission of other crimes more likely.'[78] In many jurisdictions, especially those following common law traditions, the doctrine of conspiracy is one tool to create liability for people involved in criminal organisations,[79] especially those 'who plan and organise crimes but take no part in their actual commissions'.[80]

One purpose of the conspiracy offence is to extend liability 'backwards' beyond attempts by criminalising the planning (or 'agreement') stage of a criminal offence. Conspiracy is a more preliminary crime than attempt; it creates liability even if no preparation of the contemplated offence has begun.[81] As such, prosecuting conspiracy can serve to prevent crime and allows law enforcement agencies to intervene (and enables charges to be laid) some time before an offence is actually attempted or completed.[82]

Conspiracy has a further dimension in that it allows for the criminalisation of multiple persons involved in a criminal enterprise. The offence attaches liability to agreements to

---

77 Ibid, pp. 29–30; Vlassis, 'The United Nations Convention against Transnational Organized Crime and its Protocols', p. 92; Freedman, 'The New Law on Criminal Organizations in Canada', p. 197; Clark, 'The United Nations Convention against Transnational Organized Crime', pp. 170–171; Orlova and Moore, ' "Umbrellas" or "Building Blocks"?', pp. 286–287; *Legislative Guides*, pp. 21–22; McClean, *Transnational Organized Crime*, pp. 61–62.

78 M. Joutsen, 'International Cooperation against Transnational Organized Crime: Criminalising Participation in and Organized Criminal Group', *UNAFEI Resource Materials*, 2002, vol. 59, p. 417, p. 419.

79 Cf. C.M. Powell, 'Conspiracy Prosecutions', *Criminal Law Quarterly*, 1970, p. 34, p. 42.

80 L. Waller and C. Williams, *Criminal Law*, 11th edn, Sydney, NSW: Lexis Nexis, 2009, para. 10.66.

81 *R v Trudel* (1984) 12 CCC (3d) 342 (Quebec Court of Appeal).

82 P. Gillies, *The Law of Criminal Conspiracy*, 2nd edn, Sydney, NSW: Federation Press, 1990, pp. 4–13. Cf. *DPP v Nock* (1978) 67 Cr App R 116, pp. 126–127.

commit crime. This enables the prosecution of persons who organise and plan crime, rather than execute it.

Elements of Article 5(1)(a)(i)

Article 5(1)(a)(i) combines elements of conspiracy (the agreement to commit a crime) with the additional requirement of a purpose of obtaining a financial or other benefit.

For criminal liability to arise, the material or physical elements (*actus reus*) of Article 5(1)(a)(i) require proof of:[83]

- an agreement to commit a serious crime (as defined in Article 2(b), see above);
- between two or more persons; and
- where required by domestic law, proof of an overt act in furtherance of the agreement.

The mental or fault elements (*mens rea*) under Article 5(1)(a)(i) require proof:

- that the purpose of agreement or the crime committed was to obtain a financial or other material benefit; and
- of the accused's intention to enter the agreement (see Article 5(1), châpeau).

In essence, liability under Article 5(1)(a)(i) arises when two or more persons deliberately enter into an agreement to commit a serious crime for the purpose of obtaining some material benefit. Unlike liability for attempt at common law, there is no requirement to demonstrate that the accused came close ('proximate') to the completion of the substantive (serious) offence.[84]

The offence in Article 5(1)(a)(i) centres predominantly on the agreement to commit a serious offence as defined in Article 2 of the Convention. The agreement must be made between at least two people; an agreement with oneself is not possible.[85] Common law suggests that while the agreement cannot exist without communication between the conspirators, there is no requirement that the parties to the agreement know each other. All that is required is that each conspirator is committed to the agreed objective(s). There is no requirement regarding the level of involvement of a conspirator in the agreement. The agreement may envisage that all conspirators equally take some action towards the agreed goal, but a conspirator may also be part of the agreement without carrying out any conduct towards the common objective.[86]

The agreement between the conspirators imports an intention that the unlawful act or purpose of the agreement be carried out.[87] To prove the existence of a conspiracy, it must be shown that the alleged conspirators were acting in pursuance of a criminal purpose held in

---

83 Cf UNODC, *Model Legislative Provisions against Organized Crime*, Article 7 (option 1), p. 30, p. 31.
84 G. Williams, *Criminal Law: the General Part*, London: Stevens, 2nd edn, 1961, p. 710.
85 *R v O'Brien* (1954) 110 CCC 1 (Sup Ct of Can); *Peters v R* (1998) 192 CLR 49.
86 Cf. S. Bronitt and B. McSherry, *Principles of Criminal Law*, 3rd edn, Sydney, NSW: Thomson Reuters, 2010, pp. 416–424; D. Brown *et al.*, *Criminal Laws: Materials and Commentary on Criminal Law and Process in NSW*, 4th edn, Sydney: Federation Press, 2006, pp. 1092–1103; D. Lanham *et al.*, *Criminal Laws in Australia*, Sydney: Federation Press, 2006, pp. 469–470, pp. 471–475.
87 *R v Rogerson* (1992) 174 CLR 268; *R v O'Brien* (1954) 110 CCC 1 (Sup Ct of Can).

common between them. This requirement is reflected in the châpeau of Article 5(1) which expressly states 'when committed intentionally'.

An important addition to the traditional common law concept of conspiracy is the requirement that the purpose of the agreement between the conspirators is directed at obtaining financial or material benefits. This element is both reflective of the overall purpose of UNTOC and, as mentioned previously, one of the main characteristics of organised crime. The effect of this added requirement is that it eliminates from Article 5(1)(a)(i) those conspiracies that are aimed at committing non-profitable crimes. Material benefits are, however, understood quite broadly and may also include non-financial advantages such as sexual gratification.[88]

At common law, jurisdictions are divided over the requirement to prove some overt physical manifestation to take place after the agreement. Many jurisdictions add the 'overt act' element to ensure that the conspirators actually put their plans into action and that agreements that are no more than bare intent or wishful thinking do not fall within the scope of criminal liability.[89] Most United States and some Australian jurisdictions require that at least one of the parties to the agreement commit an overt act pursuant to the agreement.[90] In English common law,[91] Canada,[92] New Zealand,[93] and some parts of Australia,[94] the 'overt act' is not a formal requirement of conspiracy. In these jurisdictions, liability for conspiracy may also arise without any physical manifestation of the agreement between the conspirators. In practice, however, some overt act usually has occurred before conspiracy is charged.[95]

The Convention accommodates those jurisdictions that under their domestic law require proof of an overt act in furtherance of the agreement.[96] The experience of those countries that have adopted the 'conspiracy model' set out in Article 5(1)(a)(i) of the UNTOC has also shown that most conspiracy charges are based on evidence of an overt act, even if this is not a formal requirement. This is because it 'may be difficult for the prosecution to prove what occurred in a private meeting between conspirators'[97] and because 'the

---

88 See also *Legislative Guides*, p. 24; McClean, *Transnational Organized Crime*, p. 63.

89 D. Stuart, *Canadian Criminal Law*, 5th edn, Toronto: Thomson Carswell, 2007, p. 705; Joutsen, 'International Cooperation against Transnational Organized Crime', pp. 420–421.

90 Sections 11.5(2)(c) *Criminal Code* (Cth), 48(2)(c) *Criminal Code* (ACT), and s 107 *Penal Code* (Singapore). See also McClean, *Transnational Organized Crime*, p. 67.

91 'It is not necessary in order to complete the offence that any one thing should be done beyond the agreement': *R v Aspinall* (1876) 2 QBD 48 at 58 *per* Brett JA. *Poulters' Case* (1611) 77 ER 813.

92 See *Belyea v R* (1932) 57 CCC 318; *Cameron* (1935) 64 CCC 224 at 230; *Harris* [1947] OR 461 at 466; *Deal* (1956) 114 CCC 325 at 331. '[I]t is immaterial that there was no effort towards achieving the common purpose once agreement is proved.' Stuart, *Canadian Criminal Law*, pp. 688–689.

93 *R v Gemmell* [1985] 2 NZLR 740 at p. 743. Cf. *R v Johnston* (1986) 2 CRNZ 289; *R v Sanders* [1984] 1 NZLR 636.

94 Sections 541, 542 *Criminal Code* (Qld); Section 321(1), (2) *Crimes Act* 1958 (Vic).

95 'The overt acts taken to carry out the agreement are merely evidence going to prove the agreement': *R v Douglas* (1991) 63 CCC (3d) 29; *Kouftis v R* [1941] SCR 481, p. 488; *R v Gudgeon* (1995) 133 ALR 379.

96 See also Article 5(3), Convention against Transnational Organized Crime. Cf. UNODC, *Model Legislative Provisions against Organized Crime*, Article 7(2) (option 1), p. 30; *Legislative Guides*, p. 23; Clark, 'The United Nations Convention against Transnational Organized Crime', p. 171; McClean, *Transnational Organized Crime*, pp. 62–63, pp. 66–67.

97 B. McSherry and B. Naylor, *Australian Criminal Laws*, Melbourne: Oxford University Press, 2004, p. 390.

authorities generally do not learn of the conspiracy until it has been transacted, wholly or partly'.[98]

Article 5(2) recognises that in some legal systems it is permissible to use circumstantial evidence to establish the mental elements of criminal offences. Accordingly, the purpose and intention elements of Article 5(1)(a)(i) may be inferred from objective factual circumstances, thus lowering the threshold of the burden of proof placed on the prosecution.[99]

Observations

One of the practical advantages of conspiracy – and thus of Article 5(1)(a)(i) – is that it offers an avenue to target the masterplan of criminal activities, i.e. the agreement, rather than limiting liability to isolated substantive offences.[100] Conspiracy recognises the connection between different individuals and different crimes by allowing the merging of the prosecution of several charges against multiple persons.[101] 'The conspiracy prosecution', remarks Clay Powell, 'has the great advantage of combining all the isolated acts to put together the full picture.'[102] The difficulty resulting from this combining of offences and offenders is the complexity of conspiracy prosecutions and trials. Douglas Meagher notes: 'Where the number charged exceeds five or six, the trial tends to become unmanageable.'[103]

While the essence and rationale of conspiracy captures many features of organised crime, proving the elements of conspiracy can be difficult for certain people involved in criminal organisations. First, conspiracy cannot be used as a charge against persons who are not part of the agreement. The agreement element, 'in the sense of a meeting of two or more minds, does not accord with the common experience and how people actually associate in a criminal endeavour',[104] note Michael Levi and Alaster Smith. 'Each defendant in a single conspiracy indictment has to be shown to be party to the same agreement and its terms are usually indirect. It is thus often difficult to distinguish related or sub-conspiracies.'[105] In practice, this may exclude from liability low-ranking members of criminal organisations who are not privy to the agreement and are not involved in the planning of criminal activities.[106] Mere knowledge or recklessness in regard to the agreement does not suffice to establish liability for conspiracy.[107] Furthermore, some criminal organisations engage in a diverse range of illegal transactions that cannot be tied together as a single common agreement.[108]

98 P. Gillies, 'Secondary Offences and Conspiracy', *Criminal Law Journal*, 1991, vol. 15, p. 157, p. 161.

99 UNODC, *Model Legislative Provisions against Organized Crime*, pp. 41–2.

100 Cf. *R v Shepherd* (1988) 37 A Crim R 303, pp. 309–310.

101 Cf. ibid., p. 162.

102 Powell, 'Conspiracy Prosecutions', p. 43.

103 D. Meagher, *Organised Crime*, Canberra: AGPS, 1983, p. 65.

104 M. Levi and A. Smith, *A Comparative Analysis of Organised Crime Conspiracy Legislation and Practice and their Relevance to England and Wales*, London: UK Home Office, 2002, p. 16.

105 Ibid., p. 148.

106 Cf. Meagher, *Organised Crime*, p. 64.

107 *R v Alexander* (2005) 206 CCC (3d) 233; *R v Roche* (2004) 192 CCC (3d) 557.

108 See, for example, *US v Elliot* 571 F.2d 880 (5th Cir. 1978), a case in which the members of the criminal group engaged in a criminal activity such as murder, fencing of stolen goods, arson, and the sale of illicit drugs. The Fifth Circuit Court argued that conspiracy could not have been used successfully in this case because a single conspiracy, tying all defendants together, could not be established.

Second, in those jurisdictions that require proof of an overt act – and many jurisdictions do – it becomes difficult, if not impossible, to target high-ranking members of criminal organisations that mastermind and finance the criminal activities, but that are not involved in executing their plans and thus do not engage in any overt acts. Peter Hill remarks:

> Typically, those at the higher end of the hierarchy will attempt to dissociate themselves from direct participation in criminal activity, especially crimes which carry a high risk of arrest. As these higher-echelon figures often receive much of their income from taxes, tribute, or dues paid by their subordinates, they are effectively insulated from indictment.[109]

Many countries that have adopted the offence set out in Article 5(1)(a)(i) also require proof of some overt act in furtherance of the agreement. In August 2008, the Conference of the Parties to the United Nations Convention against Transnational Organized Crime noted that:

> Of those States which criminalised the agreement to commit a serious crime, approximately one half reported that the definition of that offence included, as allowed by article 5, the additional element of an act committed by one of the participants in furtherance of the agreement or the involvement in an organized criminal group, while 33 States indicated that no additional element was required.[110]

A third problem with this offence stems from the fact that senior members of criminal organisations may give instructions about the general type and nature of criminal activity to be carried out, but the planning and organisation these persons are involved in may not, or not always, involve specific details about individual operations. 'Conspiracy contemplates an agreement to engage in conduct which relates to one or a series of closely related crimes, it does not contemplate the activities of a multi-faceted criminal enterprise.'[111]

A fourth issue is that conspiracy charges often fail in practice because the law is so overly complex, because the cases involve a great number of defendants and are very resource-intensive, and because some jurisdictions have created procedural obstacles (such as approval by Attorneys-General) to limit the use of conspiracy charges.[112]

Although Article 5(1)(a)(i) does not resolve these issues, the drafters of UNTOC included the conspiracy model, mindful of the fact that some countries would oppose legislation (and thus the Convention) that creates liability for mere participation in, or association with a criminal group,[113] which can be found in the alternative offence under Article 5(1)(a)(ii).

---

109 P. Hill, *The Japanese Mafia: Yakuza, Law, and the State*, Oxford: Oxford University Press, 2003, pp. 148–149.

110 UN, Conference of the Parties to the United Nations Convention against Transnational Organized Crime, Implementation of the United Convention against Transnational Organized Crime: consolidated information received from states for the first reporting cycle, UN Doc. CTOC/COP/2005/2/Rev.2, 25 August 2008, para. 7.

111 Levi and Smith, *A Comparative Analysis of Organised Crime Conspiracy Legislation and Practice*, p. 16.

112 B. Hocking, 'The Law of Criminal Conspiracy: Uses, Abuses and Potential', PhD thesis, Brisbane: The University of Queensland, 1998, p. 377.

113 McClean, *Transnational Organized Crime*, p. 60.

Article 5(1)(a)(ii): the participation model

The Convention against Transnational Organized Crime offers a second, different type of organised crime offence in Article 5(1)(a)(ii) which is based on the *'association de malfaiteurs'* laws developed in several civil law countries, chief among them Italy, where special legislation aimed at the role of members in a criminal organisation emerged in 1982.[114] A further influence in the development of Article 5(1)(a)(ii) were moves within the European Union in the late 1990s to agree on a framework for greater harmonisation of anti-organised-crime laws. In 1998, a Joint Action on making it a criminal offence to participate in a criminal organisation in Member States of the European Union (98/733/JHA) was issued. This document is widely considered to provide 'the first internationally agreed upon definition of organised crime'.[115] The Joint Action also provided a codification of the offence of 'participation in a criminal organisation', though an Action Plan for the prevention and control of organised crime issued in 2000 shifted the focus away from this offence, instead calling on Member States to criminalise certain types of conduct usually associated with organised crime.[116]

In contrast to the conspiracy offence under paragraph (i), the offence under Article 5(1)(a)(ii) adopts a model that makes the participation in a criminal organisation a separate offence. States Parties may implement this second type as an alternative to the offence under paragraph (i), or they may – as has been done in some jurisdictions – implement both types cumulatively.[117]

Elements of Article 5(1)(a)(ii)

To establish liability under Article 5(1)(a)(ii), the physical elements of the offence require that the accused is 'taking an active part in' either (a) the criminal activities of the organised criminal group, or (b) other activities of that group.

The mental elements of Article 5(1)(a)(ii) require that the accused:[118]

- intended to take an active part (Article 5(1) châpeau); and
- had knowledge of either

  ○ the aim and general criminal activity of the organised criminal group, or
  ○ the organised criminal group's intention to commit crimes.

- If the participation relates to other, non-criminal activities of the organised criminal group, Article 5(1)(a)(ii)(b) further requires knowledge that such participation will contribute to achieving the criminal aim.

---

114 Articles 416, 416bis *Penal Code* (Italy). See further E. Wise, 'RICO and its Analogues: A Comparative Perspective', *Syracuse Journal of International Law and Commerce*, 2000, vol. 27, p. 303, pp. 314–320.

115 F. Calderoni, *Organized Crime Legislation in the European Union*, Berlin: Springer, 2010, p. 23. See also C. Harding, 'The Offence of Belonging: Capturing Participation in Organised Crime', *Criminal Law Review*, 2005, p. 690, p. 691; Joutsen, 'International Cooperation against Transnational Organized Crime', p. 423.

116 See further E. Symeonidou-Kastanidou, 'Towards a New Definition of Organised Crime in the European Union', *European Journal of Crime, Criminal Law and Criminal Justice*, 2007, p. 83, pp. 87–88.

117 See Article 5(1)(a): 'either or both'.

118 Cf. UNODC, *Model Legislative Provisions against Organized Crime*, p. 34.

According to Article 5(2) the intention and knowledge required under Article 5(1)(a)(ii) may be inferred from objective factual circumstances.

Liability under Article 5(1)(a)(ii) requires that an accused 'takes active part in' certain activities of an organised criminal group (as defined in Article 2(a)). The participation has to be 'active' in the sense that it makes an actual contribution to the group's activities and is not completely unrelated to them. This also renders the participation different from the attempt or completion of the criminal acitivity itself. The accused's participation may be (a) in the group's criminal activities or also (b) in other, non-criminal activities if the accused knows that his/her contribution will contribute to achieving a criminal aim.[119] The physical elements of the offence thus limit liability to conduct that contributes to the criminal activities or criminal aims of the group. For example, as Matti Joutsen notes,

> an accountant knowingly working for an organized criminal group would fulfil this definition, even if he or she in no way engages in illegal accounting practices or in money laundering; merely helping the group with its accounts would seem to be sufficient.[120]

Participation such as providing food to an organised criminal group would probably not be sufficient. Whether or not acts such as supplying a firearm, fixing a criminal group's motorbikes, or being a look-out man at a burglary would (or should) be enough to meet these requirements is less certain.[121]

The mental elements of Article 5(1)(a)(ii) restrict liability to persons who intentionally participate in the above-mentioned activities and who have actual knowledge of the aims and activities or the criminal intentions of the organised criminal group.[122] This, according to Gerhard Kemp,

> requires convincing proof that the accused intended to join the association for the purpose of supporting the group's criminal conduct. Furthermore, this principle requires proof that the accused had sufficient knowledge of the association's past, present and continuing criminal activity and that he or she joined the organisation in support or sustenance of that activity.[123]

The mental elements exclude from liability any person who may unwittingly contribute to a criminal organisation or who is recklessly indifferent about the nature and activities of the group. Under Article 34(3) States Parties to the Convention are, however, at liberty to lower the *mens rea* requirement and expand liability to recklessness, negligence, or even strict liability without proof of a fault element.[124]

Observations

In essence, Article 5(1)(a)(ii) attaches criminal liability to deliberate, purposeful contributions to criminal organisations, not in the pursuit of a preconceived plan or agreement.

---

119 Freedman, 'The New Law on Criminal Organizations in Canada', p. 198; Clark, 'The United Nations Convention against Transnational Organized Crime', p. 172.
120 Joutsen, 'International Cooperation against Transnational Organized Crime', p. 426.
121 McClean, *Transnational Organized Crime*, p. 64.
122 See further, *Legislative Guides*, p. 24.
123 Kemp, 'The United Nations Convention against Transnational Organized Crime', p. 155.
124 McClean, *Transnational Organized Crime*, p. 62.

Participation does not require proof of an accused's membership or of any ongoing role in the organisation or any 'meeting of the minds'.[125] Article 5(1)(a)(i), in contrast, requires that the accused is a co-conspirator and part of the agreement.

The application of Article 5(1)(a)(ii) thus allows for the criminalisation of persons who are more remotely connected to criminal activities. For liability under this offence to arise, it is not required that any criminal offences have been planned, prepared, or executed. Article 5 (1)(a)(ii) attaches criminal liability to events that occur well before the preparation (and sometimes before the planning) of specific individual offences. A person may be liable under paragraph (ii) merely for contributing to activities that are ultimately designed to achieve a criminal aim but without being criminal activities themselves. This would include, for instance,

> the conduct of someone who rents a property or a hotel room to criminals or who provides a bookkeeping service to an organized criminal group, provided that he or she knows that that conduct is supporting the activities of the organized criminal group.[126]

Paragraph (ii) thus creates an avenue to hold low-level 'enhancers' and facilitators of organised crime groups criminally responsible for their contributions. There is also no requirement to show an overt act, which, as mentioned earlier, limits the application of the conspiracy offence in some jurisdictions. Article 5(1)(a)(ii) thus renders organisers and financiers of criminal organisations liable who are not physically involved in the organisations' criminal activities, but who control, plan, and 'mastermind' these operations.

Extensions to liability

Article 5(1)(b)

Liability for involvement in organised crime is further extended by Article 5(1)(b) of the Convention to include intentionally 'organizing, directing, aiding, facilitating or counselling the commission of serious crime involving an organised criminal group'.

This criminalises secondary liability for persons who provide advice or assistance to serious crimes committed by an organised criminal group. The purpose here is to extend liability beyond persons who participate directly in the (criminal) activities of criminal organisations (as captured by Article 5(a)(ii)). 'Aiding, facilitating or counselling' covers secondary parties and accomplices who are not themselves principal offenders.[127]

'Organising' and 'directing', on the other hand, are extensions not commonly found (and defined) in national laws prior to the development of UNTOC. To that end, Article 5(1)(b) 'is intended to ensure the liability of leaders of criminal organisations who give the orders but do not engage in the commission of the actual crimes themselves'.[128] Article 5(1)(b) enables the prosecution of leaders, accomplices, organisers, and arrangers as well as lower levels of

---

125 D. Stuart, 'Politically Expedient but Potentially Unjust Criminal Legislation against Gangs', *International Review of Penal Law*, 1998, vol. 69, p. 245, p. 249.
126 UNODC, *Model Legislative Provisions against Organized Crime*, pp. 34–35.
127 McClean, *Transnational Organized Crime*, pp. 64–65.
128 *Legislative Guides*, p. 25; UNODC, *Model Legislative Provisions against Organized Crime*, p. 39; McClean, *Transnational Organized Crime*, p. 64.

participants that assist criminal organisations in their activities.[129] This provision, notes Guymon, 'takes a significant step in recognising that those chiefly responsible for organised crime are often not the perpetrators alone, but the other links in the hierarchical chain of command'.[130] What is not clear from Article 5(1)(b) is whether liability for organising and directing requires proof that a serious crime has been committed by an organised crime group or whether this provision also captures serious crimes that have only been planned and perhaps prepared, but have not yet been executed.

Corporate liability

Article 10 of the Convention serves as a tool to hold commercial enterprises responsible for assisting the operations of criminal organisations and for laundering the assets derived from crime, for corruption, and for the obstruction of justice.[131] The Legislative Guides note that:

> Complex corporate structures can effectively hide the true ownership, clients or partic-
> ular transactions related to crimes ranging from smuggling to money-laundering and
> corrupt practices. Individual executives may reside outside the country where the offence
> was committed and responsibility for specific individuals may be difficult to prove. Thus,
> the view has been gaining ground that the only way to remove this instrument and shield
> of transnational organized crime is to introduce liability for legal entities. Criminal
> liability of a legal entity may also have a deterrent effect, partly because reputational
> damage can be very costly and partly because it may act as a catalyst for more effective
> management and supervisory structures to ensure compliance.[132]

As the Convention was written at a time when corporate criminal liability was less developed and less widely recognised than it is today, Article 10(2) allows States Parties to choose whether the liability of legal persons is criminal, civil, or administrative (or any combination thereof). Measures to hold legal persons liable are designed as an additional, not an alternative tool to the criminal liability of natural persons who have committed offences under the Convention. Article 10(3) states that: 'When an individual commits crimes on behalf of a legal entity, it must be possible to prosecute and sanction them.'[133]

Observations and experiences

The offences established under Article 5 of the Convention against Transnational Organized Crime, along with the other provisions relating to criminalisation, law enforcement, international cooperation, and prevention – if implemented and enforced properly – can serve as

---

129 *Legislative Guides*, p. 25. Cf. Clark, 'The United Nations Convention against Transnational Organized Crime', pp. 172–173; McClean, *Transnational Organized Crime*, pp. 64–65.
130 Guymon, 'International Legal Mechanisms for Combating Transnational Organised Crime', p. 95.
131 Cf. Articles 6, 8, 23, Convention against Transnational Organized Crime. See further Clark, 'The United Nations Convention against Transnational Organized Crime', p. 176; McClean, *Transnational Organized Crime*, pp. 126–129.
132 *Legislative Guides*, p. 116.
133 Ibid., p. 120.

prophylactic tools to prevent the commission of criminal offences by organised crime groups. This is an important goal in the worldwide 'war' against transnational organised crime that is achieved primarily by extending criminal liability beyond existing concepts of inchoate and accessorial liability.

The development of UNTOC was led by the realisation that disrupting criminal activities and arresting individual offenders does not dismantle the criminal organisations that stand behind these illegal activities. 'As the law stands now', remarked Michael Moon in 1999, 'the Crown may prosecute and eliminate individual members, but the organisation continues; new people move into the vacated spot, and the enterprise carries on.'[134] 'Previous efforts against organised crime have failed because the focus has been on individual prosecutions rather than on organisational foundations', adds Goldsmith.[135]

The penalisation of the criminal organisation is justified on the basis of crime prevention: it reduces the risk that the organisation will engage in criminal activity. It allows law enforcement agencies to intervene earlier, long before a criminal group commits specific offences. 'From the perspective of crime prevention', notes Estelle Baker,

> logic suggests that an approach aimed at the level of the organization is likely to produce greater crime reduction dividends than one which requires dissipated law enforcement efforts across a spectrum of individual end behaviour offences.[136]

The extensions of criminal liability created by UNTOC are significant, but not without controversy:

> In all countries, even in those that do not formally accept the concept, there has been similar internal debate about the desirability and the contours of a crime based on membership in a criminal association. Concern has been expressed about the compatibility of such a crime with . . . traditional principles of criminal law which are supposed to require focusing attention on the concrete specific act of a specific individual at a specific moment in time and on that individual's own personal guilt, not on that of his associates. . . . Every system of law has had to grapple with the problem of defining the appropriate limits to doing so which derive from a common fund of basic ideas about what is entailed in designating conduct as criminal – the requirements of an act, of harm, of personal individual culpability.[137]

In essence, the extensions to criminal liability are achieved by reducing the requirements that relate to the physical involvement in a criminal offence. Liability for the offences under Article 5 arises on the basis of loose associations, agreements, and intentions, rather than on the basis of proven damage, harm, or other physical results or conduct. Thus UNTOC's Article 5, notes Frank Verbruggen, breaks

134 M. Moon, 'Outlawing the Outlaws: Importing RICO's Notion of "Criminal Enterprise" into Canada to Combat Organized Crime', *Queens Law Journal*, 1999, vol. 24, p. 451, p. 459.

135 M. Goldsmith, 'RICO and Enterprise Criminality: A Response to Gerard E Lynch', *Columbia Law Review*, 1982, vol. 88, p. 774, p. 775.

136 E. Baker, 'The Legal Regulation of Transnational Organised Crime: Opportunities and Limitation', in A. Edward and P. Gill (eds), *Transnational Organized Crime: Perspectives on Global Security*, London: Routledge, 2003, p. 183, p. 187.

137 Wise, 'RICO and its Analogues', p. 321.

with the classical theory that states should not intervene in human relations with a blunt instrument like criminal law unless damage has been done to a specific 'legally proscribed interest', 'a common good' like property, sexual integrity or life and limb. . . . The Convention confirms unambiguously that those classical theories no longer apply. . . . Instead, criminal law becomes a tool to prevent the damage from ever happening, by making endangerment the threshold for intervention and sanctioning.[138]

'In seeking to address [organized crime] problems', notes Dorean Koenig,

the solutions themselves have become problems. They have threatened to change the nature of the system of criminal justice . . . by greatly increasing the reach of the criminal law and enhancing sentences, while lessening the mens rea requirements.[139]

One weakness of the international system is that UNTOC leaves responsibility for the adoption and design of measures against organised criminal groups to individual States Parties; it neither predetermines a particular conceptualisation of the offence, nor does it establish an offence under international law, nor does it spell out any limitation for the extensions of criminal liability. The definition of 'organised criminal group' in Article 2(a) of the Convention is also ambiguous and open to manipulation insofar as it relates to 'serious crimes' that are determined by States Parties and may vary greatly between jurisdictions.

The main practical and conceptual concern that stems from the offences in Article 5 and the definition of 'organised criminal group' in Article 2(a) of the Convention – and that is perpetuated by the provisions relating to law enforcement, international cooperation, and prevention – is the fact that UNTOC does not definitively resolve the question of where criminal liability for participation in an organised criminal group ought to begin and where it should stop. It may not be surprising – but it is nevertheless disappointing – that the development of UNTOC, including the definition of 'organised criminal group' and the offences under Article 5, was motivated and heavily influenced by national interests and political considerations of the negotiating States, rather than by a genuine desire to understand the organisation and operation of organised crime and by thorough, empirical research about the best and most effective ways to combat it.

On the other hand, it has to be remembered that the creation of the Convention against Transnational Organized Crime 'marks a turning point in the commitment of the community of states to cooperate against transnational crime'.[140] The UNTOC

focuses attention on the problem, legitimises stiffer domestic law enforcement measures, provides aspirational standards and expectations, facilitates smoother cooperation among states willing to make agreements by increasing harmonisation, and has great symbolic force. [The Convention] exerts a kind of 'peer pressure' on countries around the world that have not yet developed effective modalities to combat organised crime.[141]

---

138 F. Verbruggen, 'On Containing Organised Crime Using "Container Offences"', in H. Albrecht and C. Fijnaut (eds), *The Containment of Transnational Organised Crime: Comments on the UN Convention of December 2000*, Freiburg: Edition Isucrim, 2002, p. 113, p. 130.

139 D. Koenig, 'The Criminal Justice System Facing the Challenge of Organised Crime', *Wayne Law Review*, 1998, vol. 44, p. 1351, p. 1377.

140 Militello, 'Participation in an Organised Criminal Group as International Offence', p. 97.

141 Guymon, 'International Legal Mechanisms for Combating Transnational Organised Crime', p. 98.

The framework proposed by the Convention offers a new set of tools that can assist investigators, courts, and prosecutors in addressing many aspects of organised crime more effectively. It also allows for the universal criminalisation of organised crime. The criminal offences under UNTOC are accompanied by a set of measures that enhance investigations and law enforcement cooperation, both domestically and internationally. It is very encouraging to see that the Convention has found widespread support and adoption around the world.

The Convention is a milestone in an area where international collaboration is only in its infancy. Criminal justice is seen by many, if not most countries, as a cornerstone of national sovereignty.[142] The fact that the Convention took only two years to be developed by the UN Ad Hoc Committee, together with the fact that it has found widespread support and ratification around the world, demonstrates that most countries are serious about preventing and suppressing transnational organised crime more effectively and collaboratively. 'The success of this type of international instrument', notes David McClean, 'does not depend on the skill of the drafters, but on the political will of the government of each State Party, and the resources that can be made available.'[143]

142 Cf. Vlassis, 'The United Nations Convention against Transnational Organized Crime and its Protocols', p. 76.
143 McClean, *Transnational Organized Crime*, p. 30. See also the remarks by Kemp, 'The United Nations Convention against Transnational Organized Crime', pp. 166–167.

Part IV
Implementation

26

Implementation of transnational criminal law

Issues and challenges

Yvon Dandurand and Vivienne Chin

Introduction

The adoption over the last twenty-five years of several transnational criminal law conventions (TCLCs), whether at the global or regional levels, confronts States that are parties to these treaties and the international community as a whole with numerous challenges relating to the implementation of these instruments. The objectives of these conventions vary, but they all generally aim to promote some shared definitions of crime, some compatible criminal law procedures, and a general regime of international cooperation.

The slow and limited implementation of the TCLCs and the fairly low level of State compliance with their obligations under these instruments raise questions about the apparent lack of political will and the limited national capacity to meet these obligations. It has also led to repeated calls for more effective technical assistance and greater investments in programmes to help States achieve compliance with the TCLCs.

Previous chapters have already mentioned some of the many challenges impeding the full implementation of the TCLCs and limiting their impact and practical usefulness. The present chapter focuses on broader implementation issues that cut across the whole range of TCLCs. It addresses three main questions: what are the main implementation issues encountered by States party to these conventions and how are they being addressed? What are the reporting and review mechanisms and how much do we know about the actual implementation of these new instruments and States' compliance with their obligations? And finally, why is there so little progress in assessing the outcomes and the impact of these major international conventions?

Objectives of the criminal law conventions

Without getting into a detailed analysis of the purpose and objectives of the various new TCLCs, we can briefly consider here that TCLCs explicitly aim to mobilize the criminal law and the criminal justice system to control, prevent or otherwise address various threats against public safety or state security. Among TCLCs, there is a significant body of conventions relating to corruption, to various serious crimes committed by transnational organized criminal groups, to drug control, and to counter-terrorism. One defining feature of these conventions is their intent to promote and support criminal justice responses and international cooperation in controlling various types of crimes.

It is worth noting that some TCLCs are not entirely or exclusively relevant to criminal law or criminal justice systems. This is the case, for example, with counter-terrorism conventions which, until fairly recently, did not necessarily require the 'criminalization of terrorism' or the definition of specific terrorist acts as crimes.[1] In 2011, Security Council Resolution 1373 specifically referred to the use of criminal law as a main response to terrorism.[2] The UN Security Council threw its considerable influence behind a number of counter-terrorism measures engaging the criminal law.[3] This obviously placed a huge burden on the criminal justice system of many States. It also revealed that relying on the criminal justice system to prevent and respond to terrorism has some real limitations.[4] For instance, Laborde and DeFeo noted the obvious ineffectiveness of legal deterrents when the crime is motivated by beliefs powerful enough to provoke suicidal behaviour.[5]

It is also worth noting that several human rights conventions have direct implications for criminal justice. Their implementation requires the bringing of national criminal law, criminal justice policies, procedures and practices into compliance with a rights-based normative framework. By contrast, TCLCs tend to be very practical, to require the criminalization of specific conduct and the implementation of specific operational policies and procedures. They are concrete and often have direct operational implications. In particular, they tend to focus on how States cooperate with each other in establishing a global or regional 'regime' to interdict, control or prevent certain transnational transactions. In a sense, they are a pragmatic response to globalization, the growing deterritorialization of crime, and the internationalization of many criminal groups and their activities.[6] The contrast between these two approaches is even more evident when human rights bodies see the need to adopt resolutions or to provide guidance on the implementation of TCLCs. For example, the Office of the High Commissioner for Human Rights saw the need to express principles and guidelines on human rights and human trafficking at the time the Palermo Human Trafficking Protocol[7] was being implemented.[8]

1   See United Nations Office on Drugs and Crime, *Guide for the Legislative Incorporation and Implementation of the Universal Anti-terrorism Instruments*, New York, United Nations, 2006.
2   Security Council Resolution 1373, para. 2(e), of 28 September 2001.
3   K. Roach, *The 9/11 Effect: Comparative Counter-Terrorism*, Cambridge: Cambridge University Press, 2011. Roach's study describes and compares various national approaches to the implementation of counter-terrorism measures and their impact on criminal law and criminal justice. See also A. Bianchi, 'Security Council's anti-terror resolutions and their implementation by member states – An Overview', *Journal of International Criminal Justice*, 2006, vol. 4, pp. 1044–1073.
4   Y. Dandurand/UNODC, *Handbook on Criminal Justice Responses to Terrorism*, New York: United Nations, 2009.
5   J.-P. Laborde and M. DeFeo, 'Problems and Prospects of Implementing UN Action Against Terrorism', *Journal of International Criminal Justice*, 2004, vol. 4, p. 1087, p. 1088.
6   United Nations Office on Drugs and Crime. *The Globalization of Crime: A Transnational Organized Crime Threat Assessment*, Vienna: UNODC, 2010.
7   Protocol to Prevent, Suppress and Punish Trafficking in Persons, Especially Women and Children (Trafficking Protocol) 15 November 2000, 2237 UNTS 319, in force 25 December 2003.
8   OHCHR, *Recommended Principles and Guidelines on Human Rights and Human Trafficking*, addendum to the report of the United Nations High Commissioner for Human Rights, UN Doc. E/2002/68/Add. 1.

International cooperation: one measure of success

The goals of the TCLCs are usually stated in terms of the prevention or control of certain criminal activities or the interdiction of certain transactions. In some cases, such as the UNCAC,[9] the objectives of the convention are more far-reaching and include broad prevention measures that engage not only the criminal justice system but many other segments of society. This particular convention even includes a positively stated general objective of promoting 'integrity, accountability and proper management of public affairs and public property'. However, international cooperation is a stated purpose of all TCLCs and, since it is such a central feature and desired outcome of these conventions, it makes sense to evaluate their impact in terms of whether or not they have significantly improved international cooperation in the fight against various international threats.

In that respect, we may first observe that international cooperation has not grown fast enough to keep up with the pace of change in patterns of transnational crime, the movement of criminals and their growing technological sophistication. The main mechanisms supporting international cooperation include mutual legal assistance, extradition, transfer of proceedings in criminal matters, freezing and confiscation of proceeds of crime, protection of witnesses, exchange of information and intelligence, and transfer of prisoners, as well as a number of less formal measures. Many of these cooperation strategies have been in place for some time, while others are relatively new and untested. Their eventual effectiveness depends not only on various treaties, but also, to a large extent, on the enabling provisions of national law.

Numerous practical, legal and political factors hamper international cooperation in criminal matters. The most common ones include differences in cultural and legal traditions, languages or political orientations. To these we must add state sovereignty, the absence of enabling legislation, the absence of channels of communication for the exchange of information and intelligence, divergences in approaches and priorities, and corruption of public officials. The proliferation of cooperation arrangements, however necessary, is not an appropriate substitute for a more comprehensive, integrated international legal framework for cooperation in criminal matters, one in which the separate modalities of cooperation are used in a more effective and complementary manner.[10] A collaborative and coordinated effort is required to translate different policing and prosecution capacities and capabilities into an effective multilateral cooperation mechanism.

Over the last two decades, fledgling international cooperation mechanisms have indeed been put to the test. In some cases, they have produced noticeable results, having contributed to public safety and countered some significant international threats. In other instances, they were revealed as quite inadequate. Some observers have also noted with concern the emergence of national and international entities and processes, together with specialist liaison networks, functioning outside existing governance and accountability frameworks.[11]

By most accounts and in most parts of the world, this international cooperation regime remains very weak, fragmented and capricious. Existing multilateral tools have not been

9 United Nations Convention against Corruption, New York, 31 October 2003, 2349 UNTS 41, in force 14 December 2005.
10 Y. Dandurand, G. Colombo and N. Passas, 'Measures and Mechanisms to Strengthen International Cooperation Among Prosecution Services', *Crime, Law and Social Change*, vol. 47, 2007, p. 261, p. 288.
11 See e.g. C. Harfield, 'The Organization of "Organized Crime Policing" in its International Context', *Criminology and Criminal Justice*, 2008, vol. 8, no. 4, p. 483, p. 498.

adapted and frequently fail to provide a sufficient return on the investment. With the possible exception of the European Union, which has developed its own international cooperation regime with unique mechanisms (such as the European arrest warrant or the mutual recognition of court orders), the TCLCs have not yielded their expected dividends in terms of effective international cooperation. As is periodically emphasized during the World Summits of Attorneys General, Prosecutors General and Chief Prosecutors, much remains to be done at the national and international levels to strengthen that regime.

State parties to some of the TCLCs have also had to admit that the expected results of cooperation in the recovery of criminal assets, particularly the return of assets obtained through corruption, have not yet fully materialized.[12]

International cooperation is based on reciprocity and trust, and that trust is not built by treaties or legislation. Confidence, trust and mutual respect can take a long time to develop but can be undermined quickly by incompetence or corruption within the ranks of participating agencies.[13] This has led State parties to ask what kind of measures can be taken to help build confidence and trust among national agencies or among agencies of different States.[14]

Finally, as we have argued elsewhere, many of the measures adopted in recent years to combat terrorism and organized crime or facilitate international cooperation can have an unintended detrimental effect on the situation of groups vulnerable to the tactics of criminal organizations.[15] For all these reasons, it may be time, therefore, to re-evaluate the effectiveness of existing TCLCs in building the desired international cooperation regime.

Frequent implementation challenges and issues

The issues

The implementation of TCLCs has proved difficult, slow, and often problematic. There are many issues with the process of implementation. Some of them may be technical or logistical, but others have much more to do with the States' motivation and capacity. Some real limitations are imposed by the limited capacity of many States to actually implement the TCLCs.[16] Some States lose interest in implementing certain treaties once they understand

---

12 Conference of the States Parties to the United Nations Convention against Corruption, Report of the Conference of the States Parties to the United Nations Convention against Corruption on its fourth session, held in Marrakesh, Morocco, from 24 to 28 October 2011, Vienna, November 11, 2011, CAC/COSP/2011/14, p. 12.

13 See e.g. Y. Dandurand and UNODC, *Corruption and Migrant Smuggling: Issue Paper*. Vienna: UNODC, 2013.

14 Conference of the Parties to the United Nations Convention against Transnational Organized Crime, Working Group of Government Experts on Technical Assistance, Establishing Capacity-Building Programmes For Prosecutors and Members of The Judiciary and Law Enforcement Agencies – Discussion Paper by the Secretariat, Vienna, 7 August 2013, p. 2.

15 Y. Dandurand and V. Chin, 'Human Security Objectives and the Fights against Transnational Organized Crime and Terrorism', in S. Okubo and L. Shelley (eds), *Human Security, Transnational Crime and Human Trafficking*, Abingdon: Routledge, 2011, p. 36, p. 47.

16 Y. Dandurand, V. Chin, C. Griffiths, M. Lalonde, R. Montgomery and B. Tkachuk, *Programming Opportunities in the Justice and Security Sector in the Caribbean*, Vancouver: International Centre for Criminal Law Reform and Criminal Justice Policy, 2004.

the magnitude of the task or realize that the rewards for doing so, such as development assistance, financial aid or technical assistance, are not forthcoming. The resources allocated by donors to support the implementation process are often insufficient. The following are other issues encountered through the treaty implementation process.

Political motivation

It has been easy to observe over the past many years that States often viewed the formal ratification of a convention as a 'final destination' rather than as a 'starting point'.[17] In these instances, once a convention had been ratified, no further action was taken. Compliance was merely symbolic and no effective implementation process was ever put in place.

States ratify conventions for all kinds of reasons. In some cases they feel compelled to do so as a result of the pressures exerted by other more powerful or influential States. This is particularly likely when a State depends on various forms of assistance from donors. A State may ratify a convention mainly in order to continue to access development assistance or to qualify for technical assistance. Some donors have indeed tied their assistance to the ratification and at least the minimal implementation of certain conventions by recipient States.[18]

Some conventions contain features which make them attractive to States that may or may not have the means or the will to fully implement the convention as a whole. This is true, for example, of the UNCAC, which was initially met with great interest by States from the Global South. These States do not generally regard the effective implementation of TCLCs as a priority. However, the extraordinarily early and high rate of ratification of that convention by these States, in particular in Africa, showed that there was a different kind of interest for the convention's provisions relating to the return of misappropriated assets.[19]

The urge to cooperate internationally in criminal matters is sometimes stronger among States facing similar problems or sharing borders. This is why there is in these situations a deeper and more lasting commitment to fully implement the relevant bilateral or regional treaties. This is often true, for example, of extradition and mutual legal assistance treaties concluded at the bilateral or regional levels to reflect the nature of local or regional law enforcement and security challenges. This may explain why much more progress in facilitating cooperation in criminal matters has been achieved within the European Union than in other regions of the world.

The situations in which different States find themselves with respect to particular types of transnational crime are often asymmetrical. As a result, their respective reasons for becoming party to a particular convention may be quite different. Consider for example the fact that developing countries frequently find it difficult to take measures to prevent illegal

---

17 V. Chin and Y. Dandurand, *National Programs to Prevent, Punish and Eradicate Violence against Women in Ten Caribbean Countries*. Washington: Commission of Women, Organization of American States, ILANUD and ICCLR, 2000.

18 This is what is achieved, for example, by the Trafficking in Persons (TIP) Reports which the United States Department of State is required by law to submit each year to the US Congress. It is ostensibly a measure to help eliminate severe forms of human trafficking. However, the reports assesses States' efforts to prevent human trafficking, and those that fail to satisfactorily meet the 'minimum standards' set by the US Government can be placed on a watch list or denied non-trade-related assistance.

19 N. Passas, 'The Impact of UNCAC on Governance: Opportunities and Risks', in N. Passas and D. Vlassis (eds), *The United Nations Convention against Corruption as a Way of Life*, Milan, International Scientific and Professional Advisory Council of the United Nations Crime Prevention and Criminal Justice Programme, 2006, p. 85, p. 89.

immigration and the smuggling of migrants. These States are typically under pressure from 'destination countries' to curb illegal immigration, the smuggling of migrants and trafficking in persons. However, the States' economic dependency on foreign remittances and the fact that large segments of their population aspire to emigrate make it difficult for politicians to take measures to prevent their own citizens from looking for a better future abroad.[20]

In addition, there often is a fundamental asymmetry of means and capacity among States facing a common transnational threat, even if they are both parties to the same convention. States manifestly do not all have the same priorities when it comes to crime control. They obviously do not have the same crime control capacity or the same capacity to cooperate internationally.

Mobilizing the relevant agencies and stakeholders

The commitment made by a central government to implement a new treaty is not necessarily perceived as a priority by every level of government or by all criminal justice agencies in that country. For example, in federal States, the central government is typically responsible for the country's foreign policy and holds the authority to undertake international obligations on its behalf, sometimes without any significant internal consultation. This has raised the problem of having significant policy decisions affecting the future of a country's criminal law and criminal justice system made without proper input by those who will be charged with their implementation.

The process of negotiating treaties and reporting on their implementation often raises issues of coordination and consultation. In countries like Canada, where responsibility for the administration of justice is shared by different levels of government, the question is often a sensitive one. For example, a Senate Committee review in 2007 of Canada's implementation of the Convention on the Rights of the Child led the Committee to make several critical comments about the current process as it relates to human rights treaties. 'At the heart of the problem', the Committee observed, 'is the fact that there is no modern, transparent, and democratic treaty implementation process understood and accepted in Canada. No institution has ultimate responsibility for ensuring that international human rights conventions are effectively implemented.'[21] The Committee could just as easily have been talking about TCLCs, and Canada is obviously not the only country which finds itself in that situation.

Consequences of non-compliance

Efforts to establish consequences for a State's non-compliance with its treaty obligations have not been very successful. It seems that this threat of consequences is applied too sporadically and erratically to have a real impact except perhaps in the most blatant and defiant cases of

---

20 Y. Dandurand, 'International Cooperation', in J. Winterdyk, B. Perrin and P. Reichel (eds), *Human Trafficking: Exploring the International Nature, Concerns, and Complexities*, London: CRC Press, 2012, p. 207, p. 224.

21 Standing Senate Committee on Human Rights, *Children: The Silenced Citizens – Effective Implementation of Canada's International Obligations with Respect to the Rights Of Children*, Ottawa, Parliament of Canada, 2007, p. 226.

non-compliance.[22] In short, in the area of transnational criminal law, there are very few real consequences for a State's non-compliance with its obligations under a treaty it ratified.

Compliance of national law with the treaty requirements

State parties to TCLCs must take the necessary measures, including legislative and administrative measures, in accordance with fundamental principles of their domestic law, to ensure implementation of their obligations under these conventions.[23] In particular, the TCLCs are meant to help State parties to move towards a common legal basis for criminalizing various conducts, something that is often referred to as the harmonization of criminal definitions. The legal definitions adopted by each State reflect not only its own culture and legal tradition, but often also some local political compromises.

Even when a definition has been duly adopted in strict compliance with the requirements of a convention, the courts may take a different view and influence how that definition is interpreted and implemented. For example, in the case of the offence of migrant smuggling as defined in Canada's Immigration and Refugee Protection Act,[24] the offence was judged in the Supreme Court of British Columbia to have been defined too broadly, and thus to infringe section 7 of the Canadian Charter of Rights and Freedoms. It was therefore declared of no force and no effect.[25]

States have different approaches to the implementation of international treaties. Each State must opt for what it considers the most appropriate implementation mechanism. In some States, a treaty has no domestic application until implemented by a domestic law. This is often referred to as the 'dualist tradition', in which international law and domestic law are considered two separate systems. By contrast, in monist States, once a treaty is ratified, it is automatically incorporated into domestic law and most of its provisions become self-executing.

Some States, because of domestic law or as a matter of policy, will not adopt a treaty until legislation is in place that permits the fulfilment of all its international obligations. In practice, States often achieve different levels of compliance with the legal requirements of a convention before it is even adopted. The implementation of a treaty usually requires a comprehensive review of national criminal law and its relevant provisions, followed by amending legislation. In some cases, the review can serve to identify how the requirements of many conventions can be met at once.[26]

---

22 For example, the Financial Action Task Force (FATF) used to publish a list of 'non-cooperative countries or territories' (the 'black list'). Since 2008, the FATF has installed a more analytical process of identifying jurisdictions deficient in their anti-money laundering (AML) and anti-terrorist financing regimes. On the basis of the results of the review by the International Co-operation Review Group (ICRG), jurisdictions may be publicly identified in one of the two FATF public documents that are issued three times a year. Similarly, the INCB can take measures under Art. 14 of the Single Convention on Narcotic Drugs of 1961, 30 March 1961, 520 UNTS 151; in force 13 December 1964, as amended by the Protocol amending the 1961 Single Convention on Narcotic Drugs, 25 March 1972, 976 UNTS 3; in force 8 August 1975.
23 See for example the text of Art. 34(1) of the United Nations Convention against Transnational Organized Crime, 15 November 2000, 2225 UNTS 209, in force 29 September 2003 (UNTOC).
24 Immigration and Refugee Protection Act, SC 2001, C. 27, s. 117.
25 *R v Appulonappa*, 2013 BCSC 31.
26 See e.g. Ministry of Justice of Vietnam, *Improvement of Vietnam's Criminal Law and Policies in the Context of Globalization and Economic Integration*, Hanoi, Criminal and Administrative Legislation Department, 2009.

Some States, like China, may not have constitutional dispositions or basic laws on the status of treaties in their domestic legal system. In these cases, substantive treaty obligations are typically incorporated into special national laws. China, for example, has prescribed most transnational crimes as criminal offences under its national criminal law and established its jurisdiction over many offences. Article 9 of the Criminal Law of the People's Republic of China, as revised in 1997, ensures that when a treaty to which China has become a party requires parties to establish jurisdiction over certain criminal offences, the Chinese courts can exercise criminal jurisdiction over such crimes.[27]

The actual legislative process to bring national criminal law into compliance with the requirements of a particular treaty can be quite complicated. In some instances, for example, it may prove difficult to convince legislators to criminalize certain forms of conduct. Illicit enrichment, which is prescribed as an offence in the Inter-American Convention against Corruption (IACAC), the African Union Convention on Preventing and Combating Corruption (AUCPCC) and the United Nations Convention against Corruption (UNCAC), is not universally accepted as a valid anti-corruption measure and continues to generate extensive debate and controversy.[28] On the technical side, however, model laws and model bilateral treaties can be and have been developed to assist the process.[29] Various legislative and technical guides have also been produced to provide guidance.[30]

Beyond paper compliance

For many States the implementation of a convention, to achieve more than mere 'paper compliance', represents a major undertaking, including not only legislative action but also institution building, capacity building and organizational change. The implementation process is much more than a mere technical and mechanical process. Beyond legislation and technical measures, long-term success may depend on attitude adjustments and on whether the convention's substantive principles and messages are well known to all and converted into a way of life.[31] The success of reforms and capacity-building initiatives in the criminal justice sectors depends, in large measure, on whether they reflect a local consensus, a commitment to action, and some level of effective mobilization. That level of mobilization of stakeholders often tends to be missing from the implementation strategies designed to give effect to the TCLCs.

---

27 See H. Xue and Q. Jin, 'International Treaties in the Chinese Domestic Legal System', *Chinese Journal of International Law*, 2009, vol. 8, no. 2, p. 299.

28 L. Muzila, M. Morales, M, Mathias and T. Berger, *On the Take: Criminalizing Illicit Enrichment to Fight Corruption*, Washington: World Bank and UNODC, 2012.

29 For example, the UNODC model laws on 'Assistance in Criminal Matters' (2007), 'Extradition' (2004), 'Against the Smuggling of Migrants' (2010), 'Against Trafficking in Persons' (2009), etc.

30 UNODC, *Legislative Guides for the Implementation of the United Nations Convention against Transnational Organized Crime and the Protocols Thereto*, New York, United Nations, 2004. UNODC, *Legislative Guide for the Implementation of the United Nations Convention against Corruption, Second Revised Edition*, New York, United Nations, 2012. Also, UNODC, *Technical Guide to the United Nations Convention against Corruption*, New York, United Nations, 2009.

31 N. Passas, 'Introduction', in N. Passas and D. Vlassis (eds), *The United Nations Convention against Corruption as a Way of Life*, Milan, International Scientific and Professional Advisory Council of the United Nations Crime Prevention and Criminal Justice Programme, 2006, p. 9, p. 10.

The need for comprehensive approaches to implementation

Given the complexity of the TCLCs, there are frequent calls for the development of national strategies to implement them.[32] Some States found it beneficial to develop national action plans relating more broadly to crime prevention, countering corruption or countering terrorism. Some States have also developed strategies and action plans for specific forms of organized crime. Such strategies typically cover various aspects of the treaty implementation process: threat assessment, specific objectives to be achieved or targets to be met, the establishment of an institutional framework (including national coordinating committees to operationalize the strategy and monitor action plans), revision of existing legal frameworks, public education and awareness raising, or the mobilization of various stakeholders.

Capacity issues

The most intractable implementation issue is often the limited capacity of a State's criminal justice system. Many States lack even the capacity to identify what legislative changes and other programme initiatives are required in order to implement a particular convention. They require technical assistance even at that early stage of implementation. They even require help to assess their own laws and their compliance with the requirements of a given convention or a set of conventions.[33]

The TCLCs usually call for State parties to put in place various mechanisms to implement the international cooperation measures, forgetting unfortunately that they are not dealing with a 'level playing field'. These cooperation mechanisms presuppose that the State parties involved already have a somewhat efficient or even functional criminal justice system. Clearly this is not always the case. Furthermore, many States are quite incapable of implementing international cooperation measures because of the blatant weaknesses of their own justice systems. In most States, the capacity of law enforcement and prosecution services to successfully investigate and prosecute organized crime, corruption or terrorist activities usually requires substantial enhancement of the capacity for prosecution services before they can effectively cooperate internationally.

It is unfortunately true that it is those States that are most vulnerable to transnational threats that are least capable of facing them on their own. Some of the States facing the greatest challenges with respect to transnational crime have the weakest and most corrupt criminal justice institutions. In fact, given the criminalization and corruption of some weak governments, some innovation may be required, as suggested by Shaw and Reitano, in order to create a means to prosecute traffickers and other criminals outside of the legal frameworks of weak States.[34]

---

32 For example, Conference of the Parties to the United Nations Convention against Transnational Organized Crime, Working Group of Government Experts on Technical Assistance, Development of National Strategies to Address Transnational Organized Crime, Note by Secretariat, CTOC/COP/WG.2/2012/2, Vienna, 1 August 2012.

33 One example among many is the assessment conducted for the Ministry of Justice of Vietnam: Ministry of Justice of Vietnam, *Assessment of the Legal System in Vietnam in Comparison with the United Nations Protocols on Trafficking in Persons and Smuggling of Migrants*, Hanoi: Department of Criminal and Administrative Law, Ministry of Justice, UNODC and UNICEF, 2004.

34 M. Shaw and T. Reitano, *The Evolution of Organized Crime in Africa*, Pretoria: Institute for Security Studies, 2013, p. 4.

Many States are also at a very real disadvantage when it comes to participating in a global cooperation regime. This is so for 'fragile States', where governments are weak and unable to control what happens on their territory. Such weakness can create a void that criminal organizations may exploit to their own advantage.[35] Small States are also at a disadvantage. Their vulnerability, including their economic vulnerability, is something that must be well understood as part of international efforts to institute an international regime of interdiction, control or law enforcement cooperation. For many small States, the burden of participating in the increasingly internationalized regime of crime control and prevention places a heavy demand on already weak institutions. Overcoming vulnerabilities arising from factors such as globalization, environmental degradation, international corruption or transnational organized crime is a constant challenge for these States. They are at risk of becoming the 'weakest links' in the global regime to prevent transnational crime, money laundering, corruption or terrorism.[36]

Resistance

The implementation of TCLCs, just like rule of law reforms in general, is partly a technical but more fundamentally a political process. As noted by many observers, the greatest obstacles to the necessary reforms are not so much technical and financial as they are human and political.[37] In the case of anti-corruption measures, for example, reforms represent a significant risk for those who benefit from the status quo: corruption benefits well-connected people, who do not surrender their advantage easily.[38] As explained by Rachel Kleinfeld, even the simplest technical reform is likely to create winners and losers. The losers are often well aware of their potential loss and will attempt to prevent or even sabotage change. Power structures and cultural norms must therefore be affected if the outcome of reforms is to be achieved.[39] The implementation of TCLCs tends to require deeper changes in cultural norms and traditions.

For example, State parties to the UNTOC Convention have had to reflect on how resistance at senior levels within law enforcement agencies can be more directly addressed in technical assistance projects. They have also been looking for ways to minimize inter-agency struggles for power and competition for government resources during capacity-building initiatives.[40]

35 M. Shaw and W. Kemp, *Spotting the Spoilers: A Guide to Analyzing Organized Crime in Fragile States*, New York: International Peace Institute, 2012.

36 Y. Dandurand, 'Capacity Building and Technical Assistance in Small States', in M. Shaw and Y. Dandurand (eds), *Maximizing the Effectiveness of Technical Assistance Provided by Member States in Crime Prevention and Criminal Justice*, Helsinki: HEUNI, 2006, p. 42.

37 T. Carothers, 'The Rule-of-Law Revival', in T. Carothers (ed.), *Promoting the Rule of Law Abroad*, Washington: Carnegie Endowment for International Peace, 2006, p. 4.

38 M. Johnston, *Syndromes of Corruption: Wealth, Power, and Democracy*, Cambridge, Cambridge University Press, 2005, p. 195.

39 R. Kleinfeld, *Advancing the Rule of Law Abroad: Next Generation Reform*, Washington: Carnegie Endowment for International Peace, 2012.

40 Conference of the Parties to the United Nations Convention against Transnational Organized Crime, Working Group of Government Experts on Technical Assistance, Establishing Capacity-building Programmes for Prosecutors and Members of the Judiciary and Law Enforcement Agencies – Discussion paper by the Secretariat, CTOC/COP/WG.2/2013/3, 7 August 2013, p. 2.

Broadening the circle – beyond the role of State parties

The implementation of conventions is now understood to involve not only State parties but also other actors and stakeholders. The concept of 'shared responsibility' applied to the implementation of TCLCs underscores the need to engage much more than the criminal justice system in that process. It calls for realistic and practical measures in which all State and non-State actors may move in concert to achieve the aims of a convention.[41] In fact, it can be argued that the growing 'precautionary nature' of international criminal law, whether it is in relation to corruption, human trafficking or crimes against the environment, and its emphasis on preventive measures inevitably requires a much broader social and institutional implementation effort.[42]

Technical assistance

The duty to collaborate with each other and, when possible, to offer technical assistance to requesting State parties is specifically mentioned in the TCLCs.[43] Much hope is being placed on the role of technical assistance in ensuring the implementation of the TCLCs. However, there are some fundamental issues with the way that much of the current and often considerable technical assistance in the field of criminal justice, often in support of treaty implementation, is designed and delivered. It is becoming abundantly clear that our methods of providing technical assistance are themselves quite weak and ineffective.[44] For example, the report of the working group on technical assistance of the Conference of Parties to the UNTOC Convention referred to the need for meaningful and cost-effective technical assistance and underlined the need to carry out assessments of technical assistance projects. It emphasized the need for assistance to build the basic capacity of the police and prosecutorial services.[45] It also referred to the need to ensure better coordination among donors in the provision of technical assistance.[46]

It is widely recognized that more of the same kind of assistance will not be sufficient to bring the wide range of reforms necessary to build capacity and to fully implement TCLCs. As Thomas Carothers has convincingly argued, we have not yet developed a good understanding of how significant changes to criminal justice systems can be effected.[47] Finally,

---

41 International Narcotics Control Board, 'Shared responsibility in international drug control', Report of the International Narcotics Control Board for 2012, New York, United Nations, 2013, pp. 1–8.

42 On the 'precautionary logic' behind such laws, see: T. Arnoldussen, 'Deus sive Natura: Investigating the Axioms of Precautionary Logic', in M. Hildebrandt, A. Makinwa and A. Oechmichen (eds), *Controlling Security in a Culture of Fear*, The Hague: Boom Legal Publishers, 2010, p. 75.

43 See e.g. Art. 29 of the UNTOC Convention and Arts 60 to 63 of the UNCAC.

44 See M. Shaw and Y. Dandurand (eds), *Maximizing the Effectiveness of Technical Assistance Provided by Member States in Crime Prevention and Criminal Justice*, Helsinki, HEUNI, 2006. See also C.T. Griffiths, Y. Dandurand and V. Chin, 'Development Assistance and Police Reform', *The Canadian Review of Policing Research*, 2005, p. 101.

45 Conference of the Parties to the United Nations Convention against Transnational Organized Crime, Working Group of Government Experts on Technical Assistance, Establishing Capacity-building Programmes for Prosecutors and Members of the Judiciary and Law Enforcement Agencies – Discussion Paper by the Secretariat, CTOC/COP/WG.2/2013/3, 7 August 2013.

46 Conference of the Parties to the United Nations Convention against Transnational Organized Crime, Working Group of Government Experts on Technical Assistance, Report on the Meeting of the Working Group of Government Experts on Technical Assistance held in Vienna on 17 and 18 October 2012, CTOC/COP/WG.2/2012/4, Vienna, 14 November 2012, p. 3.

47 T. Carothers, 'The Rule-of-Law Revival'.

there are very few evaluations of current technical assistance activities and, thus, little systematic knowledge about the impact of that assistance and the return on the large investments made to provide this kind of assistance.[48]

Monitoring and review mechanisms

Introduction

The respective attitudes of States towards the implementation of TCLCs vary considerably. Some of them are reluctant to ratify a new convention until they have achieved compliance or near-compliance with all their main obligations under that convention. Others rush forward, for political, symbolic or other reasons, without having given much thought to implementation issues or to the capacity of their own institutions to comply with these new obligations.

It is difficult to find out exactly how much progress has really been achieved by States in implementing the conventions they have ratified. Few States systematically monitor their own progress and, indeed, many of them do not even systematically gather much data on the operation of their own criminal justice system.

We must therefore rely on the formal reporting mechanisms and sometimes, although relatively rarely, on the monitoring activities performed by civil society.

Reporting mechanisms

Establishing effective mechanisms to monitor the implementation of international treaties lies at the heart of the effectiveness of the treaties themselves. All TCLCs provide some kind of reporting mechanism.[49] Unlike some human rights treaties where other bodies or organizations can also report on a State party's compliance with its obligation under the treaty, most TCLCs are careful to limit this responsibility. As might have been expected, State parties jealously preserved their ownership over the review process and the responsibility for reporting on the implementation of these treaties belongs exclusively to them. There is even, among State parties, some disagreement over the general transparency of the process and the extent to which the national reports should be made public.

The reporting provisions provided for in a convention are negotiated just as carefully and cautiously as any other provision of that convention. The modality of each reporting mechanism is sometimes left to be negotiated among parties once the convention in question has come into force.

The purpose of reporting is often referred to and even sometimes specifically defined in the conventions themselves. These purposes typically include: assessing compliance and whether parties are living up to their legal obligations under the convention; promoting international cooperation and supporting operational activities; identifying and sharing best

---

48 Y. Dandurand, 'Evaluating the Effectiveness of Technical Assistance', in M. Shaw and Y. Dandurand (eds), *Maximizing the Effectiveness of Technical Assistance Provided by Member States in Crime Prevention and Criminal Justice*, Helsinki: HEUNI, 2006, p. 104.

49 In the cases of the UNTOC and UNCAC, the reporting mechanisms were not specifically defined in the conventions and had to be determined later by the conferences of parties.

practices in achieving the aims of the convention or implementing some of its provisions; and identifying issues with the conventions and offering suggestions for improving the instrument. The last of these can sometimes be the starting point of the convention review and amendment process.

State parties to TCLCs tend to agree that the review of the implementation of the conventions must be an 'ongoing and gradual process'.[50] In that sense, compliance is expected to be achieved over a long period of time and not necessarily before or immediately after treaty ratification.

Reporting on the implementation of an international treaty is clearly a challenging task for many State parties to TCLCs. Obtaining information from them in a timely and reliable manner is made difficult by several factors, including: a lack of financial, human or technical resources; administrative and technical difficulties; personnel changes and languages; the complexity of the information required; the absence of information management systems; and a lack of clarity on the nature, scope and relevance of the information requested.

In the case of the UNCAC and the UNTOC conventions, both Conferences of Parties debated the question of the reporting process. There are a variety of methods to gather information at different stages of any review process. The Conferences could have adopted any of them in order to discharge their functions, based on the relative advantages and disadvantages of each method. The Conference of Parties to the UNCAC eventually adopted and implemented a self-assessment checklist.

Resolution 1 of the first session of the Conference of Parties to UNCAC formulated the following principles to guide the review process.[51] It stated that the review mechanism should: (1) be transparent, efficient, non-intrusive, inclusive and impartial; (2) not produce any form of ranking; (3) provide opportunities to share good practices and challenges; and, (4) complement existing international and regional review mechanisms (and therefore seek to avoid duplication of reporting efforts). Within the confines of these principles, the Conference of Parties worked to determine implementation review mechanisms that would enable it to identify implementation gaps and issues, assess needs for technical assistance, establish priorities in the provision of such assistance, establish benchmarks and assess trends over the longer period of time. There is also an attempt to make greater use of technology; for example, the reporting mechanism for UNCAC is supported by software to assist in using the self-assessment checklist.

Reporting issues

States often face a proliferation of reporting requirements, sometimes even on a single criminal justice issue. In many instances, States are parties to more than one treaty dealing with the same subject. That is often the case where a State is party to similar conventions, with similar but not identical reporting requirements, at both the regional and global levels. A similar situation also occurs once a State has contracted several reporting obligations relating to the same issue, as is the case for measures to prevent money laundering addressed by the Financial Action Task Force (FATF), the UNTOC Convention and the UNCAC. It can also

---

50 See e.g. Res. 1/1 of the Conference of State parties to the UN Convention against Corruption, available at https://www.unodc.org/unodc/en/treaties/CAC/CAC-COSP-session1-resolutions.html (accessed 9 April 2014).

51 Ibid.

occur when a number of multilateral treaties are adopted over the years, creating different reporting requirements and sometimes different oversight bodies, as in the case of the UN international drug control conventions[52] with the evolution over the years of the respective roles of the International Narcotics Control Board (INCB) and the UN Commission on Narcotic Drugs (UNCND). This multiplication of reporting requirements on a particular criminal justice issue represents not only an extra burden on national governments, but potentially also a lot of unnecessary duplication and confusion.

Review mechanisms

Most TCLCs have established bodies to review their implementation. These bodies, with the consent of a State party, can adopt procedures and mechanisms for reviewing and evaluating their compliance with the requirements of a convention. This is clearly a delicate matter. The mechanisms established to assess and monitor compliance are not always defined in great detail in the text of the treaty. Sometimes this is left to be determined at a later stage.

At this point in time, State parties to the UNTOC have not yet agreed to a formal mechanism for the review of the implementation of that convention and the protocols thereto. The Conference of Parties has established an open-ended intergovernmental working group on the review of the implementation of the convention. Progress has been slow.[53] In the case of the UNCAC, the Conference of State Parties established an implementation review and made it also responsible for reviewing technical assistance initiatives, thus linking technical assistance discussions to the findings of the review mechanism.[54]

Sometimes the review process needs to be re-energized. For example, in 2009, the UN's Commission on Narcotic Drugs (CND) adopted the 'Political Declaration and Plan of Action on International Cooperation towards an Integrated and Balanced Strategy to Counter the World Drug Problem'.[55] It reaffirms the principal role played by the CND as one of the United Nations organs with prime responsibility for drug control matters. In 2014, the CND will conduct a high-level review of the implementation of the Political Declaration and Plan of Action, and the outcome of that review will be submitted to the General Assembly for its consideration in 2016.

At the regional level, some effective multilateral review mechanisms have also been established. The Inter-American Drug Abuse Control Commission (CICAD) created in 1986 by the Organization of American States (OAS) established in 1998 a multilateral evaluation mechanism to make periodic recommendations to Member States on improving their capacity to control drug trafficking and abuse and enhance multilateral cooperation. Another example is provided within the Council of Europe by the Group of States against Corruption

---

52 Specifically, the Single Convention on Narcotics Drugs of 1961 as amended by the 1972 Protocol, above note 22; the Convention on Psychotropic Substances, Vienna, 21 February 1971, 1019 UNTS 175, in force 16 August 1976; and the United Nations Convention against Illicit Traffic in Narcotics Drugs and Psychotropic Substances, Vienna, 20 December 1988, 1582 UNTS 95; in force 11 November 1990.

53 Conference of the Parties to the United Nations Convention against Transnational Organized Crime, Report of the Conference of the Parties to the United Nations Convention against Transnational Organized Crime on its sixth session, held in Vienna from 15 to 19 October 2012, CTOC/COP/2012/15, Vienna, 5 November 2012

54 See UNODC, *Mechanism for the Review of Implementation of the United Nations Convention against Corruption: Basic Documents*, New York: United Nations, 2011.

55 New York: United Nations, 2009.

(GRECO), which has its own reporting requirements and process. It undertakes evaluations that involve the collection of information through questionnaires, on-site country visits enabling evaluation teams to solicit further information during high-level discussions with domestic key players, and drafting of evaluation reports. These reports, which are examined and adopted by GRECO, contain recommendations to the evaluated States on how to improve their level of compliance with the provisions under consideration. Measures taken to implement recommendations are subsequently assessed by GRECO under a separate compliance procedure. Compliance reports are prepared and made publicly available on the Council of Europe's website.[56]

Amendment mechanisms – challenging existing treaties

With the consent of State parties, any TCLC can be amended as necessary.[57] Rules of Procedures are typically adopted concerning the amendment process.[58] However, in spite of the weaknesses that may have already been discovered in the TCLCs, delays in implementing adequate review processes make it unlikely that amendments to these conventions will seriously be proposed or considered in the near future.

Even when some of the dispositions of a particular convention are being questioned by some State parties, the process of change is quite laborious. For example, in the case of some of the drug control treaties, where there is a growing consensus across the world, and especially in the Americas, that policies reflected in these conventions have caused more harm than good, it is not clear how existing policies can be reversed. Given the consensus-based nature of the international system, there is a lack of appetite among States parties to the relevant conventions to renegotiate them. Some States are now actively looking at different scenarios, including legal experimentation, and are hoping to find some flexibility to improve national and regional policies within the framework of existing international conventions.[59]

Conclusion

Western nations have poured hundreds of millions of dollars into developing an international cooperation regime and providing technical assistance to States that have lacked a basic capacity to cooperate. Unfortunately, the results of these efforts have been generally disappointing. Treaties may represent a good starting point, but it is becoming increasingly clear that international cooperation remains an empty promise unless States are prepared to seriously address some very real obstacles to it and develop a genuine capacity to work together across borders. The primary obstacles to international cooperation are clearly not always

---

56 See GRECO, Third Evaluation Round Reports, available at http://www.coe.int/t/dghl/ monitoring/greco/evaluations/round3/ReportsRound3_en.asp (accessed 3 April 2014).

57 For example, Art. 39(1) of the UNTOC provides for the possibility of amendments to the Convention (five years after the entry into force of the Convention). A similar provision is found in UNCAC (Art. 69). The amendments are themselves subject to ratification by State parties (UNTOC, Art. 39(3)) or State parties' Acceptance to be bound by it (UNCAC, Art. 69(5)).

58 See for example: UNODC, *Rules of Procedure for the Conference of the Parties to the United Nations Convention against Transnational Organized Crime*, New York: United Nations, 2005.

59 Organization of American States, *Report on the Drug Problem in the Americas*, Washington: OAS, 2013; and Organization of American States, *Scenarios for the Drug Problem in the Americas 2013–2025*, Washington: OAS.

technical or financial, but also political and human. There is therefore no substitute for strong political will to implement such a regime. On that point, the asymmetries which characterize the respective situations of State parties will continue to make international cooperation in criminal matters a very challenging task and should be explicitly taken into account. This is perhaps also to say that the sharing of practical experience and lessons learned among professionals as well as among Member States is more important than ever in order to perfect cooperation strategies and develop a capacity to implement them successfully.

Index

Figures in *italics* refer to tables